How the U.S. Securities Industry Works

Updated and Expanded in 2004

By

Hal McIntyre

ISBN: 0-9669178-1-2

Printed in the United States of America

Published and distributed by The Summit Group Press, a division of The Summit Group.

For general information on The Summit Group Press or for permission to photocopy items for corporate, personal or educational use, please call our Wall Street Office at (212) 328-2500.

Cover photo and design: Lee Titone

Introduction

This book is the updated and extended version of a book that I first wrote in 1999-2000. While much has changed in the last five years, it is remarkable how much has remained the same. There have been significant advances in trade processing and in clearing and settlement, and slow but steady progress in many other areas.

Where possible, I've tried to retain a bridge between the previous book and this one to minimize confusion and to continue my belief that to understand how things work today you should understand how they have evolved. Also, I have deliberately included some repetition between chapters when it was important to talk about the same activity in a different context.

I would like to thank the staff of The Summit Group and Securities Operations Forum for their support, and would especially like to recognize the continuous editing and feedback provided by Scott Porter, Kim McIntyre and Eileen Haeger.

Since most of this book is based upon our first edition, I would like to re-thank the people who helped previously. Many of the Securities Operations Forum instructors provided important input to the first edition, including Abe Mastbaum, Barry Kipnis, Mike Curley and Jerry O'Connell. Several other industry experts also provided input and reviewed sections of this book, including Laura Mah, Gus Schwarz, Joe Rosen, Rosanna Perez, Bob Carney and John Coker.

Much of the review for this book came from industry experts who are members of ISITC-IOA, including Kevin Smith, Denise Adams, Stephen Lachanga, Frank DiMarco, Ed O'Toole, Mike D'Ambrisi, Genevy Dimitrion, Sandy Throne, June Biner, Lorraine Morrison and Adrienne Jacobs.

Other significant contributions were made by Dannette Buddecke, Debbi McKindles, Al Howell, Rob McIassac, Al Durso, Linda Fuller, William Vandenburgh, Scott Fiata, Jose Manso, Louis Lepore, Anthony Leone and Nicole Goodnow.

I would particularly like to thank a few people who went above and beyond in providing support. Chuck Wiley practically re-wrote the section on SWIFT, Harry Lopez who reviewed the sections on CUSIP and standards, Denise Adams who added major portions to the chapter on Investment Management operations, Frank DeMarco who provided valuable input to the chapter on brokerage processing, Ed O'Toole who thoroughly reviewed the chapter on Issuance and Alyssa Gilmore for her very useful clarifications on Omgeo.

The contributions of all of these people were invaluable in producing a book of this scope. Any errors are mine alone. [1]

Hal McIntyre	THE SUMMIT GROUP
Managing Partner	48 Wall Street / 4th Floor
hal@tsgc.com	New York, NY 10005
June 1, 2004	(212) 328-2500

---

[1] I also note that TSG Securities and TSG Bank and Trust Company, which are identified in many of the examples in this book, are fictitious firms, and are used merely to illustrate various documents.

Forward

The following forward was written by Bill Jaenike in 2000, as he was retiring as chairman of the DTC, for the original edition of this book. As we revised and updated the book we started to consider a new forward; however, upon reflection, what Bill wrote in 2000 is as valid today as it was then. The DTC and NSCC have merged and continued to evolve, and increased automation is still the only solution to reduce costs and errors, as well as to improve client service.

Therefore, we have reprinted the Forward in its entirety:

*****

"How does the securities industry work?" Not too long ago, many industry professionals might have answered such a question by saying, 'it is a marvel that it does.'

Of course, as a result of looking at the industry through today's perspective of advanced technological systems, innovative product development and centralized support infrastructure, the cause for such cynicism is not readily apparent.

When I first started at The Depository Trust Company (DTC) in 1974, the securities industry was dramatically different than it is today. The vast array of financial products that currently exist, such as exchange listed options, futures and the many varieties of other derivatives, had either not been created or were not distributed effectively in the marketplace. Investing in foreign securities was a rare occurrence and owning stock was solely the domain of institutional investors or wealthy individuals. As a result, daily trading volumes were only a small fraction of the billion shares days that are regularly experienced today, and the general profitability of the industry as a whole paled in comparison to today's marketplace.

It is easy to look back upon that time and dismiss its significance. However, the growth and prosperity enjoyed today would not be possible had it not been for the infrastructure that was assembled in the 1970's. For example, not until the Banking and Securities Industry Committee (BASIC) was formed in 1970, had there been any effort made toward establishing a centralized inter-industry depository for post-trade securities processing. Although volumes increased fourfold from 1960 to 1970, trading remained paper-based, standards were non-existent and settlement continued to be a long, drawn out manual process. As a result, in the two years concluding with BASIC's formation, over 100 firms were forced out of business because of losses resulting from failed settlement of trades, and the New York Exchange was forced to curtail its daily trading hours even to the extent of closing each Wednesday. Clearly, the industry was trying to grow, but the infrastructure just could not support it.

Gradually throughout the 1970s, these limitations were eliminated. In 1972, Securities Industry Automation Corporation (SIAC) was formed to provide the exchanges and their member-brokers with automation and data processing services. The next year, DTC was created from what had been the NYSE's Central Certificate Service and in 1977, and National Securities Clearing Corporation was formed through a merger of the clearing subsidiaries of the major markets. Subsequent rules issued by self-regulatory bodies and approved by the SEC mandated the use of these institutions, setting in motion an industry infrastructure that, today, has the capacity to handle multi-billion share days. As a result, few sectors of the economy have grown and diversified as rapidly as the financial services industry.

The purpose of this history lesson is not merely to reflect upon how far the industry has come, but to suggest just how far it can continue to go. After all, in order to understand and prepare for the future we need to understand where we are and how we got here. Consider what the industry would be like today if DTC and NSCC had not been created when they were. Imagine the trillions of dollars that flow into mutual funds today from all corners of the globe. Would this have been possible without an efficient system to process and settle all of the underlying trades?

It appears as if the activity in the financial markets will expand at an accelerated rate. However, the industry will be able to sustain its impressive growth only for as long as it is supported by a strong operating infrastructure comprised of knowledgeable people and innovative systems. If firms are going to be successful in their efforts to expand their client base, products and distribution systems, they need to automate costly, error-prone back office processing, streamline operating procedures, reduce costs and minimize risk.

While readers would agree that the need for strong and efficient back office systems is self-evident, it is now more than ever that the industry must gear up for that by adopting Straight Through Processing (STP). STP, or the real-time settlement of transactions without manual intervention, must be the rallying cry for the industry as it enters the 21st century.

It is my hope that this book will prove to be a resource that will assist you in both understanding the industry and appreciating the history which has brought it to this point - a past and a present which should provide you with insight into a more efficient future.

William F. Jaenike
Chairman and CEO of DTC, Retired

CONTENTS

I. Introduction

This book is designed to provide an overview of the major aspects of the securities industry and to help the reader establish a framework from which he or she can acquire additional details about specific topics. As the framework is developed, the reader should increasingly understand the terminology of the industry and by the end of the book should have acquired a significant additional vocabulary.

It is important to remember that this book presents the basics of the industry, and the goal is to introduce a variety of topics and define their relationships to other topics. There are many different aspects to the U.S. securities industry, and although this book is designed to expose the reader to the major points, it is not designed to explain every topic in detail.

In addition, by its nature, a book is out of date by the time it is printed. So while this book forms a framework and defines the industry's processes at a point in time, additional sources of information, such as newsletters and conferences, should be used to stay current.

To help, Securities Operations Forum has established a daily online newsletter that presents topics of interest regarding the securities industry and has developed a series of eLearning courses. To find out more, go to www.soforum.com.

Also, the book does not cover the administrative systems and processes that are needed by every firm, such as Human Resources, General Accounting, Premises Management, etc.

This book has been divided into the following five sections:

Section I – The Marketplace	1. Introduction
	2. Securities Industry Participants
	3. Regulators and Legislation
Section II – Making the Deal	4. Creating New Securities
	5. Account Opening
	6. Buying and Selling Securities
Section III – Securities Processing	7. Post-Trade Processing, Clearing and Settlement
	8. Post Settlement Processing
	9. Broker Processing
	10. Bank Processing
	11. Investment Manager Processing
	12. Mutual Fund Processing
Section IV – Types of Securities Instruments	13. Equity-Related Instruments
	14. Fixed Income Instruments
	15. Mutual Fund Instruments
	16. Other Products
Section V – Industry Support	17. Vendors
	18. Industry Owned Organizations

A. FINANCIAL MARKETS

The primary role of banks, brokers, investment managers and mutual funds in the securities industry is to act as financial intermediaries.

The role of a financial intermediary is to satisfy the financial needs of borrowers and lenders; that is, to participate in matching individuals or firms who need *additional* funds for their business or personal use, with other businesses or individuals who have *excess* funds and wish to obtain a return on their investment.

- Borrowers either take out a loan or issue securities in order to get the funds they need.

- Investors seek opportunities to invest their excess funds into areas that will provide the greatest return possible for the level of risk they are willing to take.

Financial intermediaries also help issuers create new securities and process the transactions that move funds and securities from borrowers to lenders and vice versa.

All of this activity is performed within a complex industry infrastructure of exchanges, depositories, and clearinghouses, and within a regulatory environment of laws, regulations and rules.

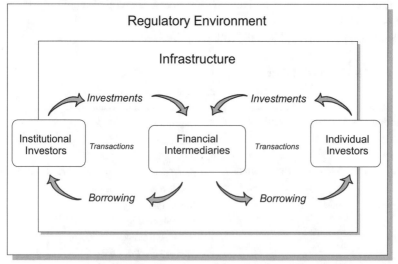

Figure 1 - Role of Financial Intermediaries

In later chapters we will talk about:

- Various types of investors
- Types of instruments in which they invest
- Different kinds of financial intermediaries
- Firms that form the industry's infrastructure
- Functions performed by these firms
- Regulations that guide the industry

B. VALUE CHAIN

The steps that investors go through when they make a trade are based upon the different phases of the trade life cycle, which is also called the industry's value chain. Figure 2 introduces many of the concepts that will be explained in more detail throughout the book.

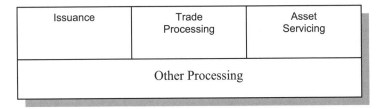

Figure 2 - Trade Life Cycle

The different phases of the life cycle are summarized in the following sections, and are described in detail later in this book.

Issuance

The trade life cycle starts with the creation of an instrument through a process called issuance, or underwriting, which often involves the creation of a new security that is distributed through an Initial Public Offering (IPO). There are several different types of activities involved in the issuance of new securities. Later chapters describe how a security is issued, as well as the major roles of firms participating in the issuance and processing of securities, such as the paying agent, the registrar and the transfer agent.

Trade Processing

There are five major activities in post-trade processing:

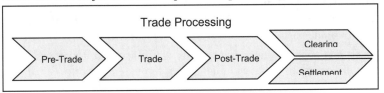

Figure 3 - Trade Processing Activities

Pre-Trade

After a security has been created, it is available for trading in the secondary market, where it is examined by investors during the pre-trade phase of the trade life cycle. At this point, investors can gather market information, conduct research, perform different types of analytics or modeling on their portfolio, and evaluate the overall risk of their portfolio as well as the impact of the trade under consideration. The chapter on Buying and Selling Securities will discuss the research function, how firms analyze investment alternatives and risk management.

Trade

Once an investor knows what he wants to do, he must find a counterparty. This takes place in the trading phase. At this point all of the various parties to the trade monitor the trade's progress as it either goes to an exchange, to the over-the-counter market, or directly to an Electronic Crossing Network as the trader looks for a counterparty.

Post-Trade

After the trade has been completed, both sides wish to confirm that the trade they made was identical to what their counterparty thought was accomplished. This process occurs in the post-trade phase through the functions of matching, confirmation and affirmation.

After both parties to the trade have agreed on the details, two separate processes take place.

Clearing

The broker to broker portion of the trade (which is called the street-side of the trade) is entered into a U.S. clearing system that nets all of the trades made by all of the brokers throughout the day. This process is called Continuous Net Settlement (CNS).

Throughout each trading day, CNS nets each participant's security obligations (purchases and sales) into one net position for each issue and one overall net cash position. The process for monitoring the cash side of the trade, which also occurs throughout the trading day, is called Daily Net Money Settlement.

Settlement

The final exchange of securities for cash is called settlement.

For brokers, the settlement of the street-side of the trade occurs at the depository at the end of the day by using the net amounts that were calculated during the clearing process.

Institutions and individuals (which form the client-side of the trade) settle on a trade-by-trade basis.

If a firm is unable to deliver a security that it has sold it may have to borrow them in order to settle with the buyer through a process called securities lending, which is described in the chapter on Post Trade Processing.

If a client does not have sufficient cash to pay for a purchase the client might be able to temporarily borrow from the broker through a process called margin lending, which is discussed in the chapter on broker processing.

Issue Servicing

After the trade is settled, the post-trade process begins, which includes functions such as:

- Income Collection
- Corporate Actions
- Pricing
- Reporting, etc.

Once again, we will discuss all of these activities in more detail at various points throughout the book.

Summary

As individual and institutional investors prepare to buy or sell, they all go through a similar set of steps. Investors must gather information about the markets, sectors, and companies before they make an informed decision. Then, whether they are buying or selling, they must find a counterparty for each trade. After the brokers on each side of the trade reach an agreement, the details of their trade must be matched to ensure that they both understood the same thing.

As the street-side of the trade moves into the clearing stage, the brokers involved on each side of the trade inform the appropriate clearing agency about the trade. The details are matched again and the information about the trades is netted by the clearing agency. The net amount for each security traded by each broker is transmitted to the depository for the final exchange of securities for cash.

Finally, after the trade has been settled, the process of maintaining the position in a portfolio begins. This is where the broker or custodian keeps track of the value of the position, any income that should be collected and any corporate actions that could affect the position.

C. FIRMS IN THE U.S. INDUSTRY

There are many different types of firms involved in the securities industry. Some are directly involved in trading or processing trades, while others support these firms or are involved in the issuance of securities.

Investors

Banks, brokers, mutual funds, corporations and investment managers can all be involved at different times as investors. We will talk more about the different types of investors in the chapter on Industry Participants.

Issuers

Issuers consist of corporations, agencies and governments that wish to raise funds. They are supported by the banks, brokers and investment banks that offer underwriting services.

Infrastructure

The U.S. infrastructure consists of the exchanges, depositories and clearing corporations, as well as governmental agencies such as the Fed and SEC, international organizations such as SWIFT and ISITC-IOA that support U.S. activities and industry associations that provide information to their members.

Vendors

There are many different types of vendors that support the securities industry and provide services, such as:

- Applications
- Hardware
- Consulting
- Processing Services
- Information

Each of these types of participants is discussed in detail in the next chapter, and vendors are covered in a separate chapter later in the book.

With this quick overview of the industry in mind, we can now start to look at the reasons people invest and some of the major concepts that support the securities industry.

D. INVESTOR OBJECTIVES

To begin understanding the securities industry, we should understand why investors (retail and institutional) want to invest, and what they consider as they decide between the available alternatives.

When making investments, institutions and individual clients consider the risk of the investment vs. the potential reward (or return) on the investment. The greater the risk, the greater the required return in order to attract investors.

Figure 4 - Investment Risk vs. Reward

There are several categories of risk that investors should consider:

- Loss of all or a portion of the investment – if the value of the investment declines

- Lower return than with other investments – if the investor picks an investment that does not keep up with the rest of the available alternatives

- Inflation is greater than the return – if the rate of inflation increases after a long-term fixed rate investment is made, then the final value of the investment could be less than the value of inflation-adjusted instruments

- Changes in taxation that affect locked-in investments – if legislation changes and tax exempt or tax deferred investments are no longer allowed

This combination of risk and reward is also influenced by the length of time that an investment is open. Generally, the longer the term of the investment the greater the risk that the investment will not be repaid. With this thought in mind, the *standard yield curve* is derived. This shows that investors require a higher return for longer-term investments to compensate them for the time-value of their risk and the potential for inflation.

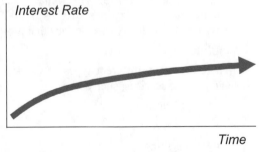

Figure 5 - Standard Yield Curve

The following chart shows an actual example of interest rates at two points in time, and reflects the Standard Yield Curve.

Key Rates	June 28, 2004	June 28, 2003
Money Market Funds	0.62%	0.75%
90 Day Treasury Bills	1.30%	0.88%
2 Year Treasury Notes	2.79%	1.74%
10 Year Treasury Notes	4.72%	3.36%
30 Year Treasury Bonds	5.40%	4.40%

Figure 6 - Key Interest Rates

Occasionally, we have a circumstance where the short-term fears of inflation are greater than long-term fears, and the result is an *inverted yield curve*.

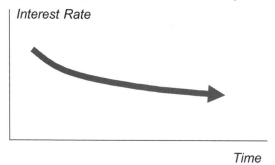

Figure 7 - Inverted Yield Curve

There are also other ways to look at yields.

Bond Yield Comparisons

The yields on different types of bonds can also be compared to each other.

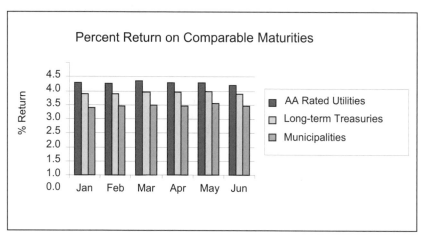

Figure 8 - Yields on Comparable Maturities

This chart shows the difference in yields for three categories of bonds that have different risk profiles. This is not a yield curve; it is a comparison of yields for three different types of instruments at specific points in time. The chart can be read as follows:

- The long-term Treasuries stayed flat during this period of time
- Municipals also stayed flat, and also had a slightly lower yield since they are tax-free
- Double-A rated utility bonds had a higher yield than U.S. Treasuries since they are considered to have slightly more risk

These different curves reflect the differences in the risk and taxability of these investments.

Investor Needs

As they invest, investors are looking for an environment where they have access to a variety of investments, with accurate and timely information, along with a level playing field and liquidity.

- A range of investment types, with different risk profiles is necessary to satisfy the various and changing requirements of investors
- Accurate and timely information is necessary for investors to make informed decisions.
- The level playing field concept is based on the premise that all investors should have equal access to information and equal access to the markets so that no one category of investor has an advantage.
- Liquidity is important because if an investor wishes to sell a security and there are no buyers, the security is actually worthless at that point in time, except for any income that it might provide.

The investment styles of individuals and institutions determine how they buy and sell securities and the types of instruments that interest them. Individuals and institutions can either be investors (with a long time horizon and a focus on the intrinsic value of the firm) or traders (who wish to profit by short-term movements in the price of the security).

Investors can focus on an entire sector such as technology stocks, a geographic region such as Asia, or they can decide to look for the best value from a single stock from any sector such as technology or financial firms.

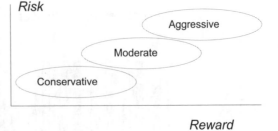

Figure 9 - Investment Alternatives

Investors are looking for a return on their investments, and that return can include current income, capital gains, or both. While some categories of investors need current income, others do not need the money today and prefer to have the value of their investment increase over a period of time.

The challenge for investors has been to identify specific companies and specific instruments, including equities and bonds, which will meet these different needs.

Traders look to make a profit on the short-term movement in the price of specific securities, and are not as concerned about the fundamental value of the underlying company as they are about changes in the prospects for a particular firm. Although trading has historically been an institutional function, individuals can participate in the market as day traders.

To meet all of these needs, corporate finance specialists have created a range of products (or instrument types) that have different risk/reward profiles. And, the industry has defined alternative ways to organize investments. As shown in Figure 8, some instruments have a low risk to meet the needs of certain types of investors and these investments have a low return. The higher the reward, the higher the risk.

Asset Allocation

The concept of asset allocation has become universally accepted as investors understood that if they have a mix of instrument categories, each of which has its own risk profile, they will be in a better position to withstand long-term market risk.

An asset allocation model is based upon an examination of the history of movements in the securities markets. On average, and over the long run, investors have had the best returns by investing in equities. However, there have been many points in time where equities were not the best possible investment. To accommodate these shifts in returns, the concept of asset allocation was created.

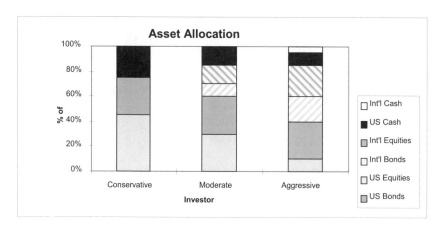

Figure 10 - Sample Asset Allocation Model

The theory behind asset allocation states that investors can reduce their overall level of risk by putting a percentage of their investments into different categories of securities. The theory states that at different points in time, investors should have some percentage of their assets invested in equities, a percentage in bonds, and some in cash.

There is no single answer as to what the optimum asset allocation mix should be. Different firms have different views about the best asset allocation at the same point in time. For instance, at any one point in time, different brokers could recommend the following allocations:

Firm	% Stocks	% Bonds	% Cash	% Other
Broker A	75	25	0	0
Broker B	40	55	5	0
Broker C	57	27	13	3
Broker D	65	20	0	15

Figure 11 - Asset Allocation Recommendations

But, this basic asset allocation model is too simple for most situations. The next example shows how this concept is used for more complex investment objectives.

Risk-Adjusted Allocation Model

Individual investors do not retain the same investment profile forever. As people age their ability to recover from risky investments decreases since they have less time to recover. Generally, an individual investor becomes more conservative over time.

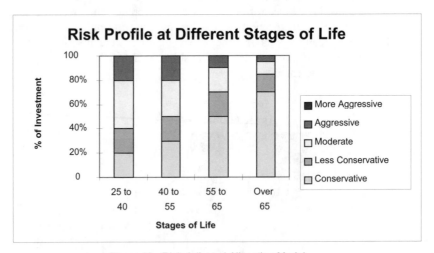

Figure 12 - Risk-Adjusted Allocation Model

Regardless of an investor's risk profile, there are a few concepts that are important to anyone with a long-term investment view.

Stock Returns Over Time

The average return for the time period shown below (1977 to 2003) was 12.56%. In this twenty-year period, there were nine times when the annual return was less than the twenty-year average, but the S&P 500 only had a negative return four times.

This is good for investors, but only if the investor picks the bottoms as the times to invest and the peaks as the times to sell. Investors have not been able to consistently do this over the long-term.

% Change in the S&P 500

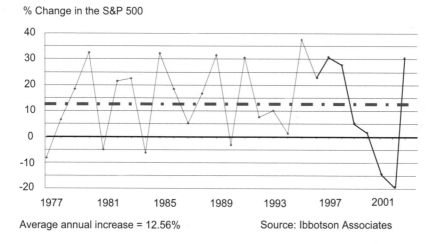

Average annual increase = 12.56%   Source: Ibbotson Associates

Figure 13 - Stock Returns Over Time

To accommodate this inability to constantly pick the peaks and valleys, the investment community has identified the concept of dollar cost averaging.

Dollar Cost Averaging

Dollar cost averaging occurs when an investor invests the same amount at regular intervals, regardless of whether the market is up or down. By so doing, more shares are bought when the market is down and the portfolio is worth more when the market is up.

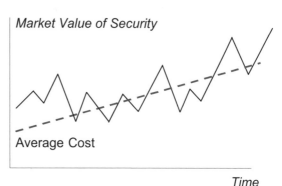

Figure 14 - Impact of Dollar Cost Averaging

Since the equity market has historically risen over the long-term, the dollar cost averaging investor will buy during the ups and downs of the market and as long as the investment does not have to be extracted when the market is depressed, the portfolio will show a long-term gain.

Investment Considerations

Investors have several general considerations that they make as they decide what to buy or sell:

- Goals – What are the investors' individual goals, such as retirement, meeting ROI targets, etc.?

- Time Horizon – How long before the money is needed?

- Risk Propensity – How much risk are they willing to take?

- Financial Circumstances – Can they afford to tie up the money for a long period of time, or to possibly lose it altogether?

E. BUSINESS CONCEPTS

The key participants in the securities industry are firms such as banks, brokers, investment managers, mutual funds and vendors. Each of these types of firms will be discussed in more detail in the next chapter on Securities Industry Participants; however, the next section presents a high level comparison of how these businesses function and how people in these firms behave.

Brokers

Brokerage firms have been established to help investors access the securities markets. Brokers can either self-clear or can clear through a correspondent clearing firm. In this context, clearing refers to the entire back office process, and a firm either clears its own trades or hires another brokerage firm to process for them. If a firm does its own processing, it can either run the necessary systems in-house or use a service bureau. If it runs systems in-house, the systems can either be developed by the firm or acquired from a software vendor.

Large brokers are frequently also dealers, and are called broker/dealers. In this book we will use the term brokers to mean brokers as well as broker/dealers, except where it is necessary to differentiate between the types of firms.

A brokerage firm is frequently a principal to the trade.

- A brokerage firm can become a principal to the trade when it becomes responsible for the settlement of a client's trade.

- A broker can also be a principal to the trade when it acts as a dealer and completes a trade by buying or selling from its own positions. A dealer can also be called a market maker in OTC securities when it marks-up a purchase price or marks-down a sale price as it resells the security to its client.

- When a broker uses a correspondent clearer, the correspondent clearer also becomes a principal to the trade, and its role in the processing of the transaction must be clearly disclosed to the client. Confirmations and statements must be clearly marked to show the role of the broker and the involvement of any correspondent clearer.

Banks

Banks typically only act as an agent for their client and normally process their own transactions. When they use another bank for processing the service is usually called Private Label (or White Label) processing, and the processor acts as an agent for the initiating bank. The fact that there is another bank involved in the transaction does not have to be disclosed to the client, and confirmations, advices and statements only show the name of the initiating bank.

One important service provided by banks is securities custody. Many types of clients prefer to keep their assets in one central point, and not with a broker. Banks offer a full range of services that can safekeep and maintain these security assets on behalf of a client. The bank acts as an agent and the securities are registered in the client's name. If the assets remained at a brokerage firm, the assets would be in the broker's name, with the client as the beneficial owner.

For several years, banks were able to establish their own brokerage firm under Section 20 of the Glass-Steagall Act if the bank was organized as a Holding Company. A Section 20 brokerage firm acted like a regular broker.

In November, 1999, significant parts of the Glass-Steagall Act and the Bank Holding Company Act were repealed. Banks, brokerage firms and insurance companies are now allowed to merge and to sell each other's products.

Investment Managers

Investment managers usually define themselves in terms of the type of investment advice they provide. For instance, a manager may only focus on small-cap stocks or may only invest in U.S. based technology stocks, etc.

Investment managers also manage portfolios for pensions, institutions and/or mutual funds. Because the regulations are different for each of these categories of clients, there are different requirements for the manager. These differences will be discussed in the chapter on Investment Manager Processing.

Mutual Funds

Mutual Funds are characterized by their investment strategy, and overall the industry is exhibiting rapid growth with a wide diversity of investments. Mutual Funds were initially conceived as a way to simplify individuals' investment decisions. Now there are more Mutual Funds available than there are equities traded on the NYSE and the task of deciding between mutual fund alternatives has become complex.

Mutual Funds are discussed in the chapter on Mutual Fund Processing and in the chapter on Fund Products.

F. PEOPLE CONCEPTS

Another way to distinguish between these firms is to describe the way that people work in the firms.

- People in a brokerage firm normally have a very detailed experience in a small number of functional areas. They know a lot about a few topics, and they have a compensation plan that involves a reasonable base salary with the potential for a significant bonus if the firm does well. This makes brokers very well informed about their areas of responsibility and very cost conscientious.

- Bankers typically are moved around their firms more frequently, and therefore tend to know something about many topics. Bankers also usually receive a higher base salary, but have a limited bonus potential, so they tend to have a broader understanding of the securities business and have less incentive to worry about costs as long as they are within their budget.

- Investment Managers are frequently owner-managed, which makes them very cost conscious, and the firm is increasingly compensated based upon its investment performance. For many years, managers received a set fee that was calculated as a percentage of the assets held for managing a portfolio, regardless of whether it did well or poorly. If the portfolio's return beat an industry average, or dropped below the average, the manager received the same compensation.

Institutional clients for these services now typically require that the manager share in the risk, and will allow the manager to share in the gain. This means that while a manager might receive a small fixed fee to manage the portfolio, a major portion of the manager's compensation can come from the performance of the portfolio. If the return on the portfolio beats the specified averages, then the manager gets to share in the success; but if it fails to beat an average, the manager may not receive any additional compensation. This helps the manager to focus very clearly on the performance of the portfolio.

Investment managers are usually smaller than the banks and brokers they use, but their staff still has to be knowledgeable in many different areas.

- Mutual Funds have a unique set of processing requirements since they are often investment managers themselves, plus they have to keep track of the amount each investor has made into each fund.

G. Purpose of Securities Instruments

There are a variety of instruments that are designed to meet the issuer's need for funds and the investors' need to balance risk and return.

- Equity provides some ownership, which could result in dividends and participation in the growth of the firm.
- Debt carries a promise to repay the principal and a defined amount of interest for a specified period of time.
- Derivatives are based upon the value of some other financial instrument, and since they generally are financially leveraged they offer a very high potential return (along with high risk).

All securities instruments are created as a contract that gives the investor some rights that are granted by the issuer in exchange for their investment.

Most of the securities that are created follow some standards that are used in the market. For instance, if a firm creates a new common stock issue, the terms of that issue are typically standard throughout the market. However, issuers can also create a unique instrument within the existing laws, where the terms of the investment are specifically and perhaps even uniquely defined.

H. Trade Processing Summary

The full trade life cycle consists of five distinct steps:

1. Pre-Trade

In the pre-trade process, individual and institutional investors determine what they want to buy or sell.

2. Trade Order and Execution

The trade process starts when a buy or sell instruction is given to a broker. The broker enters the order into his system, and the trade is then passed on to the trading areas for execution.

An order is executed when a counterparty agrees to the trade. At that time the trade date is established, and a contract to settle on a specified date is also established. The minimum required data is:

- Securities identifier
- Execution price
- Trade amount
- Trade date
- Parties to the trade

The confirmation contains the details of the trade, and is sent via paper for a retail client, and electronically through one or more of the approved confirmation methods for institutional trades.

3. Clearing

Brokers settle between themselves using a process called clearing, which results in a net settlement.

4. Settlement

Settlement is the final exchange of securities for money.

- Individuals deal with brokerage firms on a cash basis.
- Institutions deal through the DTCC on a Deliver vs. Payment (DVP) basis.

After a trade has been settled, the event is recorded in the firm's books and in the client's portfolio.

- Settlement date accounting is used by most retail clients.
- Trade date accounting is generally used for portfolio managers and institutional investors who are managing pension funds.

Settlement can either be contractual or actual.

- Actual settlement occurs when the trade actually settles, and some forms of record keeping are based upon the actual date.
- Contractual settlement is used when a firm records a settlement on the date when it is contracted to settle, rather than the date when it actually does settle. Pension funds and mutual funds generally use this process to recognize that they have incurred a financial obligation when the trade is made.

5. Asset Servicing

After the trade has been settled, the process of servicing the asset begins, and continues for as long as the investor holds the security.

II. Securities Industry Participants

There are a variety of categories of participants in the securities industry. These participants can be divided into the following categories:

- Issuers
- Individual Investors
- Institutional Investors
- Financial Intermediaries

Except for the individual investors, the participants are usually organized in one of the following business structures:

- Sole Proprietorship
- Partnership
- Limited Liability Corporation
- Corporation

In this chapter, we will examine the characteristics of individual and institutional investors, and the business structures that are used most often by the firms in the industry.

A. INDIVIDUAL INVESTORS

The total amount that individuals have invested in securities has grown significantly over the past twenty years.

The majority of these investments have gone into mutual funds, but there has also been a strong growth in the volume of purchases and sales of other specific securities.

In addition to the total amounts invested, the percentage of individual assets that are invested in securities has also grown significantly. In 1998 the amount that individual households invested in securities exceeded for the first time the amount invested in their primary residence.

Individual investors, also called retail investors, have several specific characteristics that distinguish the type of account they open and the type of securities they will purchase.

- Most of the retail investors who purchase securities directly, rather than through a mutual fund, buy a small number of shares or bonds at any one time.
- Individual investors are required by their broker to pay on or before the settlement date for a purchase. The settlement date is the day on which the securities and cash are actually exchanged.
- Individuals usually have only one account or a few accounts.
- Since most individuals buy in small amounts, they are not able to negotiate a better commission, and typically pay fixed rates or a spread imposed by the broker/dealer.
- For most retail clients, the buying broker usually holds the investor's securities.

Individual Investors – Types of Individual Investors

Different types of people have different investment styles based upon a variety of factors including their propensity for risk.

- Professional Management
- Stock Pickers
- Mutual Fund Investors
- Day Traders

Individual Investors - Professional Management

Individuals with sufficient assets can obtain professional money management for their portfolio.

Stock Pickers

Some individuals believe that they can select individual stocks for long term investment on their own. There are a variety of web-based tools that are now available for individuals.

Mutual Fund Investors

Most individuals do not have sufficient liquid assets to obtain individual professional money management, nor sufficient time or inclination to invest on their own. These people generally select Mutual Funds.

Day Traders

Another category of individual investor is a day trader. Day traders are retail clients who lease access to a broker's transaction processing systems, and try to trade like an institutional professional. Over 100 firms in the U.S. now offer their facilities to individuals who wish to trade actively. It was estimated that in mid-1999 at least 5,000 people in the U.S. were active Day Traders. The number peaked in early 2000 and then dropped significantly along with the stock market. Day Trader activity started to return in mid-2003 although will probably not become as frantic as it was in the late 1990s.

Traders are required to open an account with at least $50,000, and are normally not allowed to hold any positions overnight, thus the derivation of their name. Day traders must close out all of their positions by the end of the day to avoid overnight risk.

Day traders are different from retail clients who use their own equipment and the Internet to buy and sell securities. As many as 5,000,000 people in the U.S. occasionally buy and sell using the Internet from their homes or offices. At its peak, these trades accounted for 15% of the NASDAQ volume.

B. BUSINESS STRUCTURES IN THE SECURITIES INDUSTRY

There are several different types of business structures that can open securities accounts, but not all of them can issue equity or debt securities. In this section we will look at each type of business structure and how each type of business can raise capital or invest their excess funds.

Sole Proprietor

A sole proprietor is the owner/operator of what is normally a small business. This is typically the owner of a small store, a taxi driver or an independent consultant. If the sole proprietor gets sick or doesn't work, no revenue is earned.

Raising Capital

As a result, a sole proprietor is very limited in his opportunity to raise capital. To cover their risk, if a bank lends the owner money, the bank may require the owner to take out a disability insurance policy or a life insurance policy for the duration of the loan at the sole proprietor's expense. It is almost impossible for a sole proprietorship to raise capital in the securities market.

Invest Excess Funds

Unlike other businesses, sole proprietors usually invest as individuals.

Partnership

There are regular partnerships and a special form of partnership called a Limited Partnership. In a regular partnership, each partner owns a specified share of the business and is liable up to the amount of their ownership. Limited Partnerships have two classes of partners:

General Partner

The General Partner (GP) manages the business, is usually an expert in the field and contributes little, if any, money to the firm although the GP is personally liable.

Limited Partner

The Limited Partner (LP) usually supplies all of the money, and may receive most of the profits. However, the LP's liability, and risk, is limited to the amount of his investment.

Partnerships do not directly pay any taxes. Profits and/or losses are passed on to the individual partners, and the activity of the partnership is reported on the personal tax returns of the individual partners.

Raising Capital

A partnership form of business is slightly better than a sole proprietorship from the point of raising capital since there are two or more people sharing common goals, profits and losses, and banks are slightly more willing to lend money.

There are different types of risks and benefits in this form of business.

- If one partner gets sick, the other partner can continue the business, and the business doesn't close for the day. However, if one of the partners leaves or dies, the partnership is dissolved, and a new one has to be established.

- The general partners can be sued, even for their personal assets; however, a new form of partnership has been created that has the tax advantages of a partnership, but with the legal liability limited as with a corporation. It is called a Limited Liability Corporation, or LLC, and is described separately in this chapter.

Invest Excess Funds

A partnership can open a business securities account by filling in the appropriate forms as is shown in the chapter on Account Opening.

Limited Liability Corporation

A new type of legal entity, called a Limited Liability Corporation (LLC), has been defined that includes some of the tax rights of a partnership and the legal protection of a corporation.

Raising Capital

The LLC currently has the same limited ability as a regular partnership to raise capital in the securities markets.

Invest Excess Funds

The LLC can open a business account for securities by filling in the appropriate forms, which are discussed in the chapter on Account Opening.

Corporations

A corporation is the most common form of business structure for institutional investors in the securities industry.

In order to begin conducting business as a corporation, the firm must first properly complete the required forms and register with the Secretary of State in the state in which the business will be incorporated. The Secretary of State issues a certificate of incorporation. With this official document, the corporation is considered a legal entity and does business as a result of this license.

The type of business that a corporation can conduct is defined in its corporate charter, which includes several types of information.

Identification

The name and address of the corporation are identified, and the names and addresses of the officers and directors of the corporation are listed.

Purpose

The specific purpose of the business is identified in a charter, along with other intentions/possibilities for future activities. The charter is designed to cover everything that the firm may wish to do in the future so that the firm does not have to keep amending its charter.

Capital Statement

The capital statement is the numerical description of how the firm is capitalized. Capital consists of equity and debt.

The charter normally allows corporations to open bank and securities accounts in the name of the corporation and to issue equity and debt on behalf of the corporation.

Raising Capital

There are two kinds of stock that represent the ownership of the corporation: common and preferred. By law, the firm must maintain these two categories of equity as separate types of capital. We will talk more about these different types of equity in the chapter on Equities.

A firm's total amount of either common or preferred shares that are authorized is defined in the firm's Certificate of Incorporation. When a firm gives or sells shares, those shares are considered to be *authorized and issued*. Any authorized shares that remain are considered *authorized and unissued*.

There is also another type of equity that is known as treasury stock. This is common or preferred stock that has been issued by a corporation, but was re-acquired by the corporation through purchases or donations. Treasury stock receives no dividends and has no right to vote. Since the holder of treasury stock (the corporation) does not share in the profits, this class of stock is not used to calculate the earnings per share, which improves earning per share.

The corporate float is that amount of *issued and outstanding* stock that is in the hands of the public. The public is defined as those shareholders that are not part of management. A public issue of stock is considered to be thin if a large percentage of the stock is held by the managers of the corporation. Management-held stock tends to stay in the hands of management.

Invest Excess Funds

Corporations can open accounts in their own name and conduct business in the name of the corporation. This requires specific documentation, which is discussed in the chapter on Account Opening.

Trusts

A trust is a legal entity that requires an agreement defining the terms of the trust, a trustee who has specific responsibilities, and a beneficiary who has specific rights. A trust can be established in any one of three categories:

- Personal Trust – a trust that is established to benefit one or more individuals
- Institutional Trust – a trust that has been established to hold the investments for activities such as pensions, foundations, etc.
- Corporate Trust – the type of trust that is established by a bank to manage the activities that are involved when equities and bonds have been issued to the public

These three categories of trust are described in more detail later in this chapter.

The trust is formed through a trust agreement, which is a legal contract that can range from tens to hundreds of pages. Each agreement can have many unique clauses, and that is what makes administering a trust account so difficult and costly.

A trust agreement defines exactly how a trust account will work. It defines:

- How funds will be received, invested and disbursed
- Required reporting
- The role of the trustees
- Payment of legal, trustee, and other fees
- Liability of trustees

Any individual or legal entity can be a trustee and the trustee has a fiduciary responsibility for a trust. The trustee is responsible for receipts, disbursement, and investing the trust's assets. When a bank acts as a trustee, it can act as an agent or as a fiduciary. When it acts as a fiduciary, it takes on specific legal responsibilities.

As defined by the Employee Retirement Income Security Act (ERISA), which is described later in this chapter, a fiduciary is "one who occupies a position of confidence or trust and who exercises any power or control, management, or disposition with respect to monies or other property of a fund or who has authority or responsibility to do so." The fiduciary responsibility includes several specific requirements.

- The fiduciary must be loyal to the trust, not to himself or to his firm.
- Trusts are conservative by nature and the trustee is required to try to preserve the trust's assets.
- The trustee must ensure that the principal of the trust is segregated from the income it receives since the original principal is not taxable when it is distributed since it normally would have been taxed before it was placed in the trust. The trust's income is taxable to the beneficiary when the income is withdrawn.
- The trustee must be careful in how he performs his duties, and is legally accountable. A trustee can be sued for failure to properly perform his duties, and there are criminal penalties if the trustee engages in fraud.
- Trusts also specify how the income of the trust is to be distributed, and the trustee must ensure that this is done in accordance with the trust agreement.

Trusts contain assets, which can include:

- Financial Assets, such as securities and cash
- Real Property
- Business(s)

When a trust makes investments, it must be authorized to do so by the trust agreement. This authorization is discussed in the chapter on Account Opening.

If a firm has investment discretion over a trust account, the firm must have a clear investment policy that is auditable. The Office of the Comptroller of the Currency (OCC) will review these policies under Regulation 9.

The account administration of a trust is complex because of the potential customization of every account. The record keeping for the trust must be very clear and maintained for the life of the trust, which can involve generations.

Raising Capital

A trust does not raise capital in the market. The funds that are put into a trust come from individuals or institutions and the funds usually have already been taxed.

Invest Excess Funds

Personal and institutional trusts are normally engaged in investing their assets and may open accounts for this purpose. Opening a trust account requires some specific documentation that is discussed in the chapter on Account Opening.

C. INSTITUTIONAL INVESTORS

The Securities accounts that can be opened by these businesses, which are also called institutional investors, have several common characteristics.

- An institutional investor is an institution that has a pool of funds that can be invested in a range of assets. These assets can include securities, real estate, commodities, derivatives, etc. Institutional investors include banks, mutual funds, charitable institutions, universities and employee benefit plans.

- These accounts can be a standard investment account (also called a custody account or a safekeeping account) that is similar to an individual's cash account, or they can be trust accounts that could be used for pensions or estates. Each of these types of accounts has specific rules associated with it.

- Accounts opened in the name of a partnership are generally opened as standard investment accounts, although different forms are required.

- Investments are typically in large amounts, with block trades common.

- Institutional clients often use investment managers to make purchase and sale decisions for their portfolios.

- Most trades are made as Deliver vs. Payment (DVP), with a custodian bank involved in the settlement.

- Clients typically have multiple accounts and may have multiple investment managers.

- Soft Dollar arrangements are common.

In addition to their common characteristics, there are several things that make each institutional investor structure unique.

D. ISSUERS

Issuers consist of corporations, agencies and governments that wish to raise funds. They are supported by the banks, brokers and investment banks that offer underwriting services.

The role of Issuers is discussed in detail in the chapter on Creating New Securities.

E. CATEGORIES OF FINANCIAL INTERMEDIARIES

Financial Intermediaries are the banks, brokers, mutual funds, insurance companies and investment managers who help bring together investors and issuers.

Banks

Banks have been traditionally considered to be a safe place to put money, while receiving a modest return. Banks also have provided a number of processing services for individuals and institutions, including:

- Checking accounts (also called demand deposits)
- Savings accounts
- Time deposits, including Certificates of Deposit
- Unsecured lending
- Secured lending
- Funds transfers from one bank to another
- Foreign exchange

Trends

Several trends in the financial services industry have caused the traditional banking business to decline for many years.

- Disintermediation has been caused by the introduction of products such as Commercial Paper (CP). The bank's role as a financial intermediary can be eliminated when the bank's traditional clients begin dealing directly with other bank clients as they do with CP.

- The retail investors' shift towards mutual funds and away from the non-interest bearing checking accounts and low yielding savings accounts that have been traditionally provided by banks has eliminated a key source of low cost funding for banks.

- The introduction of the Cash Management Account by brokerage firms attracted assets that were historically held in banks. This type of account is described in the section on brokers.

- Increased competition between banks and the large number of bank mergers has resulted in significantly lower margins.

Because of these trends, in the last twenty-five years the amount of personal assets held by banks has declined from 36% of an individual's personal assets to 17%. The money has generally moved from bank checking and savings accounts to brokerage firms and other investments.

According to industry legend, bankers used to engage in a business strategy called 3-3-3. The bankers planned to take deposits from their local community on which they paid 3% interest. They marked this up by 3% and made long-term mortgage loans to people who lived in their town. Then, they were on the golf course by 3 p.m.

In the early 1980's, Walter Wriston, then the chairman of Citibank, which was at that point the largest bank in the world, saw the coming end of this golden age, and said "I have seen the future of banking, and it is Merrill Lynch." When he said this, he was recognizing that the future of banking would no longer be the safe and profitable business where banks could easily make very large spreads between deposits and loans. Banks would have to begin to try to survive in the very competitive world of investments and securitized products.

More recently, another Citibank alumnus, Richard Kovacevich, now the President and CEO of Wells Fargo & Company has said, "Banking is necessary, banks are not." He saw that the traditional competitors are being challenged by non-traditional competitors who can provide the services that banks provide without the restrictions and inefficiencies that hamper banks.

These trends have reduced the number of commercial banks in the U.S. from 13,000 in 1988 by over one-third in the last fifteen years, to about 8,000 banks in 2003. This downward trend has continued.

Regulations

To survive, banks have attempted to migrate towards delivering investment products. Now there are several different types of complex and competitive securities functions performed by banks. However, many of these functions were provided via trust accounts or special purpose subsidiaries, called Section 20 Brokerages because of the Glass-Steagall Act.

For over sixty-five years the 1933 Glass-Steagall Act required this separation of activities. This law was passed after the 1929 market crash to prevent certain of the excesses that led to the depression. It required that banks, brokers and insurance companies not operate within a single business entity with mingled cash and risks. Major parts of this law were repealed in 1999, which once again allows banks to operate full brokerage subsidiaries.

The McFadden Act further restricted the market that a bank could cover to a single state. This led to banks initially being focused on specific types of services and to a limited geography within the U.S. Other commercial banks tried to satisfy their state's requirements and eventually grew to cover neighboring states. These banks came to be known as Regional Banks.

Since there were no U.S. restrictions on what a bank could do outside of the U.S., some banks began to market to their state and to the rest of the world. These banks came to be known as Money Center Banks since most of them were operating out of what was considered to be *the* money center for the world, New York City. Today, many banks outside of NYC are act as Money Center Banks.

Categories of Banks

In addition to the geographic differences, there are several different types of banks, based upon the types of clients they serve:

- Retail Banks
- Commercial Banks
- Custodian Banks
- Trust Banks
- Private Banks

Retail Banks

Retail Banks deal primarily with the banking and investment needs of individuals, which include:

- Secured and unsecured loans - Secured loans offered by banks for the purpose of buying securities are similar to the margin loans offered by brokers and are called purpose loans.
- Checking and savings accounts
- Electronic funds transfers
- Purchase and sale of mutual funds and securities through specific-purpose subsidiaries
- Bank investment products such as Certificates of Deposit

Commercial Banks

Commercial Banks provide a variety of services to institutions, including:

- Loans to commercial firms that may be secured or unsecured
- Loans to brokerage firms to help the brokers finance their positions

- Underwriting services through the bank's corporate finance department
- Supporting the international purchase and sale of goods and materials
- Clearing of U.S. government securities
- Securities custody services

Custodian Banks

Custody is the safekeeping and administration of securities and cash on behalf of others. This function can be either the primary purpose of the firm or one department in the bank. The administrative activities can be as agent or as a fiduciary. The servicing activities can include:

- Trade Processing
  - Monitoring the purchase and sale of securities via brokers
  - Receiving and delivering of securities (settlement)
  - Advising clients of every movement in the account (reporting)
  - Accounting for every possible type of securities and derivative (accounting)
  - Safekeeping of shares through a central depository or in a vault if necessary
- Post Settlement Processing
  - Income Collection
    - Collecting dividends and interest
  - Corporate Actions
    - Collecting principal and revenue at maturity
    - Supervising drawings, lotteries, etc.
    - Responding to offers (tenders, exchanges, exercises, etc.)
    - Registering securities and processing nominee functions
  - Cash Management
    - Offering STIF (Short-Term Investment Funds)
    - Processing foreign exchange
    - Providing credit against collateral
  - Pricing of positions and maintaining reference data
  - Accounting
  - Reporting
    - Providing periodic statements of the account
    - Delivering electronic information
  - Client Servicing
  - Advisor Communications
  - Reconciliations
  - Performance Measurement

- Securities Lending

A custodian may perform its services for institutions, or for individuals who are usually very wealthy private clients, called High Net Worth Individuals (HNWI), through legal entities or departments typically called Private Banks.

- Domestic Custodians process U.S. securities for U.S. firms and for international firms. The custodians are responsible for coordinating their clients' transactions between brokers, investment advisors and the appropriate U.S. depository.

Domestic Custodian	2003 Assets	
State Street	6,959	
The Bank of New York	6,176	
JPMorgan	4,864	
Mellon Group	2,760	
Citigroup	2,130	
Northern Trust	1,476	
SIS Segaintersettle AG	965	
Investors Bank and Trust	869	
Wachovia	847	
HSBC	786	
Sub-total	27,832	85.6%
Top 25 Domestic Custodians	32,514	100.0%

Figure 15 - Domestic Custodian Rankings

- Global Custodians co-ordinate the movement of information between their clients, their clients' investment manager(s) and the appropriate sub-custodians in the countries where their clients have investments. A global custodian actually re-enters every transaction into its own systems and re-processes the transaction to build the appropriate records in a consistent fashion.

Global Custodian	2003 Assets	
State Street	9,400	
The Bank of New York	8,577	
JPMorgan	7,098	
Citigroup	6,381	
Mellon Group	3,500	
UBS AG	2,398	
Northern Trust	2,300	
BNP Paribas	2,167	
HSBC	1,483	
Société General	1,165	
Sub-total	44,469	82.2%
Top 25 Global Custodians	54,106	

Figure 16 - Global Custodian Rankings

This book does not go into any detail regarding the role and functions of a global custodian.

Trust Banks

A bank can perform custody directly for its institutional or private clients, or it can perform these services for a trust. There are several different types of trust that are discussed on the following pages.

Personal Trust

Personal trusts are established for the benefit of a single individual or a small number of individuals. These beneficiaries may receive the principal from the trust, the income, or both, according to the terms of the trust.

Personal trust accounts involve a trust agreement that defines the terms of the trust, a trustee (or fiduciary) who is legally responsible to enforce the terms of the trust and a beneficiary (or beneficiaries) who receives money from the trust.

The trustees can be individuals or institutions such as a bank. Within a bank's personal trust activities, the bank may also offer an investment service where investment decisions are made on behalf of the client.

These discretionary accounts grant the portfolio manager the right to buy and sell securities at his own discretion, usually within some boundaries. The portfolio manager is typically not allowed to move cash out of the account. Many personal accounts are non-discretionary, and the manager (or broker) acts only as an advisor.

Institutional Trust Services

The most common form of institutional trust is for employee benefit programs, which are retirement plans. These plans fall into two major categories:

Defined Benefit Plans

A defined benefit plan is usually funded by the corporation, and the retiree is promised a specific amount upon retirement based upon factors such as number of years of service, last average salary, etc.

Defined Contribution Plans

The individual and/or the employer may fund a defined contribution plan. Retirees do not know how much money will be in the plan when they retire since each person is responsible for making personal investment decisions, and the value of the plan will be the result of these decisions. The person only knows how much they put into the plan.

Personal trust and institutional trust activities support accounts that hold securities for individual or institutional investors. There is another type of trust service that is provided by banks for the issuers of securities and the investors.

Corporate Trust

A corporate trust department provides a variety of services for investors regarding the issues that they hold. In this case, the bank acts as an agent for the holders of the debt instrument, but the bank is paid by the issuer.

There are several different types of agent functions that can be performed by a bank's corporate trust department. These functions will be discussed in the chapter on Bank Processing.

Private Banking

The private banking business was initiated in Europe as a very personalized form of banking service reserved for the very wealthy. The clients of these services could expect the bank to do everything in its power to keep them happy, to protect their assets and to help them make more money. Over the years, the private banking business has expanded rapidly as many more banks got into this business and many more people had increasing sums of investable funds.

Today, there are many different levels of private banking services, some for individuals with as little as $100,000 in investable assets. Most, however, establish a minimum threshold of $1 million or $5 million. The clients, called high net worth individuals (HNWI), are provided with banking and securities services that frequently combine traditional banking and brokerage services, along with a significant level of hand holding. This is a very personalized service.

Broker/Dealers

While there are many different types of brokerage firms, the primary roles of a brokerage firm are to:

- Assist clients in buying and selling securities, commodities and other financial instruments
- Provide a custody service for the assets
- Provide periodic statements of the assets in the account

In general, brokers constitute the *sell-side* of the business (whether they are buying or selling securities), and the investment managers constitute the *buy-side*.

Trends

There are several categories of trends that are affecting brokers

Business Focus

Decimalization has had and continues to have a serious impact on the profitability of broker/dealers. Firms are finding it more difficult to maintain their profits through the spreads they receive on their trades as a market maker. By reducing their inventory they can reduce their capital costs and will rely more on commissions and fees.

Competition increases with traditional competitors and non-traditional competitors. The full impact of the repeal of Glass-Steagall was delayed because of the financial recession of 2000, but has been increasing over the last year. This repeal causes the distinctions between banks, brokers and insurance companies to become very blurred.

Client Confidence that declined as a result of the numerous corporate scandals and perceived ties between underwriters and issuers has not yet returned. Until small investors return in large numbers the trade volume will tend to have significant increases and decreases as all of the 'experts' react in a similar fashion.

Technology

Through the last years of the century, firms were concerned about how to maximize their use of the interest and browser technology. Technology investment was extensive as firms were afraid of being left behind. As the internet bubble burst, volumes declines, new issues disappeared, and technology investment plummeted. It is only now starting to increase again after several years of actual year-to-year declines.

Since the internet frenzy, the focus was on T+1 and the related requirement for Straight Through Processing. Without sufficient investment capital, the industry determined that it really didn't understands the business case for T+1, and the definition of STP changed to include incremental improvements.

Now, we are seeing another wave of demand flow through the industry that includes increased attention to compliance, new opportunities for electronic trading, and a suddenly obvious need for client relationship management applications. All of these technical needs require improved connectivity and standards.

Trading

The trading process has been changing significantly over the last few years as a number of vendors have provided new alternative trading systems (ATS) and electronic connectivity networks (ECN) that have opened up many opportunities for more efficient equity trading. In the last year, fixed income traders are finally getting new automated alternatives that will cause numerous change sin how fixed income trading is conducted.

Regulation

In a legislative reaction to the scandals, firms are faced with a major wave of new regulation that must be attended to, regardless of whether it makes processing more efficient or increases profitability. This trend is likely to continue for several years as regulations are enacted and revised.

Regulations

Broker/Dealers are closely regulated by the SEC and multiple Self-Regulatory Organizations. The primary regulations are the '33 Act and the Exchange Act and the subsequent amendments that are discussed in the chapter on Regulators and Legislation.

Brokers vs. Dealers

Despite these differences, we still usually talk about these firms as being brokers or broker/dealers. In fact, brokers and dealers are different businesses.

Broker

A broker is any person or firm buying and selling securities for a client's account as part of his regular business. Brokers act an agent for their clients, and execute client orders to buy/sell securities.

Brokers generally get their revenue from the commissions they charge.

Dealer

A dealer is any person or firm making securities transactions for his own account, and which therefore acts as a principal to the trade.

Dealers invest their own capital to purchase/sell securities from/to clients and profit from the mark-up they charge on purchases or the mark-down charged on sales, which is called the spread.

A dealer in the over-the-counter market is called a market maker.

There is a special type of dealer called a Primary Dealer, which is discussed separately in this chapter.

The largest brokerage firms are often brokers and dealers and are therefore called broker/dealers, although the two functions must be kept separate by law. But, like everyone else, in this book we will usually just say broker to encompass all of these concepts.

Categories of Broker/Dealers

The two major types of brokerage firm are:

- Full Service Firms
- Discount Firms

Full Service Firms

Full service firms offer investment advice to their clients along with execution and transaction processing services. These firms typically charge minimum account fees to clients who do not trade above a minimum level. Almost all of the full service firms are adding electronic online accounts, which are described later in this chapter.

Discount Firms

Discount firms have not historically offered investment advice along with their execution and transaction processing services, and are rapidly shifting to online accounts. As they move to online and Internet-based delivery, many firms are beginning to purchase investment advice from full service firms and are delivering this information to their online clients.

Discount firms were first established when commissions were deregulated in 1975. Prior to that time, all brokers charged the same commissions and provided very similar services.

Once fixed rates were abolished, each firm could set its own rates, which were theoretically negotiated with the client. In effect, retail rates were still set by each broker, although some chose to eliminate some services and charge minimal discount rates. Institutions, due to their larger buying power, could actually negotiate rates.

Over time, the differences between full service firms and discounters have tended to disappear as full service firms now offer discounted electronic accounts and discount brokers add more research to their product offering.

Market Focus

Another way of looking at brokers is along the following dimensions. Both full service and discount firms can be any one or more of the following types of firms.

Member Firm

A member firm is a member of one or more registered stock exchange(s), with a basic business of buying and selling securities for its clients on the stock exchanges of which it is a member.

Investment Banking Firm / Underwriter

An investment banking firm creates and distributes new securities to the public. It frequently buys issues from a corporation, and then sells the securities to the public at a price that includes the firm's profit.

Over-the-Counter (OTC) Firm

An OTC firm does not buy and sell securities on an exchange. Instead, it buys and sells securities *over-the-counter*, which is the purchase and sale of securities on NASDAQ or directly between brokers.

Most large securities firms do business in all three of these areas.

Functional Focus

Brokerages can also be described by the various functions they perform, which can be:

Introducing Broker

The introducing broker is the firm that owns the relationship with the client. This function is either performed by an independent broker or the sales office of a brokerage firm.

Executing Broker

The executing broker is a firm that has a seat on an exchange, or which is a dealer or market maker for its own account. This function is the one where the broker finds a counterparty for the client's trade, either by finding another broker or using his own positions.

When an executing broker settles a trade by buying or selling the securities directly, they are acting as a dealer.

Clearing Broker

A clearing broker is a firm that has its own back office processing functions. The clearing broker might have his own system (either developed, purchased or leased) or use a time-sharing service provided by a firm such as ADP.

Although there are thousands of brokers in the U.S., only a few hundred either clear for themselves (self-clearing) or clear for others (correspondent clearers).

Electronic Brokers

Due to the increasing commoditization of the retail trade function, nearly one-third of all retail trading is already conducted via some form of online access. It is also estimated that about 60 million households in the U.S. use the Internet as of 2004 and 4.3 million already have portfolios over $100,000, so there will probably be considerable growth of online accounts in the next few years.

The number of brokers that provide electronic services in the U.S. has continued to increase in the past few years, despite the industry slowdown. According to a variety of surveys, the top online brokers in 2004 are:

- Charles Schwab & Co.
- Fidelity Brokerage Services
- CSFBdirect (formerly DLJ Direct)
- Datek Online
- Ameritrade
- Merrill Lynch Direct

Primary Dealer

There are a limited number of Primary Dealers, which are broker/dealers that have been granted a special status to act as a dealer in the government securities market.

Prime Broker

When a broker acts as a prime broker for their client, they are taking on the responsibility to consolidate the assets in one place. The prime broker or other brokers could execute the trades, but all of the assets are settled with the prime broker.

The prime broker provides settlement, safekeeping, asset servicing and financing support to their clients, regardless of which broker executed the trades.

Correspondent Clearing

When a broker sells its excess processing capacity to another broker it is acting as a correspondent clearer. There are over 120 brokerage firms in the U.S. clearing for other firms. The five largest clearers in the U.S. in terms of the number of accounts serviced are Bear Stearns, Pershing, Wexford Clearing, Spear, Leeds & Kellogg, and First Clearing/Wexford. As shown in the chart, of the top 25 clearing brokers, the top five serve 66% of the correspondent brokers.

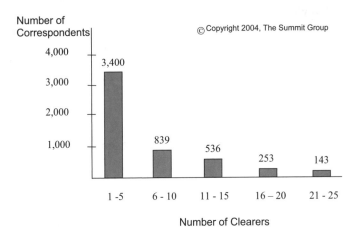

Figure 17 - Distribution of Correspondent Clearers

A correspondent clearer actually becomes a party to the trade, and accepts some of the trading risk. Several years ago the brokerage firm Hanover Sterling became insolvent, and due to the size of its debts, its correspondent clearer (Adler Coleman) was forced into bankruptcy along with Hanover Sterling.

Many brokers have chosen to use correspondent clearers since the cost to upgrade technology to keep up with the changes in the industry has become greater than many firms can absorb. And, as technology becomes commonly available, it is increasingly difficult for firms to differentiate themselves with an efficient back office.

The move to a shorter settlement period in 1995 caused many firms to rethink their processing strategy and to decide that a clearer was a more efficient option. As the number of regulations climbs and the cost to constantly upgrade technology increases each year the Correspondent Clearing business continues to grow.

Once again, the largest firms can provide all of these functions.

Insurance-Affiliated Brokers

There are some unusually features for most broker that are part of insurance companies, supporting the company and their clients.

Securities products that are sold by an insurance company can only be sold by agents who are registered representatives (who have passed the appropriate Series license exams). Insurance agents may be required to pass the Series 6, 7, 65 and 66 exams in order to sell their companies' products.

Most of the insurance companies' products are considered to be 'check and app' products, where the application and check are received and often are processed on to the product manufacturer.

The primary products offered by an insurance company that are broker-related are:

Mutual Funds

Most Mutual Funds that are sold by insurance agents who are also registered representatives are pass-throughs, where the purchase or sale of mutual fund shares are processed through the broker/dealer, but are not maintained in a client brokerage account. Once purchased, the primary relationship is between the mutual fund and the client. The mutual fund knows the client and sends the statements directly to the client.

Stocks and Bonds

Most insurance agents do not attempt to sell individual stocks and bonds, although that may be possible through their captive broker/dealer. Because of this, Insurance broker/dealers do not have to maintain a large number of client brokerage accounts, and usually do not self-clear.

Since they use a correspondent clearer, most brokers have only a few internal applications. They will probably have a books and records application that will manage the flow of information into and from the clearer, and commission applications that will allow the broker to calculate its commission on a transaction as it passes it to the product manufacturers.

Variable Annuity and Variable Life

The NSCC and DTC have recently develops some applications that specifically support the Variable Life and Variable Annuity products. Information flows through the broker/dealer to the NSCC and the completed transaction is verified back to the insurance company.

Broker/dealer subsidiaries of insurance companies have to work with the securities regulators to ensure that the regulators understand the nuances of their business. For instance, recently the NASD asked all brokers to provide information at the client level regarding the charges for mutual funds. It was very difficult for most insurance companies to comply since they do not keep the detailed client records – these are maintained by the mutual fund company in the normal course of business between an insurance company and a mutual fund provider. Most brokers would have recorded the transactions in a client brokerage account, while the insurance companies do not normally do so.

Broker Organization

Historically, brokers have been organized around a front office that has client contact and a back office that processes transactions.

The back office was originally organized to process paper transactions, and has retained that organizational flavor since trading began. In the 1960's the process of automating the back office began with the use of the available technology (batch processing), while automating one department after another. Those systems were eventually electronically linked, but much of the code that was written in the 1960's remains today in complex legacy systems.

As one way to move away from these legacy systems, firms have been establishing and expanding a new entity, the middle office.

The middle office, which typically combines some of the functions that have historically been conducted by the front office and/or the back office, usually consists of functions such as:

- Investment Accounting
- Risk Management
- Decision Support
- Trade Processing
- Client Services, etc.

There is no definitive line that divides the front from the middle, and the middle from the back.

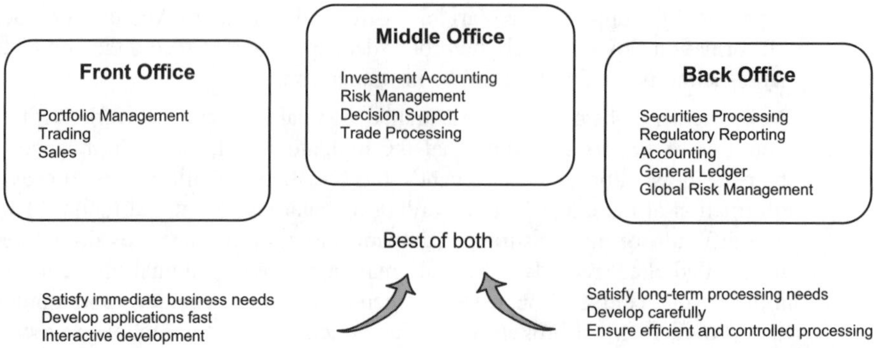

Figure 18 - Middle Office

- The front office technology units established a reputation in the 1980's for responding quickly and satisfying the immediate needs of the firm, often by using emerging technologies in a creative way.

- The back office has typically satisfied the firm's long-term processing needs with a highly structured systems development process, and an efficient and controlled processing environment.

Plan Sponsors

When a business wants to create a *defined benefit* retirement plan for its employees, it establishes the program under Department of Labor legislation called the Employee Retirement Income Security Act (ERISA). These rules require the firm, called the Plan Sponsor, to adequately fund the plan in order to meet the retirement obligations of the plan.

These plan sponsors select investment managers to make purchase and sale decisions within certain investment parameters, and select a custodian bank to safekeep the plan's assets and make periodic reports as required by ERISA.

When ERISA was established in 1974, it drove a large amount of business towards the banks as custodians. This business has become increasingly automated over the last ten years and is increasingly competitive.

When a firm establishes a *defined contribution program* for its employees, a third party administrator generally administers this program. The beneficiary typically invests in a limited range of mutual funds that are selected by the plan's trustees, who are usually the senior managers of the firm.

Investment Managers

Investment managers can be organized as sole proprietorships, partnerships or corporations, and these entities are regulated by the SEC under the Investment Advisors Act of 1940.

Investment managers, also commonly referred to as asset managers, are generally considered to be the buy-side of the industry since they buy services from brokers.

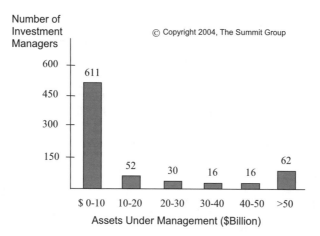

Figure 19 - Distribution of Investment Managers

Investment managers typically manage money for pension funds, mutual funds, high net worth individuals or other institutions. When they are supporting a pension fund, the plan sponsor chooses the custodian, and if the manager has multiple pension fund clients, they may have to deal with multiple custodians.

When the manager supports a mutual fund, it usually only supports a small number of fund administrators, and may deal with only one custodian.

Although the managers are not always able to direct their clients to a single custodian, which would reduce their costs and risks, they are able to direct their brokers (who see the manager as the client) towards various vendors of software. When the manager selects a vendor, the broker may have to also buy some software from the same vendor.

Investment managers can perform a variety of roles:

- Research and portfolio management
- Trading for their own account or for client portfolios when they have discretionary authority
- Providing investment advice when they do not have discretion to invest on their own

There are many different ways a traditional investment manager can make a profit, including:

Management/Advisory Fees

Management and Advisory Fees are charged to the client for managing the portfolio, which is typically a certain percentage of the assets under management.

Custodian/Administrative Fees

Custodian/Administrative Fees are charged to the client for custody and administrative services related to the account. Sometimes these fees are charged separately or included with the management fee.

Trading Commissions

If the investment manager's organization performs trading, the IM can receive a certain percentage of the trading commissions.

Performance Fees

If an investment manager reaches a certain targeted return a performance fee can be earned. Some performance fees are based on the investment manager reaching a minimum return (e.g., hurdle rate) before the performance fee begins to accrue. Traditionally, hedge funds are known for charging performance fees.

Challenges

Investment management firms generally have relatively fixed costs with good upside potential. Some of the current challenges that investment management firms face are as follows:

Obtaining Competitive Returns

In order to attract new business and maintain their existing clients, managers must obtain investment returns that are better than the averages and better than their competitors. This is measured by comparing against certain benchmarks.

Pay for Performance

Most firms now have an additional incentive to perform well since their compensation is frequently tied directly to their performance in the market. Firms that do not beat the averages may not receive very much compensation for their efforts.

Business Continuity

With the events of September 11th, there has been significant emphasis on organizations reviewing their business continuity/resumptions plans to ensure that if there was a catastrophic event, their organizations are prepared to get their businesses back up and running for critical business operations.

Pressure on Fees Charged

As clients become more sophisticated and investment manager services become more competitive, there tends to be a downward pressure on fees. So investment managers need to continue to differentiate themselves in the marketplace to maintain their client base.

Growth of Index Funds

The growth of index funds as a form of passive investment has removed a significant amount of investment capital from active managers.

Plan sponsors have been forced to allocate a portion of their investment assets in passive forms of investment since, on average, more than half of the managers do not beat the averages. The plan sponsors have a fiduciary responsibility to the plans and have not been able to justify investing all of their assets with active managers based upon the overall returns of the managers in the industry.

Growth of Exchange Traded Funds (ETF)

ETF's are similar to index mutual funds, but are traded more like a stock. As their name implies, Exchange Traded Funds (ETFs) represent a basket of securities that are traded on an exchange. ETFs are discussed in more detail in the chapter on Fund Product.

Controlling Costs

Investment managers must control their costs, since these costs are deducted from their clients' returns, while constantly upgrading their technology in order to remain competitive and to attract talented portfolio managers, analysts and traders.

Investment managers can also be involved in raising capital for their own use and in investing excess funds for their own use and for their clients' use.

Raising Capital

An investment management firm that is organized as a corporation may raise capital in the securities market just like any other corporation. Investment managers can also be involved in raising capital for their own use and in investing excess funds for their own use and for their clients' use.

The primary role of investment managers is to find investment alternatives for their clients and themselves. An investment manager may open an account in the firm's name, or in the name of the clients. The forms used are the same as for other accounts; however, if an investment manager directs trades in a client's accounts, the manager must have been granted discretion to invest by the client.

Managed Investment Companies

Managed Investment Companies were established to allow groups of investors to pool their money to invest in equities, bonds, money market instruments, etc.

The first mutual fund was created in 1924, in Boston, before there were any significant regulations regarding the funds. This first fund, the Massachusetts Investors Trust, was established with only $50,000 in assets and while it invested in only 45 stocks, it offered a significant innovation whereby individual investors could redeem their shares in the fund at the value of the underlying shares. Prior to this, investment pools had been created, but they were all established as closed end funds and there was not a direct relationship between the price of the underlying shares and the price of the pool.

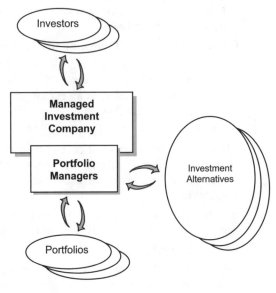

Figure 20 - How a Mutual Fund Works

Within a few months State Street Research opened its own fund, and the first Fidelity fund was established in 1930.

In 1972, the Reserve Fund created the first Money Market Fund (MMF) and Fidelity added a checking account feature to a MMF in 1974.

A mutual fund is created by a managed investment company that hires the portfolio managers and manages the administration of the funds. As shown in the diagram, a managed investment company will usually have more than one mutual fund, with each fund having a specific investment purpose. One portfolio manager may have responsibility for more than one portfolio, and investors can invest in more than one mutual fund at a time.

The different categories of investment banks are described in the chapter on Fund Products.

Investment Banks

The term investment bank is one that can be used in a variety of ways. A firm can be established as a brokerage firm or a bank and call itself an investment bank if it performs all of the functions that are normally performed, such as:

- Underwriting (creating new instruments)
- Research (evaluating investments and making recommendations)
- Portfolio management (having the right to invest on behalf of a client)
- Trading (trading for its own account or for a client)

- Sales (selling portions of its inventory to clients)
- Brokerage (acting as a client's agent in buying and selling securities)

A commercial bank can also call itself an investment bank if it performs these same functions.

Investment banks provide services in every segment of the securities industry. They create products and their different divisions are on either the buy-side or the sell-side.

Investment banks have a variety of ways to make revenue. They can earn underwriting fees, receive a management fee on portfolios, commissions on securities transactions that they broker, and a spread on securities that they hold in their own account.

Insurance Companies

Insurance companies are active in the securities market through their treasury functions and through their investment management activities. Many of the products offered by an insurance company are backed by various securities investments, including:

- Annuities
- Mutual funds
- Life insurance policies

When these products have a securities component, they have to be registered as a security.

Categories of Insurance Companies

There are three basic types of insurance companies.

Mutual Companies

A mutual insurance company is owned by the policy holders.

Stock Companies

A stock insurance company is owned by shareholders just as any other corporation.

Hybrid Companies

In a hybrid insurance company, and if it is allowed in the state of domicile the ownership is held in a mutual holding company. The policy holders own 51% of the stock, and sells 49% to the general public in order to raise capital.

Sales Process

In order to sell securities products, insurance companies have established insurance-affiliated broker/dealers that can be a legal conduit for the products. The brokers' registered representatives have to pass the same NASD exams as other RRs; however, the insurance-affiliated RRs still have a primary focus on their relationships and tend to work for the long term. This contrasts with the regular brokers' RRs who focus exclusively on selling securities and tend to be more transaction oriented.

Each insurance company's agents tend to be organized on one of two ways:

General Agency System

General agents are independent agents who can exclusively sell one insurance firm's products or can, in some cases, sell the products provided by other firms as well.

Each general agent manages their business in their own way. Support is provided by their primary insurance provider but they only have contractual obligations to the provider.

Agency System

The agency system involves agents who are employees of the insurance company. Their processes are far more consistent than the general agent's since these regular agents can be directed to work in a specific way.

Pricing

Insurance companies are in the spread business, where the spread is the difference between what the company earns on their assets and what the company payouts on their liabilities. The spread must provide for expense, risk and profit.

Some considerations that impact the investment manager of an insurance company are as follows:

- Asset Liability Management (ALM) – the timing and coordination of an insurer's investments (maturities or cash availability) and policy liabilities (e.g., policy payouts). This requirement cause insurance companies to have more of a buy and hold strategy

- Risk Based Capital (RBC) – "RBC requirements are used for evaluating the adequacy of an insurer's capital and surplus based on the insurer's size and riskiness of its assets and operations." [2] This requirement helps protect the policyholders in case the insurance company goes bankrupt by ensuring that there will be enough capital to pay policyholder claims.

Processing

Insurance companies follow the same investment process as other investment managers; however, insurance companies' investment philosophies and considerations differ when managing assets. For insurance companies, assets can be segregated into the four main categories as follows:

General Account

A general account is an undivided account in which life and health insurers maintain funds from guaranteed insurance products such as ordinary life insurance. [3]

Separate Account

In the United States, an investment account is maintained separately from an insurer's general investment account to help manage the funds placed in variable life insurance policies and variable annuities. [4]

---

[2] LOMA's Glossary of Insurance Terms, Third Edition

[3] ibid

[4] ibid

Advisory Account

A portfolio that is actively managed for the direct benefit of another party may be a Separate Account or an Advisory Account. Advisory Accounts differ from Separate Accounts when a company manages a portfolio of assets rather than managing funds received from the sale of specific insurance products. These assets are not owned by the company and therefore are not reported as the Company's assets. These accounts are reported annually on the Form ADV.

Other Accounts

This category represents accounts that do not fall under any of the other three categories listed above.

Trends

Demutualization

Mutual insurance funds are looking to change from a mutual structure to a stock (or hybrid) structure for two reasons:

- To raise capital for the expansion into activities such as brokerage and banking that is necessary for insurance companies to complete in a post Glass-Steagall world.

- To prepare for the inevitable consolidation that occurs as insurance products become commoditized.

Regulatory Focus

Most of the new regulations that are drafted are established with regular broker/dealers in mind, not with insurance-affiliated brokers. In order to avoid regulations that are unfair to the insurance-affiliated brokers, the insurance companies work to get involved early and ensure that the regulators understand the business nuances for insurance securities products.

Regulations

Insurance-affiliated brokers and investment managers must follow the same rules as all other brokers and investment managers when they are dealing in the securities markets. This means that they have to follow the federal guidelines and the firm and the RRs register in each state in which they do business, like other brokers.

In the insurance markets, there are no federal laws or regulations; however, each state has the authority to regulate its own insurance businesses so insurance companies must meet each state's requirements.

Reporting

In terms of reporting, insurance companies have a third reporting basis, in addition to GAAP and tax, called statutory reporting, which is provided to the National Association of Insurance Companies (NAIC) on a quarterly basis with more detailed information provided on an annual basis.

Some examples of statutory reporting requirements include financials, notes to the financials, insurance related activity, investment activity and investment holdings.

III. Regulators and Legislation

This chapter will identify how the regulators have established an underlying set of rules and regulations that affect the entire industry and how, within this environment, there are financial markets, depositories, clearinghouses and vendors working together to serve the investment community.

Rules are often defined by the participants in an activity to ensure fair relations between themselves. However, it is usually necessary to establish some form of enforceable legislation to ensure that people outside the group are treated fairly.

Regulations, which are usually based upon some legislation, are established to ensure that everyone in the securities industry conducts business in a similar way to protect the investor.

The securities industry has both kinds of governance:

- **Rules** that are developed by groups of industry participants (called Self-Regulatory Organizations) which must conform to the regulations established by the agencies
- **Regulations** that are established by government agencies

It is not the purpose of this book to identify the details of each law; however, it is important to know these laws exist and that they regulate the industry's activities.

A. SECURITIES INDUSTRY REGULATORS

There are five major U.S. government agencies that govern the securities industry: the Federal Reserve System, the Securities Exchange Commission, the Office of the Comptroller of the Currency, the Department of Labor and the Commodities Futures Trade Commission.

Federal Reserve System

The Federal Reserve System, the central bank of the United States, is a government institution created by Congress in 1913 to administer the nation's credit and monetary policies, and oversee the banking industry as well as certain aspects of broker activity such as credit.

The Fed was established as a result of the *Rich Man's Panic* of 1907 to provide the U.S. with a safe, flexible and stable monetary and financial system. In 1907, banks were basically unregulated, and without a central bank to support the banking system. In the event one bank failed, a single large bank failure could affect the entire market. At that time, investors in the stock market were generally the wealthy, and when the market fell, only they were affected.

The Fed is responsible for establishing and enforcing monetary policy in the U.S. and for regulating the amount of credit outstanding. It does this by establishing the bank discount rate and the rules for credit. The market's response to the Fed's determination to control inflation by raising and lowering the discount rate affects long-term interest rates, which have a significant impact on the securities markets.

Today, the Federal Reserve's duties fall into four general areas: [5]

- Conducting the nation's monetary policy by influencing the money and

---

Source: Federal Reserve System

credit conditions in the economy in pursuit of full employment and stable prices

- Supervising and regulating banking institutions to ensure the safety and soundness of the nation's banking and financial system and to protect the credit rights of consumers

- Maintaining the stability of the financial system and containing systemic risk that may arise in financial markets

- Providing certain financial services to the U.S. Government, to the public, to financial institutions, and to foreign official institutions, including playing a major role in operating the nation's payments system.

The Fed uses the Federal Open Market Committee (FOMC) to manage the three major methods that are used by the Fed to control interest rates:

Purchasing/Selling Government Securities

The Federal Open Market Committee determines whether the economy should have more money in circulation by buying back Treasury Bills (T-bills) and Government Bonds; or, selling T-bills and Bonds that absorb excess funds and reduce liquidity.

Selling government securities absorbs money from the money supply, and therefore acts to slow down spending. When the Fed buys their securities back, they are adding money to the money supply and stimulating the economy.

Reserve Requirements

Depending on the size of a bank's deposits, the bank must deposit reserves with the Fed which earn no interest and cannot be loaned out to clients. For large banks this can range from 3% to 22% of their assets.

Consequently, increases or decreases in the Fed's reserve requirements have a dramatic effect on the interest rates charged by banks and therefore changes are infrequently instituted.

Discount Rate

The discount rate is the rate at which the Fed's member banks borrow money overnight from the Federal Reserve System. This base interest rate is used by member banks and other financial firms to set their short-term rates. As this rate goes up, other short-term rates follow.

The Fed Funds rate is the rate at which member banks lend money to each other overnight.

The Fed also provides processing for loans, currency transfers, check clearing and electronic funds transfers for its member banks.

Securities and Exchange Commission (SEC) [6]

The Securities and Exchange Commission (SEC) is the primary regulatory body that administers the securities industry. Created by Congress through the Securities Exchange Act of 1934, the SEC is an independent, bipartisan, quasi-judicial agency of the United States Government. The laws administered by the SEC deal with securities and finance and seek to provide protection for investors

---

[6]   Source: Securities and Exchange Commission

in their securities transactions.

The SEC:

- Sets the overall rules for the industry and reviews the procedures established by the Self Regulating Organizations (SROs) to ensure that they are in compliance with the letter and the spirit of the securities law

- Reviews new securities registrations to determine if they comply with the laws established by Congress

- Is extremely concerned with protecting the rights of individual investors, and managing the securities marketplace to avoid any serious disruption in the U.S. financial markets

The primary laws administered by the SEC are the:

- Securities Act of 1933

- Securities Exchange Act of 1934

- Public Utility Holding Company Act of 1935

- Trust Indenture Act of 1939

- Investment Company Act of 1940

- Investment Advisers Act of 1940

Organization

The executive body is composed of five commissioners, including the chairman, who are appointed by the president of the United States with the consent of the senate for five year terms of office. No more than three commissioners may be from the same political party.

The commission is headquartered in Washington, DC and operates regional offices around the country.

Region 1 - Northeast Regional Office

Region: Connecticut, Delaware, District of Columbia, Maine, Maryland, Massachusetts, New Hampshire, New Jersey, New York, Pennsylvania, Rhode Island, Vermont, Virginia, and West Virginia

Region 2 - Southeast Regional Office

Region: Alabama, Florida, Georgia, Louisiana, Mississippi, North Carolina, Puerto Rico, South Carolina, Tennessee, and Virgin Islands

Region 3 - Midwest Regional Office

Region: Illinois, Indiana, Iowa, Kentucky, Michigan, Minnesota, Missouri, Ohio, and Wisconsin

Region 4 - Central Regional Office

Region: Arkansas, Colorado, Kansas, Nebraska, New Mexico, North Dakota, Oklahoma, South Dakota, Texas, Utah, and Wyoming

Region 5 - Pacific Regional Office

Region: Alaska, Arizona, California, Guam, Hawaii, Idaho, Montana, Nevada, Oregon, and Washington

Responsibilities

The SEC sets the overall rules for the industry and reviews the procedures established by the Self Regulating Organizations (SROs) to ensure that they are in compliance with the letter and the spirit of the securities law.

The SEC also reviews new securities registrations to determine if they comply with the law.

The SEC is extremely concerned with protecting the rights of individual investors, and managing the securities marketplace to avoid any serious disruption in the U.S. financial markets.

EDGAR

The Electronic Data Gathering, Analysis, and Retrieval system (EDGAR) was established to support the automated collection, validation, indexing, acceptance, and forwarding of forms submitted by companies and others who are required by law to file forms with the SEC.

Office of the Comptroller of the Currency (OCC) [7]

The OCC was created by a law passed in 1863 and regulates national banks. The OCC must approve the establishment of new national banks, bank mergers involving national banks and liquidations of national banks.

When a national bank provides discretionary investment management services for its clients, the OCC uses Regulation 9 to inspect and ensure that the bank has the appropriate policies in place and is following the policies.

The Comptroller of the Currency is appointed by the president and confirmed by the senate for a term of five years. The OCC's principal function is the supervision of the national banking system. A staff of over 1,800 bank examiners performs the statutorily required regular examinations of the approximately 2,200 banks that are subject to the Comptroller's supervision.

In regulating national banks, the OCC has the power to:

- Examine the banks.

- Approve or deny applications for new charters, branches, capital, or other changes in corporate or banking structure.

- Take supervisory actions against banks that do not comply with laws and regulations or that otherwise engage in unsound banking practices. The agency can remove officers and directors, negotiate agreements to change banking practices, and issue cease and desist orders as well as civil money penalties.

- Issue rules and regulations governing bank investments, lending, and other practices.

---

[7] The title "Comptroller of the Currency" was established by the National Bank Act of 1864, which said that currency issued by national banks was the official currency of the U.S. and the Comptroller exercised the monetary control functions. Today, the Comptroller's Office has a very minor role in the administration of currency in the U.S.

Functions of the OCC Law Department [8]

The Law Department, which is managed centrally by the Chief Counsel's office, consists of eight legal practice areas located in the Washington DC headquarters office and six general practice offices in each of the six district office locations. The eight practices are:

- Administrative and Internal Law Division
- Bank Activities and Structure Division
- Community and Consumer Law Division
- Counselor for International Activities
- Enforcement and Compliance
- Legislative and Regulatory Activities
- Litigation
- Securities and Corporate Practices

Districts

Each of the Law Department's offices in the six OCC district locations is managed by a district counsel. The district legal staff is the primary source of legal advice and counsel for the field examiners and district management, providing general interpretive advice on the full range of banking and securities law issues. The district legal staff also is responsible for handling a wide range of enforcement actions including civil money penalties and cease and desist orders.

There are also several other government departments that are involved in regulating specific aspects of the securities industry.

Department of Labor (DOL) [9]

The U.S. Department of Labor is responsible for the administration and enforcement of over 180 federal statutes. These laws and the regulations produced to implement them cover a wide variety of workplace activities for nearly 10 million employers and well over 125 million workers, including protecting workers' wages, health and safety, employment and pension rights; promoting equal employment opportunity; administering job training, unemployment insurance and workers' compensation programs; strengthening free collective bargaining and collecting, analyzing and publishing labor and economic statistics.

The DOL is also responsible for administering the Employee Retirement Income Security Act (ERISA), which regulates employers who offer pension or welfare benefit plans for their employees. It preempts many similar state laws and is administered by the Pension and Welfare Benefits Administration (PWBA).

Under the ERISA statute, employers providing a retirement plan must also protect the retirement benefits, by making insurance premium payments to the Federal government's Pension Benefit Guaranty Corporation. Pension plans must meet a wide range of fiduciary, disclosure and reporting requirements.

---

[8]   Source: Office of the Comptroller of the Currency

[9]   Source: Department of Labor

Employee welfare plans must meet similar requirements.

Commodity Futures Trading Commission (CFTC) [10]

The Commodity Futures Trading Commission (CFTC) was created by Congress in 1974 as an independent agency to regulate futures and option markets in the United States. The agency protects market participants from manipulation, abusive trade practices and fraud. Through oversight and regulation, the CFTC enables the futures markets to provide a mechanism for price discovery and a means of offsetting price risk.

The CFTC is responsible for the following exchanges, most of which trade commodities as well as financial instruments.

- American Commodity Exchange - ACE
- AMEX Commodities Corporation - ACC
- Chicago Board of Trade - CBT
- Chicago Mercantile Exchange - CME
- Chicago Rice & Cotton Exchange - CRCE
- Coffee, Sugar & Cocoa Exchange - CSCE
- COMEX Division of New York Mercantile Exchange - COMEX
- Kansas City Board of Trade - KCBT
- MidAmerica Commodity Exchange - MCE
- Minneapolis Grain Exchange - MGE
- New York Cotton Exchange - NYCE
- New York Futures Exchange - NYFE
- New York Mercantile Exchange - NYMEX
- Philadelphia Board of Trade - PBOT
- Pacific Commodity Exchange - PCE
- Pacific Futures Exchange - PFE
- Twin Cities Board of Trade - TCBT

Contract Review and Market Surveillance

To ensure the financial and market integrity of the U.S.'s futures markets, the CFTC reviews the terms and conditions of proposed futures and option contracts. Before an exchange is permitted to trade a futures and option contract in a specific commodity, it must demonstrate that the contract reflects the normal market flow and commercial trading practices in the actual commodity. The Commission conducts daily market surveillance and can, in an emergency, order an exchange to take specific action or to restore orderliness in any futures contract that is being traded.

Regulation of Futures Professionals

Companies and individuals that handle client funds or give trading advice must apply for registration through the National Futures Association (NFA), a

---

[10]   Source: Commodity Futures Trading Commission

self-regulatory organization approved by the Commission. The CFTC also seeks to protect clients by requiring:

- Registrants to disclose market risks and past performance information to prospective clients
- Client funds be kept in accounts separate from those maintained by the firm for its own use
- Client accounts to be adjusted to reflect the current market value at the close of trading each day

In addition, the CFTC monitors registrant supervision systems, internal controls and sales practice compliance programs.

The commodity exchanges' rules complement Federal regulation rules that cover clearance of trades, trade orders and records, position limits, price limits, disciplinary actions, floor trading practices and standards of business conduct. A new or amended exchange rule may be implemented only with the approval of the CFTC, which may also direct an exchange to change its rules or practices. The CFTC also regularly audits each exchange's compliance program.

CFTC Organization

Commissioners

The CFTC consists of five commissioners, appointed by the President with the advice and consent of the Senate to serve staggered five year terms. The Commission develops and implements agency policy and direction. One of the commissioners is designated by the president to serve as chairperson.

Major policy decisions and Commission actions, such as approval of exchange designations, adoption of agency rules and regulations, and the authorization of enforcement actions, must be approved by a majority vote of the commissioners. Most Commission meetings are open to the public.

The CFTC closely monitors markets and market participants by maintaining, in addition to its headquarters office in Washington, offices in cities that have futures exchanges (New York, Chicago, Kansas City and Minneapolis). For enforcement purposes, the Commission also maintains an office in Los Angeles.

State Insurance Departments

Broker/dealers that are subsidiaries of insurance companies will also have to ensure that they are in compliance with the rules established by the State Insurance Departments in the states in which they are authorized to conduct business.

Each state has its own rules, but they try to coordinate and maintain some commonality by working through the National Association of Insurance Commissioners which is discussed in Chapter XVIII – Industry Owned Organizations.

Office of Thrift Supervision (OTS) [11]

The Office of Thrift Supervision, the successor to the Federal Home Loan Bank Board, was established by Congress in 1989 as the primary Federal regulator of all Federal and state-chartered savings institutions across the nation that belong to the Savings Association Insurance Fund (SAIF).

The OTS headquarters is in Washington, D.C., but OTS staff work out of local offices that are organized into five regions where they examine and supervise savings institutions throughout the country. Its OTS functions include:

- Serving as the primary regulator of all Federal and state-chartered savings institutions

- Issuing federal charters for savings and loan associations and savings banks

- Adopting and enforcing regulations to ensure that both Federal and state-chartered thrift institutions operate in a safe and sound manner

B. LEGISLATION

The Securities Acts are Federal laws passed by the U.S. Congress. They are designed to protect investors and are enforced by the Securities and Exchange Commission.

Securities Act of 1933

The Securities Act of 1933 governs new issues, and the Securities Exchange Act of 1934 (described in the next section of this chapter) covers most of the other major legislation relevant to the securities industry.

The need for regulation was clear after the stock market crash led to the depression of the 1930's. The stock market went up throughout the 1920's as a result of many factors, including:

- Low interest rates made borrowing to buy stocks profitable

- Low margin rates made it easy to buy even speculative issues on margin

- High capital gains tax rates made it unattractive to sell securities after they rose in value, so while demand increased, the supply was low

- Wall Street insiders were able to manipulate stock prices in the absence of laws

- Banks had brokerage subsidiaries and were encouraged to make loans so that the bank would make money on the interest and the brokerage departments would make money on the commissions

When the speculative bubble began to burst, many investors were subjected to margin calls. Since they were fully invested, they had to sell some securities in order to raise the money necessary for the margin calls. This selling drove the market down even further, and additional margin calls were made. The result was a rapidly dropping market with few buyers.

The 1933 Act was passed to address some of these concerns by preventing fraud in the issuance of securities, and is often called the *Full Disclosure_Law* or the

---

[11]   Source: Department of the Treasury

Truth in Securities Law. This law has two basic objectives:

- To require that investors are provided with material information concerning securities offered for public sale

- To prevent misrepresentation, deceit, and other fraud in the sale of securities

The Act requires a registration statement to be filed with the SEC outlining all of the details of a new issue. This information is then given to the prospective purchaser in a document called a prospectus in order to make investment decisions. A copy of the prospectus must be given to potential investors no later than when the confirmation of the purchase is sent to the investor.

The SEC never approves an issue. It just makes sure that there is sufficient information for the investor to make a decision regarding the suitability of the investment.

While the Act is very comprehensive, the following types of securities are exempt from the filing requirements of the Act:

- U.S. Government Obligations

- Municipal Securities

- Offerings by Charitable Institutions

- Commercial Paper

- Bankers Acceptances

- Certificates of Deposit

- Insurance Policies

- Fixed Annuities

Securities Exchange Act of 1934

The Securities and Exchange Act of 1934 created the SEC, and granted more authority to the Federal Reserve System's Board of Governors who are now responsible for establishing and monitoring margin requirements. The 1934 Act regulates securities exchanges that operate interstate with the regulations that are designed to prevent inequitable and unfair practices within these exchanges and markets.

The 1934 Act also governs factors such as:

- The lending of money by brokerage firms

- The short-sale (up tick) rule

- Regulations regarding insiders or controlled persons

This Act was designed to protect the public against unfair and inequitable practices in securities transactions and related activities after issuance. An amendment to the '34 Act, the Maloney Act of 1938, established Self Regulating Organizations (SROs). SROs, an essential segment of the securities industry, are owned by their participants and are allowed to establish the specific rules that govern how their industry segment will function. SROs are described in more detail later in this chapter.

Securities Amendment Act of 1964 [12]

Thirty years after the '34 Act was voted into law, the Securities Act Amendments of 1964 extended disclosure and reporting provisions beyond the exchanges to equity securities in the over-the-counter market. This included hundreds of companies with assets exceeding $1 million and more than 500 shareholders.

Corporate Reporting

Companies seeking to have their securities registered and listed for public trading on an exchange must file a registration statement with the exchange and the SEC. Companies with equity securities that are traded over-the-counter and which meet the minimum asset size and number of shareholders must file a similar registration form. SEC rules prescribe the content of these registration statements and require certified financial statements, which are generally comparable to, but less extensive than, the disclosures required in Securities Act registration statements.

Following the registration of their securities, companies must file annual and other periodic reports to update information contained in the original filing. In addition, issuers must send certain reports to shareholders requesting information. Since May 1996, virtually all corporate filings are available electronically as well as on the SEC's website.

Proxy Solicitations

Another provision of this law governs soliciting proxies (votes) from holders of listed and over-the-counter registered securities for the election of directors and/or for approval of other corporate actions. Solicitations, whether by management or shareholder groups, must disclose all of the material facts concerning the matters on which holders are asked to vote. Shareholders also must be given an opportunity to vote *yes* or *no* on each matter.

Where a contest for control of corporate management is involved, the rules require the disclosure of the names and interests of all the participants in the proxy contest.

In addition, the rules permit shareholders to submit proposals for a vote at the annual meetings.

Tender Offer Solicitations

In 1968, Congress amended the Exchange Act to extend its reporting and disclosure provisions to situations where control of a company is sought through a tender offer or other planned stock acquisition of over 10% of a company's equity securities. Commonly called the Williams Act, this amendment was further amended in 1970 to reduce the stock acquisition threshold to 5%.

These amendments, and SEC rules under the act, require the disclosure of pertinent information by anyone seeking to acquire over 5% of a company's securities by direct purchase or by a tender offer.

---

[12]   Source: Securities and Exchange Commission

Insider Trading

Insider trading prohibitions are designed to curb misuse of material confidential information that is not available to the general public. This includes:

- Buying or selling securities to make profits or avoid losses based on material non-public information

- Telling material non-public information to others so that they may buy or sell securities before such information is generally available to the market

The SEC has brought numerous civil actions in Federal court against people whose use of material non-public information constituted fraud under the securities laws.

Section 16 of the Exchange Act requires that all officers and directors of a company and beneficial owners of more than 10% of its registered equity securities must file an initial report with the Commission, and with the exchange on which the stock may be listed, showing their holdings of each of the company's equity securities. Thereafter, they must file reports for any month during which there was any change in those holdings.

In addition, the law provides that profits obtained by them from purchases and sales or sales and purchases of these equity securities within any six-month period may be recovered by the company or by any security holder on its behalf. This recovery right must be asserted in the appropriate U.S. District Court. Such *insiders* are also prohibited from making short sales of their company's equity securities.

Margin Trading

Margin trading in securities also falls under certain provisions of the Exchange Act. The Board of Governors of the Federal Reserve System is authorized to set limitations on the amount of credit that may be extended for the purpose of purchasing or carrying securities. The Federal Reserve periodically reviews these limitations, which are contained in Regulations T, U and G.

The objective of the margin trading rules is to prevent the excessive use of credit for the purchase or carrying of securities. While the credit restrictions are set by the Fed, investigation and enforcement is the responsibility of the SEC.

Trading and Sales Practices

Securities trading and sales practices on the exchanges and in the over-the-counter markets are subject to provisions that are designed to protect the interests of investors and the public. These provisions have been established to prevent misrepresentations and deceit, market manipulation, and other fraudulent acts and practices. They also strive to establish and maintain open, fair, and orderly markets.

The SEC is responsible for promulgating rules and regulations which, among other things:

- Define acts or practices which constitute a "manipulative or deceptive device or contrivance" prohibited by the statute
- Regulate short selling, stabilizing transactions, and similar matters
- Regulate hypothecation (which is the use of clients' securities as collateral for loans)
- Define the financial responsibility safeguards for brokers and dealers

Regulations such as these were designed to curb the many abuses that occurred, and which were encapsulated in a short rhyme popular at the time:

> He that sells what isn't his'n
>
> Must buy it back or go to prison.
>
> *Daniel Drew*

Registration with the SEC

The Exchange Act requires registration with the Commission of:

- National securities exchanges (unless the SEC grants a limited securities trading volume exemption)
- Brokers and dealers who conduct securities business in interstate commerce
- Transfer agents
- Clearing agencies
- Government and municipal brokers and dealers
- Securities information processors

To register, exchanges must show that they are organized to comply with the provisions of the statute as well as the rules and regulations of the SEC. The registering exchanges must also show that their rules contain just and adequate provisions to ensure fair dealing and to protect investors.

Broker/Dealer Registration

The registration of brokers and dealers engaged in soliciting and executing securities transactions is an important part of the regulatory plan of the act. Brokers and dealers must apply for registration with the SEC and amend registrations to show significant changes in financial conditions or other important facts. Applications and amendments are examined by the SEC. Brokers and dealers must conform their business practices to the standards prescribed by the law and the SEC regulations for protecting investors, and to rules on fair trade practices of their association. Additionally, brokers and dealers violating these regulations risk suspension or loss of registration with the SEC (and thus the right to continue conducting an interstate securities business) or of suspension or expulsion from a SRO.

Securities Acts Amendments of 1975

In 1975, Congress approved additional amendments to the Securities and Exchange Act of 1934. Known as the Securities Act Amendments of 1975, the new legislation established a variety of statutory standards for the governance of national securities exchanges, including guidelines for various membership and commission criteria.

The amendments also established guidelines for securities information processors and broadened the SEC's authority to impose regulations on institutional investment managers and issuers of municipal securities. In addition, the legislation also encouraged the utilization of new data processing and communications techniques in the securities industry.

The National Market System for Securities, National Market Advisory Board, and the Municipal Securities Rulemaking Board were all created as a result of the amendments.

Investment Company Act of 1940

This Act, commonly called the '40 Act, defined investment companies, which do not include banks, insurance companies, brokerage firms and bank holding companies. The Act defined three categories of investment companies:

- Face Amount Certificate Company
- Unit Investment Trust Company
- The Management Company

Each of these categories is described on the following pages.

40 Act - Face Amount Certificate Company

As with a bond, the Face Amount Certificate Company, which is the issuer, states the amount of the investment on the certificate. The investor puts in a lump sum or a stated amount in installments, which the company guarantees will be repaid at maturity, which is at least two and usually ten to fifteen years away. The company guarantees a pre-determined interest rate and a cash surrender value should the investor redeem early. If the company does well there may be extra returns.

The investments consist mainly of U.S. government municipals, prime real estate, mortgages and the highest quality equity securities. This type of company looks very much like an insurance company, and some states assign the State Insurance Commissioner to oversee them as opposed to the securities regulator.

40 Act - Unit Investment Trust Company

A Unit Investment Trust (UIT) is an investment company that offers an investment, denominated by units, in a fixed portfolio of securities. The securities are usually self-liquidating and do not have to be managed, which lowers the cost of administering the portfolio.

UITs have Shares of Beneficial Interest (SBI), which are established for a specific purpose and for a specific period of time, after which the trust must be liquidated. The proceeds of the portfolio may not be re-invested. They must be distributed on a proportionate basis to unit holders. The investors' capital goes into either a fixed trust or a participating trust.

Fixed Trust

In a fixed trust there can be no purchase/sale activity after the start up of the trust and there is no investment fee. The investor buys the securities and holds them until they mature or the trust is dissolved. While there is no management fee, there are other fees, and this form of investment is very profitable to the broker that creates one.

Participating Trust

In a participating trust, investors participate in the activity of other investment companies that are organized as management companies. The investors hold units of the participating trust that they invest in the other management companies.

40 Act - The Management Company

The management company is established under a corporate charter that is administered by a board of directors. It offers redeemable or non-redeemable shares of stock. This form of investment company is more popularly called a mutual fund. Mutual funds are described in the chapters on Securities Industry Participants, Mutual Fund Processing and Fund Products. Management companies must:

- Register with the SEC
- Have net assets worth at least $100,000
- Adhere to a decision to be diversified or not
- Have outside audits twice a year
- Restrict their borrowing, and they may not buy stock on margin
- Restrict their investment in other investment companies
- 40% of the board for a load fund must be comprised of outsiders

Investors have the right to elect directors and approve contracts with management companies. No changes in the fund's objectives can be made without at least a 50% affirmative vote.

Investment Advisors Act of 1940 [13]

People and firms engaged in providing investment advice were brought under the jurisdiction of the SEC by the Investment Advisors Act of 1940. The Act prohibits contracts that compensate the advisor for a client's capital gains and prohibits the defrauding of clients. Advisers who have more than 15 clients are affected by the Act and must register with the SEC.

This law regulates the activities of investment advisers, including advisers to investment companies, private money managers, and most financial planners. With certain exceptions, it requires persons or firms that are compensated for providing advice about investing in securities to register with the SEC and conform to statutory requirements designed to protect their clients.

Provisions of the Act

The most significant of the statutory provisions is the Act's broad prohibition against fraudulent conduct, which has been interpreted by the U.S. Supreme Court as prohibiting violation of the fiduciary duties of an investment adviser to its clients. Among other things, this provision requires an adviser to disclose to clients material facts concerning any conflict of interest the adviser may have with the client, to refrain from taking advantage of the position of trust the adviser occupies without the client's informed consent, and to comply with specific prohibitions the SEC has adopted by rule that are designed to prevent

---

[13]   Source: Securities and Exchange Commission

fraudulent conduct.

The Act requires investment advisers registered with the SEC to maintain books and records according to SEC rules. The agency conducts periodic examinations of investment advisers during which these books and records are reviewed to determine whether the adviser is in compliance with the Act as well as the other Federal securities laws.

The SEC has the authority under the Act to deny, suspend, or revoke an investment adviser's registration based on a violation by the adviser of the Act or of other laws prohibiting fraud, theft, or other kinds of financial misconduct. In addition, the SEC may impose various forms of sanctions on an investment adviser, including substantial fines, and it may issue a cease and desist order or seek an injunction in Federal court prohibiting further violation of the law. The SEC may also recommend criminal prosecution by the U.S. Department of Justice for violation of the act.

Investment Advisers Act Fiduciary Responsibility

"Unlike some of the other securities laws, the Advisers Act does not contain detailed rules governing the way advisers conduct their business. Rather, the Act broadly prohibits fraud and holds advisers to rigorous fiduciary standards when dealing with clients. Investment advisers have two choices under the Act:

- They must rid themselves of all conflicts of interest with their clients - conflicts that might influence them to act in their own best interest rather than in the best interest of their clients.

- Or, they must fully disclose any conflicts to clients and prospective clients"

SEC Chairman Arthur Levitt (April 5, 2000)

Fiduciary Responsibility

"An investment adviser (IA) is required to act solely in the best interests of the client and to make full and fair disclosure of all material facts, particularly where the adviser's interests may conflict with the client's."

SEC v. Capital Gains Research Bureau, 375 U.S. 180 (1963)

Some examples of potential conflicts in fiduciary duty are:

- Where the IA is compensated, directly or indirectly, from a source other than a client for recommending a security

- Where the IA receives a fee or commission for recommending an investment from someone other than the client

- Where the IA owns or is affiliated with a broker through which client transactions are traded

- Where the IA, or its employees, buys or sells the same securities as a client

- Where the IA or a related party compensates a third party for referring a client

Duties of a Fiduciary

Some of the duties of a fiduciary are:

- Duty to have a reasonable, independent basis for its investment advice
- Duty to obtain the best execution for clients' securities transactions
- Duty to ensure that investment advice is suitable to the client's objectives, needs, and circumstances
- Duty to refrain from effecting personal securities transactions that are inconsistent with client interests
- Duty to be loyal to clients
- Duty to treat clients fairly and not to favor one client over another

Sherman Antitrust Act

The Sherman Antitrust Act of 1890 makes it illegal to establish actual and attempted monopolization and agreements (or conspiracies) that unreasonably restrain trade or commerce.

This statute is enforced both by the government and by private parties. Criminal violations of the Sherman Act are felonies punishable by fines (up to $11 million per violation for corporations and $350,000 per violation for individuals) and, in the case of individuals, imprisonment.

In addition to government enforcement, those injured by anticompetitive conduct may sue to recover treble damages and all their attorneys' fees. The Federal Trade Commission Act, which is enforced by the Federal Trade Commission and state attorneys general, makes unlawful:

- Unfair or deceptive acts or practices
- Unfair methods of competition

These acts are considered unlawful even if they are engaged in by only one person or entity.

Glass-Steagall Act of 1935

One result of the Securities Act of 1933 was to prevent any one financial firm from engaging in multiple lines of financial business. Banks, brokers and insurance companies could not be owned by the same entity.

This legislation, which was written to provide regulations to prevent what many people at that time considered to be the root causes of the depression, defined the securities activities banks may or may not perform until it was repealed.

On November 12, 1999, President Clinton signed into law the Gramm-Leach-Bliley Act, which repealed the Glass-Steagall Act and which is discussed later in this lesson. One impact of this repeal is that certain advisory activities of the banks are now regulated by the Investment Advisor Act of 1940.

Section 20

This section originally said that banks could not have security affiliates, which were common in the 1920s and early 1930s. An affiliate, according to the Act was "any corporation, association, business trust or other organization engaged principally in the issue, floatation, underwriting, public sale, or distribution of wholesale or retail through syndicate participation of stocks, bonds, debentures, notes or other securities."

In 1971, a Supreme Court ruling on the Glass-Steagall Act was used to justify that bank holding companies could be formed to separate banking and brokerage activities in separate corporations. As these banks began to set up separate brokerage entities, these entities came to be known as Section 20 brokerage firms.

Section 16

This section defined what banks could do in the securities business, but the areas were extremely vague beyond the ability for banks to offer financial advising. Banks could also deal in government and municipal securities and underwrite municipals.

Overall, the effect of the act was to separate banking, brokerage and insurance into separate businesses. The Glass-Steagall Act was repealed with the passage of the Financial Services Modernization Act of 1999.

McFadden Act

The McFadden Act placed another regulatory hurdle in front of banks by restricting their geographic range. Banks were limited by this Act to maintain their activities within a specific state.

By using a bank holding company, banks have been able to expand throughout the U.S.

Financial Services Modernization Act

Passed in 1999, the Financial Services Modernization Act, also called the Gramm-Leach-Bliley Act (GLBA), repealed parts of the Glass-Steagall Act of 1933 and the Bank Holding Company Act of 1956. This Act removes the barriers for banks, brokers and insurance companies to merge and cross sell their products.

The GLBA is discussed later in this chapter.

Other Related Federal Legislation

Public Utility Holding Company Act of 1935 [14]

Interstate holding companies that are involved in the electric utility business or in the retail distribution of natural or manufactured gas are subject to regulation under this act. Today, fifteen systems are registered. These systems must register with the SEC and file initial and periodic reports.

Detailed information concerning the organization, financial structure, and operations of the holding company and its subsidiaries is contained in these reports. However, if a holding company or its subsidiary meets certain specifications, the SEC may exempt it from part or all of the duties and obligations otherwise imposed by statute. Holding companies are subject to SEC regulations on matters such as structure of the system, acquisitions, combinations, issuing and sales of securities.

Issuance and Sale of Securities

Proposed security issues by *any* holding company must be analyzed and evaluated by the staff, and approved by the SEC, to ensure that the issues meet the following tests under prescribed standards of the law:

---

[14] Source: Securities and Exchange Commission

- The security must be reasonably adapted to the security structure of the issuer and of other companies in the same holding company system
- The security must be reasonably adapted to the earning power of the company
- The proposed issue must be necessary and appropriate to the economical and efficient operation of the company's business
- The fees, commissions, and other remuneration paid in connection with the issue must not be unreasonable
- The terms and conditions of the issue or sale of the security must not be detrimental to the public or investor interest

Subject to satisfaction of certain conditions, the issuance of securities by subsidiaries of registered holding companies are, for the most part, exempt from the requirement for prior Commission approval.

Holding Company Act - Issuance and Sale of Securities

Proposed security issues by any holding company must be analyzed and evaluated by the staff, and approved by the SEC, to ensure that the issues meet the following tests under prescribed standards of the law:

- The security must be reasonably adapted to the security structure of the issuer and of other companies in the same holding company system
- The security must be reasonably adapted to the earning power of the company
- The proposed issue must be necessary and appropriate to the economical and efficient operation of the company's business
- The fees, commissions, and other remuneration paid in connection with the issue must not be unreasonable
- The terms and conditions of the issue or sale of the security must not be detrimental to the public or investor interest

Subject to satisfaction of certain conditions, the issuance of securities by subsidiaries of registered holding companies are, for the most part, exempt from the requirement for prior Commission approval.

Maloney Act of 1938

By a 1938 amendment to the Exchange Act, congress also provided for the creation of a national securities association. The only such association, the National Association of Securities Dealers (NASD), is registered with the SEC under this provision of the law. This Association is responsible for preventing fraudulent and manipulative acts and practices, and for promoting just and equitable trade principles among over-the-counter brokers and dealers. The establishment, maintenance, and enforcement of a code of business ethics by the NASD is one of the principal features of this provision of the law.

Each exchange and national securities association is a self-regulatory organization (SRO). Its rules must provide for the expulsion, suspension, and other disciplining of member broker/dealers for conduct inconsistent with just and equitable principles of trade. The law intends that SROs shall have a full opportunity to establish self-regulatory measures that ensure fair dealing and investor protection.

The SEC must approve all proposed SRO rule changes to ensure that they are consistent with the other standards of the Exchange Act. In addition the SEC has the authority by rule to amend the rules of SROs if necessary to implement the purposes of the Exchange Act.

However, most rule changes are proposed by the SROs and generally reach their final form after discussion between representatives of both bodies and an opportunity for the public to comment.

Trust Indenture Act [15]

Passed in 1939, the Trust Indenture Act defines the securities *indenture* as an agreement under which any debt for public sale must be issued. This Act applies to bonds, debentures, notes, and similar debt securities offered for public sale and issued under trust indentures with more than $7.5 million of securities outstanding at any one time. Even though such securities may be registered under the Securities Act, they may not be offered for sale to the public unless the trust indenture conforms to the statutory standards of this Act which safeguards the rights and interests of the purchasers, and:

- Prohibits the indenture trustee from conflicts of interests which might interfere with the performance of its duties on behalf of the securities purchasers

- Requires the trustee to be a corporation with minimum combined capital and surplus

- Imposes high standards of conduct and responsibility on the trustee

- Precludes, in the event of default, preferential collection of certain claims that are owed to the trustee by the issuer

- Provides that the issuer supply to the trustee evidence of compliance with indenture terms and conditions (such as those relating to the release or substitution of mortgaged property, issue of new securities, or satisfaction of the indenture)

- Requires the trustee to provide reports and notices to security holders

Other provisions of the Act prohibit impairing the security holders' right to sue individually for principal and interest, except under certain circumstances. It also requires the trustee to maintain a list of security holders for their use in communicating with each other regarding their rights as security holders.

Investment Company Act of 1940

This Act defined investment companies, which do not include banks, insurance companies, brokerage firms and bank holding companies.

The Act defined three categories of investment companies.

Face Amount Certificate Company

As with a bond, the face amount certificate company, which is the issuer, states the face amount on the certificate.

---

[15]   Source: Securities and Exchange Commission

The investor puts in a lump sum or a stated amount in installments, which the company guarantees will be repaid at maturity, which is at least two and usually ten to fifteen years away. The company guarantees a pre-determined interest rate and a cash surrender value should the investor redeem early. If the company does well there may be extra returns.

The investments consist mainly of U.S. government municipals, prime real estate, mortgages and the highest quality equity securities.

This type of company looks very much like an insurance company, and some states assign the State Insurance Commissioner to oversee them as opposed to the securities regulator.

Unit Investment Trust Company

A Unit Investment Trust (UIT) is an investment company that offers an investment, denominated by units, in a fixed portfolio of securities. The securities are usually self-liquidating and do not have to be managed, which lowers the cost of administering the portfolio.

UITs have Shares of Beneficial Interest (SBI), which are established for a specific purpose and for a specific period of time, after which the trust must be liquidated.

The proceeds of the portfolio may not be re-invested. They must be distributed on a proportionate basis to unit holders.

The investors' capital goes into either a fixed trust or a participating trust.

Fixed Trust

In a fixed trust there can be no purchase/sale activity after the start up of the trust and there is no investment fee. The investor buys the securities and holds them until they mature or the trust is dissolved.

While there is no management fee, there are other fees, and this form of investment is very profitable to the broker that creates one.

Participating Trust

In a participating trust, investors participate in the activity of other investment companies that are organized as management companies. The investors hold units of the participating trust that they invest in the other management companies.

The Management Company

The management company is established under a corporate charter that is administered by a board of directors. It offers redeemable or non-redeemable shares of stock.

This form of investment company is more popularly called a mutual fund. Mutual funds are described in the chapters on Securities Industry Participants, Mutual Fund Processing and Fund Products.

Management companies must:

- Register with the SEC
- Have net assets worth at least $100,000
- Adhere to a decision to be diversified or not

- Have outside audits twice a year
- Restrict their borrowing, and they may not buy stock on margin
- Restrict their investment in other investment companies
- 40% of the board for a load fund must be comprised of outsiders

Investors have the right to elect directors and approve contracts with management companies. No changes in the fund's objectives can be made without at least a 50% affirmative vote.

Investment Advisors Act of 1940 [16]

People and firms engaged in providing investment advice were brought under the jurisdiction of the SEC by the Investment Advisors Act of 1940. The Act prohibits contracts that compensate the advisor for a client's capital gains and prohibits the defrauding of clients. Advisers who have more than 15 clients are affected by the Act and must register with the SEC.

This law regulates the activities of investment advisers, including advisers to investment companies, private money managers, and most financial planners. With certain exceptions, it requires persons or firms that are compensated for providing advice about investing in securities to register with the SEC and conform to statutory requirements designed to protect their clients.

The most significant of the statutory provisions is the Act's broad prohibition against fraudulent conduct, which has been interpreted by the U.S. Supreme Court as prohibiting violation of the fiduciary duties of an investment adviser to its clients. Among other things, this provision requires an adviser to disclose to clients material facts concerning any conflict of interest the adviser may have with the client, to refrain from taking advantage of the position of trust the adviser occupies without the client's informed consent, and to comply with specific prohibitions the SEC has adopted by rule that are designed to prevent fraudulent conduct.

The Act requires investment advisers registered with the SEC to maintain books and records according to SEC rules. The agency conducts periodic examinations of investment advisers during which these books and records are reviewed to determine whether the adviser is in compliance with the Act as well as the other Federal securities laws.

The SEC has the authority under the Act to deny, suspend, or revoke an investment adviser's registration based on a violation by the adviser of the Act or of other laws prohibiting fraud, theft, or other kinds of financial misconduct. In addition, the SEC may impose various forms of sanctions on an investment adviser, including substantial fines, and it may issue a *cease and desist* order or seek an injunction in Federal court prohibiting further violation of the law. The SEC may also recommend criminal prosecution by the U.S. Department of Justice for violation of the act.

Federal Bankruptcy Reform Act of 1978

The National Bankruptcy Act of 1898 (repealed and passed again in 1978 as the Federal Bankruptcy Reform Act) identified the priority of claims in the event of a corporate bankruptcy, which are, in this order:

---

[16]   Source: Securities and Exchange Commission

- Secured creditors when collateral has been defines
- Administrative Claims (lawyers regarding the bankruptcy)
- Middleman Debts (Debts after the filing but before the order for relief)
- Unpaid wages up to $4,300
- Employee Benefit Claims (up to 180 days before filing)
- Deposits by individuals for consumer goods up to $1,950
- Alimony and Child Support claims
- Unpaid Taxes (Federal and state income tax and state sales taxes)
- Unsecured Bondholders (Bond issues may be subordinated to other bond issues)
- Common stockholders (Common shares are subordinate to preferred shares, and possibly to other common shares)

The Act also established a bankruptcy-court system, which has the following process for bankruptcy.[17]   Reorganization proceedings in the U.S. Courts under Chapter 11 of the Bankruptcy Code are begun by a debtor, voluntarily, or by its creditors. Federal bankruptcy law allows a debtor in reorganization to continue operating under the court's protection while it attempts to rehabilitate its business and work out a plan to pay its debts. If a debtor corporation has publicly issued securities outstanding, the reorganization process may raise many issues that materially affect the rights of public investors.

Chapter 11 of the Bankruptcy Code authorizes the SEC to appear in any reorganization case and to present its views on any issue. Although Chapter 11 applies to all types of business reorganizations, the SEC generally limits its participation to proceedings:

- Involving significant public investor interest
- Protecting public investors holding the debtor's securities
- Participating in legal and policy issues of concern to public investors

The SEC also addresses matters of traditional SEC expertise and interest relating to securities. Where appropriate, it comments on the adequacy of reorganization plan disclosure statements and participates where there is a SEC law enforcement interest.

Under Chapter 11, the debtor, official committees, and institutional creditors negotiate the terms of a reorganization plan. The court can confirm a reorganization plan if it is accepted by creditors for:

- At least two-thirds of the amounts of allowed claims
- More than one-half of the number of allowed claims
- At least two-thirds of the amount of the allowed shareholder interest

The principal safeguard for public investors is the requirement that a disclosure statement containing adequate information be transmitted by the debtor or plan proponent in connection with soliciting votes on the plan. In

---

[17]   Source: SEC

addition, reorganization plans involving publicly held debt usually provide for issuing new securities to creditors and shareholders which may be exempt from registration under Section 5 of the Securities Act of 1933.

Securities Investor Protection Act of 1970

This Act created the basis for the Securities Investors Protection Corporation (SIPC), which resembles the FDIC in that it insures investors against the liquidation of a brokerage firm, rather than the failure of a bank. SIPC is discussed in more detail later in this chapter.

Bank Secrecy Act 1970

The Bank Secrecy Act (October 1970) was enacted to fight money laundering and other financial-related crimes conducted through financial institutions. The Act initially only covered banks, but was later expanded to include other financial services firms.

Some of the Bank Secrecy Act's compliance requirements include:

- File Currency Transaction Report (CTR) for each deposit, withdrawal, exchange of currency more than $10,000 in cash
- CTR must be filed and completed with the government within 15 days of the transaction in currency
- File a CTR if smaller cash transaction report on a single day by the same person amounts to more than $10,000
- File a CMIR (Currency or Monetary Instrument Report) for international of currency and/or monetary instruments in excess of $10,000
- File a SAR (Suspicious Activity Report) for any suspicious transaction relevant to a possible violation of law or regulation
- Maintain records of all taxpayer identification numbers (SSN or EIN) for all account holders
- Keep records of all individuals who buy checks, money orders and traveler's checks of amount $3,000 to $10,000
- Maintain data documenting of both the sender and receiver of funds

Penalties

Some of the potential penalties are:

- $50,000 for negligent activities
- $1,500 per report for recordkeeping violations such as filing an incorrect CTR
- Up to $1,000 per day for non-compliance
- $250,000 or imprisonment for five years for willful violation of the Act

Employee Retirement Income Security Act of 1974 (ERISA)

ERISA was passed in 1974, following revelations that employees lost benefits because of inadequate information about their pensions. This Act was designed to ensure that employees have a right to the funds in the pension even after leaving a job, and under some conditions, allows them the opportunity to invest the funds in an IRA within 60 days of terminating the job.

It also requires those employers who provide a pension to submit an annual report to the employees and the Department of Labor.

Commodity Futures Trading Act of 1974

This Act established the Commodities Futures Trading Commission (CFTC), which oversees procedures and regulations for trading futures. The Act gives the CFTC the right to regulate all commodity futures and requires any persons involved in futures trading to register.

Securities Acts Amendments of 1975

In 1975, Congress approved amendments to the Securities and Exchange Act of 1934. Known as the Securities Act Amendments of 1975, the new legislation established a variety of statutory standards for the governance of national securities exchanges, including guidelines for various membership and commission criteria.

The amendments also established guidelines for securities information processors and broadened the SEC's authority to impose regulations on institutional investment managers and issuers of municipal securities. In addition, the legislation also encouraged the utilization of new data processing and communications techniques in the securities industry.

The National Market System for Securities, the National Market Advisory Board, and the Municipal Securities Rulemaking Board were all created as a result of the amendments.

Insider Trading Sanctions Act of 1984

The Insider Trading Sanctions Act, which was signed into law on August 10, 1984, allows the SEC to impose fines up to three times the profit gained (or loss avoided) by use of material non-public information.

This Act increased the fines and punishment against those who benefit from insider trading, and allows the SEC to seek up to three times the amount gained from insider information in fines.

Shareholder Communications Act of 1985

The Shareholder Communications Act of 1985 allowed the SEC to regulate proxy processing by fiduciaries. Although broker/dealers were required to forward proxy information and related documentation to the beneficial owners of securities prior to the law, those functioning in a fiduciary capacity were not.

As a result of the Act, regulations now define how and when the material must be provided to the beneficial owner. Additionally, the fiduciary now has a legal obligation to reveal the name, address and position held by the beneficial owner if requested by the issuer.

Government Securities Act of 1986

The Government Securities Act was established as a result of the many losses caused by unregulated dealers in the government securities market during the 1980s. As a result of the Act, all brokers and dealers of government securities must inform all of the appropriate regulatory agencies that they are functioning in this capacity, including those that were previously unregulated. Consequently, government securities dealers, with few exceptions, are subject to this Act. The Act includes regulations about the safekeeping of the securities as well as the reporting and record keeping that must be performed by the broker/dealer institution.

Insider Trading and Securities Fraud Enforcement Act of 1988

This Act is a Federal law that is meant to discourage and decrease the amount of insider trading. It allows rewards to be given to individuals who provide information about insider trading activity.

Gramm-Leach Bliley Act (GLBA) 1999

The Gramm-Leach-Bliley Act (GLBA) (1999) protects non-public personal information. GLBA applies to all financial institutions.

Also known as Financial Services Modernization Act, GLBA requires banks and financial institutions to ensure that client information is protected from cyber criminals and to provide detailed security policies to clients and regulators.

Section 101 of the Act repealed Section 20 of the Glass-Steagall Act which established limits for the services offered by banks, brokers and insurance companies.

Some of the Gramm-Leach-Bliley Act's compliance requirements include:

- Adopt and disclose privacy policies
- Create 'opt-out' choice for consumers while sharing their information with third parties for marketing purposes
- Abstain from obtaining or disclosing an individual's financial information under false pretenses
- Involve the board of directors to promulgate, approve, implement and review information security programs
- Assess internal and external threats that might threaten client information
- Ensure sufficient and sound strategies to manage and control identified risks
- Train employees on information security programs
- Test security programs regularly for any internal/external hazards
- Establish appropriate oversight of relationships with outsourcing vendors
- Adjust information security practices continuously to keep up with the latest industry trends
- Report to board/committee annually on the status of security programs

Penalties

For non-compliance with administrative, technical or physical safeguards requirements, the firm could be penalized:

- Fines up to $1 million
- Termination of FDIC (Federal Deposit Insurance Act) insurance
- Removal or permanent termination of members of the management board
- Imprisonment for five to ten years

Federal Deposit Insurance Corp. Improvement Act (FDICIA)

Chapter 112 of FDICIA was signed into law in May, 1993. This law requires banks to annually certify that management is responsible for their financial statements, and that controls are in place and that the bank is in compliance with regulations. This forces the banks to constantly assess the effectiveness of their procedures and their compliance with regulations.

Regulation ATS

Regulation ATS defines Alternative Trading Systems as "any organization, association, person, group of persons, or system that constitutes, maintains, or provides a market place or facilities for bringing together purchasers and sellers of securities or for otherwise performing with respect to securities the functions commonly performed by a stock exchange within the meaning of Rule 3b-16 under the Securities Exchange Act of 1934...and that does not:

- Set rules governing the conduct of subscribers other than the conduct of such subscribers' trading on such organization, association, person, group of persons, or system; or

- Discipline subscribers other than by exclusion from trading."

Alternative Trading Systems are designed to bring together buyers and sellers without using an exchange or NASDAQ. If an application is designed to connect buyers and sellers, and unless the volume is very low or the application trades only government securities and certain other related instruments, the application is subject to Regulation ATS.

An ATS can only be offered by a broker/dealer registered under section 15 of the Act, and is therefore subject to the broker/dealer regulations, as well as some specific additional regulations, including:

- Fair Access
- Fee Prohibitions
- Processing Capacity, Integrity, and Security
- Self-Examinations
- Reporting

In addition, an alternative trading system must comply with applicable state laws relating to the offer or sale of securities or the registration or regulation of persons or entities effecting transactions in securities.

Regulation NMS

A national market system was mandated by the Securities Act Amendments of 1975 to the Exchange Act to connect the growing number of different markets. The national market system consists of two main parts:

- The Intermarket Trading System (ITS) includes nine markets (the American, Boston, Cincinnati, Chicago, New York, Pacific, Philadelphia stock exchanges, the Chicago Board Options Exchange (CBOE), and the NASD over-the-counter market) that are linked electronically to allow traders at any exchange to seek the best available price on all other exchanges where a particular security is eligible to trade.

- The consolidated electronic tape, which combines last-sale prices from all markets into a single stream of information.

The current rules for the national market system are based upon Section 11A of the Securities Exchange Act of 1934 ("Exchange Act").

There is currently a difference in the transaction speeds between floor exchanges and electronic markets. When an ECN order must be sent to an exchange, the transaction speed slows as the floor becomes involved. This has led to the idea of fast vs. slow markets. To resolve this, the floor-based exchanges are adding fast alternatives whereby certain orders can by-pass the floor while retaining the best possible price, but in order to allow and regulate these changes, some of the rules must be adapted.

In 2004, the SEC began proposing four modifications to the rules which it calls Regulation NMS:

- Uniform trade-through rules that would affirm the fundamental principle of price priority, so that orders must be executed at the best price available

- Establishing a de-minimis standard for intermarket linkages that would modernize the terms of access to quotations and execution of orders in the NMS

- A sub-penny quoting rule establishing the penny as the minimum quoting increment for a security, unless the security trades at less than $1.00

- Changes to the rule governing market information that would modify the formulas for allocating net income to reward markets for more broadly based contributions to public price discovery

USA PATRIOT Act [18]

The full name of the USA PATRIOT Act is Uniting and Strengthening America by Providing Appropriate Tools Required to Intercept and Obstruct Terrorism Act of 2001.

The USA PATRIOT Act was enacted on October 24, 2001 to amend the Bank Secrecy Act and is a comprehensive anti-terrorism law that was passed as a result of the events of September 11, 2001.

The Anti-Money Laundering provisions of the law seek to combat money laundering and terrorist financing and have broad ramifications for financial institutions, which now have additional requirements for detecting and preventing money laundering which is estimated to include $1 trillion annually, with 50% of the funds passing through the U.S. at some point of time.

The definition of financial institutions with anti-money laundering responsibilities was expanded to include brokers and dealers of securities, mutual funds, insurance companies, money service businesses, gaming establishments, travel agencies and others. These institutions are now required to have Anti-Money Laundering training programs and establish procedures for reporting suspicious activity.

---

[18]   Source: HR 3162 RDS, Federal Reserve System

- The Act increases the strength of United States measures to prevent, detect, and prosecute international money laundering and the financing of terrorism for fighting international money laundering and blocking terrorist access to the U.S. financial system.

- The Act is far-reaching in scope, covering a broad range of financial activities and institutions. The provisions affecting banking organizations are generally set forth as amendments to the Bank Secrecy Act (BSA).

- These provisions relate principally to U.S. banking organizations' relationships with foreign banks and with persons who are resident outside the United States.

- The Act, which generally applies to insured depository institutions as well as to the U.S. branches and agencies of foreign banks, does not immediately impose any new filing or reporting obligations for banking organizations, but requires certain additional due diligence and recordkeeping practices.

Some requirements take effect without the issuance of regulations. Other provisions are to be implemented through regulations that will be promulgated by the U.S. Department of the Treasury, in consultation with the Federal Reserve Board and the other federal financial institutions regulators.

The Act requires every financial institution to establish an anti-money laundering program that includes, at a minimum:

- Development of internal policies, procedures, and controls

- Designation of a compliance officer

- Ongoing employee training program

- Independent audit function to test the program

One of the main provisions enforces the 'know your client' rule for all financial institutions.

Some of the other USA PATRIOT Act requirements include:

- Examine data of all the clients from sources, both internal and external to the organization

- Determine the client's behavioral patterns that might affect business and national security

- Appoint a compliance officer to lead the anti money-laundering (AML) program

- Create internal AML policies and procedures and institute training programs

- Create an independent audit process to test internal procedures

- Establish minimum procedures to identify verifications when new clients open accounts

- Cross-check account holder names against all government lists of known or suspected terrorist organizations

- Record owner of account, originator of a transaction, person who approved the transaction and any other individual involved in approving an account

Penalties

- Regulatory fines up to $1 million
- Potential criminal charges against officers for rules violations
- The Tower Group reports that U.S. brokerages will spend $700 million through 2005 to comply with the Act.

Sarbanes-Oxley Act of 2002

The Sarbanes-Oxley Act (SOX) defines the rules and processes for corporate accountability regarding financial statements and disclosures with the objective: "to protect investors by improving the accuracy and reliability of corporate disclosures made pursuant to the securities laws". The law makes violations of these rules the same as a violation of the '34 Act, and imposes the same penalties.

The Act requires financial management areas of public companies to be aware of the new responsibilities of chief executive officers and chief financial officers, who are now required to personally certify their company's financial statements. Corporate audit committees are specifically responsible for hiring, compensating and overseeing the independent auditors and there are new requirements regarding enhanced financial disclosures.

The Act is organized into eleven titles, although sections 302, 404, 401, 409, 802 and 906 are the most significant for compliance and internal control.

SOX applies to all publicly traded firms on any U.S.-based financial exchange, regardless of their domicile. The law firm of Foley & Lardner estimated that annual compliance cost will go up from $1.3 million before SOX to $2.5 million with SOX.

The Act requires that the annual report of a publicly traded firm to contain an internal control report, which:

- Identifies who is responsible for establishing and maintaining the internal control structure and procedures for financial reporting
- Assesses the effectiveness of the internal control structure and the financial reporting procedures

Some of the Sarbanes-Oxley Act's compliance requirements include:

- Disclose all financial and non-financial reports
- Public certification of financial reports and internal controls by the CEO and CFO
- Update investors with all the latest changes inside the organization, both financial and non-financial
- Report company securities trading within two business days
- CEOs, CFOs must certify that they are responsible for establishing and maintaining disclosure controls and procedures

- Engage independent and preeminent legal counsel and a registered public accounting firm
- Elect a professionally competent Board of Directors that is truly independent - psychologically as well as legally
- Attract and retain a loyal foundation of shareholders

Penalties

Some of the penalties are:

- Criminal penalties for records destruction, securities fraud and failure to report fraud.
- Failure to maintain all audits or review papers for at least five years may result in jail terms of ten years. Penalties may again go up to twenty years for destroying documents in a federal or bankruptcy investigation while penalty for securities fraud is twenty-five years.
- A CEO or CFO who knowingly certifies non-complying financials can be fined up to $1 million and imprisoned for ten years.

State Legislation

Blue Sky Laws are state laws that define specific state regulations for many areas, such as mutual funds and securities. The laws are passed by individual states with the power to:

- Authorize state commissions
- Require licensing of firms and representatives
- Mandate filing on new securities
- Define trade practice standards
- Define and prohibit frauds

The rules can be different for each state.

C. REGULATION OF CREDIT

The Fed controls the regulation of credit, and regulations have been established for a variety of circumstances:

Fed Regulation G

Regulation G governs credit for margin securities that has been extended by parties other than banks, brokers and dealers.

Fed Regulation T

Regulation T governs credit for margin securities extended by securities brokers and dealers to their clients.

Fed Regulation U

Regulation U governs lending of money using securities as collateral by banks to their clients.

D. SELF-REGULATORY ORGANIZATIONS

An amendment to the 1934 Act, the Maloney Act of 1938, established the right for participants in the U.S. securities industry to establish their own rule making organizations, which are called Self Regulating Organizations. A Self Regulating Organization must be approved and supervised by the SEC. SROs present their rules and rule changes to the SEC for final approval.

An SRO can be an exchange, an association, a clearing agency or a depository and has the following general functions:

- Defines rules, qualifications for membership, record keeping, etc.
- Monitoring compliance with the SRO's rules
- Representing the industry to regulatory agencies
- Enforce fair, ethical and efficient practices

In addition to their rulemaking and enforcement activities, most SROs are also responsible for processing securities in some way. The SROs regulatory responsibilities are discussed in this chapter and processing responsibilities are covered in the chapters on Buying and Selling Securities and on Post-Trade Processing, Clearing and Settlement.

Some of the leading SROs are:

American Stock Exchange (AMEX or ASE) [19]

As a self-regulating organization, the American Stock Exchange has established and published rules, policies, and standards of conduct for its members and member organizations. As a self-regulatory organization registered with the SEC, the American Stock Exchange is required by the federal securities laws to have rules and regulations in place to:

- Prevent fraudulent and manipulative practices
- Promote just and equitable principles of trade
- Protect investors and the public interest

The Exchange also must have the ability to enforce compliance by its members and member firms with the provisions of the federal securities laws, the rules and regulations of the SEC, and the Constitution and rules of the American Stock Exchange.

The primary tasks of monitoring trading in markets by member firms and their clients, and enforcing compliance with the securities laws and our Constitution and rules is the responsibility of the Member Firm Regulation Division.

The Member Firm Regulation Division is among the larger divisions of the American Stock Exchange with a professional staff comprised of attorneys, investigators, trading analysts, and financial and sales practice examiners.

The Division is divided into three functional areas:

- Market Surveillance
- Examinations
- Enforcement

Chicago Mercantile Exchange (CME) [20]

Founded as a not-for-profit corporation in 1898, the CME became the first

---

[19]   Source: American Stock Exchange

[20]   Source: Chicago Mercantile Exchange

publicly traded U.S. financial exchange in December 2002 when the Class A shares of the parent company, Chicago Mercantile Exchange Holdings Inc., began trading on the New York Stock Exchange under the ticker symbol CME.

The CME Rulebook is a comprehensive guide that provides the rules, definitions and regulations for trading at CME.

A division of the CME Clearinghouse, the Audit Department is an essential component of the Exchange's financial safeguard system. Through direct surveillance and information programs such as reporting and inspection, the Audit Department ensures the financial integrity of CME's clearing firms and their adherence to the CME's Rules.

Chicago Stock Exchange (CHX) [21]

The Chicago Stock Exchange opened on May 15, 1882, and initially, the 52 stocks and 82 bonds traded at the CHX were primarily regional issues.

- In 1949, the CHX merged with the St. Louis, Cleveland and Minneapolis-St. Paul exchanges to become the Midwest Stock Exchange (MSE).

- In 1959, the New Orleans Stock Exchange also merged with the MSE.

- Chicago's subsequent emergence as the "Exchange Capitol of the World" prompted the CHX to return to its original name on July 8, 1993.

Today, the Chicago Stock Exchange trades more than 3,500 NYSE, AMEX, NASDAQ and CHX-exclusive issues.

The Chicago Stock Exchange currently consists of approximately 200 member organizations (holding 450 seats) and a staff of over 200. It is a self-regulatory organization under the oversight of the U.S. Securities and Exchange Commission (SEC).

Depository Trust Company (DTC) [22]

The Depository Trust Company (DTC), a member of the U.S. Federal Reserve System, is a limited-purpose trust company under New York State banking law and a registered clearing agency with the Securities and Exchange Commission. The depository retains custody of approximately two million securities issues, effectively "dematerializing" most of them so that they exist only as electronic files rather than as paper, and provides the services necessary for the maintenance of the securities it has in custody.

The DTC has a series of rules that guide its member's activities when dealing with the depository.

Emerging Markets Clearing Corporation (EMCC) [23]

Emerging Markets Clearing Corporation (EMCC) provides automated trade comparison, settlement and risk management of transactions involving Brady Bonds, sovereign debt and related transactions in emerging-market economies. One of the first clearing corporations in the world to guarantee cross-border trading activity, EMCC currently clears trades of securities representing issues

---

[21]   Source: Chicago Stock Exchange

[22]   Source: Depository Trust Company

[23]   Source: Emerging Markets Clearing Corporation

from more than 50 countries. In 2001 the value of transactions EMCC processed averaged $1.3 billion each trading day.

The EMCC has established a set of rules that are available online.

Fixed Income Clearing Corporation – GSD [24]

The Government Securities Division clears, settles and nets a broad range of U.S. Government securities transactions for its 104 member firms (brokers, dealers, banks and other financial institutions) and more than 400 correspondent firms that clear through these members. These transactions include original auction purchases of Treasury and Freddie Mac securities, buy/sell and repo transactions in Treasury and Government Agency securities, and GCF Repo transactions in certain mortgage-backed securities.

As an SRO, the GSD has established a series of rules (FICC Rulebook) that guide the activities in the government securities clearing and settlement process.

The Government Securities Division also maintains strict membership standards to ensure that firms with an increased risk profile or chance of failure are excluded from the GSD's process. The GSD has four types of membership:

Comparison-Only

The Comparison-Only category is open to any type of entity that can benefit from the GSD's comparison services.

Netting

The Netting category is open only to:

- Banks
- Two categories of dealers
- Two categories of futures commission merchants (FMCs)
- Two categories of inter-dealer brokers (IDBs)
- Insurance companies
- Issuers of Government securities
- Registered clearing agencies
- Registered investment companies (RICs)

Repo Member

GSD offers comparison and netting services for overnight and set-term repo trades involving the GSD-eligible securities to members already meeting the requirements for buy/sell comparison netting membership, provided the GSD qualifies the member for participation.

Clearing Agent Bank

The Clearing Agent Bank category is open to members of the Federal Reserve System that are regularly engaged in the business of providing clearing services in eligible securities for members and that have agreed to provide the GSD, upon request and under mutually agreeable terms, with clearing services.

---

[24] Source: Government Securities Division

Fixed Income Clearing Corporation – MBSD [25]

The Mortgage-Backed Securities Division operates two primary business units:

- Clearing services, which include trade comparison, confirmation, netting, and risk management

- Electronic Pool Notification (EPN) services, which allow clients to transmit/retrieve MBS pool information in real-time as opposed to standardized message formats.

Mortgage-backed securities are bought and sold in the over-the-counter cash, forward and options markets. The key participants in these markets, the nation's original secondary markets for loan assets, are mortgage originators, government sponsored enterprises, registered broker/dealers, inter-dealer brokers, institutional investors, investment managers, mutual funds, commercial banks and insurance companies.

The FICC Rules include the MBS Division's Clearing Rules and the MBS Division's EPN Rules.

Municipal Securities Rulemaking Board (MSRB) [26]

The Municipal Securities Rulemaking Board (MSRB) was established in 1975 by Congress to develop rules regulating securities firms and banks involved in underwriting, trading, and selling municipal securities, including bonds and notes issued by states, cities, and counties or their agencies to help finance public projects. The MSRB is a self-regulatory organization that sets standards for all municipal securities dealers and has the authority to make rules regulating the municipal securities activities of banks and securities firms only. It does not have authority over issuers of municipal securities or investors and is subject to oversight by the Securities and Exchange Commission (SEC).

The MSRB Board consists of fifteen members including five representatives of bank dealers, five representatives of securities firms, and five public members not associated with any bank dealer or securities firm. Board members serve staggered three-year terms and each year five new members are elected. The MSRB's chairman and vice-chairman serve one-year terms.

National Association of Securities Dealers (NASD) [27]

Under federal law, virtually every securities firm doing business with the U.S. public is a member of NASD. Roughly 5,200 brokerage firms, over 95,000 branch offices and more than 661,000 registered securities representatives come under our jurisdiction.

The Securities Exchange Act of 1934 gave the exchanges the right to self-regulate, but never mentioned the OTC Market. The SEC has granted the NASD the right to be a Self Regulating Organization, and the NASD has created a series of rules to guide firms as they conduct business in the over-the-counter market.

The National Association of Securities Dealers (NASD) is the rule making body

---

[25]   Source: Mortgage-Backed Securities Division

[26]   Source: Municipal Securities Rulemaking Board

[27]   Source: National Association of Securities Dealers

that governs the over-the-counter brokerage industry. As an SRO the NASD is organized to "adopt, administer, and enforce rules of fair practice and rules to prevent fraudulent and manipulative acts and practices, and in general to promote just and equitable principles of the trade for the protection of investors."

NASD registers member firms, writes rules to govern their behavior, examines them for compliance, disciplines those that fail to comply and operates the largest securities dispute resolution forum, along with arbitration and mediation programs, in the world.

Enforcement is a fundamental part of NASD's mission. It encourages compliance and punishes wrongdoing, but also helps the vast majority of our members who obey the rules and have a strong interest in maintaining the industry's reputation.

National Futures Association (NFA) [28]

The National Futures Association (NFA) was established in 1982 with the stated mission of protecting the public investor by maintaining the integrity of the future's marketplace.

NFA's board of directors consists of elected representatives of every category of membership and by representatives from U.S. futures exchanges and non-futures industry Board members.

The Board serves as a governing body that is responsible for interpreting the mission of the organization, developing policy and ensuring a sound financial structure. An Executive Committee, elected from the Board, supervises the implementation of NFA's policies and rules.

The NFA has four congressionally mandated responsibilities:

- To screen all firms and individuals wishing to conduct business with the investing public
- To develop a wide range of investor protection rules and monitor all members for compliance
- To provide investors with information needed to make educated financial decisions
- To offer a fast, efficient method for settling disputes

The Commodity Futures Trading Commission (CFTC), established by Congress in 1974, is the Federal regulator responsible for overseeing the commodity futures markets in the United States, and futures contracts may only be bought and sold on exchanges licensed by the CFTC. As a self-regulatory organization authorized by the CFTC, NFA has established extensive rules to govern the conduct of its members, which include:

- Futures Commission Merchants
- Introducing Brokers
- Commodity Pool Operators
- Commodity Trading Advisors

---

[28]   Source: National Futures Association

Investors considering participation in the futures markets can use NFA's online Background Affiliation Status Information Center (BASIC) to review the registration status and disciplinary history of the firm or individual with whom they may be working. BASIC is available through NFA's web site, www.nfa.futures.org/basic/about/asp.

National Securities Clearing Corporation (NSCC) [29]

National Securities Clearing Corporation (NSCC) is the largest of the U.S. clearing corporations, processing in 2001 an average of nearly 14 million transactions each day. NSCC provides clearing and settlement, risk management, central counterparty services and a guarantee of completion for all trades involving equities, corporate and municipal debt, money market instruments, American depositary receipts, exchange traded funds, unit investment trusts, mutual funds, insurance products and other securities.

NSCC also nets trades and payments among its participants, reducing the volume and securities and payment that need to be exchanged by an average of 95% each day. NSCC generally clears and settles trades on a T+3 basis.

The NSCC has established a series of rules for its members.

New York Stock Exchange (NYSE) [30]

The NYSE's independent governance structure separates the Exchange's regulatory function from its marketplace function and from influence by members and member organizations. Chief Regulatory Officer Richard Ketchum and the NYSE Regulation group report directly to Regulatory Oversight and Regulatory Budget Committee of the NYSE Board of Directors. Among other responsibilities, this committee - now consisting solely of independent directors - determines the Exchange's regulatory plan, programs, budget and staffing proposals annually.

NYSE Regulation consists of three divisions:

- Member Firm Regulation
- Market Surveillance
- Enforcement

The NYSE is the examining authority for the major securities firms in the U.S., including more than 250 member firms that deal with the public and which account for more than 85 percent of broker/dealer client accounts.

There are several sections to the NYSE's rules, including:

- General Rules
- Dealing and Settlement
- Admission of Members
- Operations of Member Organizations
- Communication with the Public
- Disciplinary Rules

---

[29] Source: National Securities Clearing Corporation

[30] Source: New York Stock Exchange

- Listing and Delisting Securities
- Arbitration
- Off-Hours Trading Rules

Pacific Exchange (PCX) [31]

The Pacific Exchange (PCX) is a marketplace where individual and institutional investors, professional broker/dealers, and registered member firms meet to buy and sell options on more than 1,200 stocks. It is one of the world's leading derivatives markets.

The PCX is also the regulator of the Archipelago Exchange (ArcaEx), a fully electronic market for securities listed on the New York, American stock exchanges, the Pacific Exchange, and the NASDAQ Stock Market. The PCX provides all market surveillance, member firm financial and operating compliance monitoring, and enforcement services for ArcaEx, which is operated by Archipelago Holdings, LLC (www.tradearca.com). ArcaEx began trading operations on March 22, 2002.

The *Pacific Stock Exchange Guide* is made available as a service to members and the public by the Pacific Exchange, Inc.

Philadelphia Stock Exchange (PHLX) [32]

The Philadelphia Stock Exchange (PHLX) trades approximately 2,000 stocks, 1,200 equity options, 16 index options and 8 currency options and 6 currency futures.

Founded in 1790, the PHLX was the first stock exchange to be established in the United States and continues in that tradition of innovation through the products and services it offers today.

The *Philadelphia Stock Exchange Manual* is made available as a service to members and the public by the Philadelphia Exchange, Inc.

---

[31] Source: Pacific Exchange
[32] Source: Philadelphia Stock Exchange

E. SECURITIES LICENSING

In order to work in many of the jobs in the securities industry, people need to prove that they have a sufficient understanding of the industries rules and practices. There are two ways that people can demonstrate this proficiency: Passing Specific Licensing Exams or being certified by some recognized industry association.

Licensing Exams[33]

The primary licensing exams in the U.S. for securities professionals are divided into a number of specific examinations:

Registered Principal

Persons associated with a member, who are actively engaged in the management of the member's investment banking or securities business, including supervision, solicitation, conduct of business, or the training of persons associated with a member for any of these functions are designated as principals. Such persons include sole proprietors, officers, partners, managers of offices of supervisory jurisdiction, and directors of corporations.

Series	Securities Test
23	General Securities Principal Qualification Examination Sales Supervisor Module
24	General Securities Principal
27	Financial and Operations Principal
28	Introducing Broker/Dealer Financial and Operations Principal
26	Investment Company Products/Variable Contracts Limited Principal
39	Direct Participation Programs Limited Principal
4	Registered Options Principal
53	Municipal Securities Principal
51	Municipal Fund Securities Principal
9, 10	General Securities Sales Supervisor

Figure 21 - Registered Principal Tests

---

[33]   Source: NASD

Registered Representative

Persons associated with a member, including assistant officers other than principals, who are engaged in the investment banking or securities business for the member including the functions of supervision, solicitation, or conduct of business in securities or who are engaged in the training of persons associated with a member for any of these functions, are designated as representatives.

Series	Securities Test
7	General Securities Representative
6	Investment Company Products/Variable Contracts Limited Representative
22	Direct Participation Programs Limited Representative
62	Corporate Securities Limited Representative
72	Government Securities Limited Representative
82	Limited Representative-Private Securities Offerings Representative
55	Equity Trader Limited Representative
42	Registered Options Representative
52	Municipal Securities Representative
11	Assistant Representative - Order Processing

Figure 22 – Registered Representative Tests

Other Examinations Administered by NASD

Series	Securities Test
5	Interest Rate Options Examination
15	Foreign Currency Options Examination
3	National Commodity Futures Examination
30	Branch Managers Examination - Futures
31	Futures Managed Funds Examination
32	Limited Futures Exam - Regulations
33	Financial Instruments Examination
63	Uniform Securities Agent State Law Examination
65	Uniform Investment Adviser Law Examination
66	Uniform Combined State Law Examination
14	Compliance Officer
16	Supervisory Analyst

Figure 23 - Other NASD Tests

Industry Credentials

There are several different certifications and credentials that are available in the securities industry, including:

Chartered Financial Analyst (CFA)

The CFA designation is awarded to individuals who meet the standards of the CFA institute (formerly AIMR) and pass a test of their knowledge of the investment process.

Training programs are provided by various vendors to prepare individuals for the tests.

Securities Industry Professional (SIP)

The SIP credential is awarded to securities industry operations, technical and administrative professionals who complete a series of eLearning courses and pass a rigorous test of their knowledge of the overall securities industry. The SIP program is sponsored by ISITC-IOA and delivered by Securities Operations Forum.

SOF provides the eLearning courses that are designed to prepare each professional for the tests that are administered by SOF.

Certified Securities Operations Professional

The American Bankers Association, through their subsidiary, the Institute of Certified Bankers, has developed the CSOP program. The CSOP program covers the Trust segment of the securities industry, including Types of Securities, Regulation and Compliance, Controls, Reconciliation and Audit, and Industry Structures.

CSOP education is available through Cannon and other vendors.

F. REGULATORY INFLUENCERS

In addition to the SROs, there are numerous industry associations that assist firms in achieving a consensus opinion that they present to the regulators on topics of mutual interest. These associations are then often very active in lobbying for or against regulation when the association feels it is in the best interests of its members.

Industry Associations are covered in the Chapter on Industry Owned Organizations.

G. INDUSTRY MANDATED INSURANCE

Federal Deposit Insurance Corporation (FDIC)

The Banking Act of 1933 established this independent agency to insure depositors for up to $100,000 at banks that are entitled to Federal Deposit Insurance. Banks pay the FDIC fees that are based upon the total amount of deposits in the bank.

The FDIC also has supervisory powers over banks, along with the Federal Reserve System, the Office of Thrift Supervision, and the Office of the Comptroller of the Currency.

FDIC insurance is different from SIPC insurance.

The Securities Investor Protection Act (SIPA)

The Securities Investor Protection Act was originally a fund established by the NYSE for its members. In 1970, Congress passed the Act that established the Securities Investor Protection Corporation (SIPC), which is not a government agency. SIPC is a federally chartered, non-profit corporation.

All brokers must be members, and the members were initially assessed until the fund reached $150,000,000. SIPC now has a line of credit at the U.S. Treasury of $1 Billion. SIPC Insurance covers accounts that are held by SIPC members that include cash and most securities, including mutual funds and Money Market Funds.

SIPC protects a maximum portfolio value of $500,000 per client (not per account), not more than $100,000 of which can be in cash. For amounts in excess of $500,000, the client will become a general creditor of the broker; however, most firms purchase additional insurance for their clients.

When a firm fails, SIPC assigns a trustee. The day the trustees arrive is the date the portfolio values are determined, and creditors are given six months to present their claims. The trustee will transfer as many of the client accounts as possible to another qualified broker, and if an account cannot be immediately transferred, SIPC will purchase securities to cover the clients' positions at the current market value.

Settlement Guarantee Fund

The Settlement Guarantee Fund is managed by the NSCC to ensure that in the event an NSCC participant fails during the clearing process, the clients will not lose their securities or their cash. If a broker fails after the security has been settled, the investor is protected by SIPC.

Municipal Default Insurance

Municipal Default Insurance is available for issuers from private insurance agencies. The cost of this insurance is borne by the investors, who receive approximately 25 basis points in reduced yield.

IV. Creating New Securities

Businesses and governments raise capital or obtain funds through the securities market in order to expand, restructure their business, pay for public projects, etc. In this chapter, we will discuss the roles of the different participants involved in creating securities, the relevant legislation, the types of processes used, and the profit dynamics of underwriting.

A. FIRMS IN THE ISSUANCE PROCESS

There are two categories of firms involved in the issuance of securities:

- Issuers are the firms that need to raise capital or acquire funds by issuing securities.
- Other financial intermediaries support the issuance of securities by helping issuers create and distribute new issues.

Issuers of Securities

Firms issue securities in order to raise capital by selling equity or debt, and increasingly to establish the value and liquidity of the shares held by the original owners. In recent years the percentage of the firm offered to the public through an equity IPO has dropped to an average of 31% of the shares authorized. Some of the dot.com issues in the late 1990s offered as little as 10% of their authorized shares to the market, and the remaining shares are held by the firm, management, initial investors and venture capitalists.

Any corporation or U.S. Governmental entity can issue securities in the U.S. to raise capital, as long as it follows the U.S. laws and regulations.

- Corporations can issue debt or equity as long as there are investors who are willing to risk their money.
- Governments can issue debt to finance projects and the Federal government also uses the issuance of debt as one way to control the amount of money in circulation. The various types of government offices that can issue debt are:
  - U.S. Government
  - U.S. Government Agencies and Quasi-government Agencies
  - States
  - Counties
  - Municipalities

Within the general categories of debt and equity there are several different types of securities that can be issued. There is more information concerning the different types of securities that can be issued in the chapters on the various types of products.

Firms Supporting the Issuance of Securities

Several categories of financial intermediaries are involved in supporting the issuance of securities, including:

Investment Banks

Investment banks, which have been described earlier in this book, help define, create and distribute new securities through the process of underwriting. Firms act as underwriters when they assist issuers in identifying and distributing the type of security that will best meet the issuer's financing needs, and which will be attractive to some investing segment of the market.

Underwriters help firms evaluate their current capital structure and the type of securities that will best satisfy the firm's short- and long-term need for funding. Underwriters can recommend simple equity or debt, or create an entirely new type of instrument if required. Underwriters also must understand what investors are willing to buy and how much they are willing to spend. The goal of the underwriter is to maximize the value of the new issue for the issuer.

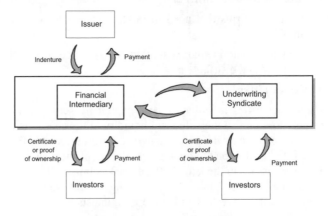

Figure 24 - Creating New Securities

An underwriter can either buy a new security from the issuer, and then sell (distribute) the securities to the public at a price that includes the underwriter's profit, or it can act as an agent and receive a fee from the issuer.

Broker/Dealers

Broker/dealers can participate through their own investment banking activities or by helping the underwriter sell the new security to the broker/dealer's clients.

Corporate Trust Departments

The corporate trust department of a bank, which was described in the chapter on Securities Industry Participants, helps the underwriter create the certificate and place it in a depository if the security meets the depository's criteria. The corporate trust department will also be involved in recording the ownership of the securities in its role as a registrar or transfer agent, and it may perform other services if selected by the issuer.

Exchanges / NASDAQ

If the new issue meets the criteria of an exchange or NASDAQ, and if the issuer wants to list, the exchange or NASDAQ will become involved in creating a new listing. Also, new U.S. issues will be listed on the Luxembourg Stock Exchange if offered globally, and all Global that are eligible for Clearstream and Euroclear will be listed on the Luxembourg Stock Exchange.

Depository

If the new issue meets the criteria established by the depository, it can be entered as an eligible security, and investors can settle their trades in the security through a U.S. depository. It will also be made eligible by Euroclear in Brussels and Clearstream in Luxembourg if the issue is offered globally

Firms can issue additional shares or bonds for an existing issue, which is called a primary distribution or a primary offering, or they can create a totally new issue. These totally new offerings can be made to the public through various forms of private placements or initial public offerings.

Additions to an Existing Issue	New Issues
Primary Distribution, also called a Primary Offering	Initial Public Offering
	Private Placement

Figure 25 - Issuance Methods

The typical form of corporate underwriting involves a process called a *negotiated underwriting*, where the issuer selects a lead underwriter based upon the underwriter's perceived ability and then works with the underwriter to define the issue, terms, price, etc. The other form of underwriting is a *competitive underwriting*, which is most often used by municipalities, and which allows various lead underwriters to make an offer to underwrite the issue. Both of these processes are described later in this chapter.

B. UNDERWRITING ROLES

There are several different roles for investment banks and brokers as they support the issuance of securities:

Advising

The investment banker, or the corporate finance department of a commercial bank, may help the issuer decide the form of the issuance. This issuance may be a part of a complete reorganization of the firm's capital structure, or it could be a specific issuance of debt or equity.

The advisor will also normally assist the firm in registering with the SEC and in presenting this new investment opportunity to investment managers around the country.

Pricing

Once the decision has been made regarding what to issue, the underwriter has to assist the firm in establishing the price at which the security will be offered. This is based upon the underwriter's experience and current market conditions. The lead underwriter may be assisted in this task by other underwriters.

Processing

After a new issue has been defined by the underwriters, the issue is turned over to the Syndicate Operations Department of the lead manager in order to assign a CUSIP number, lodge the issue in a depository, etc., and to a corporate trust agent for the actual issuance of the certificate.

Lead manager notifies the syndicate operations department which initiates the IPO process, which includes getting a CUSIP number, lodging the security in the depository, and co-coordinating with the Corporate Trust provider.

Purchasing

The underwriter may participate singly or as a part of a syndicate, as an agent or as a principal to the deal.

Principal

An underwriter can make a firm commitment to purchase all or a part of the security by itself, or through a syndicate, which is a group of underwriters. A syndicate has a lead manager and co-managers who jointly agree on how they will support the issuance of this new security.

Agent

An underwriter can act as an agent for the issuer. In this case, the underwriter does not take a position, and only acts on behalf of its client. There are two main types of agency underwriting:

- A Best Efforts underwriting is when the underwriter will do its best to sell whatever it can, and gets compensated based upon the number of shares actually sold.
- If an All or None distribution is in place, everything must be sold or the agent will not be paid since the distribution would be cancelled.

Distributing

The underwriter, acting alone or as a member of a syndicate, will distribute the issue into the market. In some cases, additional brokers are recruited to participate in a selling group, and they are compensated based upon the number of shares or bonds sold.

In summary, there are several different underwriting functions performed as shown in the following chart.

	Underwriter	Syndicate	Selling Group	Corporate Trust
Advising	X			
Pricing	X			
Purchasing	X	X		
Distributing	X	X	X	
Processing				X

Figure 26 - Underwriting Functions

C. UNDERWRITING REGULATION

The Securities Act of 1933, also called the Full Disclosure Act and the Truth in Securities Act, governs new issues, and requires the issuer to provide complete and accurate information to the potential buyers. The 1933 Act is also discussed in the chapter on Regulators and Legislation.

Although responsible for enforcing the 1933 Act, the SEC never approves an issue; it just ensures that there is sufficient information for investors to make an informed decision regarding the suitability of the investment.

The Act covers all public offerings of securities issued and traded in the U.S., with some exceptions that are described later in this chapter, regardless of whether or not the issuer is a U.S. entity.

Types of Public Offerings

Initial Public Offering (IPOs)

When a firm creates and distributes a specific issue for the first time, it is distributed to the general investing public through the primary market as an IPO. After the security has been issued, any subsequent trading occurs in the secondary market. Any subsequent issues of the same security are considered a primary distribution or a primary offering, not an IPO.

The '33 Act protects investors by mandating full disclosure of all material information connected with a new security. One of the disclosure rules requires that issuers file a registration statement and preliminary prospectus (called a 'red herring') with the SEC.

After the registration statement and preliminary prospectus are filed with the SEC, a 20 day cooling-off period begins. During this period the proposed new issue may be discussed with potential buyers, but brokers may not send any materials other than the preliminary prospectus to potential clients to obtain "indications of interest." An indication of interest does not obligate or bind the client to purchase the issue when it becomes available, since all sales are prohibited until the security has cleared registration.

A final prospectus is prepared and distributed when the registration statement is accepted by the SEC. The final prospectus contains all of the information contained in the preliminary prospectus including the final price of the issue, and the underwriting spread. The acceptance does not indicate that the SEC approves of the issue, merely that all of the necessary information has been filed.

Primary Offering

A primary offering occurs when the issuer already has securities outstanding and wishes to issue additional securities of the same type through the primary market.

Shelf Registration

New issues can also be issued as a shelf registration, which is used when a corporation knows that it will need additional funds over a period of time and wants to minimize its underwriting preparation expenses by issuing all of the securities at one time and then distributing them at various points in time. In this situation, all of the shares or bonds that have been approved should. "...reasonably be expected to be sold within a two year period..." (SEC Rule 415).

While most issuers of securities are covered by the 1933 Act, there are a variety of exemptions. However, regardless of whether the securities are registered or exempt, the anti-fraud provisions of the Act apply to all sales of securities involving interstate commerce or the U.S. mail.

Exempt Securities

The following categories of securities are exempt from the SEC's filing requirements:

- U.S. Government Obligations
- Municipal Securities
- Offerings by Charitable Institutions
- Commercial Paper
- Bankers Acceptances
- Certificates of Deposit
- Insurance Policies
- Fixed Annuities

Exemptions for some of these categories of securities are available only when certain other conditions are met. These conditions include the use of an offering circular that must contain certain basic information.

Some other categories of exemptions include:

Private Placement

The private placement of securities (stocks or bonds) includes private offerings to a limited number of persons or to institutions who:

- Have access to the kind of information that is required to be included in an SEC registration, as opposed to the general investing public, who would need the formal prospectus to find out the same information
- Do not plan to redistribute the securities in the open market

There are several different forms of private placement that are exempt from the regular provisions of the 1933 Act:

Regulation D

With a private placement regulated under Regulation D, the issuer must register the issue with the SEC, but the process requires less time and expense. The offer is described in an offering memorandum, and neither the issuer nor the investment bank may make any public advertisement of the offering.

Purchasers of this form of private placement must be an accredited investor, which means that they either must have a net worth of at least $1,000,000, or gross income of at least $200,000 per year for the last two years and anticipate that they will continue at this level of income.

The offering can be made to no more than 35 investors in a twelve-month period and each buyer must sign an investment letter stating that the securities were purchased for investment and there are no current plans to sell them. The stock must be held a minimum of two years; however, additional stock acquired in the open market is not subject to the two year requirement.

Rule 144

Under Rule 144, an *individual* investor holding either restricted or controlled stock in publicly traded corporations must notify the SEC when he or she intends to sell.

- Restricted stock is not registered with the SEC and is normally acquired through a private placement. Restricted stock must be held for at least two years, and the owner must notify the SEC when the sell order is placed with his/her broker.

- Control stock is that which is acquired in any way by an officer or a director of the firm issuing the stock. When a control person sells these shares, he must do so under the provisions of Rule 144, which requires that the control person notify the SEC when he has placed the sell order with his broker.

Rule 144A

Rule 144A describes and allows a form of sale of restricted stock between *qualified institutional buyers (QIBs)*, which are defined as firms having at least $100 million in financial assets. Securities that are already listed on an exchange can not be covered by this rule.

These securities have not been registered under the Securities Act of 1933 and may not be offered or sold in the United States except in accordance with the resale restrictions applicable thereto. These securities having been previously sold, this announcement appears as a matter of record only.

$86,250,000

Aspen Technology, Inc

5.25% Convertible Subordinated Debentures
due June 15, 2005

Price 100%

Plus accrued interest, if any, from June 17, 1998

Certain of these securities have been sold in the United State in private offerings that included sales pursuant to Rule 144A under the Securities Act of 1933

Joint Lead Managers

Goldman, Sachs & Co. NationsBanc Montgomery Securities LLC

William Blair & Company

July 9, 1998

Figure 27 - Tombstone for 144A

Firms require some evidence that the investor is a QIB, and often ask the client to complete a form such as the following.

Attention: Compliance Department

Gentlemen:

We certify, to enable you to make offers and sales of securities pursuant to Rule 144A under Securities Act of 1933 (the "Act"), that we are a qualified institutional buyer in that we satisfy the requirements of one or more of paragraphs (i) through (v) hereof (CHECK APPLICABLE BOX(ES)).

(i)   We are an entity referred to in sub-paragraphs (A) through (G) hereof and in the aggregate owned and invested on a discretionary basis, for our own accounts and the accounts of other persons, at least the amount of securities specified below (not less than $100 million), calculated as provided in Rule 144A, as of the date specified below. (Please check one of the following boxes).

(A) ☐ Corporation, etc. A corporation (other than a bank, savings and loan or similar institution referred to in (ii) below), partnership, Massachusetts or similar business trust, organization described in Section 501©(3) of the Internal Revenue Code, Small Business Development Company licensed by the U.S. Small Business Administration under Section 301© or (d) of the Small Business Investment Act of 1958, or business development company as defined in Section 202(a)(22) of the Investment Advisers Act of 1940; or

(B) ☐ Insurance Company. An insurance company as defined in Section 2(13) of the Act; or

(C) ☐ ERISA Plan. An employee benefit plan within the meaning of Title I of the Employee Retirement Income Security Act of 1974; or

(D) ☐ State or Local Plan. A plan established and maintained by a state, its political subdivisions, or any agency or instrumentality of a state or its political subdivisions, for the benefit of its employees; or

(E) ☐ Trust Fund. A trust fund, whose trustee is a bank or trust, whose participants are exclusively plans specified in sub-paragraph © or (D) above (but not including trust funds having IRAs or Keough plans as participants).

(F) ☐ Investment Company. An investment company registered under the Investment Company Act of 1940 or any business development company as defined in Section 2(a)(48) of the Act; or

(G) ☐ Investment Adviser. An investment adviser registered under the Investment Advisers Act of 1940.

(ii) ☐ Bank or Savings and Loan. We are a bank as defined in Section 3(a)(2) of the Act, a savings and loan association or other institution referenced in Section 3(a)(5)(A) of the Act, or a foreign bank or savings and loan association or equivalent institution that in the aggregate owned and invested on a discretionary basis, for our own account and the accounts of other persons, at least the amount of securities specified below (not less than $100 million), calculated as provided in Rule 144A, as of the date specified below and had an audited net worth of at least $25 million as of the end of our most recent fiscal year. (This paragraph does not include bank commingled funds, except as noted in (i)(E) above).

(iii) ☐ One of a Family of Investment Companies. We are an investment company registered under the Investment Company Act of 1940 that is part of a "family of investment companies", as defined in Rule 144A , that owned in the aggregate at least the amount of securities specified below (not less than $100 million), calculated as provided in Rule 144A, as of the date specified below.

(iv)   We are dealer registered under Section 15 of the Securities Exchange Act of 1934, and we are one of the following.

(A) ☐ Dealer QIB. We owned or invested on a discretionary basis, for our own account and the accounts of other persons, at least the amount of securities specified below (not less than $10 million), calculated as provided in Rule 144A, as of the date specified below.

(B) ☐ Dealer/Riskless Principal or Agent. We are acting either on a riskless principal basis for simultaneous resale to a qualified institutional buyer or as agent for one or more qualified institutional buyers.

(v)   ☐   **Entity Owned by Qualified Buyers.** We are an entity, all of the equity owners of which are qualified institutional buyers (each satisfying one or more of (i) through (iv) above including as applicable the $100 million test).

In calculating the amount of securities owned or invested by an entity as provided in Rule 144A; (a) repurchase agreements, securities owned by subject to repurchase agreements, swaps, bank deposit instruments, loan participants, securities of affiliates and dealers unsold allotments are excluded; and (b) securities are valued at cost, except that they may be valued at market if they are reported in financial statements at market and no current cost information is published.

Each entity, including a parent or subsidiary, must separately meet the requirements to be qualified institutional buyer under Rule 144A. Securities owned by any subsidiary are included as owned or invested by its parent entity for purposes of Rule 144A only if (1) the subsidiary is consolidated in the parent entity's financial statements and (2) the subsidiary's investments are managed under the parent entity's direction (except that a subsidiary's securities are not included if the parent entity is itself a majority-owned consolidated subsidiary of another enterprise and is not a reporting company under the Securities Exchange Act of 1934).

We further certify that we will purchase securities under Rule 144A from or through you only for our own account or for the account of another entity which is a qualified institutional buyer including, if we are an insurance company, our separate accounts. We will not purchase securities for another entity under Rule 144A unless it satisfies one or more of paragraphs (i) through (v) above including as applicable the $100 million test.

We agree to notify you of any change in the certifications herein, and each purchase by us of securities under Rule 144A from or through you will constitute a reaffirmation of the certification herein (as modified by any such notice) as of the time of such purchase.

Complete blanks as indicated:

Assets under Management or $_____   _____

Assets Owned: Name of Entity (Print or Type)]
      (DO NOT specify amount of transaction)

Date of Most Recent Fiscal year-end: _____   By: _____
                                            [Signature of Chief Financial Officer
                                            or other Executive Officer]

Date Owned/Invested: _____   Name: _____

(complete only if this date is after most recent   (Print or Type)
fiscal-year end)

                                            Title: _____

                                            (Print or Type)

                                            Address of Entity:
                                            _____

Figure 28 - Sample Qualified Institutional Buyer Form

Regulation A (Small Issue Registration)

Securities that are issued under Regulation A must be registered with the SEC, and an offering circular must be given to potential investors. These securities may only be issued under this exemption if they are U.S. or Canadian firms with an offering that does not exceed a total of 100,000 shares and a value of $5,000,000 in a twelve month period of time.

This form of registration is less expensive and less time consuming than a full registration.

Rule 147

Rule 147 provides a registration exemption for offerings that are restricted to residents of the state in which the issuing company is organized and conducting business.

Exempt Issuers

The securities issued by municipal, state, Federal, and other domestic governmental entities as well as charitable institutions and banks are exempt from the full provisions of the Act.

Municipal Issuance

Municipalities issue debt in the form of bonds and notes in order to borrow money to finance projects, cover short-term cash flow requirements, etc., and can use negotiated or competitive underwriting to issue these securities. Each of these methods is described in more detail later in this chapter.

While a more complete explanation of the types of debt securities issued by municipalities can be found in the chapter on Fixed Income Instruments, the two major categories are General Obligation Bonds and Revenue Bonds.

General Obligation Bonds

When a municipality wishes to raise funds with a General Obligation Bond (GO), it generally uses the process of competitive underwriting.

The sale of municipal GO bonds requires a notice to be posted in an approved publication. The following notice is an example of when a municipality wants to receive bids from potential underwriters, who are usually brokers which make a market in this type of security.

NOTICE OF INTENTION TO SELL BONDS

$10,000,000

CITY OF BERKELEY

1997 General Obligation Bonds (Election of 1996, Series A)

General
Obligation
Bonds

NOTICE IS HEREBY GIVEN that the City of Berkeley, intends to offer for public sale on Tuesday, May 20,1997 (or on such subsequent Tuesday as is communicated by the Clerk of the City of Berkeley through The Municipal News no less than 24 hours in advance) at the hour of 10:00 a.m., California time, at the office of Brown & Wood LLC, 565 California Street, 50th Floor, San Francisco, California 94104 $10,000,000* principal amount of general obligation bonds of the City designated "City of Berkeley 1997 General Obligation Bonds (Election of 1996, Series A)" (the "Bonds"). Within 24 hours of said date and time, the Director of Finance of the City will consider the bids received and, if an acceptable bid is received, award the sale of the Bonds on the basis of the lowest true interest cost. In the event that no bid is awarded by the designated time, proposals will be received the following Tuesday at the same time and place specified above and each Tuesday thereafter until such time as a bid is awarded notice to the contrary is given.

NOTICE IS HEREBY FURTHER GIVEN that the Bonds, dated June 1, 1997, will be offered for public sale subject to the terms and conditions of the Official Notice of Sale which, along with a Preliminary Official Statement relating to the Bonds, will be furnished upon request to Project Finance Associates, LLC, 1491 Indian Valley Road, Novato, California 94947, telephone: (415) 897-9943, the financial advisor to the City for the Bonds.

Dated: May 2,1997

CITY OF BERKELEY

By:/s/ Francis David

Director of Finance

* Preliminary, subject to change.

Figure 29 - Example of Municipal Notice of Sale

Revenue Bonds

Most Revenue Bonds are given to an underwriter on a negotiated basis, which does not include any competitive bidding.

U.S. Government Issuance

The different categories of U.S. government securities are discussed in the chapter on Fixed Income Instruments.

The process of issuance is different for U.S. government securities than for municipal issuance. The Treasury Department does not select a lead underwriter but performs that function itself. Well-capitalized broker/dealers are allowed to participate as Government Dealers in a periodic auction of government securities.

The U.S. Treasury auction process, called a Dutch Auction, permits authorized government dealers to place bids for a specific amount of securities. In the auction, each dealer makes a bid for a specific amount of securities at the price they are willing to pay.

- Prior to 1992, the Treasury Department used a multiple-price auction format, in which successful competitive bidders were awarded securities at the yields specified in their bids. The dealer with the highest bid got all they asked for at the price specified, and the next highest bidder received what they requested, and so on until all of the securities were sold.

- In 1992, the Treasury changed the format to a Dutch Auction single-price method, where all successful bidders (in the two-year and five-year note auctions) would receive the securities at the average price bid. In this method, the Treasury uses the bids to determine which dealer will get the securities, and uses the average bid of all of the successful bidders as the closing price.

Individuals are allowed to participate in the auction process; however they do not propose a price. Individuals can tell the Fed that they wish to purchase a certain amount of securities, and the Fed will sell them that amount at the average price established by the government dealers during the auction itself.

Asset Backed Securities Issuance

Asset Backed Securities, which are described in the chapter on Products, are generally issued by a few government sponsored agencies, which are responsible for purchasing, packaging, pricing and distributing the securities. When the issuer purchases a group of substantially similar mortgages and forms a pool of mortgages, the process of issuing a new security begins.

The process of issuing this type of security is substantially different from the normal underwriting process, and is not addressed in this book.

D. UNDERWRITING FOR SPECIFIC CATEGORIES OF ISSUERS

Although the laws apply equally to all forms of underwriting by corporations, there are some differences that are employed in creating new instruments for some specific categories of issuers.

Issuance by a Corporation

Corporations can issue equity or debt. While the details of these categories of instruments can be found in the various chapters on instrument types, there are two specific types of equity that should be mentioned in addition to the issuance of regular common or preferred shares:

Rights

A right can be issued by a corporation and given to current shareholders. It gives the shareholder the right to buy additional shares at a pre-determined price within a specific period of time. Once a right has been issued, it can be traded on an exchange or over the counter just like an equity.

A special type of underwriting, called a stand-by underwriting agreement (or stand-by registration) can be used if the issuer of an existing issue wishes to raise additional capital by issuing rights, but is unsure if there is enough market demand for the entire issue. In this case, the underwriter *stands-by* to purchase any of the shares that are not bought by investors exercising their rights.

Warrants

A corporation can also issue warrants, which are sold by the corporation to investors, and which allow investors the right to buy shares at a specific price for a specific period of time. This time period is usually longer than the time offered to rights holders.

More information about rights and warrants can be found in the chapter on Equities.

Mutual Fund Issuance

Mutual funds create securities that are sold to investors and which represent ownership of the managed investment company. Mutual funds are described in more detail in the chapter on Mutual Funds; however, there are two basic types that are involved as fund shares are issued.

Open End Fund

An open end mutual fund is one where the fund agrees to continue to sell shares in the fund as long as there are interested investors. The price of the fund is calculated as the Net Asset Value (NAV) of the Fund, and the shares are sold by the fund to the investors either directly or through brokers. Therefore, after the initial offering of an open end fund, shares continue to be issued.

Closed End Fund

A closed end fund is one where the fund managers decide at the time the fund is created what the maximum amount of the fund will be. When the fund is fully subscribed, the market price is no longer directly related to the NAV. Instead, the fund is bought and sold at whatever value investors believe it to be. Therefore, after the initial offering of a closed end fund, no additional shares are offered and all of the existing shares trade in the secondary market.

The types of mutual funds are presented in more detail in the chapter on Mutual Fund Instruments.

Issuance of Derivatives

Various forms of derivatives are issued by firms and, in the case of options, by individuals. The Options Clearing Corporation is the official issuer of all options listed on U.S. securities exchanges.

When an option is created (or written) by the seller, the process is also managed by OCC, which is described later in this book.

E. NEGOTIATED UNDERWRITING PROCESS

The first step in the issuance of securities in a negotiated underwriting occurs when the issuer registers its intent to issue securities by filing a registration form and a prospectus with the SEC.

Registration

There are different registration forms for various types of companies; however, the forms generally contain information such as:

- Business description and properties held
- Amount of shares held by officers, directors and underwriters
- Names of each investor holding over 10% of the shares
- Biographical information on the officers and directors

- Certified financial statements
- Description of the security being offered for sale
- Capitalization of the firm and the impact of this issue on the firm's capitalization
- How the money collected will be used

The registration of new issues with the SEC is intended to ensure that information disclosed to the investing public is adequate and accurate, and contains material facts concerning the company and the securities it proposes to sell. With this information, investors may make an informed and realistic appraisal of the value of the securities and then exercise their judgment to determine whether or not to purchase them.

The 1933 Act prohibits false and misleading statements under penalty of fine, imprisonment, or both. Investors who purchase securities and have financial losses have specific recovery rights through state or federal courts if they can prove that there was incomplete or inaccurate disclosure of material facts in the registration statement or prospectus. If such misstatements are proven, various entities involved in the sale of the securities could be found liable, including the:

- Issuing company
- Issuing company's responsible directors and officers
- Underwriters
- Company's controlling interests
- Sellers of the securities

Registration statements are examined by the SEC for compliance with the disclosure requirements of the 1933 Act. If a statement appears to be incomplete or inaccurate, the company is usually informed by letter and given an opportunity to file correcting or clarifying amendments. However, if the SEC concludes that the material deficiencies in the registration statement stems from a deliberate attempt to conceal or mislead, or that the deficiencies do not lend themselves to correction through the informal letter process, the SEC may decide that it is in the public interest to conduct a hearing to determine if a *stop order* should be issued which would stop or suspend the issuance.

The SEC may issue stop orders after the sale of securities has been commenced or completed. A stop order is not a permanent bar to the completion of the registration statement or to the sale of the securities. If amendments are filed correcting the statement in accordance with the stop order decision, the order must be lifted and the statement declared effective.

Prospectus

The Prospectus is required by the SEC, which specifies certain categories of information that must be included in the document. The prospectus must be approved by the SEC before an issue may be distributed.

The prospectus can come in two forms. Usually the prospectus is initially published with a specific disclaimer, called a *No Approval* clause, printed on the cover in red ink that says that the issue has not yet been approved by the SEC for sale. The preliminary prospectus, also called a red herring, does not have a price printed on it since the price will not be determined until later in the process after the registration has been approved by the SEC.

The prospectus is the only document that may be placed in the hands of the client. No securities representative can make copies of any magazine article, or any other document that refers to the company that is listed in the prospectus. Registered representatives have gotten into trouble by giving clients additional information. The rule is so strict that even underlining or highlighting the prospectus is not permitted.

There is an industry legend about a specific firm's registered representative who ran out of red herrings. According to the legend, he made copies of the front page and put it, along with his business card, under windshield wipers in a shopping mall. When the SEC found out about this, it said that the firm had to drop out of the syndicate since the SEC classified the solicitation as one where the broker did not provide a full disclosure.

The actual offering of the IPO is only made by the final prospectus that is issued after the red herring. The final prospectus does not have the disclaimer, and does have the actual price printed on it.

The SEC approves an issue if the registration form and the prospectus are complete and do not appear to contain any misleading information.

A final prospectus must be provided to any investor who purchases a new security listed on a registered stock exchange during the 25 days immediately after the issue has become effective. If the issue is an IPO and is only being traded over-the-counter, the prospectus must be provided for 90 days.

PROSPECTUS

SUBJECT TO COMPLETION, DATED APRIL 1, 1996

10,788,219 Shares

Class A Common Stock

Of the 10,788,219 shares offered hereby, 10,000,000 shares will be sold by Planet Hollywood International, Inc. (the "Company") and 788,219 shares will be sold by certain Selling Stockholders. The Company will not receive any of the proceeds from the sale of shares by the Selling Stockholders. See "Principal and Selling Stockholders."

A total of 8,630,575 shares (the "U.S. Shares") are being offered in the United States and Canada (the "U.S. Offering") by the U.S. Underwriters and 2,157,644 shares are being offered outside the United States and Canada (the "International Offering") by the Managers. The initial public offering price and the underwriting discounts and commissions are identical for both the U.S. Offering and the International Offering (collectively, the "Offerings").

Prior to the Offerings, there has been no public market for the shares. It is currently anticipated that the initial public offering price will be between $14.00 and $16.00 per share. See "Underwriting" for a discussion of the factors considered in determining the initial public offering price. Up to 1,000,000 of the shares will be reserved for sale to approximately 100 persons who are directors, officers or employees of, or are otherwise associated with, the Company and who have advised the Company of their desire to participate in its future growth. In addition, 1,610,584 shares will be reserved for sale to a principal stockholder of the Company. See "Underwriting."

The Class A Common Stock has been approved for trading on The Nasdaq Stock Market's National Market under the symbol "PHII," subject to official notice of issuance.

See "Risk Factors" beginning on page 9 for certain considerations relevant to an investment in the Class A Common Stock.

THESE SECURITIES HAVE NOT BEEN APPROVED OR DISAPPROVED BY THE SECURITIES AND EXCHANGE COMMISSION OR ANY STATE SECURITIES COMMISSION NOR HAS THE SECURITIES AND EXCHANGE COMMISSION OR ANY STATE SECURITIES COMMISSION PASSED UPON THE ACCURACY OR ADEQUACY OF THIS PROSPECTUS. ANY REPRESENTATION TO THE CONTRARY IS A CRIMINAL OFFENSE.

	Price to Public	Underwriting Discounts and Commissions (1)	Proceeds to Company (2)	Proceeds to Selling Stockholders (3)
Per Share	$	$	$	$
Total (4)	$	$	$	$

(1) See "Underwriting" for indemnification arrangements with the U.S. Underwriters and the Managers.
(2) Before deducting expenses payable by the Company, estimated at $
(3) Before deduction of $7,882 ($.01 per share) to be paid to the Company upon the exercise of Warrants relating to the shares to be sold by the Selling Stockholders.
(4) The Company has granted to the U.S. Underwriters and the Managers 30-day options to purchase in the aggregate up to 1,618,233 additional shares of Class A Common Stock solely to cover over-allotments, if any. If the options are exercised in full, the total Price to Public, Underwriting Discounts and Commissions and Proceeds to Company will be $, $ and $, respectively. See "Underwriting."

The U.S. Shares are offered by the several U.S. Underwriters, subject to prior sale, when, as and if delivered to and accepted by them and subject to certain conditions, including the approval of certain legal matters by counsel. The U.S. Underwriters reserve the right to withdraw, cancel or modify the U.S. Offering and to reject orders in whole or in part. It is expected that delivery of the U.S. Shares will be made against payment therefor on or about   , 1996, at the offices of Bear, Stearns & Co. Inc., 245 Park Avenue, New York, New York 10167.

Bear, Stearns & Co. Inc.
Montgomery Securities
Schroder Wertheim & Co.
Smith Barney Inc.
, 1996

Figure 30 - Example of a Red Herring

PROSPECTUS

10,788,219 Shares

Class A Common Stock

Of the 10,788,219 shares offered hereby, 10,000,000 shares will be sold by Planet Hollywood International, Inc. (the "Company") and 788,219 shares will be sold by certain Selling Stockholders. The Company will not receive any of the proceeds from the sale of shares by the Selling Stockholders. See "Principal and Selling Stockholders."

A total of 8,630,575 shares (the "U.S. Shares") are being offered in the United States and Canada (the "U.S. Offering") by the U.S. Underwriters and 2,157,644 shares (the "International Shares") are being offered outside the United States and Canada (the "International Offering") by the managers of the International Offering named herein (the "Managers"). The initial public offering price and the underwriting discounts and commissions are identical for both the U.S. Offering and the International Offering (collectively, the "Offerings").

Prior to the Offerings, there has been no public market for the shares. See "Underwriting" for a discussion of the factors considered in determining the initial public offering price. Up to 1,240,645 of the shares have been reserved for sale to approximately 100 persons who are directors, officers or employees of, or are otherwise associated with, the Company and who have advised the Company of their desire to participate in its future growth. In addition, 1,910,000 shares have been reserved for sale to a principal stockholder of the Company. See "Underwriting."

The Class A Common Stock has been approved for trading on The Nasdaq Stock Market's National Market under the symbol "PHII," subject to official notice of issuance.

See "Risk Factors" beginning on page 9 for certain considerations relevant to an investment in the Class A Common Stock.

THESE SECURITIES HAVE NOT BEEN APPROVED OR DISAPPROVED BY THE SECURITIES AND EXCHANGE COMMISSION OR ANY STATE SECURITIES COMMISSION NOR HAS THE SECURITIES AND EXCHANGE COMMISSION OR ANY STATE SECURITIES COMMISSION PASSED UPON THE ACCURACY OR ADEQUACY OF THIS PROSPECTUS. ANY REPRESENTATION TO THE CONTRARY IS A CRIMINAL OFFENSE.

	Price to Public	Underwriting Discounts and Commissions(1)	Proceeds to Company(2)	Proceeds to Selling Stockholders(3)
Per Share	$18.00	$1.08	$16.92	$16.92
Total(4)	$194,187,942	$11,651,277	$169,200,000	$13,336,665

(1) See "Underwriting" for indemnification arrangements with the U.S. Underwriters and the Managers.
(2) Before deducting expenses payable by the Company, estimated at $1,825,000.
(3) Before deduction of $7,882 ($.01 per share) to be paid to the Company upon the exercise of Warrants relating to the shares to be sold by the Selling Stockholders.
(4) The Company has granted to the U.S. Underwriters and the Managers 30-day options to purchase in the aggregate up to 1,618,233 additional shares of Class A Common Stock solely to cover over-allotments, if any. If the options are exercised in full, the total Price to Public, Underwriting Discounts and Commissions and Proceeds to Company will be $223,316,136, $13,398,968 and $196,580,502, respectively. See "Underwriting."

The U.S. Shares are offered by the several U.S. Underwriters, subject to prior sale, when, as and if delivered to and accepted by them and subject to certain conditions, including the approval of certain legal matters by counsel. The U.S. Underwriters reserve the right to withdraw, cancel or modify the U.S. Offering and to reject orders in whole or in part. It is expected that delivery of the U.S. Shares will be made against payment therefor on or about April 24, 1996, at the offices of Bear, Stearns & Co. Inc., 245 Park Avenue, New York, New York 10167.

Bear, Stearns & Co. Inc.
Montgomery Securities
Schroder Wertheim & Co.
Smith Barney Inc.

April 18, 1996

Figure 31 - Example of a Final Prospectus

A prospectus can be a very detailed, complicated document. The preliminary prospectus shown on the previous page, which was used to raise approximately $30 million, consisted of 12 chapters and 77 pages. The document is used to identify the risks facing the investor, and how the money will be used by the company. There is an extensive analysis of the company's financial data, including the prior year results and future expectations.

Subject To Completion, Dated May 22, 1997

PROSPECTUS

2,300,000 Shares

Common Stock

All of the 2,300,000 shares of Common Stock offered hereby are being sold by New Era of Networks, Inc. ("NEON" or the "Company"). Prior to this offering, there has been no public market for the Common Stock of the Company. It is currently estimated that the initial public offering price will be between $10.00 and $12.00 per share. See "Underwriting" for a discussion of the factors to be considered in determining the initial public offering price. The Company has applied to have the Common Stock approved for quotation on the Nasdaq National Market under the symbol "NEON."

The Common Stock offered hereby involves a high degree of risk. See "Risk Factors," beginning on page 6.

THESE SECURITIES HAVE NOT BEEN APPROVED OR DISAPPROVED BY THE SECURITIES AND EXCHANGE COMMISSION OR ANY STATE SECURITIES COMMISSION NOR HAS THE SECURITIES AND EXCHANGE COMMISSION OR ANY STATE SECURITIES COMMISSION PASSED UPON THE ACCURACY OR ADEQUACY OF THIS PROSPECTUS. ANY REPRESENTATION TO THE CONTRARY IS A CRIMINAL OFFENSE.

	Price to Public	Underwriting Discounts and Commissions(1)	Proceeds to Company(2)
Per Share	$	$	$
Total (3)	$	$	$

1. For information regarding indemnification of the Underwriters, see "Underwriting."
2. Before deducting expenses of the offering payable by the Company, estimated at $850,000.
3. The Company has granted the Underwriters an option, exercisable within 30 days from the date hereof, to purchase up to 345,000 additional shares of Common Stock on the same terms and conditions set forth above, solely to cover over-allotments, if any. If such option is exercised in full, the total Price to Public will be $, the Underwriters' Discounts and Commissions will be $ and the Proceeds to Company will be $. See "Underwriting."

The shares of Common Stock offered by the Underwriters are subject to prior sale, receipt and acceptance by them and are subject to the right of the Underwriters to reject any order in whole or in part and certain other conditions. It is expected that delivery of such shares will be made through the offices of UBS Securities LLC, 299 Park Avenue, New York, New York, on or about   , 1997.

UBS Securities   Cowen & Company

, 1997

Figure 32 - Example of a Preliminary Prospectus

The prospectus also discusses the market in which this company will operate and their competition. The chapters included in this prospectus were:

- Risk Factors
- Use of Proceeds
- Dividend Policy
- Capitalization and Dilution
- Financial Data
- Management's Discussion of Finances and Operations
- Prior Year Results
- Description of the Business
- Management
- Principal Stockholders
- Description of Capital Stock
- Report of Independent Public Accountants

Process

The registration statement and prospectus become public immediately after they are filed with the SEC; however, if the issuer has never issued stock before, the issuer must wait 20 days after filing the registration with the SEC (or 20 days after the final amendment) before the actual offer to potential investors can occur. This is known as the cooling-off period.

During this time, the SEC examines the registration form for completeness, and may ask for changes or additional information. While the SEC is responsible for reviewing the prospectus, it will never offer an opinion as to whether this is a good investment or not. If the SEC wants more information, it will send a Deficiency Letter, and if concerned, may issue a Stop Order.

During the 20 day period, a syndicate is officially established. A syndicate is a group of underwriters that will work together to distribute the issue to investors. There is always a lead manager, and there may be co-managers as well as different levels of co-managers, based upon the amount of risk they are willing to take. Additional brokers can be included to help in the distribution but who do not take any investment risk, and are called the Selling Group.

During this period, the issuer will also register the security in each state where the underwriter intends to distribute the issue, which normally means all 50 states. These registrations are made under each state's Blue Sky Laws, which are state-specific laws that extend Federal laws. There are three methods of potential registration in each state, at the state's discretion:

- Formal *notification* by the issuer by filing a registration with the state
- A process of *coordinating* the state and Federal registration at the same time
- An issuer can be *qualified* by the state if it meets the state's requirements after the SEC has approved the registration

When the syndicate has been formed, the lead manager is required to publish a

Tombstone, which is an advertisement that is placed in a newspaper so that Wall Street will know that the security might soon be available.

Tombstone

There are several required portions of the tombstone.

- At the top of every tombstone is the disclaimer that is required by the SEC that states that the offer of these securities can only be made by the prospectus.

- In the center of the tombstone the actual issue is described. The issue shown below is for common stock.

- The names of the underwriters of this issue are printed at the bottom of this tombstone. In this example they are identified as joint lead managers.

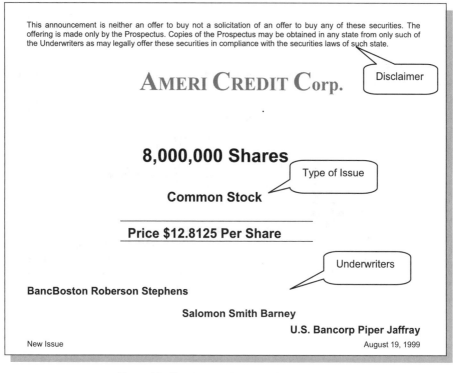

Figure 33 - Tombstone (Common Stock)

The tombstone shown in the following example is one that was published for a new issue of common shares for Iron Mountain Inc. [34]

This tombstone shows that Iron Mountain Incorporated is offering 4,025,000 common shares at a price of $34.75 per share. The three lead managers are shown in larger type at the bottom of the tombstone, and the co-managers are shown in smaller type. If there were multiple classes of co-managers based upon their participation in the offering, the different classes would be identified by different sizes of type.

This announcement is neither an offer to buy not a solicitation of an offer to buy any of these securities. The offering is made only by the Prospectus Supplement and the related Prospectus.

NEW ISSUE

4,025,000

 IRON MOUNTAIN INCORPORATED

Common Stock
Price $34.75 Per Share

Copies of the Prospectus Supplement and the related Prospectus may be obtained in any state in which this announcement is circulated from only such of the Underwriters, including the undersigned, as may lawfully offer these securities in such state.

Bear Stearns & Co. Inc.

        William Blair & Company

                Prudential Securities Incorporated

Allen & Company	Chase Securities Inc.	Merrill Lynch & Co.	PaineWebber Incorporated
Wasserstein Perella Securities, Inc.	Blackford Securities Corp.	Cantor, Weiss & Friedner, Inc.
John Dawson & Associates	First Analysis Securities Corporation	Sanders Morris Mundy

Figure 34 - Tombstone

---

[34] Iron Mountain is a records depository that is used by many financial firms. It is located in upstate New York, and is actually in a cave that has been carved out of a mountain.

Soliciting Investors

After the registration and prospectus have been filed with the SEC, the syndicate is permitted to begin to solicit public interest by issuing offer letters.

```
New Era of Networks, Inc.
Directed Securities Program
Page 1


May 30, 1997

TO: Friends of New Era of Networks, Inc.

New Era of Networks, Inc. ("the Company") recently filed a registration statement
with the Securities and Exchange Commission with respect to the proposed initial
public offering of 2,300,000 shares of common stock. The managing underwriters of
the initial public offering are UBS Securities, LLC and Cowen & Co.

In connection with this offering, the management of the Company has asked the
underwriters to make a certain number of shares available for employees and friends
of the Company.

The probable price range of this offering is estimated between $ 10 and $ 12 per
share. The approximate date on which it is anticipated the proposed offering of
these shares will commence is the week of June 16, 1997.

Since a limited number of shares are available, we request that the shares be
purchased only for your account. The deadline for submitting the attached
Indication of Interest and accompanying documentation to the UBS Securities LLC
Restricted Stock Group is Monday, June 9, 1997.

Prior to making a decision to submit your indication of interest in this initial
public offering, please review the preliminary prospectus as there are risks
associated with investing in any initial public offering and in the stock market as
well. A copy of the preliminary prospectus is enclosed.

A registration statement relating to these securities has been filed with the
Securities Exchange Commission but has not yet become effective. No offer to buy
the securities can be accepted and no part of the purchase price can be received
until the registration statement has become effective, and any such offer may be
withdrawn or revoked, without obligation or commitment of any kind, at any time
prior to notice of its acceptance given after the effective date. An indication of
interest in response to this correspondence will involve no obligation or
commitment of any kind. This communication shall not constitute an offer to buy nor
shall there be any sale of these securities in any state in which such offer,
solicitation or sale would be unlawful prior to registration or qualification under
the securities laws of any such state.

Please read the New Era of Networks, Inc. Directed Securities Program's
instructions which are attached. If you have any questions concerning any of the
attached documents, please call Linda Lund at (415) 352-5696

Sincerely,

//Original Signed//

Gregory R. Miller
Vice President




                                                          UBS Securities LLC
```

Figure 35 - Letter Soliciting Investors

When an IPO is established, there are several categories of potential investors:

- Employees of the company
- The underwriting syndicate
- Retail clients
- Institutional clients
- Friends of the company

The letter that is shown on the previous page is an example of a letter that was offered to friends of the company.

IPO Indication of Interest

In addition to the offer letter, the prospective investor is required to confirm their interest in the IPO. A sample of an Indication of Interest letter is shown on the next page.

This letter allows potential investors to request a certain number of shares and to acknowledge that they:

- Have received a copy of the preliminary prospectus
- Might not get all of the shares they requested
- Agree to pay for whatever they get
- Agree to let the underwriter tell the firm about the purchase
- Were not recipients of any inside information

It is important to point out that an individual who requests a certain number of shares is not automatically entitled to them. In many cases, the IPO is over-subscribed and the investor may only receive a portion of those requested.

New Era of Networks, Inc.
Directed Securities Program
Page 5

INDICATION OF INTEREST

I/We hereby indicate my/our interest in purchasing _____ shares of the New Era of Networks, Inc. (the "Company") common shares at the Initial Public Offering.

By signing below, I/We agree to and certify the following:

1. I/we have received and read the Preliminary Prospectus and fully understand the risks associated with the investments in the stock market generally and with these securities in particular;

2. I/we understand and agree that, because the amount of securities available as part of the New Era of Networks, Inc. Directed Securities Program is limited and subject to certain conditions, the number of shares I/we am/are interested in purchasing may be reduced without further consultation with me/us and, furthermore, that there is no assurance I/we will be able to participate in the program or to purchase any shares;

3. I/we agree to pay for whatever amount of shares is finally allocated to me/us within three(3) business days of the Offering Date;

4. I/we hereby authorize UBS Securities, LLC, to release to Company information about the number of shares allocated to me/us;

5. I/we agree and acknowledge that I/we have not received or relied upon any investment advise from UBS Securities LLC, and that my/our decision to invest in the Company's securities was made independently, based upon my/our own investment analysis and/or that of my/our investment advisors.

(X)_____   (X)_____
Client Signature/Date   Client Signature/Date

_____   _____
Print Name   Print Name

Figure 36 - Indication of Interest Letter

IPO Questionnaire

In addition to the subscription request, the potential investor is also required to attest to certain conditions that are required by the SEC in order to prevent insider trading. The questionnaire shown on the next page requires potential investors to identify if they are:

- Employees (including immediate family members) of a broker
- Finders related to the deal
- A fiduciary
- An employee (including immediate family members) of a bank

And, if they are any one of the above, are they acting in accordance with their normal investment practice.

Due Diligence

Approximately ten days after the prospectus has been filed with the SEC, a due diligence meeting is held by the underwriting syndicate. This meeting is also called an information meeting.

This meeting is called by the Lead Manager and the participants are the financial officials of the corporation and the other syndicate members. At this time, price may be discussed, but the price is not yet formally set.

On the 20th day an official price meeting is held. Once that meeting is held and a price has been determined, it is printed on the final prospectus. If the price is too high the issue won't sell, and if it is too low the company doesn't get the money it is worth.

At this point, although the price has been determined, the issue does not have to be immediately sold. It can be held until market conditions are favorable.

The difference between the issue price and the amount the issuer gets is called the spread, which goes to the syndicate. Typically, for every dollar of the spread, the lead manager gets $.30, whether he sells the shares or not. The co-managers that sell the shares get $0.70 on every dollar of the spread, as does the lead manager on the shares he sells.

The example of a final prospectus shown earlier in this chapter showed that the underwriter received $1.08 per share.

The lead manager does not usually distribute all of the shares to the co-managers. Approximately 25% of the issue is held to be allocated to the selling group, institutional purchasers and friends of the company.

The selling group gets a *selling concession*, which is a professional discount of $0.25 cents per share to cover their distribution costs and their profit.

Unless the SEC has objected, the twentieth day after the filing is the effective date of the issue. Any time after the effective date, the issuer can establish the public offering date.

New Era of Networks, Inc.
Directed Securities Program
Page 4

DIRECTED SECURITIES QUESTIONNAIRE

The rules of the National Association of Securities Dealers, Inc. ("NASD") require that we obtain certain information about you and your "immediate family," which the NASD defines as:

> your "**parents, mother-in-law or father-in-law, husband or wife, brother or sister, brother-in-law or sister-in-law, son-in-law or daughter-in-law, and children,**" as well as "**any other person who is supported, directly, or in directly, to a material extent**" by you or other members or you immediate family.

This information is needed to ensure that neither you nor we engage in transactions prohibited by the NASD. Please complete the following questionnaire by checking the appropriate boxes below and sign and date where requested.

1. Are you or a member of your immediate family an officer, director, general partner, employee or agent of, or otherwise associated with, a securities broker or dealer?   Yes   No

2.

(a) Are you or any member of your immediate family a finder in respect to the public offering contemplated hereby, or   Yes   No

(b) Are you or any member of your immediate family acting in a fiduciary capacity to any of the managing underwriters (including as an attorney, accountant, or financial consultant)?   Yes   No

(c) Are you or any member of your immediate family a senior officer of a   domestic or foreign bank savings and loan institution, insurance company, investment company, investment advisory fund or other institutional account (such as a hedge fund, investment partnership/corporation or investment club), or do your or any member of your immediate family's activities directly or indirectly involve or influence the buying or selling of securities for any such entity?   Yes   No

3. If you answered "YES" to any of the questions in 2 above, are you purchasing these securities in accordance with your **"normal investment practice,"** which the NASD describes as investments of approximately the same size, frequency and dollar amount during the last year or several years? Please note that the purchase of mainly "hot issues" (primary offerings that trade at a premium in the secondary market) can not be considered to constitute normal investment practice   Yes   No

(X)_____   (X)_____
Client Signature/Date   Client Signature/Date

_____   _____
Print Name   Print Name

Figure 37 - Directed Securities Questionnaire

Listing on an Exchange

In 1983, the NYSE developed specific procedures to help companies list on the NYSE concurrently with their initial public offerings. One of the main advantages to listing immediately on an exchange is that the companies receive an exemption from most states' blue-sky registration requirements, which saves time and expense.

The issuers wishing to list on the NYSE concurrently with their IPO must meet all the NYSE's listing standards. The exchange will accept a statement from the company's underwriter that the offering will meet or exceed NYSE standards regarding the market value of the shares and the number of shareholders.

Companies that wish to list in conjunction with their IPO are required to submit the following documents to the NYSE:

- Corporate Charter and By-Laws

- Draft Prospectus or Registration Statement, including financial statements

Once these are received, the NYSE process consists of the following steps.

- A confidential eligibility review is requested by the issuer, which begins when the eligibility package is received by the exchange. It takes about two weeks for the exchange to complete their review.

- The issuer receives verbal and written communication from the exchange regarding its eligibility clearance and notification of any listing conditions that might exist. The issuer may file its application when it received the eligibility clearance, or at any time in the next six months.

- The issuer files an original listing application at any time within the six-month period following its eligibility clearance. An acknowledgment of the clearance will appear in the NYSE Weekly Bulletin on the first Friday following the receipt of the application.

- The NYSE authorization of the listing, which recognizes the receipt of all of the critical documentation, and the SEC's certification also take about two weeks.

- The issuer's securities are admitted to trading, and the original listing date is established at the issuer's convenience and can be set for any day after the effective date of the registration.

Distributing the Underwriting

Underwriters and the Corporate Trustee/ Transfer Agents are increasingly using the DTC's FAST (Fast Automated Security System) system to distribute shares during an IPO. This system allows the corporate trustee or transfer agent to hold the master certificate in their own custody rather than in the vaults at DTC, which also indemnifies the DTC for any loss, fire, fraud etc

The following graph shows the growth in the number of issues distributed by FAST.

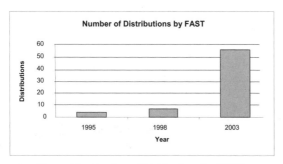

Figure 38 - Number of Distributions by FAST

Procedures for Hot and Weak Issues

Immediately after an issue's public offering date, either demand will exceed supply and the price will rise, or the supply will exceed the demand and the price will fall.

Bid Stabilization for Weak Issues

When a new security is issued, the managers want to ensure that the price either goes up or at least remains stable, so they establish an artificial bid stabilization period, which usually lasts about two weeks.

Stabilization is a form of price manipulation that is allowed by the SEC. Since not every new issue is in demand, and since falling prices damage the confidence of the market, the managing underwriter can issue a standing bid for the purchase of the issue at, or slightly under, the offering price in order to keep the price from falling.

During this period, the syndicate managers are willing to buy the security at the issue price to artificially maintain the price level. This artificially prevents the price from dropping in the first weeks after a distribution.

The underwriters and the selling group also encourage investors to hold the securities rather than look for a fast profit or to sell immediately after the purchase.

- This encouragement applies primarily to retail high net-worth individual clients. Brokers will tell these retail clients that if they want to continue being considered for new issues, they should hold the stock. The members of the selling group are also encouraged to control their retail clients since the syndicate can penalize the broker and not pay the broker's distribution commission if the broker's clients sell their shares too quickly.

- This message is not presented as strongly to the institutions that purchase a large number of shares. Since the underwriters need their continued support, they do not complain automatically if the institutional clients begin to sell immediately after a new issue is distributed to take a fast profit.

For both types of clients, the Underwriting community and the DTC developed an IPO Tracking system to track "flippers" so that the syndicate member selling to that institution would be penalized by taking back the selling concession that was awarded for that sub-allocation. The syndicate member could then decide whether or not to allocate future IPOs to that institution.

Hot Issues

A hot issue exists when there is an over subscription and the demand exceeds the supply. That usually means that the trading immediately after issuance drives the price of the stock up.

The following categories of investors are not allowed to invest in hot issues:

- Broker/dealer's cannot buy hot issues for their own account

- Officers and directors of the issuing firm and their immediate families

- Senior officers and employees of the securities departments of banks and insurance companies

An underwriter can legally over-sell the offering by up to 15% by anticipating cancellations. If the underwriter has to buy in the after-market to satisfy subscriptions after the price has gone up, the losses are pro-rated to all of the members of the syndicate.

Free Riding

Free riding occurs when a firm holds securities that have been issued, even though it has orders, so that the demand pushes the price up. Free riding is not allowed by the exchanges or the NASD.

> Principal Jack A. Alexander of Poway, CA, was suspended for five days. Without admitting or denying the allegations, Mr. Alexander consented to findings that he purchased shares of a new issue that traded at a premium in the immediate aftermarket, in contravention of the NASD Board of Governors Free-Riding and Withholding Interpretation.
>
> Source: Wall Street Journal

Figure 39 - Example of Free Riding

Quiet Period

The SEC also imposes a quiet period for twenty-five days after the IPO where brokerage firms cannot issue research reports. As soon as this period is over, firms begin to publish investment options.

F. COMPETITIVE UNDERWRITING PROCESS

Competitive underwriting, also called competitive bidding, is a process employed by municipalities in order to try to get the best possible price for their debt. The process allows multiple lead underwriters to create a syndicate to bid on the issue. The potential lead underwriters each prepare a bid to distribute the issue, the municipality compares the bids that it receives and then selects the winning underwriter or syndicate.

Municipal underwriting also involves the use of additional categories of experts:

Financial Advisors

A financial advisor assists the municipality in determining the type of bonds to issue (GO or Revenue Bonds), the maturity, insurance, call provisions, etc.

Bond Counsel

Municipal issues require a legal opinion by an attorney who functions as the bond counsel. The counsel certifies that the issue meets all of the applicable laws, and that all of the required documentation is property maintained.

G. U.S. UNDERWRITING TRENDS

The leading underwriters are shown in the league tables that are compiled by Dealogic/ COMMSCAN in the next two sections. These tables are used by the firms to promote their own underwriting experience and to attract additional clients.

Leading U.S. Bond Underwriters

In 2003, ten firms accounted for 59% of the over $1 Trillion in bonds that were introduced to the market, as shown in this table.

Rank	Bookrunner	Deals	Amount ($ Billions)	Market Share %
1	Citigroup	1,445	441,118.72	8.57
2	Lehman Brothers	1,510	331,745.39	6.45
3	Morgan Stanley	1,455	328,503.54	6.38
4	Credit Suisse First Boston	1,158	318,748.38	6.19
5	Deutsche Bank	1,465	317,478.60	6.17
6	JP Morgan	1,177	294,814.47	5.73
7	Merrill Lynch	1,726	287,792.63	5.59
8	UBS	1,237	275,828.77	5.36
9	Goldman Sachs	854	254,638.35	4.95
10	Banc of America	1,745	196,858.56	3.82
	Subtotal	11,679	3,047,527.40	59.21
	Total	27,429	5,146,901.39	100

Source: Dealogic/ COMMSCAN

Figure 40 - Leading U.S. Fixed Income Underwriters

Leading U.S. Equity Underwriters

Also, in 2003, ten firms accounted for 71% of the nearly $455 Billion in new equities that were brought to the market in the U.S., as shown in the following table.

Rank	Bookrunner	Deals	Amount ($ Billions)	Market Share %
1	Goldman Sachs	170	48	11.04
2	Citigroup	237	44	10.05
3	Morgan Stanley	154	40	9.21
4	JP Morgan	162	37	8.24
5	Merrill Lynch	160	32	7.29
6	Deutsche Bank	128	32	7.13
7	UBS	187	31	7.01
8	Credit Suisse First Boston	138	23	5.15
9	Lehman Brothers	94	15	3.32
10	Nomura	118	12	2.77
	Subtotal	1,231	316	71.21
	Total	4,131	444	100

Source: Dealogic/ COMMSCAN

Figure 41 - Leading U.S. Equity Underwriters

H. UNDERWRITING PROFIT DYNAMICS

Underwriting can be very profitable, and there are many different ways for firms to make money. Firms throughout the securities industry want to participate in underwriting, and that is why commercial banks are shifting towards the securities industry as their traditional banking business dissolves.

	Fees	Spread	Commission
Principal	X	X	
Agent	X		
Selling Group			X

Figure 42 - Sources of Underwriting Revenue

The underwriting spread on equities can be as much as 7%, while the spreads on bonds are usually closer to 0.7%, with municipals as little as 0.1%. When the relative size of the bond vs. the equity market is factored in, the revenues received from bonds and equities by the underwriters are approximately equal.

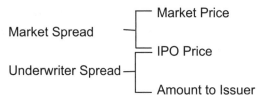

Figure 43 - Source of Spread Revenue

Underwriters charge fees for their services and may also purchase a block of the shares or bonds and attempt to resell it at a higher price. In this circumstance, the underwriters are compensated by the market spread, which is the difference in the IPO price and the selling price.

Brokers typically receive commissions of about 4% when they serve as a member of a selling group, in addition to their professional discount.

V. Account Opening

In order to buy and sell securities, have a bank act as a custodian or trustee, or to have an investment manager manage a portfolio, an investor must open a securities account. This process is different for different types of clients and for the different types of accounts that can be opened for these clients. In this chapter, we will discuss how individuals and institutions open various types of securities accounts.

The clients for securities products can be individuals, corporations, partnerships or trusts. There are different types of securities accounts available for each category of client which can be opened by a broker, bank or investment manager. This chapter describes the different types of clients that can open securities accounts, the differences in the accounts available and what is needed to open these different types of accounts.

The primary objectives for firms during the account opening process are:

- Ensure that all of the required documentation is correct in order to protect the firm
- Know your client in order to avoid fraud and to comply with increasingly strict regulations such as the USA PATRIOT Act
- Ensure that the client understands the terms of the account

The secondary objective during account opening is to process the account opening efficiently.

A. INDIVIDUAL ACCOUNTS

When a client opens an individual account (also called a retail brokerage account) to buy and sell securities, the account agreement between the client and the broker defines what the client can and can not do, and limits the liability of the broker.

To open a retail account, several types of forms are needed, which include:

- Account Opening Form
- Client Agreement
- Signature Cards
- Tax Forms

These forms are discussed throughout the rest of this chapter.

Account Opening Form

An account opening form is used to identify the person or persons opening the account and to begin the processing of evaluating their credit history and their ability to invest in complex instruments.

Accounts are opened by a representative of a financial firm.

- In a brokerage firm, these representatives who passed the Series 7 licensing exam and are registered by a sponsoring firm are Registered Representatives. Increasingly they are also called account executives or investment consultants, which are more client-oriented terms.
- In a bank, the historic term for a client representative in the securities business has been account executive or relationship manager. When helping a client initiate a securities transaction, these individuals must also have passed the Series 7 exam and be registered by their firm.

In all firms, the account opening form, which has been filled out by the client and reviewed by the firm's registered representative, goes to a processing unit that verifies the information. This is an important step since it is a critical function to protect the firm *and* the client.

Clients are protected since this reduces the chance that an unscrupulous broker will try to get an uninformed person to invest in complex instruments. And the firm is protected from clients who have a history of fraud or financial insolvency.

- NYSE Rule 405, and similar rules on other exchanges, requires brokers to be able to prove that they know enough about their clients' investment requirements and financial positions to know the suitability of each investment for the client. NYSE Rule 405 states, in part, "Every member organization is required ...to use due diligence to learn the essential facts relative to every client, every order, every cash or margin account accepted ... and every person holding power of attorney over any account..." [35]

- NYSE Rule 407 also requires that employees of other brokerage firms, exchanges, etc., obtain a written consent from their employer to open an account with another financial firm. Additionally, a duplicate account statement and confirmations must be sent directly to their employer from the other financial firm. Rule 407 states, in part, "No member shall, without the prior written consent of the employer, open a securities or commodities account [if the account opener is]:
  - An employee of another firm
  - An employee of an exchange
  - A director or officer of a publicly traded firm" [36]

Because of these rules and the need to fully *know the client*, some of the main points that are covered in the retail account opening form are:

- Identification of the client so that the person's credit history can be checked, which includes:
  - Full name and address
  - Social security number or taxpayer ID number
  - Age
  - Employment status
  - Marital status and number of dependents
- Financial History (Net worth)
- Investment History (Experience and Objective)
- Potential Insider Trading Conflicts
  - Affiliations with securities firms
  - Officer or director of publicly held firms
  - Significant shareholder of a publicly traded firm

The following form is an example of a form that is used to acquire new accounts

---

[35] Source: New York Stock Exchange

[36] ibid

information.

New Account Information Form (please complete and sign at the bottom)

Title of Account (if joint, include both names)

Home Address (do not use P.O. Box)

Street Address

Street Address

City, State, Zip

Home Telephone Number

Business Address (do not use P.O. Box)

Street Address

Street Address

City, State, Zip

Home Telephone Number

**Address for all ___ Home   ___ Business   ___ Other (fill out below)
communications:**

Other Address:

Street Address

City, State, Zip

Citizen of U.S.   Yes ___   No ___   Marital Status   Individual ___   Married ___

Social Security Number	Date of Birth	Country of Legal Residence
Employer	Position	Occupation

Spousal Information:

Name	Employer	Position

Financial Information (for joint accounts, use combined financial numbers)

Bank Reference (Bank Name)	Other Brokerage Accounts
Annual Income (Approximate)	Net Worth (excluding home)

Investment Objective (check one)   Capital Preservation___   Income ___   Growth ___   Speculation ___
Investment Experience (check one)   None ___   Limited ___   Good ___   Extensive ___
Investment Knowledge (check one)   None ___   Limited ___   Good ___   Extensive ___

Specify any security(s) firms in which you (or any joint account holder) are affiliated:

Specify all publicly traded companies with which you (or any joint account holder) have been in the last 3 months a 16-b officer, director, or 10% shareholder:

Joint Account Holder

Citizen of U.S.   Yes ___   No ___

Social Security Number	Date of Birth	Country of Legal Residence
Employer	Position	Occupation
Home Telephone Number		Business Telephone Number

Client agrees to notify Firm of any changes in this information

Account Holder Signature   Date

Joint Account Holder Signature   Date

To Be Completed By Registered Representative

RR Registered in State of Client's Residence?   Yes ___   No ___   Account Number _____

Client Introduced By _____   How Long Have Your Known Client _____

Signature of Registered Representative)   (Date)   (Signature of Branch Office Manager/Principal)   (Date)

Figure 45 - Sample Account Opening Form

Account Agreement

The actual account agreement that is used is a legal contract between the brokerage firm and the account opener, and the terms are based upon the type of account that is opened. There are several types of accounts that are available for retail clients. Some are only used by individuals for accounts that have a single owner and some can also be used by other types of clients.

The type of account that is selected depends upon the financial circumstances of the individual investor and his level of financial knowledge. Certain types of accounts allow the investor to assume additional risk in the hope of higher returns.

There are several general account terms, however, that are common to most of the different types of accounts.

- The account contract gives the firm the right to hold the investor's securities in book-entry form in the firm's name at a depository.

- Individual accounts with a brokerage firm typically give the broker the right to use the account holder's securities for securities lending without compensating the account holder. For larger individual and institutional accounts, firms will normally negotiate a split of the revenue received from the lending activities.

- The account form identifies who has the signing authority over the account.

- A power of attorney is sometimes used to give someone other than the owner of the account the right to make decisions regarding the account.
    - A limited power of attorney normally permits the person managing the account to enter buy and sell orders, but not to move money out of the account.
    - A full power of attorney permits the person managing the account to deposit and withdraw securities and cash in addition to buying and selling securities.

- The agreement will also be used to identify any investment constraints that may have been placed on the account.

TSG
Securities

TSG Securities LLC
Subsidiary of The Summit Group

CLIENT CASH ACCOUNT AGREEMENT
(Please read agreement and sign on page 3)

In consideration for TSG Securities LLC ("TSGS") opening or maintaining one or more accounts (the "Account") for the undersigned (the "Client"), the Client agrees to the terms and the conditions contained in this Agreement. The heading of each provision of this Agreement is for descriptive purposes only and shall not be deemed to modify or qualify any of the rights or obligations set forth in each such provision. For purposes of this agreement, securities and other property means, but is not limited to, money, securities, financial instruments and commodities of every kind of nature and related contracts and options, except that the provisions of paragraph 22 herein (the arbitration clause) shall not apply to commodities accounts. This definition includes securities or other property currently or hereafter held, carried or maintained by you or by any of your affiliates, in your possession or control, or in the possession or control of any such affiliate, for any purpose, in and for any of my accounts now or hereafter opened, including any account in which I may have an interest. This agreement shall not become effective until accepted by TSGS in its New York office. Acceptance may be evidenced by internal records maintained by TSGS.

1.   APPLICABLE RULES AND REGULATIONS

All transactions in the Client's Account shall be subject to the constitution, rules, regulations, customs and usages of the exchange or market, and its clearinghouse, if any, where the transactions are executed by TSGS or its agents, including its subsidiaries and affiliates. Also, where applicable, the transactions shall be subject to (a) to the provisions of (1) the Securities Exchange Act of 1934, as amended, and (2) the Commodities Exchange Act, as amended; and (b) to the rules and regulations of (1) the Securities and Exchange Commission, (2) the Board of Governors of the Federal Reserve System and (3) the Commodities Futures Trading Commission.

2. AGREEMENT CONTAINS ENTIRE UNDERSTANDING/ASSIGNMENT

This Agreement contains the entire understanding between the Client and TSGS concerning the subject matter of this Agreement. Client may not assign the rights and obligations hereunder without first obtaining the prior written consent of TSGS.

3. SEVERABILITY

If any provisions of this Agreement are held to be invalid, void or unenforceable by reason of any law, rule, administrative order or judicial decision, that determination shall not effect the validity of the remaining provisions of this Agreement.

4. WAIVER

Except as specifically permitted in this Agreement, no Provision of this Agreement can be, nor be deemed to be, waived, altered, modified or amended unless such is agreed to in writing signed by TSGS. TSGS' failure to insist at any time upon strict compliance with this agreement or with any of its terms or any continued course of such conduct on Broker's part shall not constitute or be considered a waiver by Broker of any of its rights.

5. DELIVERY OF SECURITIES

Without abrogating any of TSGS' rights under any other portion of this Agreement and subject to any indebtedness of the Client to TSGS, the Client is entitled, upon appropriate demand, to receive physical delivery of fully paid securities in the client's account.

6. LIENS

All securities and other property of the Client in any account in which the Client has an interest, and the proceeds thereon, shall be subject to a lien for the discharge of any and all indebtedness or any other obligation of the Client to TSGS. All securities and other property of the Client shall be held by TSGS as security for the payment of any such obligations or indebtedness to TSGS in any Account that the Client may have an interest, and TSGS subject to the applicable law may, at any time and without prior notice to the Client, use and/or transfer any or all securities and other property interchangeably in any Account(s) in which the Client has an interest (except regulated commodity Accounts). In enforcing its lien, TSGS shall have the discretion to determine which securities or property is to be sold and which contracts are to be closed.

7. PLEDGE OF SECURITIES AND OTHER PROPERTY

Within the limitations imposed by applicable laws, rules and regulations, all securities and other property of the Client may be pledged acknowledged and hypothecated and rehypothecated by TSGS from time to time, without notice to the Client either separately or in common with such other securities and other property of other bona fide Clients of TSGS, for any amount due to TSGS, in the Client's Account(s). TSGS may do so without retaining in its possession or under its control for delivery a like amount of similar securities or other property.

8. CANCELLATION OF ORDERS

The Broker is authorized, at the Broker's discretion, should the Client die or should the Broker for any reason whatever deem it necessary for the Broker's protection, without notice, to cancel any outstanding orders in order to close out the accounts of the Client, in whole or in part or to close out any commitment made on behalf of the Client.

9. EXECUTION OF TRANSACTIONS

Any sale, purchase or cancellation authorized hereby may be made according to the Broker's judgment and at the Broker's discretion on the exchange or other market where such business is the usually transacted, or at public auction, or at private sale without advertising that same and without any notice, prior tender, demand or call, and the Broker may purchase the whole or any part of such securities free from any right of redemption, and the Client shall remain liable for any deficiency. It is further understood that any notice, prior tender, demand or call from the Broker shall not be considered a waiver or any provision of this Agreement.

custagre (5-14-97

Figure 46 - Client Agreement (Page 1)

Cash Accounts

For U.S. retail brokerage activity, a cash account is the most common form of account. This account type has several characteristics:

- Only cash transactions are permitted, and no credit is provided
- All securities purchased must be paid for in full on settlement date, which is currently three days after the trade for most types of U.S. securities
- The client retains full ownership of the securities, and the client's rights are defined in a general account agreement

The key points in a typical cash account agreement are shown in the agreement that is reproduced in this chapter. The information in the following paragraphs has been extracted from the previous example which begins on the next page. Although every firm creates its own account opening agreement, some terms are required by the industry while others are defined by each firm.

1. Applicable Rules and Regulations

"All transactions in the Client's Account shall be subject to the constitution, rules, regulations, customs and usage of the exchange ... the transactions shall be subject to:

(a) the provisions of the Securities Exchange Act of 1934 and the Commodities Exchange Act

(b) the rules of the Securities and Exchange Commission, the Fed's Board of Governors and the Commodities Futures Trading Commission."

2. Agreement Contains the Entire Understanding

"This Agreement contains the entire understanding between the Client and the Broker ..."

3. Severability

"If any provisions of this Agreement are ... invalid ... that ... shall not effect the validity of the remaining provisions ..."

4. Waiver

"... no provision of this Agreement can be ... waived, altered, modified or amended unless such is agreed to in writing [and] signed by the Broker. ..."

5. Delivery of Securities

"... the Client is entitled ... to receive physical delivery of fully paid securities in the client's account."

6. Liens

"All securities and other property of the Client ... shall be subject to a lien for the discharge of any and all indebtedness ... of the Client to the Broker. ...

In enforcing its lien, the Broker shall have the discretion to determine which securities or property is to be sold ..."

7. Pledge of Securities and Other Property

"... all securities and other property of the Client may be pledged ... and hypothecated ... by the Broker ... without notice to the Client ..."

8. Cancellation of Orders

"The Broker is authorized ... without notice, to cancel any outstanding orders in order to close out the accounts of the Client ..."

9. Execution of Transactions

"Any sale, purchase or cancellation ... may be made according to the Broker's judgment and at the Broker's discretion on the exchange or other market where such business is the usually transacted ..."

10. Satisfaction of Indebtedness

"The Client agrees to satisfy ... any indebtedness or balance owing, including interest and commissions and any costs of collection, including attorneys' fees, and to pay any debit balance remaining when the Client's Account is closed ..."

11. Transactions and Settlements

"All orders for the purchase or sale of securities ... will be authorized by the Client and executed with the understanding that an actual purchase or sale is intended and that it is the Client's intention and obligation in every case to deliver certificates or commodities to cover any and all sales or to pay for any purchase ..."

12. Sales by Client

"The Client understands and agrees any order to sell *short* will be designated as such by the Client, ..."

13. Broker as Agent

"The Client understands that the Broker is acting as the Client's agent, unless the Broker notifies the Client, ... that the Broker is acting as a dealer for its own account or as agent for some other person."

10. SATISFACTION OF INDEBTEDNESS

The Client agrees to satisfy, upon demand, any indebtedness or balance owing, including interest and commissions and any costs of collection (including attorney's fees), and to pay any debit balance remaining when the Client's Account is closed, either partially or totally. Client Account(s) may not be closed without Broker first receiving all securities and other property for which the Account is short and all funds to pay in full for all securities and other property in which the Account(s) are long.

11. TRANSACTIONS AND SETTLEMENTS

All orders for the purchase or sale of securities and other property will be authorized by the Client and executed with the understanding that an actual purchase or sale is intended and that it is the Client's intention and obligation in every case to deliver certificates or commodities to cover any and all sales or to pay for an) purchase upon TSGS' demand. If TSGS makes a short sale of any securities and other property at the Client's direction or if the Client fails to deliver to TSGS any securities and other property that TSGS has sold at the Client's direction, TSGS is authorized to borrow the securities and other property necessary to enable TSGS to make delivery and the Client agrees to be responsible for any cost or loss TSGS may incur, or the cost of obtaining the securities and other property ii TSGS is unable to borrow it. TSGS is the Client's agent to complete all such transactions and is authorized to make advances and expend monies as are required.

12. SALES BY CLIENT

The Client understands and agrees any order to sell "short" will be designated as such by the Client, and that TSGS will mark the order as short. All other sell orders will be for securities owned ("long"), at that time. By the Client by placing an order designated long, the Client represents that he owns the securities and affirms that he will deliver the securities on or before the settlement date.

13. BROKER AS AGENT

The Client understands that TSGS is acting as the Client's agent, unless TSGS notifies the Client, in writing before the settlement date for the transaction, that TSGS is acting as a dealer for its own account or as agent for some other person.

14. CONFIRMATIONS AND STATEMENTS

Confirmations of transactions and statements for the Client's Account(s) shall be binding upon the Client if the Client does not object, in writing, within ten days after receipt by the Client. Notice or other communications including margin and maintenance calls delivered or mailed to the address given in the New Account Information Form executed by the Client shall, until TSGS has received notice in writing of a different address, be deemed to have been personally delivered to the Client whether actually received or not.

15. RESTRICTIONS ON TRADING / TERMINATION

Client understands that TSGS may in its sole discretion prohibit or restrict trading of securities or substitution of securities in any of the Client's accounts. The Client further agrees that TSGS has the right to terminate any of the Client's accounts (including multiple owner accounts) at any time by notice to the Client.

16. ORAL AUTHORIZATIONS

The Client agrees that TSGS shall incur no liability in acting upon oral instructions given to it concerning the Client's accounts, provided such instructions reasonably appear to be genuine.

17. CREDIT INFORMATION AND INVESTIGATION

The Client authorizes TSGS and each of its affiliates to obtain reports concerning the Client's credit standing and business conduct at TSGS' discretion. Upon the Client's request, TSGS will inform the Client of the name and address of each consumer reporting agency from which it obtained a consumer report, if any. The Client also authorizes TSGS and each of its affiliates to share any information they may have or obtain about the Client for any legitimate business purpose.

18. SUCCESSORS

Client hereby agrees that this Agreement and all terms thereof shall be binding upon Client's heirs, executors, administrators, personal representatives and assigns. This Agreement shall endure to the benefit of the Broker's present organization, and any successor organization, irrespective of any change or changes at any time in the personnel thereof, for any cause whatsoever.

19. CHOICE OF LAWS

THIS AGREEMENT SHALL BE DEEMED TO HAVE BEEN MADE IN THE STATE OF NEW YORK AND SHALL BE CONSTRUED, AND THE RIGHTS AND LIABILITIES OF THE PARTIES DETERMINED, IN ACCORDANCE WITH THE LAWS OF THE STATE OF NEW YORK, WITHOUT GIVING EFFECT TO THE CONFLICT OF LAW PROVISIONS THEREOF.

20. CAPACITY TO CONTRACT, CLIENT AFFILIATION

By signing below, the Client, represents that he/she is of legal age, and that he/she is not an employee of any exchange, or any of corporation of which any exchange owns a majority of the capital stock, or of a member of any exchange, or of a member firm or member corporation registered on any exchange, or of a bank, trust company, insurance company or of any corporation, firm or individual engaged in the business of dealing, either as a broker or as principal, in securities, bills of exchange, acceptances or other forms of commercial paper, and that the Client will promptly notify TSGS in writing if the Client is now or becomes so employed. The client also represents that no one except the Client has an interest in the account or accounts of the Client with you.

21. ARBITRATION DISCLOSURES

- ARBITRATION IS FINAL AND BINDING ON THE PARTIES.
- THE PARTIES ARE WAIVING THEIR RIGHT TO SEEK REMEDIES IN COURT, INCLUDING THE RIGHT TO JURY TRIAL.
- PRE-ARBITRATION DISCOVERY IS GENERALLY MORE LIMITED THAN AND DIFFERENT FROM COURT PROCEEDINGS.
- THE ARBITRATORS' AWARD IS NOT REQUIRED TO INCLUDE FACTUAL FINDINGS OR LEGAL REASONING AND ANY PARTY'S RIGHT TO
- APPEAL OR TO SEEK MODIFICATION OF RULINGS BY THE ARBITRATORS IS STRICTLY LIMITED.

THE PANEL OF ARBITRATORS WILL TYPICALLY INCLUDE A MINORITY OF ARBITRATORS WHO WERE OR ARE AFFILIATED WITH THE SECURITIES INDUSTRY.

Figure 48 - Client Agreement (Page 2)

14. Confirmations and Statements

"Confirmations of transactions and statements ... shall be binding upon the Client if the Client does not object, in writing, within ten days after receipt by the Client. ..."

15. Restrictions on Trading / Termination

"Client understands that the Broker may ... prohibit or restrict trading of securities or substitution of securities in any of the Client's accounts. ..."

16. Oral Authorizations

"The Client agrees that the Broker shall incur no liability in acting upon oral instructions ... provided such instructions reasonably appear to be genuine."

17. Credit Information and Investigation

"The Client authorizes the Broker and each of its affiliates to obtain reports concerning the Client's credit standing ..."

18. Successors

"Client hereby agrees that this Agreement ... shall be binding upon Client's heirs, executors, administrators, personal representatives and assigns. ..."

19. Choice of Laws

"This agreement shall be deemed to have been made in the State of New York."

20. Capacity to Contract, Client Affiliation

"By signing below, the Client, represents that he/she is of legal age, and that he/she is not an employee of any exchange, ... or of a member of any exchange, or of a member firm ... or of a bank, trust company, insurance company or of any corporation, firm or individual engaged in the business of dealing ..."

21. Arbitration Disclosures

- "Arbitration is final and binding on the parties.
- The parties are waiving their right to seek remedies in court, including the right to a jury trial .
- Pre-arbitration discovery is generally more limited than ... court proceedings ...
- ... Any party's right to appeal or seek modification of rulings by the arbitrators is strictly limited.
- ... minority of arbitrators ... are ... affiliated with the securities industry."

22. ARBITRATION

THE CLIENT AGREES AND BY CARRYING AN ACCOUNT FOR THE CLIENT TSGS AGREES THAT ALL CONTROVERSIES WHICH MAY ARISE BETWEEN US CONCERNING ANY TRANSACTION OR THE CONSTRUCTION, PERFORMANCE, OR BREACH OF THIS OR ANY OTHER AGREEMENT BETWEEN US PERTAINING TO SECURITIES AND OTHER PROPERTY, WHETHER ENTERED INTO PRIOR, ON OR SU13SEQUENT TO THE DATE HEREOF, SHALL BE DETERMINED BY ARBITRATION. ANY ARBITRATION UNDER THIS AGREEMENT SHALL BE CONDUCTED PURSUANT TO THE FEDERAL ARBITRATION ACT AND THE LAWS OF THE STATE DESIGNATED IN PARAGRAPH 19, BEFORE THE NEW YORK STOCK EXCHANGE, INC. OR AN ARBITRATION FACILITY PROVIDED BY ANY OTHER EXCHANGE OF WHICH TSGS IS A MEMBER, OR THE NATIONAL ASSOCIATION OF SECURITIES DEALERS, INC., OR THE MUNICIPAL SECURITIES RULEMAKING BOARD AND IN ACCORDANCE WITH THE RULES THEN IN EFFECT OF THE SELECTED ORGANIZATION. THE CLIENT MAY ELECT IN THE FIRST INSTANCE WHETHER ARBITRATION SHALL BE BY THE NEW YORK STOCK EXCHANGE, INC. OR OTHER EXCHANGE OR SELF-REGULATORY ORGANIZATION OF WHICH TSGS IS A MEMBER, BUT IF THE CLIENT FAILS TO MAKE SUCH ELECTION, BY REGISTERED LETTER OR TELEGRAM ADDRESSED TO TSGS AT TSGS' MAIN OFFICE, BEFORE THE EXPIRATION OF TEN DAYS AFTER RECEIPT OF A WRITTEN REQUEST FROM TSGS TO MAKE SUCH ELECTION, THEN TSGS MAY MAKE SUCH ELECTION, THE AWARD OF THE ARBITRATORS, OR OF THE MAJORITY OF THEM, SHALL BE FINAL, AND JUDGMENT UPON THE AWARD RENDERED MAY BE ENTERED IN ANY COURT, STATE OR FEDERAL, HAVING JURISDICTION. NO PERSON SHALL BRING A PUTATIVE OR CERTIFIED CLASS ACTION; OR WHO IS A MEMBER OF A PUTATIVE CLASS WHO HAS NOT OPTED OUT OF THE CLASS WITH RESPECT TO ANY CLAIMS ENCOMPASSED BY THE PUTATIVE CLASS ACTION UNTIL: (i) THE CLASS CERTIFICATION IS DENIED OR; (ii) THE CLASS IS DECERTIFIED; OR (iii) THE CLIENT IS EXCLUDED FROM THE CLASS BY THE COURT, SUCH FORBEARANCE TO ENFORCE AN AGREEMENT TO ARBITRATE SHALL NOT CONSTITUTE A WAIVER OF ANY RIGHTS UNDER THIS AGREEMENT EXCEPT TO THE EXTENT STATED HEREIN.

23. DISCLOSURES TO ISSUERS

Under rule 14b-l(c) of the Securities Exchange Act of 1934, we are required to disclose to an issuer the name, address, and securities position of our clients who are beneficial owners of that issuer's securities unless the client objects. Therefore, please check one of the boxes below:

___ Yes, I do object to the disclosure of such information.

___ No, I do not object to the disclosure of such information.

THIS AGREEMENT CONTAINS A PRE-DISPUTE ARBITRATION CLAUSE AT PARAGRAPH 22.

Client Signature	Date		Client Signature *(for joint accounts)	Date

Account Number	

*If joint account, all clients must sign.

**Please indicate Preference in Paragraph 23.

***Please return original executed copy to TSG Securities LLC and retain a second copy for your files.

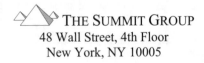

THE SUMMIT GROUP
48 Wall Street, 4th Floor
New York, NY 10005

Figure 49 - Client Agreement (Page 3)

22. Arbitration

"The client agrees … that all controversies which may arise … shall be determined by arbitration. …"

23. Disclosure to Issuers

"… we are required to disclose to an issuer the name, address, and securities position of … beneficial owners of that issuer's securities unless the client objects. …"

Margin Account

When a retail client wants to take more risk and increase his potential profit, he often considers opening a margin account. When a client establishes a margin account with a brokerage firm a secured credit relationship is established. A margin account allows the account holder to use the securities that are in the account as collateral to purchase additional securities.

- A credit account includes a margin agreement, which defines the terms for any loan.
- The client puts up part of the cash needed for purchases and the broker lends the rest, using the securities in the account as collateral.
- The ratio between the loan and the value of the collateral is established by the Fed and the broker. The Fed sets the maximum loan ratio, e.g., listed U.S. equities can receive a margin loan up to 50% of the current market value of the position. The broker can decide which securities it will or will not allow for margin, and can implement standards that are stricter than the Fed's maximums.
- The client pays interest on the loan, which is usually a very competitive market rate.

Many of the terms included in a margin agreement are similar to those in a cash agreement. The following contract from another broker includes specific additional paragraphs for margin accounts along with clauses that are needed by the broker as it acts in its capacity as a clearing broker.

The paragraphs that are different from those in a standard cash account are:

4. Deposits on Transactions

"… [the broker] may require you … to deposit cash or collateral immediately in your account prior to … settlement date."

6. Execution Fees and Service Charges

"… your account will be charged brokerage commissions or mark-ups/ mark-downs in connection with the execution of transactions … and may be charged certain other fees …"

Client Agreement

PLEASE READ CAREFULLY, SIGN AND RETURN

THE SUMMIT GROUP SECURITIES LLC
48 Wall Street, 4th Floor
New York, NY 10005

This agreement ("Agreement") sets forth the terms and conditions on which subsidiaries of The TSG Securities Companies Inc. will open and maintain account(s) in your name and otherwise transact business with you.

1. PARTIES. You hereby agree that the parties to this Agreement shall consist of you and each and every subsidiary of The TSG Securities Companies LLC, whether now existing or hereafter created (each such subsidiary being referred to hereinafter as a "TSG Securities entity" and all such subsidiaries being collectively referred to hereinafter as "TSG Securities").

2. APPLICABLE LAWS, RULES AND REGULATIONS. All transactions shall be subject to the applicable laws, rules and regulations of all federal, state and self-regulatory authorities, including, but not limited to, the rules and regulations of the Board of Governors of the Federal Reserve System and the constitution, rules and customs of the exchange or market (and clearinghouse) where such transactions are executed.

3. SECURITY INTEREST AND LIEN; REGISTRATION OF SECURITIES. As security for the payment and performance of all of your obligations and liabilities from time to time outstanding to any TSG Securities entity, whether under this Agreement or otherwise, each TSG Securities entity shall have a continuing first lien and security interest in (i) all property in which you now have or hereafter acquire an interest which is now or hereafter held by or through any TSG Securities entity, including, but not limited to, any and all accounts, instruments, documents, contract rights, commodities and commodity futures contracts, commercial paper and other securities, monies, deposit accounts and general intangibles, and (ii) any and all rights, claims or causes of action you may now or hereafter have against any TSG Securities entity. You hereby acknowledge and agree that all such property of yours held by or through any TSG Securities entity is held as collateral by such TSG Securities entity as agent and bailee for itself and all other TSG Securities entities. You represent that all of the above-described collateral shall at all times be free and clear of all liens, claims and encumbrances of any nature other than the security interest created hereby. In addition, in order to satisfy any of your outstanding liabilities or obligations to any TSG Securities entity, TSG Securities may, to the fullest extent permitted by law, at any time in its discretion and without prior notice to you, use, apply or transfer any and all securities or other property (including, without limitation, fully-paid securities and cash). You hereby agree that, except as otherwise specifically agreed in writing, TSG Securities may register and hold the securities and other property in your accounts in its name or the name of its designee.

4. DEPOSITS ON TRANSACTIONS. Whenever TSG Securities, in its sole discretion, considers it necessary in order to assure the due performance of your open contractual commitments, it may require you, and you hereby agree, to deposit cash or collateral immediately in your account(s) prior to any applicable settlement date.

5. BREACH, BANKRUPTCY OR DEFAULT. Any breach of or default under this Agreement or any other agreement you may have with any TSG Securities entity, whether heretofore or hereafter entered into, or the filing of a petition or other commencement of a proceeding in bankruptcy or insolvency, or the appointment of a receiver, by or against you or any guarantor, co-signer or other party liable on or providing security for your obligations to any TSG Securities entity, or the levy of an attachment against your or any such other party's account(s) with any TSG Securities entity, or your death, mental incompetence or dissolution, or any other grounds for insecurity, as determined by TSG Securities in its sole discretion (including, without limitation, any indication of your refusal or inability to satisfy promptly any mar- gin call or other deposit requirement hereunder), shall constitute, at TSG Securities' election, a default by you under any or all agreements you may then have with any TSG Securities entity, whether heretofore or hereafter entered into. In the event of any such default, each TSG Securities entity shall have all of the rights of a secured party upon default under the New York Uniform Commercial Code and other applicable laws, rules and regulations, including, without limitation, the right, without prior notice to you: to sell any and all property in which you have an interest held by or through any TSG Securities entity, to buy any or all property which may have been sold short, to exercise any and all options and other rights, to accelerate, cancel, terminate, liquidate, close out and net the settlement payments and/or delivery obligations under any or all outstanding transactions and/or to purchase or sell any other securities or property to offset market risk, and to offset any indebtedness you may have (either individually or jointly with others), after which you shall be liable to TSG Securities for any remaining deficiency, loss, costs or expenses incurred or sustained by TSG Securities in connection therewith. Such purchases and/or sales may be effected publicly or privately without notice or advertisement in such manner as TSG Securities may in its sole discretion determine. At any such sale or purchase, any TSG Securities entity may purchase or sell the property free of any right of redemption. In addition, each TSG Securities entity shall have the right, at any time and from time to time, to set off and otherwise apply any and all amounts owing by such TSG Securities entity to you or for your account or credit against any and all amounts now or hereafter owing by you to any TSG Securities entity (including, without limitation, any indebtedness in your accounts), whether matured or unmatured, fixed, contingent or otherwise and irrespective of whether any TSG Securities entity shall have made any demand therefore. TSG Securities agrees to notify you of any such set-off and application; provided, how- ever, that the failure to give such notice shall not affect the validity of any such set-off and application.

6. EXECUTION FEES AND SERVICE CHARGES. You understand that your account(s) will be charged brokerage commissions or mark-ups/ mark-downs in connection with the execution of transactions ("Execution Fees") and may be charged certain other fees for custody

Figure 50 - Margin Account Agreement (Page 1)

8. Debit Balances; Truth in Lending

"... interest will be charged on any debit balances in your account ..."

9. Clearance Accounts

"If ... [the broker acts]... as clearing agent for your broker, ... it may accept ... orders ... and any other instructions ...

... [the broker] shall have no responsibility or liability ..."

10.   Collection and other Account Related Costs

"You hereby agree to pay ... all reasonable ... costs ..."

11. Impartial Lottery Allocation

"... you will participate in the impartial lottery allocation system for such called securities ..."

13.   Free Credit Balances

"You hereby authorize [the broker] to use any free credit balance ... and to pay ..."

14. Restrictions on Credit

"... may restrict or prohibit trading of securities or other property in your account and may terminate your account, and you shall ... remain liable for all of your obligations ..."

17. Margin and other Collateral Requirements

"... deposit and maintain such margin in your margin accounts ... as [the broker] may ... require, and you agree to pay ... on demand any debit balance ...

... you further agree to deposit promptly and maintain ..."

26. Telephone Conversations

"... you hereby authorize [the broker] ... to monitor and/or record any or all telephone conversations or electronic communications between you and [the broker]."

and other services furnished to you ("Service Fees"). All such fees shall be determined by TSG Securities unless your account(s) is (are) introduced to TSG Securities by another broker, in which case all Execution Fees and certain Service Fees shall be determined by such other broker. You further understand that Execution Fees may be changed from time to time without prior notice to you and Service Fees may be changed from time to time upon thirty days' prior written notice to you, and, in each case, you agree to be bound thereby.

7. TRANSACTION REPORTS AND ACCOUNT STATEMENTS. Reports of the execution of orders shall be conclusive if not objected to in writing by you within the shorter of the applicable settlement cycle of the subject transactions or three business days after such documents have been transmitted to you by mail or otherwise. Statements of account shall be conclusive it not objected to in writing with- in ten days after transmission.

8. DEBIT BALANCES; TRUTH-IN-LENDING. You hereby acknowledge receipt of TSG Securities' Truth-in-Lending disclosure statement. You understand that interest will be charged on any debit balances in your account(s) in accordance with the methods described in such statement or in any amendment or revision thereto which may be provided to you. Any debit balance that is not paid at the close of an interest period will be added to the opening balance for the next interest period.

9. CLEARANCE ACCOUNTS. If any of your accounts is carried by any TSG Securities entity as clearing agent for your broker, unless such TSG Securities entity receives from you prior written notice to the contrary, it may accept from such introducing broker, without any inquiry or investigations (a) orders for the purchase or sale of securities and other property in your account(s), on margin or other- wise, and (b) any other instructions concerning your account(s) or the property there- in. You understand and agree that TSG Securities shall have no responsibility or liability to you for any acts or omissions of your broker, its officers, employees or agents. You agree that your broker and its employees are third-party beneficiaries of this Agreement, and that the terms and conditions hereof, including the arbitration provisions, shall be applicable to all matters between or among any of you, your broker and its employees and TSG Securities and its employees.

10. COLLECTION AND OTHER ACCOUNT-RELATED COSTS. You hereby agree to pay, on demand, all reasonable direct and indirect costs, liabilities and damages incurred by TSG Securities (including, without limitation, costs of collection, attorneys' fees, court costs and other expenses) in connection with (i) enforcing its rights hereunder, (ii) any investigation, litigation or proceeding involving your account or any property therein (including, without limitation, claims to such property by third parties), (iii) your use of or access to any TSG Securities or third-party system or (iv) TSG Securities' acting in reliance upon your instructions or, if your account is introduced to TSG Securities by another broker, the instructions of such other broker. In each case and whether or not demand has been made therefore, you hereby authorize TSG Securities to charge your account(s) for any and all such costs, including, without limitation, costs incurred in connection with the liquidation of any property held in your account(s).

11. IMPARTIAL LOTTERY ALLOCATION. You agree that, in the event TSG Securities holds on your behalf securities in its name, in the name of its designee or in bearer form which are called in part, you will participate in the impartial lottery allocation system for such called securities in accordance with the rules of the New York Stock Exchange, Inc. or any other appropriate self-regulatory organization. When any such call is favorable, no allocation will be made to any account in which, to the knowledge of TSG Securities, any officer, director or employee of TSG Securities has any financial interest until all other clients have been satisfied on an impartial

12. WAIVER, ASSIGNMENT AND NOTICES. Neither TSG Securities' failure to insist at any time upon strict compliance with this Agreement or with any of the terms hereof nor any continued course of such conduct on its part shall constitute or be considered a waiver by TSG Securities of any of its rights or privileges here- under. Any assignment of your rights and obligations hereunder or your interest in any property held by or through TSG Securities without obtaining the prior written con- sent of an authorized representative of TSG Securities shall be null and void. Each TSG Securities entity reserves the right to assign any of its rights or obligations here- under to any other TSG Securities entity without prior notice to you. Notices and other communications (including, without limitation, margin calls) delivered, faxed, sent by express delivery service or mailed to the address provided by you shall, until TSG Securities has received notice in writing of a different address be deemed to have been personally delivered to you. Margin calls may also be communicated orally, without subsequent written confirmation.

13. FREE CREDIT BALANCES. You hereby authorize TSG Securities to use any free credit balance awaiting investment or reinvestment in your account(s) in accordance with all applicable rules and regulations and to pay interest thereon at such rate or rates and under such conditions as are established from time to time by TSG Securities for such account(s) and for the amounts of cash so used.

14. RESTRICTIONS ON ACCOUNT. You understand that TSG Securities, in its sole discretion, may restrict or prohibit trading of securities or other property in your account(s) and may terminate your account(s), and you shall nevertheless remain liable for all of your obligations to TSG Securities under this Agreement or otherwise.

15. CREDIT INFORMATION AND INVESTIGATION. You authorize TSG Securities and, it applicable, your introducing broker, in its or their discretion, at any time and from time to time, to make or obtain reports concerning your credit standing and business conduct. You may make a written request for a description of the nature and scope of the reports made or obtained by TSG Securities and the same will be provided to you within a reasonable period of time.

16. SHORT AND LONG SALES. In placing any sell order for a short account, you will designate the order as such and hereby authorize TSG Securities to mark the order as being "short." In placing any sell order for a long account, you will designate the order as such and hereby authorize TSG Securities to, mark the order as being "long." The designation of a sell order as being for a long account shall constitute a representation that you own the security with respect to which the order has been placed, that such security may be sold without restriction in the open market and that, if TSG Securities does not have the security in its possession at the time you place the order, you shall deliver the security by settlement date in good deliverable form or pay to TSG Securities any losses and expenses it may incur or sustain as a result of your failure to make delivery on a timely basis.

Figure 51 - Margin Account Agreement (Page 2)

17. MARGIN AND OTHER COLLATERAL REQUIREMENTS. You hereby agree to deposit and maintain such margin in your margin accounts, if any, as TSG Securities may in its sole discretion require, and you agree to pay forthwith on demand any debit balance owing with respect to any of your margin accounts. In addition. You further agree to deposit promptly and maintain such other collateral with TSG Securities as is required by any other agreement or open transaction you may have with any TSG Securities entity. Upon your failure to make any such payment or deposit, or if at any time TSG Securities, in its sole discretion, deems it necessary for its protection, whether with or without prior demand, call or notice, TSG Securities shall be entitled to exercise all rights and remedies provided in paragraphs 3, 5 and 27 hereof. No demands, calls, tenders or notices that TSG Securities may have made or given n the past in any one or more instances shall invalidate your waiver of the requirement to make or give the same in the future. You further acknowledge and agree that any positions in your margin account(s) shall be deemed "securities contracts' within he meaning of Sections 555 and 741(7) of the U.S. Bankruptcy Code and any successors thereto. Unless you advise B at Stearns in writing to the contrary, you represent that you are not an affiliate (as defined in Rule 144(a)(1) under The Securities Act of 1933) of the issuer of any security held in any of your accounts.

18. CONSENT TO LOAN OR PLEDGE OF SECURITIES IN MARGIN ACCOUNTS. Within the limits of applicable law and regulations, you hereby authorize TSG Securities to lend either to itself or to others any securities held by TSG Securities in any of your margin accounts, to convey therewith all attendant rights of ownership (including voting rights) and to use all such property as collateral for its general loans. Any such property, together with all attendant rights of ownership, may De pledged, repledged, hypothecated or rehypothecated either separately or in com- -non with other property for any amounts due to TSG Securities thereon or for a greater sum, and TSG Securities shall have no obligation to retain a like amount of similar property in its possession and control. You hereby acknowledge that, as a result of such activities, TSG Securities may receive and retain certain benefits to which you will not De entitled. In certain circumstances, such loans may limit, in whole or in part, your ability to exercise voting and other attendant rights of ownership with respect to the loaned or pledged securities.

19. LEGALLY BINDING. You hereby agree that this Agreement and all of the terms hereof shall be binding upon you and your estate, heirs, executors, administrators, personal representatives, successors and assigns. You further agree that all purchases and sales shall be for your account(s) in accordance with your oral or written instructions. You hereby waive any and all defenses that any such oral instruction was not in writing as may be required by any applicable law, rule or regulation.

20. AMENDMENT. You agree that TSG Securities may modify the terms of this Agreement at any time upon prior written notice to you. By continuing to accept services from TSG Securities thereafter, you will have indicated your acceptance of any such modification. If you do not accept such modification, you must notify TSG Securities in writing; your account may then be terminated by TSG Securities, after which you will remain liable to TSG Securities for all outstanding liabilities and obligations. Otherwise, this Agreement may not be modified absent a written instrument signed by an authorized representative of TSG Securities.

21. GOVERNING LAW. THIS AGREEMENT SHALL BE DEEMED TO HAVE BEEN MADE IN THE STATE OF NEW YORK AND SHALL BE CONSTRUED, AND THE CONTRACTUAL AND ALL OTHER RIGHTS AND LIABILITIES OF THE PARTIES DETERMINED, IN ACCORDANCE WITH THE LAW OF THE STATE OF NEW YORK WITHOUT GIVING EFFECT TO ANY CONFLICTS OF LAW PRINCIPLES THEREOF.

22. ARBITRATION. YOU AGREE THAT CONTROVERSIES ARISING BETWEEN YOU AND YOUR INTRODUCING BROKER AND I OR TSG SECURITIES, AND ANY OF YOUR OR THEIR CONTROL PERSONS, PREDECESSORS, SUBSIDIARIES, AFFILIATES, SUCCESSORS, ASSIGNS AND EMPLOYEES, SHALL BE DETERMINED BY ARBITRATION. WITH RESPECT TO THE RESOLUTION OF ANY SUCH CONTROVERSY, YOU FURTHER ACKNOWLEDGE THAT:

• ARBITRATION IS FINAL AND BINDING ON THE PARTIES.

• EXCEPT AS OTHERWISE PROVIDED HEREIN, THE PARTIES ARE WAIVING THEIR RIGHT TO SEEK REMEDIES IN COURT, INCLUDING THE RIGHT TO JURY TRIAL.

- PRE-ARBITRATION DISCOVERY IS GENERALLY MORE LIMITED THAN AND DIFFERENT FROM COURT PROCEEDINGS.

- THE ARBITRATORS' AWARD IS NOT REQUIRED TO INCLUDE FACTUAL FINDINGS OR LEGAL REASONING AND ANY PARTY'S RIGHT TO APPEAL OR TO SEEK MODIFICATION OF RULINGS BY THE ARBITRATORS IS STRICTLY LIMIT- ED. - THE PANEL OF ARBITRATORS WILL TYPICALLY INCLUDE A MINORITY OF ARBITRATORS WHO WERE OR ARE AFFILIATED WITH THE SECURITIES INDUSTRY.

- NO PERSON SHALL BRING A PUTATIVE OR CERTIFIED CLASS ACTION TO ARBITRATION NOR SEEK TO ENFORCE ANY PRE-DISPUTE ARBITRATION AGREEMENT AGAINST ANY PERSON WHO HAS INITIATED IN COURT A PUTATIVE CLASS ACTION OR WHO IS A MEMBER OF A PUTATIVE CLASS WHO HAS NOT OPTED OUT OF THE CLASS WITH RESPECT TO ANY CLAIMS ENCOMPASSED BY THE PUTATIVE CLASS ACTION UNTIL: (I) THE CLASS CERTIFICATION IS DENIED; (II) THE CLASS IS DECERTIFIED; OR (III) THE CLIENT IS EXCLUDED FROM THE CLASS BY THE COURT. SUCH FORBEARANCE TO ENFORCE AN AGREEMENT TO ARBITRATE SHALL NOT CONSTITUTE A WAIVER OF ANY RIGHTS UNDER THIS AGREEMENT EXCEPT TO THE EXTENT STATED HEREIN.

- ANY ARBITRATION UNDER THIS AGREEMENT SHALL BE HELD AT THE FACILITIES AND BEFORE AN ARBITRATION PANEL APPOINTED BY THE NEW YORK STOCK EXCHANGE, INC., THE AMERICAN STOCK EXCHANGE, INC. OR THE NATIONAL ASSOCIATION OF SECURITIES DEALERS, INC. OR, IF THE TRANSACTION WHICH GIVES RISE TO SUCH CONTROVERSY IS EFFECTED IN ANOTHER UNITED STATES MARKET WHICH PROVIDES ARBITRATION FACILITIES, BEFORE SUCH OTHER FACILITIES. YOU MAY ELECT ONE OF THE FOREGOING FORUMS FOR ARBITRATION, BUT IF YOU FAIL TO MAKE SUCH ELECTION BY REGISTERED MAIL OR TELEGRAM ADDRESSED TO TSG SECURITIES CORP., 48 Wall Street, NEW YORK, NEW YORK 10005, ATTENTION CHIEF LEGAL OFFICER (OR ANY OTHER ADDRESS OF WHICH YOU ARE ADVISED IN WRITING), BEFORE THE EXPIRATION OF TEN DAYS AFTER RECEIPT OF A WRITTEN REQUEST FROM TSG SECURITIES TO MAKE SUCH ELECTION, THEN

Figure 52 - Margin Account Agreement (Page 3)

TSG SECURITIES MAY MAKE SUCH ELECTION. FOR ANY ARBITRATION SOLELY BETWEEN YOU AND A BROKER FOR WHICH TSG SECURITIES ACTS AS A CLEARING AGENT, SUCH ELECTION SHALL BE MADE BY REGISTERED MAIL TO SUCH BROKER AT ITS PRINCIPAL PLACE OF BUSINESS. THE AWARD OF THE ARBITRATORS, OR OF A MAJORITY OF THEM, SHALL BE FINAL, AND JUDGMENT UPON THE AWARD RENDERED MAY BE ENTERED IN ANY COURT, STATE OR FEDERAL, HAVING JURISDICTION.

23   SEVERABILITY. If and to the extent any term or provision herein is or should become invalid or unenforceable under any present or future law, rule or regulation of any sovereign government or regulatory body having jurisdiction over the subject matter of this Agreement, then (i) the remaining terms and provisions hereof shall be unimpaired and remain in full force and effect and (ii) the invalid or unenforceable provision or term shall be replaced by a term or provision that is valid and enforceable and that comes closest to expressing the intention of such invalid or unenforceable term or provision.

24. EXTRAORDINARY EVENTS. TSG Securities shall not be liable for losses caused directly or indirectly by government restrictions, exchange or market rulings, suspension of trading, war, strikes or other conditions beyond its control.

25. HEADINGS. The headings of the provisions hereof are for ease of reference only and shall not affect the interpretation or application of this Agreement or in any way modify or qualify any of the rights provided for hereunder.

26. TELEPHONE CONVERSATIONS. For the protection of both you and TSG Securities, and as a tool to correct misunderstandings, you hereby authorize TSG Securities, at TSG Securities' discretion and without prior notice to you, to monitor and/or record any or all telephone conversations or electronic communications between you and TSG Securities or any of TSG Securities' employees or agents. You acknowledge that TSG Securities may determine not to make or keep any of such recordings and that such determination shall not in any way affect any party's rights.

27.   CUMULATIVE RIGHTS; ENTIRE AGREEMENT. The rights of each TSG Securities entity set forth in this Agreement and in each other agreement you may have with any TSG Securities entity, whether heretofore or hereafter entered into, are cumulative and in addition to any other rights and remedies that any TSG Securities entity may have and shall supersede any limitation on or any requirement for the exercise of such rights and remedies that is inconsistent with the terms of this or any other such agreement (including, without limitation, any requirement that time elapse or notice or demand be given prior to the exercise of remedies). The provisions of this Agreement shall supersede any inconsistent provisions of any other agreement heretofore or hereafter entered into by you and any TSG Securities entity to the extent that the subject matter thereof is dealt with in this Agreement and the provisions of such other agreement would deny any TSG Securities entity any benefit or protection afforded to it under this Agreement. You hereby appoint TSG Securities as your agent and attorney-in-fact to take any action (including, but not limited to, the filing of financing statements) necessary or desirable to perfect and protect the security interest granted in paragraph 3 hereof or to otherwise accomplish the purposes of this Agreement. Except as set forth above, this Agreement represents the entire agreement and understanding between you and TSG Securities concerning the subject matter hereof.

28. CAPACITY TO CONTRACT, AFFILIATIONS. You represent that you are of legal age and that, unless you have notified TSG Securities to the contrary, neither you nor any member of your immediate family is: (i) an employee or member of any exchange, (ii) an employee or member of the National Association of Securities Dealers, Inc., (iii) an individual or an employee any corporation or firm engaged in the business of dealing, as broker or principal, in securities, options or futures or (iv) an employee of any bank, trust company or insurance company. If the undersigned is signing on behalf of others, the undersigned hereby represents that the person(s) or entity(ies) on whose behalf it is signing is/are authorized to enter into this Agreement and that the undersigned is duly authorized to sign this Agreement and make the representations herein in the name and on behalf of such other person(s) or entity(ies).

If this is a Joint Account, both parties must sign. Persons signing on behalf of others should indicate the titles or capacities in which they are signing.

BY   SIGNING   THIS   AGREEMENT,   YOU ACKNOWLEDGE THAT-

1. THE SECURITIES IN YOUR MARGIN ACCOUNT(S) AND ANY SECURITIES FOR WHICH YOU HAVE NOT FULLY PAID, TOGETHER WITH ALL ATTENDANT OWNERSHIP RIGHTS, MAY BE LOANED TO TSG SECURITIES OR TO OTHERS; AND

2. YOU HAVE RECEIVED A COPY OF THIS AGREEMENT.

THIS AGREEMENT CONTAINS A PRE-DISPUTE ARBITRATION CLAUSE AT PARAGRAPH 22.

THIS AGREEMENT IS DATED AS OF _____, 19 __

_____
(Account Number)

_____
(Typed or Printed Name)

_____
(Signature)

_____
(Typed or Printed Name)

_____
(Signature)

ACCEPTED AND AGREED TO: _____
THE SUMMIT GROUP HOLDINGS INC AND ITS SUBSIDIARIES

Figure 53 - Margin Account Agreement (Page 4)

Third Party Accounts

Third Party Accounts are designed to support situations where the account holder wishes to give some investment discretion to another party, or when the account holder cannot legally make decisions regarding the account.

Discretionary retail brokerage accounts can allow the registered representative, or another individual or firm, to buy and sell securities without receiving specific instructions from their client, usually within some boundaries. If the registered representative has been granted any discretion, it is typically a limited discretion and the RR is not allowed to move cash out of the account.

Discretionary trading by a registered representative requires:

- Prior written consent from the client
- Acceptance of the account by the brokerage firm in writing
- Marking each order *Discretion* and having all orders reviewed by the Branch Office Manager
- Frequent reviews by the brokerage firm's compliance staff (This protects the account owner against churning the account, which occurs when a registered representative buys and sells to generate commissions, rather than to help the client profit from the trades.)

There are two types of trading authorization.

- In an account with a full trading authorization, the person granted discretion is allowed to remove cash from the account.
- With a limited trading authorization, the authorization allows the person with discretion to only buy and sell securities. They *cannot* remove cash from the account.

Full Trading Authorization

An account owner can designate another individual who has the authority to make trades on their behalf and to move money in and out of the account. This is called a full trading authorization.

In the following example of a full trading authorization the account owner can designate an individual to act as the agent and *attorney in fact* for the account.

This person will be able to:

- "… buy, sell (including short sales) and trade in stocks, bonds, options … and any other securities or commodities…"
- "… on margin or otherwise …"
- "… to direct deliveries of securities or payment of monies to the agent or others …"

The account holder also indemnifies the brokerage firm against any losses, costs or expenses.

TSG
Securities

THE SUMMIT GROUP SECURITIES LLC
48 Wall Street, 4th Floor
New York, NY 10005

FULL TRADING AUTHORIZATION
WITH PRIVILEGE TO WITHDRAW
MONEY AND SECURITIES

Account Title: _____   Account Number(s): _____

_____   _____

The undersigned hereby authorizes _____ as the undersigned's agent

(Print Name of Agent and Attorney-in-Fact)

and attorney-in-fact (the 'Agent') with full power and authority on the undersigned's behalf to buy, sell (including short sales) and trade in stocks, bonds, options (including uncovered option writing), and any other securities and commodities, and contracts relating to the same (including foreign futures and foreign options contracts), on margin or otherwise, and to enter into securities repurchase and securities reverse repurchase transactions in accordance with your terms and conditions, and to direct deliveries of securities and payment of monies to the Agent or others, for the undersigned's account(s) and risk, and in the undersigned's name or number on the books of TSG Securities LLC ("TSG Securities") a subsidiary of The Summit Group Holdings, Inc.. Inc. ("TSG"). If more than one Agent is designated, the under- signed authorizes each Agent to act severally; that is, each Agent alone shall be able to exercise the powers conferred hereby.

In all such purchases, sales or transactions, or deliveries of securities or payment of monies, TSG Securities and whenever applicable, TSG (hereinafter sometimes referred to collectively as the "Brokers") are authorized to follow the instructions of the Agent in every respect concerning the undersigned's account(s) with TSG Securities. The Agent is authorized to act for the undersigned and in the undersigned's behalf, in the same manner and with the same force and effect as the undersigned, with respect to such purchases, sales or transactions in the account(s).

The undersigned hereby agrees to indemnify and hold each of the Brokers, their successors and assigns (the "Indemnified Parties") harmless from, and to pay the Indemnified Parties promptly on demand, any and all losses, costs or expenses incurred in connection with the

use of this trading authorization, including any debit balance in the undersigned's account(s). This authorization and indemnity is in addition to (and in no way limits or restricts) any rights which any of the Indemnified Parties may have under any other agreements) between the undersigned and any of the Indemnified Parties. This authorization and indemnity is a continuing one which shall not be affected by the subsequent disability or incompetence of the under- signed, and shall remain in full force and effect until revoked by the undersigned by a written notice received at the TSG Securities office at 48 Wall Street, New York, New York 10005, or until TSG Securities receives actual notice of the death of the undersigned (or if two clients sign, the death of either one), and shall enure to the benefit of each of the Brokers and any of each of their respective successor firm or firms.

Because TSG Securities is acting as clearing agent for a correspondent broker/dealer, and/or commodities Introducing Broker or Futures Commission Merchant (hereinafter referred to as 'IB" and "FCM", respectively), this authorization and indemnity shall enure likewise to the benefit of the undersigned's broker/dealer, and/or IB or FCM, their successors and assigns, and all references herein to the Brokers shall be deemed references to both the Brokers and the undersigned's broker/dealer, IB and FCM. The foregoing notwithstanding the undersigned acknowledges and agrees that if the Agent designated herein is an employee or agent of a correspondent broker/dealer, IB, or FCM, such Agent is neither an agent of nor under the control of the Brokers and the Brokers shall bear no liability for any transactions effected pursuant to the authority granted herein. **The terms of this authorization shall be governed by the laws of the State of New York.**

_____   _____   _____
(Date)   (Client Signature)   (Joint Party's Signature)

_____   _____
(Print Client Name)   (Print Joint Party's Name)

THIS QUESTION MUST BE ANSWERED: Is the Agent a person associated with any member, allied member or member organization of any securities or commodities exchange or a person associated with any broker/dealer or financial institution?

_____   _____
(Yes or No)   (Name of Firm)

Authorization Accepted: _____

STATE OF _____ , COUNTY OF _____
On   19   before me personally came

to me known, and known to be the individual(s) described herein, and who as a client(s) of (name of correspondent broker- dealer and/or commodities Introducing Broker and/or Futures Commission Merchant, executed the foregoing FULL TRADING AUTHORIZATION, and duly acknowledged to me that he executed the same.

_____
Notary Public

2000-107B (Full Authorization-Rev. 6/95) PO# 130129 7/97   **COMMODITY CLIENTS ALSO MUST COMPLETE REVERSE SIDE**

(PO#45911 7/93)

Figure 54 - Full Trading Privileges

Limited Trading Authorization

The Limited Trading Authorization is used when the account owner wishes to designate another party to make trading decisions for the account but does not wish this party to be able to move money in or out of the account.

It is a very serious offense for a broker who does not have discretionary authority over an account to make decisions for the account without obtaining prior written approval from the account owner. In this example the designated agent would be authorized to buy or sell securities only.

TSG
Securities

THE SUMMIT GROUP SECURITIES LLC
48 Wall Street, 4th Floor
New York, NY 10005

Trading Authorization Limited to
Purchases and Sales of
Securities, Commodities and Options

Account Title: _____

Account Number(s): _____

_____

_____

The undersigned hereby authorizes _____ as the undersigned's agent

(Print Name of Agent and Attorney-in-Fact)

and attorney-in-fact (the "Agent" with full power and authority on the undersigned's behalf to buy, sell (including short sales) and trade in stocks, bonds, options (including uncovered option writing), and any other securities and commodities, and contracts relating to the same (including foreign futures and foreign options contracts), on margin or other- wise, and to enter into securities repurchase and securities reverse repurchase transactions m accordance with your terms and conditions, for the undersigned's account(s) and risk, and in the undersigned's name or number on the books of TSG Securities LLC. ("TSGS'), a subsidiary of The Summit Group Holdings, Inc. ("TSG"). If more than one Agent is designated, the undersigned authorizes each Agent to act severally; that is, each Agent alone shall be able to exercise the powers conferred hereby.

In all such purchases, sales or transactions, TSG Securities and whenever applicable, TSG (hereinafter sometimes referred to collectively as the "Brokers") is authorized to follow the instructions of the Agent in every respect concerning the undersigned's account(s) with TSG Securities. The Agent is authorized to act for the undersigned and in the undersigned's behalf, in the same manner and with the same force and effect as the undersigned, with respect to such purchases, sales or transactions in the account(s).

The undersigned hereby agrees to indemnify and hold each of the Brokers, their successors and assigns (the "Indemnified Parties) harmless from, and to pay the Indemnified Parties promptly on demand, any and all losses, costs or expenses incurred in connection with the use of this trading authorization, including any debit balance in the undersigned's account(s).

This authorization and indemnity is in addition to (and in no way limits or restricts) any rights which TSG Securities and any of the Indemnified Parties may have under any other agreement(s) between the undersigned and TSG Securities and any of the Indemnified Parties.

This authorization and indemnity is a continuing one which shall not be affected by the subsequent disability or incompetence of the undersigned, and shall remain in full force and effect until revoked by the undersigned by a written notice received at the TSG Securities office at 63 Wall, New York, New York 10005, or until TSG Securities receives actual notice of the death of the undersigned (or if two clients sign, the death of either one), and shall enure to the benefit of the Brokers and any successor firm or firms, and the assigns of the Brokers or any of their respective successor firm or firms.

Because TSG Securities is acting as clearing agent for a correspondent broker dealer and/or commodities Introducing Broker and/or Futures Commission Merchant (hereinafter referred to as "IB" and "FCM" respectively), this authorization and indemnity shall enure to the benefit of the undersigned's broker/dealer, and any of the Indemnified Parties and assigns, and all references herein to the Brokers shall be deemed references to both the Broken and the undersigned broker/dealer IB and/or FCM. The foregoing notwithstanding, the undersigned acknowledges and agrees that if the Agent designated herein is an employee or agent of the undersigned broker/dealer, IB, and/or FCM, such Agent is neither an agent of nor under the control of the Brokers and the Brokers shall bear no liability for any transactions effected pursuant to the authority granted herein. **The terms of this authorization shall be governed by the laws of the State of New York.**

_____   _____
(Client Signature)   (Joint Party's Signature)

_____   _____
(Print Client Name)   (Print Joint Party's Name)

_____   _____
(Date)   (Date)

THIS QUESTION MUST BE ANSWERED: Is the Agent a person associated with any member, allied member or member organization of any securities or commodities exchange or a person associated with any broker/dealer or financial institution? _____   _____

(Yes or No)   (Name of Firm)

Authorization Accepted: _____

2000-2227 (7/92) (THIRD PARTY AUTHORIZATION)   COMMODITY CLIENTS ALSO MUST COMPLETE REVERSE SIDE
(PO#45911 7/93)

Figure 55 - Account Opening Form for Limited Trading Authorization

There are several types of third party accounts for specific purposes:

Custodial Accounts

Custodial accounts are established when there is one custodian and one minor in each account. These are usually parent/child accounts, and are often established under the rules of the Uniform Gift to Minor's Act (UGMA).

All States permit *reasonably prudent* investments on behalf of the minor. Being *reasonably prudent* does not include margin accounts, short sales and commodities, so only cash accounts are allowed. All of the assets placed into the accounts are irrevocably the property of the minor.

In a custodial account, the custodian may not:

- Pledge or lend out custodial property
- Commingle personal and custodial funds
- Use custodial property to answer margin calls or make temporary loans to personal accounts
- Use custodial property to finance normal out-of-pocket expenses in raising children

Fees

While reasonable fees can be charged, no fee can be charged if the donor is the custodian. Some states such as New York only allow a bank or a trust company to charge a custodial fee.

Tax Consequences

All tax liabilities for custodial property belong to the minor.

Death of a Minor

All property becomes part of the minor's estate.

Reaching Majority

When the minor becomes an adult he assumes legal responsibility for his accounts. Once the age of majority has been reached, securities can be re-registered in a new personal account.

Joint Accounts

In a joint account, two or more individuals share in the ownership of the account. The different forms of ownership have estate tax implications.

Joint Account - With Right of Survivorship (JAWROS)

A JAWROS is another form of custody account that is also called a Tenant by the Entity Account. It is a specific type of account that is usually established between a husband and wife. Upon the death of one account holder, the entire account becomes the property of the survivor.

Joint Account - Tenants in Common

When a joint account is opened as Tenants in Common, it is as if the account is a partnership. The death of one account holder has no effect on the survivor's percentage of ownership in the account, and the assets owned by the deceased become a part of their estate.

Tenants in common account holders are required to identify their share of ownership in the account. The following is an example of this type of agreement.

TSG
Securities

THE SUMMIT GROUP SECURITIES LLC
48 Wall Street, 4th Floor
New York, NY 10005

TENANTS IN COMMON (T.I.C.)

_____
ACCOUNT NUMBER

Gentlemen:

In consideration of your carrying a Tenants-in-Common ("T.I.C.") account for the undersigned, the undersigned jointly and severally agree that each of them shall have authority on behalf of the account to buy, sell and otherwise deal in, through you as brokers, stocks, bonds, listed options (including uncovered writing) and other securities and commodities, on margin or otherwise (including short sales); to receive on behalf of the account demands, notices, confirmations, reports, statements of account and communications of every kind, and to dispose of same; to make on behalf of the account agreements relating to any of the foregoing matters, and to terminate or modify the same or waive any of the provisions thereof, and generally to deal with you on behalf of the account as fully and completely as if each alone were interested in said account, all without notice to the other or others interested in said account. The authority hereby conferred shall remain in force until written notice of its revocation, addressed to you, is delivered at your office at 48 Wall Street, New York, NY 10005.

for any of the rights and remedies you otherwise would have.

Because each of us is interested in the subject-matter of the authority hereby conferred upon the other, we jointly and severally agree, on our own behalf and on behalf of our respective estates, that the authority hereby conferred by each of us upon the other(s) shall survive our respective deaths.

In the event of the death of either or any of the undersigned, the interests in the account as of the close of business on the date of the death of the decedent (or, if such date is not a business day in New York City, on the next following business day), shall be as follows: (Name of participant) _____ or his or her estate _____ %

(Name of participant) _____ or his or her estate _____ %
(Name of participant) _____ or his or her estate _____ %
(Name of participant) _____ or his or her estate _____ %

Note: Total of Percentages must equal 100%

The foregoing authorizations shall enure to the benefit of TSG Securities LLC ("TSGS"), its controlling persons, successors and assigns. Because TSG Securities is acting as clearing agent for a correspondent broker/dealer or for a commodities futures commission merchant or introducing broker (hereinafter "FCM" or "IB"), all references herein to you shall be deemed references to both TSG Securities and the undersigned's broker/dealer, FCM or IB. Subject to the provisions hereof, all notices or communications for the undersigned in respect of the joint account are to be directed to:

NAME AND ADDRESS _____

_____ Very truly yours,

ALL TENANTS   X _____   X _____
MUST SIGN.   X _____   X _____

Dated at _____ On ___/___/___

3000-465 (Rev 7/91)

Figure 56 - Account Opening Form for Tenants in Common

Option Agreement

Since Options are considered to be a sophisticated form of investment because of the risk involved, the client is usually required to complete an additional account opening form to identify their investment capabilities and experience.

This front of the agreement is designed to find out more about the client's investment experience than was captured on the standard account opening form. Specifically, the broker needs the following information to evaluate whether this client should be allowed to invest in options:

- Income level
- Other types of investments held
- Investment objectives
- Degree of investment experience

The reverse side of the account agreement contains the terms that are specifically required for an option account. The terms that differ from the standard cash and margin agreements are:

- "All options transactions shall be subject to the ... rules of the Options Clearing Corporation ...
- I have received from you the current Options Risk Disclosure Document and Special Statement for Uncovered Writing and have read and understood the contents...
- I have read and understand the document ... *Exercise and Assignment* ...
- [the broker] shall have responsibility to notify me when an option in my account is nearing expiration ...
- If I engage in uncovered option writing, I agree to maintain sufficient cash reserves in my account ..."

OPTIONS INFORMATION FORM AND AGREEMENT

Account # _____

Dear Client: Exchange rules require us to request the following information from all clients who intend to effect transactions in options. The information is intended to assist us in making recommendations that are appropriate to your investment objectives. We would appreciate your completing the form. TSG Securities may, on the basis of the information provided, decline to accept any account for option activity or may limit such account to specific activities.

NAME _____   PHONE # _____

ADDRESS _____
IF ACCOUNT IS IN NAME OF MORE THAN ONE INDIVIDUAL, PLEASE
SUPPLY INFORMATION FOR ALL OWNERS.

OCCUPATION _____	EMPLOYER _____
TYPE OF BUSINESS _____	YEARS THERE _____
AGE _____ MARITAL STATUS _____	DEPENDENTS _____
APPROXIMATE _____ INCOME	SPOUSE'S INCOME _____
	APPROXIMATE LIQUID NET WORTH
APPROXIMATE NET WORTH	(Cash, Securities, Other) _____
(Do Not Include Residence)	

CHECK BOX

OTHER INVESTMENTS: ___ REAL ESTATE   ___ TAX SHELTERS   ___ SAVINGS

INVESTMENT OBJECTIVES: ___ INCOME   ___ GROWTH   ___ TRADING PROFITS

PAST INVESTMENT EXPERIENCE: _____ ACTIVITY _____

	YEARS EXPER.	NONE	LIMITED	MODERATE	EXTENSIVE
STOCK/BONDS	_____	_____	_____	_____	_____
OPTIONS	_____	_____	_____	_____	_____
COMMODITIES	_____	_____	_____	_____	_____

INVESTORS SHOULD NOT PURCHASE PUT OR CALL OPTIONS UNLESS THEY ARE ABLE To SUSTAIN A TOTAL LOSS OF THE PREMIUM AND TRANSACTION COSTS, OR WRITE UNCOVERED OPTIONS UNLESS THEY ARE ABLE TO SUSTAIN SUBSTANTIAL FINANCIAL LOSS.

PLEASE CHECK (SELECT) ONE OR MORE OF THE OPTION STRATEGIES YOU MAY WISH TO EMPLOY:

COVERED CALL WRITING   _____

PUT/CALL SPREADS PUT/CALL BUYS (SPECULATIVE WRITING   _____

PUT WRITING (SPECULATIVE)   _____

UNCOVERED CALL   _____

(THIS IS A HIGHLY SPECULATIVE ACTIVITY)

ATTENTION CLIENT: PLEASE SIGN THIS FORM ON THE BOTTOM RIGHT HAND SIDE AFTER
READING THE AGREEMENT. THANK YOU.

Date _____   R.R. Signature _____

Date _____   Approved Equity Options _____

Date _____   Approved For Currency Options _____

Date _____   Approved Interest Rate Options _____

Date _____   Approved (Registered Options Principal) _____

_____   _____
Date disclosure document sent   Date statement of risks for uncovered options writers sent

3000-349 (REV.1 1/93) CON @122310)

Figure 57 - Account Opening Form for Options

With respect to any transaction effected by you on my behalf, I hereby agree and represent as follows: 1. All options transactions shall be subject to the constitution, rules, regulations, customs and usages of the Options Clearing Corporation and any exchange or other marketplace where executed. 1, alone or in concert with others, will not violate the position or exercise limits of the exchanges, which may change from time to time.
2. As security for payment of all my obligations and liabilities to TSG Securities LLC ("TSG Securities"), I agree that TSG Securities shall have a lien upon and continuing security interest in all of my property held in any account at TSG Securities, including but not limited to securities, commodity futures contracts, commercial paper, monies and any after acquired property. In case of my insolvency, death, the attachment of my property or the occurrence of any event that gives you grounds for insecurity as you determine in your sole discretion, or my breach of this Agreement, you may take such steps as you may consider necessary or appropriate to protect yourself against loss with respect to any open options contract positions refuse to accept orders for the establishment of any new options positions, sell any and all property in my account(s), buy any property that is short in such account(s) to cancel any outstanding transactions all to offset any indebtedness due and owing to you; I will continue to be liable to you for any remaining deficiency. Such purchases or sales may be effected publicly or privately with or without notice, in such manner as you in your sole discretion determine to be appropriate under the circumstances.
3. I have received from you the current Options Risk Disclosure Document and Special Statement for Uncovered Writing and have read and understood these documents. I have noted particularly those sections of the Options Risk Disclosure Document summarizing the risk factors involved in options trading, and I have determined that, in view of my financial situation and investment objectives, options trading is not unsuitable for me.
4. I have read and understood the section of the Options Risk Disclosure Document entitled "Exercise and Assignment". I am aware that if I fail to give instructions to the contrary by expiration date, any option I may hold which is in the money by three quarters of a point or more at expiration will be exercised automatically by the Options Clearing Corporation. I am also aware that I may not receive actual notice of an exercise or assignment until the week following expiration date.
5. TSG Securities shall have no responsibility to notify me when an option in my account is nearing expiration, and I will have no claim for damage or loss arising out of the fact that an option in my account was not exercised unless I have instructed TSG Securities to exercise such option at or before the time established by TSG Securities.
6. If I engage in uncovered option writing, I agree to maintain adequate cash reserves to meet reasonably foreseeable margin calls and will, upon your request, immediately deposit cash reserves in my account that you deem to be required under the circumstances.
7. ARBITRATION
Arbitration is final and binding on the parties.
The parties are waiving their right to seek remedies in court, including the right to jury trial.
Pre-arbitration discovery is generally more limited than and different from court proceedings.
The arbitrators' award is not required to include factual findings or legal reasoning and any party's right to appeal or to seek modification of rulings by the Arbitrators is strictly limited.
The panel of arbitrators will typically include a minority of arbitrators who were or are affiliated with the securities industry.
No person shall bring a putative or certified class action to arbitration, nor seek to enforce any pre-dispute arbitration agreement against any person who has initiated in court a putative class action or who is a member of a putative class who has not opted out of the class with respect to any claims encompassed by the putative class action until:
(i) The class certification is denied: (ii) The class is decertified; or (iii) The client is excluded from the class by the court. Such forbearance to enforce an agreement to arbitrate shall not constitute a waiver of any rights under this agreement except to the extent stated herein.
You agree, and by maintaining an account for you TSG Securities agrees, that controversies arising between you and TSG Securities, its control persons, predecessors, subsidiaries and affiliates and all respective successors, assigns and employees, whether arising prior to, on or subsequent to the date hereof, shall be determined by arbitration. Any arbitration under this agreement shall be held at the facilities and before an arbitration panel appointed by the New York Stock Exchange, Inc., The American Stock Exchange, Inc., or the National Association of Securities Dealers, Inc. (and only before such exchanges or association). You may elect one of the foregoing forums for arbitration, but it you fail to make such election by registered mail or telegram addressed to TSG Securities LLC, 48 Wall Street, New York, New York 10005, Attention: Chief Legal Officer (or any other address of which you are advised in writing), before the expiration of ten days after receipt of a written request from TSG Securities to make such election, then TSG Securities may make such election. For any arbitration solely between you , sue and a broker for which TSG Securities acts as clearing agent, such election shall be made by registered mail to such broker at its principal place of business. The award of the arbitrators, or of the majority of them, shall be final, and judgment upon the award rendered may be entered In any court, state or federal, having jurisdiction.
8. THIS AGREEMENT AND ITS ENFORCEMENT SHALL BE GOVERNED BY THE LAWS OF THE STATE OF NEW YORK. Its provisions, including the arbitration provision, shall be continuous and shall inure to the benefit of TSG Securities, its controlling persons and their respective successors and assigns, and it shall inure to the benefit of and shall be binding upon my estate, executors, administrators and assigns. Because TSG Securities is acting as a clearing agent for a correspondent broker/dealer, the terms of this agreement, including the arbitration provision, shall inure likewise to the benefit of my broker/dealer, its successors and assigns, and all references to TSG Securities shall be deemed references to both TSG Securities and my broker
9. I am aware that exercise assignment notices for option contracts are allocated among client short positions pursuant to a procedure which randomly selects from among all client short option positions, including positions established on the day of assignment, those contracts which are subject to assignment. All short option positions are liable for assignment at any time. A more detailed description of TSG Securities random allocation procedure is available upon request.
10. This agreement supplements any Client Agreement that I may have signed, the terms of which shall, where inconsistent, supersede the terms set forth herein. Except as specifically amended by this agreement, all of the terms and conditions thereof shall remain effective.
11. I HEREBY CERTIFY THAT THE BACKGROUND INFORMATION AND FINANCIAL DATA PROVIDED HEREIN IS ACCURATE, AND I AM AWARE THAT THE INFORMATION AND DATA WILL BE RELIED UPON TO SERVICE MY ACCOUNT. I WILL ADVICE YOU IMMEDIATELY IN WRITING OF ANY CHANGES IN SUCH INFORMATION OR DATA OR IN MY OPTIONS INVESTMENT OBJECTIVES.
I ACKNOWLEDGE THAT THIS AGREEMENT CONTAINS A PRE-DISPUTE ARBITRATION CLAUSE ON THIS PAGE AT PARAGRAPH 7.

_____ X _____
Date   Signature of Client

_____ X _____
Name of Account   If account of more than one principal (i.e. joint
(please print or type)   account) all principals to the account must sign.

Figure 58 - Account Opening Form for Options (Back)

Tax Forms

The account owner(s) must provide the brokerage firm with a Social Security Number (SSN) or a certification of tax eligibility. U.S. citizens and residents are required to provide their SSN, and non-resident aliens must file a W-8 form in order to avoid mandatory 20% withholding on interest and dividends.

Form **W-8**

(Rev. February 1991)

Department of the Treasury

Internal Revenue Service

Certificate of Foreign Status

Name of beneficial owner (if joint account, also give joint owner's name) | U.S. taxpayer Identification number (if any)

Permanent Address (See Specific Instructions.) (include apt. or suite no.)

City, province or state, postal code and country

Current Mailing Address, if different (Include apt. or suite no., or P.O. Box if mail is not delivered to street address.)

City, town or post office, state, and ZIP code (if foreign address, enter city, province or state, postal code and country.)

List account information here (Optional, see *Specific instructions*.) | Account number(s) | Account type

Notice of Change in Status.-To notify the payer, mortgage interest recipient, broker or barter exchange that you no longer qualify for exemption, check here ___ If you check this box, reporting will begin on the account(s) listed.

Please Sign Here

Certification. – (Check applicable box(x)). Under penalties of perjury, I certify that:
___ For **INTEREST PAYMENTS**, I am not a U.S. citizen or resident (or I am filing for a foreign corporation, partnership, estate, or trust); **AND**
___ For **BROKER TRANSACTIONS** or **BARTER EXCHANGES**, I am an exempt foreign person as defined in the instructions below.

Signature | Date

General Instructions

(Section references are to the Internal Revenue Code unless otherwise noted.)

Purpose of Form.-Use Form W-8 or a substitute form containing a substantially similar statement to tell the payer, mortgage interest recipient, middleman, broker, or barter exchange that you are a nonresident alien individual, foreign entity, or exempt foreign person not subject to certain U.S. information return reporting or backup withholding rules.

Caution: Form W-8 does not exempt the payee from the 30% (or lower treaty) withholding rates.

Nonresident Alien Individual.-For income tax purposes, the term **nonresident alien individual** means an individual who is neither a U.S. citizen nor resident.

Generally, an alien is considered to be a U.S. resident if:
o The individual was a lawful permanent resident of the United States at any time during the calendar year, that is, the alien held an immigrant visa (a 'green card"), or o The individual was physically present in the United States on:
(1) at least 31 days during the calendar year, and

(2) 183 days or more during the current year and the 2 preceding calendar years (counting all the days of physical presence in the current year, 1/3 the number of days of presence in the first preceding year, and only 1/6 of the number of days in the second preceding year).

See **Pub. 519**, U.S. Tax Guide for Aliens, for more information on resident and nonresident alien status.

Exempt Foreign Person.-For purposes of this form, you are an **exempt foreign person** for a calendar year in which:
o You are a nonresident alien individual or a foreign corporation, partnership, estate or trust, and
o You are not engaged, or plan to be engaged during the year, in a U.S. trade or business that has effectively connected gains from the broker or barter exchange, or your country has a tax treaty with the U.S. that exempts your transactions from US taxes.

Who May Not File.-If you are a nonresident alien individual married to a U.S. citizen or resident and have made an election under section 6013(g) or (h), you are treated as a U.S. resident and may not use Form W-8.

When To File.- Form W-8 or substitute form should be filed before a payment is made. Otherwise, the payer may have to withhold and send 20% of the payment to the Internal Revenue Service (see Backup Withholding below). This certificate generally remains in effect for three calendar years. However, the payer may require you to file a new certificate each time a payment is made to you.

Where To File.-File this form with the payer of the qualifying income who is the withholding agent (see Withholding Agent on page 2). You may wish to keep a copy for your own records.

Backup Withholding.-A U.S. taxpayer identification number or Form W-8 or substitute form must be given to the payers of certain income. If a taxpayer identification number or Form W-8 or substitute form is not provided or the wrong taxpayer identification number is provided, these payers may have to withhold 20% of each payment or transaction. This is called "backup withholding."

Reportable payments subject to backup withholding rules are:
o Interest payments under section 6049(a).
o Dividend payments under sections 6042(a) and 6044.
o Other payments (i.e., royalties and payments from broker and barter exchanges) under sections 6041, 6041A(a), 6045, 6050A and 6050N.

If backup withholding occurs, an exempt foreign person who is a nonresident alien individual may get a refund by filing **Form 1040NR**, U.S. Nonresident Alien Income Tax Return, with the Internal Revenue Service Center, Philadelphia, PA 19255, even if filing the return is not otherwise required.

U.S. Taxpayer Identification Number.-The Internal Revenue law requires that certain income be reported to the Internal Revenue Service using a U.S. taxpayer identification number (TIN). This number can be a social security number assigned to individuals by the Social Security Administration or an employer identification number assigned to businesses and other entities by the Internal Revenue Service.

(Continued on back.)

Form W-8 (Rev. 2-91)

Figure 59 - IRS Form W-8

B. INSTITUTIONAL INVESTOR ACCOUNTS

The process of opening an institutional account is similar to the process for individuals, but the forms are different to reflect the legal status of the institution.

- For corporations, the account must be formally authorized in the by-laws of the corporation or its corporate charter, and the corporate charter must specifically allow the purchase of securities. A specific corporate resolution must be passed that identifies who has what level of authority over the account.

- And, specialized accounts, such as those with a fiduciary responsibility, will need specific documents such as the Trust Agreement, etc.

The forms required to open a corporate institutional account include:

- Institutional Account Opening Form
- Corporate Documentation
- Account Agreement
- Signature Cards

These forms are discussed throughout the rest of this chapter.

Institutional Account Opening Form

To open an institutional account, the corporation must present a copy of its certificate of incorporation, a corporate resolution, and complete an institutional account opening form. The following is one example of a form that is used to open a corporate account at a bank for a small corporation.

Business & Professional
Brokerage Cash and Margin Account Application
For Corporation, Unincorporated Association, Partnership, Investment
Club, Trust and other Business & Professional accounts.

If you have questions or need assistance completing this application please call 212-238-2500 or 800-555-5200. For Text Telephone Service (TTS) for the hearing impaired, call TSG Investment Services at 800-555-3405. *TSG Investment Services can not approve this application unless all information is completed and a Business & Professional Clients Certification and, if necessary, a Trustee Certification of Investment Powers is attached.* Please print or type.

1. How Would You Like the Title of Your Account to Appear?

Your Brokerage Account may be linked to a TSG Insured Money Market Account or checking account for the settlement of your brokerage transactions. The name you use for your Brokerage Account must be identical to the title of the TSG Transaction Account you select.
For a Business & Professional Account
Exact Title of Account _____

Taxpayer Identification Number or Social Security Number _____

2. What is the Address and Telephone Number for This Account?

Address		
City	State	Zip Code
Telephone Number(s)		

___ Check here if you do not want your name, address and securities positions disclosed to the companies in which you own securities that are held in your Brokerage Account.

3. Your TSG Account May Be Used as a Linked Transaction Account.

You may use a TSG Insured Money Market Account (IMMA) or checking account for the settlement of your brokerage transactions and automatic deposits of interest and dividends. Please indicate the account number below, and remember, the title of your Brokerage Account must be identical to the le of the TSG Transaction Account you select.

TSG Transaction Account Number	What type of account is this? ___ IMMA ___ Checking

If you wish to open a TSG Transaction Account please see a TSG branch representative.

4. Please Provide Us With a Bank Reference.

Name of Bank Reference
Branch Address
Telephone Number (   )

5. Tell Us About Your Organization and Your Financial Objective.

Please complete all items below. This information is required by the New York Stock Exchange and the National Association of Securities Dealers.

A. Check the appropriate box to indicate the type of ___ Securities Brokerage Firm ___ Stock Exchange Other (please specify) business in which your organization is engaged:

B. What is your financial objective? (check at least one.) ___ Capital Appreciation ___ Income ___ Safety ___ Speculation

C. What is your organization's approximate: Net Worth $ _____   Liquid Assets $ _____

D. If you are a corporation, what is your corporation's federal tax bracket? _____ %

TSG Investment Services Use Only Brokerage Account Number	TSG Use Only Transaction Account Number Bank Branch #
Investment Consultant Signature Date	Accepted by: (Name Stamp) Date/Time Stamp
Principal Approval BHC Approval (for Margin Acct.)	

Discount Services Division

Figure 60 - Page 1

The first page of the example identifies the person who is authorized to open the account and defines the institution's investment objectives.

The next page of the example allows the account opener to select a margin account and identify their tax status.

6. Are You Interested in Opening a Margin Account?

If you would like to open a Margin Account along with your Cash Account, please sign in this section and sign in Section 8. By signing in this section you acknowledge:

__ You have read, understood and agreed to the terms of the Margin Account Agreement provided with this application.

__ Securities Loan Consent: You consent to having your securities lent to BHC Securities, Inc. or lent out by BHC Securities, Inc. to others according to the Lending Agreement terms of the Margin Account Agreement.

Authorized Signature	**Remember:** *You must sign again in Section 8*	Date	Authorized	Signature	Date

7. Please Certify Your Tax Status

By signing this application below you will be certifying Section I. If you are a nonresident foreigner, check the box for Section II and complete the information d to certify you are an exempt person. A certification is required by law.

I. Tax Certification for U.S. Citizens or U.S. Residents

I hereby certify under penalties of perjury that:

(1) The number provided on this application is my correct Taxpayer Identification Number (Social Security Number or Employer Taxpayer Identification Number).

and

(2) I am not subject to backup withholding either because I have not been notified by the Internal Revenue Service that I am subject to back withholding due to under reporting of interest or dividends, or the IRS has notified me that I am no longer subject to such backup withholding.

Please note. It the IRS has notified you that you are subject to backup withholding because of underreporting and has not terminated that notice, you must strike out part (2) above before signing.

II. Tax Certification for Nonresidents

I hereby certify under penalties of perjury that:

(1) I am neither a citizen nor a resident of the United States;
(2) Unless my country has a tax treaty with the United States that exempts my transactions from United States taxes,
o I have not been and do not plan to be present in the United States for 183 days or more during the calendar year and
o I am not now and do not expect to be engaged in a trade or business in the United States during the calendar year:

(3) The information provided here is correct: and
(4) I have complied with all requirements to quality for the reduced or exempt rate of tax if a reduced rate of tax applies to interest, dividends, income from a trust, estate or investment account, or any other income received under my Brokerage Account.

Please note'. This certification generally remains in effect for the current and two subsequent calendar years. However, we may ask you for a new certification from time to time in order to verity your status. It your status or residency changes. you must notify us in writing within 30 days. If you cease to be a nonresident foreigner of the United States. you must provide us with a Taxpayer Identification Number and tax certification within 30 days in order to prevent backup withholding. It you have a Taxpayer Identification Number, you must provide the number to us. If you are a resident of a country that has an income tax treaty with the United States, by completing and signing this form, you claim the reduced or exempt rate of tax under the treaty for your Brokerage Account. It you become ineligible for the tax treaty benefits, you must notify us in writing. You certify that this account is an Individual, Trust, Estate, or Investment Account (if not, identity type here: _____).

Complete Your Resident Address Outside the United States Below: For an Individual or Joint Account, give your complete permanent address: for a corporation or partnership, show the principal off ice: and for any estate or trust, show the permanent residence or principal off ice of any fiduciary. If this is a joint account, all account owners must certify by signing the application in Section 8.

My permanent residence is:

Number and Street

City   Country

It you do not provide a complete resident address in a foreign country, we will presume that you are not entitled to treaty benefits.

8. Please Indicate Your Acceptance by Signing Below.

By signing below you acknowledge:
• You are providing a tax certification statement under penalties of perjury in Section 7 above;
• You have read, understood, and agreed to the terms of the Cash Account Agreement provided with this application; • You understand that all transactions will be cleared through TSG Securities, Inc., member NYSE/SIPC;

• You understand your Cash Account cannot be activated until this application has been accepted by TSG Investment Services; and you understand your Margin Account cannot be activated until this application has been accepted by TSG Securities LLC ("TSGS")

    I You have received a copy of and agree to be bound by the predispute arbitration clauses found on page 2 paragraph 3 and page 3 item 17 of the Brokerage Cash Account and Margin Account Agreements, respectively.

Name of	Authorized Person	Title
Signature		Date
Name of	Authorized Person	Title
Signature		Date

Please note: A Business & Professional Clients Certification and, it necessary, a Trustee Certification of Investment Powers must be included with your application.

Accounts carried with TSG Securities, Inc., Member NYSE/SIPC.

Figure 61 - Institutional Account Opening Form (Page 2)

This portion of the example requires the proper signers to authorize the opening of the account.

Applicant (All Applicants must complete this section.)

Name of Business Entity (As shown on Account Opening Form) _____

Legal Address, do not use P.O. Box _____   State of Organization _____

Applicant is a: ___ Corporation/Unincorporated Association   ___ Single Stockholder/Officer Corporation ___ Partnership/Investment Club ___ Other _____

To TSG Investment Services & TSG:

The following named persons, none of whom are less than eighteen years of age, are currently all the officers/trustees/general partners/other authorized signatories of Applicant, and any one of them (the "Authorized Person") is currently authorized under the applicable governing document to act with full power to enter into the TSG Investment Services Agreement for Business & Professional Accounts and the Supplemental Margin, Lending and Option Agreements, to establish a TSG Investment Services Brokerage Account under the Agreements (the "Account"), to appoint TSG Investment Services as agent of Applicant in forwarding orders for securities transactions to TSGS, to operate the Account for Applicant, and to execute and deliver any instrument necessary to effectuate the authority hereby conferred:

Name of Authorized Person:	Title:	Signature of Authorized Person

TSG Investment Services may, without inquiry, act upon the instruction of any person purporting to be the Authorized Person named in the notification from last received by TSG Investment Services. TSG Investment Services shall not be liable for any claims, expenses (including counsel fees) or losses resulting from TSG Investment Services having acted upon any instruction reasonably believed by it to be genuine.

For Corporations and Unincorporated Associations Only

I, _____, Secretary of Applicant, do hereby certify that at a meeting on _____ at which a quorum was present through the board of directors of the corporation/the membership, board of trustees or directors of the association duly adopted a resolution, which is in full force and effect, in accordance with Applicant's charter and by-laws, and which resolution did the following:

In witness whereof I have this day subscribed my name and, if a corporation, affixed the seal of the corporation.

(Affix Corporate Seal)   1. empowered each above-named Authorized Person to open cash, margin and option accounts and effect securities transactions for the Applicant On the terms described above and in accordance with all related account agreements;
2. authorized the Secretary to certify from time to time the names and titles of the officers of Applicant and to notify TSG Investment Services when changes in office occur: and
3. authorized the Secretary to certify that such a resolution has been duly adopted and will remain in full force and effect until TSG Investment Services receives a subsequent certification revoking or modifying such resolution and shall have sufficient time to act thereon.
Signature of Secretary _____

Signature of other Officer of the Corporation or Unincorporated Association who certifies that the foregoing instrument has been signed by the Secretary of the Corporation/Association.

Print Name _____   Title _____

For Single Stockholder/Officer Corporations Only

I, _____, President of the above-named Applicant do hereby certify that;
(Affix Corporate Seal)   1. if Applicant is a business in New York State, Applicant is incorporated pursuant to Section 402 of New York's Business Corporation Law;
2. the undersigned is the owner and holder f all of the issued and outstanding stock of the Applicant entitled to vote thereon;
3. the undersigned is the sole director of the Applicant and neither the certificate of incorporation nor by-laws thereof requires the election of more than one director;
4. the undersigned is President and the sole officer of Applicant and no one occupies the office of Secretary thereof.

The undersigned does hereby authorize each above-named Authorized Person to open cash, margin and option accounts and effect securities transactions for Applicant on the terms described above and in accordance with all related account agreements. In witness whereof I have this day subscribed my name and affixed the seal of the corporation.

Signature of President/Director/Sole Stockholder _____

For Partnerships and Investment Clubs Only

We, _____, individually, and as general partners of Applicant, represent and warrant that despite any dissolution or termination of Applicant or any modification or termination of authority of any partner, TSG Investment Services may act hereunder and rely hereon until written notice to the contrary shall be received by TSG Investment Services and TSG Investment Services shall have had sufficient time to act thereon; each above-named Authorized Person is authorized to open cash, margin and option accounts and effect securities transactions for Applicant on the terms described above and in accordance with all related account agreements. In witness whereof we have this day subscribed our names.

Signature of General Partner	Signature of General Partner	Signature of General Partner

For Sole Proprietorships and All Other Business and Professional Clients

I (We) hereby certify that each above-named Authorized Person is authorized to open cash, margin and option accounts and effect securities transactions for applicant and the terms described above and in accordance with all related account agreements.

Signature of Certifying Others	Print Name	Signature of Certifying Others	Print Name

ACCOUNTS CARRIED WITH TSG SECURITIES, INC. ("TSGS"), MEMBER NYSE/SIC

Securities and annuities transactions are through TSG Investment Services, member NASD/SIPC, a licensed insurance agency and a subsidiary of TSG Holdings, Inc. **and annuities are not bank products or FDIC insured, are not obligations of or guaranteed by TSG or TSG Investment Services and involve risk to principal.**

Figure 62 - Institutional Account Opening Form (Page 3)

The following example requires specific signatures for other categories of investment.

SECURITIES INVESTMENT ACKNOWLEDGMENT

Securities transactions are through TSG Investment Services, a member NASD/SIPC, and a subsidiary of TSG Holdings, Inc. When purchasing any security, I understand that securities:

> Securities transactions are through TSG Investment Services, member NASD/SIPC, and an affiliate of TSG Holdings, Inc.. Investment products are not bank deposits or FDIC Insured are not obligations of or guaranteed by TSG Holdings, Inc. or TSG Investment Services, and are subject to investment risks, including the possible loss of the principle amount invested.

MUTUAL FUNDS / INVESTMENT TRUSTS

When investing in mutual funds or unit investment trusts, I understand the following:

• **Sales Charges.** The prospectus that I received discloses any front or back-end sales charges. If I am purchasing a mutual fund with a back-end load (also known as a contingent deferred sales charge), I have discussed with an Investment Consultant the choice between such a fee and the alternative of a front-end sales charge and I acknowledge that the back-end sales charge is most appropriate for me.

• **Funds with No Loads, Sales Charges, or Transaction Fees.** If I am purchasing a fund (other than a Money Market Mutual Fund) with no load or sales charge and I am not paying a transaction fee, I understand that I may be charged a transaction fee of 1% of any amount I redeem within 90 days of purchase.

• **Share Value Fluctuates.** The value of my shares will fluctuate. If I redeem my shares, I may receive more or less than I paid depending upon the market value of the securities in the fund or trust at the time of redemption.

• **Past Results Are Not a Guarantee of Future Performance.** Yield or performance fluctuates and reflects past results. Yield quotations or a fund's past performance should not be considered an indication or guarantee of future yield or results.

• **TSGSelect portfolios and TSGFunds**   (The "Funds"). When purchasing shares of TSGSelect portfolios or TSGFunds, I understand that TSG acts as investment manager or investment advisor to the Funds, and that the Funds are made available by CFBDS, Inc., as distributor, which is not a TSG company.

• **U.S. Government Funds.** Although payment of principal and interest on securities in U.S. Government funds is guaranteed to the fund, the market value of the shares will fluctuate with rising or declining interest rates.

STOCKS AND BONDS

When purchasing or selling stocks or bonds, I understand the following:

• **Commission Charges.** I understand that a commission will be charged when I purchase or sell shares of stock. I understand that the price and yield quoted to me on a bond may include a mark-up or will have a separately identified commission added to it.

• **Value Fluctuates.** The value of my stocks and bonds will fluctuate. If I sell my stocks, or if I sell my bonds before maturity, I may receive more or less than I paid depending on prevailing market conditions.

Non-Resident Aliens: There may be mandatory withholding on dividends. distributions from a fund or trust, or sales proceeds.

For Retirement Accounts: I understand that I am not opening a discretionary account and that I am solely responsible for making investment decisions for my individual retirement account. I further understand that TSG Investment Services is acting solely as broker in each transaction, not as an investment adviser, and does not control the holdings of my portfolio or automatically monitor its performance.

By signing below, I confirm that I have read and understood the above.

PRINT NAME OF CLIENT (1)	DATE	PRINT NAME OF CLIENT (2) (NON-IRA ONLY)	DATE
PRINT NAME OF CLIENT (1)	DATE	PRINT NAME OF CLIENT (2) (NON-IRA ONLY)	DATE

	IC NUMBER:	OFFICE NUMBER:
BROKERAGE ACCOUNT NUMBER:		

ITEM 321059 (NIK 201 (L) REV 8/98 PKG 100

OFFICE COPY

Figure 63 - Institutional Account Opening Form (Page 4)

Corporate Documentation

The corporate documentation that is required consists of the certificate of incorporation and a corporate resolution to the corporation's by-laws, which is also called the corporate charter.

Certificate of Incorporation

When a corporation is formed, the incorporators must obtain a Certificate of Incorporation from the Secretary of State in the state in which they wish to establish the company. Some of the key information provided on the certificate is:

- Corporate name
- Number of shares authorized
- Par value of the shares
- Incorporator

A company that has been established in one state can do business in other states, but they must register in each state in which they conduct business.

When opening an account, the firm must submit a copy of the certificate of incorporation which proves that the corporation has been opened and has general powers that allow the officers to buy and sell securities, trade on margin, etc.

DELAWARE REGISTRY, LTD.
CERTIFICATE OF INCORPORATION

OF

THE SUMMIT GROUP, INC.

FIRST.   The name of this Corporation is   THE SUMMIT GROUP, INC

SECOND. Its registered office in the state of Delaware is to be located at 2316 Baynard Boulevard, County of New Castle. The Registered Agent in charge thereof is DELAWARE REGISTRY, LTD., 2316 Baynard Boulevard, Wilmington, Delaware 19802.

THIRD.   The purpose of this corporation is to engage in any lawful act or, activity for which corporations may be organized under the General Corporation Law of Delaware.

FOURTH. The amount of the total authorized capital stock of this corporation is ___-------___ Dollars ($ ___-----___) divided into ___1500___ shares, of ___- NO PAR VALUE -___ each.

FIFTH. The names and mailing addresses of each of the incorporator or incorporators are as follows.

NAME   **MAILING ADDRESS**

LEILA F. FOGG 2316 Baynard Boulevard, Wilmington, Delaware 19802

SIXTH. Provisions for the management of the business and for the conduct of the affairs of this corporation and provisions creating, defining, limiting and regulating the powers of this corporation, the directors and the stockholders are as follows:

(1) The board of directors shall have the power to make, adopt, alter, amend and repeal the bylaws of the corporation without the assent or vote of the stockholders, including, without limitation, the power to fix, from time to time, the number of directors which shall constitute the whole board of director's of this corporation subject to the right of the stockholders to alter, amend and repeal the bylaws made by the board of directors.

(2) In addition to the powers and authority hereinbefore or by statute expressly conferred upon them, the board of directors of this corporation are hereby expressly empowered to exercise all such powers and to do all such acts and things as may be exercised or done by this corporation; subject, nevertheless, to the provisions of the statutes of the State of Delaware and of the Certificate of Incorporation as they may be amended, altered or changed from time to time and to any bylaws provided, however, that no bylaw so made shall invalidate any prior act of the board of directors which would have been valid if such bylaw had not been made.

SEVENTH: A director of this corporation shall have no personal liability to the corporation or its stockholders for monetary damages for breach of fiduciary duty as a director, provided that this provision shall not eliminate the liability of a director (i) for any breach of the director's duty of loyalty to the corporation or its stockholders, (ii) for acts or emissions not in good faith or which involve intentional misconduct or a knowing violation of law, (iii) under Section 174 of the Delaware General Corporation Law, or (iv) for any transaction from which the director derived an improper personal benefit.

I/WE. THE UNDERSIGNED, for the purposes of forming a Corporation under the laws of the State of Delaware, do make, file and record this Certificate, and do certify that the facts herein stated are true, and I/we have accordingly hereunto set my/our respective hand(s) and seal(s).

DATED: __3/19/92__   INCORPORATOR:
__//Signed//_____

Figure 64 - Certificate of Incorporation

Corporate Charter

Once a corporation is formed and has its certificate of incorporation, the next step is to establish a Corporate Charter which defines the business of the corporation and the guiding policies for the corporation.

If the corporate officers are allowed to open a cash or a securities account with the bank or a broker, the corporate charter must specifically authorize them to do so.

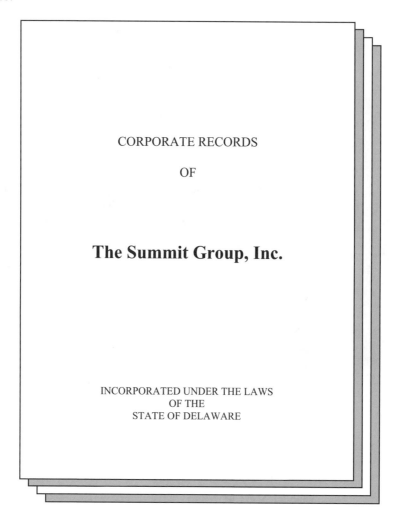

CORPORATE RECORDS

OF

The Summit Group, Inc.

INCORPORATED UNDER THE LAWS
OF THE
STATE OF DELAWARE

Figure 66 - Example of Corporate Records

Corporations may also be asked to pass a specific corporate resolution that allows the firm to open the account and identifies who can sign on the firm's behalf. A corporate resolution is a document signed by the directors, empowering certain persons to act on their behalf. These acts can include: opening accounts, giving buy/sell orders, signing securities, etc.

This resolution can be in the form of a paragraph added to the corporation's by-laws or by using a form supplied by the securities firm. An example of this paragraph is:

> RESOLVED, that the officers of this corporation be authorized and directed to open a securities account in the name of the corporation, in accordance with a securities account opening form attached to these minutes.

Figure 67 - Example of Corporate Resolution

Account Agreement

Institutional accounts can be either cash or margin accounts, and can be opened by a variety of different types of entities, including:

• Corporations	• Investment Clubs
• Broker/Dealers	• Trusts
• Joint Accounts	• Testamentary Trusts
• Estates	• Mutual Funds
• Partnerships	• Hedge Funds
• Banks	• IRAs
• Insurance Companies	• Keoghs

Custodial Account for Corporations

When a corporation wants to buy and sell securities it can open an account directly with a broker or, if required by law as in the case of pension funds, it may open a securities custody account with a bank. Brokers typically do not specifically charge for their custodial services if the account holder conducts sufficient buying and selling in the account to compensate the broker for the services through their commissions. Banks, however, charge for their custodial services since they do not receive any commission on the purchase and sales.

The custodial services banks perform were discussed in the chapter on Securities Industry Participants and generally include settlement support and asset servicing after the trade has settled.

When a bank is involved in providing custody for institutional clients, there are usually three parties involved in every trade:

- Institutional Investor
- Broker
- Bank Custodian

The settlement process is simplified by the systems provided by the Depository Trust Company. The DTC's systems connect all three parties and also inform other interested parties of the transaction. In addition, the custodian assumes responsibility for all of the asset servicing and reporting functions that are required by the client or by law.

The settlement process and the asset servicing functions are discussed in more detail in the chapter on Post-Trade Processing, Clearing and Settlement.

Fiduciary Account

A trust account is a special type of account where the account holder is the trust itself. Trusts can be established for a variety of reasons, and in each case the account agreement must identify the:

- Trust name and location
- Purpose of the trust
- Conditions of the trust
- Names of beneficiaries
- Names of fiduciaries

Trusts can contain any form of assets, which can include:

- Real Property
- Financial Assets
- Business

Each trust follows formats prescribed by law and precedent; however, each trust is a unique document. Trusts are described in more detail in the chapter on Securities Industry Participants.

CERTIFICATE OF TRUSTEES REGARDING INVESTMENT AUTHORITY

TSG
Securities

THE SUMMIT GROUP SECURITIES LLC
48 Wall Street, 4th Floor
New York, NY 10005

Account Title: _____

Account #: _____ Social Security # or Tax ID: _____ Date of Trust: _____

Names of Trustees: _____
_____

Names of Beneficiaries: _____
_____

THE UNDERSIGNED TRUSTEES HEREBY CERTIFY THAT:

1. Investment Decision Making. The trust agreement for the trust authorizes investment decisions to be made by:

   (please check one)

   __ Any trustee individually   __ A majority of the trustees jointly   __ The following trustees jointly   __ All trustees jointly

   (print names): _____   _____   _____

   __ The account executive for this account who has discretion over the account.

   __ The following independent investment adviser (print name):

2. Permitted Investments. The trust is authorized to trade in the securities and other financial instruments specified below:

   (please check all that apply)   __ U.S. Governments   __ U.S. Agencies   __ Municipal Bonds
                                    __ Corporate Equities   __ Corporate Bonds   __ Mutual Funds
                                    __ Limited Partnerships   __ Certificate of Deposits __ Covered/Long Options
                                    __ Uncovered Options   __ Commodity Options   __ Commodity Futures
                                    __ Physical Commodities   __ Other _____

3. Borrowing Money and Pledging Collateral. The trust: (please check one) ____ is   ____ is not expressly authorized to borrow against the loan value of the marginable securities in its account and to pledge such securities as collateral.

4. Buying Securities on Margin. The trust: (please check one) ____ is   ____ is not expressly authorized to open and maintain a margin account and, in conjunction therewith, to buy any of the above-indicated financial instruments on margin.

5. Selling Securities Short. The trust: (please check one) ____ is   ____ is not expressly authorized to sell short any of the above-indicated financial instruments

6. Employee Retirement Income Security Act of 1974 (ERISA). The trust: (please check one) ____ is   ____ is not an employee benefit plan covered under ERISA.

The undersigned trustees further represent that the certifications contained herein are true, accurate and consistent with the purposes and investment objectives of the trust. The undersigned trustees jointly and severally agree to indemnify TSG Securities and hold it harmless from any loses, expenses, penalties, claims or liabilities (including reasonable attorney's fees) that may arise out of TSG Securities' acting in reliance on the representations contained in this certification. This indemnification shall survive the termination of the trust or the trust account.

TSG Securities may rely upon this certification unless and until the trustees advise it in writing to the contrary. This certification supersedes any prior certifications, documents or other written or oral information provided to TSG Securities regarding the trust.

Signatures of Trustees (All trustees must sign this certification)

_____   _____   _____
          (signature)   (signature)   (signature)

_____   _____   _____
          (print name)   (print name)   (print name)

Notarization (required)

Figure 68 - Authorization To Open A Trust Account

Limited Liability Companies (LLC)

The general terms and conditions for LLCs are very similar to those for corporations. Because of the legal structure of the firm there are some differences in the documents.

Account Number _____

CERTIFICATE OF TRADING AUTHORITY FOR LIMITED LIABILITY COMPANIES

1, _____, being a duly authorized representative of _____ a limited liability company formed under the laws of _____ and having a principal place of business at _____ (the "Company"), hereby certify that, the Company is authorized and directed to establish and maintain one or more accounts (including margin accounts) (each, an "Account"), and to engage in any of the transactions hereinafter described, with or through, TSG Securities LLC ("TSG Securities"), through an Account or otherwise. TSG Securities is authorized to act as principal or agent in such transactions.

I FURTHER CERTIFY THAT, the Company is authorized and empowered to purchase (including on a forward or when-issued basis or on margin), hold, finance, pledge, exercise, convert, tender, redeem, exchange, transfer, assign, sell (including short, when-issued and forward sales), enter into, write, issue and otherwise deal and trade, singly or in combination, in the following:*

• Securities (General): any and all forms of securities, trust certificates, evidences of interest, participation or indebtedness of any kind whatsoever, whether publicly registered or exempt from registration, for example as a private placement or exempt security including without limitation, the securities, instruments and transactions listed in the categories set forth below;

• Debt Securities: any and all forms of bonds, debentures or notes of any coupon (including "zero coupon") or maturity, including but not limited to obligations issued or guaranteed by the United States Government or any of its agencies or instrumentalities, Government Sponsored Enterprises, foreign sovereign nations, corporations or other entities, including special purpose entities, whether investment grade, unrated or high yield or secured or unsecured;

• Equity Securities: any and all forms of common and preferred stock, scrip, warrants and rights;

• Mortgages, Mortgage-Backed and Other Asset-Backed Securities: whole mortgage loans and interests and participations in mortgage loans, whether residential or commercial or multi-family; mortgage- backed, mortgage-related or mortgage-derived securities or instruments of any kind whatsoever including, but not by way of limitation, any tranches of, collateralized mortgage obligations, REMICs, mortgage pass-through certificates and participation certificates, whether issued or guaranteed by or backed by collateral of a Government agency, Government Sponsored Enterprise or a private issuer, including but not limited to planned or targeted amortization, interest- only, principal-only, floating rate, inverse floating rate or zero coupon classes, interest-only or principal-only strips or mortgage residuals or any combination of the foregoing; all forms and tranches of asset- backed securities, including but not limited to, securities backed by auto, truck, boat, home equity, credit card loans, and any other form of consumer debt or business debt, lease payments, any form of bank debt, and interest in and debt instruments issued by entities whose principal assets are any of the foregoing and any asset-backed residual:

• Repurchase, Reverse Repurchase and Securities Lending and Similar Transactions: repurchase and reverse repurchase transactions, securities lending, bonds borrow pledge, dollar rolls, buy forward sale and other similar transactions involving cash or any kind of security, asset-backed interest or participation or other financial instrument;

• Money Market Instruments; Bank Notes and Bank Loans: money market instruments, including but not limited to bankers acceptances, certificates of deposit and commercial paper, deposit notes and other bank notes and corporate, commercial or sovereign loans or obligations;

• Foreign Exchange: spot and forward transactions in foreign currencies, currency futures contracts, and listed or over-the-counter options on foreign currencies;

• Commodities and Futures: commodities and financial futures contracts and listed over-the-counter options on commodities and financial futures;

• Options and Certain Derivative Securities: any and all forms of listed or over-the-counter options (whether or not "covered") on, and securities whose performance is linked to, individual securities, groups or indices of securities, currencies, interest rate indices, commodity indices, financial instruments, or any other transaction type whether or not described in this resolution;

• Interest Rate Currency and Other Swap Transactions: swap transactions, including but not limited to interest rate swaps, basis swaps, commodity swaps, rate protection transactions, serialized interest rate options, interest rate futures, caps, collars, floors, corridors, and forward rate agreements, currency swap agreements, cross-currency rate swap agreements, or equity or equity index swaps, or any similar transaction or combination thereof whether on a forward basis or otherwise, including any option to enter into any of the foregoing; and

• International Securities and Transactions: each of the above itemized securities, obligations, instruments and other transaction types may be dealt in regardless of whether such security, obligation, instrument or other transaction type is issued by, the obligation of, or related to, a foreign person, enterprise or sovereign, is denominated in a foreign currency or trades or is settled on or through a foreign market, ex- change or clearinghouse.

*INVESTMENTS OR TRANSACTIONS NOT AUTHORIZED ARE CROSSED OUT.

Figure 69 - Trading Certificate for LLCs (Page 1)

Each of the following persons or entities is hereby individually authorized for and on behalf of the Company (1) to give to and receive from TSG Securities oral or written instructions, confirmations, notices or demands with respect to any Account or transaction; (2) to have complete authority at all times to bind the Company to the performance of any transaction or agreement, amendment or modification thereof, relating to any Account or transaction involving the Company; (3) to lend or borrow money or securities and to secure the repayment thereof with the property of the Company; (4) to pay in cash or by check or draft drawn upon the funds of the Company any sums required to be paid in connection with any Account or transaction; (5) to order the transfer or delivery of any securities, funds or other property to such person or entity or to any other person or entity; (6) to order the transfer of record of any securities, funds or other property to any name and to accept delivery of any securities, funds or other property; (7) to direct the sale or exercise of any rights with respect to any securities or other property; (8) to sign for and on behalf of the Company all releases, assignments, powers of attorney or other documents in connection with any Account or transaction; (9) to agree to any terms or conditions affecting any Account or transaction; (10) to endorse any securities or other property in order to pass title thereto (or to any interest therein); (11) to direct TSG Securities to surrender any securities or other property for the purpose of effecting any exchange or conversion thereof or otherwise; (12) to appoint any other per- son or persons to do any all things which such named person or entity is hereby empowered to do; and (13) generally, to take all such action as such person or entity may deem necessary or desirable to implement or facilitate the foregoing trading activities:

Name of Person _____

Title/ Firm Name _____

Specimen Signature _____

Name of Person _____

Title/ Firm Name _____

Specimen Signature _____

Name of Person _____

Title/ Firm Name _____

Specimen Signature _____

The foregoing shall apply to all transactions and agreements between the Company and TSG Securities, even if such transactions and agreements were previously entered into by the Company and TSG Securities (which prior transactions and agreements are hereby ratified in 0 respects) and shall remain in full force and effect in all respects until the close of business on the day after TSG Securities receives written notice of the modification or revocation thereof at its offices located at 48 Wall Street, 4th Floor, New York, NY 10005, Attn: Chief Legal Officer.

TSG Securities is instructed to direct all notices or communications including demands, notices, confirmations, reports and statements of account for the Company, in connection with the Account (s), as follows:

Name: _____

Address: _____

Phone: Fax: _____

Please provide the portion of the Company's Operating Agreement or other document authorizing the person signing this Certificate on behalf of the Company to do so. In the absence of such a document, please have all members/managers sign on the attached sheet.

(Signature) Name: _____

Date: _____

Name: _____

Address: _____

Phone: _____

Fax: _____

Please provide the portion of the Company's Operating Agreement or other document authorizing the person signing this Certificate on behalf of the Company to do so. In the absence of such a document, please have all members/managers sign on the attached sheet.

_____
(Signature)

Name: _____
Date: _____
By: _____

Name: _____
Date: _____
By: _____

Name: _____
Date: _____
By: _____

Name: _____
Date: _____
By: _____

Figure 70 - Trading Certificate for LLCs (Page 2)

C. INVESTMENT MANAGER ACCOUNTS

An investment manager is usually organized as a corporation or as a partnership, and open brokerage accounts in their name (if the account belongs to the investment firm) or in their clients' names (with each client's consent) with brokerage firms.

If the brokerage account has been established in the client's name, the account opening forms must identify the level of discretion that has been granted to the investment manager's employees as well as any other special instructions or limitations.

Institutional accounts also typically need a custodial account with a bank, and the client generally opens this account directly and instructs the bank regarding the level of authority the investment manager has and any limitations on the investments.

D. NEW ACCOUNT PROCESSING

The processing of these new account forms by brokers is described in the chapters on Broker, Bank and Investment Manager Processing.

VI. Buying and Selling Securities

To buy or sell securities, retail clients conduct research, analyze the information they gather and then make an investment decision. That decision is generally relayed to a registered representative, who is an employee of a brokerage firm and who enters the order into the broker's system. The order will then normally either go to an exchange or NASDAQ to be executed, to a trader who will find a counterparty for the trade, or to be filled from the broker's own inventory.

Institutional clients go through the same process of research, analysis and decision making, although with more sophisticated tools and techniques. Their decision is usually relayed to a broker/dealer's salesman or trader for execution. The trader will normally go to an exchange or NASDAQ, fill from the trader's own inventory, or find a counterparty in the market.

A. FINANCIAL MARKETS

When most people in the U.S. talk about the *market*, they are usually only referring to the Dow Jones Industrial Average (DJIA), which reflects the activity of thirty large stocks on the NYSE. The thirty stocks, selected by the Dow Jones Company to reflect the overall industrial base in the U.S., as of April, 2004 are:

Company Name	Ticker Symbol
ALCOA Inc.	AA
American Express Co.	AXP
American International Group Inc.	AIG
Boeing Co.	BA
Caterpillar Inc.	CAT
Citigroup Inc.	C
Coca-Cola Co.	KO
Dupont Co.	DD
Exxon Mobil Corp.	XOM
General Electric Co.	GE
General Motors Corp.	GM
Hewlett Packard Co.	HPQ
Home Depot	HD
Honeywell International Inc.	HON
Intel	INTC
International Business Machines Corp.	IBM
J.P. Morgan Chase & Co.	JPM
Johnson & Johnson	JNJ
McDonalds Corp.	MCD
Merck & Co.	MRK
Microsoft	MSFT
Minnesota Mining & Manufacturing Co.	MMM
Pfizer Inc.	PFE
Phillip Morris Co.	MO
Procter & Gamble Co.	PG
SBC Communications, Inc.	SBC
United Technologies Corp.	UTX
Verizon Communications Inc.	VZ
WalMart	WMT
Walt Disney Co.	DIS

Figure 71 - Dow Jones Components

We often use the DJIA as a proxy for the *market*, when, in fact, there are multiple markets, and the DJIA only represents a small portion of market activity.

Historically, only including NYSE equities, it now includes two stocks from NASDAQ.

There is a primary market and a secondary market that will be discussed in the next section. There are also markets that are made by each of the exchanges, and by the over-the-counter market. And, there are more financial markets in the U.S. than just securities-oriented markets. There is a commodities market, an options and futures market, the money market and the FX (foreign exchange) market; and these markets can be further subdivided into the spot, cash, and forward or futures markets.

There are various settlement periods that can be used for different circumstances, which are also referred to as markets.

The regular way to settle most of the securities in the U.S. involves a three-day process. Some other instrument types settle in one day (options, government securities and some money market instruments) and others settle on a specific day each month (mortgage backed securities).

Although the vast majority of trades in the U.S. settle in the regular way, if both brokers agree, the settlement date can be any date after the trade date.

The cash or spot market involves instruments that are traded and settled on the same day (foreign exchange and some money market instruments).

The futures and forward market involves trades made today that will settle at a mutually agreed upon time in the future (foreign exchange and commodities).

Primary Market

Firms offer their securities to the public through the primary market. As discussed in the chapter on Creating New Securities, these offerings, called initial public offerings (IPOs), are distributed to institutional and individual buyers through underwriters and participating brokers. Issues that are brought into the primary market are often called *When, As and If Issued* securities.

After an issue has been brought to the market in an IPO, all of the subsequent trading is conducted in the secondary market.

The primary market involves a commitment to buy a security before the security is actually available, and the trade date can only be established when the security is issued. The actual settlement of a security sold in the primary market will then usually occur in the regular way for that security type.

Secondary Market

The secondary market includes the exchanges and over-the-counter markets where securities are bought and sold after they were brought to the market through an original issuance in the primary market.

The U.S. secondary market consists of the regulated U.S. exchanges and the U.S. over-the-counter market. There are two other markets that are really subsets of the secondary market, which are called the third and the fourth markets.

Third Market

The third market is a dealer market that is used for trading blocks of shares or bonds. Dealers contact other dealers in order to assemble the blocks without alerting the market to the fact that they are buying.

Fourth Market

The fourth market is an electronic market that allows institutions to locate other institutions that want to trade a specific security.

There is a dramatic increase in the number and use of electronic trade matching systems, which are also called Alternative Trading Systems (ATS).

An ATS can be used for different instrument types:

- In the debt and standardized OTC derivative markets, electronic trading systems are moving the markets from bilateral telephone trading to more centralized multilateral screen trading.

- In equity markets, the new trading systems have added competition for exchanges that had previously enjoyed near monopolies.

- Electronic trading systems are also being developed in the non-standardized OTC derivative markets.

ATSs and another form of electronic counterparty matching through Electronic Communications Networks (ECN) are discussed in the chapter on Vendors. These systems and networks were established to allow investment managers to see each other's proposed purchases or sales, without disclosing who are interested in buying or selling. The networks must pay a recognized SRO to monitor and audit their activity, and they must keep a very detailed audit trail.

One of the goals of these ATSs and ECNs is to provide an auction service like the floor of an exchange over an electronic network. If they can do this effectively for all of the types of investors, the exchange floors could become unnecessary. Despite the rapid growth in the use of ATSs, it is unlikely that they will ever completely eliminate the need for a broker for large transactions; however, ECNs will reduce the need for floor exchanges.

B. U.S. TRADING MODELS

Brokers can either act as an agent or as a principal to the trade.

- When a broker trades as an agent, he represents the buyer or the seller but is not a principal to the trade.

- When a broker trades as a principal, he is usually buying or selling from his own inventory.

There are three basic trading models in the U.S., all of which are discussed in more detail in later sections of this book:

Exchange Trading

Transactions on an exchange involve agency trading in an auction environment, all of which are subject to the rules of the Intermarket Trading System. An auction involves multiple people who can simultaneously bid/offer for a security.

Many exchanges, including the NYSE are preparing to add some level of electronic trading that would by-pass the floor in order to compete with some of the purely electronic markets.

Stocks, bonds, options, futures and commodities are all traded on various exchanges in the U.S.

NASDAQ Trading

NASDAQ provides a platform that supports agency trading in a negotiation environment for stocks. Negotiated trading involves one potential buyer and one potential seller who agree at a price.

Over-The-Counter

OTC transactions that occur off of NASDAQ also involve trading as agent or principal in a negotiation environment. When trading as a principal, the dealer is called a market maker.

These trades are primarily made by telephone and increasingly via Alternative Trading Systems.

All types of securities can be traded OTC.

C. STOCK AND BOND EXCHANGES

An exchange has historically been a centralized market with a specific location, called a floor, which supports the trading of listed equities, bonds and options. Exchange traders have traditionally used a process of open outcry to participate in an auction, where the prices of all trades must be disclosed to the market.

Because an exchange has historically been organized around a physical place, it has had regular hours established for trading. For instance, the NYSE is currently open from 9:30 a.m. to 4:00 p.m. In recent years, as exchanges have begun serving investors from around the world, there has been increasing pressure to extend the hours. The NYSE has been considering extending its hours and/or adding an evening session, but has met with some resistance by its members who feel that they might have to work longer hours for the same trade volume.

However, competition from other forms of matching buyers and sellers, as well as international competitors, may force the exchanges to add hours. Some brokers have begun to provide access for their clients to after hours trading on several of the Electronic Crossing Networks that are described in the chapter on Vendors.

Exchange Functions

There are several functions common to most U.S. exchanges:

Listing Securities

Each exchange establishes its own rules for listing securities. These rules include the size of the company's capitalization, the number of shareholders and whether or not the exchange's clients would be interested in buying or selling the issue.

The types of securities that are listed on exchanges are:

- Equities
- Corporate Bonds
- Options
- Futures

Securities that are listed on one exchange (or NASDAQ) can also be traded on other exchanges under the provisions of the Unlisted Trading Privileges (UTP).

Centralizing Buying and Selling

An exchange provides a central place for its members to meet so that they can purchase and sell securities. The NYSE began when brokers in New York started meeting at a Buttonwood tree on Wall Street in 1791. The AMEX also began when the New York Curb Market moved indoors in the early 1920s.

Reporting trading activity

Each exchange is required to report every trade in its listed securities, whether the trade was conducted on the exchange or off of the exchange.

Avoid Arbitrage

Since any one issue can be listed on more than one exchange, the exchanges want to avoid price discrepancies that could allow brokers to take advantage of momentary differences in the price of a single issue on the various exchanges by buying on one exchange and selling on another exchange within seconds, if not simultaneously. The U.S.'s national and regional exchanges are linked by the Intermarket Trading System (ITS), which allows members on each exchange to see prices on commonly traded securities.

Monitoring compliance

Each exchange is responsible for ensuring that its members comply with the exchange's rules, and for punishing firms and individuals violating these rules.

Arbitration

The exchange provides an arbitration method to resolve disputes between brokers as well as between brokers and their clients.

Trade Processing on an Exchange

When a client's order is to be executed on an exchange, it goes through several steps as shown below.

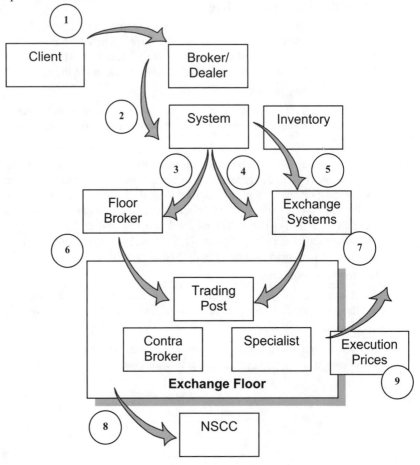

Figure 72 - Trading Using an Exchange

1. The client contacts his registered representative, usually by telephone, and gives instructions to buy or sell a specific security. Increasingly, clients are able to use a broker's online system or the Internet to enter a trade.

2. The registered representative or a designated assistant enters the order into the broker's system, unless the order goes through an online input application or the Internet.

3. The broker's system determines whether the order goes to the floor of the appropriate exchange, or

4. … to an electronic application such as the NYSE's SuperDOT system (Designated Order Turnaround system), or

5. ... to the firm's inventory. If the broker uses their own inventory for the trade, they will notify the appropriate exchange of the transaction.

6. If the order goes to the floor, the floor trader goes to the appropriate trading post for that security and looks for a counterparty. If no counterparty is available at the post, the broker may deal with the specialist, who is an independent broker responsible for maintaining an orderly market in the security.

7. If the order goes to an automated execution system, the order will be routed to the specialist's electronic book where it will probably be matched electronically.

8. Orders that were matched on the floor or by the automated systems are recorded and sent to the NSCC for clearing.

9. Prices are reported electronically.

Execution Environments

Each exchange has an automated system that supports the automatic execution of orders at the market price through either the specialist or a market maker. These automated execution systems are:

- SuperDOT - Designated Order Turnaround (NYSE)
- AOF - AMEX Order File (AMEX)
- SuperMontage (NASD)

Trades are also reported when the floor broker/trader is involved in an execution. In order to match the trades, they will provide specific details about the trade, which includes:

- Execution details
- Counterparty
- Price
- Trade/settlement date
- Time of execution

Once the trades have been captured automatically or entered by the floor staff, the exchange's internal system processes the execution details. This information is relayed to the clearinghouse and to the brokers involved in the trade, which process the data in their own systems. These systems manage the steps of the process.

- The broker's system performs a match of the original order and the execution, which is usually based upon the order number that was assigned by the broker when the order was received.

- The registered representative or the salesperson is first advised of the trade execution, and may then notify the client directly about the trade and any money available to the client or due to the broker.

- The broker's Purchase & Sale (P&S) department is advised of the trade execution and a confirmation is created that will be sent to the client.

Types of Trade Comparisons

In order to process the street-side of the trade, the brokers representing both sides of the trade attempt to match their trade information before the information is sent to the clearinghouse. There are several different types of trade comparisons.

Locked-in Process

A trade is considered locked-in when the comparison is made as part of the trade execution. This type of trade is available on the automated execution systems that were listed on the previous page.

These systems eliminate the need for any other comparison processing.

Two-Sided Process

In a two-sided process, both brokers report their trades to their exchange, which matches the trades and reports discrepancies to the participants. This type of trade is available on several systems:

- OCS   -   Overnight Comparison System (NYSE)
- IDCE   -   Inter Day Comparison (AMEX)
- TARS   -   Trade Accounting Reporting (NASD)

These systems report on each of three categories of trades:

Matched Trades

The trades submitted by the brokers match.

Unmatched Trades

A trade submitted by a broker *does not exactly* match the trade submitted by the counterparty.

Advisory Trades

The trade submitted by a broker *does not* match any trade submitted by any other broker.

One Sided Process

In a one-sided process, one of the brokers, usually the seller reports the trades to the exchange, and the buyer can review them.

Exchange Regulations [37]

While every exchange has its own specific regulations, they are all in compliance with SEC guidelines and are therefore very similar. Some of the major regulations that apply to exchanges are:

Advertisement

Registered representatives cannot advertise independently. The only advertisements that are allowed go through the brokerage firm.

Bunching Orders (NYSE Rule 411)

"A member … shall not combine the orders given by several different clients to buy or sell odd lots of the same security, into a round lot order without the prior approval of the clients…"

---

[37]   Source: New York Stock Exchange

Correspondence

All incoming mail, including personal mail received at the branch, must be opened by the branch manager or their delegate. Business related mail received at home should be turned over immediately to the branch manager.

All outgoing correspondence also must be reviewed and approved by the branch manager or their delegate.

If the registered representative wants to write a letter showing the success of his selections, *all* of the recommendations that were made in the past twelve months must be shown, including the date and the price when the security was recommended for purchase and/or sale.

Death of a Client

Upon the notice of a death of a client, the broker must:

- Cancel all open orders
- Change account title to *John Doe*, deceased
- Block the account from further trades pending receipt of the following:
    - A copy of the Death Certificate and a copy of the Will
    - A copy of the court appointment of the executor or administrator, which establishes the executor or administrator's right to act for the estate
    - A copy of any tax waivers, which establish that no further estate tax claims will be made against the property
    - A copy of the affidavit of domicile, which establishes the state of legal residence at the time of death and therefore identifies which laws apply

Directorships

Registered representatives can hold up to three directorships in non-financial organizations with their employer's approval. The NYSE must approve directorships in financial companies.

Discretion (NYSE Rule 408)

"No member ... shall exercise any discretionary power in any client's account or accept orders for an account from a person other than the client without first obtaining written authorization."

Due Diligence (NYSE Rule 405)

Brokers must "Use due diligence to learn the essential facts relative to every client, every order, every cash or margin account accepted or carried by such organization and every person holding power of attorney over any account accepted or carried..."

Front Running

All of the exchanges and the over-the-counter regulations prohibit a broker from front running, where they hold client orders until they have completed any orders for their own account, in the hopes that the clients' order will move the market higher or lower.

A third NYSE floor broker has pleaded guilty to illegal trading on the exchange floor - including trading to benefit himself ahead of trades in the same stocks as his clients, or "front running."

Michael Frayler pleaded guilty to unauthorized trading and securities fraud ... He also admitted to ... capitalizing on his heightened access to information about market developments to reap illegal trading profits.

According to government, Mr. Frayler took a client's order to buy AT&T, then executed buy orders for AT&T for his own account at a more favorable price before he was finished executing his client's orders.

... He could receive a maximum of 20 years in prison and a fine of $ 1 million, though his sentence will likely only be a fraction of those amounts...

Source: Wall Street Journal

Figure 73 - Example of Front Running

Guaranteeing Against Loss

Brokers are not allowed to guarantee their clients against investment losses.

Keeping a Book

The registered representative must keep a record of all of their clients' transactions (although they are normally supported by the firm's systems). Transactions should be posted on the day the registered representative receives the confirmation of the trade.

Outside Employment

The registered representative must devote full time to their job as a registered representative, and any outside employment requires the prior written consent of their employer.

Proper Supervision of Accounts

Brokers must ensure that all accounts are properly supervised and that all of the appropriate rules are being followed for every account.

Rebating Commissions

Brokers are not allowed to rebate any part of a commission to a client or other firm.

Statements to Clients (NYSE Rule 409)

"...member organizations shall send their clients a statement of account showing security, and money positions and entries at least quarterly to all accounts having an entry ... during the preceding quarter."

Suitability

NYSE firms are required to ensure that all investments made by their clients are suitable for the client, regardless of whether the firm recommended the investment or the client selected it.

Teaching Activities

Registered representatives may teach at a recognized school as long as the teaching does not interfere with the regular business day.

Transferring Accounts (NYSE Rule 412)

"When a client... wants to transfer [their] entire account to another member organization ...both member organizations must expedite and coordinate [the transfer]."

Cost of a Seat on an Exchange

The cost of a seat on the major exchanges varies according to market conditions and the competitive prospects for the exchange. The following chart indicates some of the potential volatility.

	Dec, 1998	June, 2004
NYSE	$1,350 K	$1,500 K
AMEX	450 K	114 K
NY Mercantile	600 K	1,650 K
CBOT	495 K	885 K
Pacific Exchange	N/A	42 K

Figure 74 - The Cost of a Seat on Various Exchanges

Exchanges in the U.S.

There are many different stock exchanges in the U.S.:

National Exchanges

There are two national exchanges in the U.S. for stocks, bonds and options:

- American Stock Exchange
- New York Stock Exchange

These two exchanges are discussed in more detail later in this chapter.

NASDAQ is not currently an exchange, although it has initiated a process with the SEC to become registered as a stock exchange and it is generally included in the same category as the national exchanges.

Regional Exchanges

A regional exchange differs from a national exchange in that its listings tend to come from firms in the region or are related to an industry that is principally domiciled in the region.

These five exchanges are discussed in more detail later in this chapter.

- Boston Stock Exchange
- Chicago Stock Exchange
- National Stock Exchange (formerly the Cincinnati Stock Exchange)

- Pacific Exchange (Including the Archipelago Exchange)
- Philadelphia Stock Exchange

Electronic Exchanges

While Alternative Trading Systems (ATS) can help brokers or investment managers find a counterparty, only the Electronic Communication Network (ECN) segment of the ATSs might have to be listed as an exchange. ATSs and ECNs are discussed in more detail in the chapter on Vendors.

Options, Futures and Commodity Exchanges

In addition to supporting stocks and bonds, many of the exchanges also offer options and other financial instruments. The options, futures and commodity exchanges are described later in this chapter.

Trends Involving Exchanges

Some of the relevant trends are:

Increase in ECNs

There has been a continuing increase in the number and market share of ECNs, and this trend is anticipated to continue. Since these methods of trading involve lower commissions for many trades and faster execution, this will reduce broker profitability.

Electronic Communications Networks are described in the chapter on Vendors.

Regulatory Changes

In order to make the markets more efficient and provide better value to retail investors, the SEC is evaluating several changes to the National Market System and the trade-through rule. Changes to these rules would respond to the increased number of electronic trading platforms and the trade matching that been provided by the ECNs.

One of the issues that the SEC is examining is the disparity between the time it takes to execute on the electronic exchanges vs. a floor exchange. The SEC, and the industry, would like to find a way to maintain the advantages of the floors while allowing electronic exchanges to run at the fastest possible speeds.

National Market System

The National Market System (NMS) was required by the Securities Act Amendments of 1975. The NMS consists of three major systems:

- The Consolidated Tape System (CTS) collects trade data from the NYSE, AMEX and regional exchanges and distributes this information to vendors and news media for commercial distribution.
- The Consolidated Quote System (CQS) collects quote data from the NYSE, AMEX and regional exchanges and distributes this information to vendors and news media for commercial distribution.
- The Intermarket Trading System (ITS) began operation in 1978 and electronically connects the U.S. exchanges. ITS allows traders at any exchange to seek the best available price for a security that is traded on

multiple exchanges. ECNs that are registering as exchanges will be allowed to connect to ITS.

The NMS coordinates the trading at all eight U.S. exchanges.

- American Stock Exchange
- NASDAQ Stock Market
- New York Stock Exchange
- Boston Stock Exchange
- Chicago Stock Exchange
- National Stock Exchange
- Pacific Stock Exchange
- Philadelphia Stock Exchange

In the next section, we will review additional details of the leading exchanges in the U.S.

American Stock Exchange (AMEX or ASE) [38]

The American Stock Exchange, located at 86 Trinity Place, New York, NY is one of the U.S.'s leading exchanges with the second highest volume of any auction exchange in the U.S. with over 700 listed equities. The exchange originated when brokers wishing to by-pass the New York Stock Exchange met on the street to trade. The exchange was first called the curb exchange to reflect these roots.

To position itself for the perceived future dominance of electronic markets, AMEX merged with NASDAQ in 1998. The merger did not meet either party's expectations, and they are expected to de-merge.

As an agency auction market, prices on the American Stock Exchange are determined by public bids to buy and offers to sell, which are executed on the floor and electronically. The order flow is centralized on the trading floor, with a priority to public orders. Orders are executed by price and time sequence regardless of size or source, and investors trade on a level playing field and are ensured the best available price. Orders for AMEX are processed through its own systems, which are different from the NYSE.

Another difference between the AMEX and the NYSE is that option contracts are traded on the American exchange both in crowds on the floor of the exchange, and via a systemic order routing system. Similar to equity floor trades, both the buyer and seller of an option contract traded on the floor of the AMEX must also report the trade for comparison. Option contracts executed on the floor of the AMEX are submitted to the exchange's IDC comparison system. Comparison details are transmitted from the exchange to the Options Clearing Corporation (OCC).

---

[38]   Source: American Stock Exchange

AMEX Goals

AMEX's goals are to provide a market that is:

Liquid

A liquid market provides buyers and sellers with:

- Depth (Ability to buy and sell reasonable volumes of securities)
- Continuity (Provide prices at or near previous trades)
- Minimize Volatility (Ensure sufficient liquidity to reduce volatility)

Efficient

Trades should be transacted at the lowest possible cost to the investor.

Fair

Ensure that the interests of investors come first by providing the best price available and *transparency*, which means that all buyers and sellers have an equal opportunity to receive the best price.

AMEX Products

The AMEX's processing has been shifting rapidly from equities to options and other instruments, and now includes the following categories:

- Equities
- Options
  - Equity Options
  - Index Options
  - Exchange Traded Fund Options (ETF) [39]
  - HOLDRS Options (Holding Company Depository Receipts) [40]
  - Leaps
  - Flex Options
- Corporate Bonds (20 issues)
- Government Securities (Bills, Notes and Bonds)
- Closed End Funds (145)
- Structured Products [41]
- Unlisted Trading Privileges (UTP) [42]

---

39   Each ETF is a basket of securities that is designed to generally track an index - broad stock or bond market, stock industry sector, or international stock - yet trades like a single stock.

40   HOLDRS (HOLding Company Depositary ReceiptS) are securities that represent an investor's ownership in the common stock or American Depositary Receipts of specified companies in a particular industry, sector, or group. HOLDRS allow investors to own a diversified group of stocks in a single investment that is highly transparent, liquid, and efficient.

41   Structured Products, which may be based on a single equity, a basket of stocks, an index, a commodity, a debt issuance or a foreign currency, are designed to meet the specific needs of investors and offer unique risk/return characteristics.

AMEX Participants

The American Stock Exchange's primary participants are:

Specialists

AMEX specialists are members of the American Stock Exchange, and are responsible for maintaining a fair and orderly market in their securities. They have four principal roles:

- Specialists serve as *facilitators*, using their knowledge of the market in a specific security to support buyers and sellers, especially with large blocks orders.

- Specialists act as *auctioneers*, equally representing the interests of buyers and sellers ensuring that trading proceeds smoothly and efficiently.

- Specialists serve as *dealers* when there is insufficient public interest to accommodate buyers or sellers at prices close to the last trade. In these instances, specialists buy or sell from their own account to maintain price continuity and liquidity. They also participate as dealers on all odd-lot orders.

- Specialists act as *agents*, holding limit orders entrusted to them by brokers on behalf of clients. These away-from-the-market orders constitute their "book" and specialists must execute these orders when the market reaches the specified limit price.

While performing these functions, specialists are obligated to:

- Maintain a fair quotation spread
- Stabilize prices for their securities
- Seek price improvement on all orders entrusted to them

AMEX specialists are regulated in several ways and are limited to the specified roles so that they:

- Remain unbiased
- Are willing to buy or sell whenever necessary to enhance liquidity or manage price swings

Registered Traders

Registered traders are members of the exchange and are the market makers who provide an additional source of liquidity for AMEX securities. As part of the AMEX crowd, they trade for their own account and help maintain price continuity and liquidity.

Floor Brokers

Floor brokers can be either commission brokers or independent brokers. As AMEX members, they participate in the trading crowd to get the best price

---

42   The American Stock Exchange trades NASDAQ stocks on an unlisted trading privileges (UTP) basis. The AMEX provides an auction marketplace for NASDAQ-listed securities, deep liquidity for large, institutional size order, and competitively priced Exchange fees and specialist commissions.

for their clients. Other AMEX members send orders to either their firm's floor broker or an independent broker for execution on the trading floor.

AMEX Automated Order Processing System [43]

The AMEX's Automated Order Processing System provides a computerized conduit for orders, execution reports and administrative messages between member firms and the exchange's trading floor.

These systems electronically link brokers and specialists, replacing the paper created by the manual handling of orders, reports and administrative messages by clerks, brokers and specialists.

Acceptable order types for equities are:

- Day Orders
- Good 'Til Cancelled / Executed Orders
- Odd Lot Orders
- Round-lot Market Orders and Mixed-lot Market Orders
- Limit Orders

The AMEX order processing systems include the following functions:

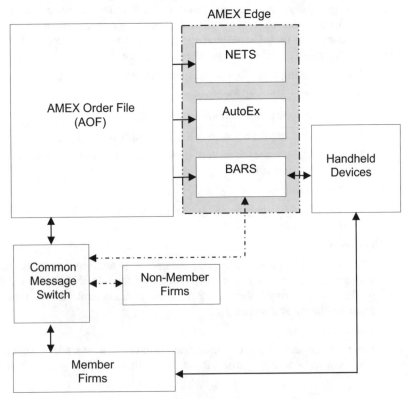

Figure 75 - AMEX Automated Order Processing Systems

---

[43]   Source: American Stock Exchange

AMEX Order File (AOF)

The AMEX Order File system:

- Accepts orders from the Common Message Switch (CMS) destined for the AMEX's order processing systems
- Validates incoming messages
- Retains order and administrative message details
- Assigns a unique turnaround number to incoming orders
- Routes incoming messages and orders to the appropriate AMEX execution service (NETS, BARS or Auto-Ex)
- Applies adjustments to open orders on file for dividends, splits, etc., and provides new orders for specialists
- Purges day orders at the end of each day's trading
- Deletes open orders on file as a result of a symbol removal, expiration of an option series, a reverse split, suspension of an issue, or at the request of the originating firm
- Acts as the host for such features as automatic cancellation and administrative message processing
- Provides order and transaction details for reports produced during after-hours for member firms, floor brokers and specialists
- Routes trade reports to the market data systems for dissemination to the national market systems
- Serves as the main tool used by the service desk for researching inquiries and the tracking of order flow

Booth Automated Routing System (BARS)

BARS is an automated order routing and management system that electronically captures and reports member firm transactions that take place on the trading floor of the Exchange, gives member firms more flexibility in order flow management, and provides a robust order inquiry capability.

Member firms can direct eligible system orders, and orders larger than the electronic order size parameters, through CMS to specific booths on the trading floor. Using a touch-screen terminal, booth clerks have the option of re-directing these orders to a floor broker's wireless hand-held terminal, back through AOF for automatic routing to one of the AMEX execution services, or to a local printer for manual handling by a floor broker.

Common Message Switch (CMS)

CMS is the portal member firms use to direct orders to the Exchange. CMS also provides validation of a firm's access rights, clearing information, message formats, and message terms.

AUTO-EX

AUTOmatic order EXecution (AUTO-EX) offers automatic execution of retail client market and executable limit orders, with a guarantee of a single price at the AMEX quoted market.

AUTO-EX provides full protection of clients' orders on the specialists' limit order book and automatically matches both sides of a trade and reports it directly to the IDCE system.

Retail client market orders and limit orders are automatically executed at prices equal to or better than the bid/ask quotation prevailing at the time the orders are received. Executions are reported back via computer and the sale price is automatically disseminated to the public through various vendors' quotation systems.

New Equity Trading System (NETS)

NETS is an enhanced specialist display book that has accelerated the trading process and provides greater functionality and automation than ever before for updating and matching orders, quoting and reporting trades, regulating, and researching order details.

AMEX Options Trading

AMEX New Trading Environment (ANTE)

ANTE is AMEX's new options trading platform that combines the price discovery of an auction market system with the speed and efficiency of an electronic trading platform. ANTE facilitates tighter markets and allows AMEX clients to access the full advantages of a screen-based trading system without sacrificing the outstanding liquidity traditionally provided by the AMEX trading floor.

ANTE is replacing essentially all previous options trading technology, including AMEX Options Display Book (AODB), Automatic Execution (Auto-Ex) system, and options pricing system (XTOPS). The system will handle incoming orders from the Common Message Switch (CMS), the Booth Automated Routing System (BARS) and the new ANTE trading application.

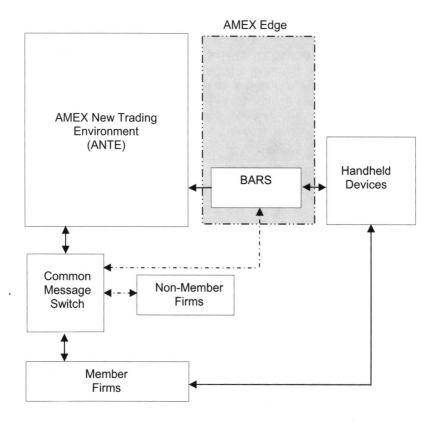

Figure 76 - Options Trading

Order Types

ANTE supports the following order types:

- Limit
- Market
- Stop
- Stop limit
- Market on close orders

Display Book

The display book shows selected incoming orders to the floor specialists and market makers. The central book stores all booked orders and quotes and is where ANTE's automatic matching occurs. Incoming orders are routed either to the display book or to the central book depending upon the trading session participant, account type, and market conditions.

Orders routed to the display book are not immediately executed. While they are pending, they are displayed to all trading application users. Orders in the display book can be cancelled, cancelled/replaced, or partially cancelled by their originator or the specialist. Specialists can book these orders into the central book.

During the opening trading session, marketable orders routed to the central book during the pre-opening trading session are automatically matched with specialist and market maker quotes and orders in the central book. Orders that are not immediately executed remain in the central book until they are traded, cancelled, or expired. Central book orders can be cancelled, cancelled/replaced, or partially cancelled.

ANTE Trading Sessions

Pre-opening

- No trading occurs
- All incoming orders are automatically booked and can be viewed by all trading application users

Opening

- Specialists set opening prices, enter their quotes, and open their options
- Market makers can enter limit orders or quotes, or mirror the specialist quote in order to participate in the opening transactions
- While the opening is in progress, the book is frozen and incoming orders are queued
- All trading application users can view important attributes of the opening

Continuous Trading

- AMEX Best Bid/Offer (ABBO) is published
- Incoming orders are routed to either the display book or the central book
- Trading and automatic execution occurs

Closing

- Order entry is stopped
- Trading and automatic execution stops
- Specialist sets price for closing rotation
- Market makers can enter quotes or mirror the specialist quote in order to participate in the closing transaction

Post Closing

- Specialist has executed the close and the trading day is complete

AMEX Trade Comparison Processing

Trade Comparison Processing involves the daily matching of tens of thousands of buy and sell transactions in equities and options, and is the first step in clearance and settlement processing.

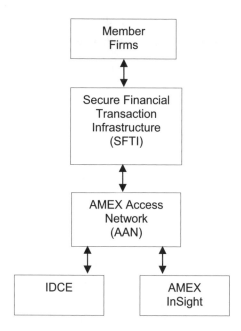

Figure 77 - AMEX Access Network

AMEX Access Network (AAN)

The AAN provides IP connectivity between AMEX production networks and the networks of member firms and market data vendors via SIAC's Secure Financial Transactions Infrastructure network (SFTI).

Secure Financial Transaction Infrastructure (SFTI) [44]

SIAC's SFTI network replaced the way member firms connect to the AMEX Access Network (AAN). SFTI is a high capacity infrastructure that improves the overall resilience of the financial industry's data communications connectivity. This highly reliable infrastructure offers firms access to the trading, clearing and settlement, market data distribution and other services SIAC provides on behalf of most of the U.S. securities industry's exchanges and utilities.

SFTI currently offers local connectivity to firms in the Northeast, Midwest and New England, and replaces point-to-point circuitry with a highly redundant infrastructure that facilitates the move from legacy communication protocols to TCP/IP connections.

Intraday Comparison Systems for Equities (IDCE)

IDCE allows AMEX members to match trades during the day and transmit compared trades on a real time basis and offers the following features:

- A browser-based interface on the user's terminal
- Matching trades

---

[44]   Source: SIAC

- Resolving uncompared trades and advisories
- Making corrections to trades and inputting new ones

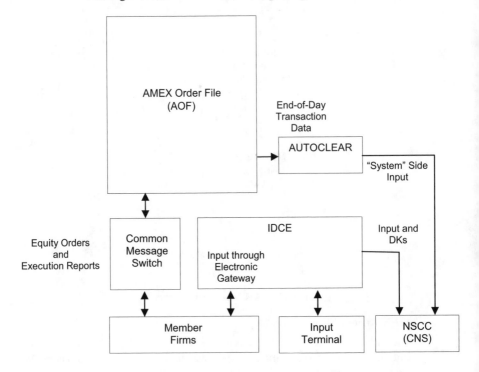

Figure 78 - Intraday Comparison System for Equities (IDCE)

AUTOCLEAR

AUTOCLEAR automatically reports order executions as matched trades to the National Securities Clearing Corporation (NSCC).

The primary advantages of AUTOCLEAR include:

- The trade match guarantee, where the originator of an order is guaranteed a compared trade even if the opposing broker fails to report the trade terms correctly
- Unique trade clearing names to further facilitate the trade resolution

Intraday Comparison (IDC) for Options

The Intraday Comparison system for options has several functions, including:

- Adds new efficiencies to the job of comparing trades by providing a real-time trade correction facility and intra-day comparison of buy and sell trade data for options
- Provides Exchange members with the ability to quickly assess and control risk

- Accepts input directly from member firms' systems through an electronic gateway (CPU to CPU) eliminating lost data and duplication
- Effectively reduces paper through the use of ROTNs (Rejected Options Trade Notices) and results in cost savings to members
- Has moved comparison closer to the point of execution and to the members' home systems
- Is the foundation for nearly instant trade comparison and the elimination of *out-trades* for options in the not-too-distant future

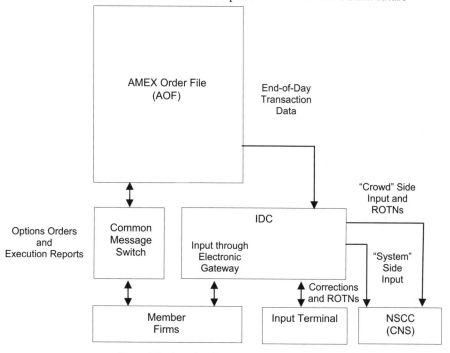

Figure 79 - Intraday Comparison for Options

AMEX InSight

AMEX InSight allows clients to access three types of data:

- **AMEX BookView** - Depth of book data for the top 100 AMEX listed securities. This predominantly includes data for AMEX-traded exchange traded funds (ETFs). The top ten levels will be displayed for both the buy and sell sides.
- **AMEX Depth Quote** - Quotes that show available liquidity at a price for NASDAQ stocks traded at the AMEX.
- **Order Imbalance Service** - Alerts users of auxiliary opening order imbalances and closing order imbalances for NASDAQ stocks traded at the AMEX.

AMEX Market Data Reporting

The AMEX's Market Data Reporting systems for equities, options and debt issues process, validate and disseminate prices and volume information via SIAC to locations around the globe on trades as they occur. They also provide for trade corrections, sales, and end-of-day summaries to market data vendors and the press.

AMEX sale and quotation reporting systems link with other U.S. exchange systems to form the Consolidated Tape Association (CTA) for securities and the Options Price Reporting Authority (OPRA) for options.

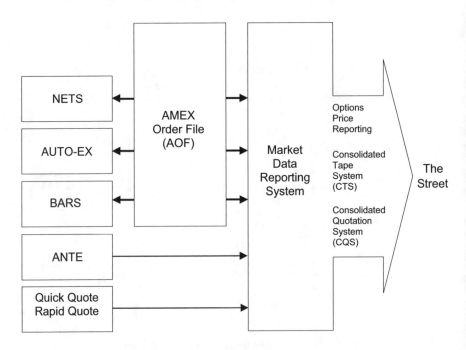

Figure 80 - Market Data Reporting

Quick Quote, Quick Trade, Rapid Quote, Electronic Entry

Quick Quote, Quick Trade, Rapid Quote and Electronic Entry are reporting tools operated by AMEX reporters that utilize computerized touch screens to enter both sale and quotation information in options or equities. Touch screens are installed at each post on the trading floor to provide for easy access and rapid transmission.

Direct Sale Reporting (DSR)

Direct Sale Reporting (DSR) reports sale information to electronic ticker tapes and investors desktop terminals around the world.

AMEX is also considering the establishment of a new futures trading exchange.

Archipelago Exchange (ArcaEx)

Archipelago opened the U.S.'s only fully electronic stock exchange in 2002 by combining the Archipelago trading platform with the Pacific Stock Exchange.

All of the Pacific Stock Exchange's stocks were converted in 2002 and options were converted in 2003. As of early 2004, ArcaEx offered over 8,100 issues for electronic trading.

The electronic trading process consists of three primary activities:

Opening Session

The Opening Session consists of two single-price Dutch auctions that match buy and sell orders at the price that maximizes the amount of tradable stock. The primary difference between the two is that the Market Order Auction will allow market orders, which require special accommodations because they are not priced. The Market Order Auction is the bridge between the Opening Auction and the Core Trading Session.

Core Trading Session

The Core Trading Session is based upon the ArcaEx Book, which displays and matches orders. The ArcaEx book is divided into four components, called Processes:

- Directed Order Process
- Display Order Process
- Working Order Process
- Tracking Order Process

Closing Session

The Closing Auction is also a single-price Dutch auction that matches buy and sell orders at the price that maximizes the amount of tradable stock.

Boston Stock Exchange (BSE) [45]

Originally founded in 1834 as a market center for local New England brokers to trade regional stocks, today the BSE is one of seven national equities exchanges in the country with individual and institutional clients throughout the United States and the world. The BSE's primary function is to operate a specialized and competitive marketplace that serves member-firm clients, their clients, and listed public companies.

Originally, the Exchange traded stocks in local area banks, railroads, insurance companies, mills and canals. The BSE currently has over 200 members, lists 160 primary companies, and trades approximately 2,000 nationally listed securities in competition with other market centers. The BSE also trades over 200 high growth company issues that are solely listed on the BSE or dually listed with another exchange.

Since 1990, trading activity on the exchange has increased at an annual rate of over 21%. In 2003 the average daily share volume reached 45.4 million shares per day, while the average number of trades daily was 68,139.

---

[45]   Source: Boston Stock Exchange

Chicago Stock Exchange (CHX) [46]

The Chicago Stock Exchange opened for trading on May 15, 1882, with an initial list of 82 bonds and 52 stocks, which were highly concentrated on regional issues, including Chicago Gas Light & Coke Company (now People's Energy) and First National Bank of Chicago. Many railroad companies became early listings on the exchange as Chicago became the rail hub of the United States.

In 1949, The Chicago Stock Exchange merged with the stock exchanges in St. Louis, Cleveland, and Minneapolis-St. Paul to form the Midwest Stock Exchange. The New Orleans Stock Exchange joined a decade later.

On July 8 1993, the Exchange returned to its original name. Today, the Chicago Stock Exchange has more than 3,500 issues available for trading.

The membership of The Chicago Stock Exchange is composed of 450 seats representing over 200 broker/dealers located throughout the United States. Once a prospective member's application is approved, membership may be acquired through a sale or lease agreement with an existing member. About one-third of all active memberships on The Chicago Stock Exchange are leased arrangements.

A CHX membership provides access to the Exchange and its trading systems, in addition to all other U.S. equity markets through the Intermarket Trading System.

CHX members receive daily notices announcing stock offerings, reorganization notices, stock splits, dividend declarations, and reinvestments concerning the stocks traded on The Chicago Stock Exchange.

There are three types of memberships:

Floor Brokers

Floor brokers represent buy and sell orders as agents for outside individual investors and institutions wishing to trade stocks.

Co-specialists

Co-specialists are members who are accountable to the Exchange and the investing public for the quality of the Exchange markets in their assigned securities. Co-specialists are responsible for fostering and acting to maintain liquid and continuous two-sided markets in those securities.

Market Makers

Market makers are members who provide added depth and liquidity to securities in which they are registered. They coordinate their activities with co-specialists to maintain fair and orderly markets.

National Stock Exchange (NSX) [47] *formerly the Cincinnati Stock Exchange (CSE)*

The Cincinnati Stock Exchange (CSE), established in 1885, existed as a traditional auction-based regional exchange for ninety years. In 1975, the CSE

---

[46]   Source: Chicago Stock Exchange

[47]   http://www.cincinnatistock.com/

underwent a significant restructuring that included the replacement of its centralized physical trading floor with an electronic trading floor.

The changes made by CSE were revolutionary at the time and resulted in the development of the first competing specialist system that could automatically execute client orders. The changes undertaken at CSE are credited with helping to bring about greater pricing efficiency in the market as a whole.

Exchange membership is limited to registered broker/dealers. Only broker/dealer members and their associated persons are eligible to execute trades on the CSE. No other individuals, businesses or corporations can apply for membership or use the Exchange to execute trades.

The CSE was one of the five regional stock exchanges that, along with the three primary exchanges, comprise the National Market System.

Now known as the National Stock Exchange, the Exchange is headquartered in Chicago's financial district, which is home to many of its members. However, the replacement of the physical trading floor with an electronic network means that each member receives the same efficiency and timeliness in quote dissemination, trade execution and trade reporting, regardless of where they are located.

New York Stock Exchange (NYSE)

The New York Stock Exchange remains the premier stock exchange in the United States, although that leadership is being constantly challenged by other entities. The NYSE processes a significant portion of the transactions in the U.S. every day: [48]

- $48 billion in securities is traded every day (April, 2004)

- Nearly 1.5 billion shares change hands each day in nearly 3.6 million trades

- 3,583 companies are listed on the NYSE

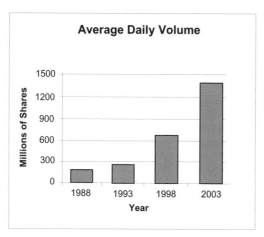

Figure 81 - NYSE Average Daily Share Volume

---

[48]   Source: NYSE

The New York Stock Exchange is the primary stock market in the U.S. Located at 11 Wall Street in New York City, the NYSE is a not-for-profit corporation that was founded in 1792 under a Buttonwood tree at 68 Wall Street, and which exists under a written constitution that was completed in 1817.

The NYSE is an agency auction market. This means that trading takes place by the exchange of open bids and offers by exchange members. Prices are determined by factors of supply and demand. The exchange is probably going to have to shift to a hybrid mode so that it combines a floor exchange along with an electronic market in order to compete with electronic markets. Today, only 10% of the trades on the NYSE are completed electronically. If that increases, it will shift volume (and revenue) away from the current floor-based process that is used by most of the members of the exchange.

Seats on the exchange may be bought and sold. Requirements for membership and securities listing are strict, which continues to make the NYSE the most prestigious exchange in the U.S.

Each listed security is assigned to a 'Trading Post.' Each post is managed by a security 'Specialist'. The Specialist is responsible for maintaining an orderly auction market for a particular security – or group of securities. Orders from floor brokers to buy and sell a particular security are maintained in the Specialist's 'book'.

Liquidity is provided by individual and institutional investors, member firms trading for their own accounts, and assigned specialists. The NYSE is linked with other markets trading listed securities through the Intermarket Trading System (ITS).

NYSE Organization

The board of directors of the NYSE consists of 26 people, elected to a two-year term, and the directors elect the chairman for a variable term.

As a result of a compensation scandal involving the previous chairman, John Reed, the former chairman of Citigroup, was appointed interim chairman and chief executive officer of the New York Stock Exchange on Sept. 21, 2003.

On January 15, 2004, John A. Thain, was appointed as the chief executive officer of the New York Stock Exchange, with John Reed remaining as the interim chairman.

NYSE Membership

Purchase of a membership permits the member to have a *seat* on the exchange.

NYSE Features

There are several main features of the NYSE, which are similar on most other exchanges:

NYSE Listing Requirements [49]

To be listed on the New York Stock Exchange, a company is expected to meet certain qualifications and be willing to keep the investing public informed on the progress of its affairs.

---

[49] Source: NYSE

The NYSE has several very specific requirements for firms that wish to list their securities on the exchange, as shown in the following table.

	U.S. Initial	On-Going	Non-U.S. Initial	On-Going
Earnings	$ 2.5 Million	$ 600,000	$100 Million in last 3 years	$25 Million
Net Assets	$ 16 Million	$ 8 Million	$100 Million	
Market Value Of Common Stock Publicly Held	$ 8 Million	$ 2.5 Million	$100 Million	
# of Publicly Held Shares	1,000,000	600,000	2,500,000	
# of Round Lot Shareholders	2,000	1,200	5,000	
OR				
All Shareholders, with an average trading volume in the last 6 months of:	2,200 / 100,000 shares			
OR				
All Shareholders, with an average trading volume in the last 6 months of:	500 / 1,000,000 shares			

Figure 82- NYSE Listing Requirements

In determining the firm's listing eligibility, the exchange considers:

- The degree of national interest in the company
- The company's relative position and stability in the industry
- Whether the company is engaged in an expanding industry, with prospects of at least maintaining its relative position

Outside Directors

New York Stock Exchange companies must have a minimum of two outside directors.

Audit Committee

Each domestic listed company must have an Audit Committee comprised solely of directors independent of management and free from any relationship that would interfere with the exercise of independent judgment as a committee member.

New York Stock Exchange Listing Procedures

For companies that meet the quantitative listing standards, the first step toward listing on the New York Stock Exchange is a confidential review of eligibility that is performed by the NYSE at the request of the listing candidate. This review is free and does not require a commitment to list.

When the review is completed, the NYSE will provide the company with both a verbal and a written response regarding its official listing status and itemize any conditions that would have to be satisfied in order to list. Assuming that there is no significant change in the status of the company, this clearance is effective for six months.

The information required by the exchange includes:

- Corporate Charter and By-Laws
- Sample of stock certificates
- Annual Reports to stockholders for each of last three years
- Latest available prospectus covering a public offering
- Latest Form 10-K and Interim 10-Q filed with the SEC (two copies of each)
- Proxy statement for the most recent annual meeting
- A stock distribution schedule
- Identification of the number of holders by the size of the holding, the ten largest holders of record, and the geographic distribution of holders
- Recent analyst reports, if available
- Summary, by principal group, of stock owned or controlled by officers, directors and their immediate families, other concentrated holdings of 10% or more and shares held under investment letters, and the Proxy or Prospectus may be referenced if it is current
- Estimate of number of non-officer employees owning stock and the total shares held
- Company shares held in profit sharing, savings, pension, or other similar funds or trusts established for benefit of officers, employees, etc.

NYSE Listing Fees

A summary of the listing fees charged by the NYSE is shown in the following chart.

	U.S. Firms	Non-U.S. Firms
Initial Fees	*As of 8/4/95*	*As of 9/8/89*
Original Listing Fee	$36,800	$36,800
Shares Issued Fees	Shares Issued: Per Million 1st & 2nd million $14,750 3rd & 4th million 7,400 5th to 300 million 3,500 300 million + 1,900	Shares Issued: Per Million 1st & 2nd million $14,750 3rd & 4th million 7,400 5th to 300 million 3,500 300 million + 1,900
Minimum Fee		$100,000
Annual Fees	*As of 8/4/95*	*As of 1/1/94*
Shares Issued Rates	Per Share Rates: Per Million 1st & 2nd million $1,650 2 million + 830	Per Share Rates: Per Million 1st & 2nd million $1,650 2 million + 830
Maximum Annual Fee	$500,000	$500,000

Figure 83 - NYSE Listing Costs

Historically, the NYSE has made it very difficult, under NYSE Rule 500, for firms to de-list. A recent revision to the rule makes it easier, although it is still not automatic. The new rule to withdraw requires:

- Agreement by a majority of the Board of Directors
- Agreement by a majority of the Audit Committee
- A 45-day notice

NYSE Floor

The main floor of the NYSE consists of trading booths that are used by the brokers to communicate with their firms and trading posts. There are several different categories of people who are allowed to be on the floor, including members and employees.

Members

Members can be:

- Partnerships such as Goldman Sachs & Co.
- Corporations such as Merrill Lynch, Bear Stearns, etc.
- Proprietorships established by individual floor traders, etc.

The 328 members firms (1,366 seats) of the exchange must possess certain minimum requirements, such as not having been barred from the securities industry, and must have sufficient capital to perform their functions. There are several different categories of brokers working within the exchange, which include:

Floor Broker

A floor broker is a member of the exchange who is authorized to trade on behalf of their clients on the floor of the exchange.

Each floor broker counterparty is required to report the transaction independently. If the two submissions agree, the trade is passed to the NSCC. If the inputs do not agree on the important key elements, the trade is returned to the counterparties for reconciliation and resolution.

Floor Trader

A floor trader is a person who is a member of the exchange who trades only for his or her own account.

Commissions House Broker

A commission house broker is a person who executes orders on the exchange floor for their firm and for their firm's clients who are usually brokers that are not members of the exchange.

Independent Broker

An independent broker, previously called a *two-dollar broker*, is a floor broker who executes orders for other exchange members and charges a fee or commission for each trade.

The historic name *two-dollar broker* refers to the $2 per trade flat fee that this type of broker used to charge. Today, these transactions are no longer based on a flat fee. However, the name *two-dollar broker* is commonly used.

Specialists

A specialist, or a specialist firm, is a member of an exchange who is required to maintain a market in the securities assigned to him and who acts as a broker's broker, with the following functions:

- Maintain current bid and asked prices for their assigned stocks, which are electronically published
- Act as an agent for floor brokers and execute trades, such as limit orders, for them
- Buy or sell for their own accounts when there is a temporary shortage of either buyers or sellers
- Bring buyers and sellers together

Specialists are required to place and execute public investor orders ahead of their own, and if there are not enough buyers or sellers, the specialist must make the market as liquid as possible by using their own capital or inventory to complete a transaction.

Historically, the specialist used a paper-based book, called the specialist book, to record the purchases and sales of specific securities. In the 1980's this book was automated and integrated with the exchanges' other automated systems.

There are seven regular firms employing 443 specialists who specialize in more than 2,800 stocks. When specialists fail to meet their obligations, they can be fined and their securities can be reassigned to other specialists, as shown in this example.

Big Board Sets Disciplinary List for Violations

Gavin Benton & Company, of New York, a firm conducting a specialist business, consented without admitting or denying guilt to findings that, among other things, it failed to maintain a fair and orderly market on six occasions in five Big Board-listed securities, and failed to reasonably supervise its specialist activities. The misconduct, by four specialist members of the firm, occurred between October, 1991 and March 1993, the exchange said.

The exchange reassigned the common stock of Manufactured Home Communities, Inc. to another specialist firm and fined Gavin Benton $100,000.

Source: Wall Street Journal

Figure 84 - Example of Disciplinary Action

Employees

Floor Official

A floor official is an employee of an exchange who supervises trading floor activities.

Floor Reporter

A floor reporter is an employee of an exchange who collects transaction data and inputs it into the exchange's price reporting system.

NYSE Trade Execution

Trades executed on the New York Stock Exchange are executed as either:

- Crowd Trades
- System Trades

Securities bought and sold by Floor Brokers are called 'Crowd Trades'. Crowd trades are executed verbally between two brokers, or between the broker and a Specialist. The trade is recorded on a Floor Report which becomes the firm's official record of the trade. Crowd Trades are often referred to as 'Hand Held' trades because the Floor Report used to be written by hand.

The paper floor reports have been replaced by mobile hand held devices which allow the floor brokers to both receive orders and record executions electronically. The Floor Brokers automatically report the executed trade to the specialist and to the NYSE OCS System.

How the NYSE Auction Market Works [50]

The NYSE is an agency auction market where trading occurs with open bids and offers by exchange members, acting as agents for institutions or individual

---

[50]   Source: NYSE

investors. Buy and sell orders come together on the trading floor and prices are determined by the interplay of supply and demand.

NYSE members bring their orders for NYSE-listed stocks to the exchange floor either electronically or through a floor broker. Each listed stock is assigned to a single trading post where the specialist manages the auction process. When an investor's transaction is completed, the best price will have been exposed to a wide range of would-be buyers and sellers.

This stream of orders is one of the great strengths of an exchange. It provides liquidity, which is the ease with which securities can be bought and sold without wide price fluctuations.

The trading floor is where all NYSE transactions occur. It is a 36,000 square foot facility that has been designed to support the centralized auction, where market professionals, supported by advanced technology, represent the orders of buyers and sellers to determine prices according to the laws of supply and demand.

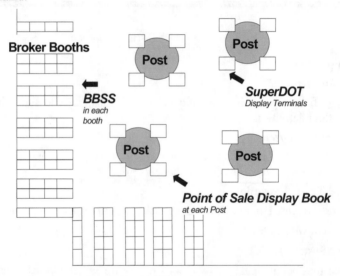

Figure 85 - NYSE Partial Floor Plan

The trading floor houses 17 trading posts (several of which are shown in the diagram), each manned by specialists and specialist clerks. Every listed security is traded in a unique location at one of these posts and by one specialist, which ensures that all trading interest in the security is centralized. All of the buying and selling takes place at these posts. Computer monitors above each specialist location show which stocks are traded there, and display data about each stock, including the last price of the stock and whether that price represents an increase or a decrease from the previous price.

There are approximately 1,500 trading booths along the perimeter of the trading floor where brokers obtain orders. Orders are transmitted to broker booth locations from off the floor either by telephone or electronically through the Broker Booth Support System (BBSS). Once a broker receives an order, he represents that order as an agent in the trading crowd of that stock.

When member firms send orders electronically from off the floor directly to the specialist through the NYSE SuperDOT system, the specialist represents these orders as an agent in the trading crowd.

NYSE Exchange Floor Technology

Retail orders that are destined for the floor of the New York Stock Exchange arrive there either through a phone call to the floor trader, the floor trader's system, or more frequently through the exchange's systems. Those automated processing systems receive orders from various brokers that route the orders to the specialist location for execution. After the trade has been completed and a counterparty identified, the details of those trades are forwarded to the ticker system and to the clearinghouse.

Common Message Switch (CMS)

CMS is the communications hub between the member firms and the NYSE systems, providing reliable communications to our clients. CMS formats and routes messages orders, cancels and execution reports.

This is the same system that was discussed with the American Stock Exchange.

Display Book

The Point of Sale Display Book is an application that maintains information on limit orders and new market orders.

Orders can be executed against:

- Another market order on the book
- Specialist's inventory
- Floor broker's order

An order execution message for all or a part of a trade is called a report. Reports are sent from the specialist via SuperDOT back to the ordering broker, who issues a confirmation to their client.

Broker Booth Support System (BBSS)

The Broker Booth Support System (BBSS) is an order-management system that enables member firms to quickly and efficiently process and manage their own orders. BBSS allows member firms to selectively route orders electronically to either the trading post or their booth on the NYSE Trading Floor.

BBSS electronically supports the following broker functions:

- Receiving orders
- Entering orders
- Re-routing orders
- Issuing reports
- Research
- Viewing other NYSE services via MS Windows

NYSE e-Broker

The NYSE e-Broker moves information to and from the point-of-sale with greater speed and accuracy than manual tickets. Through this mobile hand held order management tool, brokers are able to receive orders, disseminate reports, and send market "looks," in both data and image formats, from anywhere on the trading floor.

Consolidated Tape System (CTS)

The Consolidated Tape System (CTS) is an integrated, worldwide reporting system of price and volume data for trades in listed securities in all markets in which the securities trade.

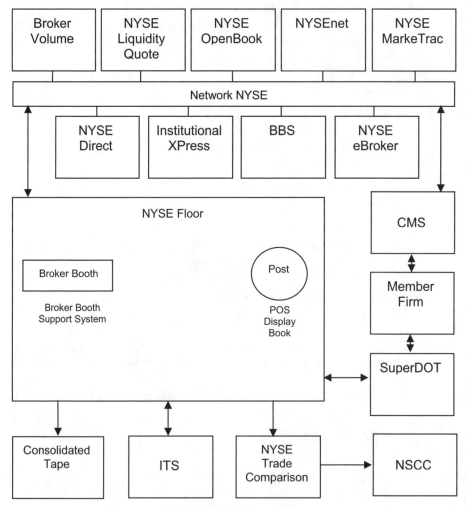

Figure 86 - NYSE Process Flow

After the trade has been executed, information is received from the specialists as well as from the counterparties to the trade. The information is matched and sent out on the ticker system that is also called the consolidated tape, and to the comparison cycle at the NSCC.

Super DOT

The SuperDOT (Designated Order Turnaround) system is the primary system used to route trades to the specialist and to brokers and to electronically match client equity orders.

The majority of trades executed on the NYSE never reach the crowd on the exchange floor. Both Market Orders and Limit Orders under 100,000 shares that are received from members are electronically entered into SuperDOT and sent directly to the appropriate trading post. [51]

Upon execution, the trade details are transmitted back to the broker along the same electronic network.

SuperDOT can currently process about 25 billion shares per day.

Network NYSE

Network NYSE brings investors closer than ever to the point-of-sale through a hybrid of traditional and electronic execution services, which include:

NYSE Direct+

NYSE Direct+ is an automatic-execution service for limit orders up to 1,099 shares, which enables users to opt for an immediate execution at the best bid or offer. The average execution time is 1 second. NYSE Direct+ executes 7% of consolidated volume in NYSE-listed equities, which is more than that executed by all ECNs combined.

More than 99% of NYSE orders are delivered electronically to the trading floor.

Institutional XPress

Institutional XPress is an electronic gateway designed specifically for the needs of NYSE member firms and their institutional clients, consisting of:

- XPress Quotes, which are bid or offer quotes for 15,000 shares or more that have been on the book for at least 15 seconds and have been "opened" for electronic execution using the XPress Order type

- XPress Orders, which provide clients greater assurance that block orders greater than 15,000 shares are immediately executed whenever a quote is in place for at least 15 seconds

Anonymous SuperDOT (ADOT)

ADOT, which enables member firms to entitle their institutional clients to route orders directly to the NYSE for electronic execution without having their identities revealed.

NYSE Bond Trading

Bonds are also traded on the New York Stock Exchange using the exchange's Automated Bond System (ABS). ABS is an electronic bond trading system

---

[51] The predecessor to SuperDOT was the DOT system (Designated Order Turnaround).

that matches bond sellers with bond buyers. Trade executions generated on ABS are routed to the NSCC for comparison and settlement.

NYSE Trade Comparison

The NYSE matches all of its trades at the marketplace level through the Exchange's Online Comparison System (OCS) and no longer uses the NSCC's trade comparison (matching) services.

NYSE Transaction Example [52]

Helen, a recent college graduate, lives in Atlanta. John, a young engineer, lives in Seattle. They don't know each other; but, at nearly the same moment, they've reached opposite decisions on the same subject: the stock of XYZ corporation (a hypothetical company whose shares are listed on the NYSE).

Helen has decided to buy stock in XYZ. By so doing, she believes she'll earn dividends that will give her more money for graduate school in a few years. John, on the other hand, has decided to sell his XYZ shares. He needs some additional cash for renovating his apartment.

John and Helen telephone their brokers at the NYSE member firms that handle their brokerage accounts. "I like the analysis you sent me on XYZ," Helen tells Peter, her broker. "I want to buy one hundred shares." "Do you want to buy at the market," Peter asks, "or do you want me to enter a limit order for you?"

"What's XYZ selling at?" Helen asks her broker. "The last sale in XYZ was 40 1/8," Peter says, "and the current bid and offer are 40 to 40 1/8." This information tells Helen that, at the moment, buyers are willing to pay $40 per share, but sellers are asking 40 1/8, or $40.125.

"Buy it at the market," Helen says. "I'll be out of the office for the rest of the day, so we can confirm the exact price tomorrow." "I may be able to confirm pretty quickly," Peter says. "If you'll be at your desk a few minutes longer, I'll call back."

Before hanging up the phone, Helen says, "I'll be traveling next month. Can I protect myself against a sudden drop in the price of XYZ while I'm away?" "You can check regularly with any of our local offices and they could easily handle a sale for you," Peter says. "But you can also place a limit order now that will automatically trigger a sale if the price of XYZ reaches any level you specify."

Helen decides on a limit order price, and Peter sends it to the firm's order room for immediate transmission, together with her buy order, to the NYSE Trading Floor. At about the same time, John tells his broker in Seattle to sell his 100 shares of XYZ *at the market*.

Helen's buy order and John's sell orders are printed out almost immediately at the two firms' order booths on the perimeter of the Trading Floor. As the floor broker representing Helen's order enters the crowd gathered at the XYZ trading post, he observes that XYZ has been trading quite actively. He also discovers that XYZ's market price has been rising steadily.

---

[52]   Example provided by the NYSE

"How's XYZ?" he asks the specialist. "40 1/8 to 40 3/8, ten by ten. The last sale was at 40 1/4," responds the specialist.

This market shorthand tells Helen's floor broker that, at any moment, the highest price anyone is willing to pay for XYZ shares is 40 1/8, and the lowest price at which anyone is willing to sell is 40 3/8. The phrase *ten by ten* tells him that buyers want a total of 1,000 shares and sellers are offering a total of 1,000 shares. The broker evaluates this information in light of the specialist's statement that the market price of XYZ has been raising steadily and that the last sale occurred at 40 1/4.

John's floor broker arrives at the trading post and hears the specialist's quote. Flat-panel display screens at each post display current quotes for each stock traded there, but floor brokers generally ask the specialist for the quote anyway - a question that traditionally begins the auction process. Any broker in the crowd can participate in the trading.

"100 at 40 1/4 ", John's broker says, offering to sell one hundred shares at that price - 1/8 point below the lowest quoted offer. "Take it!" Helen's broker replies, accepting the offer. In the auction process, brokers must act quickly or risk missing the market. For example, if Helen's broker had hesitated, another broker in the crowd could have bought one hundred shares from John's broker at 40 1/4. And that trade might have triggered another, pushing the price higher.

Within seconds the trade is entered into the NYSE's Market Data System, which flashes it onto electronic displays and market information inquiry systems around the world.

Peter, Helen's broker in Atlanta, phones her and says, "You just bought 100 shares of XYZ at 40 1/4." At almost the same moment, John's broker in Seattle says. "We've sold your 100 shares at 40 1/4."

The same electronic system that reports the transaction to the tape also creates the electronic bookkeeping entries that will update the records of the two brokerage firms. These entries enable the NYSE to reconstruct details of the trade if any question about it should arise in the future.

Within three business days Helen's account will be adjusted to show that she now owns 100 shares of XYZ. The transfer of shares - a complex procedure involving several steps - is almost completely automated. In fact, about the only pieces of paper involved in the transaction are order tickets, which are filled out by the brokers in the branch office, and a trade confirmation, which is mailed to both the buyer and seller immediately after the trade is executed. The confirmation includes details of the trade, such as price, number of shares, and terms and conditions.

Pacific Exchange (PCX) [53]

The Pacific Exchange is a regional marketplace where broker/dealers and registered member firms meet to buy and sell options on more than 1,200 equities. The stocks and bonds that were previously traded on PCX were moved to ArcaEx in 2002-03, which was described earlier in this chapter.

---

[53]   Source: Pacific Exchange

Founded in 1862, the Pacific Exchange has always seen itself as a technology leader.

- It was the first exchange in the world to build and operate an electronic trading system.

- It developed a new, more efficient method of clearing and settling securities trades that has been adopted by exchanges worldwide.

- It was the first U.S. stock exchange to demutualize, establishing PCX Equities, Inc. as a for-profit, corporate subsidiary of the Pacific Exchange in 1999.

The PCX is also the regulator of the Archipelago Exchange (ArcaEx). The PCX provides all market surveillance, member firm financial and operating compliance monitoring, and enforcement services for ArcaEx, which is operated by Archipelago Holdings, LLC.

Philadelphia Stock Exchange (PHLX) [54]

The PHLX, opened in 1790, was the first stock exchange in the U.S. It is a regional stock exchange that specializes in the trading of listed options, and has innovated around market availability:

- In September, 1987, Philadelphia was the first securities exchange in the United States to introduce an evening trading session, chiefly to accommodate increasing demand for foreign currency options in the Far East.

- In 1988, the exchange was the first to implement an electronic trading system to accommodate options trading. PHLX also was the first to offer around-the-clock trading on currency options, although it has since scaled back its trading hours.

- In January 1989, the exchange responded to growing European demand by adding an early morning session.

- In September 1990, Philadelphia became the first exchange in the world to offer around-the-clock trading by bridging the gap between the night session and the early morning hours. Although the exchange subsequently scaled back its trading hours, its current hours from 2:30 a.m. to 2:30 p.m. (Philadelphia time) are longer than any other open outcry auction marketplace.

The exchange currently lists individual equity issues, equity and index options, and foreign currency options. PHLX uses its PACE (Philadelphia Automated Communication and Execution) system for equity trading and UCOM (United Currency Options Market) for currency options.

PHLX has also demutualized.

---

[54]   Source: Philadelphia Stock Exchange

D. SECURITIES OVER-THE-COUNTER MARKET

The decentralized over-the-counter market has three ways to trade: counterparties can find each other either by telephone, through NASDAQ, or via an Alternative Trading System (ATS) or Electronic Communications Network (ECN).

The over-the-counter market is different from the exchanges in that there is no single physical location, and instead of using specialists, the OTC market uses market makers that negotiate a price rather than derive a price through the exchanges' auction mechanism.

A market maker is required to respond to any request with a bid and an offer price, which is considered a quote. The market maker must make this quote without knowing whether the person requesting the quote is a buyer or a seller. The market maker makes their profits on the spread, or the difference between the bid and the offer. Some of the leading market makers are:

CODE	FIRM NAME
GSCO	Goldman, Sachs & Co.
MLCO	Merrill Lynch, Pierce, Fenner & Smith Inc.
MSCO	Morgan Stanley & Co., Incorporated
BEST	Bear, Stearns & Co. Inc.
FBCO	Credit Suisse First Boston Corporation
PWJC	PaineWebber Incorporated
MASH	Mayer & Schweitzer, Inc.
NITE	Knight Securities, Inc.
SBSH	Salomon Smith Barney Inc.
SLKC	Spear Leeds & Kellogg Capital Markets
HRZG	Herzog, Heine, Geduld, Inc.
LEHM	Lehman Brothers Inc.
DLJP	Donaldson, Lufkin & Jenrette Securities Corporation
JPMS	J.P. Morgan Securities Inc.
WARR	Warburg Dillon Read LLC

Figure 87 - Partial List of Leading Market Makers

The OTC market is very large, and its volume now exceeds that of the New York Stock Exchange. There are four levels to the OTC market:

- The NASDAQ National Market has 2,648 listings as of April 2004
- NASDAQ Small Cap Market has 655 listings
- The OTC Bulletin Board, which is also run by NASDAQ, has 3,305 listings that are also reported on the weekly pink sheets. Information on these securities can also be found at www.otcbb.com.

- The Pink Sheets do not have any automatic dissemination of quotes

The types of instruments that are traded on the OTC include:

- OTC Equities (i.e., equities not traded on an exchange)
- Government & Agency Debt
- Municipal Debt
- Corporate Debt not traded on an exchange
- Collateralized Mortgage Obligations
- Asset backed Securities
- Mutual Funds not traded on an exchange

Trade Processing Over-the-Counter

When a client contacts a broker with an OTC order, the broker's system will route the trade either to NASDAQ or to the firm's own traders who will fill the order from the firm's own account or look for a counterparty, which is usually a market maker.

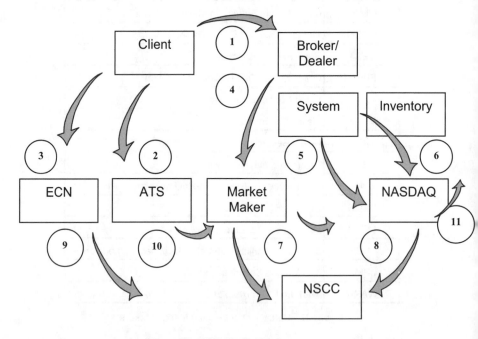

Figure 88 - OTC Trade Flow

To initiate an OTC order, a client today has options:

1. The client can contact their broker with an order, or
2. … enter the order to an Alternative Trading System, or
3. … enter the Order into an Electronic Communications Network
4. If the broker received the order, they will either contact the appropriate market maker for a bid or offer, or

5.   ... enter it into their system which would normally route the order to NASDAQ, or

6.   ... use their own inventory if they make a market in this security. In this case the broker would notify NASDAQ of the transaction.

7.   If the broker went to a Market Maker, they would both notify NASDAQ of the trade and NSCC for clearing.

8.   If the broker went directly to NASDAQ, the trade would be reported to NSCC for clearing.

9.   If the client went to an Electronic Communications Network, the trade would be reported to NSCC for clearing by the ECN. The ECN also would report the trade price to NASDAQ directly.

10. If the client used an Alternative Trading System to find a counterparty, the system would be supported by a broker (or Market Maker) that would notify NASDAQ of the trade and the NSCC for clearing.

11. Electronically distribute prices.

NASDAQ

While at one time NASDAQ was considered less prestigious than the NYSE, it now has more daily volume than the NYSE, and has become very competitive. NASDAQ's initial growth was partially because it has lower listing requirements than the exchanges, and lower costs. As a result, NASDAQ attracted many of the technology stocks when they were just start-up businesses. Many of these companies chose to remain on NASDAQ even after they met the requirements of other exchanges. For example, Microsoft continues to trade on NASDAQ.

Although the listing requirements remain lower than the NYSE, they are still taken seriously, and firms that fail to maintain the NASDAQ minimums are de-listed. As of 2004, NASDAQ trades 6,679 U.S. stocks.

NASDAQ states that it processes trades in an average of 6.7 seconds, which is 2.8 times faster than the NYSE, and that the spreads on NASDAQ are 34% better than on the NYSE.

NASDAQ's success in competing with the NYSE has not been achieved in isolation. The recent emergence of Electronic Communication Networks has captured increasing volume from the exchanges and NASDAQ. The following chart shows the NASDAQ securities that were processed via NASDAQ directly and through six other exchanges in April, 2004.

Market Center	Share Volume (billions)	% of Shares	Trade Volume (millions)	% Of Trades	Dollar Volume ($ billions)	% of Dollars
NASDAQ	19.6	47.8	26.6	31.9	348.9	44.5
ADFN	0.0	0.1	0.0	0.0	0.9	0.1
AMEX	0.0	0.0	0.0	0.0	0.2	0.0
ARCX	7.7	18.8	21.9	26.2	164.6	21.0
BOSX	3.5	8.7	10.2	12.3	72.5	9.3
CINN	10.0	24.3	24.5	29.4	192.4	24.6
MWSE	0.1	0.3	0.2	0.2	3.8	0.5
TOTAL	41.0	100.0	83.3	100.0	783.2	100.0

Source: NASDAQ

Figure 89 - Exchanges Processing NASDAQ Listed Securities

NASDAQ Business Strategy

NASDAQ's previous strategy was to become a network of networks, and it planned to establish a European version of its electronic system with links to Tokyo so that it could become a single 24-hour market.

That strategy changed along with a new CEO, and the current plan is to become the leading equity market in the U.S., with the most IPOs, and constantly attracting additional listings.

The reason for this change is that corporate CEO's often select their listing exchange based upon a brand, and historically NYSE has had the better brand name. NASDAQ would like to change the focus from branding to one of performance, where it feels that it has the advantage. NASDAQ states that its trade speed is approximately 22 milliseconds while the NYSE takes 20-30 seconds.

To implement this new strategy, NASDAQ is focusing on four core businesses:

- Listing new issues
- Delivering the technology required to support trading
- Providing market data
- Developing financial products

In addition, NASDAQ would like to become a registered exchange and has had an application pending with the SEC since 2000. Since one of the definitions of an exchange is that it has to have a specified location where brokers can trade, while NASDAQ is totally electronic, the application has not been approved as of the publication of this book.

NASDAQ's more recent success has been the result of an intensive marketing campaign and a series of product innovations. Some of these recent innovations include:

- Dual Listing of Securities
- End of Day Auction Pricing
- Changes in Market Data Rules
- Trade Through Reform

NASDAQ Functionality

NASDAQ is essentially an automated bulletin board service that lists a large number of individual equities, and which:

- Lists the best overall bid and asked price from all of the brokers using NASDAQ who have established their ability to be a market maker for a particular stock
- Lists all of the market makers' bid and asked prices

Much over-the-counter trading occurs by telephone between brokers and market makers. Market makers are individual brokers, who want to trade consistently in a specific security or securities, and:

- Have an inventory of the securities in which they make a market
- Could be long or short in a position
- Are expected to post a firm bid and asked price (two-sided quotation) without knowing which side of the trade the potential client has taken

NASDAQ provides a central point for OTC market makers to post their quotes and for potential buyers and sellers to see the best available bid and offer.

NASDAQ Trading Systems

NASDAQ implemented a new trading engine in 2004 that incorporates all of its current trading applications on one integrated system that can process all NASDAQ and NYSE-listed and AMEX securities. This new trading system facilitates the trading of dual listed securities and incorporates recent NASDAQ system enhancements such as FIX, anonymity, and Multiple Participant IDs (MPID).

The newly launched system, called The NASDAQ Market Center, includes Automated Confirmation Transaction Service, CAES, ITS, SelectNet and SuperMontage.

Automated Confirmation Transaction Service (ACT)

NASDAQ's Automated Confirmation Transaction Service (ACT) is the primary trading interface used by brokerage firms to executed trades on the electronic NASDAQ market. Trade orders entered into ACT are routed to a

Market Maker for execution. Upon execution, a trade confirmation is routed back through the ACT system to the originating broker.

Trade details are also transmitted to the NSCC for trade comparison and settlement.

Computer Assisted Execution System /Intermarket Trading System (CAES/ITS)

CAES/ITS is an automatic order delivery execution system for NYSE and AMEX listed securities.

Intermarket Trading System (ITS)

ITS, operated by the Securities Industry Automation Corporation (SIAC), is a trading link between NASDAQ and U.S. stock exchanges, including:

- American Stock Exchange
- Boston Stock Exchange
- Chicago Board Options Exchange
- Chicago Stock Exchange
- Cincinnati Stock Exchange
- New York Stock Exchange
- Pacific Stock Exchange (Los Angeles and San Francisco)
- Philadelphia Stock Exchange

Only NASDAQ market makers in NYSE and AMEX listed securities can send market or marketable limit orders to exchange specialists on floors of U.S. stock exchanges. Each order must be directed to a specific exchange and can be sent by the broker/dealer in a principal or agency capacity. Exchange specialists also can place orders through ITS that are routed for execution to market makers who have the best bid or offer.

CAES

CAES allows NASD member firms (market makers and order-entry firms) to direct orders in NYSE and AMEX listed securities to market makers for near-immediate execution.

Market makers and order-entry firms enter marketable limit orders in NYSE and AMEX listed securities to be executed against other NASDAQ market makers quoting at the best bid or offer in those securities. CAES orders must be preferenced to a specific market maker and sent in a principal or agency capacity.

SelectNet

The NASDAQ SelectNet system is utilized by market makers to execute large security orders. The system provides a market maker more control over the way the order is routed to obtain the best possible pricing for large executions.

Upon execution, trade notification is sent to the originating broker. Trade details are also submitted to the NSCC for trade comparison and settlement.

SuperMontage

SuperMontage, implemented in 2002, is a fully integrated order display and execution system for the trading of NASDAQ-listed securities, which allows buyers' and sellers' orders to be displayed so that investors can see more of the orders that are available to them.

It replaced SuperSOES and portions of SelectNet, and is a faster, more efficient trading system that has handled 4,100 executions per second, which is more than twice the capacity of the SuperSOES system. [55]

Market makers can input all or part of their buy or sell interest, by name or anonymously. The buy and sell interest is available to view at five price levels, not just the best price. Individual investors' orders are protected since if a limit order is entered into SuperMontage, it will not be traded through or bypassed in a fast moving market.

SuperMontage was designed to be a network of networks for ECNs, but many of the ECNs have not connected to it.

NASDAQ Broker Membership Levels

There are three levels of NASDAQ membership for brokers.

Level I

Level I provides only the inside market on that day on each listed equity, which is the best bid and the best offer provided by all of the market markers.

Level II

Level II provides real-time access to the actual quotes of all of the registered market makers.

Level III

Level III service provides Level II service, plus the market makers can alter or change their quotes, execute orders and send information to other NASDAQ participants.

NASDAQ Sources of Revenue

NASDAQ's approximately $1Billion in revenue in 2003 comes from several activities:

- Issuance Fees   26 %
- Equity Trading   40 %
- Market Data   26 %
- Other   8 %

The National Quotations Bureau

Pink Sheet Quotes are the dealers' best bid and best offer prices for equities that

---

[55] SuperSOES, which replaced SOES, improved the speed of executions and supports greater trading volume on the NASDAQ National Market. The Small Order Execution System (SOES) was an automatic execution system for orders of 1,000 shares or less. SOES was designed to protect investors because it guaranteed that all eligible orders were executed at the best possible bid or offer price available on the electronic market at the time the order was placed.

are available to brokers, and are printed weekly by the National Quotations Bureau. A list of debt securities are published on yellow sheets.

A service called Automated Quotations is an automated version of the Pink Sheets, and this service provides instant identification of the market makers for specific securities as well as the security's current price.

Another automated listing service is the OTC Bulletin Board, which is also maintained by NASDAQ.

Over-the-Counter Terminology

The terminology that is used by the over-the-counter market is often different from that used on the exchanges. The following terms are frequently used:

Backing Away

If the retail client agrees to *buy 100 at 5*, and the market maker says that he wants a larger order, this is known as backing away, and is a violation of NASD Rules of Fair Practice.

Boiler Room

In a boiler room, the brokers use high-pressured sales tactics to convince clients to buy. This practice is discouraged.

Bucket Shop

A bucket shop will hold orders, hoping that the market goes against the client's interest. The broker then bills the client at the higher price and keeps the difference.

For instance, if the market is at $40 and going down, and the client says to sell at the market, the broker might not process the client's order immediately. Instead, the firm might sell some of its own shares at 40, and at the end of the day, when the market is at 35, they buy the shares from the client at 35.

The NASD does not allow Bucket Shop operations.

Consummating a Transaction

After a client agrees to a price, the market maker will say, "Sold to you at 5" and the trade is considered consummated.

Firm Quote

A quote without any qualifications is considered firm, and the market maker must trade at least one unit of the security that was quoted. A unit consists of 100 shares for equities and 10 bonds for fixed income securities.

Inside Quote / Inside Spread

The inside spread is the difference between the best bid and the best ask from all of the market makers quoting on a security. Therefore, the inside spread is often smaller than the spread offered by any single market maker. Inside quotes are usually only available to other brokers, and retail clients have to buy or sell using the retail quote, which is defined in the following section.

Inventory

A market maker usually maintains an inventory, or a position, in each security in which they make a market.

Mark-Up and Mark-Down

The market maker will mark-up purchases and mark-down sales to their clients. The mark is the amount they will get for the trade.

Over Trading/Highballing

The market maker is not allowed to over trade or *highball*. This means he cannot overpay for one client sale in order to get the client to buy another security with a much higher mark-up.

Positioning as Agent or Principal

Transacting as an Agent

An OTC broker acting as an agent will buy the securities at the offered price and then will add a commission or fee for performing the service. This must be shown separately on the confirmation that is sent to the client.

Transacting as Principal

An OTC broker acting as a principal deals directly with the client by buying the security from the client or selling the securities to the client at a fair bid or offer price. The fact that the broker acted as a principal to the trade must be shown on the confirmation, and the broker makes a profit by marking up or marking down the price of the security.

Retail Quotes

A normal retail quote made by a market maker to a retail client would be "4-1/2 5." This means the market maker is willing to buy stock at 4-1/2 or sell stock at 5. The difference between 4-1/2 and 5 is the spread.

If it is not a firm quote, the market maker must so state that the amount is a subject quote, approximate for valuation, etc.

Shopping the Street

A broker that is *shopping the street* is getting quotes from multiple market makers to obtain a fair and equitable price.

Subject Quote

A subject quote is made by a market maker who is unwilling to trade now at the price quoted. The market maker will typically identify a subject quote by saying, "4-1/2 to 5-1/2 subject." This means that the firm needs time to verify the price with some party the firm represents. This type of quote is not unusual in volatile securities.

Workout Market

The Workout Market is used for trades that are usually made for inactive securities, and allows the broker to search for the best deal for their client.

For example, the market maker will say, "sell 58 to 68." This means that the client should leave the order with the market maker and he will try to sell it for the client somewhere in that 10 point spread. With large orders the market maker could say "sell 40,000 shares, 10,000 sold, 30,000 workout," which means that the market maker will take 10,000 shares now and try to sell the others.

OTC Rules and Regulations

The NASD Manual must be in every broker's office, and clients have the right to use it. The broker should ensure that the information is current.

The manual, which has recently been posted on the NASD's website, has two major sections:

- Rules of Fair Practice
- Uniform Practice Code

Rules of Fair Practice

The Rules of Fair Practice were designed to provide rules for the brokers to follow in their relationships with their clients. Some of these rules are:

Accounts Not Designated as Discretionary

When the account is not established as a discretionary account, the broker may be given authority by the client as to price and time on a specific trade, and this may be verbal.

Advertising

All of the broker's advertising must be truthful, including ads in newspapers, magazines and reprints, radio, TV, motion pictures, etc. Each advertisement must be approved and initiated by a registered principal, and the firm must keep the approvals for three years.

During the firm's first year of operation or first year of advertising, the firm must submit material to the NASD for approval ten days before it appears.

Confirmation

The confirmation must include relevant information, including the capacity in which the broker is acting.

Charges

All charges must be reasonable and not unfairly discriminatory. In other words, they may be discriminatory, but they have to be fair.

Complaint File

Brokers must maintain a file containing all statements and all client correspondence involving complaints, including how the complaint was resolved.

Clients

The broker must *know your client*. It is the broker's responsibility to obtain the essential facts about a new client to determine *suitability*. Brokers are prohibited from:

- Promoting purchases beyond client's ability to pay
- Recommending speculative stock to a client who is not sufficiently sophisticated to understand the risks associated with the investment
- Churning a client's account by encouraging them to buy and sell more frequently than is necessary
- Short term trading of mutual funds

- Unauthorized discretion in a client's account, which is also known as unauthorized trading

Discretionary Accounts

The broker must obtain written authorization from the client for all discretionary accounts. The firm must accept the granting of discretion.

All orders must be marked discretionary. A registered principal must also approve each order, and this activity must be reviewed frequently to ensure that the account is not being churned.

Discretion can include buying and selling securities, as well as moving cash out of the account. Very few brokers are granted the discretion to move funds out of the account.

Disclosure of Financial Condition

The broker must provide a copy of its unconsolidated balance sheet to clients upon request.

Fiduciary

Individuals working for a fiduciary, such as a transfer agent or a registrar, are not allowed to use this information to induce a client to make a purchase or sale, and may not sell the list of stockholders.

Gifts

Brokers must not give an employee of another firm a gift of more than $25.00, and brokers should keep a record of *all* gifts.

Must Disclose Control

The broker must disclose any participation in a primary or secondary distribution.

Partial Payment

Regulation T does not allow any partial payments in margin accounts.

Segregation of Full Paid for Securities

All securities fully paid for by the client must be segregated from the firm's positions.

Suitability

While the NYSE requires that brokers subject to its rules ensure that all client transactions are suitable for the clients, the NASD rules state that the broker is only responsible if they make a recommendation. If the client selects a non-suitable security on their own, the firm is not responsible.

Supervision

The broker must have written procedures to achieve compliance. Failure to supervise is a key issue with the NASD, which has gone so far as to suspend operations personnel for providing poor supervision. This rule, however, has been primarily used for the sales staff.

Transactions with Employees of Another Broker/Dealer

Brokers must obtain written permission from the employee's firm before they can enter any order on the employee's behalf. Duplicate confirms and statements are required to be sent to the employee's firm on all transactions.

Uniform Practice Code

The Uniform Practice Code relates to the mechanics of security processing between NASD Members. The UPC rules are similar to the rules that have been established by the exchanges. Some of the rules are:

Regular Way Contract

The regular way settlement is three business days for listed stocks and bonds (including NASDAQ), and one day for government bonds and options.

Cash Trade

With a cash trade, delivery and payment take place the same day as the settlement. Settlement of a cash trade is normally occurs at 2:00 p.m.

Sellers Option

When both parties to a trade agree to settle other than the regular way, the maximum term under the seller's option is sixty calendar days.

Good Delivery of Securities

Good delivery form means that any certificates that are being bought or sold are in negotiable form and in unit denominations that are considered acceptable.

Rejection

Items can be DK'd (don't know) by the receiver upon delivery if the trade involves the wrong amount, has bad certificates, or is an unknown trade.

Reclamation

If a broker has accepted delivery and paid for the item and then discovers a problem, such as refusal to transfer by the Transfer Agent, or that the securities were stolen or a stop has been placed on them, the broker can return the certificates and demand repayment or receive negotiable securities of the same issue in exchange.

When-Distributed Securities

The settlement date for when-distributed securities will be three business days after the security is distributed and begins to trade.

Hot Issues

A stock hot issue is a new issue of stock that shows a bid of 10% or $2.00 above the fixed offering price.

A bond hot issue is a new bond issue that shows a high bid of two points or more ($20.00) over the fixed offering price.

Who can not deal in a Hot Issue?

Any officer, partner, or other employee of any domestic broker or dealer or members of such person's family, including parents, parents-in-law, spouse, children, siblings, siblings-in-law are prohibited from participating in the issue. Brokers are also strictly prohibited from participating in the issue, unless they sign a letter stating they are selling securities to clients not in the first category at the fixed offering price and without compensation for themselves.

Some people are not totally restricted, although they have some limitations. These include the finder, its accountants, attorneys, financial consultants, members of their families, officers and employees in domestic banks, commercial or savings banks, insurance companies, or registered investment companies.

NASD Self-Policing

The stock exchanges have their own regulations and methods for self-policing, as does the NASD. To enforce the uniform practice code and Rules of Fair Practice, the NASD has established district business conduct committees, methods to identify trade practice complaints, and methods to arbitrate solutions.

Employee of Another Firm

Brokers are not allowed to open accounts for the benefit of employees of another firm without reporting these accounts to the employer of the individual for whom the account is being opened

---

New York: ...

John Romano, broker of Fort Salonga, N.Y., was fined $25,000, suspended for 105 days, required to re-qualify by exam in all capabilities, and must refrain from opening a brokerage account, either for himself or his spouse, at a firm other than that of his employer for five years. Without admitting or denying the allegations, he consented to findings that he opened a securities account in his wife's name at another firm and neither notified his firm in writing that he opened the account nor advised the other firm of his association with his firm.

The findings also said Mr. Romano placed orders for the same account without giving prior written notice to his firm. Furthermore, the NASD found that Mr. Romano, with an intent to defraud his firm, knowingly or recklessly sold securities from his firm's proprietary trading account at prices substantially below the prevailing market price, to the detriment of his firm.

Source: Wall Street Journal

Figure 90 - Example of Disciplinary Action

Churning

Brokers are required to know their clients and to avoid excessive and unsuitable trading for these clients.

New York:

A former Paine Weber Inc. broker agreed to be barred from the securities industry for what the NASD alleged was excessive and unsuitable trading in two client accounts. ... She also consented to a $125,000 fine. ...

The NASD charged that in March 1985, a client opened an account with $190,000 in cash and stock. In the year that followed, the agency said, Ms. Zim's trades for that client generated gross commissions of $203,165 and a loss of $11,016. Further, the agency charged that Ms. Zim executed transactions at a rate amounting to the sale of a security in the account about every 2 1/2 weeks. ...

Source: Wall Street Journal

Figure 91 - Example of Churning

Failure to Supervise

Officers and managers of brokerage firms are required to obtain specific licenses to indicate their knowledge of the industry, and are required to maintain proper supervision over their salesmen.

Brokerage Firm in Houston is Fined $400,000 by NASD

Government Securities Corp., one of several Houston brokerage firms that sold volatile mortgage derivatives to cities, counties and other public investors around the country, was fined $400,000 by the National Association of Securities Dealers.

The NASD, the self-regulatory organization for over-the-counter securities markets, cited the firm and its chairman, Christopher L. LaPorte for failing to adequately supervise salesmen who sold derivatives to public fund investors. In addition, George L. Putnam, one of its vice-presidents, was suspended from acting as a principal of a securities firm for 90 days. ...

Source: Wall Street Journal

Figure 92 - Example of Failure to Supervise

Investor Monitoring

In addition to ensuring that the market participants follow the rules, the exchanges and NASD are required to look for inappropriate and possibly illegal investment practices. Sometimes these investments are made by market participants and sometimes investors make them.

Stock Watch is a computer system that is used by the exchanges and NASD that automatically identifies unusual volume or price changes in any listed stock which could result from manipulation or insider trading. Most large volume days or sudden price changes can be explained by company news, trends in the industry, or national economic factors; however, when no legitimate explanation is evident, the exchange or NASD staff begins to investigate the transactions.

The investigators begin by contacting the company whose stock is showing unusual activity to see if there are any pending announcements while other Stock Watch staff construct an electronic audit trail of the details of every trade in the issue.

If anything appears incorrect, the responsible broker is contacted by Stock Watch staff to obtain the names of the clients involved. These names are automatically matched against the names of officers, directors, and other corporate and non-corporate insiders of the issue to detect any possible connections. This match is conducted against a file which contains the names of over 800,000 executives, lawyers, bankers, and accountants, plus public profile data on officers and directors of approximately 80,000 public corporations and 30,000 corporate subsidiaries.

If the staff identifies suspicious trading practices by exchange members or their employees, it can take specific disciplinary action. For individuals outside of the exchange's or NASD's jurisdiction, the staff will notify the Securities and Exchange Commission for further investigation and action.

Alternative Trading Systems

Historically, all non-NASDAQ OTC trading was conducted by telephone between two broker/dealers. In the last six years the use of many different Alternative Trading Systems (ATS) for equities has become widely accepted, and in the last three years, a large number of platforms for fixed income trading have emerged and are being accepted.

This rapid growth and popularity of Alternative Trading Systems (ATS) is the result of the evolution of technology, the increasing willingness of the investment community to trade without brokers and a favorable regulatory climate. As the speed, cost efficiencies and accessibility of electronic trading have become recognized, the weaknesses of traditional trading methodologies became obvious.

While institutional traders were the initial users and they drove the initial growth of electronic trading, the increasing use of the Internet and the emergence of a broker-less retail market have also been supporting the growth of ATSs. The use of these trading methods by institutional and individual investors will change the marketplace and create an increasing demand for electronic markets.

For some industry observers, the question is not how big electronic markets will become or how much they will dominate the securities market, but *when* will they become the *only* way to buy and sell securities. Whether or not there will continue to be any role for floor-based exchanges is still subject to debate; however, it is clear that their traditional role will never be the same.

The three generic market structure types used with electronic markets are:

Continuous Limit Order Book

In an electronic limit order book, traders continuously post their bids or offers. The order book displays orders and typically ranks them by price and by time.

Single-Price Auction

In a single-price auction system, participants may submit bids and offers over a period of time, but the system executes all trades together at one price, at a single point in time. The system normally calculates the transaction price to maximize the total volume traded, given the bids and offers residing in the system. Bids and offers with prices at least as good as the system-calculated price are processed into trades, subject to a set of priority rules.

Trading System with Passive Pricing

Some electronic trading systems determine trade prices by explicitly referring to other markets' pricing and sales activity. This process is called *passive* or *derivative* pricing.

Some trading systems allow for the possibility of price improvement by assessing market conditions in the underlying market and then pricing their trades at a price better than the best quote on the underlying market available at the time of the order entry. Prices may vary through the trading session if the system operates at the same time as its associated primary market or may be fixed at a single level such as the closing price for an after-hours trading session. A system may base trade execution on different secondary priorities than those present in the primary market.

ITG operates the largest passive pricing system, called POSIT, which traded 7.7 billion shares in 2002

There are several other terms that are used to describe ATSs, many of which are often used incorrectly. An Alternative Trading System (ATS) is an electronic system that can bring together potential buyers and sellers of securities, and which may disintermediate the traditional broker's role in trading. ATSs include call markets, matching systems, crossing networks, and Electronic Communications Networks (ECNs), which are defined in the following pages.

Call Markets

ATS can batch orders for short periods and conduct regular call markets to establish a stock price that everyone uses to buy/sell at that time.

Cross-Matching Systems

Cross-matching systems generally bring both dealers and institutional investors together in electronic trading networks that provide real-time or periodic cross-matching sessions. Customers are able to enter anonymous buy and sell orders with multiple counterparties that are automatically executed when contra side orders are entered at the same price for trades.

In some cases, clients are able to initiate negotiation sessions to establish the terms of trades.

Crossing Networks

Crossing networks are used by institutions that wish to find a counterparty without using a broker for the execution. The crossing network electronically matches buy and sell orders at a pre-determined derived price, usually at one or more specific times throughout the day.

A broker is still needed for the settlement, and the network needs an SRO to audit the Crossing Network.

The different operations of three of the main crossing networks are:

- E-Crossnet, which is owned by a dozen major investment houses, needs the orders to be crossed to be automatically submitted every half hour

- Posit is owned by ITG and runs up to six crosses a day

- Liquidnet gains access to the brokers order flow and dynamically fills the order which is similar to a firms' in-house order management system

Electronic Communication Networks

ECNs are a subset of ATSs, where an ECN has registered with the SEC as either a broker or an exchange, and is required to post their quotes on NASDAQ. The similarities and differences between ATSs and ECNs are shown in the following chart.

Similarities	Differences
Matching	ECNs are registered with the SEC as either a broker or an exchange
Electronic Communication	ECNs are regulated by the NASD if they are brokers, and are SROs and regulated by the SEC if they are registered as an exchange
Post indications and each participant may find a counterparty	ATSs can be used by the principals to a trade, but ECNs only act as agents
Anonymity	ECNs automatically match trades that have been entered as limit orders
	ECNs can be connected to NASDAQ or the floor-based exchanges through the Intermarket Trading system (ITS)
	After an ATS trade has been completed, the brokers send the trade to NSCC for clearing, but the ECN can send the matched trade directly to a clearing agency
	ECNs can trade options and connect to the Options Clearing Corporation

Figure 93 - Comparison of ECNs to ATSs [56]

Despite these stated similarities and differences, the exact definitions of ECNs and ATSs are still evolving. ECNs typically provide investors with several other advantages:

- ECNs offer trade execution that is faster than an exchange or NASDAQ transaction. For example, the average execution time for an ECN is two to three seconds, compared with more than 20 seconds for an order through an exchange.

- ECNs allow brokers to see the ECN's limit order books so they can have more complete price information than traditional market centers. This information allows investors to better assess market conditions and optimize their trading strategy.

- Anonymity is supported since the ECNs display only the price and size of an order.

- An advantage provided by the ECNs is that they are generally open longer than the traditional exchanges and provide a market after the exchange has closed.

---

[56] The Summit Group prepared one of the most widely referenced white papers describing the ATS and ECN environment. This white paper is available at http://www.soforum.com/library/ecn_ats.shtml

All ECNs are regulated by the National Association of Securities Dealers (NASD), the NASDAQ's parent organization, and have access to NASDAQ; however, some are electing to become stock markets which are registered with the SEC and which could then also connect to the other U.S. exchanges through the Intermarket Trading system (ITS). So far, only Archipelago has been accepted as an exchange because of its relationship with the Pacific exchange. Other applications are pending.

Initially, ECNs were only used by institutions and broker/dealers. This meant that occasionally the prices on the ECNs were better than the prices available to the general public. In 1997, the SEC modified the Order Handling Rules to require broker/dealers to make the best prices available to clients, regardless of the source.

ECNs enable institutions, individual investors and traders a means to electronically transmit their current best buying and selling prices. Very often, these prices are very competitive with Market Maker Quotes. Recently ECN quotes and not Market Makers' often establish the best prices.

ECNs have radically altered the NASDAQ market. NASDAQ is a dealer-oriented market, while ECNs allow ALL investors and traders to trade among themselves without the help of Market Makers.

More information about ATSs and ECNs is included in the chapter on Vendors.

E. OTHER MARKETS

In addition to the securities market, there are several other markets in the financial industry.

Money Market

The money market is the over-the-counter, telephone-based process of trading short-term (less than one year) instruments. There are several different types of money market instruments used by institutions, all of which are considered short-term instruments. The most frequently used instruments are:

- Banker's Acceptances
- Commercial Paper
- Negotiable Certificates of Deposit
- Repurchase Agreements (and Reverse Repurchase Agreements)

These instruments will be discussed in more detail in the chapter on Fixed Income Instruments.

Options and Futures

This section introduces other types of exchanges that trade financial instruments.

Futures and options on futures were initially developed for commodities such as wheat, corn, oil, etc., which are not discussed in this book. Futures and options on futures were subsequently developed for financial instruments such as interest rate instruments and indexes.

Futures Trading

There are three categories of professionals involved in futures trading.

Hedgers

Hedgers are individuals and firms that make purchases and sales in the futures market for one of two purposes:

- Establishing a known price for something they intend to buy or sell at a point in the future. By using a future, the investor attempts to protect himself against the risk of an unfavorable price change in the interim.

- Using futures to lock in an acceptable differential between their purchase cost and their selling price.

Borrowers can hedge against higher interest rates, and lenders against lower interest rates. Investors can hedge against an overall decline in stock prices, and those who anticipate having money to invest can hedge against an increase in the overall level of stock prices.

Hedgers give up the opportunity to benefit from favorable price changes in order to achieve protection against unfavorable price changes.

Speculators

Speculators are individuals or firms who seek to profit from anticipated increases or decreases in futures prices. They provide the risk capital that is needed to facilitate hedging.

- Someone who expects a futures price to increase would *purchase* futures contracts in the hope of later being able to sell them at a higher price. This is known as *going long*.

- Conversely, someone who expects a futures price to decline would *sell* futures contracts in the hope of later being able to buy back identical and offsetting contracts at a lower price. The practice of selling futures contracts in anticipation of lower prices is known as *going short*.

One important feature of futures trading is that it is equally easy to profit from declining prices (by selling) as it is to profit from rising prices (by buying); and it is equally easy to lose.

Floor Traders

Floor traders, or *locals*, who buy and sell for their own accounts on the trading floors of the exchanges, play an important role as futures market participants. Like specialists and market makers at securities exchanges, they help to provide market *liquidity*.

If there is not a hedger or speculator who is immediately willing to take the other side of an order at or near the going price, there may be a floor trader who will do so in the hope of making an offsetting trade at a small profit minutes or even seconds later.

Floor traders create more liquid and competitive markets. However, it should be noted that unlike market makers or specialists, floor traders are not *obligated* to maintain a liquid market or to take the opposite side of client orders.

Types of Futures Orders

Just as there are several different types of equity orders, there are also many types of orders for options and futures, such as:

- Limit Order (Price Order)
- Stop Order
- Buy-Stop Order
- Sell-Stop Order
- Stop-Loss Order
- Stop-Limit Order
- Margin and Margin Call
- Short Selling

And, there are different ways to place an order for futures:

- Market Order
- Market-Not-Held Order
- Market-On-Close Order
- Market-On-Open Order
- Market-If-Touched Order
- Stop-Close-Only Order
- On-Better Order
- Fill-Or-Kill Order
- Good-'Til-Cancelled Order
- One-Cancels-The-Other Order

Futures vs. Options

A *futures contract* is an agreement between two parties to buy and sell in the future a specific quantity of a commodity at a specific price. The buyer and seller of a futures contract agree now on a price for a product to be delivered and/or paid for at a set time in the future on the settlement date. Although actual delivery of the commodity can take place in fulfillment of the contract, most futures contracts are actually closed out or *offset* prior to delivery.

An *option* on a commodity futures contract is an agreement between two parties which gives the buyer, who pays a market determined price known as a premium, the right (but not the obligation), within a specific time period, to exercise his option. Exercise of the option results in the person being deemed to have entered into a futures contract at a specified price known as the strike price.

While options will be discussed more at various points throughout the book, futures will not be covered in detail. Unlike options, futures have many specific characteristics and are not based on an underlying security.

Settlement

There are two types of futures contracts, those that provide for physical delivery of a commodity or other item and those which call for cash settlement. All financial futures and options are cash-based.

Commodities

Investors look for three conditions before a commodity can be traded in the futures markets:

- It has to be standardized and, in a basic, raw, unprocessed state.

- Perishable commodities must have an adequate shelf life, because delivery on a futures contract will not mature until some point in the future.

- The commodity's price must fluctuate enough to create uncertainty, which creates both risk and potential profit.

Commodity trading floors are organized into recessed pits (or rings) where traders stand on a series of steps facing each other.

In order to trade, the people on the floor must be members of the exchange.

Like the stock exchanges, the commodity exchanges provide the place to trade and the necessary facilities, such as phones and price-reporting and dissemination systems and it regulates the activities of its members.

Futures contracts have finite lives. They are primarily used for:

- Hedging commodity price-fluctuation risks

- Taking advantage of price movements

Most traders do not buy the futures contract with the intention of taking physical possession of the commodity; however, the trade is finalized by establishing a 'contract' which must be liquidated by the maturity date, or the investor must take delivery of the commodity.

The buyer of the futures contract (who establishes a long position) agrees on a fixed purchase price to buy the underlying commodity (wheat, gold or T-bills, etc.) from the seller at the expiration of the contract. The seller of the futures contract (who establishes a short position) agrees to sell the underlying commodity to the buyer at expiration at the fixed sales price. Between the trade date and the maturity of the contract the contract's price varies. This creates profits or losses for the trader. The seller gets the fixed amount regardless of the current price so their risk has been eliminated.

Each futures exchange has a relationship with a clearing organization that assist in completing the purchase or sale of the contract. Traders on the exchange must use the designated clearing organization.

Options on futures began trading in 1983 and the option pits are usually located near the futures pit. Many of the terms that apply to options also apply to options on futures.

Options, Futures and Commodity Exchanges

To be considered an official Commodities and/or Futures Exchange, the entity must be designated as a "contract market" by the CFTC. Options exchanges are either regulated by the SEC or jointly by the SEC and the CFTC, depending upon the asset underlying the option.

There are several options, futures and commodity exchanges that are active in the U.S. and many that are dormant or that have had their charter revoked or vacated.

Exchange	Abbreviation	Active	Dormant	Revoked
New York Cotton Exchange				x
American Commodity Exchange	ACE			x
AMEX Commodities Corporation	ACC		x	
Baltimore Chamber of Commerce	-			x
Cantor Financial Futures Exchange	CX		x	
CBOE Futures Exchange	CFE	x		
Chicago Board of Trade	CBT	x		
Chicago Board Options Exchange	CBOE	x		
Chicago Mercantile Exchange	CME	x		
Chicago Rice & Cotton Exchange	CRCE			x
Coffee, Sugar & Cocoa Exchange	CSCE			x
Duluth Board of Trade	-			x
Eurex U.S.	-	x		
Exchange Place Futures Exchange	-	x		
Future Com	FCOM		x	
HedgeStreet, Inc	-	x		
Hutchinson Board of Trade Association	-			x
INET Futures Exchange	IFX	x		
International Commercial Exchange	-			x
International Securities Exchange	ISE	x		
Kansas City Board of Trade	KCBT	x		
Los Angles Grain Exchange	-			x
Memphis Board of Trade	-			x
Merchant's Exchange	ME	x		
MidAmerica Commodity Exchange	MCE	x		x
Milwaukee Grain Exchange	-			x
Minneapolis Grain Exchange	MGE	x		
New Orleans Cotton Exchange	--			x
New York Board of Trade	-	x		
New York Cotton Exchange	NYCE			x
New York Futures Exchange	NYFE	x	x	
New York Mercantile Exchange	NYMEX	x		
New York Produce Exchange	-			x
NQLX	-	x		
Omaha Grain Exchange	-			x
OneChicago	-	x		
OnExchange Board of Trade	ONXBOT		x	
Pacific Commodity Exchange	PCE			x
Pacific Futures Exchange	PFE			x
Philadelphia Board of Trade	PBOT	x		
Portland Grain Exchange	-			x

San Francisco Grain Exchange	-			x
Seattle Grain Exchange	-			x
Twin Cities Board of Trade	TCBT			X

Figure 94 - U.S. Commodities Exchanges

Chicago Board of Trade (CBOT) [57]

The Chicago Board of Trade, established in 1848, is the world's oldest and largest futures and options exchange. More than 3,600 CBOT members trade 51 different futures and options products at the CBOT, resulting in 2003 annual trading volume of 455 million contracts.

The Chicago Board of Trade was established in 1848 and is the world's oldest and largest futures and options exchange. The CBOT was initially formed to trade only agricultural futures contracts, but in 1975 the listed products expanded to include financial contracts, including the U.S. Treasury bond futures contract. Today, the CBOT also trades options on futures contracts.

The role of the CBOT is to provide markets for its members and clients and oversee the integrity and cultivation of those markets. Futures exchanges provide free market prices that are brought together in open auction. The marketplace assimilates new information throughout the trading day, and translates this information into a single market price that is agreed upon by both the buyer and seller.

The primary method of trading at the CBOT is open outcry, during which traders meet face-to-face in trading pits to buy and sell futures contracts. The CBOT built a new $182 million financial trading floor, the largest trading floor in the world, to accommodate expanding business in open outcry trading. During the last decade, as the use of electronic trading has become more prevalent, the exchange has upgraded its electronic trading system several times. Most recently, on January 1, 2004, the CBOT implemented its new electronic platform, LIFFE CONNECT.[58]

As of January 1, 2004, the Chicago Mercantile Exchange is providing clearing and related services for all CBOT products. The CME/CBOT Common Clearing Link brings together two premier financial institutions and provides operating, margin and capital efficiencies, resulting in significant benefits to FCMs and end users of futures products.[59]

In 1999, CBOT reached a partnership agreement with the Deutsche TerminBorse (DTB) to use their Eurex system and replace the CBOT's current system, called Project A.

A secondary purpose of CBOT is to provide opportunities for risk management among farmers, corporations, small business owners and other market users. Risk management, or hedging, is the practice of offsetting the price risk inherent in any cash market position by taking an equal but opposite position in the futures market. Hedgers use CBOT futures markets to protect

---

[57] Source: CBOT

[58] Source: www.cbot.com

[59] ibid

their business from adverse price changes that could negatively impact the profitability of their business.

As a Self-Regulatory Organization, the CBOT also has the responsibility to provide markets for its members and clients and oversee the integrity and cultivation of those markets. The CBOT is a self-governing, membership association that serves as an umbrella organization for member firms. The governing body of the Exchange consists of a board of directors that includes a chairman, first vice chairman, second vice chairman, 18 member directors, four public directors, and the president. An executive staff headed by the president and chief executive officer administers the Exchange.

Chicago Board Options Exchange (CBOE) [60]

The Chicago Board Options Exchange, founded in 1973, revolutionized options trading by creating standardized, listed stock options. Prior to that time, options were traded on an unregulated basis. CBOE is the second largest securities exchange in the country and the world's largest options exchange. As of today, CBOE processes for more than 51% of all U.S. options trading and 91% of all index options trading.

CBOE was originally created by the Chicago Board of Trade (CBOT) but has always been managed and regulated as an independent entity. Call options on 16 underlying stocks were initiated when the exchange opened and put options were introduced in 1977. Almost immediately options became popular and other securities exchanges entered the business, and today options are traded on other U.S. exchanges.

In 1980 the CBOE responded by increasing the number of options on listed stocks and by taking steps to broaden position limits and reduce the strike price intervals. Also in 1980 the CBOE and the Midwest Stock Exchange consolidated their options business, and today the CBOE lists options on over 1,200 widely-traded stocks.

The first broad-based stock index, now known as the Standard & Poor's 100 Index (ticker symbol OEX), was introduced on March 11, 1983. The CBOE also trades options on the Standard & Poor's 500 Index (SPX), which many U.S. money managers use as a benchmark for portfolio performance.

CBOE Futures Exchange (CFE) [61]

In 2004, the CBOE established the CBOE Futures Exchange (CFE) as a subsidiary of the CBOE.

CCorp will provide the necessary post-trade execution services to CFE. CFE participants will have access to CCorp's:

- New Trade Management (NTM)
- Allocation Claim Transaction (ACT) systems
- GAINS applications
- MQM messaging through its client network

---

[60]   Source: Chicago Board Options Exchange

[61]   ibid

OCC is the main clearinghouse for CFE, and will:

- Act as guarantor
- Oversee clearing fund and margin deposits
- Facilitate margin and settlement obligations
- Manage post-trade transactions
- Process and disseminate trade data
- Offer 24-hour member support services

Chicago Board of Trade (CBOT) [62]

Organized as a grain cash market in 1848, the CBOT is generally considered to be the oldest organized futures exchange. While experts disagree about the exact date when "true" futures trading began, CBOT cash contracts evolved into what are now considered futures contracts.

Shortly before the civil war, traders at the CBOT began trading "to-arrive" contracts (i.e., forward contracts) in agricultural commodities including wheat, corn, and oats.

- In 1859, the CBOT was granted a charter by the Illinois legislature which standardized the grades of grain and provided for inspectors to be appointed by the CBOT, whose decisions were binding on members.
- In 1865, formal trading rules were instituted for margin and delivery procedures.
- In 1877 the CBOT began publishing futures prices.
- In 1883 the first clearing organization was established to clear CBOT contracts, initially on a voluntary basis

Chicago Mercantile Exchange (CME) [63]

The Chicago Mercantile Exchange (CME), often referred to as the Merc, is the second largest options and futures marketplace in the U.S. Trading on the CME takes place using both traditional open outcry methods as well as through the Exchange's GLOBEX2 electronic trading system. Products trading on the Merc include futures and options on futures within four general categories: agricultural commodities, foreign currencies, interest rates and stock indexes.

Members of the Chicago Mercantile Exchange include the world's largest banks and investment houses, as well as independent traders and brokers. These members, as well as individuals who have leased seats from members, execute trades for clients of their firms or themselves. Members also elect from among themselves a board of directors that establishes the Exchange's policy.

Four different types of memberships may be purchased on the CME:

---

[62]   Source: CBOT

[63]   Source: CME

Full Membership

The full Chicago Mercantile Exchange division membership entitles each of its 625 owners to execute trades in any contract listed on the exchange.

International Monetary Market

The International Monetary Market division membership (813 IMM seats) entitles the owner to execute trades in all IMM and IOM futures and futures options, which includes all currency futures, interest-rate futures and stock index futures, as well as futures options.

Index and Option Market

Membership in the Index and Option Market (IOM) division entitles each of its 1,287 seat holders to execute trades in all IOM futures, which include all index futures contracts, random length lumber contracts and all options on futures.

Growth and Emerging Markets

The 413 members of the Growth and Emerging Markets (GEM) division can execute trades in products related to emerging market countries.

Founded as a not-for-profit corporation in 1898, the CME became the first publicly traded U.S. financial exchange in December 2002 when the Class A shares of the parent company, Chicago Mercantile Exchange Holdings Inc., began trading on the New York Stock Exchange under the ticker symbol CME.

CME has four major product areas: interest rates, stock indexes, foreign exchange and commodities. In 2003, a record 640.2 million contracts with an underlying value of $333.7 trillion changed hands at CME, representing the largest notional value traded on any futures exchange in the world. [64]

The Exchange's Clearing House guarantees all trading on CME. The CME's Clearinghouse Division has responsibility for assuring and maintaining the financial integrity of the Exchange through a variety of functions, including matching, carrying and guaranteeing all trades; enforcing financial safeguards; and establishing and monitoring performance bond (margin) requirement levels. The Clearinghouse is discussed more in the chapter on Post Trade Processing.

Exchange Place Futures Exchange, LLC

Exchange Place Futures Exchange, LLC originally was designated as BrokerTec Futures Exchange (BTEX). BTEX ceased operations in November 2003. As of January 30, 2004, Exchange Place Futures is wholly owned by U.S. Futures Exchange LLC (USFE)

Eurex U.S.

Eurex U.S. entered the U.S. derivatives marketplace on February 8, 2004. Also called the U.S. Futures Exchange, LLC, Eurex U.S. will specialize in key benchmark U.S. Dollar-denominated fixed income futures and options on futures including:

---

[64] Source: www.cme.com

- 2 Year U.S. Treasury Note Futures (FTNS)
- 5 Year U.S. Treasury Note Futures (FTNM)
- 10 Year U.S. Treasury Note Futures (FTNL)
- 30 Year U.S. Treasury Bond Futures (FTBX)
- Option on 2 Year U.S. Treasury Note Futures (OTNS)
- Option on 5 Year U.S. Treasury Note Futures (OTNM)
- Option on 10 Year U.S. Treasury Note Futures (OTNL)
- Option on 30 Year U.S. Treasury Bond Futures (OTBX)

Eurex U.S. plans to provide access to EUR- denominated futures and options on futures, U.S. indices as well as the most liquid European equity index products, and will clear through the CCorp.

Based in Chicago, electronic trading is available 21 hours per day. Trading on Eurex U.S.'s trading platform is different from trading on traditional open-outcry markets by providing longer hours and eliminating the need to be in Chicago to participate.

Membership at Eurex U.S. is also different from most U.S. exchange models. Members do not have ownership rights to the exchange or voting rights. All exchange members may apply for a market maker status for one or more products and are then required to quote binding bid and offer prices in the products, which they support.

HedgeStreet, Inc.

HedgeStreet plans to provide for the automated trading of binary option contracts and Economic Indexes.

INET Futures Exchange, LLC (IFX)

IFX originally was designated as Island Futures Exchange to trade Security futures products. It changed its name to IFX on December 5, 2003. It has not yet commenced trading.

International Securities Exchange (ISE)

The International Securities Exchange, the world's largest equity options exchange, was founded on the principle that technology fosters and infuses new efficiencies and operational innovations into securities trading. After developing an innovative market structure that integrated auction market principles with a screen-based trading system, ISE established the first fully electronic U.S. options exchange in May 2000.

The implementation of the ISE changed the market structure for options. In the 1980s and 1990s, while other financial markets were embracing electronic trading, the U.S. options exchanges remained steadfastly committed to open-outcry trading. The options exchanges also continued the practice of exclusively listing options on most blue chip stocks on only one exchange, limiting client choice, and forcing brokerages to maintain trading operations on the floor of each exchange.

ISE, which was launched May 26, 2000, became the first registered exchange approved by the Securities and Exchange Commission since 1973, and is a member-owner of The Options Clearing Corporation.

Kansas City Board of Trade (KCBT) [65]

The Kansas City Board of Trade was formally chartered in 1876. Early trading at the exchange was primarily in cash grains. Today, grain elevators, exporters, millers and producers use the exchange to protect their cash positions by buying or selling futures and options. Stock market investors also utilize KCBT products. Nonetheless, cash grain trading is still the core business of many of KCBT's members.

More than a century later, ten billion bushels of wheat would change hands on the exchange in one year, and grain producers and users around the globe would look to Kansas City for the fair price of hard red winter wheat, the primary ingredient in the world's bread.

Over time, the exchange's leadership would extend into other markets. Indeed, it was at the Kansas City Board of Trade that stock index futures, hailed as the most innovative financial instrument of the 1980s, were born. And in 1999 the exchange extended its leadership to the Internet with ISDEX Internet stock index contracts.

Membership

The exchange offers two types of memberships:

- There are 192 Class A seats, which allow trading in any KCBT product and more than 20 Class A members are clearing members.

- Class B seats, of which there are 60, allow trading in stock index products.

Class A members carry one vote in every election; Class B members carry one-quarter vote in the annual election of officers and otherwise may only vote on items for which they are permitted to trade.

Class A membership brings another benefit. Class A members gain one share of ownership in the exchange itself. The adjusted net asset value of one seat recently exceeded $139,000, compared with the average sale price of more than $69,500.

Regulation

Market regulation at the exchange takes place in three ways.

- The members themselves oversee floor operations and conduct in each pit.

- The staff, through the Audits & Investigations Department, visually observes trading as well as conducts rigorous reviews of trading and investigations of alleged abuses.

- The Commodity Futures Trading Commission is actively involved in both day-to-day and long-term oversight.

---

[65]   Source: Kansas City Board of Trade

Members found to be in violation of the rules are subject to both exchange and federal discipline.

Merchants' Exchange (ME)

ME was originally established in 1836 as a cash commodity market known as the Merchants' Exchange of St. Louis. That designation was vacated in 1974. In 2000, the ME was designated as a contract market by the CFTC under the name Merchants' Exchange of St. Louis, operating as an electronic exchange. It changed its name to ME in January 2002.

Minneapolis Grain Exchange (MGEX) [66]

MGE was established by the Minneapolis Chamber of Commerce in 1881 as an organization designed to promote trade in grains and to prevent abuses. In 1947, it became the MGE.

Since it was established, the Minneapolis Grain Exchange has provided price discovery and risk management services to producers and consumers involved in volatile commodities markets around the world.

Trading at the MGEX is based upon open outcry trading of futures and options contracts for:

- Hard Red Spring Wheat
- Hard Winter Wheat Index (HWI)
- National Corn Index (NCI)
- National Soybean Index (NSI)

In addition to futures and options, the MGEX provides the world's largest cash market for a variety of grains, trading approximately one million bushels daily.

Membership

There are two types of membership:

- Full membership gives the member trading privileges, voting rights and the opportunity to become a clearing member.
- Delegate membership can be leased monthly for a minimum of three months. Delegate members have the right to trade their own accounts.

New York Board of Trade (NYBOT)

NYBOT was formed in 1998 when the Coffee, Sugar and Cocoa Exchange (CSCE) and the New York Cotton Exchange (NYCE) entered into a merger agreement, which was to occur in several stages. In June 2004 when the merger was completed, the CSCE's and NYCE's contract market designations were extinguished and transferred to NYBOT.

NYBOT trades coffee, sugar, cocoa, cotton, frozen concentrated orange juice, and currencies.

New York Mercantile Exchange (NY Merc) [67]

The New York Mercantile Exchange was formed in 1872 by a group of Manhattan dairy merchants and was originally called the Butter and Cheese

---

[66]   Source: Minneapolis Grain Exchange

[67]   Source: New York Mercantile Exchange

Exchange of New York. After the addition of several new products, the exchange's name was changed to the New York Mercantile Exchange in 1882.

Today, by virtue of its merger with the Commodity Exchange in 1994, NYMEX is the world's largest physical commodity futures exchange.

To safeguard trading on the exchange, NYMEX employs a fully margined clearinghouse that acts as counterparty to all transactions. Trading is conducted by open outcry.

The Exchange is a membership organization that trades through two divisions: the NYMEX Division and the COMEX Division. Combined, the Exchange has over 1,500 seats and its members include approximately 40 clearing member firms and 120 non-clearing member firms. The Exchange is owned by its members and is governed by an elected board of directors who set policy and establish the future direction and scope of Exchange activities.

NQLX [68]

NQLX is a new market for futures products. Originally known as the NASDAQ LIFFE LLC Futures Exchange, it operated as a joint venture of the NASDAQ Stock Market and the London International Financial Futures and Options Exchange (LIFFE). It is a wholly owned subsidiary of Euronext.liffe and offers a broad range of contracts, via an all-electronic derivatives exchange.

NQLX was the first U.S. exchange to be approved for the trading of single stock futures and uses LIFFE CONNECT as its trading platform.

The single stock futures contracts include the most actively traded equities on the New York Stock Exchange, American Stock Exchange and NASDAQ. NQLX's regulatory function is operated by NASDR with all trades cleared by the Options Clearing Corporation (OCC).

OneChicago [69]

OneChicago is an electronic exchange committed to becoming the global leader in futures on individual stocks, narrow-based indexes and ETFs. OneChicago is a joint venture of the following options and futures exchanges:

- Chicago Board Options Exchange (CBOE)
- Chicago Mercantile Exchange Inc. (CME)
- Chicago Board of Trade (CBOT)

The current members of CBOE, CME and CBOT are automatically members of OneChicago and can trade through existing memberships and accounts. No new membership fees or applications are required.

Philadelphia Board of Trade (PBOT)

The PBOT is a subsidiary of the Philadelphia Stock Exchange and trades currencies.

---

[68]   Source: http://www.nqlx.com/

[69]   Source: http://www.onechicago.com/

Dormant Exchanges [70]

There are several exchanges that are currently authorized but which are not active.

AMEX Commodities Corporation (ACC)

There has been no activity on the ACC since 1986.

Cantor Financial Futures Exchange (CX)

The CX is a joint venture of the NYBOT and Cantor Fitzgerald & Co. Cantor Fitzgerald was one of the firms seriously damaged on 9/11/2001 in the attack on the World Trade Center.

FutureCom (FCOM)

FCOM was designated as a contract market subject to meeting specific conditions that were not met.

New York Futures Exchange (NYFE)

NYFE originally was established as a subsidiary of the New York Stock Exchange. It was sold to the NYCE in 1994. All NYFE contracts were transferred to the NYCE on August 1, 2003 and then to the NYBOT on June 10, 2004.

OnExchange Board of Trade (ONXBOT)

ONXBOT has never commenced trading. Its business plan is to be an internet based electronic exchange.

Pacific Futures Exchange (PFE)

The PFE has never commenced trading. The only authorized contract is the PSE Technology Stock Index future.

Twin Cities Board of Trade (TCBT)

The TCBT has never commenced trading. The only authorized contract is the British Pound/Deutsche Mark Cross Rate future.

Vacated or Revoked Exchanges

The following exchanges previously were designated by the CFTC or, prior to 1975, by the Secretary of Agriculture, as contract markets under the Commodity Exchange Act. Subsequently, these designations were either vacated at the request of the exchange, pursuant to the provisions of section 7 of the CEA, or were otherwise revoked. Once the designation of an exchange is vacated, the exchange must reapply to the CFTC for contract market designation prior to listing contracts for trading.

American Commodity Exchange (ACE)

ACE was founded in 1978 and traded futures on GNMA certificates and U.S. Treasury instruments. The last futures trades were in July 1981. The exchange closed in 1981 under an agreement whereby ACE members were offered membership in the New York Futures Exchange (NYFE).

Baltimore Chamber of Commerce

No futures contracts are known to have been traded on the Baltimore Chamber of Commerce after it was designated.

Chicago Rice and Cotton Exchange (CRCE)

Originally designated as the New Orleans Commodity Exchange in 1981, the exchange moved to Chicago in 1983 and became the Chicago Rice and Cotton Exchange. The CRCE was subsequently acquired by the MidAmerica Commodity Exchange, which in turn was acquired by the Chicago Board of Trade in 1986. In 1991, the CRCE designation was vacated and its rough rice contract was transferred to the MidAm.

Coffee, Sugar & Cocoa Exchange (CSCE)

The CSCE was the product of a 1979 merger between the New York Coffee and Sugar Exchange (founded in 1882) and the New York Cocoa Exchange (founded in 1925). In 1998, the CSCE and New York Cotton Exchange (NYCE) entered into a merger agreement to form the New York Board of Trade (NYBOT), which was to occur in several stages. On June 10, 2004 when the merger was completed, the CSCE's and NYCE's contract market designations were extinguished and transferred to NYBOT.

Duluth Board of Trade

The Duluth Board of Trade, located in Duluth, MN, was founded in 1881. The last futures trade was in 1946.

Hutchinson Board of Trade Association

The exchange operated as a wheat market in Hutchinson, Kansas between 1932 and 1936.

International Commercial Exchange

Founded in 1970, and located in New York, it was the first exchange to trade currency futures, beginning on April 23, 1970, two years before the CME. It ceased operations in 1973 and former International Commercial Exchange traders were granted certain trading privileges on NYMEX.

Los Angeles Grain Exchange

The Los Angeles Grain Exchange listed futures contracts in corn, barley and grain sorghums. The last trade occurred in December 1945.

Memphis Board of Trade

Originally known as the Memphis Merchants Exchange, it was the first exchange to trade soybean meal, beginning in 1940, eleven years before the CBOT. The last futures trade occurred in 1964.

MidAmerica Commodity Exchange (MidAm)

MidAm was founded as the Chicago Open Board of Trade, probably in the late 1870s. From the beginning, it specialized in smaller contract size versions of Chicago Board of Trade (CBOT) contracts. It was originally designated in 1922 following passage of the Grain Futures Act which required grain exchanges to be designated as contract markets. It became the MidAmerica Commodity Exchange in 1972. MidAm became a subsidiary of the CBOT in 1986. Trading on the MidAm ceased in April 2003, and it was dissolved as a legal entity on July 3, 2003. In January 2004, the CBOT requested that the CFTC vacate the MidAm's contract market designation.

Milwaukee Grain Exchange

The MGE was originally designated as the Milwaukee Chamber of Commerce. Futures trading was suspended on the exchange in 1966.

New Orleans Cotton Exchange

Founded in 1871 as the New Orleans Cotton Exchange, it was first designated in 1936. The last futures trade occurred in 1964. In 1981, another entity called the New Orleans Cotton Exchange was designated as a contract market (see Chicago Rice and Cotton Exchange above).

New York Cotton Exchange (NYCE)

The NYCE was founded in 1870 to trade cotton futures. Over the years, it established various subsidiaries to trade non-cotton contracts, including the Wool Associates, the Tomato Products Associates, the Citrus Associates, and FINEX (the Financial Instruments Exchange).

In 1998, the NYCE and the CSCE entered into a merger agreement to form the New York Board of Trade (NYBOT), which was to occur in several stages. On June 10, 2004 when the merger was completed, the CSCE's and NYCE's contract market designations were extinguished and transferred to NYBOT.

New York Produce Exchange

The New York Produce Exchange was the first exchange to trade soybean oil, beginning in 1940. In 1970, it apparently merged with the International Commercial Exchange.

Omaha Grain Exchange

Founded in 1904, the Omaha (NE) Grain Exchange was primarily a cash grain market, but made several unsuccessful attempts to trade futures contracts.

Pacific Commodities Exchange (PCE)

The PCE was located in San Francisco, CA. All PCE contracts were revoked as the result of a settlement with the CFTC, after PCE had been charged with failing to enforce its rules.

Portland Grain Exchange

Located in Portland, OR, the exchange's last trade occurred in 1942.

San Francisco Grain Exchange

The SFGA was originally designated as the San Francisco Chamber of Commerce in 1922, following passage of the Grain Futures Act which required grain exchanges to be designated as contract markets. It later was designated as the San Francisco Grain Exchange on February 28, 1938. The last trade occurred in 1940.

Seattle Grain Exchange

The last futures trade occurred in 1959.

F. REPORTS OF SECURITY TRANSACTIONS

Each exchange and NASDAQ is required to report every trade made through their facilities, and to make that information available to the public. It is possible for individuals to see the actual trades through a variety of sources for free; however, this information is usually delayed by at least 15 minutes. Professional traders and investors who want real-time information can purchase this information from market data vendors. Each exchange reports every transaction using the symbol for that security, the volume of the trade, and the price of the trade.

Ticker Tape

Starting in 1867, all trades made on an exchange were sent out by telegraph and printed on a piece of paper known as the *ticker tape*. While the process has become much more automated and it is hard to even find a piece of ticker tape any more, the industry continues to call the electronic reporting of information the *tape*.

There are two types of tapes produced by the NYSE and AMEX:

The A Tape

The A Tape, which is also called the consolidated tape, reports the stocks that are listed on the NYSE, regardless of where else they are traded, and all of the trades made on other Regional Exchanges.

The B Tape

The B Tape reports the trades on the AMEX, and AMEX shares that are traded elsewhere. If a security is listed on both the NYSE and the AMEX, it will be reported on both tapes.

These tapes are distributed for a fee by the Consolidated Tape Association, which is owned by the exchanges. Market data vendors buy the right to re-sell and distribute the data to their clients for a fee.

Examples of Tape reports

Single Sale

A single sale is the sale of one round lot, 100 shares, of a security. For example, if the tape shows:

TSG	DEF
17 - ½	36 - 7/8

The tape is reporting two single trades of 100 shares each since no volume is shown. One is for TSG that traded at 17 ½ and the other for DEF at 36 7/8.

Multiple Sales

A multiple sale (meaning multiple round lots) is when between 200 and 9,900 shares are traded. The tape would look as follows:

TSG	DEF	GHI
3s 17 - ½	9s 36 - ¾	16s 22 - 5/8

This shows that TSG traded 300 shares, DEF traded 900 shares and GHI traded 1,600 shares.

Large Sales

From 10,000 shares and up, the tape prints the entire amount.

TSG
16000s 17 - ½

Sequential Trade

Since the tape can only print 900 characters per minute, it combines trades that occur just after each other. It would take too long to print the following three trades on the tape:

TSG	ABC	ABC
3s 17 - ½	10s 17 - 5/8	30s 17 - ¾

So, the tape combines the trades as follows:

TSG
3s 17 - ½. 10s 5/8. 30s ¾

This extract from the tape shows that the tape eliminates the 17 and lists the trades for the same security in order:

- 300 shares at 17 1/2
- 1,000 shares at 17 5/8
- 3,000 shares at 17 3/4

Options Price Reporting Authority (OPRA)

The Options Price Reporting Authority (OPRA) provides, through Market Data Vendors, last sale information and current options quotations from a committee of Participant Exchanges designated as the Options Price Reporting Authority.

G. Preventing Market Panic

The President's Working Group was established by President Reagan after the 1987 stock market crash and continues to meet regularly to review actions that should be taken to prevent market panic. The group consists of the heads of the SEC, the Federal Reserve, the Secretary of the Treasury, the Commodities Futures Trading Commission, and several other key members of government.

The Working Group requires that each securities firm establish a mechanism to take all client calls and complete all client trades promptly. In 1987, many retail investors were not able to reach their mutual funds or their brokers while the market continued to decline. Now, firms such as Fidelity have established elaborate contingency plans where telephone lines have been installed in their cafeterias and managers and staff who are not normally involved in taking calls have been trained in how to take and input client orders during a crisis.

Through the Fed, the Working Group has been striving to keep interest rates low, since rapidly rising interest rates cause markets to decline.

In addition, the Working Group has defined a number of trading curbs that are designed to only restrict trading or close the markets in most extreme circumstances. The curbs that have been established on the NYSE are:

Collar (NYSE Rule 80A)

The collar was originally designed to stop trading in stock index futures when the DJIA moves 50 points from the previous close. The curbs are removed if the DJIA moves back to or within 25 points of the previous day's close.

The new collars will be calculated quarterly as two percent of the average closing value of the DJIA for the last month of the previous quarter. The calculated two percent value will be rounded down to the nearest 10 points.

Circuit Breaker (NYSE Rule 80B)

A circuit breaker is a method used by the NYSE to temporarily stop trading when the DJIA falls by a specific percentage so that the market can absorb the news and respond with intent rather than react without thinking.

The current circuit breakers are:

If the Market Falls:			Trading Halts:
10 %	Before	2:00	1 Hour
10 %	Before	2:30	½ Hour
10 %	After	2:30	No Halt
20 %	Before	1:00	2 Hours
20 %	Before	2:00	1 Hour
20 %	After	2:00	Close for the Day
30 %			Close for the Day

Figure 95 - NYSE Circuit Breakers

Circuit Breaker (AMEX Rule 117)

AMEX has established its own Circuit Breaker Trigger Points and Trade Halt Durations, which are shown in the following chart.

	Before 1:00 p.m.	1:00 p.m. - 1:59 p.m.	2:00 p.m. - 2:29 p.m.	2:30 p.m. or later
1050-point decline in the DJIA	1 hour halt	1 hour halt	½ hour halt	No halt; If decline continues to 20% trigger (2,050-points), then close for day
2,050-point decline in the DJIA	2 hour halt	1 hour halt	Close for day	Close for day
3,100-point decline in the DJIA	Close for day	Close for day	Close for day	Close for day

Figure 96 - AMEX Circuit Breakers as of 4/1/2004

Circuit breaker trigger levels are based on one-day declines in the DJIA of 10 %, 20 %, and 30 %. The specific 10, 20, and 30 % trigger values are calculated at the beginning of each calendar quarter using the average DJIA closing value for the month prior to the beginning of the quarter. Each trigger is rounded to the nearest 50 points.

NASD Circuit Breaker

NASD's policy is to halt domestic trading in all AMEX securities, NASDAQ securities, and all equity and equity-related OTC securities should the New York Stock Exchange declare a market-wide trading halt, pursuant to their rules.

Major Market Moves

The percentage decrease in the market in 1987 was far greater than the decrease in 1929 that caused a full economic depression, but the impact on the economy in 1987 was far less dramatic.

That was because the SEC and the Fed had learned that liquidity was critical in time of panic, and they worked together to ensure that money continued to flow in 1987.

In absolute terms, the adjustment that occurred in October, 1997, was even greater than the drop in 1987, but since the market has gone up so much, the percentage was lower.

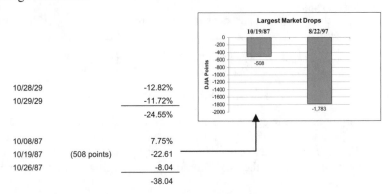

10/28/29		-12.82%
10/29/29		-11.72%
		-24.55%
10/08/87		7.75%
10/19/87	(508 points)	-22.61
10/26/87		-8.04
		-38.04

Figure 97 - Comparison of Large Market Decreases

The entire industry has become much more risk-aware since the 1987 adjustment, and firms throughout the infrastructure have prepared themselves for the increasing volumes and complexities.

H. RESEARCH

Investors usually begin their process of deciding what to buy and sell by researching the alternatives. Research is conducted to identify investment opportunities and firms that are at risk of declining in market value. There are two kinds of research:

- Primary research is used to examine the detailed information about a specific firm. The researcher tries to find out everything they can about the firm by reading, visiting, interviewing, analyzing, etc. This is the most extensive and expensive type of research.

- Secondary research occurs when an analyst or an investor uses the material that has been gathered by others to form an opinion about a specific security. This is less expensive than primary research, but it does not have the same level of detail.

There are many different sources of investment advice.

Sources of Investment Information

Secondary researchers and investors have a wealth of information available to them. This information is the result of other researchers' work, or through publications and investment advisors.

There are many different types of people who are willing to give advice, but the fact that they charge for their services does not necessarily mean that it is good advice. Also, the Internet has provided researchers and individuals with a way to directly access a wide range of raw data and information. There are already more web sites providing investor-related information than anyone could possibly visit, and more are being established each day.

Once advice and information has been collected, there are two different ways that the information is analyzed:

Fundamental Analysis

A fundamental analysis is used to focus on the basic worth of a company, relative to other firms. This is usually accomplished by the use of ratios and non-quantifiable measurements. The key question is: *what* to buy/sell? To answer this question, analysts look at:

- Product lines
- Competition
- Dividend history
- Market share
- Future plans
- Other contingencies

Since there are many different analysts reporting on the most widely held securities, firms have been established that gather this information and provide each analyst's opinion compared to the other analysts. This allows an investor to see the consensus opinion, which is provided by firms like Thomson Financial's First Call.

A fundamental analysis is useful in determining whether the long-term prospects for a specific firm are positive or negative when compared to the rest of the firm's industry or to the overall market.

Technical Analysis

Technical analysis is used to chart the performance of the firm's stock in order to see what the trends have been.

- A technical analyst looks for trends and changes in direction.
- Charts are useful in conjunction with fundamental analyses to help investors see the trends.
- The basic question that technical analysis attempts to answer is: *when* to buy/sell?

The following chart is an example of a technical chart for a security. The vertical lines show the range of trading in a given day, and the short intersecting horizontal lines show the closing price. Technical analysts look for support prices and resistance levels that provide some clues to the future potential for a security. Trends change when the overall market changes or when something changes in the company (or when some new information becomes known).

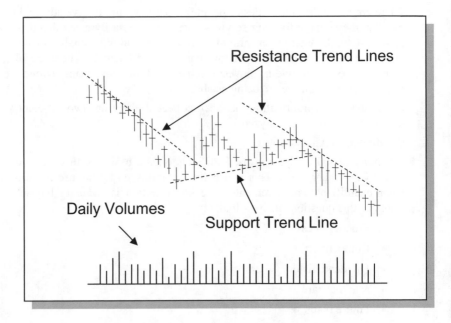

Figure 98 - Example of Technical Analysis Chart

Once someone has decided to buy or sell a security, he will either deal with a broker's registered representative, or directly with a salesperson or a trader. The roles of the registered representative, salesperson and trader are discussed later in this chapter.

I. ORDERS

There are several different types of orders that can be placed, and they all involve some processing differences. Orders can be to buy or sell.

Buy Order

A buy order is an order that is given by a client or a client's agent to a broker or a bank authorizing the purchase of a specific amount of securities or commodities. Buy orders can be day orders, good until cancelled, or good for a specific period of time.

Order Form – Buy

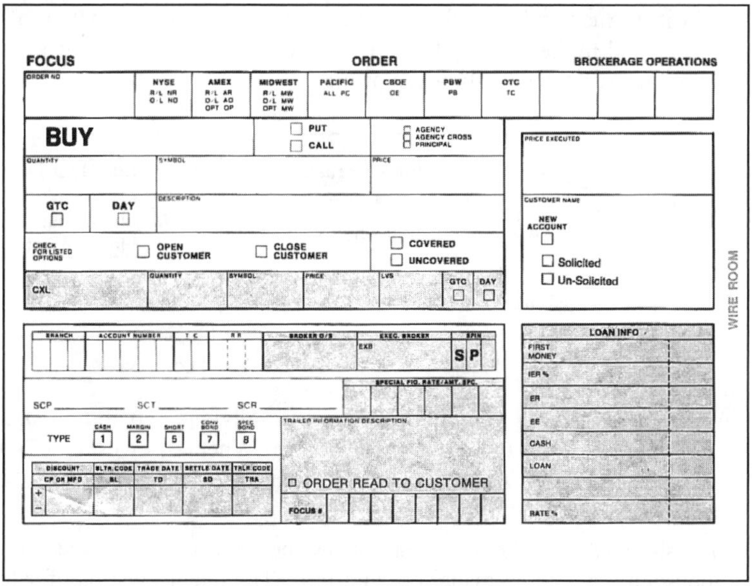

Figure 99 - Example of an Order Form to Buy

When a broker receives an order from a client who wishes to purchase or sell securities, the broker must complete an order form.

The order form identifies the client, what the client wishes to purchase or sell, and any conditions on the transaction that have been placed by the client.

Information must include:

- Name and/or number of account
- Number of shares
- Market NYSE, AMEX, OTC
- Buy or sell (If it is a sale, specify if it is long or short?)
- Security description – name or symbol
- Type of Order – market, limit, stop
- Time Qualification – day, good-'till-cancelled

Sell Order

A sell order can be given under two circumstances, where the seller either has the security or does not. When they do not have the security, this type of a sale is called a Short Sale.

Regular Sale

In a regular sale, the broker delivers the client's securities and collects the money due on settlement date.

Short Sales

A short sale is one where a security is sold by a client who does not currently own it. In most cases, a client makes a short sale in anticipation of a market decline and in the hope that the security can be bought at a lower price in the future to close their position at a profit.

When Selling	If the Price Increases	If the Price Decreases
Long	Profit when sold	Maximum loss is the investment
Short	Significant loss potential	Buy back at a lower price

Figure 100 - Impact of Short and Long Sales

When an investor is long in a position and sells, the maximum risk is that the total amount of the investment will be lost. When an investor sells short, the risk is incalculable since after the investor sells, the price can rise without limit.

In a short sale, the broker must borrow the securities that were sold so that a good delivery can be made to avoid fails. The client must pay for the cost to borrow the securities as long as a short position is held.

Section 10(a) of the Securities Exchange Act gave the SEC the authority to regulate short selling. SEC created clause 10 (a)-1, which is called the uptick rule, which states that an investor can only short a stock if the price has upticked (i.e. increased). This means that a short sale can not be made on a *down tick*. In addition, the broker processing a short sale must first borrow the shares in order to settle the trade before they process the short sale.

These rules were established because short selling is believed to have contributed to the market crash of 1929, where individuals sold more shares short than were available in the market, and they did not immediately borrow the shares to settle. This constant sales pressure drove the price of the shares down very quickly.

Order Form – Sell

When a broker receives an order to sell securities the client will either have the securities in his or her account, or will be selling short. There are some specific rules regarding short selling, and therefore the client and the broker must identify every short sale at the time of the sale. This information is recorded on the trade ticket.

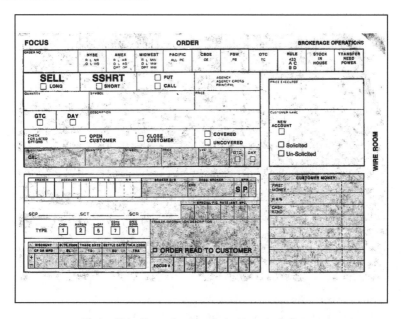

Figure 101 - Example of an Order Form to Sell

Any failure to properly identify and process short sales can result in a fine or a sanction.

NASD Disciplines Firms and Individuals

A. J. Michaels & Co., Hauppauge, NY, was fined $10,400 without admitting or denying findings that it failed to indicate on order tickets whether the sale was a long or short sale and that it failed to establish and enforce its written supervisory procedures.

In response, Michael Frev, President, said "There was no misconduct here. I only agreed to it (the fine) because it would have been more costly to fight it."

Source: Wall Street Journal

Figure 102 - Example of NASD Disciplinary Action

Orders Based Upon Execution Time

There are three types of orders for buys and sells that require an execution at a specific time:

Market Order

A market order is an order to buy or sell a security *immediately* at the best price available at the time the order is executed.

Execute at the Open

When an order is given to a broker to execute at the open, the order is transmitted to the exchange, so that it will be given, along with any other execute at open orders, to the specialist. All of the orders will be executed at the opening price.

Execute at the Close

When an order is given to a broker to execute at the close, the order is transmitted to the exchange, so that it will be given, along with any other execute at close orders, to the specialist. All available orders to buy and sell will be matched at that point, normally using the last traded price.

Orders Based Upon Duration of The Order

Orders that are given with some specific direction also need to have a time frame defined. There are two ways to define an order:

Day Orders

A day order is an order that expires at the close of the exchange or the NASDAQ trading day if it is not executed on the day the trade is entered. Investors should know that many securities can be traded in after-hours trading, and the day order would *not* be considered at that time.

Good 'til Cancelled (GTC)

Good-'til-cancelled is an open order that remains in force until it is executed or cancelled by the client. It does *not* expire at the end of the trading day.

Orders with Additional Constraints

Either the day order or the GTC order can be combined with specific instructions in orders, such as:

Limit Order

A limit order is an order where the client sets the *maximum buying* price or the *minimum selling* price that is acceptable. Buy orders may be executed below the maximum and sell orders above the minimum. A limit order could also be placed as *or better*, meaning that the client expects the broker to try to complete the trade for a price better than the buy or sell limit that has been set.

Stop Order (or Stop Limit Order)

A stop order is an order to buy or sell that becomes effective as soon as a security reaches a certain price.

Buy Stop

A buy stop order is entered above the current market price in order to limit losses or protect a profit. It is a memorandum order that becomes a buy order when the set price is reached.

Sell Stop

A sell stop order is entered below the current market price to limit losses or protect a profit. It is a memorandum order that becomes a sell order when the set price is reached.

Special Orders

In addition to the regular types of orders that we have discussed, there are some special types:

AON – All or Nothing

In trading, *all or nothing* is an instruction to fill all of the order or none of it. This is fairly common in OTC and Bond Trading.

DNR – Do Not Reduce

DNR is a formal instruction that tells the order department not to reduce the price of the order by the amount of dividends received when the corporation pays the dividend. A DNR is usually placed on buy limit, sell stop, and sell stop limit GTC orders.

DNI - Do Not Increase

DNI is a formal instruction that tells the order department to not increase the quantity of shares that has been specified on the order if a stock dividend is declared. A DNI is usually placed on buy limit, sell stop, and stop limit GTC orders.

FOK – Fill or Kill

FOK is an order that specifies that the entire order must be filled immediately, and if the entire order cannot be filled it is cancelled.

IOC – Immediate or Cancel

IOC is an order instruction type that requires the broker/dealer to immediately fill as much of the order as possible, and cancel the rest of the order.

NH – Not Held

A notation of *NH* on an order indicates that the broker or trader has discretion over the time and price, and therefore can take whatever time is needed to get a good execution.

J. PEOPLE IN THE TRADE PROCESS

Retail Investors

Retail investors are the individuals who own securities and who decide what they are going to buy or sell. They will either contact their registered representative or a broker to place their order, or go directly to an online broker to place their order.

Institutional Investor - Portfolio Managers

Portfolio managers are employed by investment managers to decide when to buy or sell securities for specific portfolios in order to meet that portfolio's objectives. As the managers of the positions, they decide what to buy or sell based upon their own research or the research of other people in the firm.

When they decide to buy or sell, portfolio managers will contact a broker directly if they are in a small investment management firm, or if they are in a larger firm, they will go through the firm's traders.

Registered Representatives

A firm's registered representatives are the people who manage the client relationships. They must be licensed and go by a variety of names, including:

- Account Executive
- Investment Counselor
- Investment Officer
- Personal Investment Counselor

While some also have good analytical skills, registered representatives are basically salespeople who develop a relationship with clients and pass along the firm's recommendations to the appropriate investors. From a trade processing point of view, the registered representative's primary role is as an order taker.

Traders - Investment Managers

The traders who are employed by investment managers have a responsibility to search for the best broker, Alternative Trading Systems or Electronic Communication Network to use. Although known as traders, their role is more that of a purchaser who will find the best vendor for a particular security.

They need to be very aware of market conditions to decide exactly when during the day to place an order, as well as where to place it.

Traders - Brokers

The orders taken by registered representatives are either electronically routed to an exchange's electronic system or NASDAQ, or are passed to a trader, who can either work in a firm's trading room, or for the firm on the floor of an exchange.

A trader will trade for their firm's own account as well as for client accounts.

In order to manage the level of risk that a firm incurs, the firm must monitor the activities of the traders very closely throughout the day and manage the end of day position. Individual traders can be assigned daylight and overnight limits, and the firm may also wish to aggregate all of their traders' activity for specific sectors, countries or counterparties to ensure that they are not too exposed in any one area.

To do this, firms need real-time information and the ability to take real-time action if there is a problem. This puts a burden on firms to acquire data quickly and to organize the data into usable information.

In most trading rooms, there is another function that works along with the trader. This is the salesperson.

Sales Person

Brokerage firms also have a category of employees who are involved in identifying the needs of the firm's large individual or institutional clients and try to help them buy and sell securities, usually from the firm's inventory. As shown in the following diagram, the salesperson works closely with the trader to ensure that the purchases or sales are at a price that is acceptable to the trader, who is responsible for the position.

Brokers will often acquire a position in a security because they want to be a market maker for that security and feel that they will be able to consistently buy it at a lower price than they can sell it for. The sales effort can be tied to the firm's primary market distribution efforts and/or to the secondary market.

Most of this effort occurs by phone and fax, and there is very little automation involved.

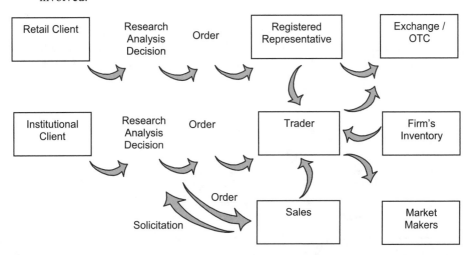

Figure 103 - Alternative Broker Sales Processes

K. TRADE ORDER AND EXECUTION – RETAIL

As shown in the next diagram, retail trades are either initiated by the client calling his or her broker or, increasingly, by using electronic forms of order entry such as the Internet. The registered representative will either receive the order electronically or will enter the order into the firm's system.

Once the order is in the broker's system it will either be routed to the broker's trader who will access market makers or electronic bulletin boards, go directly to NASDAQ, or go to the appropriate stock exchange. If the order is sent to a stock exchange such as the New York Stock Exchange it will go through the SuperDOT system and either be completed with another broker as the counterparty or with the specialist.

Once the counterparty has been identified, the identification information is entered into the broker's systems. This is the beginning of the clearing and settlement process, which is described in the chapter on Post-Trade Processing, Clearing and Settlement.

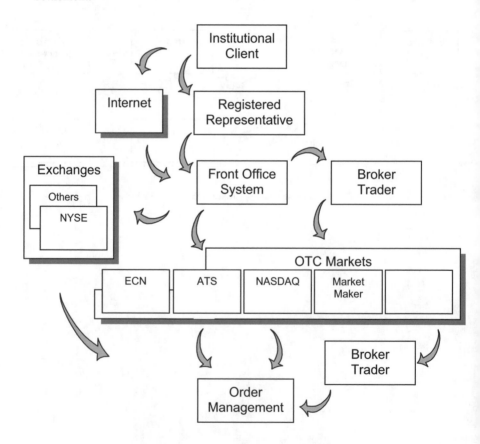

Figure 104 - Retail Trade Order and Execution

L. TRADE ORDER AND EXECUTION – INSTITUTIONAL

Institutional trades have some differences from retail trades, as shown in the next diagram. The institution can give an order to a broker, or bypass the broker completely by using an Electronic Crossing Network. If the broker receives an order it is processed similarly to the retail order, except that the broker's trader might access the third market, which is used for block trades, to find a counterparty.

As with retail trades, once the counterparty has been identified, the information is entered into the broker's system and the clearing and settlement process begins.

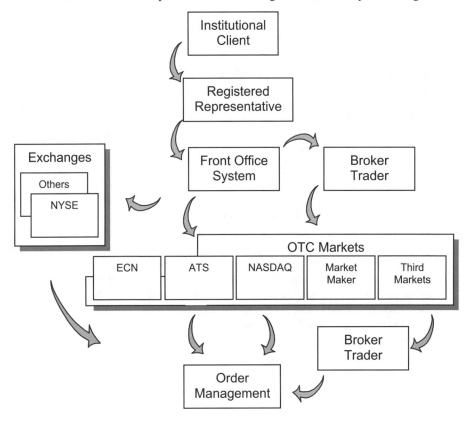

Figure 105 - Institutional Trade Order and Execution

When an institution buys or sells securities, it can either buy or sell a few thousand shares, or it can combine orders from multiple portfolios into one larger order, called a block. A block is a large purchase or sale of a specific stock, which is usually at least 10,000 shares or over $200,000, and is usually only made by institutions. Investment managers will frequently combine their requirements for multiple portfolios for the same security into a single purchase. It is important to understand the concept of the block trade at this time because it has a significant impact on how institutional trades are processed.

When an order for a large number of shares is received, a broker may have to *shop the trade* to locate several different counterparties to assemble all of the required shares without moving the market price. The assembled shares constitute the block. When the block is assembled, the broker either reports to the buyer the average cost of the shares or the individual trades that constitute the block.

Once a trade is made, whether it is a single trade or a block trade, the complexity of processing the transaction becomes apparent.

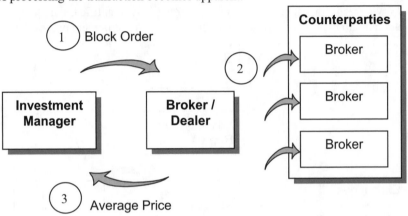

Figure 106 - Block Trading

The process of block trading is changing with the increased use of algorithmic trading, which uses computer programs to automatically split the block into potentially hundreds of small pieces and then execute all of the pieces either simultaneously over various electronic markets or to send them out at intervals throughout the day. This software has been developed by the brokers to maximize their own order flow and they are working with the Trade Order Management Systems vendors to add the functionality into these applications.

The block trade has implications for clearing and settlement, which will be discussed in the chapter on Post-Trade Processing, Clearing and Settlement.

M. CROSS BORDER TRADING

While it is not within the scope of this book to fully explain how cross-border trading is conducted, U.S. firms do interact with non-U.S. firms when investments are made outside of the U.S. The following chart shows the possible points of connectivity between the firms for institutional investors (i.e., Pension Funds, Mutual Funds, etc.), and the exact connections depend upon the choices made by the investor, the investment manager and the broker.

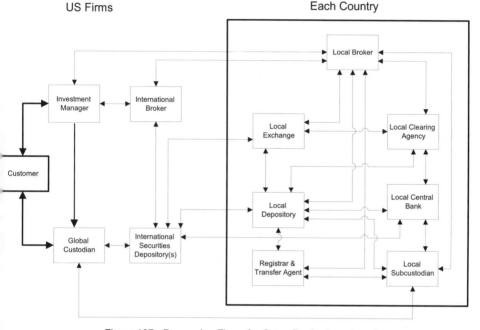

Figure 107 - Processing Flows for Cross Border Investments

This chart shows how firms buy and sell securities and introduces how they clear and settle.

The institutional client will generally select the investment manager and the custodian. The investment manager has the choice of contacting a U.S. broker that deals internationally or directly contact a broker in the market of the investment. If a U.S.-based broker is selected, that firm may have a subsidiary (or parent) in the other country, or a relationship with a local broker may exist.

The local broker will deal with the local infrastructure and find a local counterparty using a process that is specific for that country. Although the general concepts of investment and processing are the same, the details are very different for every country.

The local broker will complete the trade and notify the client's broker, who will forward the execution information to its client (the investment manager). The investment manager then notifies their client and the Global Custodian on the status of the trade.

Except for trade and settlement communications, which are not well automated and which cause a significant number of fails, the cross-border process in the local country remains the same as for domestic transactions. The transactions in the investor's country are limited to posting the transactions and moving the funds that are involved in the settlement.

Since this book focuses on the U.S. securities industry, we will not go into any more detail on cross-border buying and selling.

N. TRANSACTION CATEGORIES

One factor that makes securities processing so complicated is that there are many different circumstances applied to each transaction to process the trade.

- A client can be a retail or an institutional account and can have a cash account, a margin account, or some other type of trust or fiduciary account.

- The security might be in the broker's inventory or the firm may have to go to the street to find a counterparty.

- The transaction itself could be part of a trading strategy, such as a Wrap Account, or it could be a simple trade or a block trade.

- The security on the buy or on the sell side could be in physical form, it could be in book-entry form, or it could be part of a new registration process called the Individual Registration Option (IRO).

- And finally, each instrument type has certain characteristics that define how and where it will be settled and registered.

All of the factors shown in the Types of Transactions chart must be considered in any securities process or system. The next chapter, Post-Trade Processing, describes how these different categories of transactions affect the processing flow.

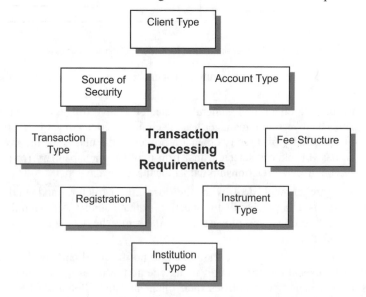

Figure 108 - Types of Transactions

VII. Post-Trade Processing, Clearing and Settlement

There are several key post-trade processing functions that are conducted by the banks, brokers and investment managers that are involved in the buying and selling of securities. In this chapter, we will identify these functions and their processing requirements.

The primary post-trade processing functions are clearing, settlement and asset servicing; however, there are several other types of functions that are more generic, and which impact the process at various points. The functions that are covered in this chapter are:

- Preparation for Clearing and Settlement
- Clearing
- Settlement

When presented with the complexity of the securities process flow, people often ask why it was made so complicated. The answer is that no one designed the *entire* system to work the way it does. Much of our current process was designed for a simpler time and the complexities evolved when the industry solved each new problem as it occurred.

In the 1920's, the U.S. settled in a manual environment in one day. Trades were simple and volume was low. As the volume and complexity of trades and instruments grew, the industry extended the amount of time provided for settlement, and by the 1960's it was a five-day manual process. At that time the volume of securities transactions exploded and the exchanges actually had to close for part of the week in order to clear the backlog. To survive, computerized automation was systematically introduced to the industry.

The back office was historically organized by function, and the automation of the back office began on a function-by-function basis. The automation of these functions was accomplished using the technology available at that time - overnight batch processing. This served to formalize the manual process, and the five-day cycle remained in place until 1995, when the U.S. industry shifted to a three-day cycle.

The three-day cycle was instituted by compressing the time frame, not by re-engineering the flow. For the most part, firms with batch systems continued to run these systems; they just ran them more frequently. If the industry eventually moves to T+1 firms will no longer be able to process with the same legacy systems in place. This will have a significant impact on the functions described in this chapter and on all firms.

Banks, brokers and investment managers all perform similar tasks in their post-trade functions, but they have different responsibilities and approach their tasks differently. This means that in order to understand how the overall industry operates and how the participants interact, we must first understand the overall flow and then focus on how each type of firm works in the later chapters on processing.

A. INTRODUCTION TO POST-TRADE PROCESSING

As we consider the processes involved in post-trade processing, it is important to note that every trade has a client-side and a street-side.

- The client-side of the trade involves the broker and their client. The client-side of the trade settles through the broker if it is for a retail client, or generally through the Depository Trust Company (DTC) if it is for an institutional client.

- The street-side of the trade involves the broker, acting as an agent for their client, and the broker's counterparty. The street-side of the trade clears through a clearinghouse such as the National Securities Clearing Corporation (NSCC). If the client's broker fills the order from their own inventory and acts as a principal to the trade, they become the counterparty and there is no street-side clearing process.

Both sides to the trade are completed in the same number of business days, which ensures that the broker's trade settles with their counterparty simultaneously with the receipt of the securities or the cash from their client.

Different types of instruments clear and settle in different time periods which will be discussed later in this chapter.

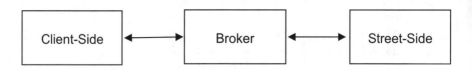

Figure 109 - Simultaneous Settlement of Street-Side and Client-Side Transactions

Regulatory Foundation for Clearing and Settlement

Section 17A of the Securities Exchange Act of 1934 (Exchange Act) was added in 1975. This section defines the establishment of a national clearing and settlement system for securities transactions, and it was established to increase efficiency and reduce risk in the U.S. clearance and settlement systems.

Depository Trust & Clearing Corporation (DTCC) [71]

The Depository Trust & Clearing Corporation is the largest financial services post-trade infrastructure in the world. DTCC is the holding company for six businesses that include a depository, four clearing corporations, and the global joint venture with Thomson Financial (called Omgeo).

Through its subsidiaries, DTCC provides clearance, settlement and information services for virtually all equity, corporate debt, municipal debt, government securities, mortgage-backed securities, and emerging market sovereign debt trades in the U.S., totaling more than $1.7 trillion daily. It is also a leading clearinghouse for mutual funds and insurance products, linking funds and carriers with distribution networks. In addition, DTCC provides custody and asset servicing for more than two million securities issues from the U.S. and 84 other countries, worth about $23 trillion.

The DTCC has five subsidiaries:

- Depository Trust Company

---

[71]   Source: www.dtcc.com

- National Securities Clearing Corporation
- Fixed Income Clearing Corporation (includes two clearing corporations)
- Emerging Markets Clearing Corporation
- Omgeo (Joint venture with Thomson Financial)

Each of these divisions is covered in the appropriate clearing and settlement section in this chapter.

Depository Trust Company (DTC)

The Depository Trust Company is the U.S.'s central securities depository for stocks and bonds. The Depository Trust Company started as a stock clearing corporation, and as a result of the paper crunch in the late 1960's split off from the clearing process to become the Central Certificate Service (CSS). To complete the immobilization process, it had to become a trust company, and the DTC did so in 1974.

As shown below, the CSS was created in 1968, during the industry's paper crisis, and the entity that was to become the NSCC was split off. The NSCC is discussed later in this chapter.

In 1973, the CSS was reorganized as a limited purpose bank called the Depository Trust Company. The DTC was reunited with the NSCC in 1999, within a new holding company called the Depository Trust Clearing Corporation (DTCC).

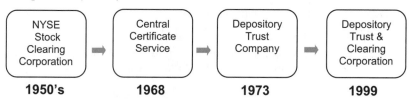

Figure 110 - History of the DTC's Organization

The DTC links over 546 participants (banks and brokers) and institutional clients, along with firms serving as transfer agents, paying agents, and exchange and redemption agents for securities issuers.

In 2003, over $105 trillion in securities were processed through the DTC's book-entry system, and the assets held reached $24.6 trillion.

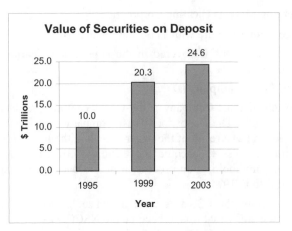

Figure 111 - Value of Securities on Deposit

DTC is owned by U.S. banks and brokerage firms and the New York Stock Exchange (which is also owned by the brokers). The mission of the DTC is to:

- Hold securities such as equities, bonds and unit investment trusts
- Arrange for the receipt and delivery of securities
- Arrange for the payments during settlement

The number of issues eligible for lodging in the DTC has grown steadily to its current level of approximately 2.2 million issues.

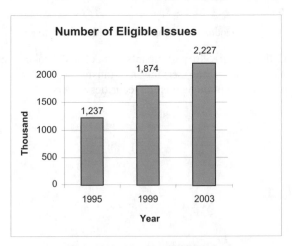

Figure 112 - Number of Eligible Issues

These functions of the DTC are discussed later in this chapter.

National Securities Clearing Corporation (NSCC)

National Securities Clearing Corporation (NSCC), a wholly owned subsidiary of The Depository Trust & Clearing Corporation (DTCC), is a central counterparty that provides centralized clearance, settlement and information services for virtually all broker-to-broker equity, corporate bond and municipal bond, exchange traded funds (ETF) and unit investment trust (UIT) trades in the U.S.

NSCC is also the main provider of centralized information services and money settlement for mutual funds and insurance and annuity transactions, linking funds and insurance carriers with their broker/dealer, bank and financial planner distribution channels.

NSCC, which today is the world's leading provider of centralized clearance, settlement and information services to the financial services industry, was established in 1976 to take over the highly paper-intensive clearance and settlement for the major stock exchanges and the over-the-counter market.

The National Securities Clearing Corporation (NSCC), established in 1976, is a clearing corporation that is responsible for netting the cash and securities transactions that occur each day between brokers in the U.S. NSCC, which is owned by the NYSE, AMEX and NASD (which are all owned in turn by the brokers), also provides trade comparison of NYSE, AMEX, and over-the-counter transactions.

Through the NSCC, brokers have established an efficient mechanism to settle among themselves called Continuous Net Settlement (CNS), and have created other processing services, including:

- Movement of cash and securities among participants
- Trade recording and processing
- Clearing and settlement
- Delivery systems
- Dividend and interest settlement services

The functions performed by the NSCC are discussed in more detail in the chapter on Post-Trade Processing, Clearing and Settlement.

In 1999, the DTC and National Securities Clearing Corporation merged within a holding company to form a consolidated firm, the Depository Trust & Clearing Corporation. The benefits of this merger, according to the participants, are:

- "Bring together or harmonize the processing systems for clearance and settlement of the institutional (buy) and broker (sell) sides of the market, thereby facilitating shortened settlement cycles, improved risk management and lower processing costs.
- Provide a centralized infrastructure to competitively position the U.S. in overseas markets.

- A single industry-driven strategy will enhance the introduction of innovative technology solutions, new products and services, and achievement of straight through processing." [72]

Fixed Income Clearing Corporation (FICC)

Fixed Income Clearing Corporation (FICC), which began operations on January 1, 2003, is DTCC's newest clearing corporation.

FICC was formed by the merger of the Government Securities Division (GSD) and the MBS Clearing Corporation (MBSCC) in order to bring greater synergies, cost reductions and efficiencies to the post-trade processing of fixed income instruments. FICC was reorganized into the Government Securities Division and the Mortgage-Backed Securities Division. These two divisions offer their own product-specific services to their own members, with each maintaining separate rules and a separate collateral margin pool.

The Government Securities Division clears, nets, settles and manages the risk arising from a broad range of U.S. Government securities transactions for its member firms (brokers, dealers, banks and other financial institutions) and hundreds of correspondent firms that clear through these members. These transactions include original auction purchases of Treasury and Freddie Mac securities, buy/sell and repo transactions in Treasury and Government Agency securities, and GCF Repo transactions in Treasury and Government Agency securities as well as certain mortgage-backed securities.

The Mortgage-Backed Securities Division operates two primary business units:

- Clearing services, which include trade comparison, confirmation, netting, and risk management
- Electronic Pool Notification (EPN) services, which allow clients to transmit/retrieve mortgage-backed securities pool information in real-time using standardized message formats

Mortgage-backed securities are bought and sold in the over-the-counter cash, forward and options markets. The key participants in these markets - the nation's original secondary markets for loan assets - are mortgage originators, government sponsored enterprises, registered broker/dealers, inter-dealer brokers, institutional investors, investment managers, mutual funds, commercial banks, insurance companies and other financial institutions.

Emerging Markets Clearing Corporation (EMCC)

Emerging Markets Clearing Corporation (EMCC), a wholly owned subsidiary of the DTCC, provides trade matching, clearance, settlement and risk management services to global dealers, interdealer brokers and correspondent clearing firms involved in emerging market debt instruments.

Established in 1998, EMCC is registered with and regulated by the U.S. Securities and Exchange Commission, and is a clearinghouse recognized for the purposes of the U.K. Financial Services Authority's Interim Prudential Sourcebook: Investment Business.

---

[72] Source: DTCC

EMCC currently provides trade services for U.S. dollar-denominated Brady Bonds and associated Value Recovery Rights (warrants), emerging markets global sovereign bonds, quasi-sovereign bonds, and selected corporate bonds. A number of additional instruments are under consideration for eligibility.

B. PREPARING FOR CLEARING AND SETTLEMENT

The U.S. industry established the current clearing and settlement process by developing four major techniques, each of which is introduced here and described in more detail later in this chapter.

Post-Trade Processing

There are several steps that must occur after the trade but before clearing or settlement can begin.

Activity	Trading/Clearing	Settlement
Matching	1	4
Confirmation		2
Affirmation		3

Figure 113 - Post Trade Activities

These steps are intended to make the clearing and settlement more efficient while reducing risk.

1. Trade Matching

2. Confirmation

3. Affirmation

4. Settlement Matching

Each of these steps is discussed in the following pages.

Trade Matching

Trade matching occurs when the counterparties to the trade match the details of completed trades, as they know them, to ensure that both sides to a trade agree in advance of the settlement. This process reduces the chances of a fail due to mismatched instructions.

Trade matching is systematically conducted by the exchanges, NASDAQ and by the brokers themselves as a part of the brokers' clearing process. Trade details are sent to the appropriate clearing agency as the trades occur. Trade matching for the clearing process results from the street-side of the trade and therefore generally involves two brokers.

Trade matching is necessary to ensure that all of the participants to a transaction agree on the trade details.

A trade match can occur at multiple points in the process, but the closer it occurs to the actual execution of the trade, the less chance for an error. The ideal situation for a trade match is to automatically capture the details of the trade when it is executed. This can occur at an exchange, NASDAQ or an Alternative Trading System (ATS).

To understand some of the characteristics of Alternative Trading Systems, you can refer to a White Paper prepared by The Summit Group titled *ECN and ATS - The Electronic Future* (http://www.soforum.com/library/ecn_ats.shtml).

There is a street-side trade match and a client-side trade match. The street-side trading match is discussed on the next pages, and the client-side trade match is discussed along with confirmations.

This process can occur in different ways, depending upon how the trade was conducted. The match itself can occur as a result of any one of the following four types of transactions:

1. Trades from broker's inventory

2. Trades on an Exchange or NASDAQ

3. Trades verbally Over-the-Counter

4. Trades via ATS

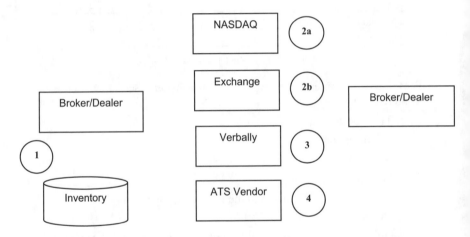

Figure 114 - Street-Side of a Trade

Each of these four methods is discussed on the following pages.

Trade Matching from Broker/Dealer's Inventory

When a broker/dealer receives an order for a security in which they are a market maker, they will normally fill the order from their own inventory and be compensated through the spread, rather than by a sales commission.

In this case, the client-side occurs within the brokerage activity of the firm and the street-side of the trade occurs within the dealer activity so there is no external matching required.

The trade details are still reported to the NYSE so that the price information can be disseminated.

Trade Matching on an Exchange or NASDAQ

When two brokers complete a trade on an exchange, the exchange records and reports the event and the trade is 'locked-in.' No further trade matching is required.

Similarly, when two brokers complete a trade on NASDAQ, the event and the trade is recorded and reported by NASDAQ, and no further trade matching is required.

Trade Matching of Verbal Executions

Verbal trades offer the greatest potential for errors. Securities that are not listed on an exchange or which are traded off an exchange for some reason such as block trades require some intervention by traders. In this case, both sides to the trade must do a post-trade match to prevent problems in settlement.

Typically, trade-related problems with verbal trades are only discovered when the counterparties receive their confirms.

Trade Matching Via Alternative Trading Systems (ATS)

Increasingly, OTC transactions are being processed through a variety of vendor applications. A number of ATSs offer firms an opportunity to find a counterparty and agree to a trade electronically, and can then report a matched trade immediately.

Confirmation

Confirmations are sent to clients to officially tell them what their broker did on their behalf. Retail clients get paper confirmations in the mail. Institutional clients can receive a paper copy if they request it, but they must receive an electronic confirmation through the DTC's automated system for instruments that are held by the DTC.

Confirmations are sent to clients to officially tell them what their broker did on their behalf.

- Retail clients get paper confirmations in the mail.
- Institutional clients can receive a paper copy if they request it, but they must receive an electronic confirmation through the DTC's automated system for instruments that are held by the DTC.

Retail and institutional clients match the trade confirmation to their original order to ensure that the broker did what was asked. If a client identifies an error on a confirm, they must notify the broker promptly.

- Retail clients manually match their orders and paper confirms
- Institutional clients often use some automated matching or reconciliation applications

Confirmation systems are used to route confirmations between investment managers, brokers and custodians. The primary institutional confirmation system used today in the U.S. is Omgeo-TradeSuite, which is based upon the DTC's original ID system.

There are other automated confirmation applications that are called Electronic Trade Confirmation Systems (ETC). ETC systems are designed to support connectivity and routing of messages between the parties to a trade, and are primarily used for local matching of cross-border transactions, although they can be used within a country as well. The U.S. ETC providers are:

Omgeo OASYS

Omgeo is discussed in detail later in this chapter.

SunGard Transaction Network (STN)

With STN, asset managers can create and route allocations to brokers, match and affirm confirmations, and research and resolve exceptions within and across institutions, around the globe.

Cross Border Exchange (CBX)

The recently formed Cross Border Exchange (CBX) is a SWIFT electronic-trade-confirmation (ETC) service provider. As a SWIFT ETC Service Provider, CBX will act as an agent on behalf of its investment manager and broker/dealer clients in exchanging electronic trade confirmation messages (orders, executions, allocations, cancellations) and sending settlement instruction messages over SWIFTNet.

In addition, there are other ETC providers that focus outside the U.S., including:

- SIA S.P.A. – Italy
- Nomura Research Institute (SmartBridge Department) – Japan
- City Networks – U.K.

Affirmation

Affirmations are required from institutional clients in order to provide a positive instruction to the custodian bank to release their funds or their securities during settlement. Without a valid affirmation of the broker's confirmation, the custodian must let the trade fail.

Institutions receive their confirmations electronically from the DTC and affirm to the DTC electronically through the same system. The DTC's automated systems are described in more detail later in this chapter.

Each trade that is made by a broker on behalf of an investment manager, and which is to settle at a custodian bank, must be affirmed by the manager before the bank will release either funds or securities to settle the trade.

Securities that are DTC eligible are usually settled through the DTC's systems, and involve a confirmation message that is initiated by the broker and that is subsequently affirmed by the manager. Institutions receive their confirmations electronically from the DTC and affirm to the DTC electronically through the same system. Without the affirmation, the trade will not settle.

Managers can notify their custodians in other ways for trades that are not settling at the DTC. This is usually accomplished by a Fax, SWIFT message or a direct file transfer. The custodian can use this instruction as their authority for releasing securities or funds.

As a part of a special contractual agreement, an investment manager can authorize their custodian to affirm their trades.

Confirmation/Affirmation Rates

There were 700,000 Average Daily Trades submitted to Omgeo in 2003.

- T+0 Confirmation Rate   85.8%

- T+0 Affirmation Rate   23.0%
- T+1 Affirmation Rate   85.0%
- T+2 Affirmation Rate   89.0%
- Unaffirmed or not affirmed through Omgeo   11.0%

Settlement Matching

Settlement matching for a single trade should occur when the investor compares the order to the confirm. Settlement matching for blocks occurs after the block is allocated and affirmed, and can also occur at the block level by matching the executed block to the order.

Settlement matching is important in order to ensure that the settlement details are correct before the actual settlement occurs. This includes the trade-related information such as security, price, and quantity, as well as settlement information such as account, place of settlement, etc.

If settlement occurs and the information was not correct, then the transaction has to be unwound and re-entered, all of which is very expensive.

Settlement matching can occur locally or centrally. The difference between local and central matching is discussed on the following pages.

Local Matching vs. Central Matching - History

Settlement matching was historically accomplished bilaterally at a local level when the two counterparties to a trade matched settlement details with each other. This matching methodology is called Local Matching, which requires a sequential process of handshakes between the counterparties as information flows back and forth (i.e., Indications of Interest, Order, Confirmation. Allocation, Affirmation).

When the industry considered shortening the settlement cycle to T+1 for most securities, the Security Industry Association's Institutional Transaction Processing Committee (ITPC) realized that the existing process would have to be significantly enhanced. This could be accomplished by additional automation within and between firms to improve the efficiency of the sequential process, or by establishing a central facility to do the matching. The central matching facility was defined as a Virtual Matching Utility (VMU) and as a central point for firms to send their trade information as it became available, rather than in the sequential form that the current process required.

To meet this need, several large brokers and custodians funded a new entity called the Global Straight Through Processing Association (GSTPA), which planned to build a new processing engine called the Transaction Flow Manager (TFM). To counter this, Thomson Financial and the DTC merged their existing post-trade applications that supported local matching and formed a joint venture called Omgeo with the intent to build a VMU.

GSTPA ultimately failed as the financial industry entered a period of lower volumes and reduced investment while Omgeo continued to build on its existing base and develop a global VMU, which it called Central Trade Matching (CTM).

Local Matching vs. Central Matching – Current Status

Today, some vendors are attacking the central matching concept and are offering new local matching automation alternatives, while other vendors are building their own VMUs. Local matching requires connectivity, standards and an in-house application, while central matching requires all of these plus a central processing application.

As the global CTM was being built, Omgeo also completed a U.S. central matching facility called TradeMatch, and Omgeo continued to offer TradeSuite as a local matching alternative.

Local Matching Alternatives

ATSs offer a central electronic point where investors and broker/dealers can find counterparties and agree on a trade. Once the trade has been agreed to within the system, it is effectively matched and can proceed to the next steps in the process.

Many of these platforms are extending their trade functionality towards settlement by supporting allocations, confirmations, affirmations and standing settlement instructions.

For instance, TradeWeb offers an allocation and matching process, TradeXpress, and an SSI called AccountNet that support local matching.

Central Matching Alternatives

Other firms have established VMUs to compete with Omgeo.

- FMC has recently implemented FMCNet II, a post-trade communication network, and will continue to support local matching.
- SunGard's STN automates the confirmation-allocation-affirmation process.

Post-Trade Communication

There are two fundamental areas that are required to make these post-trade activities work effectively:

Standards

Standards are necessary to ensure that all of the parties are talking the same language and that the words have the same definitions. There are a variety of agencies and industry associations working to establish the data elements that should be included in each type of transaction and to define the parameters for each data element.

Standards are a problem when there are too few or too many. When there are too few, each participant sends the information that they consider important, and sends it in any form they think appropriate. This significantly increases the chances for processing errors and definitely adds costs. At the other extreme, there have been periods where there have been too many agencies and associations that were working to develop competing standards and the end result is the same as with too few standards.

There is more on standards in Chapter XVIII – Industry Owned Associations.

Communication Networks

There are four primary categories of networks that are used by firms in the securities industry:

- SWIFT
- FIX
- Proprietary links
- Vendor provided links

These networks are discussed at various points throughout this book.

Clearing and Settlement

After all parties to the trade have agreed on the details, two separate processes take place:

- Clearing
- Settlement

These two concepts are often presented as if they were part of the same process, but they are distinctly different.

Clearing is the exchange of money and securities between brokers, normally using a form of netting. There are two primary forms of netting:

- Multilateral Netting
- Bilateral Netting

These two forms are discussed later in this chapter.

Settlement is the final process of exchanging money and securities between all of the counterparties to a transaction. Settlement includes the:

- End of day net transactions between brokers, when the net amounts are determined by the clearing process

- Trade-by-trade settlement of institutional account transactions at the Depository Trust Company (DTC) through their bank custodians

- Trade-by-trade settlement of retail account transactions through their brokers

The trade-by-trade process is the original form of trade settlement. Each purchase is matched to a single sale and each sale is matched to a single purchase. This process is very volume sensitive.

Clearing

The broker-to-broker portion of a trade (which is called the street-side of the trade) is entered into a clearing system that nets all of the trades made by all of the brokers throughout the day.

Clearing is the exchange of money and securities between brokers, normally using a form of netting.

Equities Clearing

For equities, this process, which is facilitated by the National Securities Clearing Corporation (NSCC), is called Continuous Net Settlement (CNS).

Throughout each trading day, CNS consolidates each participant's security obligations (purchases and sales) into one net position for each issue and one overall net cash position.

- The final position of the day for each issue is reported for a net settlement to the DTC.

- The resolution of the final cash position of the day is called Daily Net Money Settlement. It is facilitated by the DTC and cash is settled between the brokers through their respective banks.

Fixed Income Clearing

The NSCC is also responsible for clearing corporate and municipal bonds.

The Fixed Income Clearing Corporation (FICC), which consists of the Government Securities Division (GSD) and the Mortgage Backed Securities Division (MBSD), specialize in clearing U.S. government securities and mortgage backed securities respectively.

Banks also are involved in clearing and settling government securities.

Other Securities Clearing

Banks also clear money market instruments, and the Options Clearing Corporation (OCC) issues, clears, settles and guarantees options transactions.

Commodity trades are cleared through several different specialty clearinghouses.

Settlement

Settlement is the final exchange of securities for money.

Settlement is the final process of exchanging money and securities between all of the counterparties to a transaction. Settlement includes the:

- End of day net transactions between brokers, when the net amounts are determined by the clearing process

- Trade-by-trade settlement of institutional account transactions at the DTC through their custodians

- Trade-by-trade settlement of retail account transactions through their brokers

Individuals

Individuals deal with brokerage firms on a cash (or margin lending) basis, and settle each trade independently.

Institutions

For most security types, investment managers process through a custodian bank to the DTC on a Deliver vs. Payment (DVP) basis, and settle each trade independently.

For brokers, the settlement of the street-side of the trade occurs at the depository by using the net amounts that were calculated during the clearing process throughout the day.

Cash and securities must be exchanged on settlement date, and if they are not available, some form of borrowing/lending must occur.

- If a firm is unable to deliver a security that it has sold it may have to borrow it in order to settle with the buyer through a process called securities lending.

- If a retail client does not have sufficient cash to pay for a purchase they might be able to temporarily borrow from the broker through a process called margin lending.

Clearing and Settlement Periods

Different categories of securities in the U.S. clear and settle in different periods of time through different clearinghouses and depositories. The following chart shows that while the difference between the trade date and the settlement date can be different for various instruments, the majority of U.S. exchange listed securities are cleared and settled in three business days.

Security Type	Clearing	Settlement	Settlement Days
Corporate Bonds	NSCC	DTC	3
Municipal Bonds	NSCC	DTC	3
Mutual Funds	NSCC	Mutual Fund or Transfer Agent	3
Government Bonds	FICC - GSD (formerly GSCC)	Fed	T
Mortgage Backed Bonds	FICC - MBSD (formerly MBSCC)	PTC or Fed	< 45
Equity	NSCC	DTC	3
Money Market Instruments	Banks	Direct or DTC	T or T+1
Options	OCC	OCC	1

Figure 115 - Securities Clearing and Settlement Periods in the U.S.

The largest securities clearinghouse in the U.S. is the National Securities Clearing Corporation (NSCC). The Government Securities Division (GSD) Clearing Corporation (GSD) and the Mortgage Backed Securities Clearing Corporation (MBSD) are sister organizations of the NSCC and specialize in clearing U.S. government securities and mortgage backed securities respectively.

Banks are involved in clearing and settling government securities and money market instruments, while the Options Clearing Corporation (OCC) issues, clears, settles and guarantees options transactions.

The primary depository in the United States is the Depository Trust Company (DTC). In 1999, the NSCC and the DTC were merged within a new holding company called the Depository Trust & Clearing Corporation (DTCC).

The DTCC, the clearinghouses, and the other depositories are discussed later in this chapter.

SIA Guidelines for Improving Settlement

The SIA has established several guidelines that are intended to implement straight through processing and improve the settlement process. The ten recommendations are:

- Modify internal processes at broker/dealers, asset managers, and custodians to ensure compliance with compressed settlement deadlines.

- Identify and comply with accelerated deadlines for submission of trades to the clearing and settlement systems.

- Amend the National Securities Clearing Corporation's (NSCC) trade guarantee process so that the guarantee is provided on trade date.

- Report trades to clearing corporations in locked-in format and revise clearing corporations' output.

- Rewrite Continuous Net Settlement processes at NSCC to enhance speed and efficiency.

- Reduce reliance on checks and use alternative means of payment, such as automatic debits allowed by the National Automated Clearinghouse Association.

- Immobilize securities shares prior to conducting transactions.

- Revise the prospectus delivery rules and procedures for initial public offerings.

- Develop industry matching utilities and linkages for all asset classes.

- Standardize reference data and move to standardized industry protocols for broker/dealers, asset managers, and custodians.

C. CLEARING STOCKS AND BONDS

After the client has conducted research and made a buy or sell decision, and once a counterparty has been found, the brokerage firms involved in the street-side of the trade are required to exchange the security and the cash. This process is called clearing and it takes place at a clearing agency.

Clearing Rules

Several different regulations require firms to use an SEC approved clearing organization.

NYSE Rule 132

Rule 132 requires every NYSE member becoming a party to a contract to compare and settle through a fully-qualified clearing agency.

AMEX Article X.2

This article in the AMEX constitution requires that every exchange contract include payment and delivery through the National Securities Clearing Corporation or the Options Clearing Corporation.

NASD Schedule D

Part VI, Section 7 of Schedule D requires all NASDAQ market makers within twenty-five miles of a registered clearing agency to clear and settle transactions through such an agency.

MSRB Rule G-12

This rule requires municipal bond brokers and broker/dealers to compare and settle their contracts through a qualified clearing agency.

SEC Rule 15c3-3 Customer Protection Rule

The client protection rule defines the possession and control requirements and the need for segregating client assets from assets owned by the firm.

Clearing Process

In today's securities processing environment there is a delay between the trade date and the settlement date. While it varies for different categories of instruments, it is generally three days for equities and listed corporate and municipal bonds, which make up the majority of the transactions in the U.S.

As described elsewhere in this chapter, other instruments also clear in different ways through different clearing corporations, and then settle in different ways.

One of the most efficient ways of clearing is through netting.

Netting

In order to reduce the cost associated with trade processing, brokers use a technique called netting. Netting is a process of bringing together all of the trades or transactions made by the netting system's participants. The system uses all of a participant's purchases and sales for a specific security to offset each other, thereby creating a single net debit or net credit position at the end of the day for cash as well as for each security for each participant.

Firms that are participants of a common clearing agency can use the system provided by that agency to net all of their trades with each other throughout the trading day and can reduce these transactions to a single net amount for each security and for cash at the end of the day. Clearing netting can be either bilateral or multilateral.

Bilateral Netting (Daily Netting)

In bilateral netting, each broker nets all of their trades with each of the other counterparties. This process is more effective than the trade-for-trade process, but not as efficient as multilateral netting.

Multilateral Netting

In multilateral netting, all of each brokers' trades with each of the other brokers are simultaneously netted, and each broker ends the day with a single dollar position and a single net position for each security. This is the primary netting process used in the U.S. today.

In addition to netting, trades can be settled on a trade-by-trade basis. The trade-for-trade process is the original form of trade settlement. Each trade is individually matched to its counterpart, where each purchase is matched to a single sale and each sale is matched to a single purchase. This process is very volume sensitive.

While brokers in the U.S. normally net their trades with each other through the clearing agencies, they can settle individual trades if they wish.

Continuous Net Settlement

While there are several methods of netting that can be used in clearing, the most popular form used in the U.S. is a multilateral netting process. The multilateral netting process offered by the National Securities Clearing Corporation for equities, corporate bonds and municipal bonds is called Continuous Net Settlement (CNS).

In CNS, the brokers' positions are calculated and monitored continuously throughout the day by the NSCC and at the end of the day only the net amounts due from or to each broker are settled. This greatly reduces the number of individual transactions that have to be traced by the brokers, and thereby reduces the cost of trading. CNS is discussed in more detail later in this chapter.

All of the clearing corporations are owned by their members and, within the rules established by the clearing organization, process transactions for their members as efficiently as possible. The major functions of a clearing organization are:

- Trade recording and processing
- Clearance processing
- Interface to the settlement agency
- Dividend, interest and corporate actions support

The major clearing organizations in the U.S. are discussed in the following pages.

National Securities Clearing Corporation [73]

One of the cornerstone entities in the U.S.'s securities processing infrastructure is the National Securities Clearing Corporation (NSCC). The organizations that were to become the NSCC were formed in the 1960's when it separated from the DTC to concentrate on clearing for brokers. In 1999, the NSCC and DTC recombined within the Depository Trust & Clearing Corporation (DTCC) in order to achieve synergies and reduce costs.

In 2003, the NSCC processed 18 million trades per day with an average daily value of $324 billion for the following eligible securities:

- NYSE and AMEX equities and corporate bonds
- NASDAQ and over-the-counter equities
- Over-the-counter corporate bonds
- American Depository Receipts (ADRs)
- Municipal bonds
- Unit Investment Trusts (UITs)
- Mutual Funds
- Index warrants
- Country funds and other closed end funds

The NSCC, which is broker-owned, helps brokers clear their trades among

---

[73]   Source: National Securities Clearing Corporation

themselves. NSCC provides centralized clearance, settlement and information services to broker/dealers, mutual funds, banks and insurance companies.

The NSCC's primary processes are:

Trade Capture/Reporting

Trade records for NSCC member firms can be submitted to NSCC for matching, netting and settlement either at the point of execution or after the trade has been executed.

Trade Matching

The NSCC trade matching process matches the trade submission of buying firms with the corresponding trade submission of the selling firms. Trades are matched based on the following criteria:

- Trade date, settlement date and place of settlement
- The security traded
- Buy or sell
- The quantity of securities traded
- The trade execution price
- The contra broker
- Accrued Interest for fixed income securities

Matched trades are forwarded to the NSCC Settlement System. Unmatched trade records, or Uncompared Trades, are returned to the originating brokerage firms for reconciliation.

Trade Netting

Trade Netting is performed by the NSCC's CNS System, which nets each member firm's buy and sell activity for each security traded in order to establish one net settlement quantity at the end of the day.

Trade Settlement

The NSCC's Continuous Net Settlement System (CNS) is used for security and trade-related money settlements. The NSCC's Trade Netting and Settlement processing can reduce the number of share and money settlements by up to 95%.

Trade Guarantee

The NSCC provides its members with a guarantee that all trades will be settled once they are accepted by the NSCC system as a compared trade. This guarantee ensures that if one party to a compared trade becomes insolvent, and therefore is unable to meet its obligation to settle the trade, the other party is compensated.

Stock and Bond Clearing

Comparison Process

The actual comparison of trades involves a significant amount of information that is transferred back and forth between the exchanges and the NSCC. Orders are transmitted by the exchanges on trade date, with the details reported to the NSCC no later than 2 a.m. on T+1.

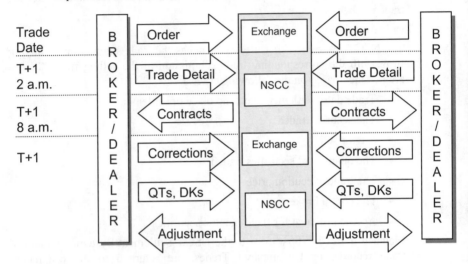

Figure 116 - NSCC Comparison Process

As shown in the previous diagram, by 8:00 a.m. on the morning of T+1, the contracts are created and reported back to the brokers. If the brokers have any corrections, questionable trades, or DK's (Don't Knows), they must notify the NSCC on T+2 so that adjustments can be made promptly, and trades can be settled efficiently on T+3.

The NYSE and AMEX have developed their own trade comparison applications and do not use the NSCC's system.

Continuous Net Settlement (CNS)

The Continuous Net Settlement (CNS) System is an automated book-entry accounting system that centralizes the settlement of compared security transactions and maintains an orderly flow of security and money balances. CNS provides clearance for equities, corporate bonds, Unit Investment Trusts and municipal bonds that are eligible at the DTC.

With CNS, the clearance process is based upon multilateral netting, and is processed throughout the day so that at any point in time the process can identify each broker's net position on each security traded.

This is the primary method used to clear brokers' trades through the NSCC. In the CNS process every transaction for every broker for each security is recorded, and the net change for each broker for each compared trade is continuously calculated.

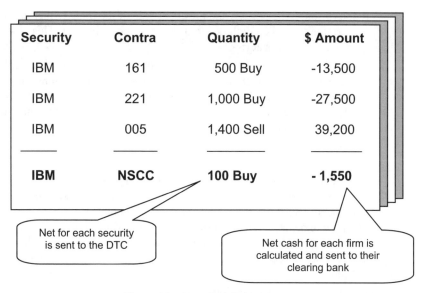

Security	Contra	Quantity	$ Amount
IBM	161	500 Buy	-13,500
IBM	221	1,000 Buy	-27,500
IBM	005	1,400 Sell	39,200
IBM	**NSCC**	**100 Buy**	**- 1,550**

Net for each security is sent to the DTC

Net cash for each firm is calculated and sent to their clearing bank

Figure 117 - How CNS Works

In the previous example, every transaction in IBM made during the day by every broker participant is recorded. The purchases and the sales are netted so that at the end of the day the broker has a net change in their securities position for a specific security (e.g., IBM) and a net amount due. The net change in the position is reported to the DTC, which makes the appropriate entries, and the net amount due, either a credit or a debit, is transmitted to the broker's bank and the appropriate cash transfers are made.

As the following chart indicates, trade details are entered into the NSCC's computers on trade date. On trade date plus one (T+1) the regular way contract sheets are created, and uncompared trades and errors are identified.

Trade Date	Enter trade details to NSCC
Trade + 1	Regular Way Contract sheets
	Compared Trades
	Uncompared Trades
	Advisory Trades
Trade + 2	Last day to reconcile trades for regular T+3 settlement
	Preparation for CNS
	Identify what will settle on T+3
Trade + 3	Exchange of securities for cash

Figure 118 - CNS Processing Flow

On T+ 2 any errors are corrected and the participants are notified that unless the NSCC is otherwise instructed, the trades will clear on T+3.

The NSCC settlement flow is similar to the DTC's settlement process that will be discussed later in this chapter and is also based on a three-day process. It is important to reiterate that the settlement of the street-side of the trade (through the NSCC) and the client-side of the trade (either at the broker or through the DTC) both occur at the same point in time. This is so that no party to the trade is at risk.

The NSCC has also established a form of self-insurance, called the Clearance Fund, which is used by the brokers participating in the CNS process. If a trade is properly compared, it is guaranteed by the NSCC to settle in the event of a participant's failure. This means that when a trade has been properly compared the NSCC becomes the contra-party to the buyer and to the seller.

Correspondent Clearing Service

The Correspondent Clearing Service is a trade-reporting service that processes equity and corporate bond transactions executed by NSCC members (Special Representatives) on behalf of other participants (Correspondents). The correspondent clearing process transfers the settlement obligations to correspondents, which eliminates the need for redeliveries and decreases the number of possible errors in accounting and settlement.

OTC Comparison Processing

The Over-the-Counter (OTC) Comparison service accepts one-sided transactions from NSCC participants and matches buyers and sellers based upon the clearing firm, executing market participant ID, CUSIP or trading symbol, share quantity, price and trade date. Once a match is established the trade is recorded and a contract is forwarded to the participants confirming the comparison. For DTC eligible securities, the trade data is also forwarded to NSCC's CNS system for settlement as well as its risk management systems for risk control.

Transactions that do not result in a match during the NSCC comparison process are also reported to participants on the night the trade was submitted. Participants can continue to try to establish a match by resubmitting the trade to the NSCC comparison process the following day directly or through the facilities of NASDAQ's Automated Confirmation Transaction (ACT) system.

The OTC comparison application accepts one-sided trade data at the end of each business day. The service then searches for a match for each submission based on a number of match criteria:

- M1 - All terms on the contract agree (exact match)

- M2 - All terms agree except trade quantity (summarized match)

- M3 - All terms agree except quantity and two executing brokers (summarized two-way match)

OTC Trade Processing

The Over-the-Counter Trade Capture and Reporting Service is a reporting service that processes domestic and foreign equity transactions executed in the NASDAQ Stock Market and by Qualified Service Representatives (QSRs). A QSR is a broker/dealer who operates an automated execution system or clears for a firm that operates an automated trading system and submits locked-in transactions on behalf of itself and other broker/dealers. A QSR must be on one side of every transaction submitted to NSCC and must adhere to NSCC's QSR rules and regulations. Over-the-Counter trade data is validated and then reported to participants on contract output files for reconciliation purposes. For securities eligible at the depository, trade data is forwarded to NSCC's Continuous Net Settlement application for settlement as well as to the risk management systems for risk control.

The Over-the-Counter Trade Capture and Reporting application accepts trade data in real-time or on a multi-batch basis. The service then validates various trade data elements and reports the trade details to NSCC participants on an intra-day and end-of-day basis. The intra-day output was created in a universal format so that all trade data is reported to participants using virtually the same record layout across all domestic marketplaces.

PC Web Direct

PC Web Direct is a browser-based data-entry and communications application that allows users direct access to some NSCC services, including:

- Automated Client Account Transfer Service (ACATS)
- Continuous Net Settlement (CNS) System
- Reconfirmation and Repricing Service (RECAPS)

Prime Broker

A prime broker transaction occurs when one party (the executing broker) executes a trade on behalf of an institutional client who directs that the trade be forwarded to another party (the prime broker) for clearance and settlement. These transactions are affirmed in DTC's system and settle at DTC. With the DTC/CNS Interface option, these transactions can net in CNS, simplifying trade processing and reducing risk to both parties.

Real-Time Trade Matching (RTTM)

NSCC members can use RTTM to match Corporate and Municipal Debt Securities and Unit Investment Trust (CMU) trades. RTTM is managed by the FICC, but the clearing and settlement of CMUs remain with the NSCC.

RTTM was first used for U.S. Government securities in 2000, and was later adapted for mortgage-backed securities in 2002. Today, about 97% of all U.S. government securities trades representing an average of about $1.8 trillion daily are now submitted in real-time, while about 74% of mortgage-backed securities trades representing an average daily value of $211 billion are submitted in real time.

As of 2004, 250 firms also are submitting corporate and municipal bond and UIT transactions to FICC's RTTM service, with an average daily value of approximately $13 billion.

Regional Exchange Trade Processing

The Regional trade Interface Operations (RIO) Trade Capture and Reporting Service is a service that processes domestic equity and corporate bond transactions from the regional markets and exercises any assigned options and expired single stock futures from the Options Clearing Corporations

(OCC). The RIO application also accepts Prime Broker transaction data from Omgeo's TradeSuite application.

Trades received from the regional marketplaces are locked-in. Once received, the trade data is validated and reported to participants for reconciliation purposes. For DTC eligible securities, the trade data is also forwarded to NSCC's CNS system for settlement as well as its risk management systems for risk control.

The RIO Trade Capture and Reporting application accepts trade data on a multi-batch basis. The service then validates various trade data elements and reports the trade details to NSCC participants on an intra-day and end-of-day basis. The intra-day output was created in a universal format so that all trade data is reported to participants using virtually the same record layout across all domestic marketplaces.

TradeSuite/CNS Interface for Prime Broker Business

The TradeSuite/CNS Interface for Prime Brokers is a settlement option that connects CNS with Omgeo's TradeSuite System.

A Prime Broker transaction occurs when a trade is executed by one party (the Executing Broker) on behalf of an institutional client who directs that the trade be forwarded to another party (the Prime Broker) for clearance and settlement. These transactions are affirmed in Omgeo's TradeSuite system and settle via DTC's PDQ service. With the TradeSuite/CNS Interface option, these transactions can net in CNS, simplifying trade processing and reducing risk to both parties.

The TradeSuite/CNS Interface allows the executing broker to continue to process Prime Broker transactions as usual in Omgeo's TradeSuite system, up to noon of T+2 (SD-1). Trades are affirmed in the TradeSuite system and then forwarded to NSCC's CNS System. Once in CNS, these transactions are netted with each broker's other trades, to produce one position per broker for each security.

Each day, Omgeo provides participants with an Eligible Trade Report of affirmed transactions. Those transactions, which are eligible for the TradeSuite/CNS Interface, are marked on the report with a special indicator, PB/CNS. These transactions are recorded by NSCC on its regional interface operations (RIO) blotters.

Early on the morning of T+2, participants receive a Cumulative Eligible Trade Report from Omgeo showing all transactions affirmed between T and noon of T+2, and forwarded to CNS for settlement on T+3.

Participants also receive a CNS Consolidated Trade Summary Report from NSCC, in which transactions forwarded from DTC carry the TradeSuite notation in the "Market of Execution" field.

Prime Brokers participating in the TradeSuite/CNS Interface can reconcile the client and street-sides of each trade by using Cumulative Eligible Trades Report and NSCC's Consolidated Trade Summary Report.

Mutual Funds

Mutual Funds Services - Fund/SERV

The NSCC's comparison process also supports mutual funds. Through the NSCC's Fund/SERV system brokers can communicate electronically with the mutual fund processors.

The process works very much like the Continuous Net Settlement system in that the NSCC keeps track of the net position throughout the day and settles only the net at the end of the day.

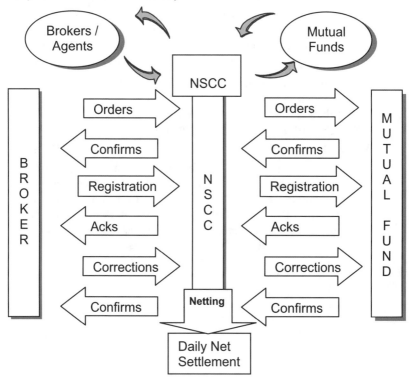

Figure 119 - Fund/SERV Processing

Mutual Funds Services - ACATS-Fund/SERV Interface

The ACATS-Fund/SERV Interface is a system that links NSCC's Automated Client Account Transfer Service (ACATS) and the Fund/SERV system.

- ACATS automates and standardizes procedures for the transfer of assets in a client account from one brokerage firm to another, which expedites the transfer process.

- Fund/SERV is an automated central processing system that standardizes mutual fund order entry and account recording procedures, which reduces the time and cost of processing transactions.

The ACATS-Fund/SERV Interface allows mutual funds to electronically update their account registrations when a client account is transferred from one broker to another.

Mutual Funds Services - Commission Settlement and Global Update Service

The Commission Settlement and Global Update Service is an automated system that facilitates the exchange of mutual fund commission-related information between brokers and funds, and centralizes the commission payments into NSCC's settlement system. With this service brokers can also provide mutual funds with global and individual update information that affects single as well as multiple accounts, e.g., when there is a change in the branch address, branch number, or account executive information.

Mutual Funds Services - Defined Contribution Clearance & Settlement

Defined Contribution Clearance & Settlement is a new service that standardizes, centralizes and automates the processing of Defined Contribution mutual fund transactions. This service uses the capabilities of NSCC's existing Fund/SERV, Networking and Mutual Fund Profile systems.

Mutual Funds Services - Mutual Fund Profile Service (MFPS)

The Mutual Fund Profile Service is an automated, centralized system that has been created to improve the flow of mutual fund information among NSCC participants. The service also enables them to exchange accurate and timely information on daily prices and dividend rates, firm and fund members, individual security identifications, processing capabilities, and projected and actual distribution declarations.

Mutual Funds Services - Networking

Networking is the NSCC's process for mutual fund client account maintenance and reporting. The automated record keeping system ensures that non-trade related client information will appear identically on the records of the firm and the fund or its transfer agent.

Networking, shown below, supports:

- Dividend information
- Net settlement information
- Registrations
- Account maintenance
- Year-end reporting

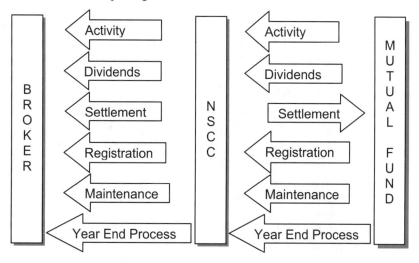

Figure 120 - NSCC Networking

Mutual Funds Services - Retirement Asset Transfer

The Retirement Asset Transfer capability is part of the Fund/SERV system and enables two mutual fund companies to initiate, acknowledge, confirm and settle the transfer of the value of mutual fund shares held in Individual Retirement Accounts (IRAs) in a centralized, standardized and automated fashion.

Mutual Funds Services - Annuity Processing Service (APS)

The Annuity Processing Service is an automated, centralized processing system that links insurance carriers with broker/dealers, banks and/or their affiliated insurance agencies that sell annuities.

Insurance

Due to the growth of the annuity market in the mid-1990s, DTCC introduced Insurance Services, which provides a suite of services that streamline the sale, servicing, and back office processing of fixed and variable annuities and life insurance

Annuity Processing Service (APS)

The Annuity Processing Service, which is designed to support the insurance industry, is an automated, centralized and standardized system that links insurance carriers with broker/dealers at various points throughout the annuity and life insurance processing cycle.

APS enables the broker/dealers to process initial applications, initial premiums, subsequent and add-on premiums and financial activity reporting for annuities.

Insurance Processing System (IPS)

As the central source for the exchange of information, DTCC combines transaction details for a specific carrier or distributor in one file and creates daily reports of all transactions submitted.

Applications & Subsequent Premiums (APP / SUB)

Applications (APP) & Subsequent Premiums (SUB) transmit annuity application and premium information from distributors to insurance carriers. They validate, format and submit applications while incorporating same-day money settlement.

Licensing & Appointments (L&A)

Licensing & Appointments automates the bilateral flow of the information that is needed to manage producer information between insurance carriers and distributors. It also provides for money settlement between parties.

Financial Activity Reporting (FAR)

Financial Activity Reporting enables insurance carriers to provide their distributors with the annuity and life insurance financial transaction information they need to help comply with the anti-money laundering provisions of the USA PATRIOT Act and general suitability regulations.

Commissions (COM)

The Commissions application transmits information regarding commissions and compensation from insurance carriers to distributors for annuity and life insurance products. It also provides same-day money settlement.

Positions & Valuations (POV)

Positions & Valuations enables insurance carriers to send annuity and life insurance contract details to their distributors on a daily, weekly, monthly or other custom basis.

Asset Pricing (AAP)

Asset Pricing enables insurance carriers to transmit the unit values for funds within annuity and life insurance products to distributors on a daily basis.

Derivative Clearing

DERIV/SERV

DTCC's Deriv/SERV is a post-trade processing matching service for credit default swaps. It automates, standardizes and brings greater certainty to this rapidly growing market. Using DTCC's existing mainframe-to-mainframe connections, Deriv/SERV's processes are conducted in real-time, are highly automated, and identify errors for correction immediately. A front-end Web interface is available for trade comparison input, online research, or management reporting.

DTCC's service is integrated with Mark-It Partners' reference entity data (RED) service and uses their data in the trade confirmation process. DTCC has thirteen of the largest dealers in credit default swaps worldwide signed on to use the service to confirm trades.

Other Services

Archival Microfiche Service

The Archival Microfiche Service provides microfiche of each firm's daily processing activity on the Automated Client Transfer Service, Continuous Net Settlement (CNS) Service, and non-CNS settlement and equity/fixed income trade comparison services.

Automated Client Account Transfer Service (ACATS)

The Automated Client Account Transfer Service (ACATS) is a system that automates and standardizes the procedures used to transfer the assets in a client account from one brokerage firm to another. Instruments handled by the system include equities, corporate and municipal bonds, unit investment trusts, mutual funds, options, cash and other investment products.

In 2003, 6.6 million accounts were transferred through ACATS, containing more than 27 million individual assets worth an estimated $345.3 billion.

Canadian Depository for Securities Link (CDS)

The Canadian Depository for Securities Link provides book-entry clearance and settlement, including custodial and institutional settlement services, to Canadian participants that trade equities and corporate bonds with U.S. participants. The CDS Link has two primary components:

- The CDS Link allows members of the Canadian Depository for Securities to use NSCC's Correspondent Clearing Service, which streamlines the processing of trades executed by one participant on behalf of another.

- The CDS Link provides CDS members access to the DTC's custodial and institutional clearance and settlement services.

Through the CDS Link, U.S. participants execute and submit trades into Correspondent Clearing on behalf of Canadian participants. The NSCC member that executes the trade is called the Special Representative, and the CDS member for whom this trade is executed is called the Correspondent.

For institutional trading activity, the CDS Link provides Canadian participants access to DTC's systems, which compare the details of trades executed for institutional investors. After these trades are reported as compared, the system routes them to an automatic book-entry settlement facility at DTC.

Commission Billing for Listed Equities Service

Commission Billing for Listed Equities Service provides an automated facility for the debiting and crediting of commissions for NSCC settling members and non-clearing members. Non-clearing firms, often referred to as commission bill firms, include the specialists and the $2 brokers who trade on the New York and American Stock Exchanges, but are not NSCC members.

Fully Paid For Account

The Fully Paid For Account is a special sub-account within CNS that assists participants in maintaining compliance with the possession and control requirements of Rule 15c3-3. The account allows participants to complete the settlement of their obligations based on anticipated activity within CNS, and third-party deliveries for credit through the Depository Trust Company's systems.

The account is available for CNS-eligible equities, corporate bonds, unit investment trusts, rights and warrants. Municipal bonds are not eligible.

DTCC's Money Settlement System (MSS)

The Money Settlement System is designed to electronically move a participant's funds in the fastest, easiest way possible.　Used by broker/dealers, banks and mutual fund companies, MSS handles billions of dollars every day, and eliminates manual processing often associated with cash management.

The process provides that:

- Payment obligations to and from each party are aggregated
- Separate standardized detailed reports are provided
- A final money settlement report that summarizes all payments and receipts obligations is available to each participant every day.　This report defines each participant's net end-of-day settlement obligation.

At the end of the business day

- Participants that are owed money receive a payment in their bank from DTCC over the Fedwire
- Participants that owe money can move their payment from their bank to the DTCC

Stock Borrow Program

The stock borrow program allows participants to lend NSCC available stocks and corporate bonds from their accounts at the DTC to cover temporary shortfalls in CNS. NSCC credits members' money settlement accounts with the full market value of securities borrowed, and members can earn overnight interest on that value by investing the funds.

Dividend Settlement Service

Dividend Settlement Service (DSS) is a centralized claims-processing system that manages the collection of dividends and interest owed to participants by other financial institutions. DSS enables users to claim funds due them by charging other DSS participants through NSCC's clearance and settlement system.

Funds Only Settlement Service

Funds Only Settlement Service (FOSS) is a system that centralizes the routing of envelopes that contain money-only charges to full-service participants located in New York City and Jersey City. Although it can also be used for other money-only charges, FOSS is used primarily for debits and credits that result from mark-to-market adjustments.

Envelope Settlement Service

Envelope Settlement Service (ESS) standardizes and controls participant-to-participant physical delivery of securities in New York City and Jersey City. The Intercity Envelope Settlement Service (IESS) standardizes and controls participant-to-participant physical delivery of securities between New York City and NSCC branch cities.

National Transfer Service

National Transfer Service (NTS) is used primarily by broker/dealers for the transfer and subsequent re-registration of securities that are not eligible at the Depository Trust Company. In addition to handling items that result from the trading cycle, NTS also delivers book-closing items and legal transfers overnight.

New York Window

The New York Window is an industry-driven platform of services that performs various operational activities, including clearance and settlement of book-entry and physical securities transactions, for brokers, dealers, custodian banks and other financial institutions. NSCC established the common processing facility in 1993 to help its participants centralize processing, reduce risk and effect savings associated with a variable rather than a fixed cost structure.

The New York Window acts as an extension of its participants' process by managing their varied securities operations. The Window today features support for:

- Equities
- Municipal and corporate bonds
- Government securities
- Mortgage backed securities
- Money market instruments, including medium-term notes, certificates of deposit and commercial paper
- Private placements
- Legal/restricted items

Fixed Income Clearing Corporation (FICC)

The Fixed Income Clearing Corporation (FICC) was formed by the January 1, 2003 merger of the Government Securities Division (GSD) and the MBS Clearing Corporation (MBSCC) to improve their common focus on processing Fixed Income securities.

FICC consists of two divisions, which each offer their own product-specific services to their own members, along with separate rules and a separate collateral margin pool for:

- Mortgage backed Securities Division
- Government Securities Division

Each of these divisions is discussed in greater detail in the next two sections of this chapter.

Mortgage Backed Securities Division (MBSD)

The Mortgage Backed Securities Division, a division of FICC, helps brokers clear mortgage backed securities (MBS) that are issued by GNMA, FNMA and FHLMC. The purpose of the organization is to aid in settlement and decrease the processing risk for mortgage backed securities. MBSD has 76 clearing members and processed $67 Trillion in 2003.

Volumes in 2003 were:

- Total Clearing Par $66,986,422,101,836.90
- EPN Current Face $11,655,107,521,109.00

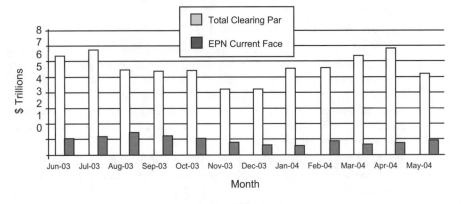

Figure 121 - MBS Volumes

Mortgage backed securities are bought and sold in the over-the-counter cash, forward and options markets. The key participants in these markets are mortgage originators, government sponsored enterprises, registered broker/dealers, inter-dealer brokers, institutional investors, investment managers, mutual funds, commercial banks, insurance companies and other financial institutions.

More information about how mortgage backed securities work is available in the SOF eLearning course on Fixed Income Instruments; however, it should be noted at this point that there are several special characteristics of this type of instrument that make them difficult to settle.

- Mortgage backed securities only settle monthly and the actual amount of a trade is usually not fixed until just before settlement.
- The value of a MBS security is based upon the market's interest rates and the time to settle is so long that there is a significant risk of price fluctuations between the time of the trade and the settlement. To

accommodate this, the process allows the seller to adjust the price of the security slightly to within 98 % - 102 % of the original trade.

- The settlement amount consists of a partial return of principal along with accrued interest.

The Mortgage Backed Securities Division operates two primary business units:

- Clearing services, which include trade comparison, matching, confirmation, netting, and risk management
- Electronic Pool Notification (EPN) services, which allow clients to transmit/retrieve mortgage backed securities pool information in real time using standardized message formats

The rules for the MBSD are available at:

http://www.ficc.com/mbs/docs/rules/mbsd.clearing.rules.pdf

MBSD Eligible Securities

The following securities are eligible for processing by the MBSD:

- All security types issued by GNMA, including all MBSs, REMICs and Platinum issues
- All REMIC securities issued by the Veteran's Administration after 6/25/92
- Certain REMIC securities issued by the FHLMC and FNMA

MBSD Services

The MBS Division provides the following services:

- Comparison
- Clearing
- Real Time Trade Matching (RTTM)
- Electronic Pool Notification

These four services are discussed on the following pages.

MBSD Comparison

Currently, FICC's Mortgage-Backed Securities Division (MBSD) conducts trade-by-trade comparisons and does not operate as a Central Counterparty (CCP), which involves stepping between trading parties and guaranteeing each side of the trade. This is different from the Government Securities Division (GSD), which does provide CCP services.

MBSD is proposing a model that would essentially create a unified CCP structure for both MBSD and GSD by leveraging FICC's existing CCP system for U.S. Government securities.

Comparison can also be performed by vendors, such as SunGard and the compared information presented to the RRTM.

MBSD Clearing Services

MBSD has two different systems for its members' clearing and confirmation requirements: a dealer-to-dealer comparison system and a broker/dealer system.

- In the dealer-to-dealer comparison system, both the selling and purchasing parties submit trade terms as principals.

- The broker/dealer system is a three-sided trade input system designed to compare inter-dealer broker trades when one of the brokers is acting for another broker.

Clearing services are intended for all brokers, dealers and institutions dealing with MBS instruments. User firms that act as a principal to the underlying trade maintain direct accounts, while omnibus users process information on behalf of others in a fully disclosed capacity. Omnibus users are typically investment managers and correspondent clearing organizations.

Participants can use several different clearing service functions, including:

- A centralized automated process to compare, match and confirm trades electronically

- Critical risk management activities to minimize financial exposure and promote safety

- Early notification of potential trade breaks

- A netting capability to reduce the overall number of receive/deliver obligations

- A sophisticated accounting system to reconcile delivery variances resulting from netting obligations

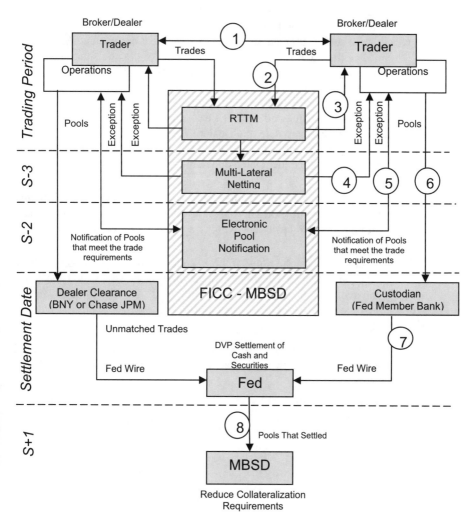

Figure 122 - MBS Clearing and Settlement at the Fed

1. MBS trading is conducted by telephone contact between buyers and
    sellers, and increasingly through the use of an ATS such as TradeWeb.
    TradeWeb connects fixed income dealers to each other and to
    institutional investors in the US and Europe.
2. Trades are then sent by the trader's internal system to RTTM, or if they
    use TradeWeb, it will send information to the trader's systems and to
    RTTM.
3. RTTM will compare the trade input and match the trades. Exceptions
    are reported back to the trading firms for resolution up to S-3.
4. On S-3, the trades are netted through the MBSD's netting application
    and exceptions are reported to the broker's settlement operations areas.
5. The trading firms who have access to the EPN systems can use it to
    notify their counterparties about the pools that they will use to meet the

trade obligations. These pools must meet the Bond Market Association's Good Delivery criteria.

6. Prior to settlement date, the broker's settlement department should notify either their Prime Dealer or custodian of the pools that will settle. If a custodian is used, they will contact their Prime Dealer, since only Prime Dealers have access to the FedWire system.

7. The Prime Dealers will transmit the trades to the Fed on settlement date. The Fed will match and settle the cash and securities side of the trade.

8. After the settlement date, the Dealer Clearing Agent notifies the broker, and the broker notifies the MBSD of the pools that settled and the MBSD can reduce the related collateralization requirements for the participants.

This chart presented the flow if one trader is a broker and settles through a Dealer Clearance Agent (normally BNY or JPMChase), and the counterparty settles through a bank custodian who is a member of the Federal Reserve System.

The next chart shows the flow if both counterparties are brokers settling through the same Dealer Clearance Agent, that agent will match the trades locally and avoid sending the transaction to the Fed. This has three advantages for the brokers:

- They avoid the incremental Fed fees for settlement

- The firm's daylight overdraft's at the Fed are calculated based upon their balances, and since these transactions do not go to the Fed the balances are lower.

- The DCAs can also act as agents for tri-party repos which are used for financing

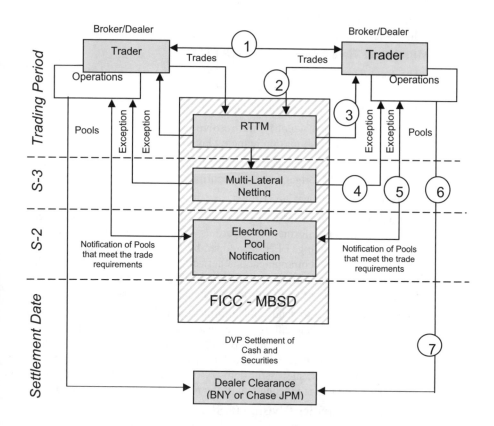

Figure 123 - MBS Clearing and Settlement at a Dealer Clearance Agent

MBSD Clearing Methodologies

MBSD has two different methodologies for its members' clearing and confirmation requirements: a dealer-to-dealer comparison system and a broker/dealer system.

- In the dealer-to-dealer comparison system, both the selling and purchasing parties submit trade terms as principals on a trade by trade basis.

- The broker/dealer system, called the Settlement Balance Order (SBO) is a three-sided trade input system designed to compare inter-dealer broker trades when one of the brokers is acting for another broker.

The majority of trades are entered into the SBO system. Trades, either net buys or sells, which cannot be paired-off, become SBO settlement obligations. Historically, the SBO process has eliminated the need to settle more than 90% of all trades submitted for netting.

At this time, the MBSD does not act as a central counterparty to the trades, as does the NSCC and the GSD. While the MBSD would like to perform this service, there are a large number of differences involved with MBS settlements that are not identified until after the settlement. A central counterparty would have difficulty dealing with this large number of small differences.

MBSD Real Time Trade Matching (RTTM)

The Real Time Trade Matching (RTTM) service was implemented in 2002 and replaced the previous twice-daily match process.

There are two key features of RTTM:

- Participants can identify and resolve trade execution differences within minutes after submission reducing both execution and market risk
- The processes between the Government securities (which also use RTTM) and Mortgage backed securities markets are standardized

Electronic Pool Notification (EPN)

The MBSD also provides an Electronic Pool Notification system that can be used to transfer information regarding the mortgage backed pools the participants are trading. EPN, developed by MBSCC in the early 1990's, is a real-time electronic communications network that allows buyers and sellers to transmit MBS pool information quickly, efficiently and reliably. Before EPN, firms relied on phones and faxes to exchange this information.

EPN users are able to send pool information and deliver the information on time, even if the recipient is not logged onto EPN. In the phone and fax environment, billions of dollars in fails occurred because of the recipient's inaccessibility, phone and fax problems, and staffing limitations. Since the introduction of EPN, successful delivery of a message is denoted by the EPN time-stamp and this is independent of the recipient's retrieval of the message.

Government Securities Division (GSD)

The Government Securities Division, a division of the FICC, clears, nets, settles and manages the risk arising from a broad range of U.S. Government securities transactions for its 125 netting member firms (brokers, dealers, banks and other financial institutions) and hundreds of correspondent firms that clear through these members.

These transactions include:

- Original auction purchases of Treasury and Freddie Mac securities
- Buy/sell and repo transactions in Treasury and Government Agency securities
- GCF Repo (General Collateral Finance Repurchase Agreements) transactions in Treasury and Government Agency securities
- Certain mortgage backed securities

GSD rules are available at http://www.ficc.com/gov/docs/rules/gsd.rules.pdf

GSD Eligible Securities

The term "Eligible Security" means a security issued or guaranteed by:

- United States
- U.S. government agency or instrumentality
- U.S. government-sponsored corporation

- Any other security approved by the Membership and Risk Management Committee

A GCF Repo Security shall be deemed to be an Eligible Security only in connection with a GCF Repo Transaction.

An Eligible Treasury Security is an unmatured, marketable debt security in book-entry form that is a direct obligation of the United States Government.

Volumes in 2003 were:

- Total Value Compared $527,987,312,759,896.00
- Total Value Settled $168,984,978,437,462.00

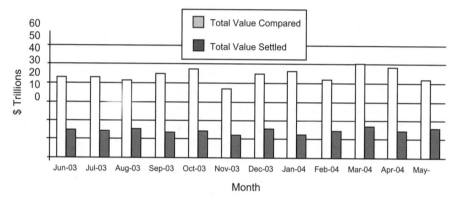

Figure 124 - Government Securities Volumes

GSD Services

GSD's basic service, Real Time Trade Matching (RTTM), includes:

- Comparison and netting of Treasury bills, notes, bonds, and zero-coupon securities
- Book-entry non-mortgage backed agency securities

GSD's clearance processing is divided into several areas, including:

- Trade Comparison
- Netting and Settlement
- Repurchase Agreements
- GCF Repurchase Agreements
- Auction Takedown
- Risk Management
- Cross-Margining

Each of these areas is discussed on the following pages.

GSD Processing - Trade Comparison Service

In order to use the Trade Comparison service, a company must become a comparison participant of GSD. Comparison participants of GSD who meet the criteria for netting membership may also become netting members.

The system involves an online, real time comparison system that monitors each trade throughout the day and nets positions. While on an average day in 2003 approximately $2.1 trillion is traded, only about $400 billion (20%) actually changes hands because most of the value is processed via the netting system.

The comparison system automatically matches the buy and sell sides of a cash transaction, or both sides of a repo. The real time comparison system provides immediate results through a GSD terminal within seconds of trade input, or after end-of-day processing. The outputs include compared and uncompared transactions, as well as advisories, which inform the participants of any trades submitted against them for which they did not make a corresponding submission.

Several vendors such as SunGard also provide a government securities matching service which delivers matched trades to the GSD.

GSD Processing - Netting and Settlement Services

GSD's Netting and Settlement Services provides centralized, automated clearance and guaranteed settlement of eligible U.S. Treasury bills, bonds, notes, strips, and book-entry, non-mortgage backed agency securities.

Through this process, GSD establishes a single net long or short position for each participant's daily trading activity in a given security, including all of their cash buy/sell, repo/reverse, and Treasury auction purchases.

GSD acts as a Central Counterparty and guarantees the settlement of all the trades entering its network by interposing itself between the original trading parties and becomes the legal counterparty for settlement purposes. Settlement is guaranteed when GSD makes netting results available to its participants, usually before 12 a.m. on the morning after transactions are compared. The net of all government securities transactions for each broker is sent to the clearing banks and for cash to either Fedwire or intra-bank.

GSD Processing - Repurchase Agreement Services

GSD also offers electronic comparison and netting services for Repurchase Agreements (repos).

The confirms that are generated by GSD constitute binding and enforceable contracts for compared repo transactions, and GSD provides a settlement guarantee for all netted repo transactions.

As part of its clearing function GSD nets repos along with the buy/sell activity for other government securities and Treasury auction purchases.

GSD Processing - GCF Repurchase Agreements

A General Collateral Financing (GCF) trade is a general collateral repurchase agreement that has been executed on a blind broker basis through the Government Securities Division.

This method of trading allows dealers and agents to trade government issued fixed income securities on a term and rate basis, rather than waiting for settlement on a trade by trade basis. This provides for faster transaction times and greater freedom of trading mobility for participating institutions.

GSD's GCF Repo service supports dealers trading general collateral repos, based on the rate, term, and underlying product, throughout the day without requiring intra-day, trade-for-trade settlement on a delivery versus payment (DVP) basis.

GSD Processing - Treasury Auction Takedown Service

GSD's Treasury Auction Takedown Service reduces the settlement risk and cost for its participants' Federal Reserve auction purchases. The service nets each participant's Treasury auction purchases along with their secondary market trades, thereby reducing securities movements and the associated costs and risk.

GSD Processing - Risk Management

The Government Securities Division provides guaranteed settlement, and to protect itself, it manages risk in several ways, including:

- Guaranteed Settlement
- Forward Margin Procedures
- Clearing Fund
- Loss Allocation Procedures
- Rules and Regulations

GSD Guaranteed Settlement (Central Counterparty)

The Government Securities Division acts as a Central Counterparty to each trade and becomes the legal counterparty to each side. This minimizes the risk to its participants since GSD guarantees settlement of all trades processed by GSD.

GSD Forward Margin Procedures

The GSD's Forward Margin procedures protect participants against potential risk by guaranteeing the settlement of forward transactions at the contract value on their settlement date. Because forward cash trades and repo close legs are guaranteed, the GSD must maintain sufficient funds to meet the settlement obligations if a participant defaults.

Clearing Fund

The GSD's Clearing Fund has been established to ensure that the GSD has sufficient liquidity to guarantee orderly settlement and provide the collateralization required to cover each participant's overall exposure.

The Clearing Fund consists of collateral deposits posted by participants in the form of cash, eligible securities, and letters of credit. Deposit requirements are based on a combination of a participant's recent trading activity and the potential impact historical market fluctuations will have on the participant's overall position in the GSD's netting system.

Loss Allocation Procedures

The Loss Allocation Procedure ensures that a systemic failure of the settlement process never occurs. If a participant becomes insolvent, the GSD would use the participant's Clearing Fund and Margin deposits to liquidate the member's positions.

If an event occurred where those deposits were insufficient to cover the liquidation of all positions, the GSD's Loss Allocation procedure would be used. The procedure allocates any remaining liabilities pro rata among the participants who most recently traded with the failed firm. This minimizes the impact such a situation would have on all Government Securities Division participants.

Rules and Regulations

Rules and Regulations were covered in the chapter on Self-Regulatory Organizations

GSD Processing - Cross-Margining

GSD's Cross-Margining service effectively links the cash for U.S. Treasury securities with related financial futures products to better manage the member's collateral requirements.

GSD and the participating Futures Clearing Organizations (FCO) provide each other with access to any proceeds arising from the liquidation of related positions and the associated collateral in the event of an eligible member's insolvency. Each clearing organization holds and manages its own collateral.

Yield-to-Price Service

GSD's Yield-To-Price Service reduces comparison costs for its participants' When-Issued trades and provides GSD's settlement guarantee before the auction date. When-Issued trades are compared on their submission date based on their yield and commission amounts, which eliminates the need for a second submission when the coupon is announced.

EMCC [74]

The Emerging Markets Clearing Corporation (EMCC), a wholly owned subsidiary of the DTCC and recently added to the FICC organization, provides trade matching, clearance, settlement and risk management services to global dealers, interdealer brokers and correspondent clearing firms involved in emerging market debt instruments.

Established in 1998, EMCC is registered with and regulated by the SEC, and is a clearinghouse recognized by the U.K. Financial Services Authority. EMCC provides automated trade comparison, settlement and risk management of transactions involving Brady Bonds, sovereign debt and related transactions in emerging-market economies. One of the first clearing corporations in the world to guarantee cross-border trading activity, EMCC currently clears trades of securities representing issues from more than 50 countries.

---

[74] Emerging Markets Clearing Corporation

Clearing of Money Market Instruments

Money Market instruments are generally cleared through banks and the interbank payment system. Banks act as agents for their clients when these instruments are issued, and then act as custodians for their clients.

Banks are also involved in the clearing function when they transfer instruments from one party to another, and make the necessary payments on behalf of their clients. To make this process work efficiently, banks open a securities account and a cash account for their money market clearing clients, and then transfer the securities in physical form (or increasingly through the DTC), and then transfer the cash from one bank to another through the interbank payments system.

D. SETTLING STOCKS AND BONDS

Settlement is the final exchange of cash for the securities in the trade. Settlement occurs directly between brokers and their retail client, through the Depository Trust Company (DTC) for institutional clients and for clearing firms utilizing net processing.

The use of DTC is required by a number of different rules, including NYSE Rule 387, AMEX Rule 423, NASD Uniform Practice Code Section 64, and MSRB Rule G-15. These rules require their members to use the Cash on Delivery privilege with the DTC.

Institutional Client Settlement Requirements

To prepare for settlement there are several other post-trade processes that must occur, some of which are different for individual and institutional clients.

In post-trade processing for retail trades, the individual client must have sufficient cash or sufficient margin credit available, and would either:

- Leave securities with the broker
- Deliver to another broker
- Take physical possession of the certificates

However, in institutional post-trade processing the investment manager generally uses a bank custodian to hold their securities rather than leave them with a broker. In addition, institutions often buy a large quantity of a specific security (block) that they then allocate across several accounts. To ensure that each trade is credited to the proper account, most accounts should be identified in a Standing Settlement Instruction (SSI) database.

Each of these three concepts is discussed in this chapter:

- Block Trades
- Allocations
- Standing Settlement Instructions

Block Trades

Investment Managers may initiate a single transaction for a single portfolio, or they may aggregate several small orders for a specific security for multiple portfolios into a single large order for a block of securities to get a better price and reduce purchase costs.

In the example, a broker had to go to three other broker/dealers to assemble the total block of 25,000 shares. If the Investment Manager had placed an order for 25,000 shares as a single order, the price would probably have been higher than the $46.2984 per share because as the perceived demand increases, so does the price. By dividing the total order into smaller orders, the true demand is hidden from the market.

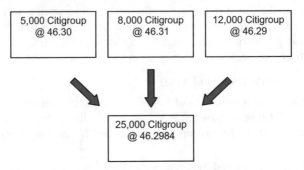

Figure 125 - Block Trade Example

Allocation

A significant percentage of investment managers' trades are blocks, which must be allocated to the appropriate portfolios.

When an investment manager buys a block of securities, those securities are usually allocated over several different portfolios, and the settlement for each portfolio requires a separate confirmation from the broker that identifies the exact account, amount and settlement instructions that are to be followed.

Some portfolio managers identify the allocation when they submit their trades to the traders, and others wait until the broker has filled all or part of the order before they decide upon the exact allocation.

In this example, the block that was acquired is distributed over four different portfolios.

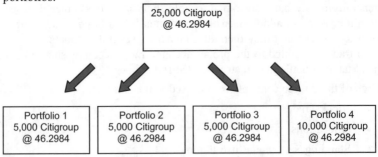

Figure 126 - Allocation Example

Allocation Communication

Originally, allocations were sent manually, often by fax – and some firms are still sending manual allocations. However, investment managers have several different ways of electronically communicating allocation instructions to their brokers, including:

Value Added Networks

- Omgeo products (TradeSuite, OASYS, CTM, etc.)
- SunGard
- FMCNet and FMCNet II

Structured Networks

- Leased or proprietary lines using FIX 4.4
- SwiftNet

Standing Settlement Instructions

Thousands of investment managers may have hundreds of thousands of accounts with hundreds of custodians. Rather than send detailed processing instructions with each transaction, it is more efficient and accurate to have a central file of settlement instructions that can be accessed by all of the participants to the trade.

To meet this need, the industry defined the concept of a Standing Settlement Instruction database (SSI).

An SSI contains the details for an account that are needed to settle a trade. Rather than re-send the same details along with each trade, the SSI can be maintained by the investment manager (or custodian) and then accessed by the broker (or custodian) and the information used to settle the trade.

In the 1990's Thomson Financial had developed an SSI application called ALERT, and DTC subsequently built a similar application called SID (Standing Instruction Database). When Omgeo was formed, it absorbed ALERT and SID and continues to support both of them.

Some Trading Networks have their own built-in SSIs, or are adding them along with support for allocations. For instance, TradeWeb has an SSI called AccountNet.

Settlement Instruction Automation

Managers have two ways of communicating settlement instructions to their brokers:

Standing Settlement Instruction Databases

Several alternative SSIs exist, including:

- SID
- ALERT
- FMCNetII
- SunGard Transaction Network (STN)
- AccountNet

Individual Transactions

Instead of using an SSI, firms can communicate settlement instructions for individual transactions by using other forms of connectivity, including:

- Leased or proprietary lines using FIX 4.4
- SwiftNet
- Fax, or other manual instructions that are sent directly to the broker

Settlement Alternatives

There are five different alternatives for settlement.

Regular Way Settlement

The regular way settlement period is generally three days for exchange listed and NASDAQ equities, and corporate and municipal bonds. The regular way settlement for listed options is one business day, and U.S. government securities and most money market instruments settle on the day of the trade.

Mortgage Backed and Asset Backed securities usually settle once a month on a specific day for each type of security.

Cash Settlement

All securities can be part of a cash trade, which settles on the same day as the trade occurs, usually at 2:00 p.m.

Next Day Settlement

A settlement that occurs on the first business day after the trade is called a next day settlement.

Seller's Option Settlement

Trades that are made as a seller's option can settle on any business day that is selected by the seller.

Buyer's Option Settlement

Trades that are made as a buyer's option can settle on any business day that is selected by the buyer.

Post-Trade Processing Example

In the next pages, we'll walk a trade through from order to settlement and show the relationships between the allocation, confirmation and affirmation processes.

Post-Trade Processing Sequence 1

In this example the investment manager has placed a single large order with a single broker/dealer that must go to additional counterparties in order to fill the client order.

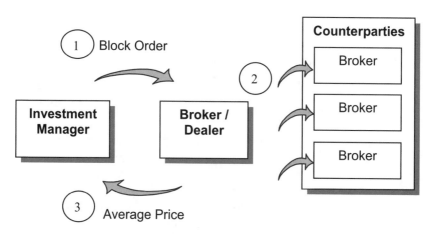

Figure 127 - Block Trading (1)

1. An investment manager submits a block order to a broker/dealer.

2. Since this is a large order, the broker/dealer locates multiple counterparties and concludes portions of the total block with each of them. In this example, three other firms are contacted and become counterparties.

3. After the broker/dealer has filled all or as much of the order as possible, the B/D informs the investment manager of either the average price or each of the actual prices of the block.

Post-Trade Processing Sequence 2

The client's broker will now have to settle each of the street-side trades with each of the counterparty brokers. The brokers each communicate their trade information to the NSCC for clearing, and the net of the transactions is reported to the DTC at the end of the day.

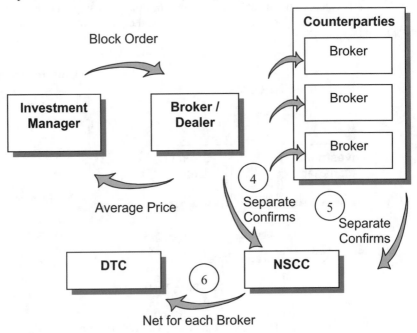

Figure 128 - Block Trading (2)

4. and 5. The separate street-side of the trade involves each of the three broker/dealers submitting a confirm to the NSCC, and a matching confirm is sent from the intermediate broker/dealer. The NSCC matches these confirms and clears the trades.

6. At the end of the trading day, the NSCC will send the net of the trades to the DTC for street-side settlement.

Both sides of the trade should settle on the same day, which is currently three days after the trade for most types of securities. If the trade is a purchase, the intermediary broker receives shares and simultaneously delivers the shares to the custodian acting as the agent for the manager. The intermediary broker receives cash from the custodian and simultaneously sends the cash to the brokers who were the counterparties to their trades.

The NSCC facilitates the street-side of the trade; while the DTC completes the client-side of the trade for institutional clients, and the final settlement of the NSCC's activity for the day.

Post-Trade Processing Sequence 3

At this point, the investment manager must identify how he wants the block spread over various portfolios by sending allocation information to the broker.

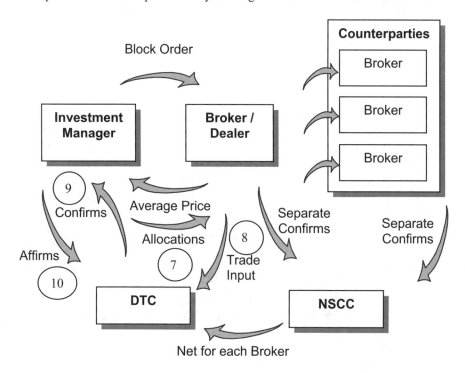

Figure 129 - Block Trade (3)

7. Based upon the amount of the order that was filled, the Investment Manager will determine which accounts should receive how much of the trade. This allocation information is sent to the broker. In the example the manager has identified four portfolios that should be allocated a portion of the trade.

8. Based upon the allocation, the broker notifies the DTC of the four trades.

9. This trade input causes the DTC to create four confirmations that the manager must individually affirm.

10. The manager affirms each of the four confirms and adds the appropriate settlement information.

While the client-side of the trade is being completed, the street-side of the trade, where the broker/dealer dealt with the other three brokers to assemble the trade, also must be completed.

Both sides of the trade should settle on the same day, currently three days after the trade for most types of securities. If the trade is a purchase, the broker receives shares and simultaneously delivers the shares to the custodian acting as the agent for the manager. The broker receives cash from the custodian and sends the cash to the brokers who were the counterparties to their trades.

The NSCC facilitates the street-side of the trade; the DTC completes the client-side of the trade for institutional clients, and the final settlement of the NSCC's activity for the day.

The client-side of these messages is sent through a confirmation/affirmation application, such as Omgeo or another vendor and ultimately to the DTC for settlement.

Omgeo [75]

Omgeo is a joint venture between Thomson Financial and the DTCC. Throughout the 1990's these two firms maneuvered for positioning in the post-trade marketplace. They merged their applications in 2001, primarily to defend against another industry initiative – GSTPA. The GSTPA ultimately failed.

Omgeo brought together two groups of software products:

- DTC's TradeSuite line of products, which included SID and DTC's Institutional Delivery (ID) application
- Thomson Financial ESG's ALERT and OASYS and OASYS Global products

The joint venture focused on merging these two product lines and ultimately creating a new overall methodology, Omgeo Central Trade Manager (Omgeo CTM) which would be needed to support any shortened settlement cycle. Although T+1 was postponed in 2001 by the industry, work on Omgeo CTM continued and it is now available to improve affirmation rates and reduce fails on global trades.

Omgeo Services

Omgeo's products and other post trade products are organized into two categories (Information Services and Transaction Services) and are described in the following pages.

Omgeo Information Services

Omgeo Information Services centralize standard account, market and settlement information that can be accessed by its users and used to enrich trade communications. Omgeo's Information Services are shared global databases for the maintenance and communication of standing settlement and account instructions (SSI). The services include:

- Omgeo ALERT
- Omgeo SID
- Omgeo ALERT-SID

Omgeo ALERT

Omgeo ALERT is a global database that helps users maintain and communicate standing settlement and account instructions (SSI). ALERT

---

[75] Source: Omgeo

reduces trade failures by enabling investment managers, broker/dealers and custodian banks to share accurate SSI automatically worldwide.

ALERT provides the following functionality:

- Ensures complete, automated communication of account and settlement instructions between counterparties using standardized formats
- Automated enrichment of allocations with SSI and account information in Omgeo Central Trade Manager, Omgeo OASYS and Omgeo OASYS Global
- ALERT's interface validates new data entered against industry standard rules to ensure accurate SSI data.
- ALERT is continually enhanced to keep pace with ISO15022 / MT54X fields for securities, and ISO7775/MT304, MT210 and MT202 messages for cash and FX trading

Omgeo SID

Formerly DTC's Standing Instructions Database (SID), SID provides automated settlement processing by electronically enriching allocations, trade confirmations and settlement messages with account and settlement data, and then routing settlement instructions to custodian banks and brokers' clearing agents.

Omgeo ALERT-SID

Omgeo ALERT-SID links Omgeo ALERT with Omgeo SID. ALERT-SID provides a single point of access to centralized Standing Settlement Instructions (SSI) for U.S. DTC-eligible trades.

ALERT-SID enables users to manage their accounts and settlement data via the ALERT user interface in both ALERT and in SID by enriching trade confirmations with ALERT account data that has been replicated in SID. After replication, clients can use ALERT to manage account and settlement information for distribution to trade counterparties. Subsequent account additions, updates and deletions result in the automatic update of both the ALERT database and SID, as appropriate.

Omgeo Transaction Services

Omgeo Transaction Services connect Investment Managers, Broker/Dealers and Custodians and help them to complete the trade allocation and confirmation/affirmation processes for cross-border and domestic trades.

Some of Omgeo's transaction products are:

Omgeo Product	Purpose
Omgeo TradeSuite	Confirm/affirm communication
Omgeo OASYS - TradeMatch	U.S. central matching
Omgeo Central Trade Manager	Global central matching
Omgeo OASYS	Communicating trade and allocation details between investment managers and broker/dealers (U.S.)
Omgeo Allocation Manager	Electronic allocation messaging
Omgeo AutoMatch	Global local matching
Omgeo TradeMatch / Omgeo NearMatch	U.S. local matching
Omgeo TradeHub	Common message switching between DTC participants

Figure 130 – Omgeo's Transaction Services

Each of these products is discussed on the following pages.

Omgeo TradeSuite [76]

The DTC's Institutional Delivery System, which was introduced in 1973, was initially developed as an electronic settlement system to link investment managers and their agent banks. The ID system was merged into a new group of products by the DTC in 1998, called TradeSuite.[77] At that time, these products provided support for over 2 million post-trade and settlement messages daily.

Institutional Delivery System (ID)

The DTC's Institutional Delivery System, which was merged into TradeSuite as TradeMessage prior to the merger of DTC's and Omgeo's products, is presented here separately to help the reader understand the evolution of the technology.

DTC's ID system was an electronic book-entry-like settlement system that was used to link the investment managers and their agent banks to the trades that were made for the managers by brokers. The system processed a huge number of transactions and the messages related to these transactions each day, and was a cornerstone of the securities industry for institutional transaction processing.

---

[76] Source: DTC

[77] In September 1998, The Depository Trust Company (DTC) announced a family of straight-through processing products called DTC TradeSuite. TradeSuite incorporated, and built upon, the Institutional Delivery (ID) System, the Standing Instructions Database (SID), and the DTC Hub.

As with Omgeo TradeSuite today, investment managers could use the ID system to initiate a single transaction for a single portfolio or they could place a large order for a block of securities that they allocated across multiple portfolios in order to get a better price and reduce purchase costs.

The transactions shown at the top of the following chart were historically completed by telephone. Today, most of the NOEs and allocation messages can be electronic and an increasing number of buy/sell instructions are being transmitted through an Alternative Trading System.

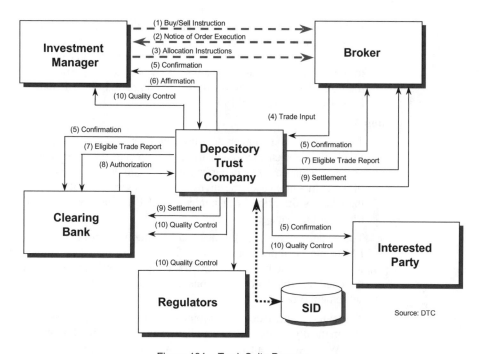

Figure 131 – TradeSuite Process

Initially, the ID cycle started with step four, where the broker informed the DTC electronically that it conducted a trade for one of its specific clients. After step four:

- The DTC sent a copy of this message as a confirmation to the manager and to their agent bank

- The manager affirmed the trade and notified the DTC by electronic message

- The DTC then completed the settlement of the trade with the agent bank

Today, TradeSuite can support the full workflow for users as shown in the following example, assuming the participant uses all of the available features.[78] The sequence of steps in this TradeSuite example does not match exactly to the sequence of messages that occur via the ID system.

Step 1

Through TradeSuite, after executing a trade, a broker submits a notice of execution to the investment manager.

Step 2

The investment manager responds with allocation messages, breaking down the block trade into individual client trades.

Step 3

Based on the allocation message from the investment manager, brokers submit trade details to TradeSuite, which then creates and forwards trade confirmations to the investment manager with copies to the broker and custodian banks, to ensure that all parties agree to the trade details. This step is normally completed on trade date or at latest by the morning of T+1.

Step 4

The investment manager acknowledges or affirms the trade. For DTC-eligible securities, an affirmation indicates that settlement may proceed. This step may occur as early as trade date or as late as noon of T+2. In some cases the investment manager will notify the bank that the confirmation is in agreement and the bank will affirm the trade for the manager.

TradeMatch eliminates the need to separately affirm confirmations. Electronic comparison of the investment manager allocation instruction to the broker dealer's trade input, allows Omgeo to create matched affirmed confirmations and via TradeSuite, initiate the settlement process.

TradeSuite provides automated settlement processing. It automatically sends to the custodian bank and clearing brokers, DTC or SWIFT settlement messages, with up-to-date client account and settlement data, from SID or ALERT.

Step 5

In the case of DTC-eligible securities, DTC sends deliver and receive instructions to the custodian bank and broker, identifying the trades expected to settle on T+3. This step occurs on the afternoon of T+2.

For DTC-ineligible securities, DTC can send settlement instructions on behalf of the broker to its clearing agent and on behalf of the investment manager to the client's global custodian. However, the global custodian must send settlement instructions to their sub-custodian, and if a depository is used for ultimate settlement, the clearing agent and sub-custodian follow that depository's procedures to complete settlement.

---

[78]   Source: DTC

Step 6

The broker or custodian bank (depending upon which party is the deliverer), instructs DTC with authorizations (or exceptions indicating which trades they do not wish) to settle automatically on T+3.

Step 7

Settlement is effected by DTC on T+3. Shares are transferred by book-entry from the depository account of the delivering participant to that of the receiving participant, with the corresponding payment being credited to the delivering participant and debited to the receiving participant.

During the end-of-day net settlement process, each DTC participant settles its net cash position with DTC by payment or receipt of a same-day funds wire via the Federal Reserve's Fed Wire System. DTC sends settlement reports to the brokers and custodian banks identifying the trades that settled on T+3 and, if a delivery did not settle, specifying the reasons. This step is completed on T+3.

When DTC's existing trade messaging and settlement services were incorporated into TradeSuite, over 10,000 institutional investors, broker/dealers and custodian banks using DTC's ID, SID, Matching, and DTC Hub services automatically became TradeSuite users, and were given the option of also using TradeSuite's new communications services.

When TradeSuite became part of Omgeo's offering in 2001, its original functionality was divided into four distinct services, which are available using a variety of standards and protocols:

- **Omgeo TradeSuite** - TradeSuite automates the exchange of post-trade messages between brokers, custodians and institutions, including block trade notices of execution, allocations, trade confirmations and affirmations.

- **Omgeo SID** - See Omgeo's Information Services

- **Omgeo TradeMatch** - TradeMatch is now a separate product and is described in more detail later in this section.

- **Omgeo TradeHub** – TradeHub is now a separate product and is described in more detail later in this section.

Omgeo OASYS-TradeMatch

Developed to increase allocation automation and central matching by U.S. trade participants, the OASYS-TradeMatch product resulted from Omgeo's formation. As of March 2004, 105 investment managers were live on Omgeo OASYS-TradeMatch, which is a central matching service for U.S. domestic securities.

- 165 Omgeo investment managers have adopted OASYS-TradeMatch

- Trade volume over OASYS-TradeMatch has grown 70% since January 2002

OASYS-TradeMatch clients are experiencing higher same day affirmation (SDA) rates, and are seeing a decrease in the number of failed trades. According to Omgeo's research, SDA rates for OASYS-TradeMatch users are routinely higher than 80%, with some clients experiencing 90% SDA compared to an industry average of 23.4%. OASYS-TradeMatch users have only 2/ 1,000 trades fail, compared to an average of 9/ 1,000 .

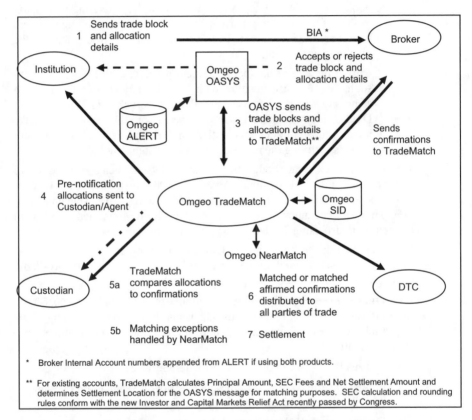

Figure 132 – Omego TradeMatch's Process

Omgeo Central Trade Manager

Introduced in 2003, Omgeo Central Trade Manager (Omgeo CTM) processes trades from execution through settlement and supports same-day or next-day settlement for global trades, for both fixed income and equity securities. CTM provides exception-only processing, real-time settlement instruction enrichment and automated settlement notification messaging, and will support U.S. domestic tradeflows in the future.

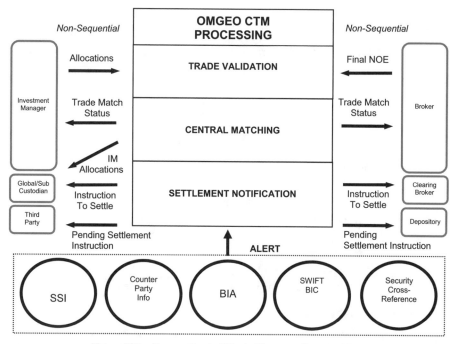

Figure 133 – Omgeo Central Trade Manager (Omgeo CTM)

As of August 2004, Omgeo CTM had:

- 23 IMs, 2 Banks, 7 Vendors live
- 46 additional clients signed and pending implementation
- More than 300 Brokers receiving allocations via a bridge to OASYS Global

Omgeo OASYS

Designed specifically for automation of allocations, *Omgeo OASYS 4.0* automates the trade allocation and acceptance process by communicating trade and allocation details between investment managers and broker/dealers.

Omgeo Allocation Manager

Omgeo Allocation Manager is a secure web-based tool that simplifies trade allocations for smaller U.S. investment managers and broker/dealers. This solution supports investment managers and counterparties who are currently processing trades manually.

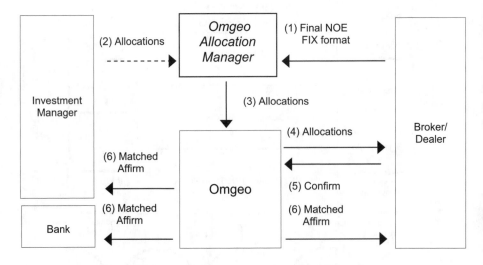

Figure 134 – Omgeo Allocation Manager Process

Omgeo AutoMatch

Omgeo AutoMatch is a global trade matching service for investment managers and Hedge Funds that automatically compares trade details submitted by their broker/dealers via Omgeo OASYS Global against order details from their own internal trade or portfolio management system.

Omgeo TradeMatch

Formerly a component of TradeSuite, Omgeo TradeMatch is a U.S. domestic trade comparison system that matches investment managers' allocations to Broker/Dealers' confirmations.

TradeMatch automates the comparison of investment managers' allocations with brokers' trade confirmations, which facilitates early trade agreement and identification of potential exceptions, while triggering settlement messaging for matched trades without the need for separate affirmations.

Omgeo Near Match

For use with TradeMatch and OASYS-TradeMatch, Omgeo NearMatch is an exception processing tool that helps investment managers identify discrepancies between unmatched allocations and unmatched confirmations. NearMatch assists investment mangers establish an exception-only process to reduce manual interaction and risk.

OmgeoTradeHub

Formerly a component of TradeSuite, TradeHub is an open messaging system for post-trade communications, transmitting settlement notification, reconciliation information, and other messages between investment managers and custodian banks. TradeHub can be accessed securely via the Web, host-to-host connection, or FTP.

Investment managers can connect to all of their custodians via a single access point and counterparties transmit messages in one agreed format. Messages can be sent in any U.S. industry-standard format (e.g., Omgeo OASYS, SWIFT, and FIX).

TradeHub provides real-time global communications services between several global networks, as well as numerous order management, portfolio management and ETC systems.

Depository Trust Company [79]

The Depository Trust Company (DTC) is the world's largest securities depository and is the primary central securities depository for stocks and bonds in the U.S. The history of the DTC was discussed in the chapter on Regulators and Legislation.

Depositories in the U.S. have several basic functions:

- Determining eligibility
- Immobilizing securities
- Re-registration in nominee name
- Book-entry movements
- End of day cash settlements
- Collecting and distributing interest income
- Collecting and distributing dividends

Depositories use three steps, representing increasing levels of automation, to eliminate paper certificates. They are immobilization followed by dematerialization, with the final step being complete book-entry.

The Depository Trust Company (DTC), a subsidiary of the DTCC, provides settlement, custody and asset servicing for more than 2.2 million securities issues from the United States and 100 other countries and territories.

The use of DTC is required by a number of different rules, including NYSE Rule 387, AMEX Rule 423, NASD Uniform Practice Code Section 64, and MSRB Rule G-15. These rules require their members to use the Cash on Delivery privilege with the DTC, which is also called Deliver vs. Payment (DVP).

DTC is organized as a limited-purpose Trust Company, owned by banks and brokerage firms, that:

- Maintains detailed records of all receipt and delivery settlement transactions that affect DTC client accounts
- Acts as a custodian for participant banks and broker/dealers to hold the book-entry and physical certificates for securities such as equities and bonds
- Arranges for the receipt and delivery of physical securities
- Arranges for the payments during settlement
- Arranges for processing of corporate actions, interest and dividends

---

[79]   Source: Depository Trust Company

Immobilization

Immobilization is the placement of certificates and financial instruments in a central securities depository to reduce the movement of physical securities in the marketplace and to facilitate book-entry transfers.

Dematerialization

Dematerialization is a process by which physical certificates are eliminated so that securities exist only as accounting records. Individual certificates are cancelled and replaced by a single certificate representing all of the shares or bonds.

Securities are initially immobilized in a depository and through the process of dematerialization can eventually become book-entry-only securities.

Book-Entry

Book-Entry is a settlement system that uses an electronic transfer of information about a security and/or cash between counterparties rather than physical delivery of the actual certificate. A receipt may be generated.

In practice, for a book-entry-like process to occur when certificates are required by law, the certificates need to be in some form of general name, or street name and immobilized in a depository.

The only truly book-entry securities in the U.S. are U.S. government securities, municipals and options for which no physical certificate exists.

DTC is organized as a limited-purpose Trust Company, owned by banks and brokerage firms, that:

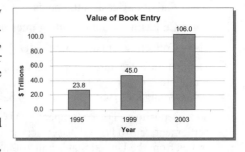

Figure 135 - DTC Book Entry Securities

- Acts as a custodian for participant banks and broker/dealers to hold the physical certificates for securities such as equities and bonds
- Arranges for their receipt and delivery of securities
- Arranges for the payments during settlement

DTC Eligible Securities

DTC eligible securities include:

- Common and preferred stocks including those traded on the NYSE, AMEX, NASDAQ, and other markets

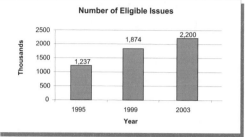

Figure 136 - DTC Eligible Securities

- Issues of both listed and unlisted corporate debt securities - Municipal bond issues (registered and bearer form)

- Certain U.S. Treasury and Federal Agency issues (including SBA issues)

- Variable Rate Demand Obligations (VRDO)

- Warrants

- Custodial Receipts

- American Depositary Receipts (ADR)

- Certificates of Deposit (Retail and Institutional)

- Certain mutual funds and closed end funds

- Certain global bonds

- Commercial paper, Medium Term Notes and other money market instruments (including Bankers Acceptances)

- Certain Canadian common and preferred stock

- Asset Backed Securities

- Certain Foreign Ordinary shares

- Brady Bonds

- Rule 144A Securities

- Regulation S Securities

- Collateralized Mortgage Obligations

The number of eligible securities has increased steadily throughout the years as new issues are created and additional instrument types are made eligible by the depository. In 2003, the total value of the securities on deposit was $25 Trillion.

DTC Services

DTC provides a variety of specific services to its participants, including the following:

- Acceptance of deposits of physical securities for custody

- Book-entry trade settlement

- Underwriting distribution

- Income collection and distribution
- Loan collateralization
- Reorganization announcements
- Same day funds settlement

Many of these services have been organized by the DTC into the following suite of products.

- Settlement Service
- Collateralization Controls
- Custody / Safekeeping Service
- Deposits Service

Each of these four services is discussed on the following pages.

DTC Settlement Service

The Settlement Service:

- Facilitates end-of-day net settlement of a participant's net settlement obligations resulting from trading activity in all DTC-eligible securities
- Ensures the collection/disbursement of a participant's net settlement obligations and credits through the Fedwire system
- Provides collateralization controls and net debit caps that protect participants against the inability of one or more participants to pay for their settlement obligations

DTC processed 225 million electronic book-entry transactions and 3.9 million physical deliveries/withdrawals in 2003.

DTC Settlement Service Process

The majority of the securities traded in the U.S. are settled in three days (T+3 = Trade Date plus three business days).

The regular settlement process is:

- Transactions that are affirmed by noon on T+2 and authorized by the seller prior to the close of business on T+2 are processed in a batch cycle during the night between T+2 and T+3.
- Transactions are effectively settled at the start of business on T+3 (SD).
- Transactions that are not affirmed prior to noon on T+2 are not included in the regular process. The exception process is that transactions must be delivered by the seller through the DTC's Night Deliver Order Processor during the night between T+2 and T+3, or during the day cycle on SD.

Deliveries that are not recognized by the receiving participant can be refused.

Participant's net cash balances for DTC settlements are re-computed with every trade; however, the net payment is not made until the end of the processing day. Final payment is made by wire transfer through the Federal Reserve Bank's funds transfer service.

Using DTC's Settlement Service, participants can:

- Settle securities transactions by processing deliver orders (DOs)
- Collect option contract premiums by processing Premium Payment Orders (PPOs)
- Collect stock loan marks-to-market on open contracts by processing Securities Payment Orders (SPOs)
- Pledge securities to pledges for collateral through the collateral loan system
- Pledge securities to the Options Clearing Corporation (OCC) to meet OCC margin requirements
- Protect client fully-paid-for positions and manage firm positions through the use of segregation and memo segregation procedures

One of the main systems involved in settlement processing is the Inventory Management System.

Inventory Management System

DTCC's Inventory Management System (IMS) allows participants to create inquiries, authorize or exempt security deliveries before transaction processing occurs.

IMS offers twelve options for managing the processing of transactions including seven inquiry options and five update options

DTC Collateralization Controls

Collateralization controls and net debit caps are employed by the DTC to protect its participants against the inability of another participant to pay for their settlement obligations.

DTC's collateralization process limits block transactions that would cause a participant's net debit to exceed the total available collateral in its account. This control protects all of the participants by ensuring that if a participant fails to pay for its settlement obligation, it will have sufficient collateral in its account to cover the settled transactions if the participant becomes insolvent.

As a backup to the collateralization control, DTC's net debit cap controls limit the net settlement debit that each participant can incur up to a specific amount, based upon its activity level, which is less than DTC's total liquidity. This ensures that DTC will have sufficient funds to complete settlement should any single participant fail to settle.

DTC Custody / Safekeeping Service

DTC's Custody Service allows DTC participants to use the depository's vaults to store some or all of the physical securities they maintain for their clients. When used with DTC's Branch Deposit Service, New York Window and/or the Restricted Deposit Service, participants can maintain control of their securities without having to handle physical securities and provide their own vault facilities.

Deposit Service – Allows participants to deliver physical securities to DTC for safekeeping

New York Window – Provided at the NSCC's location as a way to transfer physical instruments between participants

Restricted Deposit Service – Allows participants to deliver physical securities that are reviewed, imaged and transmitted to transfer agents who will remove the restrictions on the security.

Each of these services is discussed later in this chapter.

DTC Custody/Safekeeping Service Process

Deposits of securities are made using the DTC's Participant Terminal System (PTS), which notifies DTC electronically of the certificates being deposited and sent. Once the certificates arrive at DTC, a full examination of all certificates is performed by DTC's staff, including a negotiability check and verification of data received from the depositing participant firm.

DTC also performs Securities Information Center (SIC) verifications to ensure that the securities are not lost or stolen, and calls transfer agents on all SIC flags.

Ineligible issues can be made custody-eligible on a same-day basis.

All securities and accompanying documentation received by DTC are scanned for imaging. Custody-user firms can access the images through their imaging workstations, or by fax and email.

For withdrawals, DTC can make certificates available for pickup in the New York area within 45 minutes or will ship via overnight air courier outside New York City.

DTC Deposits Service

DTC's Deposits Service provides safekeeping and processing services for various types of eligible securities. The services include:

- Same day credit for transactions
- Produce automated deposit tickets
- Track deposits from a PTS terminal
- Deposit restricted securities

DTC Deposit Service Process

The Deposit Service process includes the following steps:

- After receiving deposit instructions, DTC credits deposits securities to the participant's general free account.
- The Deposit Automation Management (DAM) system allows participants to transmit details of a deposit using a PTS terminal before forwarding physical securities to DTC
- DTC's Deposits staff reviews and edits this information, and with high-value items, notifies participants of any problems or other relevant information involving the securities

NSCC New York Window

The New York Window is an industry-driven platform of services that performs various operational activities, including clearance and settlement of book-entry and physical securities transactions, for brokers, dealers, custodian banks and other financial institutions. NSCC established the common processing facility in 1993 to help its participants centralize processing, reduce risk and costs.

The New York Window acts as an extension of its participants' process by managing their varied securities operations.

The New York Window is discussed again in this chapter in the section on Physical Settlements.

Other Post-Trade Processing Vendors

Introduction to Post-Trade Processing Vendors

Although Omgeo has a central position in the post-trade process, other vendors are also developing products that support confirmations, allocations, affirmations and SSI.

Some of these vendors offer communication networks that connect the participants and provide value added post-trade applications, while others are primarily trade matching networks that are extending their functionality towards the back office.

TradeWeb

TradeWeb is a trading network that matches buyers and sellers. Recently acquired by Thomson Financial, it is currently used by 26 dealers and 1,400 managers to trade U.S. Treasuries, agencies, mortgages and commercial paper, and is adding corporate bonds.

Implemented in 1998, TradeWeb is an online trading network for fixed-income securities which the following services:

- Real time market data
- A pool of liquidity for fixed-income (U.S. Treasuries, U.S. Agencies, Commercial Paper, European Government Bonds, TBA-MBS, Pfandbriefe/Covered Bonds, Euro Supranationals/Agencies, Agency Discount Notes and ECP) products by connecting 27 primary dealers to over 1,400 buy-side institutions
- TradeXpress, which sends trade allocations to dealers and receives confirmations
- AccountNet, which is a standing settlement instruction (SSI) database

Investment managers' Trade Order Management Systems can send orders via TradeWeb to dealers. The completed trades are returned by TradeXpress to the buy-side institutions who can allocate block trades to sub-accounts.

TradeWeb states that two things are needed for successful trading networks: range of instruments and participation, and that the increased use of electronic matching networks reduces the need for a Virtual Matching Utility (VMU).

SunGard

SunGard established the SunGard Transaction Network (STN) in 2000 to connect investment managers with brokers, brokers with exchanges, exchanges with banks, and banks with settlement agents and custodians.

STN's services include:

- Routing of orders for execution
- Support for matching trades to orders
- Routing of confirmations
- Creation and routing allocations
- Generation of affirmations

These services are offered through several instrument-oriented applications:

- STN Equities
- STN Funds
- STN Fixed Income
- STN Money Market
- STN Post-Trade Services

The SunGard Transaction Network connects more than 700 banks, 1,000 money managers, 35 million 401K participants, 1,500 insurance companies, and 180 brokers.

Financial Models Company

The Financial Models Company's (FMC) trade communications network was originally established in 1990 to connect investment managers, broker/dealers, custodians and interested parties.

FMCNet was originally designed to provide local matching and was subsequently expanded to FMCNet II which offers a central matching Virtual Matching Utility (VMU).

The primary features are:

- Connects to SWIFT, DTC and CrossMar networks
- Provides a standing settlement instruction (SSI) database
- Allows managers to send allocations
- Match at multiple stages including:
    - Trade-for-Trade (Allocations to Confirmations)
    - NOE (Notice of Execution) to BON (Block Order Notification)
- Matches confirms with allocations and sends affirmations

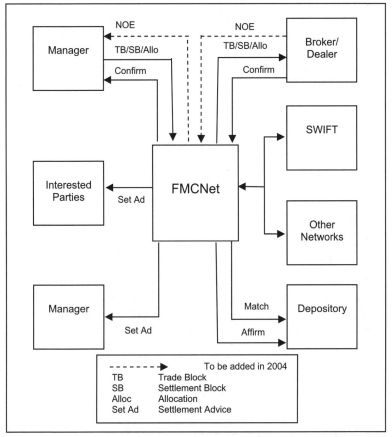

Figure 137 - FMCNet Process Flow

Fixed Income Settlement

Fixed Income Settlement occurs in different places based upon the type of fixed income security that is processed.

Security Type	Place of Settlement
Corporate Bonds	DTC
Municipal Bonds	DTC
Government Bonds	Fed
Mortgage Backed Bonds	Fed

Figure 138 -Settlement Locations

DTCC has been working for several years to develop a single application that can process all types of fixed income instruments. This application, Real Time Trade Matching (RTTM), was initiated in 2000 for U.S. Treasury securities, and was extended in 2002 to include mortgage backed securities. It is now being modified to include corporates and municipals.

Real Time Trade Matching

RTTM is a single front-end matching engine that will be used ultimately by all of the DTCC's fixed income processing activities. It is intended to reduce intra-day market and operational risk by reducing the time between when a trade is executed and when it is submitted to one of the clearing corporations.

RTTM is also a basic component of DTC's strategy for supporting any future reduction in the settlement period in the U.S. This will support the reduction to T+1 for corporates, municipals, UITs, etc., and will establish the base process for DTCC becoming the central counterparty for mortgage backed securities trades.

RTTM Process

The Access Network, jointly developed in 1998 by GSD and NSCC, serves as the single pipeline that members may use to communicate with RTTM. It provides:

- Screen access via RTTM's Terminal Service
- Interactive Messaging
- Bulk file transfer

By using the Access Network, members can access a number of applications provided by the various clearing corporations. It further enables members to connect multiple workstations throughout their organizations, providing simultaneous access to a number of services by various users in different locations.

RTTM message standards were designed to conform to the International Organization for Standardization (ISO 15022).

Federal Reserve Book Entry System (FRB)

Since July 1986, the book-entry program of the Federal Reserve System and United States Treasury has steadily replaced the physical securities issued by the U.S. government and federal agencies with book-entry processing.

Book-entry transactions make it easier, cheaper and safer to safekeep and transfer the securities between buyers and sellers.

FBE Eligible Securities

All marketable government securities held by depository institutions are eligible whether owned by them or held on behalf of correspondent banks or other clients.

U.S. branches and agencies of foreign banks and domestic depository institutions have access to book-entry conversion and wire transfer services at set prices.

FBE Services

The FBE provides the following services for eligible securities:

- Safekeeping for securities for both ordinary and pledged security accounts
- Principal and interest payments
- Book-entry facilities to depository institutions

FBE Processing

The Fed Book-entry process is:

- The delivering broker or custodian enters delivery instructions into the Federal Reserve's National Book-Entry System (NBES), which is the central securities application of the Federal Reserve System. Most financial firms use the services of a Dealer Clearance Agent such as the Bank of New York or JP Morgan Chase to process transactions with the National Book-Entry System.

- The FBE settlement delivery deadline is 3:00 p.m. Eastern Standard Time, followed by a 3:00 p.m. to 3:15 p.m. dealer time. During this fifteen minute period, only dealers recognized by the Bond Market Association may initiate deliveries.

- Authorized transactions electronically transfer securities and cash between the relevant accounts

- Once transferred, the trade is settled

Since there is no formal pre-matching of FBE instructions, exceptions can occur

- The receiving party may refuse the delivery and reverse the transaction during a 3:15 to 3:30 p.m. reclamation period

- Trade-entry cut-off extensions do occur, and the FBE participants are notified of any extension five minutes before scheduled closing

- Turnaround trades must be identified, and sell instructions must include counterparty delivery instructions

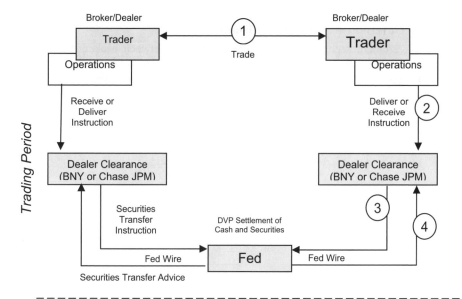

Figure 139 - U.S. Government Settlement Process

After receiving the Securities Transfer Advice from the Fed the Dealer Clearance Agent will attempt to match the advice to the Receive instruction. If it matches the transaction is completed. If it does not match, the Dealer Clearance Agent will notify the Fed that the trade is invalid. In that case, the Fed will reverse the cash and security transaction that it made.

Fedwire transfers are sent as individual transactions and are not netted. These individual trade-for-trade transactions are considered a bilateral exchange, which is also known as gross settlement.

If the trade was between two clients with the same dealer, the trade will be settled within that dealer.

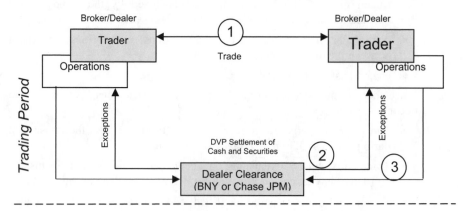

Figure 140 – Clearing and Settling Through a Dealer Clearance Agent

U.S. Government Securities Settlement

Government securities can also be transferred between brokers through the Government Securities Division (GSD), but in order to be acquired from the Fed or to be returned to the Fed, the securities and the payments must go through a bank that is a member of the Fedwire system. As of 2004, only the Bank of New York and JP Morgan Chase provide this service.

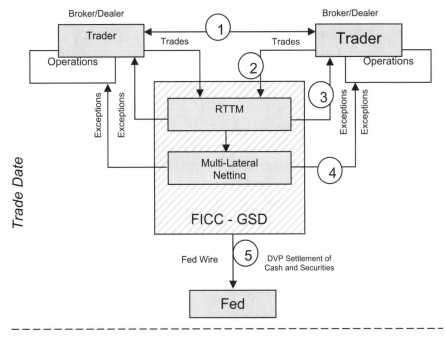

Figure 141 – Clearing and Settling Through GSD

The GSD's process consists of Real Time Trade Matching (RTTM) and the GSD's netting system. The net of the transactions is reported to the Fed for settlement.

Mortgage-Backed Securities

Mortgage-backed securities are settled through the banks that are members of the FedWire system. The banks that are involved as Dealer Clearance Agents can settle the trades internally if both sides are clearing through them, and any bank can settle directly with the Fed. This process was diagrammed in the section on clearing of MBS instruments earlier in this chapter.

Physical Settlement

Debt and equity issues that are ineligible for book-entry in either DTC or FBE must settle physically in a specified area in lower Manhattan south of Houston Street (plus Jersey City, NJ). Most banks and brokers use DTC's physical custody service in New York City, called the New York Window, at 55 Water Street.

New York Window

The New York Window, which was introduced earlier in this chapter, performs various operational activities for DTCC participants, including clearance and settlement of book-entry and physical securities transactions, for brokers, dealers, custodian banks and other financial institutions.

The Window provides support for a variety of financial instruments, including:

- Equities
- Municipal and corporate bonds

- Government securities
- Mortgage backed securities
- Money market instruments, including medium-term notes, certificates of deposit and commercial paper
- Private placements
- Legal/restricted items

New York Window's Process

The New York Window's process is:

- Sell instructions must include full information about the buyer, as well as the appropriate trade details
- Good delivery generally consists of either:
  - Certificates endorsed for sale by the registered owner, or
  - Certificates accompanied by a stock or bond power of attorney which may also need a corporate resolution that authorizes the transfer
- Payment is wired separately the same day

E. OPTIONS, DERIVATIVES AND COMMODITIES CLEARING AND SETTLEMENT

The Clearing Corporations (formerly the Board of Trade Clearing Corporation) [80]

The Board of Trade Clearing Corporation (BOTCC) was established in 1925 as the trade processing and clearing entity for the Chicago Board of Trade. In 2003, after the Chicago Board of Trade decided to shift its clearing business to the Chicago Mercantile Exchange's Clearinghouse Division, BOTCC entered an agreement to provide clearing for Eurex U.S. and changed its name to the Clearing Corporation.

On Feb. 8, 2004, The Clearing Corporation (CCorp) began processing trades for Eurex U.S., the Chicago-based electronic futures exchange that was launched by Eurex, the world's largest derivatives exchange.

The Clearing Corporation is a Delaware corporation owned by 50 stockholders, many of whom represent the world-wide derivatives marketplace participants and market makers, and is the only active independent futures clearinghouse in the world.

CCorp continuously matches every submitted trade throughout the day, by matching the clearing participant buyer with the clearing participant seller. After the trade is properly matched, the Clearing Corporation becomes the clearing counterparty to both sides of each, and thereby guarantees the performance of all of the trades it accepts, in accordance with its Bylaws, rules, policies and procedures.

The clearing process includes the following steps:

---

[80] Source: Board of Trade Clearing Corporation

- Execution of a trade through an electronic trading system such as Eurex U.S.'s trading platform

- The transaction is sent to the Clearing Corporation and immediately edited to ensure that all of the critical information required by the match process corresponds exactly on both sides of the trade

- Trades are continuously matched throughout the day

- Once a trade is matched, The Clearing Corporation's guarantee takes effect with CCorp acting as a buyer to every clearing participant seller and the seller to every clearing participant buyer

- Clearing reports are automatically transmitted to participant firms' computer systems and are available

The Clearing Corporation manages the risk of ensuring financial integrity in a variety of ways, including the collection of original margin (performance bond) at least once daily, the marking-to-market of all open positions at least twice daily, and monitoring of large trader positions and mark-to-market obligations. The Clearing Corporation's guarantee of matched trades is supported by its AAA credit rating from Standard & Poor's, a $100 million default insurance policy, a $200 million committed credit facility, and the capital contributed by its clearing members.

Chicago Mercantile Exchange Clearinghouse Division [81]

The CME's Clearinghouse Division has responsibility for assuring and maintaining the financial integrity of the exchange through a variety of functions, including matching, carrying and guaranteeing all trades, enforcing financial safeguards, and establishing and monitoring performance bond (margin) requirement levels.

The Merc's Clearinghouse employs CLEARING 21, a real-time system developed jointly by the CME and the New York Mercantile Exchange (NYMEX). Clearing 21 provides real-time processing of trades and tracks positions continuously, in real-time. Additionally, it has the flexibility to accommodate complex new product types including combinations, options on combinations, options on options, swaps, repos, etc.

CLEARING 21 also supports complex, multi-party agreements for trading and clearing linkages, cross-margining and common banking and consists of an open architecture that expands the integration between clearing member firm systems and the clearing system.

Member firm systems exchange messages with CLEARING 21 in real-time and around the clock, using a standard, message-based application programming interface.

Intermarket Clearing Corporation (ICC) [82]

The Intermarket Clearing Corporation is a wholly owned subsidiary of the Options Clearing Corporation. It was formed in 1984 to support the exchanges that were establishing futures markets and to meet the need for a cross-

---

[81] Source: Chicago Mercantile Exchange

[82] Source: Options Clearing Corporation

margining mechanism between options and futures, and is not actively used today.

Kansas City Board of Trade Clearing Corporation (KCBT) [83]

The Kansas City Board of Trade Clearing Corporation performs a variety of functions to maintain market integrity. Its seven-person Board of Directors, made up entirely of KCBT members, is responsible for managing the exchange's capital reserves, which provide protection against the financial insolvency of member firms. Since it was established in 1913, no KCBT client has suffered a financial loss because of default.

KCBT acts as a third party to all futures and options contract agreements and matches the buyer to every seller and the seller to every buyer. In this way, the traders' financial obligations are with their respective clearing firm, not with each other. Each clearing firm, in turn, is a member of the KCBT, which ensures that each firm honors its financial obligations.

New York Mercantile Exchange Clearing Division [84]

New York Mercantile Exchange's Clearing Division guarantees all of the trades that take place on the exchange, ultimately acting as the seller to every buyer and as the buyer to every seller. This is accomplished through a group of about 60 to 70 member firms called clearing members.

Acting through clearing members, all market participants are required to deposit a level of margin that will ensure that participants have sufficient funds to handle losses they may experience in the market.

When an investor buys or sells a futures contract, a deposit must be made with the clearing member that the Merc determines is sufficient to cover any one-day price move. As long as the investor holds the contract, the clearing member must maintain minimum margin funds for that position. Additional funds must be deposited if the market moves against the contract holder.

As soon as anyone buys or sells a futures contract, they must deposit with their clearing member an amount of money that the Merc determines is sufficient to cover any one-day price move. As long as that person or firm holds on to the contract, the Merc must maintain minimum margin funds for that position, with the contract holder depositing additional funds whenever the market moves against him.

As a further safeguard, the clearing members contribute to a pool of funds called a guaranty fund that can be used in the event a member or client of the Merc defaults on his obligation.

Options Clearing Corporation [85]

The Options Clearing Corporation (OCC), which was founded in 1973, is the largest financial derivative instrument clearing organization in the world. OCC, which is owned by the American Stock Exchange, the Boston Options Exchange, Chicago Board Options Exchange, International Securities Exchange,

---

[83] Source: Kansas City Board of Trade Clearing Corporation

[84] Source: New York Mercantile Exchange

[85] Source: The Options Clearing Corporation

One Chicago, NQLX, Pacific Exchange and Philadelphia Stock Exchange, is the issuer and registered clearing facility for all U.S. exchange-listed securities options. It issues put and call options on several types of underlying assets including common stocks and other equity issues, as well as stock indexes, foreign currencies and interest rate composites.

In 2003, OCC's average daily options volume was 3.6 million contracts and average daily premium settlements were $1.1 billion.

OCC has over 135 clearing members that are U.S.-registered broker/dealers and non-U.S. securities firms.

OCC was created to promote stability and financial integrity in the options markets by focusing on effective risk management. In its role as the guarantor of the trade, OCC ensures that the obligations of options contracts are fulfilled for the selling and purchasing clearing firms, regardless of the financial condition of the contra party.

OCC operates under the jurisdiction of both the Securities and Exchange Commission (SEC) and the Commodities Futures Trading Commission (CFTC).

- Under its SEC jurisdiction OCC clears transactions for put and call options on common stocks and other equity issues, stock indexes, foreign currencies, interest rate composites and single-stock futures.

- As a registered Derivatives Clearing Organization (DCO) under CFTC jurisdiction, OCC offers clearing and settlement services for transactions in futures and options on futures.

The OCC has recently signed clearing agreements with three markets formed to trade security futures: The Island Futures Exchange, NASDAQ-Liffe Markets and OneChicago.

OCC Margin Products

ENCORE

In 1988 OCC initiated the Intermarket Trade Reporting and Clearing System (INTRACS) which automated much of the clearing process. This application is being replaced by ENCORE, which is a real time processing system that will be phased in throughout 2005.

Encore will accept trade and post-trade data on a transaction by transaction basis and process that data in real time. This includes:

- Trade and Position Processing
- Margin, Collateral, Settlement

Theoretical Intermarket Margin System (TIMS)

OCC developed TIMS in response to the growing need for a risk-based margin system that balanced the conflicting forces of market liquidity versus capital requirements.

MyOCC Portal

The Options Clearing Corporation's MyOCC Portal is a web-based application for OCC clearing members, participant exchanges, retail brokers, trading desk personnel and other options industry professionals. It will replace the Options News Network (ONN) and provide a single point of access.

MyOCC will be an entry point to ENCORE via the Internet.

Other Services

Options News Network (ONN)

ONN is an online system that provides exchange and clearinghouse information including the Directory of Listed Options, statistical reports, series information and Equity Special Settlement reports.

Web Site (www/optionsclearing.com)

The OCC web site provides delayed options quotes, a directory of listed options, volume statistics, an expiration calendar, OCC's annual report and assorted educational material.

A detailed review of the operations of the OCC is beyond the scope of this book.

F. CROSS BORDER TRADE PROCESSING

While it is not within the scope of this book to fully explain how cross border trades are cleared and settled, it is useful to introduce the concepts behind this process.

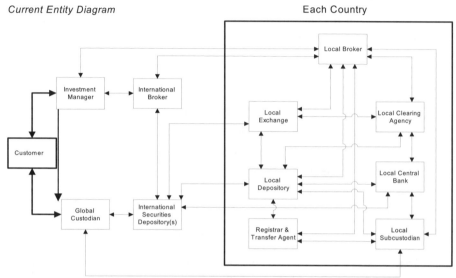

Figure 142 - Overview of Cross-Border Trading

Clearing in the local market is conducted according to the local rules, and the impact on a U.S.-based client includes:

- Time zones
- Currencies
- Local regulations and customs

The settlement usually requires a local sub-custodian who knows the local market and has the processes available to clear and/or settle trades, and who has been selected by the client's global custodian.

The local sub-custodian, which is also known as the agent bank, must be informed of the transaction and be given permission to settle the trade. When the transaction is complete, the local sub-custodian notifies the global custodian, who enters the transaction into his records and reports to the client.

The industry is working to improve cross-border clearing and settlement by promoting Straight Through Processing and by establishing cross-border clearing entities, called International Clearing and Settlement Depositories (ICSD).

Clearstream

Luxembourg-based Cedel Group was established in 1970 by 66 financial institutions from eleven countries as a neutral and independent capital markets infrastructure designed to reduce the costs and risks of settling securities transactions in the Eurobond market.

Clearstream offers settlement and custody services to more than 2,500 clients world-wide, covering over 150,000 domestic and internationally traded bonds and equities. Clearstream's core business is to deliver cash and securities between the parties to the trade, and to notify clients of the rights and obligations attached to the securities that are held by Clearstream.

Clearstream has links to counterparts in 39 domestic markets, and settles more than 500,000 transactions daily on 150,000 securities.

As of the end of 2003, Clearstream holds stocks, bonds and funds valued at approximately $7.5 trillion for their clients, and offers a range of products such as:

- Cash management and treasury services
- Cash investment services
- Same-day value withdrawal in 19 currencies
- Automatic currency conversion of income and residual balances
- Financing, lending and borrowing
- Highly featured reporting

Cedelbank also serves as the Central Securities Depository for Luxembourg.

Euroclear

The Euroclear System was originally created in 1968 to clear and settle Eurobonds using delivery versus payment. Since its inception, the Euroclear System also has provided clearance and settlement of transactions in internationally traded securities, and currently handles over 100,000 different bonds, equities and investment funds.

Market-owned and market-governed, Euroclear provides securities services to major financial institutions located in more than 80 countries.

Euroclear Bank, the ICSD, offers a single access point to securities services in over 25 equity markets and over 30 bond markets worldwide.

In addition to its role as an ICSD, Euroclear also acts as the Central Securities Depository (CSD) for Dutch, French, Irish and UK securities, a role that will soon be extended to include Belgian securities.

Emerging Market Clearing Corporation

The EMCC, as a subsidiary of DTCC, is both industry-owned and directed.

The Emerging Market Clearing Corporation (EMCC) was developed by the International Securities Clearing Corporation (ISCC) in coordination with the Emerging Markets Traders Association (EMTA) to serve as a central resource for the clearance, multilateral netting, and risk management of emerging market debt products.

Among its stated missions are to reduce counterparty risk, support the continued development of screen-based trading, and reduce dependence on individual commercial clearing organizations.

VIII. Post Settlement Processing

There are two major activities in Post Settlement Processing: Asset Servicing and Generic Post Trade Functions.

A. ASSET SERVICING

Asset servicing functions begin after the trade has settled, and are performed for as long as an investor owns a security. The brokers and custodians holding the clients' assets conduct asset servicing functions such as:

- Interest Collection – Dividends
- Interest Collection – Registered Securities
- Interest Collection – Bearer Securities
- Corporate Actions
- Reference Data
- Pricing
- Proxy
- Escheatment
- Stop Payments

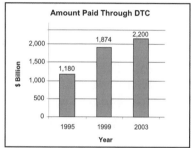

Figure 143 - DTC Payments

Each of these functions is discussed in this section.

Much of this Asset Servicing support comes from the DTC. The total value of the money processed through the DTC for principal, income and reorganization-related transactions amounted to over $2.2 Trillion in 2003.

Introduction to Income Collection

Brokers and custodians are responsible for collecting income from the DTC or the responsible paying agent and for paying the correct amount to their clients.

Stocks pay dividends and bonds pay interest. While dividends are generally granted at the discretion of the Board of Directors, interest payments are usually defined at the time the bond is created.

There are three categories of income collection:

- Dividends
- Registered Bonds
- Bearer Bonds

Income Collection - Dividends

Dividends on common shares are paid to the shareholders from corporate earnings at the discretion of the board of directors. The board may decide to keep the earnings and use them to expand the business, or to return a portion of the profits to the owners.

Some categories of firms, such as public utilities, normally do not have opportunities to expand and therefore regularly pay dividends. They tend to attract a type of investor who wishes to receive regular dividend income. Other firms, such as technology firms, have many different ways to use the earnings and tend to reinvest for future growth. Investors who buy this category of equity do not expect to receive dividends, but do expect that the asset will grow faster than a firm that regularly distributes earnings to its investors.

Once a dividend has been declared, the issuer of the equity ascertains the names of the holders by asking the transfer agent for a listing of holders. This information is then provided to the paying agent, which is responsible for transferring the correct amount of dividends from the issuer to the appropriate registered owners.

When the owner holds a physical certificate, it is registered in the owner's name; however, when the owner's broker, custodian or the DTC holds the certificate for the client, it is registered in a nominee name. A nominee is a person or legal entity that is designated by another person or legal entity to act on his/its behalf.

In securities processing, the concept of the nominee is used so that one firm can act on behalf of the beneficial owner of a security. When a security is registered in a nominee name, the nominee receives a gross payment and then must identify the beneficial owners on its own books and forward the correct amount of money to the actual owners.

Types of Distributions

There are several different kinds of distributions the stockholders can receive. The most common is a cash distribution; however, there are several different kinds of cash distributions. For example, there are normal dividends that are fully taxable, and there are partial liquidations or returns of capital, which are taxable at capital gains rates. Cash dividends can also be reinvested through dividend reinvestment programs.

A corporation's board of directors can also declare a stock dividend. This can include spin-offs, distributions of warrants, stock splits and reverse splits. This type of distribution is usually processed by the re-organization department as a corporate action since it involves a change to the clients' position.

The board of directors can also declare an optional dividend where the shareholder can decide what they want to receive. They could receive a cash dividend with an option to receive stock or a stock dividend with an option to receive cash, etc.

Regular Dividends

All dividends must be approved by the firm's board of directors, and firms that pay dividends usually attempt to do so regularly since it becomes expected by the investors. When a regularly expected dividend is passed (or not declared) the stock price usually declines.

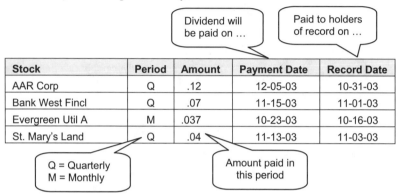

Figure 144 - Regular Dividends Presented in a Newspaper

This chart shows what is typically presented in a newspaper. The chart includes an abbreviated security name, the period of the dividend, amount of the dividend per share, the payment date and the record date.

- The payment date is the date that a dividend will be paid to eligible shareholders. Eligibility is determined by the record date.

- The record date is the day that an investor must be registered as the owner of record in order to be entitled to an announced dividend, liquidation distribution, reverse split, capital gains, etc.

This information is also available electronically through various market data vendors, and is usually provided in an overnight batch process.

Preferred Share Dividends

Preferred shares are obligated to pay dividends, based upon the covenants in the share indenture. The various forms of preferred dividends and the conditions upon which they are paid are discussed in the chapter on Equities.

The announcement could take the form as shown in the following chart, or it could be announced directly by the firm as follows.

NOTICE OF DIVIDENDS

On June 24, 1998, the board of directors of BCE, Inc. declared the following quarterly dividends, payable in Canadian dollars to holders of its shares at the close of business on the record date indicated.

Dividend Number		Amount	Payment Date	Record Date
Per Cumulative Redeemable First Preferred Shares				
Series Q	11	$0.43125	September 1, 1998	July 31, 1998
Series U	5	$0.34625	September 1, 1998	July 31, 1998
Series W	4	$0.34625	September 1, 1998	July 31, 1998
Series Y	3	$0.28750	September 1, 1998	July 31, 1998

Marc J. Ryan
Vice-President, Associate General Counsel and Corporate Secretary
BCE Inc.

Figure 145 - Dividend Notice in Newspapers

Irregular Dividends

A firm can pay a dividend at any point in time, and may choose to do so only occasionally as shown below. These become irregular dividends and are also posted in the newspapers and are available electronically.

Stock	Period	Amount	Payment Date	Record Date
Keystone	U	.085	11-06-03	12-25-03
Masabi Trust	U	.09	11-20-03	10-30-03
Northwest Equity	U	.09	11-03-03	10-27-03

U = Pay period undetermined

Figure 146 - Irregular Dividends Presented in a Newspaper

Stock Dividends

While most dividends are paid in cash, a firm can decide to issue a dividend that is paid in stock. This chart shows how firms pay in shares. A stock split is considered a stock dividend if the distribution is less than 25%. In the following chart, one issue, BNB Bancshares declared a 5% dividend. That means that a holder of 100 shares should receive an additional five shares on the payment date.

Stock	Period	Amount	Payment Date	Record Date
Bethel Bancorp	X		12-15-03	12-01-03
X – 2 for 1 split				
BNB Bancshares	U	5%	11-20-03	10-30-03
Summit Bancshares	X		11-20-03	11-06-03
X – 2 for 1 split				
Grand Casinos	X		12-28-03	12-15-03
X – 3 for 1 split				

Pay period is undetermined

Figure 147 - Stock Dividends Presented in Newspaper

Stock Splits are reported as dividends

Owners sometimes have the option to reinvest their cash dividends in the same stock, as described in the following section.

Dividend Reinvestment Programs (DRIP)

Many firms offer Dividend Reimbursement Programs, more commonly called DRIP programs, which allow stockholders to automatically reinvest their dividend into additional shares of the company that issued the dividend. When investors automatically reinvest their dividends, they increase the number of shares they own, and if the equity increases in value they can make more money than if they had held the cash, as shown in the following graph.

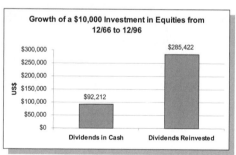

Figure 148 - Impact of Reinvesting Dividends

DRIP processors maintain records for fractional shares and do not charge any fee for their service to the clients. All charges are made to the issuer.

Issuers have supported DRIP programs in the past because the program allows the issuer to know the identity of the investor, and most DRIP investors hold their securities over a long period of time.

Dividend Check

At the client's request, dividensds can be paid by check. The corporate trust departments of banks are normally the paying agents for securities, so a check of this type could be sent by a paying agent for any one of many different companies.

Dividend Processing Flow

After a trade has been settled, the process of issue servicing begins and continues for as long as the investor owns the security. If the holder is not paid directly by the paying agent, brokers and custodians are responsible for collecting the correct amount of the dividend.

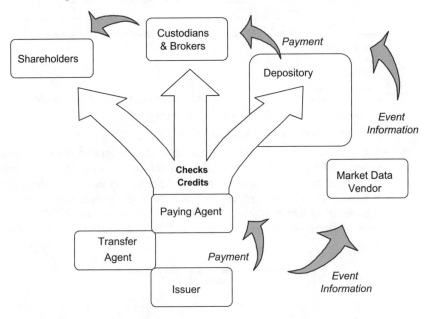

Figure 149 - Dividend Payment Process

The process begins when a corporation's board of directors declares a dividend and notifies the transfer agent and paying agent of its intent. Shortly after a dividend has been declared, a process begins to ensure that the correct dividends are distributed to the registered owner.

Frequently, a single corporate trust department will be both the transfer agent and the paying agent.

When a registered owner is a nominee name, then the nominee receives the payment and must identify its own beneficial owners and forward the correct amount of money to the actual owners.

The main steps to process a dividend are:

Event Notification

Brokers and custodians are normally notified of a dividend event by their market data vendors, through an automated interface. The information is usually provided overnight in batch.

Entitlement Determination

Brokers and custodians must process this information against their position files to see which accounts are likely to be affected, based upon the positions and the record date for the event.

Notice of the dividend's amount, record date and payment date will be placed in the firm's pending file until the payment date is reached.

Event Posting

When the execution (payment) date is reached, the firm's system will automatically make the necessary entries to each account.

On payment date, the income collection system will post the amounts that are anticipated to be received, either:

- Directly from the paying agent for securities that are held by the bank in their own nominee name
- Directly from the paying agent for physical securities that are held by the bank in their client's name
- From the DTC for the bulk of the securities which are held in the DTC's nominee name

The dividends are generally posted to the clients' accounts, and the total of these credits is set up as a receivable from the paying agent and/or from the DTC. On the payment date, the bank will receive a wire transfer from the paying agent and/or a credit from the DTC.

Simultaneously, the DTC will determine how much each bank and broker should receive in dividends and credit their account. At this point, the amount credited to the clients' accounts should equal the amount received from the DTC.

The DTC anticipates receiving an amount from the paying agent equal to the amount it pays to its participants. DTC has a 2:30 deadline for receipt of payments from the paying agents, and is prepared to reverse the credit to the participants if they do not receive their payments; however, virtually 100% of all payments to the DTC are received on time, even on peak payment days.

In 2003, DTC processed 3.4 million dividends and interest payments worth $1.2 trillion.

Reconciliation

There are many reasons why the amount expected to be received or the shares on hand do not match what the DTC thinks the position is. These differences could be in the areas of record date, payment date, rate, position, etc. In these cases, the broker or custodian must reconcile their position and investigate any differences.

When there is a discrepancy between brokers, and one broker is due funds from another broker, this is usually the result of a failed trade over record date.

Ex-Dividend Trading

In processing dividends, there are several different types of dates that are important:

Declaration Date

The declaration date is the day that the issuer announces the event. For a dividend, the declaration includes the record and payable dates, currency, and the amount of the dividend.

Ex-Dividend Date

The ex-dividend date is the day on which the buyer pays a reduced price for the security to reflect the amount of the dividend. The ex-date is usually established as two days prior to the record date so that the buyer's trade will settle after the record date for that dividend. For all trades made before the ex-date the buyer is entitled to the dividend and for all trades made on or after ex-date the seller is entitled to the dividend.

Record Date

The record date is the date on which the distribution agent will determine who will receive the dividend.

Payment Date

The payment date is the date on which the payment is actually made to the holders of record.

Impact of Ex-Dividend Processing

As shown in the following chart, when the trade date is before the ex-date, the buyer pays the $25 and sees the investment drop to $24 on ex-date; however, the buyer then receives the right to the dividend since he holds the security on record date, and will receive the money on payment date.

"ABC Directors declare a $1.00 per share dividend with a Record Date of Tuesday, 7/24."

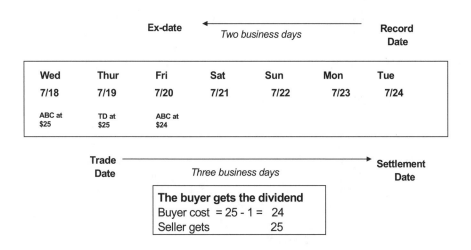

Figure 150 - Ex-Dividend Example (1)

As shown in the next chart, when the trade is on or after the ex-date, the value of the share has dropped by the amount of the dividend, and the buyer gets it for $24, and the seller gets the $24 plus the $1 dividend.

"ABC Directors declare a $1.00 per share dividend with a Record Date of Tuesday, 7/24."

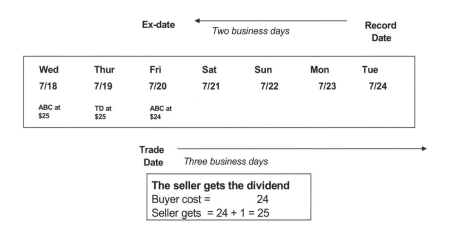

Figure 151 - Ex-Dividend Example (2)

Interest Collection – Registered Bonds

Stocks pay dividends and bonds pay interest. While dividends are granted at the discretion of the issuer's board of directors, interest payments are usually defined when the bond is issued.

When interest payments are required for registered bonds, the issuer provides the paying agent with sufficient funds to make the payments. The transfer agent notifies the paying agent of the identity of the holders it knows, including custodians and the DTC. If the bond is a variable rate bond or an indexed bond, the paying agent must verify that the rate is correct.

Interest payments are obligations of the issuer, and the bond trustee has the fiduciary responsibility to monitor whether the amount that was paid is the correct amount. If the actual name of the bondholder is registered, then the paying agent pays the owner. If a nominee holds the bonds, then the nominee receives the payment and must make the appropriate payments to the actual owners based upon the nominee's records. Bond interest can be paid monthly, quarterly, semiannually or annually. Interest is paid at the end of a period, and bond interest is an expense to the issuer.

The paying agent acts in a fiduciary capacity and is responsible to the bondholders, not to the issuer.

Interest is accrued throughout the period between payments and is paid by the buyer to the seller if the bond is sold between payment periods. The buyer will receive the full amount of the interest payment from the issuer on the next payment date. Interest is calculated differently on different types of fixed income instruments, and is defined in the chapter on Products and Instruments.

There are two key dates in interest processing:

- **Record Date** - The record date is the day on which entitlement to interest payment is established.

- **Payment Date** - The payment date is the day on which the payment of interest will be made.

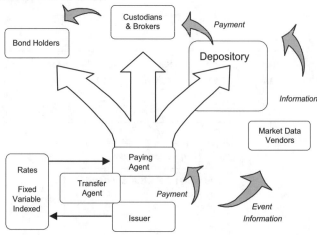

Figure 152 - Interest Processing

Interest Collection – Bearer Bonds

At one time all bonds were issued in physical form, and interest was paid when the holder presented detachable coupons to the paying agent. These were called bearer bonds because the interest and principal was paid to the bearer of the instrument. Whoever physically held the instrument was considered to be the legal owner. In 1982, congress passed a law that eliminated bearer bonds, and which required all subsequent issues to be in registered form.

Some bearer bonds that were issued prior to the law still exist, and these have physical coupons that must still be presented in order to receive interest payments.

Bearer Bond Interest Processing

The process for paying interest on bearer bonds is different from paying on registered bonds, as follows:

- The bondholder removes the coupon from the bond and presents it to an accredited paying agent or co-paying agent for that issue.

- The paying agent or the co-paying agent collects the coupon from the bondholder and pays the interest that is described on the coupon.

- A co-paying agent bundles the coupons that have been received and presents them to the paying agent for credit. The co-paying agent will be reimbursed for the amount they paid to the clients, plus a processing fee.

- The paying agent will either receive the coupons from the co-paying agent(s) or directly from the clients.

- The paying agent bundles together all of the coupons received directly from clients as well as those from co-paying agents and presents an invoice to the issuer for the total of the payments to clients, plus the co-paying agent fees and their paying agent fees.

- The paying agent will then cancel the coupons and either stores them for some defined period of time or destroys them.

Corporate Actions

Conceptually, corporate actions are easy to understand. The difficulty comes in the processing details and in making sure that everything that is supposed to happen does happen on time. Errors in processing corporate actions are very expensive for firms to correct since they may involve a financial loss for the client that the broker or custodian has to cover.

A corporate action is an event that changes the capital structure of a firm. There are several different types of corporate actions, or re-organizations, that can occur, and they can all be classified as either mandatory or voluntary.

- A mandatory corporate action is one where the issuer has the right to insist that the corporate action take place.

- A voluntary corporate action is one where the holder of the security has the right to decide whether he wants to accept or reject a proposed corporate action.

Mandatory Corporate Actions

There are several different types of mandatory corporate actions.

Merger

A merger is a combination of the assets and liabilities of two or more companies into one legal entity through the exchange of equity. The old shares are canceled and new shares are issued. The merger of Citicorp and Travelers required shareholders of both issues to present their shares, and a new equity for the new entity, Citigroup, was created.

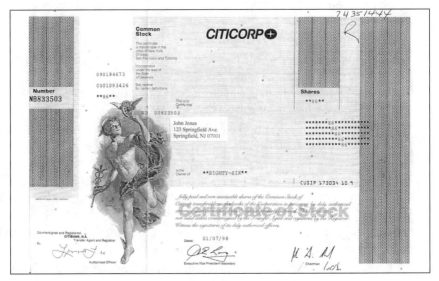

Figure 153 - Copy of Discontinued Citicorp Certificate

This is an example of a stock certificate that was registered in an individual's name. This certificate was actually created when Citicorp cancelled its DRIP program prior to the merger. The merger required the cancellation of the old certificates issued by Travelers and Citicorp, and the issuance of the new Citigroup certificates.

Acquisition

In an acquisition, the shares of one firm are cancelled and the owners of the acquired firm get new shares that are issued by the acquiring firm.

Stock Split

When a firm authorizes a stock split, it issues more shares to the existing shareholders so that while the total number of shares increases and the price per share decreases, the total market capitalization is unchanged.

For instance, if a stockholder has 100 shares of a stock with a market price of $80.00, and the issuing company announces a two-for-one split, the stockholder will now own 200 shares that are valued by the market at $40.00 each. Corporations use a stock split to reduce the price of their shares so that more potential investors will be interested in buying shares.

In the following example, the owner of 300 shares received an additional 300 shares when the stock split two for one.

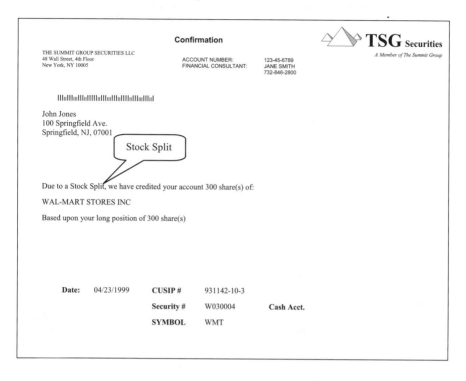

Figure 154 - Example of a Stock Split [86]

Reverse Stock Split

In a reverse split, the opposite of a stock split occurs, and the number of outstanding shares is reduced. This occurs when a firm issues new shares at a higher cost to replace the older ones. Holders of the older shares receive a smaller number of new shares.

For instance, if a stockholder has 100 shares of a stock with a market price of $2.00, and the issuing company announces a one-for-two reverse split, the stockholder will now own 50 shares that are valued by the market at $4.00 each. Corporations do this to make their stock price seem more substantial.

Stock Dividends

A firm may decide to issue a stock dividend and give additional shares to their shareholders in lieu of cash. These transactions are usually processed as a corporate action.

Calls and Redemptions

When a bond is called or matures, it is retired and redeemed for cash.

---

[86] Various types of confirmations will be used to show that each firm can establish its own format.

- A call occurs when the issuer of a bond issues a call notice in accordance with the terms of the bond indenture. A call could include all of the outstanding bonds or a portion of the outstanding issue. The owners (or the selected sub-set of the owners) of the bond must present the bond for redemption. Bonds are usually called at a premium to the current market price. Preferred shares can also be called.

- A redemption is the exchange of cash for the security. It can be the result of a call, which is mandatory, or can be a voluntary redemption if the bond indenture allows it.

- Redemptions can also occur at maturity, which is a mandatory event.

When a bond matures or is redeemed for any reason, it is usually presented to the paying agent, although a separate redemption agent can be appointed.

---

us | bank®

NOTICE TO HOLDERS OF
NEBRASKA PUBLIC POWER DISTRICT
Power Supply System Revenue Bonds, 1995 Series A

CUSIP Number*

639683 Y22	639683 Y39	639683 Y47	639683 Y54	639683 Y62	639683 Y70	639683 Y88	639683 Y96
639683 Z20	639683 Z38	639683 Z46	639683 Z53	639683 2E0	639683 z61	639683 2F7	639683 Z79

Notice is hereby given to the holders of the outstanding Power Supply System Revenue Bonds, 1995 Series A (the "1995 Series A Bonds"), of Nebraska Public Power District that there has been deposited with U.S. Bank and Trust National Association as Trustee, Investment Securities the principal and the interest on which when due will provide moneys which, together with the moneys deposited with the Trustee at the same time, shall be sufficient and available to pay the redemption price on January 1, 2005 of the 1996 Series A Bonds maturing on and after January 1, 2006, the principal of the 1995 Series A Bonds becoming due on and prior to January 1, 2005 and the interest to become due on the 1995 Series A Bonds on and prior top January 1, 2005 and that the 1995 Series A Bonds are deemed to be paid in accordance with Section 1201 of the Power Supply System Revenue Bond Resolution of the District adopted September 29, 1972.

Nebraska Public Power District
BY: U.S. BANK TRUST NATIONAL ASSOCIATION

Dated this 2nd day of July, 1998   *As Trustee*

* *No representation is made as to the correctness of the CUSIP numbers either as printed on the Bonds or as contained in this Notice.*

Figure 155 - Example of a Redemption Notice

The paying agent checks with the Securities Information Center to determine if the bond has been stolen or stopped, and if not, obtains the necessary funds from the issuer, or from a trustee if a sinking fund has been established, and pays the bondholder the amount due. The amount could be the face value of the bond, a premium or a discount.

The redeemed certificate is cancelled by punching holes into the trustee's name and signature. The bond is held for a period of time before being destroyed.

Liquidation

A liquidation is the closing of a firm and the distribution of the remaining assets. A distribution of the assets will be made to the shareholders after all of the other liabilities have been satisfied. This residual amount will be distributed proportionately to the shares held.

Spin Off

A Spin Off occurs when a portion of a company is broken off and established as a separate legal entity or when a firm owns shares in another firm and distributes them to its shareholders. The new firm, if established as a corporation, has its own capital structure.

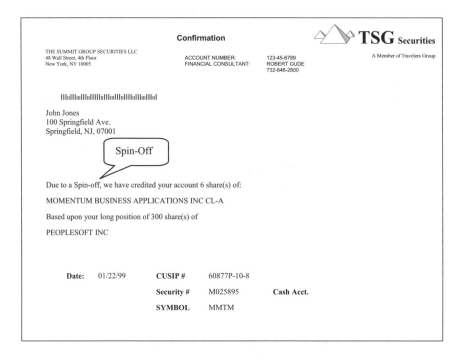

Figure 156 - Example of a Spin Off

Voluntary Corporate Actions

Voluntary corporate actions involve much more risk for custodians and brokers since they must notify their clients of the voluntary action and then collect responses within the specified period of time. Failure to properly notify the client or the issuer can result in losses for the processor.

There are numerous examples of corporate actions departments that have failed to properly process a voluntary corporate action and have taken a loss when they had to buy or sell shares on the open market to satisfy an investor's instructions. Many of these examples include a second mistake, where the manager of the corporate action department decided to *wait a few days* to see if the price of the equity would slide back down and the loss would be smaller.

This decline in price is usually expected since after the offer deadline, the premium price is generally not available. While we do not hear stories of the managers who succeeded in satisfying the client without taking a loss since they don't want their superiors to know about the original error, there are many examples where the market went against the department manager and the loss grew to the point of discovery.

There are several different types of voluntary corporate actions.

Convertible Bonds (Conversion)

A conversion occurs when one instrument is exchanged for another instrument, usually with the same company. For example, a convertible bond or preferred shares can be exchanged for common shares.

The terms of the conversion are usually defined in the original instrument, and may be allowed only within specific time periods.

Tender Offer

A tender offer is a formal offer by one company or individual to buy the shares of another company with cash, securities, or a combination of both. If either the corporation or its shareholders object, this is called an *unfriendly takeover* or a *hostile takeover*.

This is a voluntary event; however, if the target firm is acquired, the acquirer may then elect to do something else that could become a mandatory action.

The following example is a tender offer for debentures. The tombstone identifies who is making the offer and the security they wish to acquire.

This announcement is neither an offer to purchase nor a solicitation of an offer to sell the Debentures. The Offer is made only by the Company's Letter to Debenture holders dated July 10, 1998.

$150,000,000

MacMillan Bloedel Limited

and

MacMillan Bloedel (Delaware) Inc.

announce a

Fixed Spread Tender Offer

for

8 1/2% Guaranteed Debentures due January 15, 2004

Guaranteed as to Payment of Principal and Interest by MacMillan Bloedel Limited

MacMillan Bloedel Limited ('MBL') and MacMillan Bloedel (Delaware) Inc. ("MBD" and together with MBL, the "Company") have offered to purchase any and all of MBD's outstanding 814% Guaranteed Debentures due January 15, 2004 (the 'Debentures') at a price to be determined at the time the holder agrees to tender its Debentures. The purchase price for a Debenture will be calculated as the price resulting from a Yield to Maturity equal to the sum of (i) the yield on the Reference U.S. Treasury Note specified below as calculated by Salomon Smith Barney in accordance with standard market Practice, based on the bid price for such Reference U.S. Treasury Note at the time the holder agrees to tender such Debentures, as displayed only by Teler6te Page 500, plus (ii) the fixed spread specified below. In addition, the Company will pay accrued and unpaid interest to (but excluding) the settlement date. The offer is more fully described in the Letter to Debenture holders dated July 10, 1998.

Issue and CUSIP	Outstanding Principal Amount	Reference U.S. Treasury Note	Fixed Spread
8.50% due 01/15/04 554780-AA-4	$150,000,000	5.375% due 06/30/03	85 bp

In order to tender, holders must call their Salomon Smith Barney representative or call Salomon Smith Barney at the number listed below. Additional information for the offer may be obtained from MCM "CORPORATEWATCH'" Services on Telerate Page 7552, or from the Dealer Manager.

THE TENDER OFFER EXPIRES AT 5:00 p.m., NEW YORK TIME, JULY 17, 1998, UNLESS EXTENDED.

The Dealer Manager for the Offer is:

Salomon Smith Barney

Seven World Trade Center
New York, NY 10048
Liability Management Group
1-800-558-3745

Salomon Smith Barney is a service mark of Salomon Brothers Inc. Salomon Brothers Inc and Smith Barney Inc are affiliated but separately registered broker/dealers dealers under common control of Salomon Smith Barney Holdings Inc. Salomon Brothers and Salomon Smith Barney Holdings Inc have been licensed to use the Salomon Smith Barney service mark.

July 10, 1998

Figure 157 - Example of a Tender Offer

Warrants

A warrant is a certificate given to stock/bondholders by an issuer that is similar to an option, but has a longer expiration period, usually ten to twenty years. It allows the owner to purchase the issuing corporation's stock at a certain price over a stated period of time. It is a negotiable instrument and can be sold to another investor if the holder chooses not to exercise.

Warrants are often attached to another security such as a bond, as an inducement to investors, and the warrant can usually be detached and traded separately.

Right

While a right can be any form of benefit granted by a company to its stockholders, it generally refers to an opportunity to buy additional shares. Current shareholders can be given the opportunity to purchase additional equity in advance of the issue of additional shares. The document that is evidence of this privilege is called a right.

Rights are generally offered at a price below the current market price. As a result, the rights have a short-term intrinsic value and can be traded on the open market. If a right has not been exercised prior to the expiration date, it becomes worthless.

Optional Dividends

Companies can issue an optional dividend to their stockholders that allows the stockholder to select between additional shares and cash. This is most commonly used by mutual funds.

Put Bond

A put bond is a bond that is sold with an attached put that cannot be separated and traded separately from the bond. The bond can be sold back (or *put*) to the issuer at a pre-determined price within a specific time frame.

Corporate Action Processing

Although there are many different types of corporate actions, there are several distinct functions that must be performed for all of the different types.

Event Notification

Brokers and custodians are normally notified of a corporate event by their market data vendors, through an automated interface. The information is normally provided overnight in batch.

Entitlement Determination

The processor must process this information against the position files to see which accounts are likely to be affected. This is based upon the positions and the record date for the event.

- If it is a mandatory action, it will be placed in the firm's pending file until the execution date is reached.
- If it is a voluntary action, the firm must contact the client to determine what the client wants to do.

Client Notification

Voluntary corporate actions require the custodian to inform the stock/bondholder of the corporate action event and to explain the choices that the client has. The custodian must notify the client, obtain a decision from the client and notify the appropriate corporate trust agent of the decision before a deadline date.

This process must be carefully monitored and detailed records maintained. The firm must avoid the possibility of not notifying a client of a voluntary event and finding later that the client wanted to exercise his or her rights. If a loss occurs, the processor is financially responsible for this error.

Event Posting

When the execution date is reached, the system will automatically make the necessary entries to each account. This same event should be occurring at the DTC, so the positions should be balanced.

Reconciliation

There are many reasons why the amount received or the shares on hand are not what the firm's records reflect. In this case, the processor must reconcile the position and investigate any differences.

Processing Activities

For some types of corporate actions, nothing is distributed from the issuer to the stock or bondholder except information. When an issuer changes its name, the processor must recognize this information in their system simultaneously with the other processor so that the security can be accurately traded and settled. Replacement shares may or may not be issued.

In 2003, DTC processed 11,350 corporate actions valued at $1 trillion, plus 282,000 redemptions worth $858 billion.

The following types of corporate actions require an exchange of certificates, a distribution of a certificate in either physical or electronic form, or a payment in cash:

- Acquisition (Mandatory)
- Calls and Redemptions (Mandatory)
- Convertible Bonds (Conversion) (Voluntary)
- Liquidation (Mandatory)
- Merger (Mandatory)
- Put Bond (Voluntary)
- Reverse Stock Split (Mandatory)
- Rights (Voluntary)
- Spin Off (Mandatory)
- Stock Dividends (Mandatory)
- Tender Offer (Voluntary)
- Warrants (Voluntary)

The receipt or distribution of securities and/or the distribution of cash will also flow from the issuer through a corporate trust department to the processor. From there it goes to the client.

Corporate Trust Activities

Transfer agents are responsible for processing mandatory events in a timely fashion, but have not always met their processing goals. SEC Rules 17Ad-1 through 17Ad-5 require registered transfer agents to complete 90% of the routine processing within three business days. Routine processing excludes reorganizations, tender offers, exchanges, redemptions and liquidations.

The Securities Industry Association (SIA) has determined that transfer agent turnaround today can exceed thirty days and be up to 180 days, and is working to identify appropriate solutions.

Role of the Corporate Action Department

The Corporate Actions Department, also called the Reorganization (or Reorg) Department, monitors the capital structure activities of issues that are held by the firm and for the firm's clients. The primary activities that occur are:

Information Management

Receiving and using information about issues

Maintaining Issues

Updating issues automatically or based upon a new event

Restructuring Issues

Changing an issue based upon an event

Retiring Issues

Closing an issue and eliminating the line item

Typical Organization of a Corporate Actions Department

The Corporate Actions Department is often organized based upon the following categories of activities. The actual organization will depend upon the size of the department, the volumes of activity, the level of automation and the skills of the staff.

Information Management

A Corporate Actions Department must collect manual and electronic information and use it correctly to meet the objectives of the corporate actions while limiting risk to the client and the firm.

Corporate Action Types

Some firms organize their staff into teams who focus on specific categories of corporate actions. Some of these potential groupings are:

- Mandatory vs. Voluntary Actions
- Subscriptions vs. Redemptions

Control

The Control activity is responsible for ensuring that the processing is performed correctly.

International

The International activity is responsible for processing corporate actions for non-U.S. issues.

Reference Data

Reference data is relatively static information about securities (e.g., type of security, settlement method, corporate actions, paying agent, transfer agent, income payment frequency, etc.) or clients (address, payment histories, ID numbers, etc.).

New Securities

The pricing department is also usually responsible for setting up new securities on the firm's securities master file. Although there are millions of securities available in the market, most clients only invest in a small portion of the available issues. Since there is an expense associated with systemically maintaining the information about each of these securities, firms tend to only maintain a subset of the available securities.

- When a client trades an issue for the first time or when a new issue is created, that security must be promptly and properly added to the master file.

- For mutual funds, the security must be added the day it is traded in order to process the security on the trade date and to have the information about the trade available to the trust accountants.

Most firms price new securities today in a two-step process:

- Add a shell for the new security during the day in which the security is traded

- Add full information about the security during the overnight batch update

If the settlement cycle is reduced in the future, more of this process will have to be conducted in real-time.

Issues that are incorrectly set up or that have erroneous prices can cause client statements to be incorrect, and they may have to be recalculated.

Corporate Actions

Firms throughout the industry need information about new corporate action events in order to process them effectively, especially if they are voluntary actions with a deadline. This formation is gathered by many different vendors and generally made available to firms as a batch input to their corporate action processing modules.

Clients

The client master file is a critical component of the firms processing and contains information about the client that has been entered by the firm, often manually when the account was originally established.

Pricing

There are four activities that require prices:

- Real-Time Pricing
- End-of-Day Pricing

- Pricing of New Issues
- Price-Related Analytics

Impact of Pricing Errors

Errors on pricing can have an immediate impact and result in cascading errors. Some of the impacts are:

- Erroneous fund or portfolio valuations
- Incorrect trading decisions
- Incorrect confirmations and settlements

The single largest source of processing and accounting errors comes from bad data.

Real-Time Pricing

Each exchange and NASDAQ is required to report every trade made through their facilities, and to make that information available to the public. It is possible for individuals to see the actual trades through a variety of sources for free; however, this information is usually delayed by at least 15 minutes. Professional traders and investors who want real-time information can purchase this information from market data vendors. Each exchange reports every transaction using the symbol for that security, the volume of the trade, and the price of the trade.

Real-time pricing systems are connected throughout the trading day to the sources of the data, such as the stock exchanges, NASDAQ, etc. The primary focus of these applications is to present a small amount of data in messages about each trade as fast as possible to traders throughout the industry.

Trading systems receive real-time market information from a variety of sources. The front office usually needs this information in real-time since seconds count in making decisions regarding trades and initiating a trade.

End-of-Day Pricing

Custodians and brokers formally price their clients' portfolios periodically, usually monthly or quarterly. While real-time prices are used to make buy and sell decisions and to determine margin positions, securities processors typically use month-end prices to establish the value of a client's portfolio. Mutual fund processors price daily or more frequently.

While most clients expect to see a priced portfolio with their statement, some types of clients must receive this pricing service as a condition of their agreement with the broker or custodian. For example, pension funds are required to get fully priced statements from their custodians according to ERISA.

These prices are generally obtained from the exchanges or from market data vendors through a batch file that is used by the firm's application to value the portfolios. Most of the commonly traded securities can be priced electronically, based upon the last actual trade for the security on the day the issue is priced. Some categories of instruments, such as municipal bonds and partnerships, are not very liquid, and firms must acquire estimated prices from vendors that provide this service or by calling traders and asking their opinions.

Pricing departments obtain their prices from market data vendors for liquid securities and the prices are automatically entered into the bank's custody system; however, the department must typically make individual phone calls to multiple sources to find the prices for illiquid issues and private placements.

Increasingly, brokerage clients are able to see their portfolios updated online throughout the day (with at least a 15 minute delay).

End-of-day pricing systems are only connected periodically to the sources of information and receive data in batches. The file contains more information about each security, including the closing price, and it is used to update the processor's positions in a batch process.

Price-Related Analyses

Most pricing analyses are conducted by investment managers and brokers conducting research. The research process involves using new prices to update history trend files and other types of analytical files, including:

- Yields
- Duration
- Convexity

Systems that support research and analysis usually require price histories that are maintained in a time-series data base.

Proxy

A proxy is a form that is given by a shareholder to authorize someone else to vote in the shareholder's place at a shareholder's meeting. The proxy notice is the official notice of the specific issues requiring a vote by the shareholders, and a description of the shareholder's voting rights. The vote usually is held at the corporation's regular annual meeting or at a special meeting. The shareholder can place their own vote, or give their proxy to someone else to vote in their place.

When a company issues a proxy and the securities are held by the owner, the proxy information can be mailed directly to the owner. However, in most cases, the company's registrar only knows that the DTC or specific banks and brokers hold a certain number of shares or bonds. The DTC, in turn, only knows which of DTC's bank and broker participants hold securities in the DTC's nominee name, and do not know who the actual underlying clients are. It's only the brokers and the banks that know the identity of their clients.

Proxy Process

The registrar for a security knows which clients hold securities in physical form and knows the amount of securities that are held by the DTC and directly by the banks and brokers. As shown in the following chart the registrar will distribute documents in one of three ways:

- Directly to the holders of the security
- Directly to the banks and brokers
- To a proxy service that is used by the brokers to distribute material

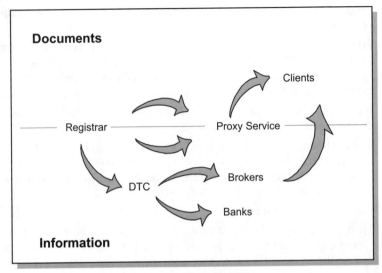

Figure 158 - Proxy Process

These proxy services receive electronic input from the brokers regarding the holders of the securities and physical documents (proxy forms, annual reports, etc.) from the issuer's agent. The services then forward the appropriate material to the security owners, collect the proxies that are returned by the holders and record the votes.

The major proxy service in the U.S. today is ADP, which bought up two of its major rivals, Independent Election Corporation and Shareholder Services.

The overall flow of the proxy process consists of the following steps:

- A corporation decides upon the issues requiring a vote
- The issuer advises the market of the event
- Depositories, banks and brokers identify shareholders based upon the record date established by the corporation
- Banks and brokers that do their own proxy processing notify the issuer of how many proxy packages they need
- Banks and brokers that outsource proxy activity provide the service with a list of the holder's names and addresses
- Banks, brokers and services all receive the number of proxy packages requested from the issuer.
- Banks, brokers and services address and mail the proxy packages to the shareholders.

Proxy Form

The following example of a proxy form shows that the holder of the security has 1,750 shares and the issues to be voted upon are listed on the left-hand side of the form.

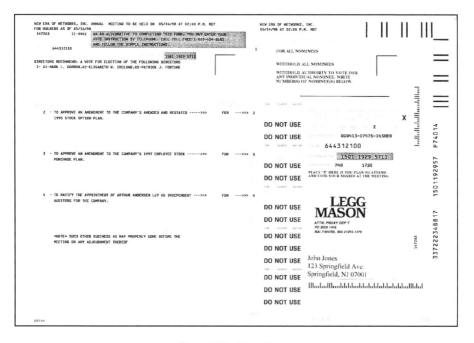

Figure 159 - Proxy Form

The issues reflected in this example are:

- Elect directors
- Approve an amendment to the employee's stock option plan
- Approve an amendment to the employees stock purchase plan
- Ratify the appointment of the independent auditors

Annual Meeting of Shareholders

Corporations hold regular annual meetings, and announcements of these meetings are sent to shareholders.

CCA INDUSTRIES, INC.

NOTICE OF ANNUAL MEETING OF SHAREHOLDERS

June 16, 1998

To The Shareholders:

NOTICE IS HEREBY GIVEN that the Annual Meeting of Shareholders of CCA INDUSTRIES, INC., a Delaware corporation (hereinafter, the "Company"), will be held on June 16,1998, at 4 p.m. at the Grand Hyatt Hotel, Park Avenue at Grand Central Station, New York, New York, for the following purposes:

Management Proposals

1. To elect directors to serve on the board of directors for the ensuing year.
2. To approve the appointment of Sheft Kahn & Company L.L.P. as the Company's independent certified public accountants for the fiscal year ending November 30, 1998.
3. To consider and vote upon a proposal to amend the Company's Certificate of Incorporation to authorize the board of directors to issue up to 20,000,000 shares of Preferred Stock in one or more series with such preferences, limitations, and relative rights as the Board may determine.

Other Matters

To transact such other business as may property come before the meeting or any adjournment thereof.

*   *   *

The foregoing items of business are more fully described in the Proxy Statement accompanying this notice.
Only shareholders of record at the close of business on May 12, 1998 are entitled to notice of the meeting, and to vote at the meeting and at any continuation or adjournment thereof.

BY ORDER OF THE BOARD OF DIRECTORS

// Original Signed //

IRA W. BERMAN,

East Rutherford, New Jersey   Corporate Secretary and Chairman of the Board

April 20, 1998

WHETHER OR NOT YOU PLAN TO ATTEND THIS MEETING, YOU ARE URGED TO COMPLETE, SIGN AND RETURN THE ENCLOSED PROXY CARD. NO POSTAGE NEED BE AFFIXED IF MAILED IN THE UNITED STATES AND IN THE ENVELOPE PROVIDED THEREFOR.

Figure 160 - Annual Meeting Notice

Proxy – Special Meeting

The following is an example of a letter notifying shareholders that a special meeting will be held to vote upon a proposed merger. This letter would have either been sent directly to the holder of a physical certificate or through a proxy service.

Registered stockholders who plan to attend the meeting may be asked for identification. If you are a beneficial owner of Citicorp stock held by a bank, broker, or investment plan (in 'street name"), you will need proof of ownership to be admitted. A recent brokerage statement or a letter from the broker or bank are examples of proof of ownership.

Fold and Detach Here   Fold and Detach Here

PROXY - SPECIAL MEETING

Special Meeting of Stockholders - July 22, 1998, 3:00 P.M., (New York City time), 399 Park Ave, New York N.Y.

The undersigned appoints P.J. Collins, J.S. Reed, and W.R. Rhodes, or any of them, proxies, each having power to substitute another person, to vote all the stock of Citicorp held of record by the undersigned on June 5, 1998 at the Special Meeting of Stockholders of Citicorp, to be held on July 22, 1998 and at any adjournment thereof. The proxies have authority to vote such stock as indicated on the reverse side hereof. The proxies are further authorized to vote such stock upon any other business that may properly come before the meeting or any adjournment thereof.

Please indicate on the reverse side of this card how your stock is to be voted. Unless you otherwise indicate, this proxy will be voted 'FOR" the proposal to approve and adopt the Agreement and Plan of Merger between Citicorp and Travelers Group Inc.

Please date and sign this proxy on the reverse side and return it promptly whether or not you expect to attend the meeting. You may, nevertheless vote in person if you do attend. We thank you for your interest.

THIS PROXY IS SOLICITED ON BEHALF Of THE BOARD OF DIRECTORS

Figure 161 -Proxy Notice

IF YOU WISH TO VOTE BY TELEPHONE
PLEASE READ THE INSTRUCTIONS
BELOW

CITICORP

Citicorp encourages you to take advantage of new and convenient ways to vote your shares for matters to be covered at the Special Meeting of Stockholders to be held on Wednesday, July 22, 1998, 3:00 P.M. (New York City time), at 399 Park Avenue, New York, New York 10043. Please take the opportunity to use one of the voting methods outlined below to cast your ballot. We've made it easier than ever.

John Jones
100 Springfield Ave.
Springfield, NJ, 07001

VOTE BY PHONE - 1-800-690-6903

Use any touch-tone telephone to vote your proxy. Have your proxy card in hand when you call. You will be prompted to enter your 12-digit Control Number that is located below and then follow the simple instructions the Vote Voice provides you.

VOTE BY MAIL –

Mark, sign and date your proxy card and return it in the postage-paid envelope we've provided or return to Citicorp, c/o ADP, 51 Mercedes Way, Edgewood, NY 11 717.

CONTROL NUMBER: 358464858977

Fold and Detach Here Fold and Detach Here

PROXY - SPECIAL MEETING

CITICORP

If you vote by phone please do not mail your proxy.

THANK YOU FOR VOTING

THE BOARD OF DIRECTORS RECOMMENDS A VOTE FOR THE FOLLOWING PROPOSAL:	FOR	AGAINST	ABSTAIN
PROPOSAL TO APPROVE AND ADOPT THE AGREEMENT AND PLAN OF MERGER DATED AS OF APRIL 5, 1998 BY AND BETWEEN CITICORP AND TRAVELERS GROUP INC. AND THE TRANSACTIONS CONTEMPLATED THEREBY	___	___	___

000109343407059 238 PLEASE MARK YOUR CHOICE LIKE THIS _X_ 3584648589 013421774029

SIGNATURE______________ DATE ______

SIGNATURE______________ DATE ______

Please sign here exactly as your name(s) appear(s) to the right. Executors, trustees, and others WARREN NJ 07059-5444 signing in a representative capacity should include their names and the capacity in which they sign.

John Jones
100 Springfield Ave.
Springfield, NJ, 07001

Figure 162 - Proxy Notice

Using Proxy's to Vote

Most small shareholders usually sign their proxy form and return it to be voted in accordance with management's recommendation.

Throughout much of the 1990's, investment managers have become increasingly involved in the governance of the firms in which they invest, and they may decide to vote against management if they do not feel that management's proposals are in their best interest. The wishes of individual shareholders usually don't get too much attention, unless they hold a significant number of shares.

While it is rare, as shown in the following excerpt, it is possible for shareholders to vote against the interests of the Board of Directors.

Talley's Chairman, a Director, Ousted in Proxy Fight, Preliminary Count Finds

In a proxy vote, shareholders of Tally Industries, Inc., ousted William Mallender as chairman and a director and Townsend Hoopes, as a director, according to a preliminary count. Mr. Mallender is expected to remain as chief executive officer.

The vote marked a victory for a group of investors calling itself "Shareholders' Committee to Remove Entrenched and Arrogant Management." The dissidents rallied shareholders of the developer of airbag technology ... to vote against the two directors in favor of their own slate. The dissident holders own about 10% of Phoenix-based Tally's 13.9 million shares outstanding.

...

Source: Wall Street Journal

Figure 163 - Results of Proxy Voting

Increasingly, shareholders are encouraged to vote electronically.

- This can be accomplished by the telephone or via the Internet. When the investor calls the telephone number to vote, they are asked a series of questions using a Computer Voice Response (CVR) system, and they enter their responses using the telephone keypad.

- Investors can also access specific web sites that have been established to record votes. One such web site can be found at www.proxyvote.com.

Escheatment

Escheatment is the process of remitting to the state any money where the beneficial owner can not be identified. The basis for the unclaimed property law originated during the colonization of America, and requires each state to maintain unclaimed funds and related owner information for claim by the rightful owner. The states must make a diligent effort to locate and refund these funds to the rightful owner, at no cost to the owner.

Since that time, states have revised and refined their various unclaimed property laws. Different states have different rules, but in general, any money that has been unidentified for three years is remitted to the state.

Unclaimed property related to the securities industry includes:

- Savings and checking accounts
- Uncashed payroll or cashiers checks
- Certificates of deposit
- Client deposits or overpayments
- Uncashed death benefit checks
- Stock and dividends
- Oil and gas royalty payments

- Contents of safety deposit boxes

In order to help banks and brokers work within the law, the National Association of Unclaimed Property Administrators was formed, with several goals in mind:

- Education regarding the laws relating to unclaimed property, abandoned property, and escheatment and the development of lectures, seminars, and training programs regarding the unclaimed property laws

- A central point for discussing questions of jurisdiction in the application of various states' unclaimed property laws

- Lobbying for uniform legislation concerning the identification, collection, and custodial function of unclaimed property

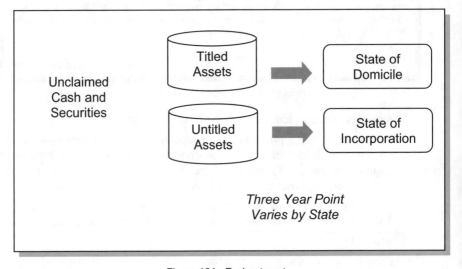

Figure 164 - Escheatment

Also, in general, as shown in the previous chart, if the assets are related to a specific person who can no longer be located, the escheatment is to the state of the person's last known residence. If the assets cannot be related to an individual, they are remitted to the state of incorporation of the brokerage firm or bank. This sometimes creates additional confusion when a firm may have its main office in one state and the firm was incorporated in another.

A firm can subsequently re-claim the escheated money if the beneficial owner is identified.

If a person, bank or broker makes a claim against a firm for assets that the firm has escheated, the escheater can submit an affidavit as shown in the following chart along with proof of the escheatment to the state to reclaim the funds.

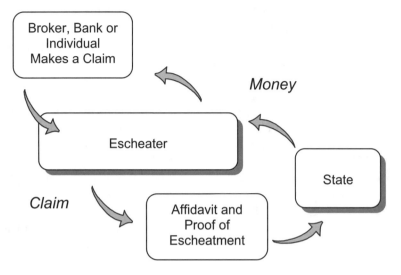

Figure 165 - Escheatment Process

Lost or Stolen Instruments (Stop Payments)

When stocks, bonds, or coupons are lost or stolen, they should be reported to the Securities Information Center (SIC), which maintains official lists. When an investor claims to have lost a certificate, the broker or custodian will check with the SIC to see if the certificate has been previously reported and if not, will record the loss. The issuing agent will cancel the old certificate in their records and issue a new certificate.

B. GENERIC POST-TRADE FUNCTIONS

In addition to asset servicing, there are several other generic functions that are performed by custodians and brokers for their clients, including:

- Record Keeping
- Cash Management
- Foreign Exchange
- Accounting
- Reporting
- Audit
- Risk Management
- Compliance
- Performance Measurement
- Securities Transfer
- Securities Lending

Record Keeping

Brokers and custodians are required to keep detailed records of their client's transactions, income collected, corporate actions, etc.

- Brokers present the results of these records in the form of confirmations, and in a monthly or quarterly statement that is sent to each client.

- Custodians will also keep detailed records and will generally prepare whatever reports their institutional clients require, so long as the client is willing to pay for them.

These records must be maintained for several years, and since the volume of paper is so great, they have historically been kept on microfiche. The problem of recovering a specific document that is needed in a short amount of time has led to vendors providing some form of electronic indexing, so that the operations staff can quickly recover a required document.

One issue is that the date for certain types of records must be stored in a non-alterable media. And, a second issue is that the regulators are insisting the archived material be quickly recoverable.

As data storage costs have dropped, electronic storage of record images has become increasingly common.

Cash Management

Cash management is used to maximize the return on liquid assets and can take two forms:

Cash Management for the Firm

A firm's objective is to have enough cash on hand to meet immediate funding requirements and regulatory obligations while simultaneously investing as much cash as possible in short term assets.

Cash Management for Clients

Cash management for clients requires banks, brokers and investment managers to have one or more of the following:

- Investment products
- Process that helps clients who manage their own accounts utilize these products
- Process that manages cash for clients where the firm has investment discretion

Different types of firms have different cash management requirements that are discussed in their respective chapters.

Cash Management Systems

Cash management systems provide information about cash positions today and cash projections of future cash requirements to cover future settlement events. For some accounts, the systems provide an automatic investment feature (often called a cash sweep) when excess cash is automatically invested overnight.

Foreign Exchange

Settlement for cross-border activities often requires an FX transaction, and may be needed for U.S. settlements. When a Global Custodian is involved, some countries require that an FX be conducted separately from the settlement and in other cases the client requests that the custodian perform the FX.

Since FX is generally related to Global Custody processing, it is beyond the scope of this book.

Accounting

One of the key roles of the back office accounting function is ensuring that the proper accounting for all transactions takes place since different types of clients and different instruments require the use of a variety of different accounting rules.

Each transaction generates debits and credits to specific accounts, which are held in sub-ledgers in the processing departments or in their systems. These sub-ledgers are then summarized into either of two major accounting documents: the General Ledger or the Income Statement.

There are several key concepts that are involved for individual types of securities.

Accruals

In accounting, an accrual is a method for recognizing an expense in the period in which it was incurred.

For bonds, interest is accrued daily at the coupon rate of the bond. Each new period starts from the last interest payment of the bond until the bond is sold, matures, is redeemed or reaches its next payment date. The buyer of a bond pays the market price plus the interest that has been accrued from the last payment to the trade date.

Expenses are also accrued when necessary to calculate the NAV for a mutual fund.

Different types of bonds accrue differently, and this topic is discussed more in the chapter on Products and Instruments.

Amortization

Amortization can be:

- The process of repaying an entire debt through a series of regular payments rather than in a lump sum

- An accounting method to regularly eliminate a balance sheet liability, deferred charge, or capital expenditure by assigning a portion of the amount as an expense in subsequent periods

- A method of pricing a Money Market Fund that determines the current NAV by calculating the current value of short-term debt instruments relative to their maturity value. For mutual funds, the alternative to amortization is for the fund to perform a daily mark to market of the positions in the fund

Accretion

Accretion is the increase in the value of certain types of fixed income instruments that occurs steadily from the time it was purchased at a discount until it is redeemed at the market value or matures at face value. For instance, a zero coupon bond accretes in value until it is redeemed at maturity.

Prior Period Adjustments

A prior period adjustment is an accounting or operational entry that is made to correct an error in a previous accounting period.

- For most clients, if an error is discovered in one period that occurred in a prior period, the broker or custodian makes the adjustment in the current period and calculates the correct amount of credit for the client.

- For pension and mutual funds, errors must be properly recorded in the period in which they occurred. That means that the fund must make an adjustment in the month the error occurred and then recalculate monthly closing balances from that point up to the current period.

Taxes

Taxes are based upon the type of:

- Client

- Account

- Security

Some accounts, such as trust accounts do not pay taxes until investment gains are distributed from the account.

In the rest of this book, the tax consequences of transactions will be discussed along with the transaction.

Cost Basis

The cost basis of a security is the accounting method that will be used to determine the cost of a security when the security is sold and the gain/loss must be calculated. There are several different types of accounting methods.

Average Cost

The most basic form of cost accounting for securities is average cost. Systems using the average cost method merely calculate the weighted average cost of the overall position when the position was acquired at different times for different prices.

Retail clients and many corporations use average cost accounting, and when some of the security is sold, the amount sold is deducted from the total, not from any specific purchase. This form of cost basis is the easiest and least costly to perform.

Tax Lot Accounting

More complicated methods involve maintaining each purchase as a separate position in the portfolio, with a separate acquisition date and a separate price. Each position is called a tax lot.

When an investor wishes to minimize taxes by using this technique when they sell a security, they will have to predefine the method they will use, and then select the specific tax lot(s) to be sold. There are two primary methods used in this more complicated way of determining gains and losses:

FIFO – First In, First Out

When a client elects to use FIFO accounting, they will sell the first lots of a position, which were presumably acquired at a lower price. Therefore, firms would have a larger realized profit, which may or may not be taxable, based upon the client's tax situation.

Non-taxable clients will generally use FIFO to maximize the reported gain.

LIFO – Last In, First Out

LIFO accounting matches the sale to the last acquired lot(s) which are assumed to have the highest cost, and usually results in a lower taxable gain.

Taxable clients will generally use LIFO to minimize tax.

Accounting Reports

The core accounting reports, which are prepared by the accounting department, are in accordance with Generally Accepted Accounting Principles (GAAP), and are:

- Daily Cash Balance and Cash Projections
- Profit and Loss Statement (P&L), also called the Income Statement
- General Ledger (and sub-ledgers)

Accounting reports are created either at a point in time to cover some period of time (day, month, quarter or year), or are created to compare one period of time to a previous period (month-to-month, quarter-to-quarter, etc).

These accounting reports show the results of transactions over a period of time.

Accounting Rules

There are several key accounting rules that are used by securities processors. Some of the most used are:

Trade Date/Settlement Date

Some categories of clients need to have their accounting based upon the actual trade date of the transaction, while other clients need the transaction to be posted on the settlement date.

Actual vs. Contractual Settlement

Securities have a pre-defined number of days after the trade in which they are scheduled to complete the settlement process. This settlement period varies by instrument type (and country) and has changed at various points in time in the U.S.'s past.

Custodians often agree to settle their client's trades on the scheduled date, regardless of when the cash and/or securities are actually available for settlement. This makes it easier for the client to reconcile positions with the custodians and ensures that the client meets their regulatory obligations. While rarely a problem in the U.S. because of the U.S.'s effective Securities Lending process, it is very useful for international trades.

Accounting Regulations

Accounting requirements are defined by a variety of laws and guidelines, including:

- FDICIA
- Sarbanes-Oxley
- SEC
- FED
- GAAP

New Accounting Report Deadlines from the SEC

When the concept of double-entry accounting and the related rules were first developed in 1494 by Luca Pacioli, an Italian monk, accounting was intended to be a cyclical process that covered certain periods of time (annually, quarterly, monthly, etc.). Accounting has become more complex and the pressure by management and the other users of financial statements to shorten the reporting cycle has increased tremendously. Most recently, the Securities and Exchange Commission (SEC) finalized rules concerning Acceleration of Periodic Report Filing Dates and Disclosure Concerning Website Access to Reports.[87]

The table below summarizes the SEC mandated changes:

For Fiscal Years Ending On or After	Form 10-K Deadline	Form 10-Q Deadline
December 15, 2002	90 days after fiscal year end	45 days after fiscal quarter end
December 15, 2003	75 days after fiscal year end	45 days after fiscal quarter end
December 15, 2004	60 days after fiscal year end	40 days after fiscal quarter end
December 15, 2005	60 days after fiscal year end	35 days after fiscal quarter end

Figure 166 - SEC Mandated Changes

By 2005, firms must be able to complete their 10-K's in sixty days and their 10-Q's in thirty-five days. For some companies this will present a huge challenge because information does not flow quickly enough into the accounting systems to allow for aggregation, management review, and audit.

The rules and penalties imposed by the Sarbanes-Oxley Act, which makes management directly responsible for the accuracy of financial statements and reporting, will be a huge source of stress for those that rely on outmoded technology and practices to complete the accounting cycle.

Reporting

There are many different types of reports that are used by firms to meet their regulatory, internal and client requirements, including:

---

[87] Final Rule: Acceleration of Periodic Report Filing Dates and Disclosure Concerning Website Access to Reports Securities and Exchange Commission. 17 CFR PARTS 210, 229, 240 and 249 [RELEASE NOS. 33-8128; 34-46464; FR-63; File No. S7-08-02] RIN 3235-AI33

- Holdings
- Strip List
- Analysis
- Performance Measurement
- Attribution
- Exposure Report
- Yields
- Risk Analysis Report
- NAV

Each type of firm in the securities industry has different reporting requirements that are discussed in their respective chapters.

Reporting Systems

Reporting systems are built around the following dimensions:

- Pre-defined vs. Ad hoc
- On-demand vs. scheduled
- As-of vs. Real-time

Different technologies are needed to meet the requirements of the different reporting applications.

Audit

An audit is a systematic examination of a firm's records and processes to ensure that the firm's transactions have been legal, accurate, and the processes are in control. When preparing for an audit, there are several predictable concerns that auditors will have, which are based upon problems that either the firm or the industry has recently experienced.

The first thing that an auditor will look for is the department's procedures. If these are not in writing, the audit is a short one, and the department fails. When the procedures do exist, the auditor uses them to ascertain if the procedures are complete and if they are being followed.

Some audit departments see their role as consultative and evaluative. They are often able to help processing areas identify weaknesses and ways to make improvements.

The other form of audit department focuses exclusively on evaluation, and to maintain an arm's length relationship will not offer an opinion or help processors change their flow.

Reconciliations

Reconciliations occur when a clerk or a system compares two different groups of information (e.g., outgoing orders vs. incoming confirmations, positions on internal books vs. positions with a custodian, income collection, etc.). The objective is to identify differences, which are often called breaks.

Reconciliations can occur daily, weekly, monthly, etc., and can be between:

- Two, or more, internal systems

- Manager to Custodian
- Broker to Manager
- Broker to a Clearing Agency
- Broker to an Exchange, NASDAQ or Alternative Trading System
- Custodian to a Depository

These different reconciliations can involve:

- Cash balances and cash transactions
- Security holdings and security transactions
- Accounting entries
- Other processing events
- Special reconciliations

In the last few years, as the requirements for reconciliations have become more complex, there has been a significant growth in the usefulness of applications that support reconciliation automation.

Purpose of Reconciliations

There are several reasons for firms to reconcile positions:

- Identify mismatches as early as possible
- Avoid problems
- Repair
- Control assets
- Control processes

Impact of Reconciliation Errors

Errors resulting from a missed reconciliation could cascade if not fixed 'immediately.'

Incorrect holdings can affect corporate actions can affect investment decisions, etc.

Determining Reconciliations Frequency

In order to determine how often reconciliation should occur, the manager should answer the following questions:

- What is the impact of an error?
- What is the potential to repair an error before it begins to cost the firm?
- How significant is the opportunity for fraud?
- Do the systems being reconciled often have differences?
- Does the external reconciling party often make errors?
- How soon will the client see errors?
- What is the cost to reconcile?
- How soon can errors be resolved?

Reconciliation Systems

Departments using these systems have to decide among several comparison parameters, such as:

- Positions or transactions
- Cash or units
- Frequency (Daily, weekly, monthly, etc.)

There are several systems that are available in the market that can help automate reconciliation.

Reconciliations are automated for several reasons, including:

- To ensure that they are applied routinely and systematically.
- To ensure that their results are permanently documented and cannot be manipulated
- Cost effectiveness – or even feasibility or performance.
- Comprehensive exception management.

Reconciliation System Functions

The primary functions of a reconciliation system are:

- External interfaces with message reformatted
- Aggregate related transactions and / or positions
- Establish running positions from transactions
- Instrument cross-referencing capability
- User defined reconciliation sequence
- Automated classification of breaks during the matching process and by user input
- Automated routing and subsequent escalation of exceptions
- Audit trails

Risk Management

Financial intermediaries are responsible for processing transactions and for managing the risk that arises from those transactions.

In order to manage something, we must first be able to define it. Once we have defined it, we can determine how to measure it. And when we can measure something, we can begin to manage it.

Risk management includes several categories of risk, which can be generally categorized as market-related risk, credit risk or operations-related risk.

Market-Related Risk

Interest Rate Risk

Interest rate risk is the risk that interest rates will change and affect the value of an investment.

Price Risk

Price risk is the risk that a price will change and affect the value of an investment.

Currency Risk (FX)

Currency risk is the risk that the exchange rates will change and affect the value of an investment.

Liquidity Risk

Liquidity risk is the risk that when an investor wishes to sell an investment, there are no buyers.

Country/Sovereign Risk

Country risk is the risk that a country will undergo a significant political or economic change that will reduce the value of investments.

Performance Risk

Performance risk is the result of potential changes in positions and the market sensitivity of the positions.

Credit Risk

Lending Risk

Lending risk is also called credit risk. It is the risk that a borrower will not make interest and/or principal payments on a loan.

Issuer Risk

Issuer risk is the risk that an issuer will default on the interest payment or redemption of a bond.

Counterparty Risk

Counterparty risk is similar to settlement risk in that it is the risk that a counterparty will fail to meet the terms of an agreement.

Operational Risk

There are several categories of operational risk.

Operations Risk

Operations risk is only one part of operational risk, and includes:

- Settlement risk
- Execution risk
- Inadequate transaction processing
- Poor documentation
- Lack of proper due diligence
- Project management
- Fraud
- Discrimination and sexual harassment
- Data quality
- Data entry
- Nostro reconciliation
- Control Settlement Breaks, exceptions and fails

Fiduciary Risk

Fiduciary risk is the risk that a fiduciary will fail to perform as required by the trust agreement.

Legal, Regulatory and Compliance Risk

Legal risks are the risks that someone will violate a law or rule and that this will affect the firm through fines or criminal actions.

Business Continuity Risk

Business continuity risk is the risk that some event (natural or man-made) will occur that presents the firm from conducting business.

Employee/Staff Risk

- Destroying, concealing or falsifying records
- Improper record keeping
- Counterfeiting/forgery
- Customer confidentiality
- Misuse of important information
- Non-disclosure of sensitive issues
- Concealing losses/problem assets
- Inflating revenue/profits
- Fraudulent misrepresentation

IT Risk

- Systems failure
- System hacking
- Inadequate systems
- Inadequate system maintenance
- Email archiving
- Data security

Facilities Risk

- Arson
- Bomb threats and explosions
- Natural disasters
- Power shortage
- Telecom outage
- Terrorism

Vendor Risk

Vendor risk is the risk that a vendor will fail to perform their contractual obligations.

Relationship and Reputation Risk

- Deceptive advertising

- Churning accounts
- High-pressure sales tactics
- Sales misrepresentation
- Violating suitability rules
- Product liability
- Unauthorized trading

Scandals have reshaped the business landscape. The securities industry is highly regulated, and improper actions are eventually found. Non-compliance is costly, so it pays to know the rules. We discussed the regulation of the industry in the chapter on Regulators and Legislation.

Operational Risk Management

Operational Risk Management used to focus on preventing the small frauds and errors that could be made by clerks. The maximum exposure was thousands to hundreds of thousands of dollars, and it really only affected a few of the people who were involved or who failed to stop the problem.

Today, the risks are significantly greater as we have seen with frauds/errors that have eliminated venerable firms and destroyed hundred of careers.

- At Barings, one person was responsible for managing operations and for trading. When Barings had a bad trade, a single trader was able to post it to an unused operational account. This would have gone unnoticed if the amount in the account had not grown to over $1 billion, which was more than the capital of the firm. Barings, a UK bank with over a 100-year history, was declared insolvent and sold to ING.

- At Daiwa, there was a similar situation. When Daiwa's New York branch opened, the trader was also the branch manager. He made a bad trade, which he was unwilling to disclose. As the branch grew he was able to hide the trade, but the dollar consequence kept growing and was also eventually nearly $1 billion. The SEC closed that firm.

We can have these kinds of problems in areas throughout the firm; in investment banking, trading, operations and systems. The reasons for these problems are simple, and they occur time after time.

- People do not always understand their job, and are afraid or unwilling to admit it and have their questions answered.

- The controls that were established may not cover every step in the process and someone will try to exploit this for personal gain or ignore a problem out of neglect.

- A lack of dual controls is a specific area where firms continually run into problems. Operations managers say that they trust their staff, or that no one would cause any mischief. History proves that this is an incorrect assumption all too often.

- Insufficient oversight occurs when a control has been established but no one looks at the reports or monitors the performance of the people.

- And finally, the one that drives most of these problems -- individual unwillingness to examine good fortune -- which is also called greed. The managers at Daiwa and Barings received significant bonuses, and although they may have felt that there was something seriously wrong with the process, they did not want to see those bonuses disappear, so they just didn't ask the right questions.

Operational risk management requires a focus on internal controls, including:

- Operational Excellence
- Predictability
- Oversight
- Accountability
- Zero Tolerance

Effective risk management includes the following concepts:

- People (Training/monitoring)
- Process (Policy/procedures)
- Supervision
- Testing (Monitoring)
- Learn From Mistakes

The risk management process includes:

- Establish the context and scope of the risk management program
- Identify the risk and opportunities for the firm
- Analyze the risks
- Develop plans to address the risks
- Communicate with all of the people involved with the process
- Monitor and report on the results of the risk management process

Compliance

The overall purpose of compliance is to monitor the performance of the firm to ensure that it is performing in compliance with laws and the rules established by the SROs.

The focus on compliance has increased dramatically in the last several years as a result of the various accounting scandals that have occurred. The passage of Sarbanes-Oxley has made it clear that the executives are responsible for all of the activities of their firm and they will be held accountable if people do not follow the rules.

Compliance is not a static process. As events occur in the industry, regulators react and establish new rules that must be implemented according to an imposed timeframe. Some of the recent areas of compliance focus have been:

- Record retention
- Archiving of emails
- Investment suitability

- Adequacy of supervision
- Anti-money laundering (AML)
- Broker/employee compliance
- Trading compliance
- Do-not-call lists

Performance Measurement

In addition to the standard reporting that all clients receive, the largest clients require an activity called Performance Measurement. This is a process whereby the portfolio's performance is compared to one or more relevant benchmarks so that the portfolio's owners can see how well their investments have performed when compared to a universe of similar investments.

Securities Transfer

The transfer of a security is required when a security is bought or sold, and it may involve the legal registration of the issue into the new name. Securities can be registered in the:

- Client's or owner's name (physical certificate)
- Depository nominee name
- Broker/Custodian nominee name

Electronic Transfers

Most securities are held in a nominee name at the DTC or are electronically recorded by their broker or custodian and are transferred by moving the record of a security from one electronic file to another.

Physical Transfers

When the owner holds securities in physical form and wishes to sell them, the physical certificate must be properly endorsed and presented to the selling broker who will forward the certificate to the contra broker. The certificate ultimately will be presented to the appropriate transfer agent. If the certificate is not in negotiable form the seller will not be compensated.

Although the industry has attempted to eliminate physical certificates, they are occasionally created, and, if sold, need to be transferred.

The following photo is an example of the back of a stock certificate. The owner is required to fill out this form with appropriate endorsements and guarantees in order to transfer the physical security to the broker or custodian so that it can be deposited in the client's account or transferred.

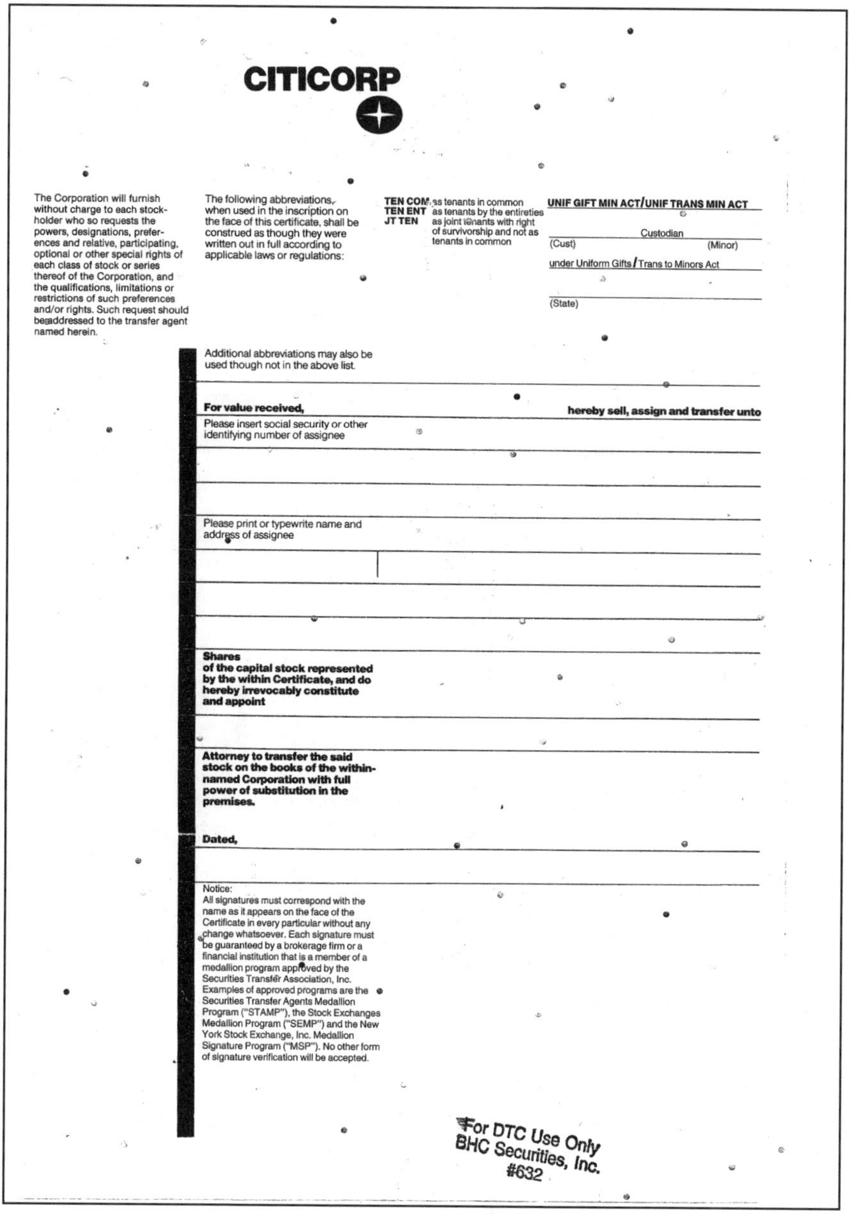

CITICORP

The Corporation will furnish without charge to each stockholder who so requests the powers, designations, preferences and relative, participating, optional or other special rights of each class of stock or series thereof of the Corporation, and the qualifications, limitations or restrictions of such preferences and/or rights. Such request should be addressed to the transfer agent named herein.

The following abbreviations, when used in the inscription on the face of this certificate, shall be construed as though they were written out in full according to applicable laws or regulations:

TEN COM — as tenants in common
TEN ENT — as tenants by the entireties
JT TEN — as joint tenants with right of survivorship and not as tenants in common

UNIF GIFT MIN ACT/UNIF TRANS MIN ACT

_____ Custodian _____
(Cust)   (Minor)

under Uniform Gifts / Trans to Minors Act

_____
(State)

Additional abbreviations may also be used though not in the above list.

For value received,   **hereby sell, assign and transfer unto**

Please insert social security or other
identifying number of assignee

Please print or typewrite name and
address of assignee

Shares
of the capital stock represented
by the within Certificate, and do
hereby irrevocably constitute
and appoint

Attorney to transfer the said
stock on the books of the within-
named Corporation with full
power of substitution in the
premises.

Dated,

Notice:
All signatures must correspond with the
name as it appears on the face of the
Certificate in every particular without any
change whatsoever. Each signature must
be guaranteed by a brokerage firm or a
financial institution that is a member of a
medallion program approved by the
Securities Transfer Association, Inc.
Examples of approved programs are the
Securities Transfer Agents Medallion
Program ("STAMP"), the Stock Exchanges
Medallion Program ("SEMP") and the New
York Stock Exchange, Inc. Medallion
Signature Program ("MSP"). No other form
of signature verification will be accepted.

For DTC Use Only
BHC Securities, Inc.
#632

Figure 167 – Back of Stock Certificate

Stock Powers

If a client submits a certificate without a proper endorsement, the firm may send a request for stock powers.

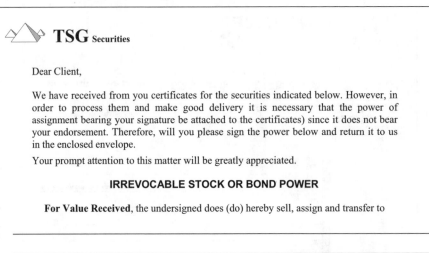

TSG Securities

Dear Client,

We have received from you certificates for the securities indicated below. However, in order to process them and make good delivery it is necessary that the power of assignment bearing your signature be attached to the certificates) since it does not bear your endorsement. Therefore, will you please sign the power below and return it to us in the enclosed envelope.

Your prompt attention to this matter will be greatly appreciated.

IRREVOCABLE STOCK OR BOND POWER

For Value Received, the undersigned does (do) hereby sell, assign and transfer to

_____

_____

_____

(SOCIAL SECURITY NUMBER OR TAXPAYER ID)

IF STOCK, COMPLETE THIS PORTION

_____ shares of the _____ stock of represented by certificate(s) No(s) _____ inclusive, standing in the name of the undersigned on the books of said Company.

IF BONDS, COMPLETE THIS PORTION

_____ bonds of _____

in the principal amount of $_____ No(s) _____ inclusive, standing in the name of the undersigned on the books of said Company.

The undersigned does (do) hereby irrevocably constitute and appoint _____ attorney to transfer the said stock or bond(s), as the case may be, on the books of said Company, with fun power of substitution in the premises.

FOR OFFICE USE ONLY

IMPORTANT: The signature(s) to this power must correspond with the name(s) as written upon the face of the certificates) or bond(s) in every particular without alteration.

_____
TITLE WHICH APPEARS ON CERTIFICATE

_____
TITLE WHICH APPEARS ON CERTIFICATE

_____
(PERSON(S) EXECUTING THIS POWER SIGN(S) HERE)

Account No. _____

Dated _____

CODE 132 REV. 3/81 PRINTED IN U.S.A.

Figure 168 - Stock Powers

Fast Automated Securities Transfer (FAST)

The DTC's Fast Automated Securities Transfer system is used to assist in transferring certificates to and from individuals, and during the issuance of new DTC eligible securities. FAST is an electronic ledger that maintains a count of the shares or bonds in the DTC's nominee name, but which is represented by a certificate that is held by the appropriate transfer agent. This reduces the need for paper certificates to move between the DTC and the various transfer agents.

Retail Account Transfer

When a retail client wishes to move an entire account from one broker to another, they initiate the transfer by filling out a retail account transfer form, such as the one shown in Chapter VIII. The actual transfer of the account takes place through an NSCC system called ACATS. The system is discussed earlier in this chapter, and the process will be presented again in the chapter on Broker Processing.

Securities Lending

Banks and brokers lend and borrow securities in order to facilitate settlement, to support arbitrage and to make a profit while they are doing it. Increasingly, Investment Managers are beginning to lend the securities they manage in order to improve their ROI.

Participants

In the securities lending business, there are borrowers and lenders. The borrowers usually have either sold short or are trying to avoid a fail to deliver, and the lenders are trying to earn some additional income on their securities through the lending process. The brokers tend to be the biggest borrowers, and the banks, with large institutional clients that essentially have static portfolios, are generally the biggest lenders.

The securities lending business has grown significantly over the years as a result of the increases in demand and the increase in the supply of securities available for loan.

Increases in demand can result from:

- Fails and short sales
- Arbitrage
- Index and options arbitrage
- DRIP

Increases in supply are the results of:

- A 1981 ruling by the U.S. Department of Labor that allowed pension plans to lend their securities
- The significant growth of mutual funds, which lend their securities

Process

At the start of each business day, the borrowers must determine what and how much they need. The securities lending market is conducted almost entirely by phone in the morning, and almost all of the trading activity is over by 10:00 a.m.

1. The firms that have securities to lend must identify what is available, and also maintain records about the firms to which their clients allow them to lend. Some lenders will also make a list of firms to whom they either will or will not lend based upon their credit evaluation.

2. When the borrowers and lenders talk on the phone, they can set the interest rate to be charged at any amount they can agree upon. If a lender has a hot security and there is much demand, the lender can charge more than for a commonly available security.

3. When they agree upon a price, the lender initiates a settlement and actually delivers the securities to the borrower through either the NSCC or the DTC. The securities remain the property of the registered owner while they are on loan and will continue to collect any interest or dividends that are due. The only complicating factor is that if a proxy is sent out, the owners must retrieve the securities in order to vote. The typical contract rules are:

    – The loan can be terminated by the lender at any time

    – Recalls are generally completed within three days

    – Cash collateral is posted by the borrower

    – Lender receives dividends and other distributions

    – Securities must be recalled in order to be voted

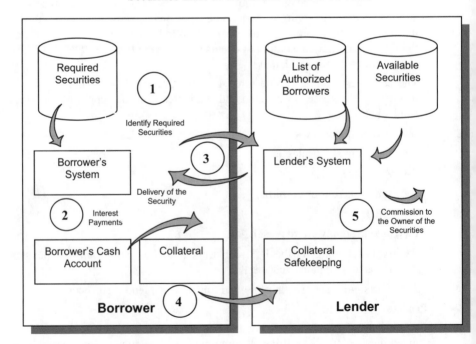

Figure 169 - Securities Lending Process Flow

4. To provide some additional stability to the market, the borrower must deliver collateral to the lender in the form of either cash or government securities. The amount of the collateral should be between 102 % and 107% of the amount of the loan. The lender will then invest the cash or receive the interest on the bonds during the life of the loan.

5. The lender will keep all of the income from the interest on both the loan and the collateral if they produced the securities from one of their retail client's accounts. If the securities came from an institutional client's account, then there is a split of the interest between the lender and the client. On some very large accounts, this activity is so profitable for the lender that they will provide custody services for free in exchange for the authority to lend.

If more than one account holds the securities that are in demand, the lender will conduct an automated lottery to select the securities that will be loaned.

Maintaining the Loan

Each loan of securities and the collateral must be priced daily in a process called mark to market. If the value of the collateral (cash or U.S. government securities) drops below 102% of the value of the loan, then the borrower has to deliver additional collateral.

The lenders have also established total credit limits on each potential borrower based upon the borrower's credit history and market conditions. The lenders must monitor the total amount lent to any one firm and ensure that they do not exceed the credit limits established by the client and/or the lender.

During the term of the loan, the borrower may find it necessary to take back their collateral, or the lender might need the securities back, and substitutions are possible.

Either side can terminate the transaction if necessary.

Closing the Loan

When the loan is closed, the borrower returns the securities and the lender simultaneously returns the collateral.

Risks

While the risks are minimal, they do exist. The biggest risk that surfaced recently was the poor use of the collateral.

In a recent event, a bank that held the collateral invested it in interest sensitive instruments, and when the interest rates changed, they actually lost a part of the principal. Although the bank initially wanted to charge this loss to the client, the other market participants convinced them that they should return the collateral in full and absorb the loss themselves, and that is what the bank finally decided to do.

IX. Broker Processing

Since securities processing is almost completely based upon the use of computers, this chapter will present how brokers process securities from a systems and an operational perspective. The architecture and information presented in this chapter is based on how firms throughout the industry handle these processes in general, and does not describe any specific firm's automation or operations environment. Each firm has its own idiosyncrasies that are based upon what functions are automated, how the automation was accomplished and when the automation was performed.

A. BROKERAGE INFORMATION SYSTEMS

Brokerage systems have been developed over the years to provide very specific automated support for activities that:

- Provide timely market information
- Interact 'immediately' with securities markets
- Process high transaction volumes
- Operate under the philosophy that after trade executions have been matched, they can be netted to eliminate the need for separate settlement transactions in the later stages of processing
- Settle only net positions between the counterparties with the DTC, not individual transactions for each client
- Post individual transactions to the client's account and create a confirmation for each transaction for each client
- Involve the extension of credit to finance purchases through a process called margin lending
- Utilize a process called Securities Lending to minimize fails to deliver

The following graphic is a high-level generic representation of the categories of systems and files that are used by brokers to support their activities. There are no definitive rules regarding which applications or functions belong in the front, middle or back office. Each firm decides based upon its own unique business, situation and processing requirements.

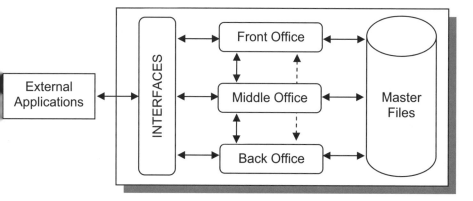

Figure 170 - Categories of Broker Systems

The rest of this section presents the master files, the interfaces and the reasons for segregating applications and functions into the front, middle and back office activities. The next section in this chapter examines each major processing function in detail.

Master Files

Applications need data to process transactions. This data is generally organized into the three major databases:

Securities Master File

The Securities Master File (SMF) contains the reference data elements that describe each security that is held or was recently held by the firm and/or its clients. This file contains descriptive information such as the name of the issue, the issuer, and the CUSIP number. It also identifies how the issue will behave under certain conditions, such as maturity, dividend declaration, interest payments, etc.

Figure 171 - Master Files

Since many firms have acquired additional applications over time, or have merged with other firms, it is not uncommon for a firm to have more than one file with information about securities. A trend in the industry is to resolve this inefficiency by developing or acquiring an application that can function as a single SMF server, and which can be used by many different applications throughout the firm. Central Security Master Files are discussed more in the chapter on Vendors.

Other firms have decided that they need multiple SMFs and have integrated them with the goal of establishing a virtual central SMF.

Stock Record

Banks and investment managers generally keep separate files for transaction history and for positions. Brokers, under regulation (SEC Rule 15c3-3), maintain one file called the stock record, which contains the position for each security at various points in time as well as the transaction history that caused the changes in the positions.

A fundamental purpose of the stock record is to segregate securities owned by the firm from securities wholly owned by the clients. Fully owned client positions in cash accounts are required to be segregated, and may not be used by the firm to finance its own activity. The broker may use client positions in margin accounts as collateral for client loans.

Client Information File

The Client Information File (CIF), also called the name and address file, contains static information about clients, such as name, address, identifying numbers and investment preferences that were gathered during the account opening process.

Most firms do not have more than one client information file unless they have acquired other firms and have not assimilated the acquired firm's systems or if the firm has established multiple, independent lines of business with separate processing applications. However, many of these CIFs were developed years ago and are not easily adapted to their current client relationship management needs.

Retail firms generally only have one CIF, while institutional firms typically have multiple CIF's that are dependent upon the instruments that are being processed.

A trend with institutional brokers is towards a single physical CIF in order to understand the clients' requirements better and to facilitate cross selling; however, many firms have decided to establish a virtual central CIF where various CIFs interact with each other when necessary.

Broker Interfaces

Brokers have a variety of interfaces to their clients, counterparties and to the industry infrastructure. Some of these interfaces are shown in the following graphic.

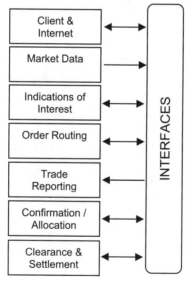

Figure 172 - External Broker Interfaces

Client Interfaces and Internet

For several years many brokers have had proprietary systems that allowed their clients to access information and even enter orders, but until the Internet allowed retail clients a way to easily access the brokers' systems, the volume was low. In the last few years, many new brokerage firms established the electronic market and captured a significant share of the retail business.

Market Data

Each firm needs to have access to a variety of different types of market data, which is either provided in real-time or in files. The various types of market data are discussed in the chapter on Vendors.

Indications of Interest

Brokers need to be connected electronically to clients who wish to use order indication software that is provided by either the broker or by vendors. This is discussed in the chapter on Vendors.

Order Routing

Once a broker receives and enters the order into its system, the order may be routed to the firm's trading floor, an exchange, NASDAQ, or ATSs and ECNs. This requires an interface to the systems used by those organizations.

Trade Reporting

A broker is required to report all of its trades in listed shares to the exchange on which it is a member.

Confirmation

Confirmations are handled differently for retail and institutional accounts.

Retail

Retail clients get a variety of paper confirmations depending upon the type of transaction and do not require any external connectivity. Examples of many of the types of confirms are presented later in this chapter.

Institutional

Once a trade has been executed for a client, it must be confirmed, and potentially allocated to the client's accounts. Much of this activity is conducted by Omgeo or other vendors providing trade processing as an add-on to their ATSs.

Clearance and Settlement Systems

Brokers use a variety of clearing corporations and the DTCC and Fed to clear and settle their transactions. Brokers often use SWIFT or central transfer functions such as Omgeo's DTC Hub to send and receive settlement related information to/from investment managers and custodian banks.

Historically, brokers' IT departments wrote dedicated programs to interface with each of the external entities. These individual interfacing programs have mostly been replaced by a category of application called middleware which is discussed in the chapter on Vendors. Middleware can be used to simplify external connectivity, and can be used to connect a firm's internal legacy systems.

Purpose of Front, Middle and Back Office Activities

As proprietary and vendor applications have added functionality and firms have used middleware to integrate their applications, the notion of a single virtual (or logical) application is closer to reality, and therefore the need for a conceptual separation of brokerage applications into front, middle and back offices systems is less important.

Although there is no clear delineation between the front, middle and back office activities, a broker's functions are often organized as shown in the following chart.

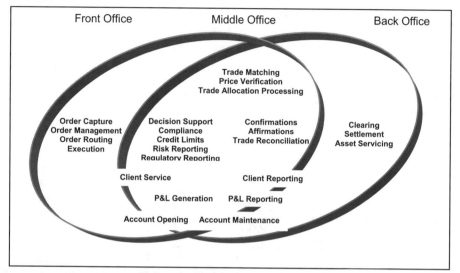

Figure 173 - Functions Arranged by Front, Middle and Back Office

There are still some generic differences between the needs of the front, middle and back office that are reflected in the way the applications have been built and in the firm's systems architecture.

Front Office

The front office applications typically provide a very interactive environment for users such as registered representatives, sales staff and traders. A large amount of information must be organized and presented in a way that can be quickly understood by the users. These applications are very time sensitive and cannot require a large number of keystrokes.

Middle Office

The middle office applications are usually more interactive with the client's applications and with the industry infrastructure. Transaction data is moved between the counterparties and the client and the clearing and settlement utilities. These applications generally are more rules-based so that they need less and less human intervention.

Back Office

Most firms have retained their mainframe-based back office applications which are usually very file intensive. The processing is far less time critical but involves retrieving, manipulating and storing large amounts of data.

The next section looks at the activities of the front, middle and back office in more detail.

Front Office Activities

Whether the firms support retail or institutional clients the primary objective is to sell the firm's services, and to do this, the broker's generally recommend securities to buy or sell and then process the orders. However, there are several differences in function and automation between the retail the institutional business.

Front Office – Institutional

The front office of an institutional broker consists of sales people and traders, along with portfolio managers and researchers.

A typical institutional broker's front office applications could consist of the following applications:

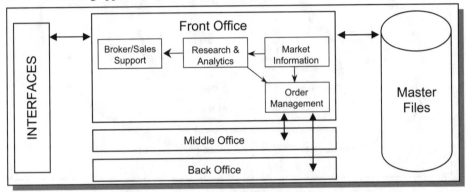

Figure 174 - Generic View of an Institutional Broker's Front Office Applications

Broker Sales Support

A firm's institutional sales representatives and traders use a Broker's Sales Support system to provide the information necessary to service their clients.

- Sales representatives and traders access information about their clients' accounts, which includes details such as name, address, investment objectives, investment experience and account restrictions. This information is gathered from the account opening form that was presented in the chapter on Account Opening. When clients are restructuring their portfolio, the sales representatives and traders also need to be able to see the client's positions.

- They must also record information about their contacts with their clients, which would include what the client has told them about the clients' investment requirements as well as what the sales representative has recommended to each client.

- Sales representatives will also access research information provided by their firm and the firm's products.

- As the client's representative, the sales representatives often initiate investigations when their clients believe that an error has been made.

This application is the main tool used by a sales representatives and is often used by the traders.

Market Information

A broker's systems receive market information from a variety of sources. The front office usually needs this information in real-time since seconds count in making decisions regarding trades, including initiating a trade. The information could include data such as:

- Current prices of securities in the marketplace
- Price history on selected securities, such as highs and lows
- Current news that could affect the registered representative's clients' positions
- Recommendations that are made by the firm's researchers

Additional information regarding market data vendors is included in the chapter on Vendors.

Order Management

The sales representative or the trader uses the order management system to enter clients' orders and to track the progress of each order as it is executed. When a trader uses this application, it provides a real-time trade blotter that reports on the trader's current position in every security he trades and on the trader's overall profit and loss.

Trades are received either electronically or manually. Electronic trades are sent to the broker using the FIX standard over proprietary lines or by an ATS using either FIX or a vendor's proprietary standard. Some U.S. brokers receive trades from their international clients via SWIFT. Electronic trades may be automatically routed to an execution point or they may be presented to the trader for action.

When these applications are used to support institutional trades, they also track the progress of assembling blocks of trades and the allocation of these blocks to portfolios.

Research and Analytics

A firm's researchers and portfolio managers use the research and analytics application(s) to develop recommendations for institutional clients to rebalance portfolios and to identify the risks in their portfolios.

These applications could be used to perform a sensitivity analysis on individual portfolios or on a group of portfolios to determine what might happen to a portfolio's rate of return if interest rates change and what available substitutions could be considered.

Front Office - Retail

The front office for a retail broker consists of the registered representatives, who talk to the clients, along with the research department, which evaluates investment alternatives and makes recommendation that the RRs present to their clients, market information systems which present the relevant data in real time, along with the portfolio managers (if any) and performance measurement (if any).

When brokerage firms first started to open branch offices, they established these new locations near to their clients. When the RR received a client's order they initially sent it by telex, which used telephone lines. These branch offices came to be known as wire rooms. When the telex was received in the main office's operations center, it was recorded and sent to the floor for execution. Executed trades were also recorded manually and sent by telex to the branch so that the RR could inform the client.

Today, branch offices are connected directly to their firm's computers, and after the RR records the receipt of a trade, the subsequent processing is automated.

A typical retail broker's front office is supported by five groups of applications as shown in the following drawing.

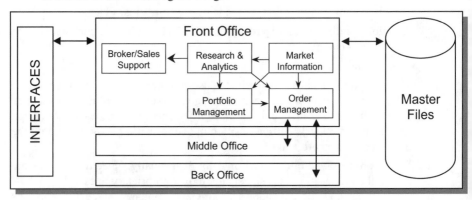

Figure 175 - Front Office Systems Functional Representation of Systems

These applications are often developed at different points in time or are acquired from several different vendors. The broker must integrate these different programs in order to move data smoothly from application to application. This is complicated by the fact that each vendor seeks to differentiate itself by creating functionality that might overlap with other categories of applications. This overlap makes it very difficult to directly compare one vendor's products to another vendor.

A retail broker's front office has on-going client contact, either directly or indirectly, and has several generic functions:

Direct Client Contact

Registered representatives have continuous client contact and need several support applications, including:

Broker Sales Support

A firm's registered representatives and their assistants use a Broker's Sales Support system to provide the information necessary to service their clients.

- RRs access information about their clients' accounts, which includes details such as name, address, investment objectives, investment experience and account restrictions. This information is gathered from the account opening form that was presented in the chapter on Account Opening.

- They must also record information about their contacts with their clients, which would include what the client has told them about the clients' investment requirements as well as what the registered representative has recommended to each client.

- RRs will also access research information provided by their firm and the firm's products.

- As the client's representative, the RRs often initiate investigations when their clients believe that an error has been made.

This application is the main tool used by a registered representative.

Market Information

A broker's systems receive market information from a variety of sources. The front office usually needs this information in real-time since seconds count in making decisions regarding trades, including initiating a trade. The information could include data such as:

- Current prices of securities in the marketplace

- Price history on selected securities, such as highs and lows

- Current news that could affect the registered representative's clients' positions

- Recommendations that are made by the firm's researchers

Additional information regarding market data vendors is included in the chapter on Vendors.

Order Management

The broker, or their assistant, uses the order management set of systems to enter retail clients' manual orders and to track the progress of each order as it is executed.

When a trader uses this set of applications, it provides a real-time trade blotter that reports on the trader's current position in every security he trades and on the trader's overall profit and loss.

Indirect Client Contact

The registered representatives are supported by several other activities that have indirect client contact, and occasional direct contact, including:

Research and Analytics

A firm's researchers and portfolio managers use the research and analytics application(s) to develop recommendations regarding asset allocation and to identify the risks in their portfolios.

The application(s) provide the researcher with the analytical tools that are needed to evaluate investment alternatives for groups of clients and for individual clients.

These application(s) could be used to perform a sensitivity analysis on individual portfolios or on a group of portfolios to determine what might happen to a portfolio's rate of return if interest rates change. It could also be used to determine the impact of adding hedging instruments to a portfolio to reduce risk.

Portfolio Management

RRs who have been formally granted the discretion to trade on behalf of their clients do not usually have access to a formal portfolio management application, but they do manage the purchase and sales of securities.

In some firms, the middle office may perform some of these functions.

Middle Office Activities

Originally, brokers had a front office that had client contact and a back office that processed and kept records about the transactions and resulting positions and balances. The need for a middle office and its evolution were described in the chapter on Securities Industry Participants.

The broker's middle office usually consists of functions such as:

Investment Accounting

The investment accounting function can be performed in the front office or the middle office. It consists of some of the functions needed for portfolio management and the support of the portfolios, as well as performance measurement.

If any of the functions supporting these activities is performed in the front office, the function usually has very little transaction activity associated with the position; whereas if it is performed in the middle office, there tend to be more processing features associated with the tasks.

Risk Management

Risk management is also a role that can be performed in the front office, although it is a classic function for the middle office. A risk management system gathers information from multiple systems in the firm, including information from geographically remote units, to give the firm's managers a broad view of the risks the firm takes in the day-to-day conduct of business.

These risks include the categories that were discussed in the chapter on Post-Trade Processing, Clearing and Settlement.

Trade Processing

The middle office is usually actively involved in order processing. Some of the functions can be performed in the front office by the order management systems and the broker's and trader's assistants; however, when the function is performed in the middle office, the firm's staff have an increased role in ensuring that each trade settles properly.

Trade processing is described in more detail later in this chapter.

Client Services

Some client service activities can be performed in the middle office, although most are performed in the front office. The middle office activities could include resolution of investigations, follow-up on new account documentation, etc.

Systems that are designed to support these functions must track the investigations and help the investigator gather the information they need to resolve the question or problem.

Compliance

While historically a middle office activity, many firms have moved compliance to the front office so that any compliance checking occurs before a trade is executed and not afterwards. The role of the compliance activity is to ensure that the firm is complying with all of the relevant laws and SRO rules that apply to each type of transaction, instrument or account.

Compliance includes:

- Policies and procedures that cover the entire range of activities
- Record the evidence that these policies and procedures are being checked and followed
- Taking action when errors are detected

Regulatory Reporting

There are many different reports that are required by SROs as a part of the SRO's enforcement responsibilities.

Back Office Activities

Brokers have a back office that has historically processed the firm's transactions and maintain assets, and which is frequently organized into several standard departments, including:

- Purchase and Sales (P&S)
- Cashier
- Transfer
- Corporate Actions / Reorganization
- Position Management (Stock Record)
- Margin
- Income
- Proxy
- Reporting / Compliance
- Accounting
- New Accounts

In the rest of this chapter, we will look at each of a typical broker's functions that are needed to process trades through the front, middle and back office and to maintain the assets.

B. BROKER PROCESSING

Brokerage processing involves several steps, and the primary processing activities that are performed by a broker's front, middle and back office. We will use the following chart as an overall roadmap as we examine each function in more detail.

There are slightly different flows for retail and institutional accounts, which is discussed later in this section. These charts only present the major functions required by brokers, and do not include administrative systems.

The boxes indicate major functions, which could also a department in some firms and which could be a separate application. When the process was first automated, most firms had a separate application for each department. Over time, some of these applications grew to incorporate the functions for multiple departments to reduce the system's complexity and to reduce processing costs. In the rest of this chapter we will refer to the thirteen boxes in the chart as 'processing activities.'

The activities outside of the large boxed area are functions that are performed outside of the brokerage firm.

Broker Processing

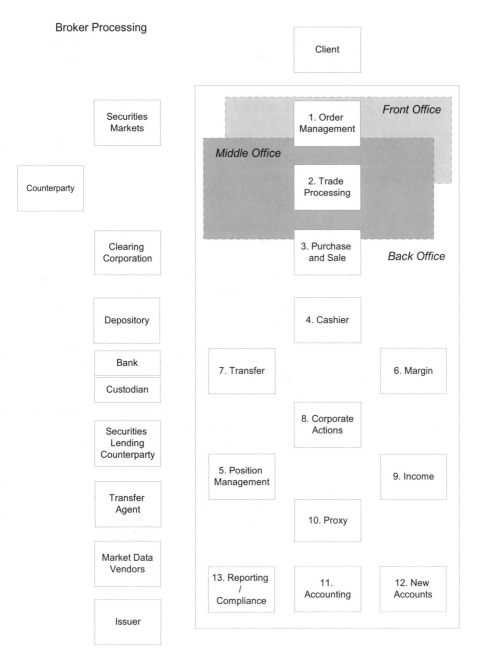

Figure 176 - Generic Brokerage Processing Activities

There are a series of basic processing steps that accompany these processing activities.

1.   The retail order is entered into the order management system (OMS), either through an internet application used by the client, or

manually by a registered representative (or their assistant).

An institutional order is either received manually and entered by a sales representative or by a trader, or electronically through a programmed interface with the client or via an ATS.

2.   The OMS creates the confirmation and sends information to the purchase and sale system for retail trades and through a trade processing function for institutional trades.

Institutional trades goes through several special steps, including allocations matching, etc.

3.   The purchase and sales system interfaces with the clearing corporations and sends information to the cashier application and to the margin system.

4.   The cashier system interfaces with the depository and updates the position management system.

5.   The position management system receives input from the cashier system and the margin system and notifies the proxy and income systems of each client's positions.

6.   The margin system keeps track of how much credit each client has and instructs other modules when adjustments have to be made.

7.   The transfer system manages the process of transferring physical securities from one registered owner to another by working with the depository and the transfer agents.

8.   The corporate action system receives information about corporate action events and works with the position management system to identify who is entitled to the action.

9.   The income system receives information about income events and works with the position management system to identify who is entitled to the income.

10. The proxy system manages the process of sending client information to third party proxy processors when proxies or other corporate notifications are required.

11. The accounting system keeps track of all of the purchases and sales for clients and for the firm's own position, as well as all income, expenses, etc.

12. The new accounts department is in charge of reviewing account applications, checking the information and actually opening the account.

13. The reporting and compliance department monitors the activities of the brokerage firm to ensure that all of the functions are being properly performed and in compliance with industry regulations and the firm's guidelines.

We will examine each of these applications and departments in detail in the rest of this chapter, after we review the differences between a retail transaction and an institutional transaction.

Retail Processing

In the chapter on Securities Industry Participants, the characteristics of retail investors were identified and are repeated here.

- Most retail investors, who purchase directly, rather than through a mutual fund, normally buy a small number of shares or bonds at any one time.
- Individual investors are required by their broker to pay on or before the settlement date for a purchase.
- Individuals usually have only one or a few accounts.
- Since most individuals buy in small amounts, they are not able to negotiate a better commission, and typically pay fixed rates.
- For most retail clients, the buying broker usually holds the investor's securities as the client-side of the trade settles between the broker/dealer and the client.
- The confirmation of the client is generally reported to the client on a paper document.

The primary processing implication of these characteristics is that retail clients must either have a margin account, keep sufficient funds in their cash account, or they are required to send in the required cash by the settlement day (SD). When the funds are not available in a cash account at the time of settlement, the broker must extend credit to the client or sell the securities to raise the funds that are needed to settle.

Brokers may automatically give the client two additional days to pay, but if the amount is not received by SD+2, the broker must contact its SRO for an extension. This involves some effort on the part of the broker plus a small fee that the broker pays to the SRO.

Institutional Processing

Processing of institutional trades is very similar to the processing of retail trades; however, there are several important distinctions. In the chapter on Securities Industry Participants, the characteristics of institutional investors were identified and are repeated here.

- An institutional investor is an institution that has a large pool of funds that can be invested in a range of assets. These assets could include securities, real estate, commodities, derivatives, etc.
- These accounts could be a standard investment or custody account, which are similar to individual cash accounts, or they could be trust accounts, which could be used for pensions or estates. Each of these types of accounts has specific rules associated with it.
- Accounts could be opened in the name of a partnership, which are generally opened as regular corporate investment accounts.
- Investments are typically in large amounts, and block trades are common.
- Institutional clients often use third-party investment managers to make purchase and sale decisions for their portfolios.
- Most trades are Delivery vs. Payment, with a custodian bank involved in

the settlement.

- Clients typically have multiple accounts and may have multiple investment managers.

- Soft Dollar arrangements are common.

These characteristics have several processing implications.

- Most institutions utilize a bank as a custodian for their securities and to hold their excess funds. Since the banks are involved in the trade process, the DTC developed a system called the Institutional Delivery system which was merged into products offered by Omgeo that connect brokers, the investment managers and the banks. This system is used to move information between the firms that are involved in a specific trade so that the custodian does not release cash or securities unless the investment manager specifically authorizes the transaction.

  When an institutional client purchases securities, it notifies its agent bank through one of several Omgeo systems or through another vendor's application to release the funds as the securities are received. When the manager sells securities, it notifies the agent bank to release the securities as it simultaneously receives the funds.

- Institutional accounts, which buy in much larger amounts than retail clients, use the Deliver vs. Payment (DVP) settlement process. With DVP, there is a simultaneous and final exchange of cash for securities. This eliminates the risk that one party delivers and the other does not. This occurs:
  - Through the DTC for equities, corporate and municipal bonds, and UITs
  - Through the Fed for U.S. government securities and MBS
  - Through the OCC for options

C. ORDER MANAGEMENT

The order management process keeps track of the orders that are sent to the various markets and of the subsequent related executions that are received.

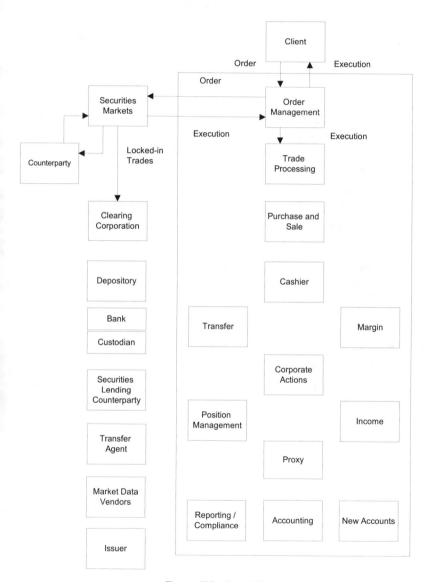

Figure 177 - Order Management

The retail order management process starts with the registered representative receiving instructions from their client to buy or sell a specific security. The RR prepares an order ticket. The order ticket, which was discussed in detail in the chapter on Buying and Selling Securities, is entered into the broker's order management system by the RR, trader, or an assistant.

The institutional order management process starts with an order from a sales person going to a trader, or an order from a client directly to a trader. The order might have been received electronically and might be passed automatically to an execution point, or it might be routed to a trader for additional work. Therefore, some orders have already been captured electronically by the OMS while others will require an order ticket form the salesperson or the trader.

After the order has been executed, the order management system posts the transaction to the firm's records, and begins the process of updating the other applications.

The functions performed by the broker's order management department are:

Capture Orders

The order is entered by the broker's staff and should include as a minimum the following information:

- Client identification
- Type of order (Buy, Sell, Short)
- Execution Instructions (Market, Limits, GTC, Day, etc.)
- Security identification
- Quantity

Route Orders

Orders can be sent by the system to:

- Any of the exchanges on which the broker is a member and the security is listed
- The broker's traders
- NASDAQ if the firm is a member and the security is listed
- To another executing broker acting as a market maker or a block trader
- Alternative Trading Systems
- Electronic Communications Networks

Track Orders

Limit orders are not immediately executed, and the broker needs to know the order's location and status at all times. These orders are maintained in a pending file until they are executed or cancelled.

The order management system keeps track of:

- Execution status
- Contra broker
- Special settlement instructions

Status Reporting

Clients also need to know the status of their order. Using the information input into the broker's order management system, the broker's registered representative could tell the client any of the following information upon demand:

- Trade status
- Execution price and venue
- Broker's role in the trade
- Changes in the order due to corporate actions, dividends, etc.
- Net funds that are due from the client

Match Orders and Executed Trades

When trades are executed, the system matches the execution information to the order. This includes the security, quantity, price, place of trade, role of the broker, etc. Any differences must be investigated immediately.

Reconcile Orders and Executed Trades

The trade reconciliation process reviews the matched orders to the executions and pending orders, and resolves discrepancies.

D. TRADE PROCESSING

Trade processing consists over several different activities that are covered in this section.

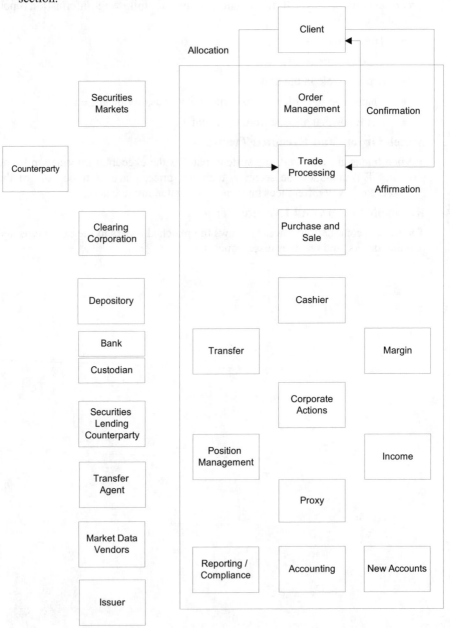

Figure 178 - Trade Processing

Trade Allocation Processing / Affirmations

Individual trades move through the process directly to the figuration function and are then enriched to include all of the information necessary to clear and settle the transaction. When an institutional trade is fully extended it is sent t the DTC for confirmation, while confirmations for retail trades are handled differently.

If the institutional trade was a block trade, the firm's system receives the allocation information and assigns the appropriate portions of the trade to the identified accounts in accordance with the allocation instructions.   After ensuring that the total of the allocated trades equals the block, each allocated trade is handled as a separate transaction.

Figuration

Figuration is the calculation of the net amount due to/from the client, including:

- Commissions
- Fees
- Taxes
- Accrued Interest

Until the industry shortened the settlement cycle from T+5 to T+3 in 1995, most firms processed their figuration in their overnight batch process. Since then, increasingly, firms are moving to calculating figuration on trade date in order to get their retail client confirmations in the mail as soon as possible and their electronic confirmations are sent out on trade date.

Prior to 1975, brokerage firms had fixed commissions and every broker charged each client the same amount, which made figuration easier to calculate. When the industry was required to shift to negotiated rates, systems had to be changed for all classes of clients to accommodate different rates.

Client Confirmations - Institutional

Confirmations for institutional trades are sent to the DTC for settlement and forwarding to the investment manager and any other interested party, such as the custodian.

Client Confirmations - Retail

When the trade management department receives an execution notice from the order management system, the trade management system creates a paper confirmation that it sends to retail clients. If the client is an institution, the institution may elect to not receive the paper confirmation and to rely solely on the electronic confirmation that is generated by the DTC.

The confirmation is used to identify potential settlement problems as early in the process as possible. Whether electronic or paper, the confirmation informs the client of information such as:

- Account
- Commission
- Interest accrued
- Security involved

- Settlement date
- Taxes, etc
- Total settlement amount
- Trade date
- Type of order
- Unit price
- Fees disclosure
- Execution Location
- Broker's role in the trade

A retail client has only ten business days (or less) to notify the broker of an error on a confirmation. This timeframe is identified in the account opening form.

Institutional clients receive their electronic confirmations through the DTC's automated system and are required to make a positive affirmation of the trade through that system before the trade is settled (or they can have their custodian affirm for them). The following examples of retail confirmations show many of the differences trading conditions that could be encountered and are reproduced in different formats that correspond to the formats used by various firms.

Retail Client Confirmation – Equity

The following example of a retail client confirmation involving an equity trade shows several points of key information about the trade, including:

- Name of the broker, who was a market maker
- Name of the client
- Description of the security
- Market or exchange for this trade
- Amount of the trade
- Amount due from the client

In this example, although the broker is a market maker and would normally charge a mark-up on this purchase, there was no markup. Instead, the broker charged a commission.

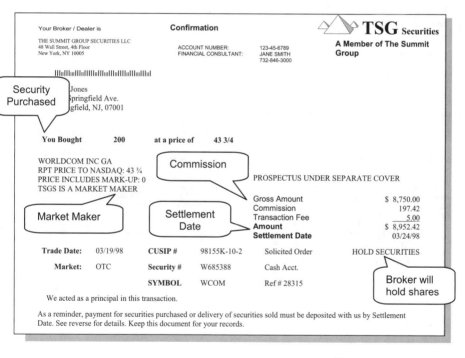

Figure 179 - Retail Client Confirmation – Equity [88]

Retail Client Confirmation – Contractual Terms

The back of that same confirm contains some contractual terms and account restrictions that exist between this broker and its clients. While many of the terms are required by the SEC and SROs, the details can vary from firm to firm.

NOTE: WE ARE REQUIRED TO REPORT NET PROCEEDS OF CERTAIN TRANSACTIONS TO THE INTERNAL REVENUE SERVICE. IF YOU ARE REQUIRED TO DOCUMENT TRANSACTIONS, THIS FORM WILL SATISFY THE PURPOSE OF IRS FORM 10996.

Please review this document carefully. If the details of any transaction are incorrect, you must notify the Branch Manager of the office servicing your account immediately. Failure to make such notification within three (3) days of receipt of this document constitutes your acceptance of the transaction(s),

Unless you have directed that the order be executed on a specified exchange or market and we have agreed to such execution, we will, at our sole discretion and without prior notification to you, execute any of your orders to purchase or sell securities on the over-the-counter market in any location or on any exchange, including a foreign exchange, where such security is traded, either on a principal or agency basis.

The firm receives remuneration for directing orders in equity securities to particular broker/dealers or market centers for execution. When such remuneration is received, it is considered compensation to the firm, and the source and amount of any compensation received by the firm in connection with your transaction will be disclosed upon request.

For NASDAQ principal transactions, any mark-up or mark-down shown on the front of this Confirmation represents the difference between the reported price to NASDAQ and your price. Your Financial Consultant receives a portion of any mark-up or mark-down as compensation in connection with these transactions, and may receive additional compensation from these transactions. Your Financial Consultant usually receives compensation from transactions that have no mark-up or mark-down.

A. When applicable, the transaction(s) set forth on the front of this confirmation constitutes an offer to the client made pursuant to the information contained in the enclosed prospectus or official statement.

B. Descriptive words in the title of any security are used for identification purposes only, and do not constitute representations.

C. The time of execution will be furnished upon written request. In transactions where The Summit Group Securities, LLC acts as agent, the name of buyer and seller wi11 be furnished on written request.

D. For Debt Securities, call features may exist in addition to those described on the front of this confirmation. Debt securities subject to call features or other redemption features such as sinking funds, may be redeemed in whole or in part before maturity. Such occurrences may affect yield. Please contact your Financial Consultant for further information. Yields on mortgage backed securities (MBS) are quoted as a Corporate Bond Equivalent Yield (BEY). Actual yield may vary based on prepayment rates. Total amount due on MBS may be subject to change after settlement date due to factor changes. Additional information will be provided upon request.

E. For Zero Coupon, Compound Interest and Multiplier securities, no periodic payments of interest or principal are generally made. These securities may be callable at a price below their maturity value without prior notice by mail to holder unless the holder has-requested these securities be held in registered form. Unless specifically requested and agreed to by TSG Securities LLC, clients' securities will not be held in registered form. Additional information will be furnished upon

request.

F. For the purpose of evaluating Federal Deposit Insurance, CDs are aggregated with all other deposits held by a client in the same legal capacity at the issuing institution. The insurance limit is $100,000 combined principal and interest for interest bearing CDs or accreted value for zero-coupon CDs.

G. If this confirmation relates to a debt obligation in bearer form, TSG Securities LLC agrees to satisfy the conditions set forth in U.S. Treasury regulation sections 1.165-12(c)(3), and covenants with you to deliver the obligation in bearer form in accordance with the requirements of paragraph (c)(1)(ii) and (iv) of those regulations. The regulations prohibit deliveries, and restrict re-sales of obligations in bearer form within the United States, and may affect the resale market for such obligations. Consult your tax advisor.

H. For certain asset backed debt securities, the actual yield may vary according to the rate at which the underlying receivables or other financial assets are prepaid. Information concerning factors that affect yield (including estimated yield, weighted average life and the prepayment assumptions underlying yield) will be furnished upon written request.

I. Rating information is provided based on good faith inquiry, but its accuracy or completeness cannot be guaranteed.

J. Structured debt securities differ substantially from standard fixed income obligations. Risks include unpredictable movements of the related index, increased volatility, reduced liquidity, and unusual call features leading to premature returns of capital that can reduce expected yield.

Figure 180 - Confirmation Terms

Retail Client Confirmation – Preferred Stock

The following example of a retail client confirmation involving preferred stock shows the same categories of information as the previous example, and shows that this was a new issue.

Some of the key points are:

- The broker solicited the order by making a recommendation to the client

- The securities will be held in the client's account with the broker

- This was sold as part of an Initial Public Offering

- Since preferred shares are not sold as often as common shares, an additional note identifying a category of risk was placed on the bottom of the confirmation.

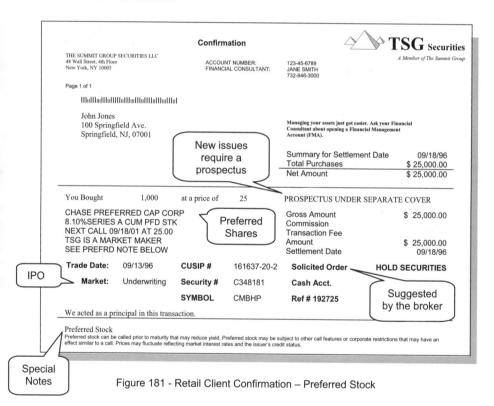

Figure 181 - Retail Client Confirmation – Preferred Stock

Retail Client Confirmation – Equity

The following is another example of a retail client confirmation involving common stock. There are several key features to this confirmation, including:

- TSG Securities was the broker, and they cleared through Bear Stearns Securities Corp., so both of their names must appear on the confirm and the statement.

- This purchase was an unsolicited order, and the broker was a market maker and charged a markup. The trade was at a price of $ 22.75 and the markup added another $ 0.65 for each share.

- This trade was conducted before the settlement cycle was shortened to three days. It shows that the trade date was on May 22 and was settled on May 29, which included a weekend.

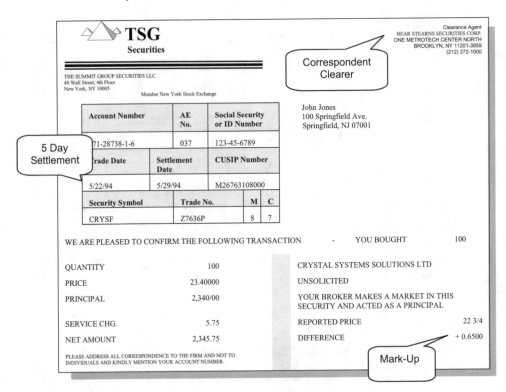

Figure 182 -Retail Client Confirmation – Equity 2

Retail Client Confirmation – Commission

The following example of a retail client confirmation shows the commission that was charged and how the commission was split between the broker and their firm on a sale of an OTC security. In this case the $ 464.00 in commission was split between the representative who received 40% and the firm, which received 60%.

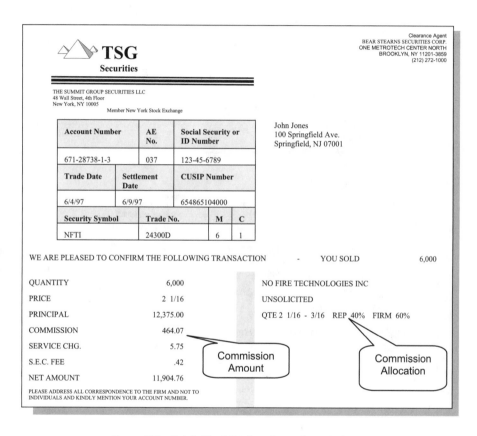

Figure 183 - Retail Client Confirmation – Commission

Retail Client Confirmation – Non-Market Maker

This retail client confirmation shows that the broker was not a market maker and that these municipal securities are only available in book-entry form.

The confirm also shows that:

- This was a bond with a 5.4% coupon rate and a maturity of 1/1/99

- The dated date is 1/1/92 and the first coupon date was 7/1/92

- Interest was scheduled to be paid on January 1 and July 1 each year

- The transaction included accrued interest that the buyer had to pay to the seller. The buyer will then recover this amount when he gets paid for the entire six-month period

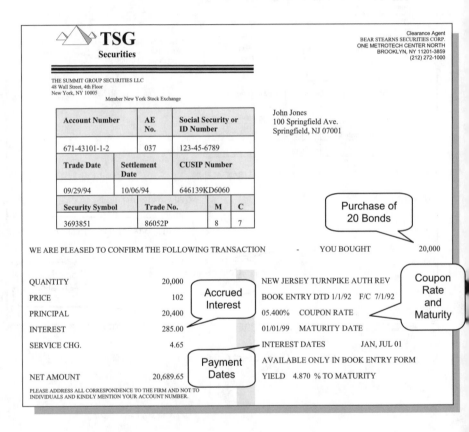

Figure 184 - Retail Client Confirmation – Non-Market Maker

Retail Client Confirmation – When, As and If Issued

This retail client confirmation is an example of a When, As and If Issued transaction. This type of transaction is used for a security that is planned to be released at a certain price at a point in the future.

The confirm shows the following points:

- Although the trade occurred on 7/16/87, the note was due to be released on 8/1/87, which is called the dated date.
- The first coupon was scheduled to be paid on 2/1/88, at a coupon rate of 6.0%.
- The trade amount has been identified, but no amount was due at the time of the trade.

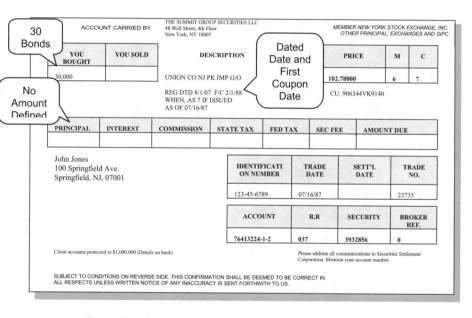

Figure 185 - Retail Client Confirmation – When, As and If Issued

Client Confirmations – Institutional

Confirmations for institutional trades are generally sent back to the clients in electronic form through DTC.

E. PURCHASE AND SALE

The purchase and sale department works closely with the appropriate clearing corporation for the instrument that was traded, and is responsible for several functions, which are shown here.

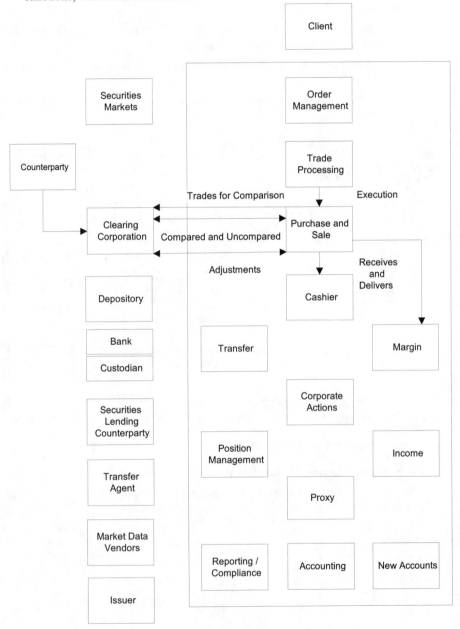

Figure 186 - Purchase and Sale

These P&S functions include:

Recording

The recording process ensures that all trade executions have been properly recorded in the firm's system.

Street Side Reconciliation

The P&S department keeps track of all transactions for all securities, and reconciles its positions with the relevant clearing organization, based upon the instrument type.

Security Type	Clearing
Corporate Bonds	NSCC
Municipal Bonds	NSCC
Mutual Funds	NSCC
Government Bonds	FICC - GSD (formerly GSCC)
Mortgage Backed Bonds	FICC - MBSD (formerly MBSCC)
Equity	NSCC
Money Market Instruments	Banks
Options	OCC

Figure 187 - U.S. Clearing Corporations

The NSCC, GSD and MBSD all operate in a similar fashion and are all managed by essentially the same organization, with similar systems.

The NSCC issues Contract Sheets on T+1 that list the trades that have been reported by the broker and by the contras brokers. The Contract Sheet has two sections:

Compared

When both counterparties to a trade report identical information, the trades are considered matched and no further action is required by either party.

Uncompared

When the trades do not match, both firms must check their trade tickets for errors, and the firm in error sends an adjustment to the NSCC no later than T+2.

The OCC and the other clearing agencies have different processes that were introduced in the chapter on Post-Trade Processing, Clearing and Settlement but all use basically the same process of identifying compared and uncompared trades.

Continuous Net Settlement

The P&S department reconciles its trades against the activity that was recorded by the clearing corporation. For the NSCC, this activity is processed through the Continuous Net Settlement (CNS) system.

The following example of the report that brokers receive from CNS shows that the broker had 238 separate purchases and 209 separate sales of Coca-Cola Co. This final page (Page 160 in this case) of the report only shows the last few trades and the totals for the day for the broker.

The report shows that although there was nearly a million dollars each in debits and credits (purchases and sales), the net amount due the broker is a credit of $68,928. With CNS, rather than settling 447 trades for this broker, there is one net deliver position for Coca-Cola that will settle at the DTC, and one cash position that will be further netted at the NSCC. The final cash settlement with the broker will occur through the broker's bank at the end of the day.

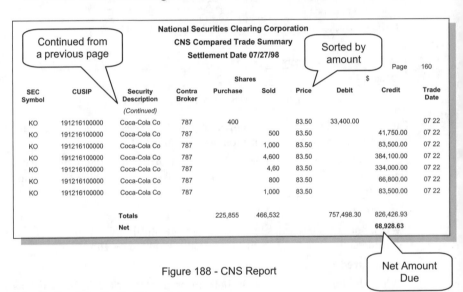

Figure 188 - CNS Report

Trade for Trade Settlement

If both sides to a trade agree, the truth can be settled outside of CNS. An indiscretion is added to the transaction that identified that this transaction will be settled trade by trade.

Balance Order Settlement

Not all securities are eligible for CNS and are processed along side CNS in a similar way. If a non-CNS trade is matched it is reported n the compared trade report and a Balance Order is issued. If it is not matched, it is listed on the non-compared report and it is handled as a break.

BOs and breaks are usually recorded in a firm's fail to receive/deliver system, where they are investigated and resolved.

F. CASHIER

The Cashier activity is responsible for a number of functions.

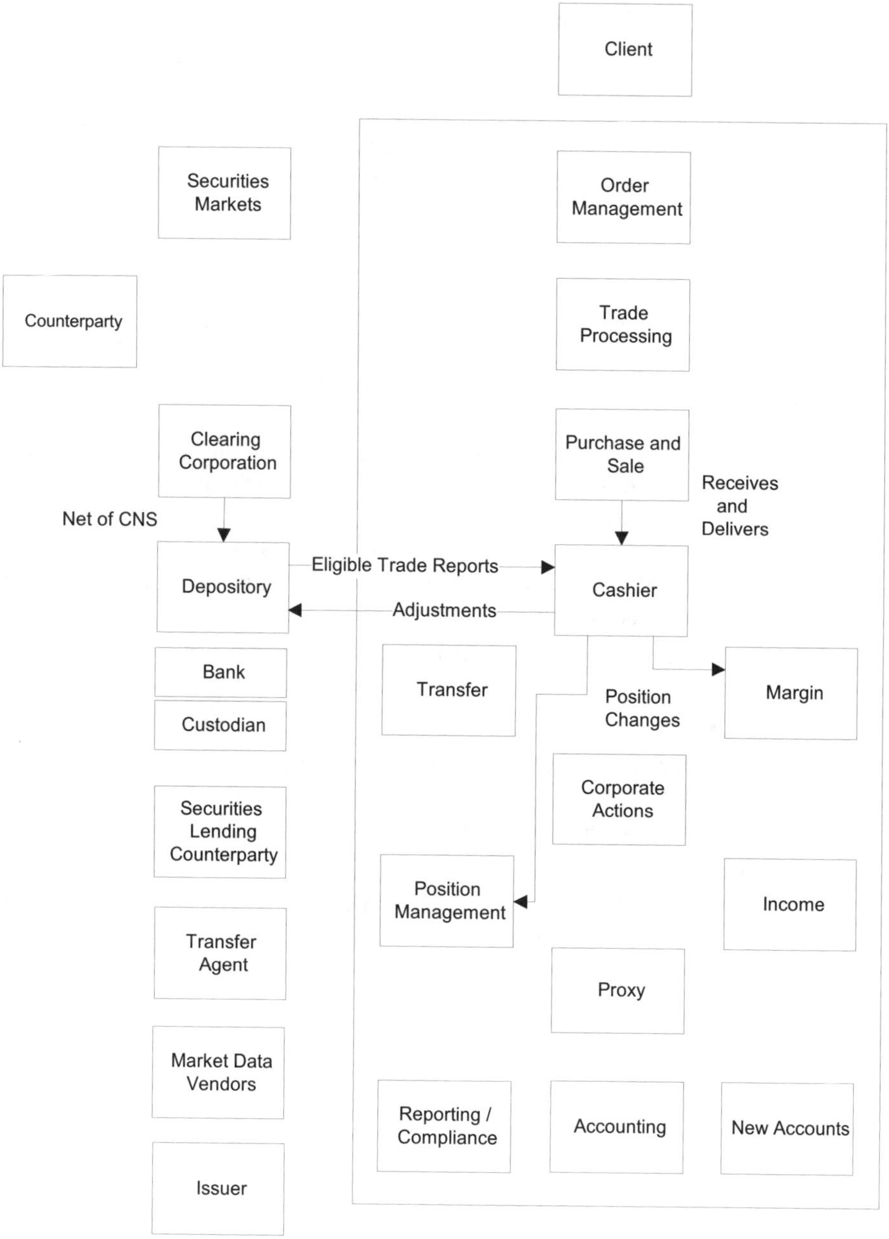

Figure 189 - Cashier

Receive and Deliver

The firm may receive/deliver securities that are either in book-entry form or physical form. Both are recorded in the cashier system. The receive and deliver function balances and reconciles the firm's positions with the DTC on a daily basis.

Balancing/Reconciliation

Any differences between the DTC's positions and the firm's positions are called breaks. Each break is researched and adjusting entries are made to resolve the problem. In some cases, the reason for the break is a failure to deliver by one of the counterparties to deliver the security they sold. Fails can be resolved through the Securities Lending process that is another function of the Cashier's department.

Vault

The vault system must keep track of all the physical receives and delivers, and record what has gone into and out of the vault. Securities that are held in the vault for clients are registered in the firm's nominee name so that the securities can be more easily transferred and cash can be more efficiently disbursed for dividends and interest.

The vault department is also responsible for ensuring that any physical instrument received is in *Good Deliverable Form*, which means that it has been properly endorsed and is a valid instrument.

Physical securities move in and out of the firm through an access point called a 'window.' The NYSE requires that all windows must in be in Manhattan south of Houston Street or in Jersey City.

DTC established a facility at its offices in lower Manhattan called the New York Window, which acts as an agent for most of the US securities firms.

Segregation

At all times, the firm must know which of the securities it holds belong to their clients and which belong to the firm. The firm is required to segregate fully paid client assets and cannot hypothecate or sell them without the client's permission.

Bank Loans

A broker may hypothecate or pledge its own securities to a bank as collateral for a loan, but may not use its client's securities unless the securities are in a margin account and are used as collateral for the client's purchases.

Smaller brokers use short-term bank loans to finance their day to day operating expenses.

Larger brokers use stock lending/borrowing to finance equities and they use structured and tri-party repos to finance fixed income transactions. These processes provide a much cheaper cost to finance the positions than bank loans.

Account Transfers

Transfers can involve individual securities or entire accounts. If an entire account is transferred, a form such as the following example is generally used. The transfer of an entire account is normally conducted through an NSCC service called ACATS, which is discussed in the chapter on Post-Trade Processing, Clearing and Settlement.

The account transfer function may be included in the Cashier's department or in very large firms may be a stand-alone department.

SECURITIES TRANSFER

THE SUMMIT GROUP SECURITIES LLC
48 Wall Street, 4th Floor
New York, NY 10005

CLIENT DECLARATION OF OWNERSHIP
MEMBER FIRM AUTHORITY TO TRANSFER AND RECEIVE ACCOUNT

TO _____   _____   ATT: CREDIT DEPT.
(FILL IN NAME OF FIRM WHERE ACCOUNT IS NOW BEING CARRIED)   (CLEARING #)   (DATE)

		FOR OFFICE USE ONLY	
(ACCOUNT TITLE)	(PRESENT ACCOUNT #)	Date Submitted	_____
		Return Date	_____

Dear Sirs:

Kindly accept this authorization to transfer my account(s) to: ___TSG Securities___, DTC # __123__, who have been authorized by me to make payment to you of the debit balance, or receive check for credit balance. I further instruct you to affix the necessary tax waivers to the certificates carried in my account, enabling: ___TSG Securities___, DTC # _123_, to transfer said certificates in their name for the purpose of sale, when directed by me.

PLEASE CANCEL ALL OPEN ORDERS FOR MY ACCOUNT ON YOUR BOOKS.

In accordance with my records, the following securities / funds are presently being held in my account with your firm.

QUANTITY	TYPE OF ACCOUNT	SECURITY DESCRIPTION (Do not use ticker symbol)	QUANTITY	TYPE OF ACCOUNT	SECURITY DESCRIPTION (Do not use ticker symbol)

NOTE: If necessary, please use additional sheet.

DEBIT BALANCE _____   _____   **or CREDIT BALANCE** _____   _____
     (AMOUNT)   (TYPE OF ACCOUNT)   (AMOUNT)   (TYPE OF ACCOUNT)

     _____   _____   _____   _____
     (AMOUNT)   (TYPE OF ACCOUNT)   (AMOUNT)   (TYPE OF ACCOUNT)

TO: ___TSG Securities___, DTC # __123__.

FOR OFFICE USE ONLY
SMA _____
Amount of Federal Call under Regulation T (if any)

Please receive my account(s) as constituted from the above mentioned firm and remit them the debit balance, or receive check for credit balance which stands in my account(s) on their books.

Yours truly,

_____
(SIGNATURE OF CLIENT – SIGN ALL COPIES)

OFFICE	NUMBER	T	BR

_____
(NAME OF NEW RR OF RECORD)

INSTRUCTIONS

In order to provide a rapid and orderly transfer of your accounts, please refer to the most recent statement of accounting received from the member firm presently maintaining your accounts. All of the information required to complete this form can be found on that document. Care should be exercised in the transcription of security description, avoiding the use of abbreviations whenever possible.

When entering the description of a bond, two lines of security description should be utilized, the first devoted to the name of the bond and the second to interest rate and maturity date.

PLEASE ENCLOSE A COPY OF YOUR LATEST BROKERAGE ACCOUNT STATEMENT

Figure 190 - Account Transfer Form

Securities Lending / Borrowing

The cashier's securities lending/borrowing function is responsible for locating stocks and bonds that the firm does not have but needs in order to settle, or it may lend out securities to other firms for a fee. The securities lending process is discussed in the chapter on Post-Trade Processing, Clearing and Settlement.

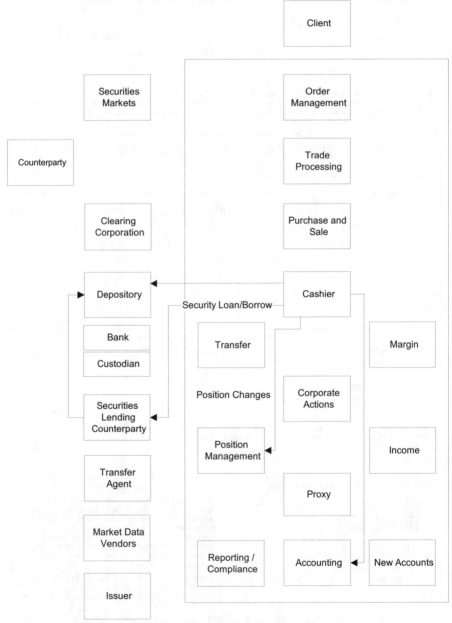

Figure 191 - Securities Lending / Borrowing

G. TRANSFERS DEPARTMENT

Any physical securities that are received by the broker need to be transferred from one owner to another when sold. The transfer process requires that specific forms be completed and signed by the relinquishing owner of the securities. The certificates are then sent to the issue's registrar to be reregistered.

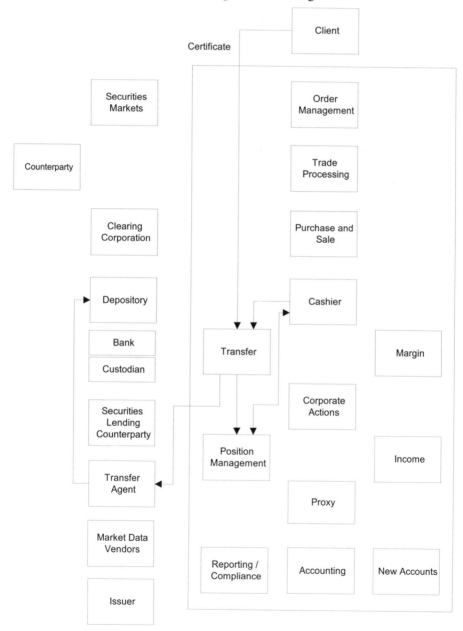

Figure 192 - Transferring Certificates

Registered securities require additional documentation and processing, including affidavits that substantiate that the restrictions have been lifted or do not apply in this case.

Dematerialization at the depository significantly reduced the scope of the Transfer Department and the introduction of Direct Registration eliminated the need for most physical securities.

Direct Registration is a process that allows the stock transfer agent to electronically record the beneficial owner of the security. Certificates are eliminated, and instead of the security being held by the DTC, broker or bank in their street name, the security is registered in the true owner's name.

Securities can be registered in a variety of names, including:

- The owner's name
- The depository's nominee name
- The broker or bank's nominee name

Transferring physical securities requires that the back of the certificate be properly completed.

H. REORGANIZATION

The reorganization department is also called the corporate actions department. This department is responsible for executing the corporate actions that affect the securities held by the firm.

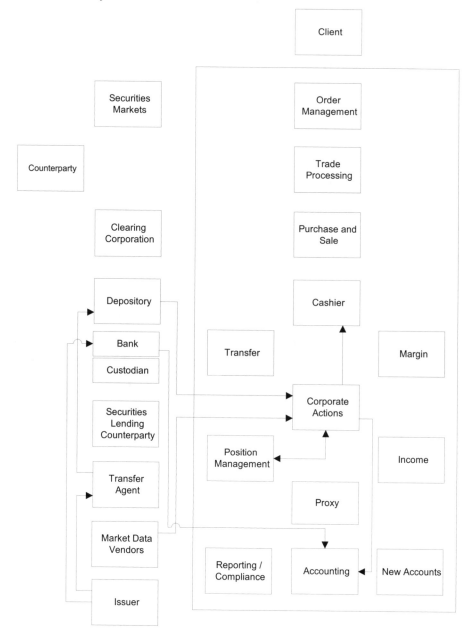

Figure 193 - Reorganization

These corporate actions affect the capital structure of the firm represented by the issuer and result in changes in the actual positions held by investors. There are a variety of corporate actions that can be initiated by the issuer or in some cases, the security's holder. These were discussed in the chapter on Post -Trade Processing, Clearing and Settlement.

The following principle processing steps for corporate actions were discussed in the chapter on Post Settlement Processing:

- Event Notification
- Entitlement Determination
- Client Notification
- Event Posting
- Reconciliation

I. POSITION MANAGEMENT

The position management process of a brokerage firm keeps track of the total number of the securities that the firm owns as well as the clients' positions. The primary method of maintaining these records is through a process called the stock record.

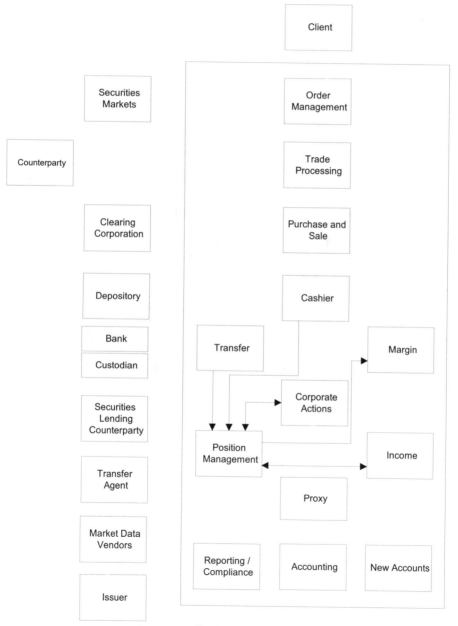

Figure 194 - Position Management

The stock record is a dual entry method of tracking the movement of securities, resulting from the following major categories of events:

- Receipt / delivery of physical certificates from clients or transfer agents
- Settlements at the relevant depository

Stock Record

The stock record is a perpetual inventory system designed to track both the ownership and location of securities and must always be in balance. It tracks all settlement activity for securities coming into and going out of the brokerage firm.

It is a dual-entry system that identifies ownership and the location of the inventory on settlement date.

- Long is *always* based upon ownership
  - *Client long* means that the client bought or otherwise acquired the security.
  - *Firm long* means the broker, for his own account and risk, has bought or otherwise acquired the security.
  - *Fail to deliver* means the firm sold securities to another broker/dealer and has failed to deliver them. The other broker owns the securities and is entitled to all the rights of ownership including dividends, proxies, etc.
  - CNS will show a long position if the broker owes securities to CNS. As far as the broker is concerned, CNS is the owner of the securities.
  - *Securities borrowed* means the firm has borrowed securities from another broker or client who retains all the rights of ownership.
  - A Reverse Repurchase Agreement is the term used in the U.S. government and mortgage-backed bond markets to describe borrowing securities. Again, the firm that lent the securities retains the rights of ownership.
  - *Dividend long* (unclaimed) means the broker has received a dividend for an unknown beneficiary and the securities must be turned over to the state (escheated) if no owner is found.

- Short is *always* based upon location or a receivable
  - An Active Box describes securities that are held physically in-house pending instructions to be delivered elsewhere.
  - Vault or Segregation refers to the physical securities that are held by the firm and are either registered in the firm's name (street name) or in the name of the beneficial owner. To the extent that these securities are client owned and are paid for as defined under SEC Rule 15c3-3 they must be segregated from the broker's securities.
  - *Fail to receive* means the firm has bought securities from another broker and the other broker has failed to deliver them.
  - *Securities loaned* means the firm has loaned securities to another broker and they are *located* at that broker.
  - *Bank loan* means the firm has pledged securities as collateral in order to obtain a bank loan. The firm has *located* the securities at the bank.

- Repurchase agreement is the term used in the U.S. government bond market to reflect either a lending of securities or the pledging of securities as collateral for a loan. The firm *locates* the securities at the firm that has either borrowed them or has accepted them as collateral.
- *Client short* means that a client has sold securities and has failed to deliver them to his broker. This position is similar to a fail to receive even if the client has *sold short* with no intentions of delivering the securities. The broker *locates* the securities with the client since he must provide the benefits of that location, including cash in lieu of dividends and all other rights of ownership.
- *Dividend short* means someone (possibly unknown) owes the broker a dividend to which the firm is entitled.
- Firm short is similar to a client selling short except that it is for the broker's own account and risk.

On the stock record, *long* (the left side) must equal *short* (the right side). That is, for every ownership there must be a location and for every location there must be an ownership.

Every department that processes the receipt/delivery of securities, or which can affect the location of a security, affects the stock record. The following example shows a stock record that reflects the previous day's closing positions (and therefore today's opening positions). This starting point will be used in an example in this chapter to illustrate what can happen during a normal trading day.

Account Number		LONG	SHORT	SEG.	NG BOX	TRANSFER
	STOCK RECORD SUMMARY for IBM					
10-12345-1	Client A	1,000		1,000		
11-23456-1	Client B	5,000			5,000	
12-34567-1	Client C	2,000				2,000
13-45678-2	Client D	3,000		1,000		
14-56789-1	Client E		2,500			
15-67891-3	Client F		1,000			
00-00161-1	DTC		2,000			
00-00172-2	NEGOTIABLE BOX		5,000			
00-00345-1	STOCK BORROW	6,500				
00-00567-1	FAIL TO RECEIVE		2,000			
00-00789-1	VAULT		3,000			
00-00891-1	TRANSFER		2,000			
General Ledger	**TOTALS**	17,500	17,500			

Figure 195 - Stock Record Example – Prior to Transactions (1 of 3)

Stock Record Takeoff

The Stock Record Takeoff, which is also called the *daily*, is a detailed listing of all trades settling, all stock record movements, and of any other journal entry made which affects a stock record position on trade date through settlement date.

- All trades must balance, reflecting a buyer for every seller.

- All movements must balance by reflecting a long for every short.

- If longs and shorts are not equal, a stock record break is created. This means that the firm either has an ownership and no location or a location with no ownership.

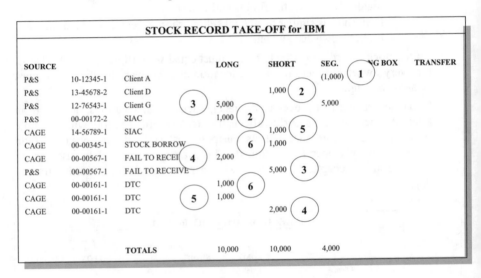

| | | | | | STOCK RECORD TAKE-OFF for IBM | | | | |

SOURCE				LONG	SHORT	SEG.	NG BOX	TRANSFER
P&S	10-12345-1	Client A				(1,000) 1		
P&S	13-45678-2	Client D			1,000 2			
P&S	12-76543-1	Client G	3	5,000		5,000		
P&S	00-00172-2	SIAC		1,000 2				
CAGE	14-56789-1	SIAC			1,000 5			
CAGE	00-00345-1	STOCK BORROW			6 1,000			
CAGE	00-00567-1	FAIL TO RECEI 4		2,000				
P&S	00-00567-1	FAIL TO RECEIVE			5,000 3			
CAGE	00-00161-1	DTC		1,000 6				
CAGE	00-00161-1	DTC	5	1,000				
CAGE	00-00161-1	DTC				2,000 4		
		TOTALS		10,000	10,000	4,000		

Figure 196 - Stock Record Example (2 of 3)

The previous example shows several transactions that occurred during the day and which affect the firm's positions. The transactions are numbered in the example.

1. On Trade Date, Client A sold 1,000 shares of IBM, with settlement three business days from today. Since the trade has not been settled, only the memo field is affected, and 1,000 shares of stock are released from segregation. Segregated transactions are released on the night of T+1 and are visible on T+2 for processing.

2. For settlement today, Client D sold 1,000 shares that were sold to another broker and cleared through CNS. Note that the short 1,000 will reduce the client's long position from 3,000 shares to 2,000 shares.

3. For settlement today, Client G bought 5,000 shares that were purchased from another broker. He paid for the purchase in full and gave instructions to hold his securities in street name. Note that the trade did not settle through CNS, but rather created a direct fail to

receive with the contract broker.

4. The fail to receive that was open from yesterday was received from the broker by crediting the firm's account at DTC.

5. Of the 2,000 shares received in DTC, 1,000 are used to deliver the firm's obligation to CNS.

6. The remaining 1,000 shares are used to return part of the stock borrowed.

The effect of these transactions is reflected in the following T-accounts, and in the Stock Record Summary, which is shown in the next section.

	Client A 10-12345-1		Client B 11-23456-1		Client C 12-34567-1		Client D 13-45678-2	
	1,000		5,000		2,000		3,000	(1) 1,000
Balance	1,000		5,000		2,000		2,000	

	Client E 14-56789-1		Client F 15-67891-3		Client G 12-76543-1		DTC 00-00161-1	
		2,500		1,000	(2) 5,000		(4) 1,000	2,000
							(5) 1,000	(3) 2,000
Balance		2,500		1,000	5,000			2,000

	N.G. Box 00-00172-2		Stock Borrow 00-00345-1		Fail to Receive 00-00567-1		Vault 00-00789-1	
		5,000	6,500	(5) 1000	(3) 2,000	2,000		3,000
						(2) 5,000		
Balance		5,000	5,500			5,000		3,000

	Transfer 00-00891-1		CNS 00-00172-2	
		2,000	(1) 1,000	(4) 1,000
Balance		2,000		0

Stock Record Summary

The Stock Record Summary is a listing of the net long and net short in each account. The following chart shows the result of the six transactions on the positions.

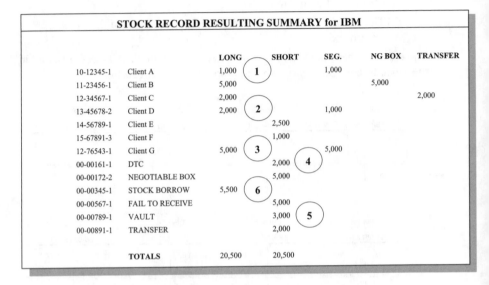

		LONG	SHORT	SEG.	NG BOX	TRANSFER
STOCK RECORD RESULTING SUMMARY for IBM						
10-12345-1	Client A	1,000 ①		1,000		
11-23456-1	Client B	5,000			5,000	
12-34567-1	Client C	2,000				2,000
13-45678-2	Client D	2,000 ②		1,000		
14-56789-1	Client E		2,500			
15-67891-3	Client F		1,000			
12-76543-1	Client G	5,000 ③		5,000		
00-00161-1	DTC		2,000 ④			
00-00172-2	NEGOTIABLE BOX		5,000			
00-00345-1	STOCK BORROW	5,500 ⑥				
00-00567-1	FAIL TO RECEIVE		5,000			
00-00789-1	VAULT		3,000 ⑤			
00-00891-1	TRANSFER		2,000			
	TOTALS	20,500	20,500			

Figure 197 - Stock Record Example (3 of 3)

For the Stock Record process to work there are several procedures that must be supported:

Account Designation

The account identification structure can be established in a system in a variety of ways. Each broker tries to develop an account identification method that ties the account to the category in which it belongs, such as cash, margin, short account, etc., and branch location, etc.

Breaks

A break occurs when there is only one side of a trade reflected in the stock record, and the record is not in balance. All breaks must be investigated and resolved, and the number of breaks is an indicator of operating efficiency.

Breaks can occur as a result of errors with:

- Trades
- Corporate Actions
- Receive Free/Deliver Free

Regulations

The primary regulations that affect the stock record are:

- SEC Rule 15c3-3. Customer Protection Rule
- SEC Rule 17a-5. Reports to Be Made by Certain Brokers and Dealers

- SEC Rule 17a-13. Quarterly Security Counts to Be Made by Certain Exchange Members, Brokers and Dealers

Among other things, these rules state that client securities that are either fully paid or in an excess margin position must be segregated from the firms assets, and that this information must be reported regularly.

Market Data

Market Data includes pricing and reference data can be part of any one of several departments (including IT), and in large firms is of a separate department.

Reference Data

Reference data, also called indicative data, includes information about the securities, the clients and the industry that does not constantly change. This information is needed by many different systems.

Pricing

Brokerage firms use pricing information in three ways:

- Brokers receive real-time pricing information that is used to help their traders make trading decisions

- Real-time pricing information is also used to help the firm's clients determine whether the they should be buying or selling

- Brokers routinely receive closing (or end-of-day) prices from market data vendors so that they can properly price liquid securities in their client's portfolios as well as perform mark-to-market on loaned securities

Brokers will maintain this pricing information either in the portfolio management system, or they may have acquired one of the central securities master file databases that are commercially available.

Brokers need real time pricing to support their trading activities and end-of-day pricing to update their portfolios and for their clients use.

Brokerage firms also provide pricing information in three ways:

- A broker's traders may be asked to establish a fair price for illiquid securities that they trade so that other firms can properly value their client's portfolios

- Some firm develop pricing matrices so that categories of securities, such as municipal securities that are thinly traded can be consistently priced

- All OTC trades and trades where the broker sell from their inventory are reported to the appropriate pricing service so that a complete record is available

J. MARGIN

The margin department is responsible for keeping track of the clients' margin accounts, the positions in these accounts, the value of these positions and the net amount of the margin loan outstanding.

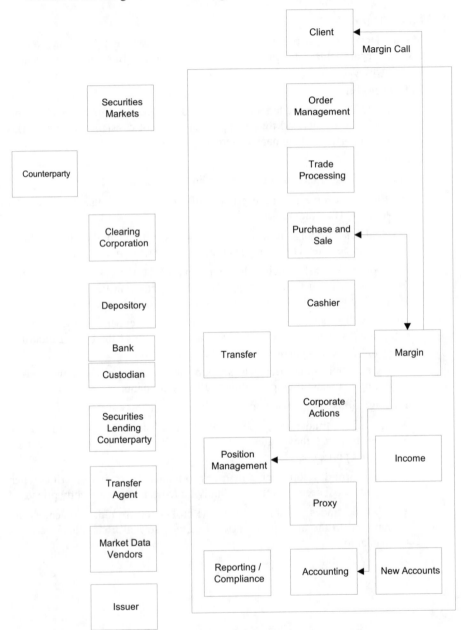

Figure 198 - Margin

Federal Reserve Board Regulation T

Regulation T was created as a result of the '34 Act to govern the granting of credit, and which:

- Identifies eligible securities and the maximum loan value that may be assigned by the broker to each type of security to initiate a margin loan and to maintain the loan
- Establishes the time frames for margin calls
- Allows SROs to grant extensions to brokers

Not all securities are eligible to be used as collateral for margin loans.

Margin Eligible Securities

The following categories of securities are margin eligible and subject to the requirements of Regulation T:

- Exchange listed equities
- OTC equities
- Listed Corporate Bonds

Other securities can be used for margin and are not regulated by Reg. T:

- U.S. Government Bonds
- U.S. Agency Bonds
- Municipal Bonds rated 'A' or better (Moody's BAA, S&P BBB or better)

Margin Policy

The margin agreement has been designed to identify the responsibilities of the firm and the client. The margin process is designed to avoid situations where the client has over extended their credit. A sample of a margin account opening form is included in the chapter on Account Opening.

Functions

The margin department manages the granting of credit to the firm's clients. This includes the following functions:

- Monitor the status of each account
- Ensure compliance with the Fed, SEC and the firm's rules and regulations
- Support salespeople as they deal with clients

To meet these goals, the margin department monitors the margin position for every client overnight and on a real-time basis. If the value of the assets in a margin account falls to below the maintenance minimums, then the margin clerk must contact the account representative who will request additional funding from the client. If additional funding is not available, the margin department will issue sell instructions so that the account can be brought back within the firm's maintenance guidelines, which are called the house guidelines.

The department is also responsible to:

- Monitor client account transfers
- Post margin interest charges
- Request extensions for client payments from the appropriate SRO

- Liquidate positions as required

Benefits of Margin

Products such as margin can benefit both the broker and the investor.

Margin lending benefits investors in two ways:

- Provides financial leverage and increased buying power
- Provides money at favorable interest rates to purchase securities

Brokers gain even more benefits from margin lending, and can:

- Earn interest on the margin loans (which should be fully collateralized)
- Hypothecate (use as collateral) up to 140% of the debit balance for the firm's own use in obtaining loans
- Earn higher commissions since margin clients tend to trade more frequently

Risks with Margin Accounts

Margin lending is not without risk. Investors take the most risk, since they must:

- Pay interest even if the market does not go up
- Provide additional funding if the market goes down, or sell off positions when the market is down

Brokers only have one risk, which is mitigated by the collateral if the broker follows proper procedures. This is the risk of a client default.

Margin's Impact on the Market

The use of margin can exacerbate a falling market by adding to the downward pressure when a declining market forces additional margin calls, and can stimulate a rising market by increasing the volume of purchases.

Margin Loan

The initial loan is made to a client who has signed a margin agreement and who is either:

- Buying securities with the intent of using some of the purchased securities as collateral for additional purchases of the same or another security
- Buying securities and using other securities that are already in their account as collateral

The maximum amount of the loan is established as a ratio of the loan to the value of the collateral, and is defined by the Fed. For example, today listed equities can be margined up to 50% of their value, while U.S. government securities can be margined up to 90%.

Each broker can make these guidelines tighter by lowering the maximum amount they are willing to loan, or by eliminating some specific securities from their list of marginable securities.

Margin Maintenance

The Fed has established certain rules under Regulation T for firms granting margin and for the maintenance of the margin requirements after the initial loan is made.

The maintenance guidelines are set slightly higher than the initial loan margin limits so that there can be some fluctuation in market prices without causing an immediate margin call. House limits can also be set lower than the Fed guidelines.

The reports used by the margin department to maintain margin accounts include information such as:

- Client Name
- Date
- Trade Date Balance
- Settlement Date Balance
- Cash Available
- Special Memo Account (This is a reserve account that preserves the buying power of the client.)
- Buying Power (This is the amount of securities the client can purchase based upon the cash in the account, the current value of the portfolio and the amount of credit already extended.)
- Equity (This defines how much of the account is actually owned by the client.)
- Non-Priced Securities
- Market Value (This is the value of all securities held in the account.)
- Federal Call (This defines the size of a margin call that is needed to meet Federal guidelines.)
- House Call (This defines the size of a margin call that is needed to meet *house* guidelines. House calls can only be equal to or more stringent than the Federal guidelines.)
- Aging (The aging section identifies the number of days outstanding of the loan.)

If the price of margined securities declines to the point where there is insufficient margin in the account, the firm issues a margin call and the account owner must either add more cash or securities to the account. If not, the firm can sell sufficient securities to cover the margin call. This is a process called buying-in.

K. PROXY

The proxy department is responsible for ensuring that all owners of securities receive the appropriate corporate announcements as they are made. The types of proxy announcements and the processing steps were discussed in the chapter on Post Trade Processing, Clearing and Settlement. This flow represents that most firms have outsourced their proxy processing activities to vendors such as ADP.

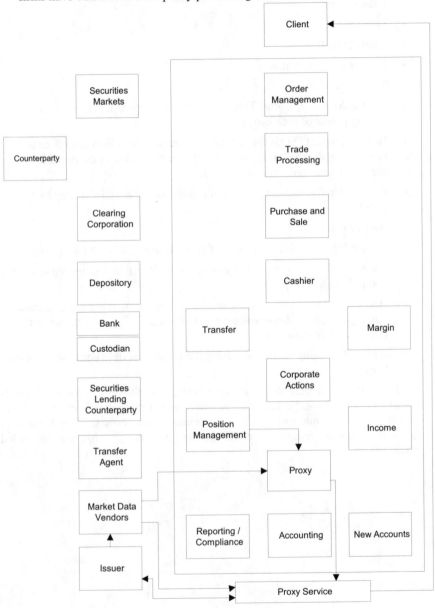

Figure 199 - Proxy

L. INCOME

The income department, as shown in the following chart, is responsible for receiving and distributing all cash dividends as well as interest payments.

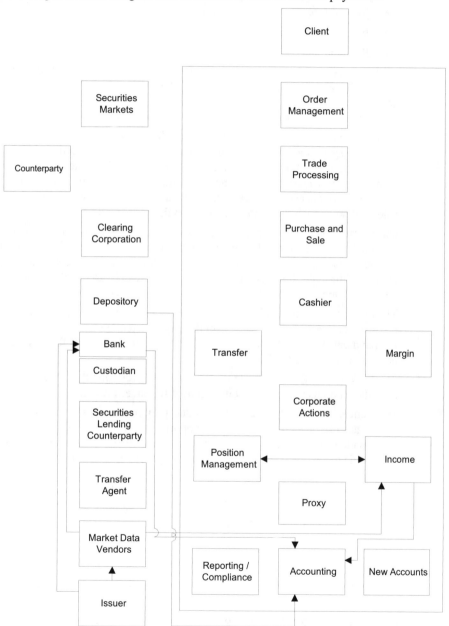

Figure 200 - Income

Dividend Collection Processing

The overall process that is involved with collecting dividends was discussed in the chapter on Post-Trade Processing, including the following three key dates:

- Record date
- Ex-dividend date
- Payment date

When the board of directors votes to pay a dividend, they notify their paying agent, who also announces the event to the marketplace. This information is gathered by market data vendors who are in business to collect and electronically relay these event notifications to firms throughout the industry.

This information is usually received in a file transfer by the broker's income collection system and is posted in an overnight batch as a pending event. This information is used to forecast actions and is held in the system until the night before the payment date for the dividend, at which time the system will determine which accounts are entitled to the dividend based upon the record date, and how much they should receive on the payment date.

On payment date, the income collection system will post the amounts that are expected to be received. The income will be received either directly from the paying agent for securities that are held by the broker in their own nominee name or through the DTC for the securities which are held in the DTC's nominee name.

The dividends are generally posted to the clients' accounts, and the total of these credits is set up as a receivable from the paying agent and/or from the DTC. On the payment date, the broker will receive a wire transfer from the paying agent and/or a credit from the DTC.

The broker must then reconcile the amounts that were distributed to their clients with the amounts that were received. Any differences must be reconciled.

Differences are usually related to a failed trade or an erroneous position. The NSCC has established the Dividend Support System (DSS) to assist in resolving any dividend (and interest) problems that are created between brokers on the street-side of the trade as a result of clearing problems on or near the record date for the issue. The DTC has its own income payment process, which is used to help resolve problems with DTC-related dividend errors.

- Fail tracking involves the DTC for equities and the Fed for U.S. Government and MBS securities
- Resolves erroneous payments
- Interest is usually manual, and some firms have their own systems

The support provided by the NSCC and the DTC is presented in the chapter on Post-Trade Processing, Clearing and Settlement.

Interest Collection Processing – Registered Bonds

The overall process that is involved with collecting interest payments was discussed in the chapter on Post-Trade Processing, Clearing and Settlement, including the following two key dates:

- Record date
- Payment date

There is no ex-date for bonds since they are traded with accrued interest.

Much of the processing of interest is similar to that for dividends, and the process sequence is the same:

- Event Generation
- Entitlement Generation
- Payment Processing
- Reconciliation

The difference between interest and dividend processing is that the interest payments are not granted at the discretion of the board of directors (although the board could vote to default on a payment). For most fixed income instruments, the amount that will be routinely paid remains the same. This is not the case for variable rate instruments and asset backed securities.

Interest Collection Processing – Bearer Bonds

Although there are fewer and fewer bearer bonds each year, some physical bonds are still in circulation. The process for paying interest on bearer bonds is different from paying on registered bonds, as was explained in the chapter on Post-Trade Processing, Clearing and Settlement

Stop Payments

Physical securities (equity and bonds) can be lost or stolen. When this occurs, the holder should immediately contact his/her broker, who will either report the event to the paying agent and to the Securities Information Center (SIC), or put the client in touch with the paying agent.

The SIC maintains a record of every lost, stolen and cancelled certificate.

The paying agent will notify the registrar and a new certificate will be issued. The old one will be cancelled in the agents' records and in the Securities Information Center records.

Claims

When a broker realizes that the amount of dividends or interest expected from the NSCC, the DTC, or the paying agent was less than anticipated, the broker generates a claim to retrieve the money. The need for a claim is usually the result of a processing error somewhere in the marketplace. If the broker has received more money than anticipated, the broker generally waits for another firm to claim.

Reasons for Claims

Claims generally occur for any one of six reasons:

- Securities Lending
- Incorrect or late information
- Fails
- Physical securities are being transferred
- Securities arrive too late to transfer

- Transfer is rejected due to incomplete information

Claim Methodologies

When a firm realizes that it has an error and should file a claim, it has three ways to do so. The broker can work with the:

- DTC Securities Payment Order process
- NSCC's Dividend Settlement Service (DSS)
- Create a claim letter that it sends to another broker.

There are three categories of DSS claims:

- Claims for physical certificates by banks or brokers that represent the new owners.
- Fail or stock loan claims for securities that sellers failed to deliver or that were out on loan on the last record date.
- Other claims on which both participants mutually agreed prior to the submission of the claim.

M. ACCOUNTING

The broker's accounting systems are responsible for all of the book keeping and accounting report production for the firm. The accounting system receives input from almost every other processing system. These other processing systems generally maintain their own detailed sub-ledgers and pass totals or net amounts to the firm's general ledger.

The major reports, which are prepared by the accounting department, are in accordance with Generally Accepted Accounting Principles (GAAP), and are:

Daily Cash Balance

The daily cash balance records all of the cash coming into and going out of the firm. The firm's cash positions with its bank and with the DTC and NSCC are reconciled daily.

Cash Management

Brokers manage cash for themselves and for their clients when they have discretion. In addition, brokers need to provide cash management alternatives for their clients who make their own decisions.

Cash Management for the Firm

Firms manage their own cash with the objective of maximizing their return.

Cash Management for Clients

Brokers manage the excess cash in their clients' accounts in order to maximize the clients' return, and provide tools for their clients that allow the clients to buy/sell short term assets or to move cash between interest bearing and non-interest bearing accounts.

Profit and Loss Statement (P&L)

The P&L statement shows the firm's overall profitability as well as the profitability by:

- Department (brokerage, trading, etc.)

- Branch (and potentially registered representative)
- Trader
- Portfolio Manager

Some firms will create P&L statements for their largest clients to determine overall client profitability.

General Ledger

The balance sheet tracks the amount in various accounts, and is used as the basis for several different types of statutory reporting. The general ledger usually contains four ranges of accounts: client, firm, street-side, and general business.

Broker Accounting

Brokers perform a variety of accounting functions on behalf of their clients and themselves.

Accounting for Institutional Clients

Brokers have to record all transactions as they occur. If an error is made, it must be promptly corrected.

Accounting for Individual Clients

Just as for institutional clients, all of the transaction for individuals must be recorded as they occur.

Accounting for the Firm

A broker, like all other businesses, has a general ledger that records all of the financial transactions that affect the firm. The general ledger records transactions as income, expenses, asset balances or liability balances.

Various processing areas are given control of specific sub-ledgers where transactions relating to the specific processing areas are recorded as they occur. The net of these transactions is reported to the general ledger.

Each department's sub-ledger, often called a proof, is used daily to record transactions and is reconciled daily to ensure accuracy.

Broker Accounting Systems

Broker systems contain detailed accounting rules that must properly calculate and record each transaction based upon the type of security, client, etc.

The accounting system receives input from almost every other processing system. Accounting systems are responsible for all of the book keeping and accounting report production for the firm.

N. NEW ACCOUNTS

All brokers need clients, and the client relationship is defined in the account agreement that was described in the chapter on account opening. When a firm opens a new account, in addition to the contractual paperwork that is required from the client, there is usually some internal paperwork that is generated to begin the process of actually opening the client's account. The new account process for retail and for institutional clients is discussed in the chapter on Account Opening.

O. COMPLIANCE DEPARTMENT

The firm's compliance department is responsible for ensuring that the firm adheres to the regulations and rules that have been established for broker/dealers. The SEC and the Fed have established these regulations, and the various Self Regulating Organizations that exist throughout the industry have defined the rules.

These regulations, rules and SROs are discussed in the chapter on Regulators and Legislation.

One of the newly important issues is data retention. The primary rules that apply to retention are:

SEC Rule 17a-4

National securities exchange members and broker/dealers are required to maintain accessible records made between specific parties for certain periods of time.

Foreign Corrupt Practices Act, 1977, 1988

To eliminate bribery and make illegal the destruction of corporate records to conceal a crime, corporations must "...make and keep books, records and accounts, which, in reasonable detail, accurately and fairly reflect the transactions and dispositions of the assets..."

Sarbanes-Oxley – Section 103

Pubic accounting firms must maintain, for not less than seven years, records including work papers and certain other documents that contain conclusions, opinions, analyses and financial data related to the audit or review of a public company. This may include emails, computational notes and instant messages relevant to the audit and financial statement review functions.

NASD 3010(d) (1)

This rule states that a broker/dealer must establish procedures in writing for how electronic correspondence between their registered representatives and the public are recorded. NASD members must preserve data in accordance with SEC 17a-3 and 17a-4.

P. RISK MANAGEMENT

Broker/Dealers are concerned about many different areas of operations where errors can occur. Some of these areas for attention are shown in the following charts:

Function	Metric
	Position Breaks
Unmatched Agent Securities	x
DTC Securities Rejection	x
Branch Processing	x
Foreign Securities Processing	x
Securities Replacements	x
Restricted Processing	x

Dividend Processing	Cash Value$ > 30days	Cash Items > 30days	Position Value$ > 30days	Position Items > 30days
Reorganization	Cash Value$ > 7days	Cash Items > 7days	Position Value$ > 7days	Position Items > 7days

DTC Recon /Trade Proof	Open Rec Items >7days
CNS Recon/Cash Trades	x
Latin America Recon	x
Settlement	Manual Input Items
Quarterly Securities Audit	Missed Box Count
Open Trans Confirmation	Unresolved Confirms
Fail Confirmation	Unresolved Confirms
Cash Forecasting	Variance (Mil$)

	Position Break Items	Cash Break Items	Cash & Position Breaks	Cost to Carry (Mil$)
DTC MBS Custody	x	x	x	x
DTC MBS Dealer	x	x	x	x
Fedwire MBS Dealer	x	x	--	x

Latin America Settlement	Fail Items		
DTC/Physical Settlement	Fail Percent (%) - Equity	Fail Percent (%) - Muni	Fail Percent (%) - Corp
Buy-In	Cost of Error $		

	T+1 Breaks	T+2 Breaks	T+3 Breaks

Corporate Clearing	x	x	x
Firm Business	x	x	Position Break Items
Listed Clearing	x	x	x
Muni Clearing	x	x	x
OTC Clearing	x	x	x
Subsidiary Clearing	x	x	x
Subsidiary Options	x	x	Position Break Items

The various types of operational risk are discussed in Chapter VIII – Post Settlement Processing.

Q. REPORTING

Brokers are required to report on transactions by issuing a confirmation to their clients, and must report their activity to various Self-Regulating Organizations.

Brokers have a variety of reporting requirements.

Client Reporting

Brokers are required to report on transactions by issuing a confirmation to their clients.

- Paper confirmations are sent to retail clients.
- Institutions receive their confirmations electronically for the instruments that are held in the DTCC, and can be supplemented by a paper confirmation if the client requires it.

Brokers must also issue a quarterly or monthly statement that lists the transactions and the resulting positions for each asset held by the broker for their client.

Regulatory Reporting

Brokers have several different types of reports that are required by their SROs, including:

- OATS
- TRACE
- DTC Regulatory Reporting
- NSCC Street-side Reporting
- Etc.

Internal Reporting

Brokers are interested in:

- Operations Reports
- Profit and Losses on trades/positions
- Cash management

R. CLIENT SERVICING

Most direct client service activities are provided by registered representatives for individual clients and by the sales staff or traders for institutional clients. They are frequently supported by assistants who do the research and consolidate the replies, or by a central investigation department for certain types of issues.

Client reporting is different for retail clients and institutional clients:

Retail Clients

Retail clients receive confirmations, monthly statements, year-end tax reports and often receive some form of monthly newsletter that provides investment advice. Increasingly advice is being provided through the firm's website.

Institutional Clients

Institutional clients receive a wider range of reports that reflect their larger volume. Most of the reports are provided in electronic form, and could include confirmations, daily transaction reports, monthly statements, quarterly evaluations, etc.

X. Bank Processing

Banks play a significant role in processing securities for all categories of institutional clients, trusts and high net worth individuals, and are increasingly establishing retail brokerage subsidiaries through holding companies.

This chapter covers the ten major roles of a bank in securities processing.

Service Provided	Role of Bank
Domestic Custody	Custodian for institutional clients investing in the U.S.
Global Custody	Custodian for institutional clients investing cross-border
Corporate Trust	Trustee for issuers
Institutional Trust	Trustee for institutional clients
Section 20 Brokerage	Brokerage for clients
Proprietary Trading	Trade for the bank's own accounts
Private Banking	Bank for high net worth clients
Personal Trust	Trustee for personal trust clients
Investment Banking	Variety of roles in creating and distributing new financial instruments
Dealer Clearance	Clearing of government securities for other financial institutions

Figure 201 - Roles of Banks in Securities Processing

Each of these ten roles is covered in the following sections.

A. DOMESTIC CUSTODY

Custody Business

As was discussed in Chapter II, a custodian may perform its services for institutions (Corporations, Insurance Companies, Mutual Funds and Pension Funds) or for individuals who are usually very wealthy private clients, called High Net Worth Individuals (HNWI), through legal entities or departments typically called Private Banks, often as a Personal Trust account.

Custodian Functions

Custody is the safekeeping and administration of securities and cash on behalf of others. This function can be either the primary purpose of the firm or one department in the bank. The administrative activities can be as agent or as a fiduciary. The servicing activities can include:

- Trade Processing and Settlement
    - Monitoring the purchase and sale of securities via brokers
    - Receiving and delivering of securities (settlement)
    - Advising clients of every movement in the account (reporting)
    - Accounting for every possible type of securities and derivative (accounting)
    - Safekeeping of shares through a central depository or in a vault if necessary
- Post-Settlement Processing

- Income Collection
- Corporate Actions
- Cash Management
- Funds Transfer
- Accounting
- Market Data
- Reporting
- Reconciliations
- New Accounts
- Dealer Clearance
- Securities Lending
- Client Servicing
- Advisor Communications
- Performance Measurement

These Post-Settlement Processing activities are covered in this chapter, and many of them are also described in more detail in Chapter VIII.

Bank Custody Clients

Custodians serve a wide variety of clients, including:

Corporations

Corporations generally invest for their own account, usually in cash equivalents for a short term in order to maximize their use of their liquid assets. To make this efficient, corporations need an ability to buy/sell on line and to see their positions throughout the day in near-real time.

Banks

A bank custodian can process for another bank, either on a disclosed or undisclosed basis.

Broker/Dealers

Banks can provide custody for broker/dealers and can provide a service called dealer clearance for government securities that is discussed in this chapter.

Hedge Funds

Banks can provide custody and accounting services for hedge funds.

Insurance Companies

Insurance Companies need custody for the investments they make in two general categories:

- Investments made on behalf of equivalents for products such as annuities, etc.
- Investments made by the insurance company to cover their general insurance liabilities.

Insurance companies have specific reporting requirements, and the systems must collect specific information to produce these reports.

Mutual Funds

Mutual Funds need the traditional functions of a custody system and need must to keep track of the fund's values and expenses in order to calculate a daily NAV. In addition to these custody functions, mutual funds also need services that can be provided by another servicing company, including the number of shareholders and the positions held by each shareholder.

Pension Funds

There are two types of pension funds (public and corporate). Custody accounts that are used to maintain public pension funds must be in compliance with ERISA and therefore are required to maintain more transactional detail, such as:

- Tax lot accounting
- Detailed accounting records for prior period adjustments
- Trade date accounting rather than settlement date accounting
- Many specific detailed reports

Banks also can provide custody for corporate pension funds that are not subject to ERISA.

Personal Trust

Personal trusts are established for the benefit of a single individual or a small number of individuals, and can require a bank to provide custody services for the trust's investments.

Personal Trust processing is introduced later in this chapter.

Bank Regulators

Banks are primarily regulated by two agencies for their traditional banking activities, by one other agency for their securities business, and by a fourth for their pension related activities:

Government Agency	Responsibilities
Federal Reserve Bank	Banking and Credit
Office of the Comptroller of the Currency	Banking
Securities Exchange Commission	Securities
Department of Labor	Pension

Figure 202 - Regulatory Responsibilities

Primary Custody Regulations

There are several regulations that affect the domestic custody business. Some of the most important are:

ERISA

If the bank is the custodian of retirement plan assets, the bank's process for accounting, reporting and receiving 12(b)(1) fees, shareholder servicing fees, or other fees must be in compliance with ERISA guidelines.

Free Riding - Regulation U - 12 CFR 221

The bank must ensure that its processes regarding free-riding are adequate. (More information regarding Free Riding can be found in Banking Circular 275, "Free Riding in Custody Accounts."

In addition to violating Regulation U which governs loans by banks, a custodian may be allowing violations of Regulation X (12 CFR 224) or Regulation T (12 CFR 220), and may be unable to recover funds advanced to a client settle a transaction.

Bank Secrecy Act (BSA) - 12 CFR 21.21 and 31 CFR 103

If a BSA review of custody services needs to be performed, the bank can refer to the "Bank Secrecy Act/Anti-Money Laundering" booklet of the *Comptroller's Handbook* for procedures.

Escheatment

A custodian must ensure that their process for escheatment of unclaimed items is appropriate. At a minimum this should include:

- Are outstanding checks aged, suspense account entries, or house accounts entries
- Whether the bank filed escheatment reports with the proper jurisdiction

Gramm-Leach-Bliley Act of 1999 (GLBA)

The Gramm-Leach-Bliley Act (GLBA), which is also known as the Financial Services Modernization Act of 1999, repealed the Glass-Steagall Act and provides limited privacy protections against the sale of private financial information. Additionally, the GLBA defines the rules against obtaining personal information through false pretenses.

Lost and Stolen Securities - 17 CFR 240.17f-1

The custodian must have written procedures to report lost and stolen securities with the Securities Information Center (SIC), including:

- Registration as a direct or indirect inquirer with SIC
- Assigned a FINS number

Overdrafts - Regulation D - 12 CFR 204

The bank must ensure that overdrafts are monitored and reported to the bank's comptroller for accurate reporting under Reg. D for reserve requirements.

U.S. Investment Company Assets - 17 CFR 240.17f

If the bank is the custodian of an investment company assets, the custodian must ensure that their processes adequately comply with the SEC's revised rule 17f-5 and new rule 17f-7.

Custody Systems

The main functions of a custody system are to:

- Collect information and instructions from clients, brokers, depositories, clearing corporations, regulators and transfer agents. This information includes a description of the assets held (positions), money received/disbursed, income collected, and trade transaction instructions.

- Provide edits and controls over transactions

- Debit/credit client's cash account for the value of the transaction and forward an appropriate advice

- Receive and deliver securities according to client instructions

- Establish master files that produce accurate and updated management and client reports

- Securities Lending (this is a value added service, but is also a component of the application)

While banks that are involved as custodians in the securities processing environment perform many of the same functions as brokers, banks always act as an agent except in their brokerage subsidiaries unless they are appointed as a trustee.

The generic functions of a custodian system are shown in the following diagram.

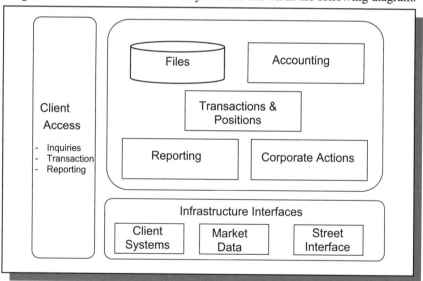

Figure 203 - Generic Bank Systems Architecture

Each of these functions is explained in the next sections; however, each function could have specific processing requirements that depend upon the type of client.

- Personal Trust systems have many more common banking functions built into them, such as bank loans, checking, etc., and must create a statement that integrates banking and brokerage activity, and which provides a clear analysis of investment performance.

- Systems that are used to maintain public pension funds must be in compliance with ERISA and therefore are required to maintain more transactional detail, such as:
  - Tax lot accounting
  - Detailed accounting records for prior period adjustments
  - Trade date accounting rather than settlement date accounting
  - Many specific detailed reports

- Insurance companies have other reporting requirements, and the systems must collect specific information to produce these reports.

- Mutual funds need the traditional functions of a custody system and need to keep track of the fund's values and expenses in order to calculate a daily NAV. In addition to these custody functions, mutual funds also need services that can be provided by another servicing company, including the number of shareholders and the positions held by each shareholder.

The activities that are performed by each of the functions shown in the generic chart shown previously are explained in the following sections.

Client Access

Client access systems allow clients and clients' investment managers to inquire and initiate transactions through:

- Increased use of the web-based browser thin client technologies

- Decreased use of dedicated workstations that provide direct access, file transfers or message based transactions

- CPU to CPU processes using file transfers or messaging, typically based upon SWIFT or vendor standards

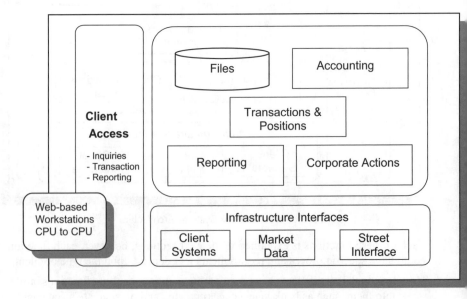

Figure 204 - Client Access Module

Transactions and Positions

The transaction and positions applications consist of a set of routines that process the different types of client transactions and properly post them to the clients' portfolios.

Domestic custody systems are only concerned about the number of units held for each investment instrument and a cash position. Cash must be divided into principle and income for trust accounts.

Global custody systems may hold securities positions and multiple cash positions for each currency, as well as foreign exchange cross rates that allow the custodian to restate the portfolio's valuations in a given base currency.

These routines also keep track of where the securities are held for each account. The locations could include:

- Central Securities Depositories (CSD)
- International Securities Depositories (ICSD)
- Physical/Vault
- Out to Transfer/Registration
- Loan/Borrow
- Collateral

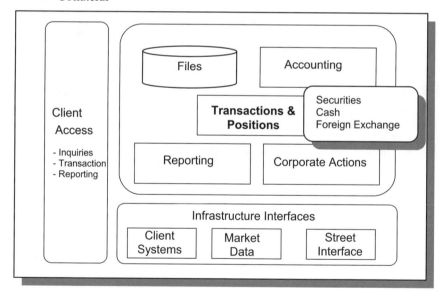

Figure 205 - Transactions and Positions Module

Trust clients require basic custody plus additional accounting and reporting services. The application must keep track of costs, tax lots, trade and settlement dates, and price the portfolio to market periodically.

Infrastructure Interfaces

Interfaces to the street are used to connect the bank's applications to the street's settlement systems, including the DTC, Fed Wire, and to clients through facilities such as the DTC Hub, FMCNet, etc.. These connections could be made through SWIFT, DTC systems,, Omgeo or other vendors, or internal links or systems used by another settlement entity.

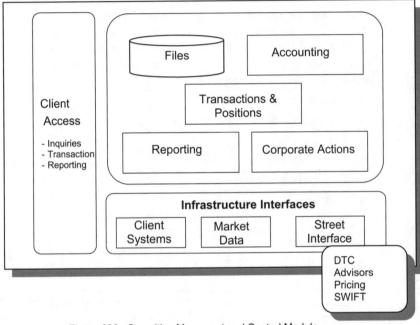

Figure 206 - Securities Movement and Control Module

These interfaces involve data moving in and out of the bank, using proprietary message, standards and networks, SWIFT, FIX, etc., as follows:

	Information comes into the bank from:	Information goes out from the bank to:
Market Data Vendors	X	
Settlement Systems CSD's/ICSD's/Local Agents	X	X
Investment Managers / Clients	X	X

Figure 207 - Sources and Uses of Data

Files

Custodian systems need files that contain details about:

- Client information including names, addresses, and other account characteristics (Client Information File)

- Securities (information) processed in the system (Securities Master File)

- Security positions and transaction history (Brokers call this the Stock Record, banks and investment managers call it Transactions and Balances)
- Cash balances and transaction history
- Industry codes such as BIC and local Market Identification Codes (MIC) (i.e., DTC, Euroclear, etc.)
- Current and historical prices for the securities held by the bank's clients

The data in these files can be either static or dynamic:

Static Information	Dynamic Information
Client Descriptions	Security positions and transactions
Security Descriptions	Cash balances and transactions
Price History	Corporate Actions
Industry Descriptions Codes (both)	Current Prices

Figure 208 - Examples of Static and Dynamic Information

An industry trend is that both Security Master Files and Client Information Files are increasingly being extracted from the firm's dedicated custody application and established as central files that are accessible by multiple applications.

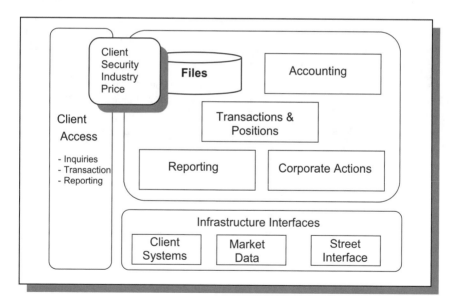

Figure 209 - File Modules

Accounting

Custody systems contain detailed accounting rules that must properly calculate and record each transaction based upon the type of security, client, etc.

These routines include tax information that is also based upon the instrument and the type of client. The global custody versions of these applications also track the tax that has been withheld by other countries for international securities so that it can be reclaimed from the country that has withheld the tax.

If the type of client requires LIFO or FIFO accounting, then the system must maintain each transaction as a separate tax lot for future use. Otherwise, the systems will calculate the average cost based upon the previous average cost and the impact of the current transaction.

For certain clients, the application must price the position and determine the profit or loss using the appropriate accounting rules. For clients requiring Performance Measurement, the data must also be audited to ensure accuracy.

The accounting system receives input from almost every other processing system. Accounting systems are responsible for all of the bookkeeping and accounting report production for the firm.

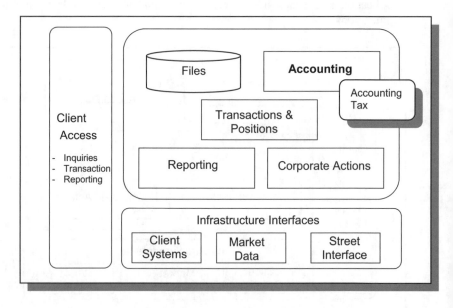

Figure 210 - Accounting Module

Corporate Actions

Custody systems usually contain an integrated corporate action and income collection module which is used to calculate entitlements, notify the holders of their entitlements, receive gross amounts of cash or securities from the paying agent and/or the depository, and allocate these amounts to the proper account.

The primary functions of a corporate action process were discussed in the chapter on Post-Settlement Processing:

- Event Generation
- Entitlement Determination
- Client Notification
- Event Posting
- Collection and Reconciliation

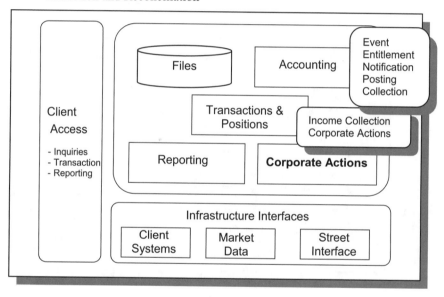

Figure 211 - Corporate Actions Module

There is additional processing required for voluntary corporate actions. The custodian must notify the owner of the securities of the action and the possible alternative responses, and then obtain their input and notify the processing agents of the client's decision within a specific time frame.

Reporting

Custody systems also contain a set of reporting modules that are used to produce the wide range of reports required by the different categories of clients, regulatory agencies, management and compliance. Reports that cover holdings and transactions activity can be formatted using industry standards and transmitted via SWIFT, the DTC Hub, Leased Line, FTP, etc.

Increasingly, custodians are creating a single process stream for transactions, regardless of the type of client and then differentiate between clients (and in their pricing) through the types of reports that are produced. This means that the application keeps track of the processing for 'plain vanilla' custody and for trust accounts, but since each type of client receives different output reports the level of service appears different and can be priced differently.

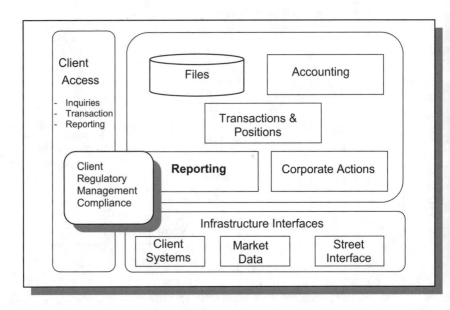

Figure 212 - Reporting Module

Bank Custodian – Major Interfaces

Banks have two generic categories of interfaces:

Client Interfaces

Most custodians have created proprietary web-based applications that institutional clients/custody clients can use to access their accounts directly, by file transfers or message-based.

However, most institutional managers have multiple custodians so they prefer information to be sent in industry standard formats via SWIFT, DTC Hub, Leased Lines, FTP or some other communication protocol.

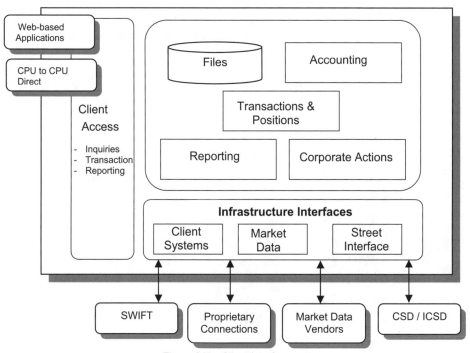

Figure 213 - Client Interfaces

Industry Interfaces

Custodians also connect to other industry participants using:

- DTC / Fed / CSD / ICSD links
- SWIFT network
- Vendor-provided networks
- Proprietary links
- Various market data vendors

These interfaces may use a variety of message structures, including industry standard formats, such as ISO15022, FIX , etc.

Custody Processing

The functions performed by the processing departments in a bank's securities operation are very similar to many of the functions performed by brokers, with the primary differences listed below:

- The custodian only gets involved after the trade has been executed
- As an agent, a custodian can not participate as a principal in any clearing corporation's netting process and must settle on a trade by trade basis
- When acting as a custodian, a bank does not have a bank-owned position in any security
- Although a custodian does not use the concept of a stock record which identifies positions, it keeps the same information in a different way

There are several different bank functions that can be organized as individual departments or into consolidated departments. The main functions are:

- Income Collection
- Corporate Actions
- Cash Management
- Accounting
- Pricing of Positions
- Maintaining Reference Data
- Foreign Exchange
- Reporting
- Client Servicing
- Advisor Communications
- Reconciliations
- Performance Measurement
- Securities Lending

Each of these functions is introduced in this chapter for Custody and in detail in the Post-Settlement Processing chapter.

Settlement Department

A bank settles directly with the relevant depository for the securities it is processing. Most of these securities are eligible at the DTC, while the depository for U.S. government securities is the Fed, mortgage backed securities are held at the MBS division of the DTCC, and options are recorded by the OCC.

DTC

Banks have multiple connections to the DTC through SMART (Securely Managed and Reliable Technology). SMART is the DTCC's technology backbone that supports clearance and settlement in the U.S. capital markets. It consists of a nationwide complex of networks, processing centers and control facilities that are designed to withstand catastrophic disasters, ensuring that time-critical activities occur.

SMART is replacing the batch processes and mainframe-to-mainframe connectivity that DTC has previously provided, and is being implemented over several years. DTCC's communication options include:

Communication Applications	Through Dec 31, 2005		Effective Jan 1, 2006	
	Direct to SMART	Via SFTI to SMART	Direct to SMART	Via SFTI to SMART
DATATRAK	ftp NDM (TCP/IP) NDM (SNA)	ftp NDM (TCP/IP)	ftp NDM (TCP/IP)	ftp NDM (TCP/IP)
AUTOROUTE	ftp NDM (TCP/IP) NDM (SNA)	ftp NDM (TCP/IP)	ftp NDM (TCP/IP)	ftp NDM (TCP/IP)
WebSphere MQ	TCP/IP VTAM/SNA	TCP/IP	TCP/IP	TCP/IP
Participant Browser Service (PBS	TCP/IP (https)	TCP/IP (https)	TCP/IP (https)	TCP/IP (https)
CCF	ftp NDM (TCP/IP) NDM (SNA) CCFUSER (VTAM)	Not supported	ftp NDM (TCP/IP)	Not supported
MDH [89]	VTAM LU6.2	Not supported	Not supported	Not supported
Participant Terminal System (PTS) [90]	SNA/SNI	Not supported	Not supported	Not supported

Figure 214 - DTCC Communications Plan

Banks receive an electronic notification from the DTC system that an investment manager has approved, or *affirmed,* a transaction to settle on a certain date. The bank will process this electronic instruction and on the settlement date will automatically make the necessary entries to move money and securities. Since the DTC is making the same entries, the bank and the DTC should have identical balances after the transactions are complete. Any differences are called breaks, and need to be investigated and resolved immediately.

Occasionally, a bank will be asked by an investment manager to conduct the affirmation process for the investment manager. In this case, the manager must submit a written instruction to the bank, either contractually for an on-going process or by fax for a single trade to the bank's Advisor Communication's Department, which is discussed later in this chapter. Once it has received a proper instruction, the bank will use the DTC system to affirm the trade on behalf of the manager.

---

[89] Replaced by WebSphere MQ
[90] Replaced by PBS

DTC's Custody Services support Safekeeping, Deposit & Withdrawal, Transfer, Restricted Transfer, Reorganization and Clearance & Settlement services through a variety of activities, including:.

- **Security** – DTC's vault and certificate-handling practices ensure security and accurate processing.

- **"Online" Vault File** – Detailed information on every certificate and document is available, including certificate number, registration, negotiability status, restricted indicator, etc.

- **Contingency** – DTC offers total system reliability including DTC's dedicated back-up site, which is available in the event DTC's main offices are inaccessible.

- **Imaging** – Images of all certificates and documents held in Custody are available through an imaging workstation.

- **Interfaces** – Participants can choose to interface with DTC's Custody Service via the available SMART protocols.

Government

Government securities are exchanged between broker/dealers acting as U.S. government securities dealers and settled through banks with the Fed through the Fed Book Entry system.

MBS

Mortgage Backed Securities and other asset backed securities are settled through the MBS division of the DTCC.

Vault

The settlement department also usually includes a vault and a physical receive/deliver window for physical securities. This area is responsible for ensuring that any item received is in good form, and is held safely in the vault. Items held in the vault are subject to the collection of income and corporate actions when appropriate.

Domestic Custody Compliance Process

The overall purpose of compliance is to monitor the performance of the firm to ensure that it is performing in compliance with laws and the rules established by the SROs.

Custodians have several compliance functions that must be performed by custodians to manage trade transactions. In this process, the custodian determines that the:

- Client's account has the securities on hand to deliver for sales

- Client's account has adequate cash or forecasted cash for purchases

- Trades are properly matched or DK'd (DK = Don't Know)

One of the most important compliance issues at this time is an increased emphasis in the Know Your Customer (KYC) requirement that has been strengthened in the USA PATRIOT Act, which is discussed in the chapter on Regulation and Legislation.

Domestic Custody Settlement Process

In summary, the custodian's process includes:

- Receiving instructions from the account owner via the DTC (or directly from the account owner)
- Ensuring that the relevant accounts have the necessary cash or securities to complete the trade
- Ensuring that the transaction is allowed by the terms of the account
- Monitoring the progress of the settlement transaction through the custodian's Securities Movement and Control System (SMAC)
- Transferring the ownership on the custodian's records on settlement date
- Reconciling with the DTC's records (possibly reconciling transactions daily and full positions monthly)
- Resolving breaks (discrepancies) that are identified as a result of the reconciliation
- Servicing the assets that are in the account

Domestic Custody Asset Servicing

Income Collection Department

Income collection consists of dividend collection and interest collection.

Dividend Processing

The overall process that is involved with collecting dividends was discussed in the chapter on Post-Settlement Processing. There are three key dates for dividend processing: record date, ex-dividend date and payment date, which were also defined in the same chapter.

There are four basic steps in dividend process, which are described in more detail in the chapter on Post Trade Processing. The steps are:

- Event Notification
- Entitlement Determination
- Event Posting
- Reconciliation

When the board of directors votes to pay a dividend, they notify their paying agent, who also announces the event to the marketplace. This information is gathered by market data vendors who are in business to collect and electronically relay these event notifications to firms throughout the industry.

This information is usually received in a file transfer by the bank's income collection system and is currently posted in an overnight batch as a pending event. Information can also be received in SWIFT format from:

- DTC
- Local Agents
- Vendors

This information is held in the system until the record date for the dividend, at which time the system will determine which accounts are entitled to the dividend, and how much they should receive on the payment date.

On payment date, the income collection system will post the amounts that are anticipated to be received, either:

- Directly from the paying agent for securities that are held by the bank in their own nominee name

- Directly from the paying agent for physical securities that are held by the bank in their client's name

- From the DTC for the bulk of the securities that are held in the DTC's nominee name, the dividends are generally posted to the clients' accounts, and the total of these credits is set up as a receivable from the paying agent and/or from the DTC. On the payment date, the bank will receive a wire transfer from the paying agent and/or a credit from the DTC.

The custodian must then reconcile the amounts that were distributed to the clients with the amounts that were received. Any differences must be reconciled and resolved.

Interest Processing – Registered Bonds

The overall process that is involved with collecting interest payments was discussed in the chapter on Post-Trade Processing, Clearing and Settlement. There are two key dates for interest processing: the record date and the payment date, which were also defined in that chapter. There is no ex-date for bonds since bonds are traded with accrued interest.

Much of the processing of interest is similar to that for dividends, and the process sequence is the same:

- Event Notification

- Entitlement Determination

- Event Posting

- Reconciliation

The difference between interest and dividend processing is that the board of directors does not grant the interest payments (although the board could vote to default on a payment). For most fixed income instruments, the amount that will be routinely paid remains the same. This is not the case for variable rate instruments and asset backed securities.

- The interest rate for variable rate instruments is usually *pegged* (associated) with a standard industry interest rate such as the Consumer Price Index, EURIBOR, etc. When that rate is known, the variable rate is calculated and paid.

- Asset backed Securities repay a portion of the principal plus interest each month. This instrument is described more in the chapter on Fixed Income Instruments.

Interest Processing – Bearer Bonds

Although there are fewer and fewer bearer bonds each year, some still remain. The process for paying interest on bearer bonds is different from paying on registered bonds, as follows:

- The bondholder removes the coupon from the bond and presents it to an accredited paying agent or co-paying agent for that issue.

- The paying agent or the co-paying agent collects the coupon from the bondholder and pays the interest that is described on the coupon.

- A co-paying agent bundles the coupons that have been received and presents them to the paying agent for credit. The co-paying agent will be reimbursed for the amount they paid to the clients, plus a processing fee.

- The paying agent will either receive the coupons from the co-paying agent(s) or directly from the clients.

- The paying agent bundles together all of the coupons received directly from clients as well as those from co-paying agents and presents an invoice to the issuer for the total of the payments to clients, plus the co-paying agent fees and their paying agent fees.

- The paying agent will then cancel the coupons and either stores them for some defined period of time or destroys them.

Reorganization Department

Corporate Action Processing

Although there are many different types of corporate actions, as described in the chapter on Post-Trade Processing, there are four distinct functions that must be performed by custodians for all of the different types, plus one additional step for voluntary actions.

- Event Notification
- Entitlement Determination
- Client Notification (Voluntary Corporate Actions)
- Event Posting
- Reconciliation

Corporate actions processing is discussed in detail in the chapter on Post-Settlement Processing.

Domestic Custodian Cash Management

Custodians manage cash for themselves and for their custody and trust clients when they have the responsibility to manage excess cash.

Cash Management for the Firm

Firms manage their own cash with the objective of maximizing their return across a variety of instruments, including:

- Cash Equivalents
- Repos
- FX

Cash Management for Clients

Custodians manage the excess cash in their clients' accounts in order to maximize the clients' return, and provide tools for their clients that allow the clients to buy/sell short term assets, often from a Short Term Investment Fund (STIF), or to move cash between interest bearing and non-interest bearing accounts.

The movement of cash into a STIF could be on a transaction-by-transaction basis, or the result of a cash sweep whereby cash over some minimum amount is moved automatically. STIF funds can be U.S. dollars or any currency.

Domestic Custodian Funds Transfer

In order to manage cash effectively, banks need to have an efficient Electronic Funds Transfer (EFT) capability. EFT uses technology within each bank along with networks and automated clearinghouses.

Accounting Department

A bank custodian has three different types of accounting that they typically perform:

- Regulatory Accounting
- General Ledger Accounting
- Client-Related Accounting
  - Custody Accounting
  - Trust Accounting
  - Mutual Fund Accounting
  - Insurance Accounting

Regulatory Accounting

Custodians have to submit regulatory reports in several areas:

- Investment activities
- Annual financial reporting
- Currency holdings
- Inward and outward remittances
- F/X conversions
- Violation of regulations (such as investment quota and share ownership)
- Online daily compliance monitoring
- Performance measurement
- Value at Risk
- Securities lending
- Regulatory Reporting of Transactions

General Ledger

A custodian bank, like all other businesses, has a general ledger that records all of the financial transactions that affect the bank. The General Ledger records transactions as income, asset balances or liability balances.

Various processing areas are given control of specific sub-ledgers where transactions relating to the specific processing areas are recorded as they occur. The net of these transactions is reported to the bank's overall ledger.

Each department's sub-ledger, often called a proof, is used daily to record transactions and is reconciled daily to ensure accuracy. Any differences are posted to a Difference and Fine account (D&F) which isolates the difference and records fines, and allows the bank's investigators to begin tracing the errors. Most firms require that items left in a D&F account over 90 days are *written off*, or expensed, as an operating loss at that time. The bank can still continue the investigation, and when resolved, the item could be *written-on* to the books.

Custody Accounting

Custodian accounting is performed for institutional accounts, and typically uses actual settlement date accounting.

Errors are corrected in the period in which they are identified and reports are usually limited to transactions and holdings reports.

Trust Accounting

Trust accounting is performed for personal or institutional trust clients. Trust accounting requires the bank to ensure that all transactions are properly recorded in *the period in which they occurred*. For most types of accounts, if an error is discovered in a period subsequent to the period in which it occurred, the bank would make an adjusting entry in the period the error was discovered. If necessary, the bank either back-values the transaction or calculates the amount of interest that the client lost and give it to the client.

With trust accounting, the adjustment has to be recorded in the period in which the original transaction occurred. This means that the previous statement has to be reopened, the transaction posted and a new closing balance recorded for that period. If the error occurred several months ago, then the statement for each month must be reopened and corrected, with a new opening and a new closing balance calculated. This is a very complex and time-consuming task, and encourages operations managers to *get it right the first time*.

Mutual Fund Accounting

If a bank is responsible for performing the accounting function for a mutual fund, the bank has to be accurate on a daily basis since open end mutual funds calculate the Net Asset Values (NAV) daily.[91] The NAV is then published each day by 4:00 and is used by investors to make their buy and sell decisions. This means that every transaction for every day must be properly recorded to avoid any errors.

---

[91] Closed end funds calculate on a weekly basis, and some funds have begun providing prices on an hourly basis.

When the custodian acts as the record keeper, they prefer to use their own chart of accounts for the accounting; however, some funds require that their own chart of accounts be used, which significantly affects the processing costs.

When the fund activity is closed each day, the fund accountants look at several different sources of information to determine the Net Asset Value (NAV), including:

- Realized gains and losses
- Unrealized gains and losses
- Interest accrual
- Income collected
- Corporate actions
- Expenses (actual and accrued)

If a mutual fund makes an error in calculating the NAV, the investors in that fund who bought or sold shares were given an incorrect price, and adjustments must be made. If the error goes undetected, the problem can compound and quickly affect a very large number of clients.

Domestic Custody Accounting Systems

Custody systems contain detailed accounting rules that must properly calculate and record each transaction based upon the type of security, client, etc.

These routines include tax information that is also based upon the instrument and the type of client. The global custody versions of these applications also track the tax that has been withheld by other countries for international securities so that it can be reclaimed from the country that has withheld the tax.

The accounting system receives input from almost every other processing system. Accounting systems are responsible for all of the book keeping and accounting report production for the firm.

Market Data

Pricing Department

The pricing department is responsible for ensuring that all positions that are held by the bank's clients are accurately priced for each statement. This also allows banks to provided audited data to their clients on the value of the portfolio. Trust and mutual fund clients need every security priced accurately, within the time parameters for their statements. While this is relatively straightforward for liquid securities that are traded actively on an exchange or NASDAQ, it can be extremely difficulty and time consuming for illiquid securities.

Pricing departments obtain their prices from market data vendors for liquid securities and the prices are automatically feed into the bank's custody system; however, the department must typically make individual phone calls to multiple sources to find the prices for illiquid issues and private placements.

- Institutional clients need completely valued custody portfolios. Recent closing prices of actively traded securities are easily obtained from several market data vendors; however, institutions frequently hold a variety of inactive instruments, including municipal bonds, partnerships, guaranteed investment contracts (GICs), etc. These instruments require more effort to value, but the custodian is still responsible for the activity.

- For mutual funds, the security must be added the day it is traded in order to process the security on the trade date and to have the information about the trade available to the trust accountants.

Issues that are incorrectly set up or that have erroneous prices can cause client statements to be incorrect, and they may have to be recalculated. When an error occurred in a previous month, that month's statement will have to be recalculated, along with all subsequent statements up to the current accounting period.

As the industry moves to STP and/or T+1 settlement, firms will have to maintain more securities in their files in order to process quickly, or develop a way to add information about a new security on the day that the security is first traded by the firm.

Reference Data Maintenance

Reference data includes several categories of fundamental data elements, including static information such as:

- Securities Master File
- Counter-parties
- Account-master files
- Clients
- Currency
- Country codes, etc.

The pricing department is also usually responsible for setting up new securities on the firm's securities master file. Although there are millions of securities available in the market, most banks' clients only invest in a small portion of the available issues. Since there is an expense associated with systemically maintaining the information about each of these securities, banks tend to only maintain a subset of the available securities. When a client trades an issue for the first time or when a new issue is created, that security must be properly added to the master file.

Domestic Custody Reporting

Custodian Banks report transactions and holdings to their clients and to various interested parties regarding these accounts, as well as to Self-Regulating Organizations.

There are several different categories of Custody Reporting:

Client Reporting

Custodian Banks have a much wider range of reporting requirements. In addition to transaction reports and monthly statements, custodians could be required to evaluate the transactions and the positions in a variety of ways. A custodian's institutional clients need their transactions and positions for reconciliation, and increasingly firms and investment managers are sending this information electronically via SWIFT or by direct transmissions using SWIFT formats.

Institutional clients need additional analytical information such as:

Realized Gains and Losses

When a client sells a position, a gain or a loss is realized. This is used to calculate the overall performance of the portfolio and may be taxable.

Realized gains and losses are taxable if the account is taxable.

Unrealized Gains and Losses

When the price of a position changes, and the client continues to hold the position, there is an unrealized gain or loss. This is also used to calculate the overall performance of the portfolio, and would be used to change the NAV if the portfolio was in a fund.

Unrealized gains and losses are not taxable, even if the account is taxable.

Market Action vs. Currency Valuation

When a firm invests internationally, there are two dimensions to gains and losses. The market action is the result of the changes in the value of the security in the currency of the issue, and the currency valuation is the difference between the currency of the issue and the base currency of the client.

These two dimensions can move together or they can move in opposite directions and cancel out portions of each other.

Pricing and Valuations

Institutions need completely valued portfolios. Recent closing prices of actively traded securities are easily obtained from several market data vendors; however, institutions (and individual trusts) frequently hold a variety of inactive instruments, including municipal bonds, partnerships, guaranteed investment contracts (GICs), etc. These instruments require more effort to value, but the custodian is still responsible for the activity.

Comparisons

Institutional clients are interested in comparing their results in the current period to their results in prior periods, on an issue by issue basis and in total.

Some clients also want to have their results compared to an index or a similar portfolio. This process is called Performance Measurement.

Custody systems also contain a set of reporting modules that are used to produce the wide range of reports required by the different categories of clients, regulatory agencies, management and compliance.

Increasingly, custodians are creating a single process stream for transactions, regardless of the type of client and then differentiate between clients (and in their pricing) through the types of reports that are produced.

Regulatory Reporting

Custodians have several different types of reports that are required by their SROs.

Internal Reporting

Custodians are interested in:

- Operations Reports
- Cash management

Domestic Custodian Reconciliation Department

The Custodian's Reconciliation department is primarily concerned with several categories of reconciliations, including:

- Ensuring that the bank's transaction and position records are the same as the records held by the various depositories
- Income collection amounts received vs. posted
- Corporate actions cash and securities received vs. posted
- Trade files from investment managers
- Custodian to sub-custodians
- Contributions and withdrawals

Any differences identified as breaks are investigated and resolved.

Risk Management

Banks are concerned about the same categories of risk management as brokers and investment managers, and are often the last line of defense in preventing errors that can affect their clients.

Operational risks are discussed in Chapter VIII - Post Settlement Processing.

New Accounts

New accounts are obtained by a sales staff contacting prospective clients and replying to client RFPs. Individual contracts are generated, which usually have a term of several years.

Dealer Clearance

When banks act as agents for broker/dealers who are active in the government securities primary market they are performing dealer clearance. To do this, the banks receive and record securities' positions and process certain types of transactions for their clients since broker/dealers cannot be members of the Federal Reserve System, and the Fed is responsible for issuing and processing government securities through the Fed Book Entry system. Secondary market transactions are cleared through the Government Securities Division (GSD).

There are high profits and high risks in the dealer clearance business since the market can experience sudden, massive increases in volume and in large dollar amounts. Over $2 trillion in government securities were traded on an average day in 2003 in 80,000 daily transactions.

Securities Lending

Brokers and banks lend and borrow securities in order to facilitate settlement, to support arbitrage and to make a profit while they are doing it.

In securities lending, there are borrowers and lenders. The borrowers usually have either sold short or are trying to avoid a fail to deliver, and the lenders are trying to earn some additional income on their securities through the lending process. The brokers tend to be the biggest borrowers, and the banks, with large institutional clients that essentially have static portfolios, are generally the biggest lenders.

At the start of each business day, the borrowers must determine what and how much they need. The securities lending market is conducted almost entirely by phone in the morning, and almost all of the trading activity is over by 10:00 a.m.

Securities lending is discussed in detail in the chapter on Post-Settlement Processing.

Client Service Department

The client service department is responsible for providing support to their clients by answering questions posed by clients and for investigating any errors that a client believes affected their account. Client service staff and all employees who have client contact must have been trained in how to deal with clients, whether the clients are retail or institutional.

Clients also frequently ask questions about the bank's processing policies and services. Client service representatives need to understand the processing policies and which services apply to which clients.

When a client believes that an error has occurred, the client will normally contact the client service department either by telephone, mail, email or fax Investigations are either handled directly by the client service representative or are passed under some form of control to the processing department that was responsible for the transaction in question. The types of transactions that generally create a client's questions regarding the bank's accuracy or timeliness are:

- Positions and fails
- Income collection
- Corporate actions
- Pricing
- Confirmations or statements
- Billing

Advisor Communications/Services Department

The adviser communications department is the primary interface between the bank and the investment managers that are employed by the bank's clients. The bank and the investment managers are normally hired independently by the ultimate client, which could be a corporation, high net worth individual, pension fund, or mutual fund. While there is no direct client relationship between the bank and the investment manager, custody banks know that it is important to work very closely with the investment managers' processing staff to ensure accurate securities processing and to satisfy their shared clients.

This unit, often called the AdCom department, will receive instructions from the managers and initiate a transaction based upon the instruction, or respond to the manager's questions regarding transactions that have been processed. The instructions could include securities/cash/foreign exchange settlements or funding transactions that are needed for settlement.

Transactions can be provided by the IM's in industry standard formats via an automated interface, via fax on through applications that are internally developed by the custodian.

Performance Measurement

Performance measurement is not performed directly by registered representatives. More typically, a separate group performs the function in a broker's organization or by banks, investment managers or third party firms.

To achieve precise performance measurement it is necessary to ensure that every transaction and adjustment is properly posted in the period in which they occurred and that all income and corporate actions have been properly accounted for in the period in which they were supposed to occur.

Most broker processing systems, however, are geared towards making adjustments in the period in which errors are discovered, whether or not the error occurred in that period. Performance measurement involves the re-posting of the transaction to a prior period through the use of a dedicated application.

Once the rate of return for the portfolio has been determined, the rate is further attributed to various investment segments so that it can be compared to a comparable universe or benchmark.

B. GLOBAL CUSTODY

The custody processing that has been discussed up to this point in this chapter has been primarily focused on U.S. securities, either for a U.S. or a non-U.S. client. Many large U.S. custody banks are also in the business of helping their clients settle trades in non-U.S. securities. This business is called global custody.

There are several functions that are performed by a Global Custodian, including:

- Multi-Currency Settlement
- Safekeeping
- Corporate Actions
- Dividend and Income Collection
- Proxy Voting
- Cash Management
- Foreign Exchange
- Withholding Tax Reclaims
- Securities Lending
- Investment Accounting
- Contractual or Actual Accounting
- Performance Measurement
- Derivative Processing
- Master Custody and Master Trust

- Physical Certificate Processing
- Multi-Currency Reporting

While it is outside the scope of this book to discuss cross-border processing, it must be noted that the role of a global custodian is an important one for some banks

Securities Operations Forum has a complete eLearning course in Global Custody Processing.

C. CORPORATE TRUST

The corporate trust department, as discussed in the chapter on Securities Industry Participants, is responsible for processing transactions that affect an overall issue, either through corporate actions or income distribution.

A corporate trust department provides a variety of services for investors regarding the issues that they hold. In this case, the bank acts as an agent for the holders of the debt instrument, but the bank is paid by the issuer. There are several different types of agent functions that can be performed by a bank's corporate trust department.

The primary agency functions performed by a corporate trustee can be:

Types of Agency	Description
Bond Trustee	A bond trustee is appointed by the issuer to ensure the proper administration of the bond issue, with specific responsibilities such as: • Certify the validity of the bond when it is issued • Ensure indenture provisions (often called covenants) are met • Monitor the payment of interest and principal to the holders • Administer a sinking fund, if applicable • Monitor the performance of any assets pledged as collateral, if applicable • Represent the creditors in the event of a default • Periodically report to the bondholders • Maintain records on all of the above
Collateral Agent	A collateral agent is responsible for safely holding the collateral presented by the issuer to support specific instruments.
Collection Agent	A collection agent receives coupons, pays the presenter for them and forwards the coupons to the paying agent.
Conversion Agent	A conversion agent has the authority to exchange one class of security for another, according to the instructions of the issuer.
Exchange Agent	An exchange agent supports corporate reorganizations when a merger or re-capitalization is involved.
Fiscal Agent	A fiscal agent can be appointed to disburse funds for interest payments, issuance and registration, and some tax withholding activities.
Forwarding Agent	A forwarding agent receives securities during a tender offer and

	then forwards the securities to the tender agent.
Issuing Agent	An issuing agent issues certificates on behalf of the issuer.
Paying Agent	A paying agent: • Receives funds from the issuer (dividends or interest) • Calculate any interest payment due to bondholders • Disburses the principal an40 • d interest payments to the holders of record as appropriate
Redemption Agent	A redemption agent is typically responsible for: • Designing, printing and mailing letters of transmittal • Receiving and processing returned letters of transmittal and certificates • Designing materials and providing investor communications, including extensive call center operations • Making appropriate payments to holders; and performing tax reporting
Registration Agent	The registration agent, also called the registrar, is responsible for registering the ownership of the securities for which they are responsible, which includes: • Record changes in the ownership of the stocks or bonds • Maintain accurate records of ownership • Ensure that the transfer agent does not issue more in outstanding shares or bonds than originally authorized
Scrip Agent	A scrip agent issues scrip for fractional shares when the firm issues a stock dividend or does a reverse stock split.
Subscription Agent	A subscription agent processes the exercise of stockholders' subscription rights.
Tender Agent	A tender agent administers the specific functions required in a tender offer, as well as for variable rate demand bonds and put bonds. Put and demand bonds are often repurchased by the issuer and resold at a new interest rate to new investors.
Transfer Agent	Transfer agents are used to change the registered ownership for stocks or bonds. • The stock transfer agent is responsible for the registration process that records the ownership of a security. • Bond transfer agents record the ownership of the bonds and manage the processing of transferring ownership from one entity to another. Transfer agent functions include: • Issue certificates • Register the transfer of the ownership of shares or bonds from one owner to another • Replace lost or stolen certificates and hold unused certificates
Mortgage Loan	A mortgage loan custodian is responsible for safekeeping the

Custodian	mortgage files and administration of the mortgages that are used to support mortgage backed securities.
Calculation Agent	A calculation agent collects information about the pools of mortgages for which they are responsible and calculating the amounts that are due to be paid to the investors.
Bond Administrator	The bond administrator makes the same calculations as the calculation agent, and performs these functions as a check on the calculation agent.

Figure 215 - Corporate Trust Functions

Changes in the Role of the Transfer Agent

Historically, stock transfer was a very profitable business for the corporate trust departments of banks; however, that has changed as profit dynamics have changed. Agents are typically paid on a transaction basis and used to receive float on payments as the dividends moved from the issuer to the stock holder; however, since most certificates are now immobilized in depositories, the majority of transfers for purchases and sales do not go through the Transfer Agent and float has been basically eliminated.

The role of the Transfer Agent also has changed significantly with the advent of Direct Registration. The Direct Registration process allows shareholders and bondholders to deposit their shares directly with the transfer agent, in their own name, rather than leaving the shares with banks or brokers where they are held in some street name, or holding the physical certificate.

Services for Municipalities

There are several special services that can be provided to municipalities, including:

Employee Benefit Plans Trustee

The EBF trustee:

- Manages investments and handles administrative duties for all kinds of employee benefit programs, including pension and profit sharing plans, 401(k) plans and employee stock ownership plans.

- Sets up the plan, introduces it to employees and follows-through to keep the plan up to date and running properly

Bond Indenture Trustee

The bond indenture trustee:

- Acts as trustee in the issuance of corporate or municipal bonds by establishing an indenture (trust agreement) that identifies the borrowing terms and the rights and duties of the lender, borrower and the trustee.

- Implements the terms of the indenture

- Invests bond sale proceeds, maintains records, provides reports on fund accounts and pays construction bills

Describing the detailed processing functions of a corporate trust department is beyond the scope of this book.

D. Institutional Trust

Banks can support the trust requirements for pension and mutual funds.

Pension Fund Processing

Pension funds are established by corporations for their employees, and are regulated by rules established by the Department of Labor. These rules are codified in the ERISA Act, which defines what the pension funds (plan sponsors), investment managers and banks must do to record the transactions, account properly and report the value of the funds. One of the most important provisions of ERISA requires employers to establish controls to ensure that the employees have a right to the funds related to their pension even after leaving a job if they are vested in the pension.

There are two major categories of pension funds:

Defined Benefit Programs

In a defined benefit program, the actual amount that a retiree will receive is pre-defined, based upon their age at retirement, years of service, and pre-retirement salary. The plan sponsor calculates how much will be needed in the future to pay retirees based upon actuarial tables, and then determines the anticipated rate of return on its investments in order to decide how much to put into the pension fund each year. A defined benefit program is a liability for a firm since it must be properly funded by the firm regardless of the rate of return on the fund's investments.

In a defined benefit program, the plan sponsor is usually the employer. The plan sponsor selects the investment manager(s) and the custody bank. The bank is assigned the task of keeping the records that shows how much each plan owns of each portfolio.

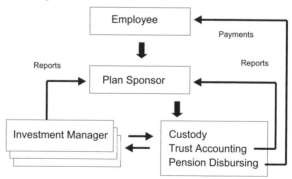

Figure 216 - Defined Benefit Plan Processing

Throughout the 1980's many large corporations were under funded and had significant liabilities due to the weak performance of the stock market. Other firms had an excess of funds in their pension programs and became takeover targets. To counter the risk associated with these two problems, firms began to rely more on another category of pension fund, a defined contribution program, which is described later in this chapter.

Master Trust

During the 1980's, as firms began merging and acquiring other corporations, it was not uncommon for one large company to have multiple defined benefit plans for its various companies, each of which invested in separately managed portfolios. This was expensive and difficult to manage, and a new methodology was created, called master trust. In a master trust, the firm establishes a small number of portfolios that invest for all of the plans. Each plan owns a portion of each portfolio.

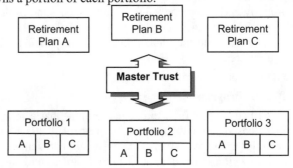

Figure 217 - Role of Master Trust

Defined Contribution Program

In a defined contribution program, which is regulated as a 403(b) or 401 (k) plan, the individual investor takes responsibility for ensuring how much he will have upon retirement. The investor decides how much to put into the program, up to some legal limits, and selects the investments from a list of alternatives provided by the sponsoring firm.

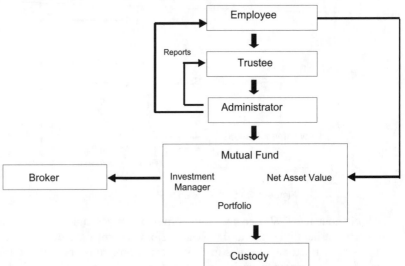

Figure 218 - Defined Contribution Processing

If the investments do well, the person has a larger amount available for retirement than if the investments do poorly. The firm sponsoring the program has no liability to the investor other than to ensure the plan is properly administered according to the law.

Types of Pension Plans

There are several different types of programs, which are based upon the type of firm and the beneficiary.

401(k)

An IRS chapter 401(k) Plan is a plan where an employee may elect to contribute up to a specific amount of pretax dollars to a qualified tax-deferred retirement plan rather than receive taxable cash as compensation or bonus.

In some cases the employer might fund the entire plan or might match the employee's contribution.

The contribution limits are:

Year	Contribution Limit	"Catch-up" contributions for individuals 50 and over Extra Contribution
2003	$12,000	$2,000
2004	$13,000	$3,000
2005	$14,000	$4,000
2006	$15,000	$5,000

Figure 219 - 401K Contribution Limits

Keogh Plans (HR 10)

Self-employed persons may deposit 25% of earned income up to a maximum of $42,000 annually, as of 2004, into any investment approved by the IRS. This limit increases by $1,000 each year

The person setting up the Keogh does not have to be exclusively self-employed.

For example, assuming a person earns $50,000 on their regular job and $20,000 as a self-employed person, under Keogh, 20% of the $20,000, or $4,000 could be put into the plan. ($4,000 is now sheltered.) Taxable earnings for the year are not $70,000, but $66,000. Any earnings on the $4,000 would accumulate tax-free until retirement.

If a person establishes a Keogh, he must provide a plan for any full-time employee if there are any other employees in the self-employed person's company. A full-time employee is anyone who has been employed for a minimum of one year and works a minimum of 1,000 hours per year.

There are three additional types of Keogh Plans, with some additional restrictions:

Profit Sharing Keogh

Annual contributions for a Profit Sharing Keogh are limited to 15% of compensation, but can be changed to as low as 0% for any year.

Money Purchase Keogh

Annual contributions to a Money Purchase Keogh are limited to 25% of compensation but can be as low as 1%, but once the contribution percentage has been set, it cannot be changed for the life of the plan.

Paired Keogh

A Paired Keogh Plan combines profit sharing and money purchase plans. Annual contributions limited to 25% but can be as low as 3%. The part contributed to the money purchase part is fixed for the life of the plan, but the amount contributed to the profit sharing part (still subject to the 15% limit) can change every year.

IRA's

Individual Retirement Act plans are established under the Employee Retirement Income Security Act of 1974. The plan provides that employed persons may contribute to an IRA on a tax-deferred basis if they meet certain qualifications.

If the person is covered by an employer-sponsored retirement plan, they may make a contribution of up to $3,000 for themselves and another $3,000 for their spouse, as long as their combined income is less than $61,000 for *married filing jointly* and $31,000 for single filers. This maximum amount will increase in the next several years.

Year	Contribution Limit	"Catch-up" contributions for individuals 50 and over Extra Contribution
2003	$3,000	$500
2004	$3,000	$500
2005	$4,000	$500
2006	$4,000	$1,000
2007	$4,000	$1,000
2008	$5,000	$1,000

Figure 220 - Increasing Contributions for IRAs

Employed persons who are not covered by an employer pension plan may make the contributions regardless of their income.

Rollovers may be made from one plan to another, but this must be done no more than 60 days after the withdrawal. Everything must be taken out between the ages of 59 ½ to 70 ½.

Roth IRA

The Roth IRA was designed to allow taxpayers to contribute funds on an after tax basis to the IRA, and to allow the investment to increase on a tax-free basis if certain conditions are met.

- The investment must remain in the IRA for at least five years.
- The taxpayer must be at least 59½ when the withdrawals begin.

Coverdell Investment (Education IRA)

The Education IRA, renamed to the Coverdell Investment, allows individuals to invest up to $2,000 per child each year. It accumulates tax-free, but is not deductible. If the money is withdrawn for educational purposes, the increase is not taxed.

Pension Plan Functions

Pension plan processing also involves three other functions, which may be performed by a bank as a trustee, or by other third-party processors:

Trustee

As described in the chapter on Securities Industry Participants, most forms of pension plans are established as a trust. Each trust needs one or more trustees. The trustees are legally responsible for ensuring the trust is properly administered.

Administration

Each pension plan needs a plan administrator. The administrator is responsible for ensuring that all of the trust reporting is properly performed, and for performing any actuarial analyses that are required to ensure that each defined benefit pension plan is adequately funded.

Pension Disbursement

Once participants in a pension plan are eligible to receive payments from the fund, some agency must be responsible for maintaining records about what each person is eligible to receive, their addresses, and their preferred methods of payment. The same agent is usually also responsible for actually making the payments either by check, wire transfer or ACH credit.

Defined contribution programs usually only use a bank as a custodian, while a defined benefit program could use the bank for several functions, including:

Custody

As a custodian, the bank will maintain additional transaction details to support the accounting requirements of the funds, as described earlier in this chapter.

Trust Administration

As a trust administrator, the bank will be responsible for performing all of the trust-related functions that were described in the chapter on Securities Industry Participants.

Pension Disbursing

As a pension disbursing agent, the bank will ensure that the appropriate beneficiary receives the correct pension payments. Banks performing this service will have to maintain records on the individuals covered by the plan (status, address, amount of benefits, etc.), as well as ensure that there are sufficient funds each month to either mail each pensioner a check or send an electronic transfer.

E. BROKERAGE

Banks were previously allowed to establish a brokerage subsidiary under Section 20 of the Glass-Steagall Act. These businesses performed their processing exactly like a regular broker.

In 1999, the Financial Services Modernization Act repealed certain parts of the Glass-Steagall Act and the Bank Holding Company Act to allow banks to merge with brokers and/or offer brokerage products.

F. PROPRIETARY TRADING

Banks trade securities for their own account, either through their treasury function in the money market, or through bond and/or equity trading rooms, usually as a supplement to their underwriting activities. These trading functions operate in a manner very similar to brokers when the brokers are trading for their own account.

G. PRIVATE BANKING

The private banking business was initiated in Europe as a very personalized form of banking service reserved for the very wealthy. The clients of these services could expect the bank to do everything in its power to keep them happy, to protect their assets and to help them make more money. Over the years, the private banking business has expanded rapidly as many more banks got into this business and many more people had increasing sums of investable funds.

Today, there are many different levels of private banking services, some for individuals with as little as $100,000 in investable assets. Most, however, establish a minimum threshold of $1 million or $5 million. The clients, called high net worth individuals (HNWI), are provided with banking and securities services that frequently combine traditional banking and brokerage services, along with a significant level of hand holding. This is a very personalized service.

The less-personalized variant of private banking that is also increasingly common today is the Cash Management Account. The CMA, which combines retail services that are usually provided separately by banks and brokers, was introduced by Merrill Lynch in the late 1970's, and has been adopted by banks and brokers throughout the world, under a variety of names.

A private banking client will expect to be able to receive all of their financial services through their private banker. Some of these services are:

Bank Services	Brokerage Services
Checking Accounts	Purchase and Sale of Securities
Bank Savings Products (CDs, etc)	Safekeeping and Reporting of Securities
Wire Transfers	Investment Advice
Credit/Debit Cards	Mutual Funds

Figure 221 - Bank and Broker Services

A private bank's operations department has to be very sensitive to the demands of these clients. The securities-related processing services are similar to those that are provided to any bank client through the bank's brokerage subsidiary, and the banking services are similar to those provided to its retail clients. The difference is in the level of personalized services, consolidation of information and the need for an even higher level of confidentiality and processing accuracy.

H. PERSONAL TRUST

Personal trust was introduced in the chapter on Securities Industry Participants. The processing requirements for personal trust accounts are very similar to the requirements for private banking clients, which are discussed later in this chapter.

Personal trust systems must also support retail banking activities such as checking, savings, sweeps, CDs, etc. Additionally, there are very strict accounting and reporting requirements, which are similar to the accounting procedures required for pension funds and mutual funds.

Personal trusts are established for the benefit of a single individual or a small number of individuals. These beneficiaries may receive the principal from the trust, the income, or both, according to the terms of the trust.

Personal trust accounts involve a trust agreement that defines the:

- Terms of the trust
- Trustee (or fiduciary) who is legally responsible to enforce the terms of the trust
- Beneficiary (or beneficiaries) who receive money from the trust.

The trustees can be individuals or institutions such as a bank. Within a bank's personal trust activities, the bank may also offer an investment service where investment decisions are made on behalf of the client.

These discretionary accounts grant the portfolio manager the right to buy and sell securities at his own discretion, usually within some boundaries. The portfolio manager is typically not allowed to move cash out of the account. Many personal accounts are non-discretionary, and the manager (or broker) acts only as an advisor.

I. INVESTMENT BANKING

The term investment bank is one that can be used in a variety of ways. A firm can be registered as a brokerage firm or a bank and call itself an investment bank if it performs all of the functions that are normally performed, such as:

- Underwriting (creating new instruments)
- Research (evaluating investments and making recommendations)
- Portfolio management (having the right to invest on behalf of a client)
- Trading (trading for its own account or for a client)
- Sales (selling portions of its inventory to clients)
- Brokerage (acting as a client's agent in buying and selling securities)

Investment banks provide services in every segment of the securities industry. They create products and their different divisions can be either on the buy-side or the sell-side.

Investment banks have a variety of ways to make revenue. They can receive:

- Underwriting fees

- A management fee on portfolios
- Commissions on securities transactions that they broker
- A spread on securities that they hold in their own account

J. DEALER CLEARANCE

When banks act as agents for broker/dealers who are active in the government securities primary market they are performing dealer clearance. To do this, the banks receive and record securities' positions and process certain types of transactions for their clients since broker/dealers cannot be members of the Federal Reserve System, and the Fed is responsible for issuing and processing government securities through the Fed Book Entry system. Secondary market transactions are cleared through the Government Securities Division (GSD).

There are high profits and high risks in the dealer clearance business since the market can experience sudden, massive increases in volume and in large dollar amounts.

There are two banks that are actively involved in providing dealer clearance for broker/dealers who are trading in government securities and MBS: Bank of New York and JP Morgan Chase. The volume that these banks individually process is such that they can often net their clients transaction so that the trades do not have to be processed through the Fed. This reduces the broker/dealer's overall costs.

XI. Investment Manager Processing

Investment managers initiate the institutional investment process, and are a fundamental segment of the securities marketplace. It is important to understand how investment managers process trade transactions and maintain positions, and how they work together with the banks and brokers to ensure accurate processing.

A. INVESTMENT MANAGEMENT BUSINESS

Investment managers manage accounts for many different types of clients and there are many different products and services that investment managers provide for their clients. These clients and products are discussed later in this chapter.

There is a significant concentration of assets among a few large firms. As of June 30, 2004, approximately 12% of the 1,944 managers in the U.S. had over $10 billion in assets. In fact, the top 1% managed 39% of the assets.

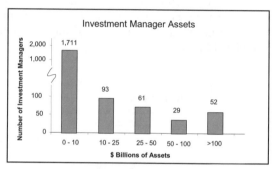

Figure 222 - Assets Managed by Investment Managers (Source: Nelson's Directory)

This concentration is important to understand since the large and small firms process differently.

- The large managers bring enough business to the brokers that they may influence which vendors' systems the brokers use. The means that the brokers may have to use multiple front-end systems in order to connect with their various clients - the investment managers.

- And, while the large number of smaller firms do not account for a significant amount of the volume, they have a disproportionate impact on the quality and timeliness of transaction processing since they usually have little automation and smaller staffs.

The investment management business is discussed in more detail in Chapter II – Securities Industry Participants.

B. INVESTMENT MANAGEMENT CLIENTS

In addition to the difference between large and small firms, investment managers may have some different processing characteristics based upon the type of clients they serve. Investment managers adjust their business model and their processing architecture to support the unique characteristics of their various types of clients. The primary categories of clients are:

- Mutual Funds

- Pension Funds
- HNWI/Families
- Individual
- Institutional
- Trusts
- Hedge Funds
- Insurance

These categories of clients are presented in more detail in the rest of this section.

Mutual Funds

When an investment manager is the manager for a mutual fund, the manager can be a separate business entity or a part of the same company as the mutual fund administrator. In either situation, the fund administrator is responsible for selecting a custodian and usually chooses a single custodian for all of the funds it administers. This makes the settlement process simpler than it is for managers supporting institutional funds.

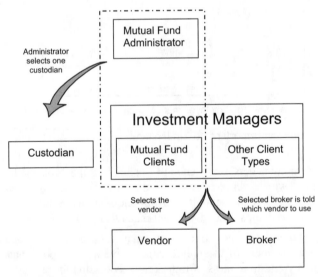

Figure 223 - Investment Manager Client Relationships

As described in the chapter on Fund Products, a mutual fund must accurately account for every trade on trade date in order for the fund accountants to calculate and publish the NAV by the end of T+1. All mutual fund trades and updates are sent continuously throughout each business day to the fund accountant to ensure accurate calculations. Investment management accounting systems should be synchronized with their custodians and fund administrators daily to ensure accuracy. Managers for mutual funds must affirm on trade date and have a very efficient method of electronic communication with their brokers and custodian.

If the fund administrator makes an error in the NAV calculation because of insufficient or incorrect data on a transaction, the fund may have to restate their shareholders' subscriptions and redemptions based on an updated NAV and that could be costly and frustrating for the shareholder. This is a rare occurrence, but can have a significant impact.

The processing sequence for mutual fund transactions is:

- IM trades on a Monday

- IM uses closing prices on Monday

- IM affirms by any time Tuesday (For Autosettle, it has to be affirmed by noon on T+2. If it is affirmed later than noon on T+2, it is a manual transaction for the custodian)

- IM adjusts Monday trades throughout the day on Tuesday, and notifies the custodian and fund accountant of all changes

- IM validates Monday's closing positions on Tuesday

- The fund accountant adds in Monday's expenses on Tuesday

- The fund accountant sends in the Monday NAV by 4:00 on Tuesday

As was described in Chapter VII - Post-Trade Processing, Clearing and Settlement, in today's three-day sequential settlement cycle, affirmations can be delayed until noon of T+2 and the trade will still settle on time; however, this is too late for efficient Mutual Fund Accounting.

Pension Funds

Investment managers typically manage portfolios for many different institutional pension funds and the plan sponsor of the pension fund usually chooses the custodian. Therefore, the manager typically deals with multiple custodians.

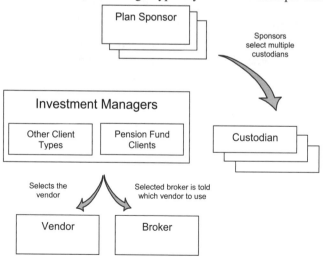

Figure 224 - Investment Manager Client Relationships

The complexity today for firms dealing with multiple custodians is that the largest managers often deal with as many as 100 custodians and each custodian is at a different point in automating their process and external interfaces. This means that even the most automated managers may have some custodians that they have to deal with occasionally by fax, or with some custodians a few instrument types may continue to require fax-based messages (e.g., Money Market trades or other Fixed Income trades, etc.)

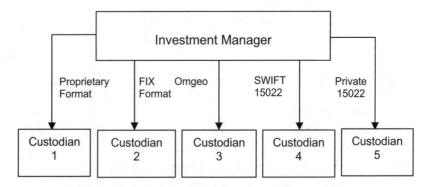

Figure 225 - Investment Managers Frequently Utilize Multiple Custodians

Custodians with well-automated systems are often in the same position when some of the large investment managers they deal with are highly automated and many of the smaller firms are less automated and require manual processing.

High Net Worth Individuals (HNWI) / Families

Investment managers often manage assets of HNWI or their Family Offices. This type of client is usually service intensive and usually requires more customized reporting. HNWI Families often establish a Family Office, staffed by professionals, who monitor the performance of one or more investment managers.

Individual Accounts

Increasingly, investment managers are reducing their minimum investment requirements in order to broaden their client base. This forces the firms to structure some form of repetitive process since every individual account cannot be completely customized. Very often this means that individual accounts have their assets invested in a legally commingled account.

The primary processing differences that are required for most other types of clients are usually based upon the following client investment requirements:

- Investment objectives
- Asset allocation
- Risk tolerances

Some of the special processing/reporting requirements that are identified in initial meetings with consultants/clients could include:

- No investing in 'sin stocks'
- Maintaining cash at a certain percentage for benefit payouts or living expenses
- Don't take losses great than $x or y%
- Reporting requirements such as communication after every transaction,

client meetings monthly, web access to reports online, etc.

Institutional Accounts

There are several different types of accounts that can be used by institutions, including:

- Corporate Plans (Includes corporation pension and profit-sharing plans and other tax-exempt corporate accounts)

- Private Management (Personal accounts for partners and key executives, including IRAs and IRA Rollovers, individual investor plans and partnership accounts, and personal trust accounts)

- Cash Management (Investments aimed at ensuring safety of principal and liquidity)

- Insurance and Captive Insurance Plans (An account of a company owned solely or in part by one or more non-insurance entities for the primary purpose of providing insurance coverage to the owner or owners)

- Municipal Plans (Accounts of government entities, including townships, villages, towns, cities, counties, and states)

- Charitable Plans (Endowment and private foundation accounts, accounts of accredited institutions for higher learning and religious organization accounts)

- Taft-Hartley Plans (Union accounts, including retirement plans and non-retirement plans)

- Health Care Organizations (Pension plans, profit sharing plans and funded depreciation plans for hospitals and health systems)

- Intermediary Alliances (Sub-advised investment products offered through a variety of partners, including retirement platforms, insurance, and financial services companies)

Trusts

Investments supporting trusts must be constantly monitored to ensure that the investments meet the objectives of the trust. For example, a trust may specify specific categories of investments or specific asset allocation/risk tolerances (sin-free stocks, 50/50 stocks/bonds with liquidity, etc.) or place some other limits/guidelines that portfolio managers must comply with, such as limits on what the assets of the trust can be used to cover (education, home, living expenses, etc.).

Hedge Funds

Although they are not regulated by the Investment Company Act of 1940, Hedge Fund portfolios require the same processing attention as other institutional portfolios. The SEC is currently evaluating whether or not Hedge Funds should be included under the Investment Company Act.

Insurance

Insurance Company portfolios require the same processing attention as other institutional portfolios.

C. INVESTMENT MANAGEMENT PRODUCTS/SERVICES

To meet the unique needs of each client, an investment manager may offer the following types of services/investment disciplines or specialty niche strategies:

- Capitalization Such as Large Capitalization, Multi and Micro Capitalization
- Geographies Such as Europe or Asian markets
- Sectors Such as Technology or Real Estate
- Instruments Such as Equities or Fixed Income
- Other focus such as passive investing or WRAP accounts [92]

D. INVESTMENT MANAGEMENT TRADING ANALYSES

The investment management process consists of four activities that lead up to the trade.

Sales

While every IM is different in nature and style, they generally identify and obtain clients in the following ways:

- Referrals from existing clients, brokers, and investment consultants
- Consultants who provide a broad range of integrated services to institutional investors
- Advertising

Clients are often supported by specialized teams of portfolio managers and client servicing managers who understand the requirements of each type of client (corporations, public funds, charitable, etc.) and are experts in their investment style or sector.

The sales team also is responsible for:

- Cross-selling
- Building strategic partnerships with insurance and financial service companies and retirement platforms
- Working with sub-advisory relationships with other investment managers
- Preparing responses to RFPs

Research

Research is conducted by the Investment Manager, by a third-party or a combination of the two. The researchers are usually focused on specific companies or groups of companies (sectors) and are responsible for making buy/sell decisions according to the investment guidelines of the IM and the client. These guidelines often include proprietary investment models that assist in the decision process.

Portfolio Management

Portfolio managers are responsible for making the buy/sell decisions for their

---

[92] A WRAP account combines custodial, accountant and legal fees into one contract, with a management fee tied to the market valuation of the portfolio at the end of each quarter.

portfolios while meeting the investment guidelines of their firm and the client. The investment decisions are often made as a result of *what-if* exercises (often called 'scenarios') that are developed through computer modeling. This allows the portfolio manager to determine the impact of events such as a change in interest rates or a restructuring of the portfolio without actually buying or selling securities.

Typically, each portfolio is "balanced" monthly or daily (based on the client's objectives) to the custodian's statement to ensure accurate performance and valuation.

The Portfolio Manager works with the client to ensure their investment policy reflects the client's investment needs and objectives. Key factors, such as time horizon, balance between growth and preservation of assets, general tolerance for risk (volatility), income needs and liquidity are continuously reviewed.

Based on the client's investment policy, an asset allocation is developed and a portfolio benchmark selected. Portfolio risk, relative to established benchmarks, is measured and monitored on a regular basis to ensure it remains consistent with the client's risk tolerance.

Client Servicing and Reporting

While the accounts/portfolios are managed by a portfolio management team, there are several other types of services that can be provided by other people, including:

- Working with other professionals associated with the client, such as actuaries, accountants, and lawyers
- Timely communications and market commentary via phone calls or email
- Education of the client (to manage expectations)

Client's receive statements/portfolio appraisals that are generally sent on a monthly basis (or quarterly), depending on the client's preference.

- The monthly report usually includes a description of all assets held, purchase price and current market values, cash projections, as well as current income.
- A quarterly communication package includes a letter from the portfolio manager with comments on the market and the individual portfolio gain/loss statements, purchases and sales transactions, and proxy voting.

E. INVESTMENT MANAGER PROCESSING

Investment manager processing involves trade processing, post-trade processing, asset servicing and a variety of support functions.

Trading Support

An investment manager's trade processing starts with the portfolio manager's decisions regarding what to buy or sell. This decision can result from:

- Some data that was developed by the portfolio management system performing 'what if' scenarios based upon research, rebalancing or modeling.
- The client's need for cash for a large redemption or available cash after

receiving routine pension payments to the portfolio

- Building the cash reserves or the client's reallocation/shift in investment strategy

The portfolio manager selects the alternative that they wish to implement and the trades are sent to the firm's Trade Order Management System.

The traders have several alternatives to execute a trade. They can either:

- Work the trade manually by calling brokers and 'shopping'
- Scan IOI applications (Indications of Interest) to see if someone has posted some indication that they are interested in trading a specific security
- Select a specific broker based upon the parameters of the trade
- Select an ATS or ECN based upon the parameters of the trade

Typically, smaller orders or orders that meet certain criteria are automatically routed to a pre-determined execution point such as specific brokers or ATSs. This decision usually is based on factors such as cost, speed of transmission, depth of markets, etc. Larger orders (blocks) are more often communicated manually to one or more brokers.

The traders use the firm's TOM System to keep track of the status of the trades on their blotter. When the trade is completed, the trader can use their application to send the trade details automatically to the firm's accounting system.

If a firm does not have this level of automation, many of the steps are manual. In that case, the trading assistants are generally responsible for entering the trades made by the traders into the firm's accounting systems, and may be involved in many different tasks and use many different applications. These people are often part of a manager's middle office.

Allocation [93]

When an investment manager buys a block of securities, those securities are usually allocated over several different portfolios, and each block requires a separate confirmation from the broker that identifies the exact account and settlement instructions that are to be followed. Some portfolio managers identify the allocation when they submit their trades to the trading desk/traders, and others wait until the broker has filled all or part of the order before they decide upon the exact allocation.

- If the order was completely filled, then the complete order is usually allocated according to the way the portfolio manager aggregated the order before it was submitted to the broker.
- If the broker was not able to obtain all of the shares the investment manager wanted, then the shares that were purchased need to be allocated in one of two ways: either each account gets a proportionately smaller amount, or the portfolio manager changes the allocation so that some accounts might not get anything and others would get the full amount.

---

[93] Allocation processing is described in detail in Chapter VII – Post-Trade Processing, Clearing and Settlement

This may be required because of the restrictions that have been placed on some of the accounts.

Investment managers have five primary ways of communicating allocation instructions to their brokers:

- Omgeo TradeSuite
- Omgeo OASYS, which is a service provided by DTC
- Electronic Trade Confirmation vendors, which are described in the chapter on Vendors
- Fax, or other manual instructions that are sent directly to the broker
- FIX protocol messages

Based upon the settlement instructions provided by the manager, the broker creates a separate confirmation for each settlement. Investment managers also have three ways of communicating settlement instructions to their brokers:

- Omgeo SID or ALERT
- Vendor provided functionality, such as Charles River or SunGard
- Fax, or other manual instructions that are sent directly to the broker

Affirmation [94]

Each trade that is made by a broker on behalf of an investment manager, and that is to settle at a custodian bank, must be affirmed by the investment manager before the custodian or broker will release either funds or securities to settle the trade. If an investment manager is using a Prime Broker, then the Prime Broker must be informed of the affirmation just as the custodian would be notified.

Securities that are DTC-eligible are usually settled through the DTC's systems, and involve a confirmation message that is initiated by the broker and that is subsequently affirmed by the manager. Without the affirmation, the trade will not settle.

Managers can notify their custodians in other ways for trades that are not settling at the DTC. This is usually accomplished by a Fax, SWIFT message or a direct file transfer using a DTC message format. The custodian can use this instruction as their authority for releasing securities or funds.

Settlement Department

The settlement function can be performed by a separate group of people or by the trading assistants depending upon the size of the investment management firm.

The investment manager must respond to the confirmation that is delivered by DTC by affirming each confirmation, unless they have outsourced this function to their custodian. If they have outsourced the function, the manager must still give a valid instruction to the custodian, which is usually either by Fax or SWIFT message.

The investment manager must also ensure that the posted transaction(s) match

---

[94] Affirmation processing is described in detail in Chapter VII – Post-Trade Processing, Clearing and Settlement

the transaction(s) most used by the custodian. Any differences must be reconciled and resolved.

One of the major areas for attention in settlement is the prevention of fails, or in receiving compensation for fails. There are different types of failed transactions, each with potential financial risk:

Custodian Errors

The bank custodian is often responsible for settlement errors and the client's account is adjusted accordingly on Trade Date. The most frequent settlement errors occur when the trade settles with the wrong price or commission. When this happens, an SPO (Standard Payment Option) charge occurs for the difference.

Broker Errors

Broker-oriented settlement errors are often the result of insufficient securities, incorrect static data, late information about the allocation and incorrect data about the transaction.

Investment Manager Error

Investment managers can contribute to settlement errors by sending incorrect or late allocation information, or incorrect settlement instructions.

Buy Fail

When a buy trade is executed (the purchase of securities against cash payments), the investment manager makes cash available for the settlement of the transaction by either selling another security for settlement on the same date or using cash reserves. The cash remains un-invested, sitting in a liquid position, until the securities are received. In the event of a fail (the securities are not received on the contracted settlement date), the investment manager has not earned additional income for a cash position that would have been otherwise invested.

Sell Fail

When a sell trade is executed (sale of securities against cash payment), the investment manager immediately invests the anticipated proceeds from the transaction. In the event of a fail (the securities are not delivered, and therefore payment is not received on the contracted settlement date) the investment manager has overdrawn its account by instructing the investment of unavailable funds. Further, with no entitlement to income from the sold securities, the investment manager does not have any earning potential on either the cash or the securities until the transaction is settled.

In addition to the interest cost, a fail of a domestic equity for more than three days could create the risk of a *buy-in*. The money difference between the original trade and the *buy-in* could be substantial, depending on market conditions. The party responsible for the fail would have to absorb this cost.

Fails of foreign trades have the additional exposure of an FX transaction where the FX rate can also change over the period of the delay.

For each failed transaction, the investment manager and custodian bank expend resources to research and determine the source of the error, and ultimately identify the party responsible for the fail. Lost income is claimed from the responsible party. If the investment manager failed to communicate a trade, it must absorb the cost of the lost interest. If the fail occurred over a weekend and/or a settlement holiday, the cost is multiplied to cover the appropriate period.

New Accounts

Investment Manager's generally establish separate account contracts for each client. The basic components of an investment advisory agreement (whether for an individual client, institutional or ERISA account) include:

- Discretionary or Non-Discretionary Authority
- Custodian (where will assets be held)
- Brokerage: Directed, Non-directed or Limited (i.e., does the client want his trades to be put through a specific firm, or traded on a best execution basis by grouping the trades with other accounts in the office to obtain the best price/lowest commission, etc.)
- Fees (fees are typically billed on the market value of the portfolio)

Reconciliation Department

Reconciliation of cash, transactions, and securities positions with each custodian is usually handled by the trading assistants, or the settlement or reconciliation departments. There are several available third-party applications that automate reconciliation through exception matching.

Departments using these applications have to decide among several comparison parameters, such as:

- Comparing positions or transactions
- Comparing on an accounting basis or units basis
- Frequency of reconciliations (Daily to identify trading errors, weekly or monthly to identify accounting differences, etc.)

Some of the reconciliations are:

- Ensuring that the bank's transaction and position records are the same as the records held by the various depositories
- Trade reconciliations including failing trades
- Income collection amounts received vs. amounts due
- Corporate actions, cash and securities received vs. amounts due, based on decisions made by the investment manager
- Cash balance reconciliation including the investigation of overdrafts and fees associated with those overdrafts
- Interest paid on cash sweeps

Pricing Department

A manager that has in-house record keeping and/or accounting must also have a pricing function similar to the one discussed in the chapters on Broker Processing and Bank Processing and Asset Servicing. An investment management firm typically chooses one or two services that complement their business practices and use these prices vs. custodian prices.

Managers will maintain this pricing information either in the portfolio management system, or they may have acquired one of the central securities master file databases that are commercially available for reference data.

The need for pricing varies with the type of activity that the investment manager is supporting:

Institutional Clients

Institutional clients need completely valued custody portfolios, normally based upon end-of-day prices.

Mutual Fund Clients

Firms that process mutual funds price daily using closing prices, or intra-day using point-in-time prices.

Trading

Traders need real-time prices.

Asset Servicing

Most Investment Managers, whether they use their own processing as their official records or use the custodian, process interest, dividend and corporate actions in order to have a record that they can use to compare with their custodian. Asset Servicing is discussed in detail in Chapter VIII – Post Settlement Processing.

Risk Management

Investment managers are concerned about a wide range of operational risks and are concerned about properly investing their clients' money.

Operational risks are discussed in Chapter VIII – Post Settlement Processing.

Accounting

Investment Managers perform a variety of accounting functions on behalf of their clients and themselves.

Accounting for Mutual Fund Clients

If an investment manager is responsible for performing the accounting function for a mutual fund, the processes uses trade date accounting and has to be accurate on a daily basis since open-end mutual funds calculate balances daily. This means that every transaction for every day must be properly recorded to avoid any errors.

When the fund activity is closed each day, the fund accountants look at several different sources of information to determine the Net Asset Value (NAV), including:

- Realized gains and losses
- Unrealized gains and losses
- Interest accrual
- Income collected
- Corporate actions
- Expenses (actual and accrued)

If a mutual fund makes an error in calculating the NAV, the investors in that fund who bought or sold shares were given an incorrect price, and adjustments must be made. If the error goes undetected for more than one day, the problem can compound and quickly affect a very large number of clients.

Accounting for Institutional Clients

Institutional clients need settlement date accounting, usually in an actual settlement date basis.

Accounting for Individuals and High Net Worth Individual Clients

Accounting for individuals and HNWI is similar to that for institutional clients, except that additional transactions information must be held at used to account for the transactions. For instance, non-US individuals (resident and on-residents) could have an accounting and the tax treatment is different than with US citizens.

Accounting for the Firm

An investment manager, like all other businesses, has a general ledger that records all of the financial transactions that affect the business. The general ledger records transactions as income, expenses, asset balances or liability balances.

Various processing areas are given control of specific sub-ledgers where transactions relating to the specific processing areas are recorded as they occur. The net of these transactions is reported to the general ledger.

Each department's sub-ledger, often called a proof, is used daily to record transactions and is reconciled daily to ensure accuracy. Some areas, such as trading may require a real-time profit and loss report.

Investment Manager Cash Management

Investment managers need to manage cash for themselves and for their clients when they manage client portfolios.

Cash Management for the Firm

Firms manage their own cash with the objective of maximizing their own investments.

Cash Management for Clients

Investment managers manage the excess cash in their clients' accounts in order to maximize the clients' return.

Compliance Department

Each investment manager has a department that is used to ensure that they are following all of the appropriate rules and regulations and which monitors investment levels.

Compliance for Client Requirements

If a firm is managing money for a client, the client may have established some guidelines regarding the firms they are willing to invest in and the firms or industries they wish to avoid. When managing money for a mutual fund, the manager must ensure that they are only buying securities that are in line with the investment objectives of the fund.

Compliance with Industry Rules

The overall purpose of compliance is to monitor the performance of the firm to ensure that it is performing in compliance with laws and with the rules established by the SROs.

Also, managers wish to avoid accumulating more than 5% of any one issuer, since that would require them to register the fact with the SEC and thereby become considered as an insider of that firm, which restricts their investment flexibility.

Compliance with Industry Regulation and Legislation

IMs must comply with the 40 Act and with new regulation as it is created, such as the USA PATRIOT Act, Sarbanes-Oxley, etc., as described in the chapter on Regulation and Legislation.

Investment Manager Reporting

Investment managers have several different categories of regulatory reporting requirements and are very focused on providing periodic statements and portfolio analyses to their investment clients.

Investment managers have a variety of reporting requirements.

Client Reporting

Investment managers have regulatory reporting requirements and are very focused on providing periodic statements and analyses to their investment clients. An increasing trend in this area is implementing applications that allow investment managers to easily customize statement packages for each client.

Regulatory Reporting

Investment managers have several different types of reports that are required by their SROs.

Internal Reporting

Investment managers are interested in:

- Operations reports (Holdings, discrepancies, etc.)
- Profit and losses on trades/positions
- Cash management and cash discrepancies
- Open trades and trade status

F. INVESTMENT MANAGER SYSTEMS

Investment managers need some of the same functions in their systems that are used by brokers and by their custodian banks. The following graphic shows the general architecture of a generic investment manager suite of applications. There are no definitive rules regarding which applications or functions belong in the front, middle or back office. Each firm decides based upon their own unique business, situation and processing requirements.

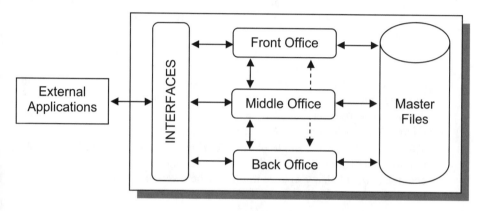

Figure 226 - Investment Manager Generic Architecture

The following sections present the master files, the interfaces and the front, middle and back office activities, and then examine each major processing function in detail.

Master Files

Applications need data to process transactions. This data is generally organized in the following major databases:

Securities Master File

The Securities Master File (SMF) contains the details that describe each security that is held or was recently held by the firm and/or its clients. This file contains descriptive information such as the name of the issue and the CUSIP number. It also identifies how the issue will behave under certain conditions, such as maturity, dividend declaration, interest payments, etc.

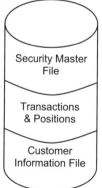

Figure 227 - Master Files

Since many firms have acquired additional applications over time, or have merged with other firms, it is not uncommon for a firm to have more than one file with information about securities. The trend in the industry is to resolve this inefficiency by developing or acquiring an application that can function as a single SMF server, and which can be used by many different applications throughout the firm. Central Security Master Files are discussed more in the chapter on Vendors.

Transaction and Position Files

Investment managers generally keep separate files for transaction history and for positions. These files are then used for reconciliation and reporting.

Client Information File

The Client Information File (CIF), also called the name and address file, contains static information about clients, such as name, address, identifying numbers and investment preferences that were gathered during the account opening process.

Firms generally do not have more than one client information file unless they have acquired other firms and have not assimilated the acquired firm's systems or if the firm has established multiple, independent lines of business with separate processing applications. However, many of these CIFs were developed many years ago and are not easily adapted to their current client relationship management needs.

The trend is towards a single physical CIF in order to understand the clients' requirements better and to facilitate cross selling; however, many firms have decided to establish a virtual central CIF where various CIFs interact with each other when necessary.

Investment Manager Interfaces

Investment managers have a number of interfaces to the rest of the securities industry as shown in the following chart.

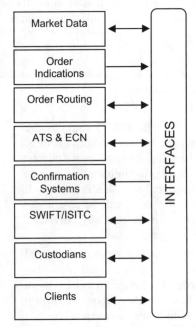

Figure 228 - Investment Manager Interfaces

Because of the complexity of the U.S. trading and settlement process, there are many individual vendors, where in order to satisfy specific niche opportunities, each vendor has focused on providing a subset of the banks/brokers/managers with a subset of required settlement functionality for a subset of instruments. Once a vendor meets some niche requirements, the next step is usually to expand the functionality in some way. This creates a larger number of overlapping products. The different categories of vendor systems that are involved in the securities process are discussed in the chapter on Vendors.

The various applications used by investment managers could be separated into the following categories, although different firms may organize these applications differently:

Front Office	Middle Office	Back Office
Indications of Interest	Compliance	Settlement Monitoring
Trade Order Management	Credit Limits	Asset Servicing
	Risk Reporting	
	Regulatory Reporting	
	Client Service	
	Client Reporting	
	P&L Generation	
	P&L Reporting	
	Account Opening	
	Account Maintenance	
	Allocations	
	Affirmations	
	Trade Reconciliation	
	Price Verification	

Figure 229 - One View of an investment Manager's Distribution of Functions

However, investment managers tend to use systems in their front office that are similar to their brokers' systems and they use applications in the back office that are similar to those used by the custodian banks. If a manager has a middle office, it generally overlaps the systems used by the front and back offices.

Front Office

In the front office, investment managers are concerned primarily with managing portfolios and trading, and in the back office they keep an accounting record of what the custodians have on their files.

For investment managers, the process begins when a portfolio manager makes a series of decisions and passes the information to the firm's traders.

The decisions could include:

- Purchases and sales of specific securities
- Cash sources for settlement or uses for the proceeds
- Timing of the purchase or sale
- Settlement requirements

The firm's traders either contact brokers to initiate a trade, or they use electronic trading networks to find a counterparty. Virtually all equity trades are handled electronically and increasingly fixed income trades are being processed through automated platforms.

The functional requirements for portfolio management and trade order management systems are tightly connected. Some applications are designed to do both, while others have greater depth of functions for either a PMS or TOMS and are designed to be easily integrated into other applications.

Market information and research applications are often used by portfolio managers and researchers, but require less integration to other processing applications.

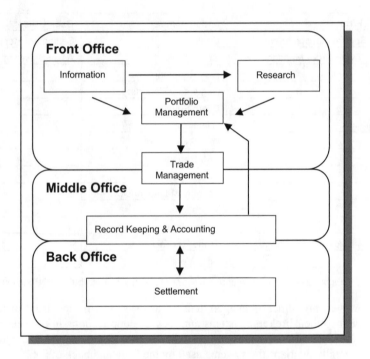

Figure 230 - Investment Manager Systems

Portfolio Management Systems (PMS)

Portfolio management systems are used to track trading, holdings, income and corporate actions, as well as fully value the portfolio. Some successful portfolio management systems that also act as the firm's settlement system have an interface to DTC for confirms, an interface to systems such as OASYS for allocations, and may have a SWIFT interface in order to send and receive electronic messages from their custodians.

A fully functioning PMS provides tools for the portfolio manager to evaluate their current positions, analyze alternatives and implement their decisions. These applications record the positions in each account and help the portfolio manager conduct *what-if* exercises (often called 'scenarios') through modeling. This allows the portfolio manager to determine the impact of events such as a change in interest rates or a restructuring of the portfolio without actually buying or selling securities.

The application can be used to evaluate the performance, or rate of return, on specific industry segments in order to help managers decide if they want to shift investments.

These applications are often designed to monitor the real-time valuation of the portfolio by applying current price information. All of them provide an end-of-day pricing process.

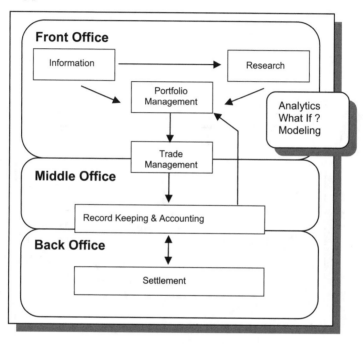

Figure 231 - Portfolio Management Systems

Investment managers often use their portfolio management systems to monitor their compliance with industry regulations, and some purchase separate systems for this purpose.

The primary architectural difference in the use of compliance applications is whether a trade passes compliance before or after the trade is sent to the broker. Clearly it is more important to ensure compliance before the trade, although with some of the older TOMS that is not possible.

Trade Order Management Systems (TOM)

An investment manager's Trade Order Management Systems are similar to the brokers' Order Management Systems. TOMS are provided by vendors that focus their resources on an investment manager's front office functions such as:

- Order Entry
- Order Tracking
- Order Routing
- Execution Tracking
- Allocation Initiation
- Broker Instructions

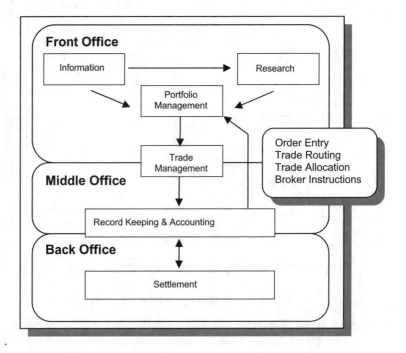

Figure 232 - Trade Management Order Systems

Most of the available Trade Management Order Systems, which are discussed in more detail in the chapter on Vendors, have been developed to support a specific instrument category, such as equity or fixed income. This means that an investment manager might have more than one TOMS.

The successful vendors present data elegantly and have robust interfaces to other applications such as:

- Portfolio Management
- Processing Systems, including
  - Settlement and Record Keeping

- Security Master Files
- Pricing, Accounting and Reporting

Middle Office

The primary objective of an investment manager's middle office is to ensure that the trades are completed and posted properly and the firm's accounting records are correct and timely.

Record Keeping and Accounting Systems

Investment managers may outsource their accounting responsibilities to their custodians or to another third-party, or they may establish their own accounting system and department to calculate their results.

As shown in the following chart, these systems have a number of functions, including:

- Transaction Posting
- Position Maintenance
- Cash Management
- Accounting
- Tax Accounting
- Asset Servicing
- Reporting

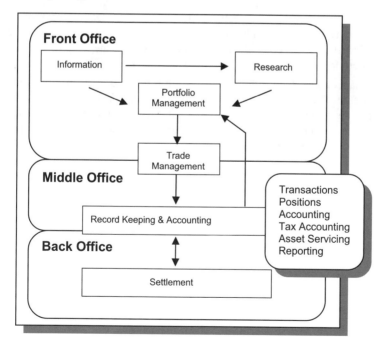

Figure 233 - Record Keeping and Accounting Systems

Firms that rely on their custodians to perform the required accounting functions also inevitably rely on their custodians to find their own processing errors. While this may be a cost efficient way to manage a process it does not increase accuracy.

Investment Management systems contain detailed accounting rules that must properly calculate and record each transaction based upon the type of security, client, etc. The accounting system receives input from almost every other processing system. Accounting systems are responsible for all of the bookkeeping and accounting report production for the firm.

Investment Management Accounting applications often include some settlement features that will help the firm reconcile their positions with their custodian(s).

Back Office

The primary objectives of an investment manager's back office is to ensure that trades are properly settled with the custodian and are maintained properly.

Settlement Systems

In some cases investment managers may delegate their settlement responsibilities entirely to their custodian, so that their custodian affirms transactions for them. If an IM delegates the responsibility, the IM must still give sufficient information to the custodian, and the IM remains responsible.

Most investment managers prefer to give allocation instructions to their custodians and track the progress of their settlements, therefore the manager must have some way of receiving electronic confirmations from the DTC and an ability to respond with an electronic affirmation. This functionality can be included in their portfolio management systems, they might use a separate system for this function or they could use the DTC's PTS terminal.

Managers also need to be able to assign a trade to a specific portfolio and to allocate block trades across their portfolios, and need an automated way to provide settlement instructions to their brokers and custodians banks. This service can be provided through Omgeo and some other vendor systems for equities, and through TradeWeb, MarketAxess and some other vendors for fixed income instruments.

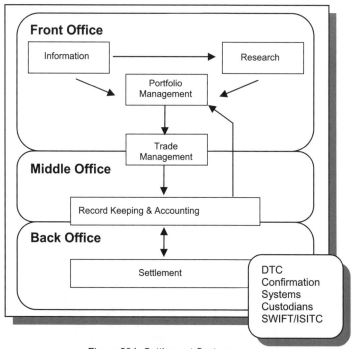

Figure 234 - Settlement Systems

Investment Manager Applications Summary

While vendors can provide very efficient solutions for their specific area of interest, they are not able to provide a comprehensive solution, and the investment managers are increasingly demanding that the applications provide interfaces with each other using industry standards such as SWIFT and FIX, which are described in the chapter on Industry Owned Organizations.

The investment management firm frequently finds itself at the center of many of these vendor interfaces. An active investment manager must get information from marketing vendors, order indication systems, order routing systems, ATSs, ECNs, confirmation systems, and probably has a direct interface with SWIFT and to one or more custody systems.

Investment managers either buy or build trading systems to manage their workflow and portfolio management systems that are used for their primary reporting and analysis. Every large manager has many distinct and different needs that are often filled by different systems. This has created a demand for middleware applications to help move all of this data between the internal applications and external firms more efficiently. Middleware is described in the chapter on Vendors.

XII. Mutual Fund Processing

Mutual funds are both a product and a type of business that processes securities. The different forms that a mutual fund business can assume were discussed in the chapter on Securities Industry Participants, and the way in which mutual funds process securities is discussed in this chapter. Mutual funds as a product are covered in the chapter on Fund Products.

Historically, clients could either buy mutual funds directly from the fund or through a broker. When a client bought directly through a fund, the fund's staff either received the client's call and entered the order into their system, or they received a written subscription from the client and manually entered the order into their back office system.

This process of ordering directly from the fund was and still is relatively simple; however, if a broker's client ordered a mutual fund through a broker, there were many more middlemen involved, and errors were plentiful. Today, when clients buy through a broker, the broker uses NSCC's Fund/SERV system to electronically send transactions to the NSCC, and the number of errors has been significantly reduced.

While clients are buying and selling shares of the mutual fund, the fund is also actively engaged in buying and selling securities for their portfolios from counterparties and settling through the DTC's automated system.

There are four major mutual fund processing functions in a managed investment company, which are shown in the following sections.

A. MUTUAL FUND FUNCTIONS

The four major functions of a mutual fund are:

Portfolio Management and Accounting

Portfolio managers must know their exact positions each day, including accruals, and are responsible for making the purchase and sale decisions that will form the basis of the fund. The portfolio manager must balance the need to have some cash available for redemptions with their normal desire to be fully invested.

The following graphic shows that the portfolio managers notify the traders of the purchases and sales they want to have made, and the traders will generally contact a broker to find a counterparty for the trade. However, an investment manager's trader could use an Alternative Trading System to find a counterparty instead of going through a broker.

The fund's traders are responsible for determining when and how the portfolio manager's decision will be implemented. The trades that are requested could be single trades, or block trades.

The mutual fund portfolio manager and the trader use processes that are the same as those that were discussed for investment managers.

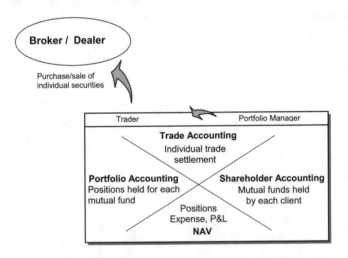

Figure 235 - Portfolio Management and Accounting

Trade Accounting

The next chart shows that when it is time to settle a trade the fund works within the U.S.'s regular settlement process, and has systems that are used to account for the securities held in the portfolio.

The processing that is required for settlement is the same as that shown in the chapters on Broker Processing, Bank Processing and Investment Manager Processing, with the mutual fund taking on the role of the investment manager, or using an external investment manager.

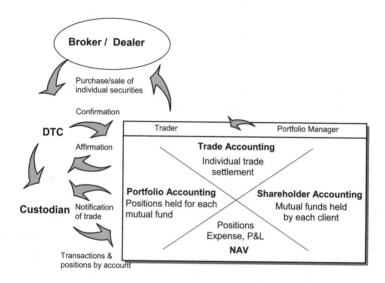

Figure 236 - Trade Accounting

Shareholder Accounting

The fund must know exactly how many shares of the fund each investor owns each day. The following graphic shows that this includes keeping track of the clients' subscriptions and redemptions (i.e., purchases and sales), as well as charges to the client, dividends, etc.

This service is either performed by the fund itself or it is outsourced to a third-party processor for the fund. If the purchase was through a broker, the broker will keep track of the ownership.

Most of the techniques used in shareholder accounting are beyond the scope of this book. However, when the actual purchase or sale of the mutual fund is conducted through a broker, the transaction can be for either a:

- Closed end fund – in which case the settlement process is the same as for any equity.

- Open end fund – in which the broker uses the NSCC's Fund/SERV system to process the transaction with the mutual fund or their transfer agent.

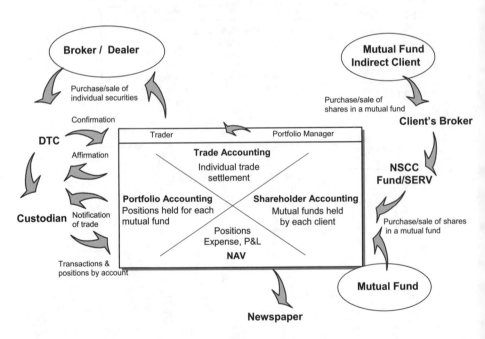

Figure 237 - Shareholder Accounting

NAV Calculations

The full mutual fund process culminates in the calculation of the NAV, which reflects the value of the fund divided by the number of shares in the fund.

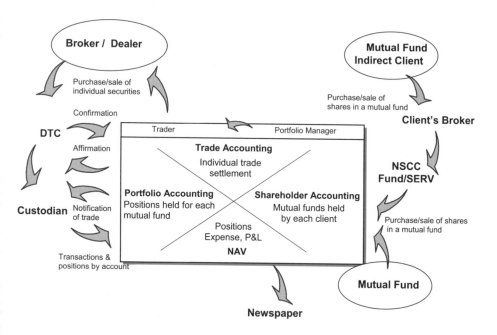

Figure 238 - NAV Calculations

Each day, the fund's accountants must price every position in the fund and determine the Net Asset Value of the fund, which is posted daily in newspapers. Clients' subscriptions and redemptions are based upon this amount.

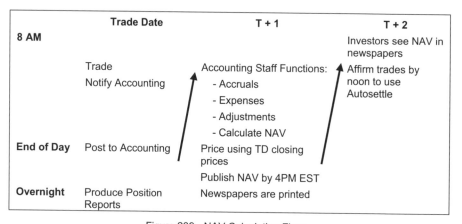

Figure 239 - NAV Calculation Flow

The closing positions on trade date are used by the fund along with TD closing prices to calculate the NAV that is posted in the newspapers, which are normally printed overnight and delivered the next day (T+2).

XIII. Equity-Related Instruments

The chapter discusses equity and equity-related instruments, including equity-based derivatives.

A. COMMON STOCK

The most frequently used type of equity is common stock.

Marketplace

Purpose

Common stock is a security that defines ownership in a corporation, which is normally represented by a certificate. With common stock, the stockholder has:

- A contract with the issuing corporation that defines the stockholders' rights
- A partial ownership position in the firm
- The right to participate in any profits earned by the firm
- A claim upon any assets that remain after all debts have been paid in the event of liquidity or bankruptcy

Stockholders do not run the company. The stockholders elect a board of directors to select the managers and to set policy. Stockholders can vote in person at a meeting or vote by proxy.

Regulators

The Securities and Exchange Commission regulates common stock in the U.S.

Issuers

The issuers of U.S. common stock are U.S. and non-U.S. based corporations.

Investors

Investors in common stock could be individuals and institutions from anywhere in the world. Investors purchase common stock with the goal of earning income through dividends and/or obtaining gains as the price of the equity increases.

Stock Certificate

Since most investors do not take possession of their stock certificates, the certificates are not often seen. The following example of a certificate was issued for a small, privately held firm.

There are several data elements that are commonly found on certificates, which are presented in this example:

Certificate Front

1. Name of the Issuing Firm

Each corporation is a unique entity with a unique name in its state of issuance.

2. Certificate Number

The certificate number is the numerical identification of the certificate. Each certificate number is unique.

3. Date of Issuance

The date of issuance is the date the certificate was issued by the registered holder to the transfer agent.

4. Class of Stock

The class of stock is the designation of the type of stock represented by the certificate. A corporation can issue any number of different classes of common stock, each of which has some unique shareholder rights, such as voting, dividend participation, claims in bankruptcy, etc.

5. Registration

The registration is the name and address of the registered holder as they appear on records of the transfer agent.

Figure 240 - Example of a Common Stock Certificate

6. CUSIP Number

The CUSIP number is a unique number that is assigned to each publicly-traded security that is issued in the U.S.

7. Script Story

The script story is an explanation of when and under what conditions the shares represented by the certificate are valid. The script story explains the terms of the issue.

8. Transfer Agent Signature

The transfer agent signature is the authorized signature of the transfer agent that validated the certificate.

9. Statement of Par Value

The statement of par value is the face value assigned to a share of stock in the charter of the corporation. This is not the same as the stock's book value or market value.

10. Numbers of Shares

The numbers of shares is the numerical notation of shares represented by the certificate.

Certificate Back

The back of the certificate is used when the holder wishes to sell the position and to transfer the certificate. The information that is required for a transfer is identified on this side of the certificate.

Figure 241 - Back of a Stock Certificate

1. Registration Abbreviations

The registration abbreviations provide an explanation of acceptable abbreviations to be used in the registration of stock certificates.

2. Stockholder Identification Number

The stockholder identification number is the social security number or other tax identification number of the person to whom the stock is being sold or transferred. Even though the shares may be registered in more than one name, only one identification number should be provided.

3. Assignment

The assignment is the information that must be furnished when selling or transferring stock certificates. The name and address of the person or firm receiving the stock is designated, along with the number of shares being sold or transferred.

4. Date

The date is the date that the assignment, or transfer, is executed.

5. Endorsement

The endorsement is the signature(s) of the shareholder(s), which must be written exactly as the name(s) appears on the face of the certificate. For the signature(s) to be valid, it (they) must be accompanied by a signature guarantee stamp from a commercial bank or brokerage firm. This is similar to, but not the same as being notarized.

Classifications

Exchange Listed Equities

Common stock can be listed and traded on a recognized U.S. exchange if it meets the requirements of the exchange.

Exchange listed securities can be sold directly from a broker's inventory to a client and can sometimes be traded directly between dealers, but the exchanges require that these transactions be reported to the exchanges in order to track every traded price for each listed security.

OTC Traded Equities

Common stock that is not listed on an exchange can be traded over-the-counter between dealers, includes NASDAQ.

Illiquid Equities

Common stock that is closely held or seldom traded is considered illiquid. Most of these securities are traded OTC, if they are traded at all.

Characteristics

Trading

Individuals and institutions generally contact brokers to buy or sell stock. The brokers either fill the orders from their own inventory or find another broker as a counterparty.

Institutions can also find counterparties by using Electronic Communications Networks, and closely held issues could be traded directly between the buyer and the seller.

There is an increasing trend to allow individuals to access some Automated Trading Systems (ATS) or Electronic Communications Networks (ECN).

Equities can only be traded on an exchange or NASDAQ when they are open. OTC securities that are not listed on NASDAQ can be traded at any time, and even exchange listed securities can be traded off of the exchange directly between brokers or on an ECN.

Transaction Costs

Transaction costs are either shown as a commission, which is separate from the traded price, or as a mark-up (for a purchase) or a mark-down (for a sale) which is combined with the reported traded price.

When stocks are traded on an exchange, an SEC fee (1/234 of 1% with a minimum of $4.50 per trade) is charged by the exchange in addition to the commission. This amount, which is adjusted semi-annually, is sometimes included in the broker's commission and is occasionally listed separately.

In November, 1999 the AMEX joined the NYSE in eliminating all of the exchange's fees on orders under 2,100 shares.

Liquidity

Exchange listed equities are normally very liquid, while OTC securities can vary from being very liquid if on NASDAQ to very illiquid.

Maturity

Common stock represents ownership in a corporation, and therefore is perpetual, so long as the corporation exists.

Par Value

The issuer selects the par value of common stock. Since it is used by the state of issuance to determine the cost of incorporation, most firms decide to select a value of zero, which is called *no par*.

Dividends

Dividends allow the shareholder to share in the profits of the company. The common stockholder can be paid a variable dividend that must be paid out of the corporation's after tax profits, and which must be voted upon and declared by the board of directors, usually at quarterly meetings. There is no requirement for common shares to pay a dividend.

When determining whether or not to pay a dividend, the board of directors must ensure that the firm has sufficient cash flow to continue operations, unless the dividend is part of a final liquidation of the firm.

Boards of directors for companies that do not have opportunities to reinvest the dividends in the growth of their company generally pay dividends to their stockholders.

Stockholder Rights

Voting

Normally, a holder of one common stock share has the right to one vote; however, different classes of shares can have different voting rights. For instance, one class (e.g., Class A) could have one vote per share while another class (e.g., Class B) might have ten votes per share.

Additionally, if a firm has three questions that must be resolved by a vote of the shareholders, each shareholder can typically vote their total number of votes for each question. This is called statutory voting.

Another form of voting is called cumulative voting. Cumulative voting was designed to give the minority shareholder a chance to change the company. In cumulative voting, each stockholder has one vote for every question that is being voted upon. The stockholder can cast all of their votes on any one issue, or distribute their votes across several questions that are up for a vote. For example, if the investor has 100 shares and there are three questions, the stockholder has 300 votes and may cast those votes however desired. Cumulative voting must be permitted specifically by the corporate charter.

Right to Transfer Shares

With a few exceptions, shareholders have the right to transfer their shares to someone else without the permission of the corporation. These exceptions generally apply to new issues, or to individuals who are considered insiders. These restrictions are discussed in the chapter on Creating New Securities.

Access to Corporate Books and Records

While the shareholders technically have the right to inspect the firm's books, the issuer usually only provides a copy of the annual report, or the same information that has already been provided to the SEC in the 10K or 10Q.

Processing

Purchases and sales of common shares on an exchange or over-the-counter are cleared between brokers on the street-side of the trade through the NSCC and settled between brokers and their client either directly through the broker or with their bank through the DTC.

Illiquid shares that are not depository eligible can be exchanged physically and re-registered through a transfer agent.

Risks

Credit

The primary credit-related risk that an investor in common stock assumes is that the issuing firm will go out of business. If the firm fails, stockholders are last in line to receive any proceeds from bankruptcy and may receive nothing.

Dividend Risk

Since the board of directors must authorize the payment of each dividend, the stockholder has a risk that the dividend will not be granted.

Market Risk

Purchasers of common stock also assume the risk that the price of the security will go down, along with other securities as the market changes. The price of an equity is based upon several factors, including:

- Performance of the company
- Price earnings ratio assigned by the market to the industry sector and to the specific firm
- Overall performance of the stock market

Taxation

Dividends

Dividends paid on common stock are taxable at the regular income tax rates of the stockholder.

Gains and Losses

Gains on securities held over a certain period of time, currently twelve months, are taxed at separate capital gains tax rates. Gains on securities held less than this period of time are taxed at regular income tax rates for the stockholder.

Losses can be offset against gains, either as regular income or capital gains, based upon the length of time they are held. Some carry-over of losses is permitted if losses exceed gains in a specific year.

Information

Common shares that are traded on a stock exchange or NASDAQ are listed in a variety of local and national newspapers. While there are differences from newspaper to newspaper, they usually look very similar to the format that is shown.

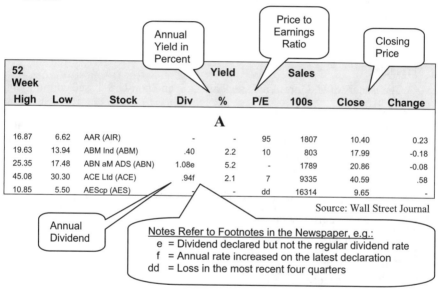

Figure 242 - Example of Equities Listed in the Newspaper

The data included in the example includes the:

- Last 52 week high and low
- Stock abbreviation
- Annual dividend per share
- Yield, which is the dividend divided by the closing price for the day
- Price-to-Earnings ratio, which is the price divided by the earnings (the actual earnings usually are not reported in the paper)
- Sales of the security in round lots of 100 shares
- Closing price for the day
- Change from the previous closing price

B. PREFERRED STOCK

Preferred stock is another form of equity representing an ownership interest in the business, but which has a *preference* over common stock. The preferences generally include guaranteed dividends and/or the distribution of assets up to a certain fixed amount in the event of bankruptcy. Preferred stockholders usually do not have voting rights, unless this right has been specifically granted by the indenture.

Marketplace

Purpose

Preferred stocks are designed to give investors a guaranteed dividend as long as the firm has enough cash to pay it, along with some opportunity to participate in the growth of the firm.

Regulators

The Securities and Exchange Commission regulates the market for preferred stock.

Issuers

The issuers of U.S. preferred stock are U.S. and non-U.S. based corporations.

Investors

Investors in U.S.-issued preferred stock could be individuals or institutions from anywhere in the world. These investors are usually looking for the guaranteed dividend, rather than significant capital gains.

Classification

The classifications of preferred shares are the same as for common shares:

- Exchange listed equities
- OTC traded equities
- Illiquid equities

Stock Certificates

Preferred shares have certificates like common shares.

Types of Preferred Shares

There are four major types of preferred shares that are issued in the U.S.

Cumulative Preferred

With a cumulative preferred issue, if a dividend cannot be paid in one period, it will accumulate, and the obligation will not be eliminated. Before the firm can pay any regular dividend, it will have to pay all of the outstanding preferred dividends.

Participating Preferred

If the company does better than expected, the holders of participating preferred shares could get an extra dividend, at the discretion of the board of directors.

Convertible Preferred

With a convertible preferred stock, the shares are convertible into a specific number of common shares.

For example, if ABC company issues a $100 Par 10% convertible preferred, which allows the holder to exchange the preferred shares for common shares at $50.00 per share, the preferred shareholder can exchange one preferred share for two common shares.

Par Value	$100	= 2 (conversion rate)
Conversion Price	$50	

If at the time it was issued, the common was selling at $40, and if the common rose to $50, it would now be trading at parity. Parity is the price at which neither a profit nor loss exists as a result of a conversion.

If the common shares trade at $55, the preferred shares should sell at $110 (Preferred x 2 = $110).

Callable Preferred

With a callable preferred issue, the issuer can *call* (or force the redemption of) the preferred shares at par or at a predefined premium over par. This is usually only allowed at certain points in time as specified in the indenture.

Characteristics

Trading

Just as with common shares, individuals and institutions contact brokers to buy or sell preferred stock. The brokers either fill the orders from their own inventory or find another broker as a counterparty.

Transaction Costs

Transaction costs are either shown as a commission, which is separate from the traded price, or as a mark-up / mark-down which is combined with the traded price.

When stocks are traded on an exchange, fees can be charged by the exchange in addition to the commission.

Liquidity

Overall, there is less of a market for preferred shares than for common shares. The exchange listed preferred equities are normally very liquid, while OTC securities can vary from being very liquid if on NASDAQ to very illiquid.

Maturity

Preferred shares can have points in time when their characteristics can change, but they continue to be an investment in the company, and are perpetual as long as the company exists.

Preferred shares could have a call feature that the firm could use to convert them to common shares. This feature could force the redemption of a portion of the issue or the retirement of the entire issue.

Par Value

Preferred shares are assigned a par value by the issuer at the time they are issued. This par value is significant for preferred shares since it is used to determine the amount of the dividend.

Dividends

Preferred shares usually pay a fixed dividend as a percentage of the issue's par value that was established at the time of the original issuance of the preferred stock. For example, different par values and different dividend rates will determine the amount of the preferred dividend.

Par	Dividend Rate		Dividend Amount
$100.00	10%	=	$10.00
$ 10.00	7%	=	$ .70

Preferred dividends are usually predetermined, and do not require the board of directors to grant the dividend each time it is due. The directors can, however, decide not to make a payment or to delay a dividend payment for preferred stock.

Rights in Liquidation

Preferred stockholders come before common stockholders but after bondholders in any liquidation.

Preferred Stock Example

This example shows several of the preferred shares that have been issued by Citigroup. The table is read similar to the common stock table that was presented earlier in this chapter.

Stock	Dividend	Yield %	Close	Change
Citigp PfF	3.18	6.1	55.02	0.30
Citigp PfG	3.11	6.0	55.48	- 0.19
Citigp PfG	1.53	6.2	24.55	-
Citigp PfS	1.50	6.2	24.55	0.16
Citigp PfV	1.78	6.8	26.18	0.13

Source: Wall Street Journal

Identifies the series of the preferred stock

The yield reflects the price and the terms of the various Issues

Figure 243 - Example of Preferred Shares Listed in the Newspaper

Firms can establish multiple issues of preferred shares, each with its own characteristics. The following table shows some of the different preferred shares issued by Citigroup at different times.

Symbol	Exchange	Issue Date	Amount Outstanding	Dividend	Par	Call Date	Call Price
NA	OTC	8/9/89	$63	7.55% 3 Yr. Treas. + 1.75% Floor of 7% Resets every 3 years Next reset 8/15/98	$100	On Any Reset Date > 8/15/04	$100 $100
NA	OTC	8/9/89	$63	8.25% 5 Yr. Treas. + 1.50% Floor of 7% Resets every 5 years Next reset 8/15/99	$100	On Any Reset Date > 8/15/04	$100 $100
CCI E	NYSE	5/24/93	$325	8.00%	$ 25	< 6/1/98 > 6/1/98	Non Call $25
CCI F	NYSE	8/30/93	$350	7.50%	$ 25	< 9/1/98 > 9/1/98	Non Call $25
CCI G	NYSE	5/9/94	$175	4.998% Index C * 84% Collar of 4.5 - 10.5% Resets quarterly Next Reset 8/31/98	$ 25	< 5/31/99 > 5/31/99	Non Call $25
CCI H	NYSE	7/22/94	$100	4.998% Index C * 84% Collar of 4.5 - 10.5% Resets quarterly Next Reset 8/31/98	$ 25	< 8/31/99 > 8/31/99	Non Call $25
CCI I	NYSE	9/26/94	$125	8.30%	$ 25	<11/15/99 >11/15/99	Non Call $25
CCI J	NYSE	2/6/95	$150	8.50%	$ 25	< 2/15/00 > 2/15/00	Non Call $25
NA	OTC	12/15/95	$125	5.86% Resets quarterly Index B + 0.5% Next Reset 2/15/06	$ 25	< 2/15/06 > 2/15/06	Non Call $25

Callout annotations: "In $U.S. Millions", "Minimum interest to be paid", "Index C is the Consumer Price Index", "Minimum rate of 4.5% and Maximum rate of 10.5%"

Figure 244 - Citibank's Various Preferred Shares at a Point in Time

Resumption of Preferred Dividends

PS INDIANA CO. CLEARS PAY OUT ON ITS PREFERRED

Public Service Co. of Indiana said its board voted to resume preferred stock dividend payments and to buy back as many as one million of the preferred shares.

Despite a massive write-off for a cancelled nuclear plant, the utility is able to pay the dividends through a rare, complicated series of accounting twists that erased an accumulated earnings deficit. That deficit prevented the dividend payments.

... Under the company's bylaws, preferred holders could have elected a majority of PS Indiana's board at its April annual meeting after four consecutive dividends had been omitted.

The Plainfield, Indiana-based utility will pay... for the first quarter ... and ... to cover the four quarterly dividends omitted last year.

... S&P said it believes the preferred dividends "will be paid on a timely basis in view of the strong internal funds generation and the retention of all common earnings until at least 1989."

Source: Wall Street Journal

Figure 245 - Article on Preferred Shares

This excerpt shows that boards can vote to stop or to reinstate a preferred dividend. In this case there was a provision for the preferred shareholders that stated if the company missed four consecutive preferred dividends; the preferred shareholders could have elected a majority of the board of directors.

Processing

Purchases and sales of preferred shares are cleared between brokers on the street-side of the trade and settled between brokers and their client either directly through the broker or with their bank through the DTC.

Risks

Credit

The primary credit-related risk that an investor in preferred stock assumes is that the issuing firm will go out of business.

Interest Rate

Preferred shareholders also assume some interest rate risk, since the value of the stock is very closely tied to interest rates and the overall credit rating of the firm. If rates go up, the price of the stock will go down, and vice versa.

Market Risk

Purchasers of preferred stock also assume some risk that the market price of the security will go down. Market risk is less important to the movement of the preferred stock price than interest rates.

Taxation

Dividends

Dividends paid on preferred stock are taxable at the regular income tax rates of the stockholder.

Gains and Losses

Gains on preferred stock held over a certain period of time, currently twelve months, are taxed at separate capital gains tax rates. Gains on preferred stock held less than this period of time are taxed at regular income tax rates for the stockholder.

Losses can be offset against gains, either as regular income or capital gains, based upon the length of time they are held. Some carry-over of losses is permitted if losses exceed gains in a specific year.

C. CONVERTIBLE BONDS

Convertible bonds are included here as a form of equity since they are usually convertible into equity. These bonds permit bondholders to exchange their debt instruments for the common stock of the corporation under certain conditions.

These bonds are usually sold at a premium over standard bonds since they will provide a fixed return along with the potential to participate in the growth of the common shares. The holder enjoys the seniority of a creditor in the event of liquidation, as well as an opportunity to participate in the potential price increase of the common stock.

The issuer benefits in several ways by issuing such a security.

- By giving the convertible feature, a lower interest rate usually is paid.
- If the stock appreciates, the company eliminates the debt without paying off the loan.
- The issuer can sometimes force the conversion by calling the convertible bond. This call provision must be stated in the covenants of the bond.

The investor also can benefit by buying a convertible.

- The investor can receive a pre-defined interest rate if the price of the equity does not go up.
- The investor can convert the bond to equity at pre-defined price if the price of the equity does go up
- The investor can receive the face value of he bond at maturity

The value of the convertible security is based upon the:

- Interest rate it pays
- Bond rating, which reflects the risk of the issuer and the specific bond
- Conversion factor to common stock
- Price of the common stock

The following is an example of a convertible subordinated debenture. The bond was convertible to common stock at $13.33 per share, but only between 1/1/55 and 1/31/58.

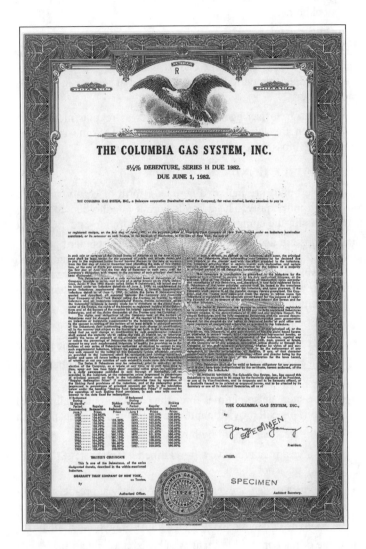

Figure 246 - Sample Bond

The general characteristics of a subordinated debenture are described in the chapter on Fixed Income Products.

D. EQUITY DERIVATIVES

A derivative is an instrument that derives its value from the value of another instrument.

There are three different equity-related derivative instruments that provide an investor with the right to purchase shares at a certain price for a certain period of time:

Warrants	Rights	Options
Issued and sold by the issuer	Issued and given to shareholders by the issuer	Issued and sold by anyone
Long Term (Up to 10 years)	Very Short Term (Weeks)	Short Term (Less than 270 days, except LEAPS)

Figure 247 - Comparison of Equity Derivative Instruments

Warrants and Rights are discussed in this section. Options are presented later in this chapter.

Warrants

A warrant is a long-term right to purchase securities at a specific price for a specific period of time. A warrant is similar to an option, except that options usually expire within nine months of issue, while warrants have a longer life. Most warrants have a life of five or ten years when they are issued, while some can have a longer life, and some, called perpetual warrants never expire. Longer term warrants may have predefined changes in the subscription price and in other conditions at specific points in time.

The following example shows a bearer warrant that allows the holder to purchase 24 common shares at a price of $5.00 per share before 3/31/77.

Figure 248 - Example of a Bearer Warrant

This warrant has its own CUSIP number (559091 12 9), which allows it to be traded and settled within the U.S. marketplace as a unique issue.

Warrants are often issued along with another security as one part of a packaged security. For example, if a corporation recognizes that the current market interest rates for newly issued bonds by other companies' with similar credit ratings is 10%, and the company only wants to pay 8%, they could add a warrant to the bond to encourage investors to buy the package.

Rights

Another form of equity is a *right*. A right can work much like a warrant, except that it is not normally sold by the issuer. Usually this right, often called a preemptive right or a subscription privilege, is granted to stockholders by the issuer's board of directors. These rights can then can be bought and sold in the secondary market.

A shareholder will normally receive one right for every share held. Rights have a value that consists of two parts:

- An intrinsic value (or theoretical value)
- A time value

A security that was issued with rights attached can trade *cum rights*, which means with rights, or *ex-rights*, which is without the rights (and in this case the rights are traded separately).

Rights usually have a very short-term. The vast majority of rights have a life of 90 days or less, and are traded as if they were an equity.

An example of a rights offering is described in the following.

Time Warner's Offer Expires; Demand is high

NEW YORK - The rights offering by Time Warner, Inc. to raise $2.76 billion by issuing 34.5 million shares expired, amid signs of heavy participation by shareholders.

Time Warner closed yesterday at $85 a share, unchanged, in composite trading on the New York Stock Exchange, comfortably above the $80-a-share price at which the rights entitled shareholders to buy new stock.

...

Source: Wall Street Journal

Figure 249 - Newspaper Article Regarding a Right

The following chart shows how the price of a right, which is denoted by the letters 'rt' after the name of the security, is reported in the newspapers.

| 52 Week | | | Sales | | | | |
High	Low	Stock	100s	High	Low	Last	Chg
10 1/2	5	Timber Ind	158	8 5/8	7 7/8	8 3/8	- 3/8
125	66 1/8	Time Warner	11402	85	84 3/8	85	--
10 3/8	2 1/2	Time Warner rt	12643	5	4 1/4	4 1/2	- 1/2
46 5/8	29 1/2	Time Warner PfC	1119	43	42 3/4	43	- 1/8
49	26 1/2	Time Warner PfD	519	48 1/2	47 7/8	48 1/2	+ 1/2

Source: New York Times

"rt" Identifies the Right

Figure 250 - Right Reported in a Newspaper

Pre-emptive Rights

Pre-emptive rights are given to existing shareholders to protect their proportionate interest or equity in the company.

For example, if a corporation has only 400 shares outstanding, and an investor holds 100 shares, the investor owns 25%. If the company issues another 400 shares and sells it to other individuals, the original investor's percentage of ownership was cut in half. To protect the current investors, the company could issue rights to existing shareholders so that they can participate in the new offering, or sell these rights to other people who want to invest.

Options

Options on equity are covered later in this chapter in the section on Options.

E. EQUITY INDEXES

A market index usually is a weighted-average price for a group of securities. As a market indicator, an index is based upon an average or a weighted-average price for a group of identified securities. The securities in the group can change, although this happens infrequently.

These averages are often quoted in the newspaper to inform people in a general way about the condition of the market for that day. The Dow Jones Industrial Averages, which are shown below are among of the best known indicators; however, there are others, such as:

- NASDAQ
- Standard & Poor's 500
- Value Line Index
- Wilshire 5000
- Russell 2000
- NYSE Composite
- AMEX Composite

STOCK MARKET INDEXES			
	Close	Chg	% Chg
DOW JONES			
30 Industrials	10139.71	+ 10.47	0.10
20 Transportation	3111.69	- 17.73	-0.57
10 Utilities	281.31	+ 1.26	0.45
65 NYSE Composite	3006.14	- 0.68	-0.02

Figure 251 - Stock Market Index as Reported in New York Times 6/13/04

Investors who wish to have an investment that matches one of these indexes, will normally purchase an Index Fund, which is described in the chapter on Fund Products.

Types of Index Calculations

Indexes may have all of the securities in the population represented by the index, such as the Russell 2,000, which includes the 2,000 equities with the largest market capitalizations. However, they may include only a sample of the securities, such as the Dow Jones Industrial Average, which only includes 30 of the industrial equities on the NYSE.

Different stock indexes are calculated in different ways as discussed in the chapter on Fund Products.

Market Value-Weighted Method (Capitalization-Weighted)

Each stock is given a weighting proportional to its market capitalization.

The market value-weighted method is the most popular way of creating an index. By giving a firm with $2 Billion in market value twice the weight of a firm with $1 Billion in market value, the market value-weighted index allows investors to best reflect total economic activity and changes in valuation of the companies in the index.

The higher weighting reflects the fact that large companies have larger revenues and profits and that any change will have a larger effect on economic activity than a change in smaller companies.

Some examples of a market value-weighted index are the S&P 500, NYSE Composite, NASDAQ Composite, Wilshire 5000, London FTSE, and MSCI Indexes.

Price-Weighted Index

Each stock is given a weighting proportional to its market price.

The main price-weighted index is the Dow Jones Industrial Average (DJIA), which was created over 100 years ago to reflect the value of twelve large companies. At that time, the index manager did not foresee how much the standard could change, and the DJIA is at 10,000 today for the 30 stocks in the index because of the unanticipated stock splits, run-offs, takeovers, mergers and acquisitions.

Equally-Weighted Index

Each stock is equally weighted in the index.

An equally-weighted index treats large and small companies the same with equal weighting. Since there are many more small companies than large ones, this strategy overemphasizes the importance of small company activity, and therefore this type of an index is not very popular in the U.S.

Total Price

The total price method adds up the prices of all of the securities in the index and divides the total by the number of securities in the index.

Price Change

The price change method identifies the daily percentage change of prices by averaging the percentage price changes of all of the securities in the index.

Classifications

An index can be established for equities, fixed income securities, foreign currencies and interest rates.

Characteristics

A stock index is typically expressed in relation to a base that was established when the index was first started.

The base may be adjusted from time to time to reflect events such as:

- Capitalization changes affecting the securities in the index
- The addition or deletion of securities to/from the index

F. EQUITY OPTIONS

A stock option is a contract where the holder has the right, but not the obligation, to buy or sell shares of the underlying security at a predefined price on or before a specific date. The seller of the option (who is also called the *writer* of the option) grants this right to the buyer.

There are two primary types of options:

- A put option gives its holder the right to *sell* a specific underlying security under certain conditions
- A call option gives the holder the right to *buy* a specific underlying security under certain conditions

Options are described in terms of their underlying security, and include the unit of trade (number of shares), strike price, and expiration date.

Marketplace

Purpose and History

Options were created initially to help investors hedge their positions, and increasingly have become speculative investments. While initially bought mostly by individuals, institutions have become increasingly involved and are now the heaviest purchasers of options.

Regulators

Although the Securities Acts of 1933 and 1934 does not formally cover options, the SEC has jurisdiction over options since they are listed on regulated exchanges.

The Options Clearing Corporation is the SRO that develops the detailed rules regarding options.

Issuers

Throughout the rest of the securities industry, the issuer of a security is the corporation upon which the security is based. With options, the issuer of the option is the person or institution creating, or *writing*, the option. The firm that is referenced by the option does not have any control over the creation of the option or any responsibility for the option.

Covered Options

Creating and then selling an option when the seller has the underlying security is called being covered. An option is considered covered, when the issuer either:

- Owns the stock

- Owns the convertible bonds

- Gets an escrow receipt from a bank

- Owns a warrant and has the money to convert the warrant

Uncovered Options

Creating and then selling an option when the seller does not have the underlying security is called being uncovered or naked.

The difference between writing covered and uncovered call positions is primarily the risk involved, where writing an uncovered call can have much more risk than writing a covered call. The writer of an uncovered call may offset some or all of their risk by holding another option as part of a spread, which is discussed later in this chapter.

Investors

An investor can be a person or firm who either buys an option or writes an option.

An investor can buy the right conveyed by the option, and hold the option until it is sold or expires. Investors generally buy an option for either of two reasons:

Protection

An investor can protect their long position in a security by buying a put or selling a call for that same security, or protect a short position by buying a call.

Speculation

A speculator can buy a call with the anticipation that the underlying security will go up, or buy a put with the anticipation that the underlying security will go down.

There are a variety of popular options strategies for investors seeking flexibility and leverage opportunities. To hedge their portfolio, individual investors will typically write covered calls or buy puts, and when they write an uncovered call or sell puts, it is usually in combination with some offsetting option position.

Institutional investors may use more complicated strategies. Since options have become better understood, and accepted, the relevant legal, regulatory and tax barriers have been eliminated.

Option Strategies

There are several basic option strategies:

- Buying calls to participate in upward price movements as part of an investment plan to lock in a stock purchase price, or to hedge short stock sales

- Buying puts to participate in downward price movements to protect a long stock position or to protect an unrealized profit in long stock

- Selling calls

  - Covered call writing (Where the writer expects the price of the underlying security to decline and wishes to lock in their current profit or minimize a loss)

  - Uncovered call writing (When the writer expects the price of the underlying security to decline and the writer wishes to participate)

- Selling puts

  - Covered put writing

  - Uncovered put writing

And, for sophisticated investors, there are several advanced strategies, including straddles, strips, straps, spreads and hedges. These techniques all involve buying and/or selling combinations of options and other instruments to manage risks, and are beyond the scope of this book, except to provide the following definitions:

- A straddle exists when an investor purchases or writes both a put and a call on the same underlying security, and when the options have the same exercise price and expiration date.

  - In a long straddle, the investor buys the put and equivalent call.

  - In a short straddle, the investor writes (or sells) the put and the equivalent call.

- A spread exists when an investor is both the buyer and writer of the same type of option (puts or calls) on the same underlying security, when the options have different exercise prices and/or expiration dates.

- A strip consists of two puts and one call on the same security and is used when the investor anticipates a declining market.

- A strap consists of two calls and one put and is used when the investor anticipates a rising market.

- A hedge exists when an investor owns a security and either buys or sells an option against the same underlying security. This has nothing to do with a Hedge Fund.

Options Compared to Common Stocks

There are both similarities and differences between options and equities that are shown in this chart.

Similarities	Differences
Both are listed on exchanges	
Orders to buy and sell both are handled through brokers	
Trading is conducted in an open, competitive auction market	
Both trade with buyers making bids and sellers making offers	For stocks, bids and offers are for shares of stock
	For options, bids and offers are for the right to buy or sell 100 shares (per option contract) of the underlying stock at a given price per share for a given period of time
Investors can continuously follow price movements, trading volume, etc.	
	An option has a limited life with a specific expiration date, but common stock can be held indefinitely
	Options that are not closed or exercised prior to its expiration date cease to exist while equities are perpetual
	The number of options is not finite, as with the number of shares issued for a firm
Book-entry trading and settlement	Stocks have certificates evidencing their ownership and the physical certificate can be traded while options do not have certificates
	Stock ownership provides the holder with: • A share of the company • Certain voting rights • Rights to dividends Option owners participate only when the stock's price moves

Figure 252 - Comparison of Stocks and Options

Contract

The underlying security is the stock that supports an options contract. An option contract is the right to buy or sell 100 shares of the underlying security at the stated strike price, up to the stated expiration date.

The prices and amounts included in the option can be changed by the Options Clearing Corporation (OCC) if the underlying stock undergoes some corporate action, such as a split, etc.

Types of Options

OTC vs. Listed Options

Options are based upon underlying equities that are either listed on an exchange or traded OTC. Additionally, the options themselves are either traded on an exchange or OTC.

OTC Traded Options

OTC traded options are informal, very cumbersome and are traditionally called conventional options. This was the original form of options, and they do not have the same level of processing regulation and protection that listed options have.

Listed Options

Listed options are those which are based upon an underlying security that is listed on any one of several exchanges, and which itself is listed on an exchange. This type of option is traded actively, and is heavily regulated, which offers some protection to investors and option writers.

Options have been traded for centuries; however, it was only in 1973 that options started to be regulated and traded on an exchange. This significantly increased the popularity and use of options by individuals and institutions.

There are several specific benefits of listed options:

Orderly, Efficient and Liquid Markets

The use of the exchanges and clearing corporations, along with specific regulation of the options market, has provided for a very orderly, efficient, and liquid option market.

Leverage

The use of options as an investment, or hedging tool, provides investors with highly leveraged potential.

Limited Risk for Buyer

The buyers of options cannot lose more than their investment, while at the other extreme the writer of an uncovered option has essentially unlimited risk.

Guaranteed Contract Performance

Listed options are settled through The Options Clearing Corporation and are governed by its rules. Trades are guaranteed by a fund established by OCC members.

Option Styles

There are three styles of options:

American Style Option

With an American style option, the holder has the right to exercise the option on or before the expiration date; and if it is not exercised, the option will expire and be worthless. All of the exchange listed stock options in the U.S. are based upon the American-style.

European Style Option

A European style option can only be exercised during a specified period of time prior to its expiration.

Capped Style Option

A capped style option gives the holder the right to exercise that option only during a specified period of time prior to its expiration, unless the option reaches a predetermine cap value prior to its expiration. If the cap is reached, the option is automatically exercised.

Options on Indexes

There are several types of options on Indexes that allow investors to participate in the price performance of an index. These options are divided into three categories:

Broad-Based Indexes

The AMEX offers a program of index options that includes:

- Major Market Index that is composed of 20 industrial companies that track the blue-chip market, allowing investors to hedge an entire portfolio against broad market risk
- The Institutional Index comprised of 75 stocks that are the most widely held by the nation's largest institutions
- S&P MidCap 400 Index
- Morgan Stanley Consumer Index
- Morgan Stanley Cyclical Index

Sector Indexes

The AMEX offers a number of indexes that are offer investors the ability to speculate or use the index to hedge investments in specific industries, including:

- AMEX Airline Index (XAL)
- AMEX Composite Index (XAX)
- AMEX Computer Hardware Index (HWI)
- AMEX Computer Technology Index (XCI)
- AMEX Deutsche Bank Energy Index (DXE)
- AMEX Disk Drive Index (DDX)
- AMEX Eurotop 100 Index (TOP)
- AMEX Gold Bugs Index (HUI)
- AMEX Institutional Index (XII)
- AMEX Interactive Week Internet Index (IIX)
- AMEX International Market Index (ADR.X)
- AMEX M S Healthcare Payor Index (HMO)
- AMEX M S Healthcare Products Index (RXP)
- AMEX M S Healthcare Provider Index (RXH)

- AMEX Major Market Index Leaps (XLT)
- AMEX Merrill Lynch Technology 100 Index (MLO)
- AMEX Morgan Stanley High Tech 35 (MSH)
- AMEX Morgan Stanley REIT Index (RMS)
- AMEX Natural Gas Index (XNG)
- AMEX Networking Index (NWX)
- AMEX North American Telecom Index (XTC)
- AMEX Oil Index (XOI)
- AMEX Securities Broker/Dealer Index (XBD)
- AMEX Tobacco Index (TOB)

Delivery Options

Options can also be defined based upon how they are ultimately settled.

Physical Delivery Options

The owner of a physical delivery option has the right, when the option is exercised, to receive physical delivery of the underlying security for a call, or to make physical delivery of the security for a put.

Cash-Settled Options

The owner of a cash-settled option has the right to receive a cash payment based on the difference between a determined value of the underlying interest at the time the option is exercised and the fixed exercise price of the option.

Most options traded in the U.S. are settled by cash and not the physical exchange of securities.

Classifications

There are several different classifications of options.

Equity Options

The issuers of the underlying equity securities do not participate in the selection of their securities for options trading. Each stock option generally covers 100 shares of the underlying security.

Index Options

An index option is an option that has the index as the underlying instrument, and which is always cash-settled.

Premiums and settlement prices for index options are more difficult to calculate than for the more commonly used equity options, and are beyond the scope of this book.

Flexibly Structured Options

Flexibly structured options do not have standardized terms. When a flexibly structured option is written, the parties to the transaction have the flexibility, with some limitations, to fix some of the option's terms, which are called variable terms. Due to this variability, the market is smaller and less active than the market for the more traditional structured and listed options.

LEAPS

Long Term Equity Anticipation Securities (LEAPS) are American-style long-term stock or index options, which are available as calls and puts, and which have expiration dates that can be up to 39 months in the future, although usually for not more than 33 months because of the way that the expiration cycle is structured.

Flex LEAP options can have a maximum term of five years.

Listed Options Characteristics

Trading

Options are traded in the U.S. at various times throughout the day, based upon the underlying security, as follows:

- Options on U.S. securities are traded during the normal day time business hours of the U.S. securities exchanges and for a short amount of time afterward
- Options on foreign currencies are traded in evening and night trading sessions

In addition, when there are unusual market conditions, a specific options market may authorize trading to continue for additional hours.

Options of the same series may be traded on more than one options market simultaneously, and are called multiple-traded options.

Internationally traded options are options that are traded on both a U.S. options exchange and a foreign options exchange.

Long and Short

The words *long* and *short* do not have the same meaning for options as with other securities.

- An investor who is long an option is the *holder* of the option
- The investor who is short an option is the *writer* of the option

Orders

An order is a purchase or sale transaction.

- An *opening order* creates a position or increases a position
- A *closing order* eliminates a position or decreases a position

Strike Price

The strike price is the pre-determined price at which a specific option can be exercised.

Pricing

Several factors determine the price of an option, including the:

- Price of the underlying stock
- Time remaining until expiration
- Volatility of the underlying stock price
- Cash dividends

- Interest rates

The value of an option has two components:

Intrinsic Value

If a selling price for the underlying security is greater than the strike price (calls) or less than the strike price (puts), the difference is called the intrinsic value of the option.

Premium

The premium is the difference between the selling price and the intrinsic value of an option plus time value. If the intrinsic price is zero, then the entire amount is the premium. Sometimes people will call the selling price the premium regardless of the intrinsic value.

Premium = Intrinsic Value + Time Value

At the Money

An option is *at the money* if the option's strike price is exactly equal to the underlying security's current market price.

In the Money

The intrinsic value of an option is the amount by which it is In the Money.

- A call option is *in the money* if the strike price is below the current market price of the underlying security.

- A put option is *in the money* if the strike price is above the current market price of the underlying security.

Out of the Money

An option is *out of the money* when the strike price is:

- Above the price of the underlying security for a call option

- Below the price of the underlying security for a put option

When an option is *out of the money*, it does not have any intrinsic value, but can still have a premium value.

Transaction Costs

The transaction costs for investing in options consist primarily of:

- Commissions which are imposed in opening, closing, exercise and assignment transactions

- Margin and interest costs in certain transactions

Liquidity

Exchange-listed options are very liquid. OTC options tend to be illiquid.

Maturity

An option that is in the money at expiration date is automatically exercised for cash, while an option that expires out of the money is worthless.

Processing

Most option holders and writers close out their option positions by offsetting closing transactions or by allowing out of the money cash options to expire. Options can be exercised prior to maturity.

If an equity option call holder decides to exercise his right to buy the underlying shares of stock (or a put holder decides to sell the underlying security), the holder must submit an exercise notice to the OCC through a broker.

While most options require that the holder take an action prior to the expiration date, capped options are subject to automatic exercise if the automatic exercise value of the underlying interest hits the cap price for the option.

Exercise Price

Exercise prices for each option series are established by the options market, and are generally set at levels above and below the market value of the underlying interest at that time. The options markets can introduce an additional series of options with different exercise prices based on changes in:

- The value of the underlying interest
- The volatility of the underlying security
- Response to investor interest
- Unusual market conditions
- Other circumstances

The exercise price depends upon the type of option:

- The exercise price of a cash-settled option is the base that is used to calculate the amount of cash, if any, that the option holder is entitled to receive upon exercise
- The exercise price (which is sometimes called the *strike price*) for a physical delivery option is the price at which the option holder has the right either to purchase or to sell the underlying interest

Expiration Date

The expiration date is the date that the option matures and becomes worthless. For listed stock options it is the Saturday following the third Friday of the expiration month.

A stock option usually begins trading up to six months before its expiration date. Normally, the longer the time remaining until an option's expiration date, the higher the option premium since there is a greater possibility that the underlying share price might move so as to put the option in the money.

The time value of an option drops rapidly in the last several weeks of an option's life.

Exercise by Exception (Ex-by-Ex)

Ex-by-Ex is the process that is used to automatically exercise cash options that are ready to expire and which are in the money, unless the client provides other instructions.

Automatic Exercise Value

A capped option has an automatic exercise value that can be evoked if the underlying security reaches a predefined point.

Option Example

This chart shows the prices for Citigroup puts and calls at a point in time. The example shows that Citigroup closed at 47 1/4 for the day, and that several different strike prices for puts and calls were available, with multiple expiration dates. Each combination of strike price, expiration date and put/call is a separate option.

Citigroup	Strike Price	Volume	Last Price	Volume	Last Price	Volume	Last Price
Close 47 1/4		Aug		Sep		Dec	
Call	40	0	--	0	--	243	9
Call	45	89	3 1/8	24	4	0	--
Call	47 1/2	246	1 9/16	0	--	0	--
Call	50	546	1 1/16	281	1 1/2	0	--
Call	55	451	1/4	0	--	195	1 7/8
Put	40	0	--	0	--	1	1 9/16
Put	45	217	15/16	557	1 3/4	0	--
Put	47 1/2	40	2	0	--	0	--
Put	50	75	3 1/2	12	4 1/4	0	--
Put	55	0	--	0	--	0	--

(Callout labels: "Number of Contracts Traded That Day" points to the Volume columns; "Exercise Month" points to the month headers.)

Figure 253 - Option Example

For example, this chart says that the Sep 50 Call closed at 1½, and there were 281 contracts sold. The next question is to look at what happens if the price of the underlying security goes up or down.

The next chart shows what would have happened if an investor bought Citigroup stock vs. three different options, and if the price of Citigroup had either gone up or down. Citigroup's NYSE ticker symbol is C.

		Buy 100 Shares of C	Buy 1 Sep Call at 45	Buy 1 Sep Call at 50	Buy 1 Sep Put at 45
If C goes up to 55	Stock Value	5,500			
	Option Value		1,000	500	0
	Cost	4,725	400	150	175
	Profit	775	600	350	(175)
	% Gain	16.4 %	150 %	233 %	(100 %)
If C goes down to 40	Stock Value	4,000			
	Option Value		0	0	500
	Cost	4,725	400	150	175
	Profit	(725)	(400)	(150)	375
	% Gain	15.3 %	(100 %)	(100 %)	215 %

Figure 254 - Option Calculations (Excluding Commissions)

The top half of this example shows that if the investor bought:

- 100 C at 47 1/4, and the stock went to 55, he would have made $725 (excluding commissions), or 16.4%.

- 1 Sep 45 Call, and the price of C went to 55, he would have made $600, or 150%.

- 1 Sep 50 Call, and the price of C went to 55, he would have made $350, or 233%.

- 1 Sep 45 Put, and the price of C went to 55, he would have lost his entire investment.

The bottom of the chart shows what would have happened if the price of Citigroup went down to 40.

Risks

Risks for Option Holders

If the price of the underlying security does not move above the strike price prior to the expiration date, or below the strike price for a put, the holder may lose his entire investment in the option.

Risks for Option Writers

An option writer can be affected by an option that may be exercised at any time during the period the option is open.

- An American-style option is subject to being exercised by the option holder at any time until the option expires.

- A European-style or capped option is subject to being exercised by the option holder only when the option is exercisable.

- A capped option is subject to being exercised by the option holder when the automatic exercise value of the underlying interest matches the cap price.

Calls

The writer of a covered call gives up the opportunity to gain from an increase in the value of the underlying instrument above the strike price, and has the risk of a decline in the value of the underlying instrument.

The writer of an uncovered call may have large losses, which are theoretically unlimited, if the value of the underlying instrument increases above the strike price.

Puts

The risk of writing put options is also considerable since the writer of a put option has a risk of loss if the value of the underlying interest declines below the exercise price, and such loss could be substantial since the price of the underlying security could drop to zero.

Taxation

Gains and losses on options are considered to be ordinary income, and are taxed at the regular income tax rates of the investor.

G. OTHER EQUITY PRODUCTS

Direct Participation Program (DPP)

The purpose of a DPP is profit *and* tax benefits. A DPP is a syndicate, group, pool or joint venture that is not a corporation, trust company or an estate through which business is conducted. The majority of DPP investments are found in oil and gas, real estate and equipment leasing.

The owners of a DPP share in the profits just like a shareholder, but may also receive tax credits and tax deduction write-offs not available to shareholders, yet at the same time, retaining limited liability.

Formation of the Limited Partnership

The document required to create this partnership is known as the Certificate of Limited Partnership. This is very much like the corporate charter and must contain information regarding the following:

- The charter must include the name and address of each general and limited partner, and the status of each person
- The amounts of contributions (investments), by contributor
- A description of how additional contributions may be made and a definition of the circumstances under which contributions may be returned
- How expenses, profits and income will be allocated
- Term of the partnership, which is usually for ten years
- How interest in the partnership may be transferred, and how new partners may be admitted
- How the partnership will be continued or dissolved in the event of the death of a general partner

The certificate must be signed by at least one general partner and one limited partner and filed with the state in which the partnership was organized. Substantial changes require amendments to the certificate.

After the partnership has been established, another document is needed, called the Agreement of Limited Partnership, which is a contract stating the rights, limitations and obligations of both the general and limited partners.

A Subscription Agreement is evidence of the purchase in a limited partnership, and includes the name, address, and social security number of the subscriber (investor). This agreement also contains a statement that the limited partner is a qualified investor as to net worth, has read the material and can accept the risk. In addition, the agreement grants a power of attorney to the general partner.

The transfer of a limited partnership is not easy since the market is not liquid and requires permission from the partnership.

Powers, Obligations and Limitations of the General Partner

The general partner has few rights and many more obligations than the limited partners do. The general partner:

- Must manage the business

- Must act as fiduciary on behalf of the limited partners
- May never act to prevent the ordinary business of the partnership
- May not compete with the partnership

Rights, Obligations and Limitations on Limited Partners

The limited partners' rights and obligations are:

- Requirement to contribute capital
- Opportunity to share in the rewards and profits of the business
- Access to business records
- Right to sue the general partner
- Limited liability
- May not engage in the day-to-day activities of partnership

XIV. Fixed Income Instruments

A. INTRODUCTION TO FIXED INCOME SECURITIES

The first section of this chapter describes the general characteristics of all fixed income securities, and subsequent sections present the details for the various primary types of fixed income securities.

Marketplace

Purpose

A fixed income security, commonly called a bond, is issued by a corporation, municipality, government or agency. It is an instrument that generally carries a specified rate of interest that the issuer agrees to pay to the bondholder, as well as a promise to repay the principal either over time, when the bond matures or when it is called. While the specified rate of interest is usually a fixed rate over the life of the bond, it could also have:

- Different fixed rates that go into effect at specified times

- A variable rate of interest that changes as some related rate changes. For example, a variable rate bond could be established as 1% over a certain index, such as the Fed Funds rate, and it could change monthly, quarterly, annually, etc.

Regulators

The Securities and Exchange Commission regulates the market for most types of fixed income securities, although some types are unregulated.

Issuers

The issuers of U.S. fixed income securities are U.S. and non-U.S. based corporations, the U.S. government, U.S. government agencies and U.S. municipalities.

Investors

Investors in fixed income securities could be individuals and institutions domiciled anywhere in the world. Tax-exempt municipals, however, tend to only be sold to taxable individuals or entities in the tax jurisdiction where the issue is tax exempt.

Certificate Form

Fixed income securities can be differentiated by the way they are issued, by the issuer, by the purpose of the issuance, and whether or not the interest payment is fixed or variable.

Bearer vs. Registered Bonds

Existing bonds can be bearer or registered; however, no new bearer bonds are allowed to be issued in the U.S. When a bond is registered, it is either registered in the bondholder's name or in a nominee name.

Bond Certificates

When a bond issue is created, at least one global certificate is established to recognize ownership. Historically, all bonds were issued in physical bearer form with detachable coupons that represented the interest due on the bond. Most bonds today do not have certificates issued.

It is possible to get physical certificates for certain types of registered bonds, and although some physical bearer bonds still exist, they are very rare.

Coupons

Coupons are physical documents that must be physically separated from the bearer bond certificate and presented to a paying agent to receive interest income.

We see very few physical coupons today because the issuance of bearer bonds has been illegal in the U.S. for over twenty-five years. The following example shown consists of four separate coupons that could have been redeemed in the 1950's and 60's to claim interest.

Figure 255 - Example of Physical Coupons

At that time, *coupon clippers* were considered to be wealthy people who used the interest from their bonds for their daily expenses. However, since the holder of the bond/coupon got the interest directly, it was very difficult for the IRS to claim income tax and/or inheritance tax. In 1982, a law was passed by congress to eliminate the creation of new bearer certificates.

Registered bonds have interest payments that accrue to the registered holder of the bond, and which are either paid directly to the registered holder or to the custodian of the bonds. The custodian, which could be a bank or broker, then pays its clients the interest that is due and collected. Banks and brokers are required to report all interest payments to the IRS so that the recipients can be taxed.

Indenture

The contractual terms of the bond are defined in the indenture, which is usually printed on the front or back of the bond certificate.

Trustee

In accordance with the Trust Indenture Act of 1939, the issuer must appoint a trustee to safeguard the public interest. The trustee is usually a commercial bank's corporate trust department, which is appointed to oversee the agreement (the indenture) and verify that the rights of the bondholders are observed.

Bond Categories

There are a number of different major categories of fixed income instruments, which include:

- Corporate Bonds
  - Fixed Rate
  - Variable Rate
- Municipal Bonds
- Government Bonds
  - U.S. Treasury Fixed Rate Bonds and Notes
  - U.S. Treasury Bills
  - U.S. Treasury Inflation Protected Bonds
- Asset Backed Securities
- Mortgage Backed Securities
  - Pass Through
  - Collateralized Mortgage Obligations
- Money Market Securities

Each of these types is discussed in this chapter.

These different instruments have different characteristics, including how they pay interest and how they repay the original investment, as shown here.

Instrument	Periodic Payments consist of:	Payment at maturity consists of:
Corporate – Fixed Rate	Pre-determined amount of interest	Face value (par) of the instrument
Corporate – Variable Rate	Variable rate of interest based upon a base rate	Face value (par) of the instrument
Municipal – Fixed Rate	Pre-determined amount of interest	Face value (par) of the instrument
U.S. Treasury – Fixed Rate Bonds and Notes	Pre-determined amount of interest	Face value (par) of the instrument
U.S. Treasury – Bills	None	Sold at a discount and redeemed at face value (par)
U.S. Treasury – Inflation Protected	Variable rate of interest based upon the CPI	Face value (par) of the instrument, adjusted for inflation
Asset Backed Securities	Variable amount of interest and principal based upon the payment pattern of the underlying assets	The remaining amount of un-reimbursed principal
Mortgage Backed Securities – Pass -Through	Variable amount of interest and principal based upon the payment pattern of the underlying mortgages	The remaining amount of un-reimbursed principal
Collateralized Mortgage Obligations	Variable principal and interest but with each tranche paid off before the next subordinate tranche is paid	The remaining amount of un-reimbursed principal
Money Market	None	Either sold at a discount and redeemed for the face value, or sold at par and redeemed for an amount equal to par plus accumulated interest

Figure 256 - Comparison of Fixed Income Instruments

Each of these types of bonds will be discussed in more detail later in this chapter; however, these different types of bonds have many common characteristics that are described in this section of this chapter.

Classifications

Secured vs. Unsecured Bonds

Bonds can be secured with some form of collateral, or they can be unsecured. Unsecured corporate bonds are called debentures.

Callable Bonds

Bonds can be issued with a call feature, which allows the issuer the right to redeem the bond at certain points in time at their discretion, possibly for a premium. For example, a possible timetable for calling bonds could be established as follows:

Time Frame	Callability		Time Frame	Callability
1 - 5 year	Non-callable		8th year	102 % of par
6th year	104 % of par		10th year	101 % of par
7th year	103 % of par		10+	100% of par

Figure 257 - Example of a Possible Call Schedule

Convertible Bonds

As was discussed in the chapter on Equity-Related Instruments, a bond can be convertible into something else, usually equity in the same firm.

Sinking Fund Bonds

A sinking fund is established when a firm promises to put a certain amount of money into an escrow account each year to provide for an annual repurchase of a portion of the outstanding bonds. For example, $1,000,000 per year could be set aside to repurchase these bonds in the open market, at market rates.

This is a positive situation for investors since they may have an opportunity to sell their bonds to the issuer if they wish, or the investors can hold the bonds longer to receive additional interest payments. Also, since the issuer's total outstanding debt is reduced each year by the amount of the repurchased bonds, the risk to the bondholder is reduced.

Since the sinking fund is used to buy back bonds that are voluntarily offered by the holder, a sinking fund works differently from a call, which is mandatory.

Bond Insurance

Bonds can also be insured against default, and there are several independent private firms that provide this type of insurance, such as:

- MBIC (The letters are used exclusively today, although they originally stood for Municipal Bond Investors Assurance)
- AMBAC (The letters are used exclusively today, although they originally stood for American Municipal Bond Assurance Corporation)
- FGIC (Financial Guaranty Insurance Company)
- FSA (Financial Services Authority)

When a bond is insured, the issuer pays for the insurance and therefore the bond pays a slightly lower yield to compensate for the decrease in risk. However, it is still possible for the bond issuer to default *and* for the insurer to default, so insured bonds are not without risk.

Bond Guarantee

A bond's promise to pay interest and/or repay principal can also be guaranteed by another legal entity. The bondholder's risk is reduced since more than one firm is legally involved, but the risk of default is not completely eliminated.

Characteristics

There are many different characteristics of bonds.

Bond Trading

Most of U.S. bonds are bought and sold OTC; however, some corporate bonds are listed on the NYSE.

Most types of bonds trade *plus accrued interest*. This means that when a bond settles, the buyer must pay the seller for market value plus the interest that has accumulated since the last interest payment. The buyer will recover this money when he or she receives the full interest payment on the next payment date.

One type of bond, called an income bond trades *flat*, which is without accrued interest, and where interest is paid to the holder only when and if the firm is able to pay.

Transaction Costs

Transaction costs are either shown as a commission, which is separate from the traded price, or as a mark-up/mark-down that is combined with the traded price.

Liquidity

The few available exchange listed fixed income securities are normally very liquid, while OTC securities can vary from being liquid to very illiquid.

Different categories of fixed income instruments also have different liquidity potential. For example, government bonds are very liquid, while municipal bonds are normally not very liquid.

Bond Pricing

A bond's price is based upon several variables, including:

• Current interest rates	• Liquidity
• Issuer's credit quality	• Maturity
• Supply and demand	• Taxable status
• Call provisions	• Sinking fund features
• Convertible features	• Expectations of inflation

When a bond is issued, it usually sells for close to its face value; however, the prices of bonds that trade in the secondary market rise and fall inversely to interest rates.

Bonds trading above their face value are considered to be trading at a *premium*, and trade at a *discount* when they trade below their face value.

Face Value vs. Market Value

The prices of bonds are more complex than for equities. Bonds have a face value, which is usually $1,000 or a multiple of $1,000, while the market value is whatever people will pay for them.

The market value of a bond is determined by its risk rating and by the prevailing interest rate in the market for that category of risk. For most bonds, the higher the market interest rate is over the bond's interest rate, the less someone will pay for the outstanding bond, because the amount the holder will receive in bond interest is set at the time of issuance and does not change.

Purchase Price

The purchase price is the price at which the issue was last purchased, either in the primary or the secondary market.

Interest Rate and Coupon Rate

Bonds generally have a specified interest rate, which is usually fixed for the life of the bond and which is related to the face value (par value), or which can also be periodically reset or linked to an index. Some bonds can be issued with a variable rate or a zero interest rate. The coupon rate on a bond is the same as the specified interest rate; however, the interest rate is different from yield, which is discussed later in this chapter.

Maturity

Unlike equities, which represent perpetual ownership in a company, a fixed income instrument represents a debt that is scheduled to be repaid in a certain period of time that can range from a day to thirty years.

A bond matures at a point in the future that is defined when the issue is created. The life of the bond is long, intermediate or short based upon its maturity date. While bonds with a life as long as 100 years exist, the IRS is arguing to have them classified as equity.

Bond maturities are generally classified in three groups:

- Short-term notes have maturities of one to four years
- Medium-term notes/bonds have maturities of five to twelve years
- Long-term bonds mature in more than twelve years

The maturity date identifies the point at which a bond *must* be redeemed. When a bond has either been called or matured and has been redeemed, it is considered retired. When a bond is retired, the certificate (if any) is physically cancelled. The cancelled certificate may be stored in an archive or destroyed.

Transfer agents are required by the SEC to maintain cancelled certificates for at least six years, and for the first six months they must be in an easily accessible place.

In general, until a bond is retired, it will continue to pay the defined interest rate, and at maturity the principal will be repaid. Some bonds repay a portion of the principal in each payment.

Bond Redemption

A bond is redeemed when the investor returns it to the issuer in exchange for cash. A redemption can occur when the bond matures, when it is called or is put.

Bond Retirement

A bond is considered retired when it matures and is redeemed.

Refunding

Refunding is the sale of a new issue, with the proceeds used to retire an old issue. The refunding must be stated in the indenture. A possible timetable for refunding bonds could be established as follows:

Time Frame	Refundability		Time Frame	Refundability
1 - 5 year	Non-refundable		8th year	102 % of par
6th year	104 % of par		10th year	101 % of par
7th year	103 % of par		10+	100% of par

Figure 258 - Example of a Refund Schedule

Interest

Interest can be paid on fixed income securities if the promise to pay interest has been defined in the bond's indenture. How interest is paid varies with the different types of bonds.

Payment Periods

Bonds generally pay interest in regular periods, which are usually quarterly, semi-annually or annually. Some bonds, however, do not pay periodic interest, while others pay a variable amount of interest along with a return of principal.

Yield

The yield on a bond is the amount of interest that is paid annually, divided by the current price of the bond. This is the actual *rate* of interest that the bondholder would receive if the bond is purchased today.

Nominal Yield

The nominal yield, also called the coupon rate, is the interest rate that is established at the time of issue, and is the same as the bond interest rate. The nominal yield is stated on the bond, and unless the bond was established as a variable rate instrument, the nominal yield does not change during the life of the bond.

If a bond has a nominal yield of 6%, the annual interest payment is $60.00.

Actual Yield

The following illustrates the various bond values, including actual yield, also called the current yield. If an investor buys a twenty year 8% bond in 1998 that was issued in 1988, and which was purchased for $800 (not including any commission or mark/up), the actual yield can be calculated as follows:

Nominal yield	8%	Shown on the bond certificate
Face value	$1,000	Shown on the bond certificate
Annual interest	$80.00	= $1,000 * 8%
Maturity	2008	Shown on the bond certificate
Actual yield	10%	= $80 / $800

Yield-to-Maturity

A yield-to-maturity is the total annualized amount of interest earned over the life of an instrument, adjusted for the purchase premium, and divided by the amount invested.

If we consider the bond that was used in the previous example, the yield-to-maturity can be calculated roughly as follows:

At maturity, the issuer will pay the investor $1,000; therefore, the investor will receive an additional $200 after 10 years, or $20 a year for the next 10 years.

$$\$80 + \$20 = \$100 \text{ in annual income}$$

The market value of the bond will increase each year towards the $1,000 that is due at maturity. The average of the market value of the period is the starting $800 plus the ending $1,000 divided by 2, or

$$(\$800 + 1,000)/2 = \$900$$

The average yield-to-maturity is the average interest divided by the average price, or

$$\$100 / \$900 = 11.11\%$$

Interest Accruals

Interest is calculated as shown here.

$$\text{Interest} = \frac{\text{Principal} * \text{Interest Rate} * \text{Days Held}}{\text{Number of Days in the Period}}$$

Figure 259 - Interest Calculation Formula

Different types of bonds have different ways to accrue interest, and settle differently, as shown below.

Type of Bond	Payments Cycles per Year	Days in Year	Days in Month	Settlement Days
Corporate	Semi-Annual	360	30	3
Municipal	Semi-Annual	360	30	3
U.S. Treasury	Semi-Annual	365/366	Actual	0

Figure 260 - Comparison of Interest Calculation Methods

This chart shows that corporate and municipal securities have very similar characteristics, but government securities are different. In addition to only settling in one day, government interest accruals are calculated using a different basis.

Corporate bonds and municipal bonds have a simplified structure for calculating accruals, while government securities continue to use the actual number of days in a month or the year.

Processing

Fixed income securities are processed in a variety of ways, depending upon their type. The processing for each type is discussed later in this chapter.

Risks

Interest Rate

The price of a fixed income security is very sensitive to changes in interest rates since the price is inversely related to changes in market interest rates.

Credit

Bonds are issued with a wide range of investor risks in mind. Investors need to judge the credit worthiness of the issuer. The highest credit quality category is for U.S. Treasury securities, which are backed by the full faith and credit of the U.S. government. The lowest credit quality bonds are those that are rated as being below investment grade and are therefore considered to be speculative.

While all investments have some degree of risk, a bond's risk is directly reflected in its rate of return, and the higher the risk, the higher the return.

Defaults

If a corporation or municipality defaults and is unable to meet its scheduled interest payment, the bondholders could force a bankruptcy. Bondholders have a higher claim than stockholders during a bankruptcy, and different classes of bondholders can have different priorities.

Credit Ratings

Bonds are rated by independent agencies in order to compare the level of risk on one issue to another. There are several rating agencies in the U.S. Although they perform a similar function, each has its own way of measuring risk and comparing one instrument to another.

Bond ratings are part of a measurement system that defines the relative investment qualities of bonds. These range from the highest investment quality (least investment risk) to the lowest investment quality (greatest investment risk).

The primary rating agencies in the U.S. are:

- Standard & Poor's
- Moody's
- Fitch
- Dun and Bradstreet

Each firm has its own measurement and reporting system. The ratings used by Standard & Poor's Corporation are shown in this chart:

Rating	Definition
AAA	Highest grade
AA+, AA, AA-	High grade
A+, A, A-	Upper medium grade
BBB+, BBB, BBB-	Medium grade
BB+, BB, BB-	Lower medium grade
B+, B, B-	Speculative
CCC+, CCC, CCC-, CC	Outright speculation
C	Income bonds paying no interest and the best defaulted bonds
D	In default, with the D symbol assigned to those issues which appear to have little recoverable value

Figure 261 - Standard & Poor's Ratings

The higher the risk, the greater the interest rate that must be paid by the issuer in order to compensate the holder for the additional risk.

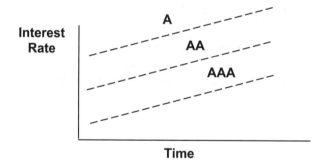

Figure 262 - Comparison of Ratings and Risk

There is additional information on the bond rating vendors in the chapter on Vendors.

Taxation

Interest

Interest paid on most forms of fixed income securities is taxable at the regular income tax rates of the stockholder. Some forms, however, are not taxable. Each type will be discussed later in this chapter.

Return of Principal

Some categories of bonds periodically return all or a part of the principal to the bondholder. A return of principal is not taxable.

Gains and Losses

Gains on securities held over a certain period of time, currently twelve months, are taxed at a separate (and lower) capital gains tax rate. Gains on securities held less than this period of time are taxed at the regular income tax rates for the bondholder.

Losses can be offset against gains, either as regular income or capital gains, based upon the length of time the security is held.

B. CORPORATE FIXED INCOME SECURITIES

When a corporation needs to raise money, it can either issue stock or borrow funds. The following chart compares equities to bonds.

Equity	Bonds
Represents ownership	Represents indebtedness
Dividends are paid at the discretion of the board of directors and paid out of after-tax profits	Interest must be paid, or the firm's credit rating will be reduced, which forces the firm to pay higher interest rates in order to attract future additional investments. Interest is paid with the corporation's before-tax dollars
The amount distributed is decided upon by the board of directors and can increase or decrease from period to period	Unless the issue is a variable rate instrument, the interest amount is fixed over the life of the loan
Perpetual agreement until the investor sells the shares or the company goes out of business	Issued for a specific period of time at which point the bond must be redeemed.

Figure 263 - Comparison of Equity to Bonds

Marketplace

There are over $3 trillion in U.S. corporate bonds outstanding and over $10 billion is traded daily. Corporates can be traded on the NYSE or OTC, and are bought and sold by institutions and individuals.

Corporate bonds are usually issued with a face value of $1,000, are sold in minimum lots of 5 bonds ($5,000) and prices are quoted as if the bond was traded in $100 increments. A bond priced at 99 refers to a bond that is being offered at $99 per $100 of face value, which is $990 per bond.

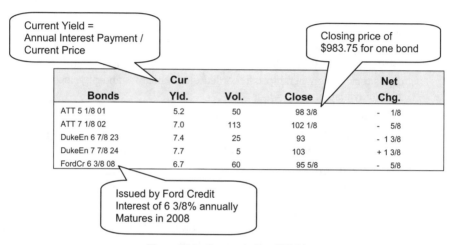

Current Yield =
Annual Interest Payment /
Current Price

Closing price of
$983.75 for one bond

Bonds	Cur Yld.	Vol.	Close	Net Chg.
ATT 5 1/8 01	5.2	50	98 3/8	- 1/8
ATT 7 1/8 02	7.0	113	102 1/8	- 5/8
DukeEn 6 7/8 23	7.4	25	93	- 1 3/8
DukeEn 7 7/8 24	7.7	5	103	+ 1 3/8
FordCr 6 3/8 08	6.7	60	95 5/8	- 5/8

Issued by Ford Credit
Interest of 6 3/8% annually
Matures in 2008

Figure 264 - Corporate Bond Yields

Purpose

Corporate bonds are issued by corporations and the proceeds are used for everything from growing the business to buying a building. Investors buy corporate bonds to receive a fixed (or occasionally variable) interest rate and a return of the initial investment that is guaranteed by the credit of the corporation.

Regulators

The Securities and Exchange Commission regulates the market for corporate bonds.

Issuers

U.S. corporate bonds can be issued by U.S. and non-U.S. private and public corporations.

Investors

Investors in corporates could be individuals and/or institutions from anywhere in the world.

Certificate Form

There are several different ways that corporate bonds can be issued:

Bearer Bonds

Bearer bonds are physical certificates that are not issued in any name, but are the property of whoever holds them. Since they could be transferred anonymously and therefore were potentially untaxable, they were banned by the Tax Reform Act of 1982. A small number of bonds that have not matured or been called remain in circulation.

Registered Bonds

Registered bonds are issued in the name of the investor or a nominee. While individual certificates can be issued, a depository, broker or custodian usually holds most of the certificates in nominee name.

Book-Entry Bonds

A book-entry bond is a registered bond that is issued without individual certificates. A single global certificate is issued which is only held in the depository. All ownership is recorded electronically, and physical certificates are not available.

Classifications

When corporate bonds are issued, they are classified according to the type of the issuer or according to the type of collateral that is used to secure them.

Issuer Classifications

There are five major categories of issuer:

Industrial Bonds

Industrial bonds are issued by corporations to increase working capital, finance expansion, or refund a previous issue.

Utility Bonds

Utility bonds are issued by regulated utilities to increase working capital, finance expansion, or refund a previous issue.

Finance Bonds

Finance bonds are issued by banks, finance companies, REITs, etc., generally to borrow at one rate and loan the funds at a higher rate.

Transportation Bonds

Railroads generally issue transportation bonds, or equipment trust bonds.

Conglomerate Bonds

Conglomerate bonds are issued by U.S. or foreign companies.

Secured Bond Classifications

Bonds are secured in order to provide additional protection for bondholders. If the issuer goes bankrupt or defaults on its debt, bondholders have a prior claim over stockholders, but different classes of bondholders have different priorities. The security is generally provided through insurance, guarantees or collateral.

A bond is not the same as a debenture.

Bonds

A bond is a fixed income instrument that is always backed by some form of collateral. Collateral can consist of physical assets such as buildings, equipment, etc., or by other securities.

Debentures

For debentures, no collateral is used, and the issue is secured only by the corporation's promise to pay. Corporations with high credit ratings usually do not have a problem issuing debentures. However, debentures usually pay a higher interest rate due to the lack of collateral and the higher risk.

Virtually all corporate convertible bonds are issued as debentures. Due to the convertible feature, it is not necessary to assign it specific collateral.

The debenture shown in the following example was issued in multiples of $1,000, and was callable.

Subordinated Debentures

A Subordinated Debenture has a lower claim on assets than other debentures in case of default. To offset this additional risk, the debenture is usually issued with a slightly higher interest rate.

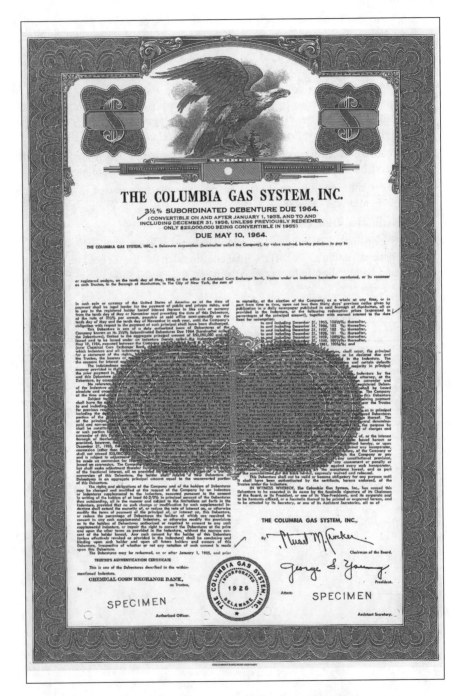

Figure 265 - Covenants of a Subordinated Debenture

Although corporate fixed income instruments can be bonds or debentures, market convention is to call them all bonds, and this book will follow that convention.

Guaranteed Bonds

A guaranteed bond is secured by a third-party. Some examples are:

- A specific issue of Western Electric bonds was guaranteed by AT&T
- Bonds issued by a subsidiary could be guaranteed by the parent company
- Bonds issued by a joint venture could be guaranteed by both parent corporations

A guaranteed bond is secured from the perspective of the issuing corporation, and is equivalent to a debenture issued by the parent firm.

Income Bond

With income bonds, interest is paid as it becomes available from the issuer. Usually these bonds are not issued as a method of obtaining original financing; instead they are issued in exchange for outstanding debt when a firm is in danger of default.

There are several different categories of secured bonds which are based upon their collateral, including:

Mortgage Bonds

A mortgage bond is secured by a mortgage on some real property, and is usually issued by utilities. This is just like an individual borrowing to buy a house by using the house as collateral. Should the corporation fail to repay, the property could be sold to repay all or part of the loan.

Open End Bond

With an open end bond, the property can be used again and again as collateral, and all of the bondholders for each issue are on an equal repayment basis. Therefore, the buyer of these bonds should make sure that the property is sufficient to cover all the debt.

Closed End Bond

A closed end bond prohibits the borrower from pledging the same collateral a second time at an equal preference in bankruptcy. This would not preclude the borrower from pledging the collateral on a subordinated basis.

Other mortgage bonds are issued as consolidated or general mortgages. In this case, the issuing corporation does not specify which items of property will serve as collateral, but pledges all of the included property.

Equipment Trust

The equipment trust bond is secured by some equipment, such as railroad cars, etc., which is normally used by the corporation in the operation of its business. These bonds are most often issued by railroads, airlines and trucking corporations using their *rolling stock*.

When the loan is made, a trustee holds title to the collateral until repayment and makes the interest distribution to the bondholders. Upon repayment, the trustee transfers title of the equipment back to the issuer.

As the agreements contain provisions for maintenance, insurance and replacement of collateral, these securities are considered high investment quality.

Sometimes these bonds are issued in *serial* form, which means that portions of the bond mature on different dates. These bonds often have a *balloon* form of repayment, with small amounts paid in the beginning, and larger amounts repaid at the end.

Collateral Trust Certificates

With a collateral trust bond, the issuer deposits securities with a trustee as a guarantee that the bonds will be redeemed and the interest paid.

This is similar to an individual who needs some private financing, and pledges stock as collateral for loans. If the borrower does not pay back the loan, the bank sells the stock and the loan is repaid.

Characteristics

Trading

Most of the corporate bond market is conducted over the counter; however, some are listed on the NYSE.

Transaction Costs

Bonds that are sold from a broker/dealer's inventory are usually sold with a mark-up, rather than a commission. If a broker/dealer goes to an exchange or to the over-the-counter market to find a counterparty, they will generally charge a commission.

Liquidity

Bonds tend to be traded less frequently than equities, and are therefore less liquid. Liquidity for corporate bonds is usually provided by broker/dealers who are market makers for specific corporate bond issues.

Pricing

Market price is related to the amount of interest paid and the demand for bonds with specific levels of risk.

When a corporate bond settles, the buyer must pay the seller for the accrued interest that has been accumulated since the last interest payment. The buyer will receive the full interest payment on the next payment date.

Income bonds trade *flat*, where interest is only paid to the bondholder if the firm earns enough money to make the interest payment.

Maturity

A bond matures at the point that is established when the issue is created. These maturities generally are classified in three groups:

- Short-term notes with maturities of one to four years
- Medium-term notes/bonds with maturities of five to twelve years
- Long-term bonds that mature in more than twelve years

In general, until a bond matures, it will continue to pay the stated interest rate, and at maturity the principal will be repaid.

Not all corporate bonds remain outstanding until they mature. Some have a call feature or a redemption feature that will affect when the principal is repaid.

Interest

There are two different types of interest rates associated with corporate bonds:

Fixed Rate

The most common form of corporate bond has a fixed interest rate. This means that the investor will receive pre-defined, regular payments for the life of the bond.

Floating (Variable) Rate

Corporate bonds can also have an interest rate that is periodically adjusted, based upon some interest rate based index. Yields for these variable rate instruments are generally lower than for comparable fixed rate bonds. They offer the investor some protection against inflation.

Payment Periods

Generally, interest on corporate bonds is paid semiannually, although it could be paid at whatever period the issuer identified in the indenture.

Yield

The yield of a bond is the relationship of the return on the investment compared to the price of the bond. Two commonly quoted yields for corporates are current annual yield and yield-to-maturity.

Current Yield

The current yield is the annual rate of return on an investment, which is a ratio of the instrument's return compared to its cost. A bond's yield is inversely related to its price, and therefore varies in relation to any changes in price. When a bond's yield drops, the price of the bond rises.

Yield-to-Maturity

A yield-to-maturity is the total annualized amount of interest earned over the life of an instrument, adjusted for the purchase premium, and divided by the amount invested. This is a more meaningful number for investors since it identifies the total return an investor will receive if they hold the bond until it matures.

Yield Curve

The yield curve is a graphical view of how interest rates relate to time. The most used yield curve is for the 30 year Treasury bond; however, separate yield curves can be constructed for corporate bond issue, based upon their relative risk.

Interest Accrual

Corporate bonds trade with accrued interest included between interest payments. Interest is usually paid semi-annually as follows:

- Jan & July
- Feb & Aug
- Mar & Sep
- April & Oct
- May & Nov
- June & Dec

For corporate and municipal bonds, the year is equally divided. Every month has 30 days, and every year has 360 days. Corporate bonds are priced either in points or in eighths or sixteenths. The par value is usually $1,000, and they can often be called early for a premium.

Processing

Corporate fixed income securities are cleared on the street-side of the trade, broker-to-broker, through the NSCC and are settled either directly between the broker and their client (for retail clients) or through the DTC (for institutional clients).

Risks

There are three primary categories of fixed income risk.

Interest Rate Risk

The price of corporate bonds, like all fixed income securities, will rise and fall in value inversely to changes in interest rates. The degree of the relationship is based upon any changes in the underlying credit worthiness of the issuer or the instrument and the length of the maturity, with longer maturities tending to be more volatile. The only points at which an investor can accurately predict the price of a bond will be at a put, call or maturity.

Credit Risk

The amount of interest that a firm must pay is based upon the perceived credit worthiness of the issuer. If the perceived credit rating of the firm or the issue changes during the life of the bond, the yield will change and the price of the bond will change accordingly although the interest payment will not change.

Junk bonds are now called high yield bonds, and are becoming popular again. A junk bond is one with a low credit rating and therefore a higher degree of risk and a corresponding higher yield. Bonds with ratings equal to or lower than the following are considered speculative or high risk:

- Standard & Poor's   BB
- Fitch   BB
- Dun & Bradstreet   BB
- Moody's   Ba

Despite this higher level of perceived risk and past notoriety, it is important to note that very few of the junk bonds of the 1980s actually defaulted, and that there is a significant premium that is paid to accommodate this risk. This increase in risk can yield as much as 7% over comparable term U.S. government bonds.

Call and Refunding Risk

A call occurs when the issuer of a bond makes a call notice in accordance with the terms of the bond indenture. A call could include all of the outstanding bonds or a portion of the outstanding issue. The owners (or the selected sub-set of the owners) of the bond must present their bonds for redemption. Bonds are usually called at a small premium to the current market price.

Although the issuer may have the right to call the bond, it may elect to not make the call. This creates uncertainty for the bondholder. However, if interest rates drop and the issuer can refinance the bonds at a lower rate, the issuer almost certainly will do so.

Because of this uncertainty, callable bonds usually have higher yields than non-callable issues, and the call itself may be issued at a premium. Bonds with calls will usually have specific times when the issuer has the right to call the issue. For instance, a bond could be issued that is:

- Non-callable for five years
- Callable at 102% from years five through ten
- Callable at 101% from year ten through maturity

Sinking Fund

A Sinking Fund is a trust fund that is established by the issuer of a corporate or municipal bond for the purpose of accumulating capital for the annual future repayment of principal. Sinking funds obligate the issuer to make periodic contributions to the trust, and are often established when the credit worthiness of the issuer is in doubt.

The portion of the outstanding bonds that are refunded each year is determined by a lottery conducted by the issuer's corporate trust redemption agent.

Puts

A put bond is one that gives the bondholder the right at specific points in time to sell the bond back to the issuer for full face value prior to maturity. Put bonds generally provide a lower yield than comparable bonds without a put privilege.

Taxation

There are three taxation concepts associated with corporate bonds:

Interest

Interest paid on corporate bonds is taxable as regular income at the Federal, state and local level, subject to the taxability of the bondholder and the taxing jurisdiction.

Gains and Losses

The actual amount of a gain or a loss on the sale of a corporate bond is taxable as regular income if it is sold in less than one year. Bonds held more than one year is subject to the lower capital gains tax. Capital gains tax rules can change from year to year.

Original Issue Discount

A security that is issued with an original issue discount (OID) is one that originally sold for less than its face value. An investor buys an OID security with the expectation that the value of the security will steadily increase as the issue approaches maturity and redemption at its face value.

The IRS taxes the annual appreciation in the bond's value as though it is regular income.

C. MUNICIPAL FIXED INCOME SECURITIES

Marketplace

Purpose

A municipal security is a debt instrument that is issued by a U.S. state or local government to fund projects such as roads, bridges and schools, or to fund operating budgets. Muni bonds are normally exempt from federal tax and are also generally exempt from state and local taxes for the investors who reside in the state or municipality where the bond is issued. A muni usually carries a fixed rate of interest, which is normally paid semi-annually.

Regulators

Prior to 1975 there were no rules governing municipal securities. At that time the industry established an independent Self Regulating Organization, called the Municipal Securities Rulemaking Board (MSRB), which was designed to establish rules for regulating the issuance, trading, clearance and settlement of munis.

The MSRB does not enforce any rules. Enforcement of the MSRB rules is accomplished by several government agencies as a part of their normal enforcement activities:

- SEC overall
- NASD for non-bank dealers
- Federal Reserve, FDIC and Comptroller of the Currency for banks

Issuers

Municipal securities are obligations of the political sub-divisions of the U.S. government, which includes U.S. states, cities, towns, etc. States have greater taxing power than their political sub-divisions (cities, towns, etc.) and can rely on corporate and personal income taxes, sales tax, gasoline, etc., to help repay the principal and interest. Since local issues don't have the taxing power of the state, they usually rely on *ad valorem* taxes, which include real property taxes.

Investors

Individuals, Mutual Funds, Money Market Funds, insurance companies, and commercial banks hold tax-exempt municipals.

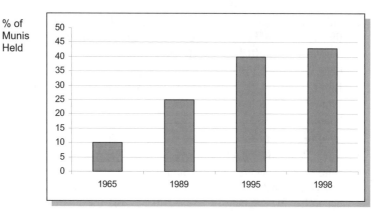

Figure 266 - Percent of Munis Held by Individual Investors

Most munis that are purchased by individuals are held to maturity and there is very little liquidity. As the graph shows, most bonds that are not held by bond traders are in the hands of individual investors.

Certificate Form

Bearer

Munis were generally issued in bearer form prior to July 1983, and now only few remain available in the market.

Registered

Since July 1983, municipal bonds have been issued only in registered form, as a result of a law passed by congress in 1982.

Book Entry

An increasing number of municipal bonds are now issued only in book entry form.

Classifications

Municipal securities consist of notes, which typically mature in a year or less, and bonds, which usually mature in more than a year.

Bonds are usually sold to finance capital projects over the longer term and are issued as either serial bonds or term bonds.

Serial Bonds

Serial bonds are issued so that the issue matures at predefined points in time. The nominal yield is usually the same for each series, but the yield to maturity will vary with the length of the maturity.

Term Bonds

All of the bonds in a term bond issue mature on a single date, and may involve a sinking fund. Term bonds may be quoted as a dollar amount, rather than a percent, and are also called *dollar bonds*.

There are two major kinds of municipal bonds: General Obligation Bonds and Revenue Bonds.

General Obligation Bonds

GOs are backed by the full faith, credit and taxing power of the municipality that issues the bonds, without any limits on the rate and amount, and are normally supported by the issuer's taxing power. General obligation bonds must be voter-approved.

Limited tax bonds are a form of GO bond and while the town may place the limit, the voters have to approve any new taxes that are required to repay the bond.

Revenue Bonds

Revenue bonds are issued to finance specific revenue producing projects such as toll roads, bridges, power plants, etc. The money raised by a revenue bond is used to construct a public facility to be used by the public. Then the revenue generated by the facility is used to pay off the interest and principal to the bondholders. The municipality does generally not guarantee these bonds and if the facility goes into default, the bondholder does not get paid.

Security for revenue bonds is established by the bond's protective covenants, which requires the municipality to maintain the revenue producing entity so that the bonds can be repaid. Some of these conditions can require that the municipality must:

- Establish rates that are sufficient to meet the on-going operation and maintenance of facility as well as generate sufficient income to repay the debt

- Have insurance to cover all contingencies

- Keep the revenue producing facility working and producing revenue

Special Tax Bonds

For special tax bonds the interest and principal due will only be paid from the proceeds of a particular tax or specific sources of funds. These bonds only tax those individuals who consume specific taxable goods and services such as cigarettes, liquor, movie tax, etc.

Industrial Revenue Bonds

Industrial revenue bonds are used to finance the construction of industrial plants, and are repaid by the lease payments that are received.

Double Barrel Bonds

On occasion, a state creates a double barrel bond. A double barrel bond is a municipal bond that is backed by a special tax or specific revenue and is also backed by the full faith and credit of the municipality.

Other Bonds

There are some other ways to categorize municipal bonds:

Housing Authority Bonds

These bonds are used to finance low-income housing and are backed by the U.S. Federal Housing Assistance Agency (FHA). The proceeds from these bonds are used to build middle and lower income housing.

Insured Municipal Bonds

Municipal bonds can be backed by insurance that is provided to reduce investment risk. If a muni defaults, the insurance company that guarantees the payment will pay the interest and principal that are due.

Variable Rate Bonds

Variable rate bonds are established with a defined relationship to a specific base rate, such as the Fed Funds rate, and are attractive in a rising interest-rate environment. These instruments are sometimes also called variable rate demand obligations (VRDO).

Deep Discount Bonds

Deep discount bonds can be issued with a zero coupon and are sold at a discount to the stated face value of the bond. Rather than receive interest payments throughout the life of the bond, the investor buys a highly discounted value and redeems the bond for the face value at maturity, or sells it prior to maturity for the value at that time.

Put Bonds

Put bonds have a feature that allows investors to redeem the bond at its face value on a specific date, or range of dates, prior to maturity.

Notes

Short-term muni debt is sometimes referred to as a municipal note. These are sold at a discount on a yield-to-maturity basis, and are generally tax-free.

Notes are normally issued by municipalities to raise money that is anticipated to be received from future taxes, state or federal aid payments, and bond proceeds and is generally used to:

- Provide funding for irregular cash flows
- Cover unanticipated deficits
- Raise immediate capital for projects until long-term financing can be arranged

Revenue Anticipation Note

A revenue anticipation note (RAN) is a form of short-term debt that is issued by a municipality, and which is designated to be redeemed with some anticipated revenue.

Tax Anticipation Note

A tax anticipation note (TAN) is a short-term debt instrument issued by a municipality that is to be repaid by the revenues that will be received from a future tax period.

Bond Anticipation Note

A bond anticipation note (BAN) is a short to medium-term debt instrument that has been issued by a municipality to fill a need prior to a new bond issue.

Municipal Derivatives

Derivatives can be created using municipal securities as the underlying instrument.

Floaters and Inverse Floaters

A municipal fixed rate bond can be used as the basis for variable interest rate derivatives called floaters and inverse floaters.

A floater is created when an underwriter commits to pay a variable interest rate that is pegged (associated) to another rate such as the Consumer Price Index (CPI).

If the fixed interest rate is 6%, and the floater is determined to yield 3.5% based upon the pegged interest rate, then the inverse floater will receive 2.5%.

Fixed Interest Rate	6.0 %
Calculated Floater Rate	- 3.5 %
Remaining Inverse Floater Rate	2.5 %

Detached Call Options

Most municipal issuers are created with a call provision. At the time of issuance, the issuer could decide to detach the call provision from the bond and sell it into the market as a separate instrument.

Once the call provision has been sold, the owner of the provision has the right to call the bond under the terms of the provision.

- In this case, if the owner of the bond buys a right to call the instrument, the investor is protected from a call by the issuer.

- If another investor buys the call, then that investor has the right to call the bond if they perceive the conditions to be the correct time to exercise the call.

Characteristics

Trading

The municipal bond market is entirely OTC and involves broker/dealers acting as market makers. Since the market for individual munis is very thin, the buy/sell price is usually determined by a few market makers, and can vary significantly from broker-to-broker.

Information on municipal bonds can be found in the *Blue List*, the *Bond Buyer* and *Munifacts*. Retail investors can see the prices for completed trades on the Bond Market Association's web-site, www.investingbonds.com.

Transaction Costs

Investors usually pay a mark-up/mark-down of between .5 to 3%, rather than a commission, and the settlement price includes accrued interest.

Liquidity

Although there are more than 2,000 banks and securities dealer firms that are registered to buy and sell municipal securities, not all will trade every security, and overall, the muni market is not very liquid. Most munis are bought and held to maturity by individual investors.

Pricing

Most tax-exempt municipal bonds and notes are issued in denominations of $5,000 and multiples of $5,000.

Maturity

A bond matures at a point in the future that is defined when the issue is created. Municipal bond maturities are generally classified in three groups:

- Short-term notes have maturities of one to four years
- Medium-term notes/bonds have maturities of five to twelve years
- Long-term bonds mature in more than twelve years

Interest

In general, until a bond matures, it will continue to pay the defined interest rate, and at maturity the principal will be repaid.

Payment Periods

Bond interest is usually paid semiannually, while interest on notes is usually paid at maturity.

When a muni is issued, it is normally dated on either the first or the fifteenth of a month. This date, called the *dated date*, determines the beginning of the interest accrual period, regardless of when the new issue is actually sold, which is called the *issue date*.

Yield

There are basically two types of bond yields for munis:

- Current yield is the annual return on the dollar amount paid for a bond
- Yield-to-maturity is the total return received by holding a bond until it matures, which includes interest and any gain or loss

Since GO bonds are fully backed by the municipality and are therefore considered safer than revenue bonds, they require a lower yield, as shown in the following graph

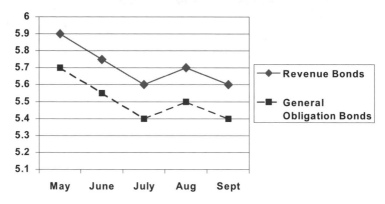

Yields as of September 5, 1997

Figure 267 - Comparison of Bond Yields

Overall, municipals pay a lower rate of interest than corporate bonds since they are generally tax-free to people who live in the taxing jurisdiction.

The comparable tax yield (or equivalent tax income) is a way to compare the yield on a taxable bond to the yield on a muni.

For example, if the muni has a 5% interest rate, and the client is in a 39.6% maximum bracket, then the comparable yield can be calculated as follows:

$1,000 x 5%	= $50.00	Interest paid
$50.00 / (1- 39.6%)	= $82.78	Tax adjusted interest paid
$82.78/$1000	= 8.3%	Comparable yield

Therefore a non-taxable yield of 5% is equivalent to a taxable yield of 8.3% if the investor is in the 39.6% tax bracket.

Interest Accrual

Generally, interest on municipal bonds is paid semiannually, although it could be paid at whatever time is defined by the issuer in the indenture. Interest is accrued between the payment periods, and a buyer must pay the accrued interest to the seller since the buyer will receive the full interest payment on the next pay date.

Example

Bonds	Coupon	Maturity	Price	Chg.	Bid Yield
Jacksonville Hth Fac	5.375	08-15-29	96 1/2	- 1/8	5.62
Jefferson Co Ala Swr	5.000	02-01-33	91 1/2	- 1/4	5.56
Mass Tpk Auth	5.000	01-01-39	90 5/8	- 3/8	5.59
Miami-Dade Co Fla Wtr	5.000	10-01-29	93 3/8	- 1/4	5.45
NJ Hlth Fac Fin Auth	5.250	07-01-29	97 1/4	- 1/4	5.44

Annual Interest Payment — *Closing Price*

Source: Wall Street Journal

Figure 268 - Interest Payments

Summary

The following excerpt is from an article that was published in the Wall Street Journal several years ago, and is a very good description of how a muni bond is issued. It identifies many of the terms that are commonly used in the muni market:

"In the municipal market, a huge proposed new issue of New York City bonds was *tentatively priced* yesterday by a *group of underwriters*, led by Goldman Sachs & Co. City officials said the issue is expected to total around $450 million of *general obligation bonds*. Proceeds will be *used to refund* previously issued bond sold when interest rates were higher.

The issue was tentatively priced to yield from 5.4% to ... according to a Goldman Sachs' spokesman.

New York officials said the sale... includes the *first insured bonds* ever issued by the city. ... That $87 million of debt will be insured by the Financial Guarantee Insurance Co. Another $65.3 million of debt, which matures from 2004 through 2006, will be insured by Bond Insurance Guarantee...

All the insured bonds are *rated triple-A* by both Moody's Investors Service, Inc. and Standard & Poor's Corp. The city expects the rest of the bonds to be *rated Baa-a by Moody's and BBB+* by S&P, the comptroller's office said."

Source: Wall Street Journal

Figure 269 - Example of Municipal Newspaper Article

Processing

Municipal fixed income securities are cleared on the street-side of the trade, broker-to-broker, through the NSCC and are settled either directly between the broker and their client, or through the DTC.

Risks

Interest Rate Risk

The price of municipal bonds, like all fixed income securities, will rise and fall in value inversely to the changes in interest rates. The degree of the relationship is based upon any changes in the underlying creditworthiness of the issuer of the instrument and the length of the maturity, with longer maturities tending to be more volatile. The only points at which an investor can predict the actual price of a bond will be at a put, call or maturity.

Market Risk

The market risk for municipal securities changes as market conditions change.

Credit Ratings

Credit ratings are established for municipalities and their issues to assist the investor and the marketplace in determining the value of specific munis.

Taxation

Interest

When the U.S. income tax was established in 1913, municipal securities were considered exempt from U.S. tax. This ruling remained in effect until the Tax Reform Act of 1986 was passed, and it was clarified that the federal government does have the right to tax municipals. However, the federal government has not elected to enact a general tax on municipals.

Instead, the Act distinguished between munis issued prior to 8/15/86, and after. Bonds issued after that date were defined in three categories:

Public Purpose Bonds

This type of bond is issued directly by the municipality to fund typical municipal projects, and is non-taxable at the city, state and federal level.

Private Activity Bonds

Private activity bonds are issued by municipalities and private firms such as sports arenas, and are subject to federal tax, but may be exempt from local and state taxation.

Non-Governmental Purpose Bonds

Non-governmental purpose bonds are issued for activities that do not support the government nor do they support private activities. They are most often used for public housing and student loan programs. These instruments are subject the Federal Alternative Minimum Tax (AMT).

Taxable and tax-exempt interest must be reported on tax returns.

Gains and Losses

Gains and losses are reported as ordinary income or as capital gains if they have been held longer than twelve months.

D. U.S. Government Fixed Income Securities

Marketplace

Purpose

The U.S. Treasury market was established over 200 years ago, and is currently the world's largest securities market with more than five times the dollar volume of the New York Stock Exchange. The U.S. government relies on this market to raise funds to pay its bills, finance any deficit and as a tool to manage the U.S. economy.

Government debt securities are direct obligations of the U.S. Government. Treasury bills, notes and bonds are generally considered nearly risk-free, and the interest rates for this class of security establish a floor, or benchmark, on interest costs for companies and consumers; however, market prices can change rapidly and frequently, resulting in the possibility of trading risks. Interest rate risks exist because government securities are very sensitive to changes in interest rates.

Regulators

Supervision of the Treasury bond market is shared between three entities:

- The Federal Reserve Bank of New York designates the primary dealers
- The Treasury Department sells the securities at auction and determines the bidding winners
- The Securities and Exchange Commission supervises the securities dealers.

In recent years, government regulation of the Treasury market was somewhat deficient and scandals occurred in the form of price manipulation and improper bidding.

Issuers

The U.S. government is the issuer of all U.S. Treasury securities.

U.S. Federal Agencies can also issue bonds, which are either regular bonds or asset backed securities, which are discussed later in this chapter.

Investors

Investors in U.S. Treasuries could be individuals and/or institutions anywhere in the world.

Certificate Form

All U.S. Treasury securities are issued in book-entry form only. When an investor purchases directly from the Treasury, they receive a receipt, but no certificate, as evidence of ownership.

Classifications

U.S. Treasury Bill

U.S. Treasury Bills are short-term instruments issued by the U.S. Government. They are extremely liquid, and have an active secondary market. Bills are issued through a Dutch auction process every Tuesday for 3 and 6-month bills, and once a month for 12-month bills.

T-Bills are issued at a discount from the face amount, in multiples of $5,000, in amounts from $10,000 to $1,000,000. They are issued in bearer form and are only available in book-entry. Yield on T-Bills is calculated on a 360-day basis, versus 365 days for the other U.S. government interest-bearing securities, and uses the actual number of days remaining until maturity.

They are quoted on a yield-to-maturity basis, where the higher the yield the lower the market value, and conversely, the higher the market value the lower the yield. This is the only situation where the reported bid is higher than the asked price. For example:

Bid	Asked
4.71	4.67

With the asked price set at a discount of 4.67%, the investor would have to pay the following for a $10,000 T-Bill that matures in 23 days:

$10,000 x .0467 x (23 days/360 days) = $ 29.836

$10,000 - $29.84   = $9,970.16

Therefore, the investor would pay $9,970.16 today and receive $10,000 in 23 days when they redeemed the T-Bill.

Treasury bills are listed in daily newspapers on a yield-to-maturity basis, which show the following information:

- The maturity date
- The number of days to maturity
- The closing bid and asked prices quoted as a discount to maturity
- The change from the previous day
- Yield-to-maturity

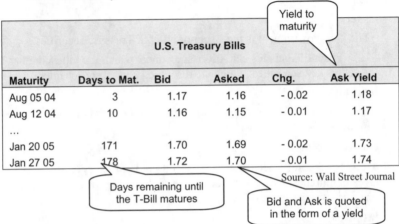

Maturity	Days to Mat.	Bid	Asked	Chg.	Ask Yield
Aug 05 04	3	1.17	1.16	- 0.02	1.18
Aug 12 04	10	1.16	1.15	- 0.01	1.17
...					
Jan 20 05	171	1.70	1.69	- 0.02	1.73
Jan 27 05	178	1.72	1.70	- 0.01	1.74

U.S. Treasury Bills

Yield to maturity

Source: Wall Street Journal

Days remaining until the T-Bill matures

Bid and Ask is quoted in the form of a yield

Figure 270 - Sample of U.S. Treasury Bills

The table shows the following information:

- The date of the maturity
- The days left to maturity
- The closing bid and asking price for the day as a yield for the day
- The change from the prior day's asking price
- The yield-to-maturity on the asking price

U.S. Treasury Notes

U.S. Treasury notes are an intermediate debt obligation of the U.S. government that is not callable. They are issued usually for one to ten years with denominations that range from $1,000 to $500,000,000.

Treasury notes are issued at *par*, with interest paid semi-annually, and are actively traded. They are quoted as a percentage of par and are traded in 32nds of a point.

U.S. Treasury Bonds

U.S. Treasury bonds are long-term debt issued by the U.S. government, with maturities from 10 to 30 years, in denominations of $1,000 to $1,000,000. The 30 year bond is an industry benchmark, and is called the long bond.

Term Bonds

Term bonds are a special type of Treasury bonds which have a double maturity date and which can be called by the government, provided they give the holder four months notice. These bonds, however, are rarely called. For example, bonds can mature in 1987 or 1992, in 1988 or 1993, or in 1989 or 1994, but they are always five years apart. The government may call the bonds at any time after the first date.

Since they can be called, they are quoted on a yield-to-call basis, rather than a yield-to-maturity.

Flower Bonds

Flower bonds were created as a special issue with the last bonds maturing in 1998. An investor could buy these bonds at a discount and, upon the death of the investor; the heirs could redeem the bonds at par to pay estate taxes.

Treasury Bonds and Notes – Examples

Treasury bonds and notes are usually listed chronologically in the same table as shown in the next table with the notes identified in some fashion. In this example, they are identified with an '*n*'.

U.S. Treasury Bonds and Notes					
Rate	Maturity	Bid	Asked	Chg.	Ask Yield
2.250	July 04 n	100.00	100.00	-	2.22
2.125	Aug 04 n	100.02	100.03	-	0.93
13.750	Aug 04	100.13	100.14	- 0.03	0.99
11.625	No	102.28	102.28	- 0.02	1.42

Source: Wall Street Journal

The 'n' indicates that this is a note.

Figure 271 - Sample of U.S. Treasury Bonds and Notes

The table shows the following information:

- The date of the maturity
- Whether it is a bond or a note
- The interest rate of the security
- The closing bid and asking price for the day as a percent of the face value. (This information is stated in 32nds; for instance, the 15 3/4 % bond is bid at 121 16/32.)
- The change from the prior day's asking price
- The yield-to-maturity

Government Agency Instruments

There are two types of government agencies that can either borrow form the government or issue securities to finance their operations:

Federally Related Institutions

These agencies are a part of the government. For example, the Government National Mortgage Association (GNMA) issues mortgage backed securities, which are discussed later in this chapter.

Government Sponsored Entities

Government Sponsored Agencies (also called Federally Sponsored Agencies or Enterprises) are not a part of the government; however, some of the securities issued by these agencies are guaranteed as to principal and/or interest and are therefore treated the same as direct obligations of the Government.

FSAs also have a line of credit at the Treasury Department, exemption from certain taxes, and favorable classifications by the Federal Reserve System. They are authorized to purchase debt directly from the Treasury for resale, which allows them access to a very cost-effective source of funding.

These corporations are chartered by the Federal government and can borrow funds in capital markets and lend them to selective sectors at favorable rates. FSAs are widely perceived as having an implicit government guarantee of their debt.

While it is beyond the scope of this book to define all of the details of these agencies, the reader should understand that there are many different issuers, each of which creates a slightly different instrument

Farm Credit Financial Assistance Corporation (FCFAC)

The Farm Credit Financial Assistance Corporation was established to provide support for the FFCBS when it began having financial difficulties in 1987.

Federal Farm Credit Bank System (FFCBS)

The Federal Farm Credit Bank System is responsible for providing loans to U.S. farms.

Federal Financing Bank (FFB)

The FFB was established by the Federal Financing Bank Act of 1973 to consolidate and reduce the government's cost of financing a variety of Federal agencies and other borrowers whose obligations are guaranteed by the Federal government. The bank is authorized to purchase any obligation that is issued, sold, or guaranteed by a Federal agency.

Federal Home Loan Savings Bank (FHLSB)

The FHLSB was established in 1932 to provide short-term liquidity and long-term credit to Savings and Loan Banks.

Federal Home Loan Mortgage Corporation (FHLMC)

The Federal Home Loan Mortgage Corporation, also known as Freddie Mac, was established in 1970 to create a national secondary market for mortgages.

Federal Land Banks (FLB)

There are 12 Federal Land Banks around the country that are made up of local farmers. The purpose of this agency is to make first mortgages to its farmer members.

Federal National Mortgage Association (FNMA)

FNMA is still considered a quasi-governmental agency since the government guarantees its bonds; however, as of 1968, Fannie Mae has been a publicly owned corporation and is traded on the NYSE.

The Federal National Mortgage Association provides a secondary market for FHA and Veteran's Administration guaranteed mortgages.

Financing Corporation (FICO)

The Financing Corporation was established in 1987 to help support Savings and Loan Associations.

Resolution Trust Company (RTC)

The Resolution Trust Company was formed in 1989 to assist the FICO deal with the problems involved with the S&L crisis.

Student Loan Mortgage Association (SLMA)

The Student Loan Mortgage Association, also known as Sallie Mae, was established in 1972 to create a secondary market for securitized student loans.

World Bank

World Bank bonds are guaranteed by the U.S. government and are fully taxable.

U.S. Treasury Derivatives

Bonds have two components, an obligation to repay the principal and an obligation to make a defined stream of interest payments for the life of the bond. In 1980, corporate finance specialists realized that there were categories of investors who wanted to purchase securities that provided one or another of these obligations, but who didn't want both.

Brokers took the opportunity to buy U.S. Treasury bonds, placed these bonds into a bank custody account as collateral, and issued two new derivative instruments:

Zero Coupon Bond

The Zero Coupon bond is a promise to repay the principal at maturity, and is consequently sold at a discount prior to maturity. A zero is sold at a deep discount and is repaid at par when it matures.

Individual brokerage firms issued their own unique securities, which included:

BEARS

BEARS is an acronym for Bonds Earning Accrued Returns.

CATs

Salomon Brothers issued these as Certificates of Accrual on Treasury Securities.

TIGRs

Merrill Lynch issued these as Treasury Investment Growth Certificates.

Although the zeros were based originally upon U.S. government securities, these broker-sponsored derivatives are issued by brokerage firms and are not backed by the U.S. Government. The investor is relying upon the issuer to repay the interest and principal.

In 1985, the U.S. Treasury established a mechanism to support the issuance of zeros that are backed directly by the Treasury, and to provide for the recombination of the zeros with their interest payments.

Strip

A Strip represents the obligation to pay a stream of interest payments until maturity. The purchaser of a strip will receive income payments regularly until the underlying instrument matures, but will not receive any repayment of principal.

U.S. Government Derivatives

The Treasury began to strip and reconstitute bonds after the market was established. With the Treasury's participation, the market for these instruments has grown significantly.

These issues are called STRIPS (Separate Trading of Registered Interest and Principal of Securities).

Debt Options

There are two kinds of Debt Options:

Price-Based Options

The underlying securities for price-based debt securities are Treasury bonds, notes and bills. Price-based options give the holder the right to purchase or sell the underlying debt security or to receive a cash settlement payment based on the value of an underlying debt. Similar to equity options, price-based calls become more valuable as the price of the underlying debt security increases, and price-based puts become more valuable as the price of the underlying debt security decreases.

Yield-Based Options

Yield-based options that are cash-settled are based on the difference between the exercise price and the value of an underlying yield.

The underlying yields of yield-based options will increase as interest rates increase, and vice-versa, therefore yield-based calls become more valuable as yields rise, and puts become more valuable as yields decrease. The value of yield-based options is based upon the relationship between interest rates or yields, and the price of a debt security.

All yield-based options are cash-settled European-style options, and the underlying yield of these options is the annualized yield-to-maturity of the most recently issued Treasury security of the specific type of Treasury bond, note or bill.

TIPs - Treasury Inflation Protection Bonds [95]

The U.S. Treasury recently offered a new type of security, a Treasury Inflation-Indexed Security, with a principal amount that is adjusted for inflation. The purpose of issuing inflation-indexed securities is to reduce interest costs to the Treasury over the long-term and increase the types of debt instruments that are available to investors in the U.S. financial markets.

These instruments tend to be bought and held, are illiquid, and are difficult to price since they are based upon the Consumer Price Index. The initial bonds were issued for ten years and will mature in 2007. The CBOT has already issued options and futures on TIPs.

Principal Amount

The principal amount of Treasury inflation-indexed securities is adjusted to reflect changes in the level of inflation. The inflation-adjusted principal amount of the securities can be calculated daily; however, the inflation adjustment will not be payable by the Treasury until maturity, when the securities will be redeemed at their inflation-adjusted principal amount or par (the principal amount of the securities on the date of original issuance), whichever is greater.

Index

The index for measuring the inflation rate is the non-seasonally adjusted CPI-U. Treasury selected the U.S. City Average *All Items Consumer Price Index for All Urban Consumers* because it is the best known and most widely accepted measure of inflation.

Interest Payments

Every six months, the Treasury will pay interest based on a fixed rate of interest determined at auction. Semi-annual interest payments are determined by multiplying the current inflation-adjusted principal amount by one-half the stated rate of interest on each interest payment date.

Example

Suppose an individual invests $1,000 on January 15 in a new inflation-indexed 10-year note with a 3% real rate of return.

- If inflation was 1% during the first six months of that year, then by mid-year the inflation-adjusted principal amount of the security would be $1,010.

- In addition, at mid-year, on July 15, the investor would receive the first semiannual interest payment of $15.15 ($1,010 times 3% divided by two).

- Suppose, then, that inflation accelerated during the second half of the year, so that it reached 3% for the full year.

- By the second semiannual interest payment date, January 15, the inflation-adjusted principal amount of the security would be $1,030.

---

[95]   Source: U.S. Treasury

- The second semiannual interest payment would be $15.45 ($1,030 times 3% divided by two).

Payment at Maturity

If, at maturity, the inflation-adjusted principal is less than the par amount of the security (due to deflation), the final payment of principal of the security by Treasury will not be less than the par amount of the security at issuance. In such a circumstance, Treasury will pay an additional amount at maturity so that the additional amount plus the inflation-adjusted principal will equal the par amount of the securities on the date of original issuance.

Maturity

Initially, the securities have been issued with a 10-year maturity; however, Treasury expects to issue other maturities over time.

Stripping

The securities were eligible for the U.S. Treasury STRIPS program as of the first issue date. Unlike the conventional STRIPS program; however, interest components that are stripped from different inflation-indexed securities, at least initially, will not be interchangeable or fungible with interest components from other securities, even if they have the same payment or maturity date.

Characteristics

Trading

Transactions often involve large amounts and the differences between bid and ask prices are often as low as 1 basis point ($25 per $ 1 million face value on a 90-day bill). Interest rate expectations and the state of the market usually determine the actual spread.

U.S. Government Dealing

Inter-dealer trading in the government securities market is highly organized, with specific brokers specializing in bringing together buyers and sellers. Most of the trading is done by phone since there is no centralized marketplace. Up to the minute prices are available electronically.

Primary Dealers

The New York Federal Reserve Bank trades government securities in the primary market with a defined list of firms, called primary dealers. Currently, there are 40 large commercial and investment banks authorized as primary dealers. These primary dealers must participate meaningfully in Treasury auctions with realistic bids.

Primary dealers can purchase government securities directly from the Federal Reserve System in return for maintaining markets in Treasury debt. Generally, each dealer must maintain average client trading volume in government securities of at least 1% of the total of all of the primary dealer's client volume. Dealers do not charge a commission on their own trades, but try to sell securities at prices above the cost of the securities.

Dealer Characteristics

Primary dealers can purchase directly from the Fed, but they must make a market in order to continue as a primary dealer. Dealers will purchase and sell for their own account and for their clients.

The market is over-the-counter, and is typically conducted by phone, with very high volume and narrow spreads. On an average day, approximately $545 billion is traded.

Transaction Costs

Investors can buy and sell U.S. Treasury instruments from/to any broker, and will generally pay a commission.

TRADES

Government dealers use the Fed's TRADES system to record the wholesale purchases of Treasury securities. Only banks can deal directly with the Fed's systems and the banks are connected to the dealers through various proprietary links.

Treasury Direct

The Treasury Direct system is used by retail investors who wish to purchase Treasury securities directly from the U.S. Treasury at a cost of only $34 per trade. This market has over 800,000 investors, 85% of whom are over 55 years old.

Until 1999, investors could walk into a Federal Reserve District office and purchase government securities. In August, that was changed so that purchases can only be made by phone or on the Internet.

Liquidity

The U.S. Treasury market is the largest and most liquid in the world.

Pricing

Transactions often involve large amounts. Differences between bid and ask prices are often as low as 1 basis point ($25 per $1 million face value on a 90-day bill). Interest rate expectations and the state of the market usually determine the spread.

Notes trade in 32nds of a point and a reported price of 97:15 means 97 and 15/32nds. Bonds also trade in 32nds of a point, while the primary dealers and other large traders may trade among themselves with spreads as little as 1/64th of a point.

Maturity

Each U.S. government security is issued for a specific period of time, up to 30 years.

Interest

Interest is paid periodically on bonds and notes, while T-Bills are sold at a discount and redeemed at par at maturity.

Payment Periods

Interest payments are made semi-annually on bonds and notes. Bills are sold at a discount and redeemed at par.

Yield

The yield curve was introduced in the beginning of this book as an academic concept. This graph shows an example of three actual yield curves for U.S. government securities at three points in time.

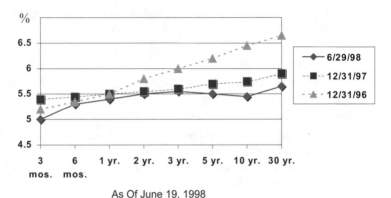

As Of June 19, 1998

Figure 272 - Yield Curve Example

This graph shows that in 1996, the Long Bond was priced at about 6.6%, but by year-end 1997 the rate had dropped to about 5.9%, and in mid-1998 was running at about 5.6%.

When the Fed begins to see inflation as a threat it will begin to increase interest rates. Since this will certainly have a negative impact on the stock market, this curve is an extremely important indicator.

Interest Accrual

U.S. Government bonds and notes also trade with accrued interest, but the calculation is based upon the actual calendar days in the month. Interest for bonds and notes is paid semi-annually, and the calculations are made using the actual number of days in the month and the year.

T-Bills trade at a discount, and do not have accrued interest.

Example

In the following example, an investor bought five $1,000 Treasury Notes at $90 maturing March 1, 2000, with a 4 ½% coupon which pays on Mar. 1 and Sept. 1. If the trade date was Jan 29, 1999, which was a Friday, interest would have been accrued and payable by the buyer to the seller using the actual number of days in each month from the last interest payment through the settlement date.

Sept.	30 Days
Oct.	31
Nov.	30
Dec.	31
Jan.	<u>30</u>
	152 Days

Government bonds and notes use the actual number of days in a regular year or a leap year to calculate interest.

In this example, the last time the owner received interest was September 1, so the buyer owes the seller interest for all of September through January 30, which was the settlement date

One bond receives $ 45.00 per year, or $ 0.1233 / day

152 days x $ 0.1233 = $ 18.74 in accrued interest

$ 18.74 x 5 bonds   = $ 88.70

Processing

Government securities settle the next business day.

Transactions by dealers in the primary market are settled through the banks that are involved in dealer clearance with the Fed.

For transactions in the secondary market, the street-side is cleared between brokers through the Government Securities Division (GSD), and the client-side of the trade is settled directly between the brokers and their client.

Risks

Credit

Government securities are generally considered to be risk-less assets; however, market prices can change rapidly and frequently, resulting in the possibility of trading losses.

Interest Rate

Interest rate risks remain because government securities are sensitive to changes in interest rates.

Taxation

Interest

U.S. Government securities are taxed at the regular Federal income tax rates of the holder, and are exempt from state and local taxes.

Gains and Losses

Gains and losses on U.S. government securities are subject to the regular tax rates of the holder, either at regular income rates if held less than one year or at the capital gains rate if held more than one year.

Original Issue Discount

Zeros are bought at a discount, and either redeemed at par at maturity or sold at a higher price by the investor. Each year that the zero is held, the price increases, or accretes, towards the par value. This annual accretion is considered to be an interest payment and is taxed at the investor's regular income tax rates.

Inflation-Indexed Securities

Federal Tax

The semiannual interest payments on inflation-indexed securities are taxable as the investor receives the payments. If the holder is a corporation or other institutional investor, the interest payments will be taxable either when received or accrued, in accordance with the holders' method of accounting.

Inflation adjustments to the principal will be taxed in the year in which the adjustments occur. Increased inflation will increase the taxable amount and decreases will reduce the amount subject to tax.

State Tax

Like all securities issued by the U.S. Treasury, inflation-indexed securities are exempt from taxation by a state or a political subdivision of a state, except for state estate or inheritance taxes and other exceptions provided in the IRS code.

E. ASSET BACKED SECURITIES

There are several different categories of Asset backed Securities; all involve the packaging of multiple consumer loans into a portfolio that is turned into a single issue of a security. While the most common type is mortgage backed securities, the other asset backed securities are:

- Fixed Rate Credit Cards
- Floating Rate Credit Cards
- Manufactured Housing
- Automobiles
- Home Equity Loans

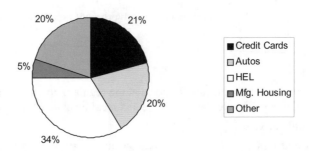

Figure 273 - Distribution of Asset Backed Securities

This chart shows the distribution of different types of asset backed securities, other than mortgage backed.

The mortgage backed process involves the securitization of retail mortgages. Similar individual mortgage loans are place into a pool, and securities are issued so that each security represents a fractional interest in the pool. The next section in this chapter goes into detail about mortgage backed securities.

F. MORTGAGE BACKED SECURITIES

Marketplace

Purpose and History

When mortgages are issued, specific property is used as the collateral for a loan. Historically, banks took in deposits from some people and businesses in their community and made mortgage loans to other people in their local community. These loans were recorded on the bank's books as assets and, by regulation, a portion of these assets had to be offset by the bank's reserves. When the amount of reserves that were required by the Fed for mortgage loans increased, these institutions were automatically encouraged to find ways to decrease the volume of mortgage loans on their books. While the banks still wanted to make the loans, they no longer wanted to maintain them.

The solution was to sell the loans to a loan consolidator that would securitize the mortgage loans and sell the new securities to investors. Initially, mortgages could only be bought and sold by financial institutions. The first mortgage security guaranteed by an agency of the U.S. government was issued in 1970.

There is a primary and a secondary market for MBSs. Mortgage backed securities are typically bought by large institutions, including dealers, when the securities are issued in the primary market, with the average trade valued up to $12 million. Dealers often then re-sell these securities to individual investors through the secondary market.

The U.S. mortgage securities market is now one of the largest financial markets in the world, with a total volume of outstanding mortgage securities well over $4.4 Trillion.

Primary MBS Market

In the primary market, while the issuers are assembling pools of mortgages in a specific category, investors (usually institutional) can begin trading these instruments before they are officially issued. These transactions are trades in what are called To Be Announced (TBA) securities. During this period of time, which can be up to 45 days, TBA securities can be traded. However, all settlement is delayed until the pool number is announced.

Once the number is announced via the mortgage backed securities Clearing Corporation's Electronic Pool Notification system, the securities are netted and settled.

Secondary Market for Dealers

After a new MBS has been distributed, it begins trading in the secondary market.

A characteristic of MBSs is that the amount of the principal constantly decreases as people make mortgage payments and pay off their loans. Since the amounts are constantly changing, a buyer can not buy a specific pool for its face value; so, for example, traders and investors cannot say that they want to buy 100 bonds. Instead they say that they want to buy a specific amount of a 7.5% GNMA, such as $1,000,000.

Regulators

The Securities and Exchange Commission regulates the market for mortgage backed securities. In addition, the MBS Division of the DTC and the MBSCC are SROs that are directly involved in setting MBS regulations.

Issuers

Mortgage backed securities can be issued by U.S. government Agencies, which are a part of the U.S. Government, and Federally Sponsored Agencies (FSA), which are independent corporations that have the backing of the U.S. Government.

- U.S. Government Agencies include departments of the U.S. government such as the Government National Mortgage Agency and the Federal Housing Administration.

- The Federally Sponsored Agencies include activities where the U.S. government may guarantee the payment of principal and interest, but the organizations may be totally independent corporations.

These issuers add liquidity to the residential mortgage market by buying mortgages from the original lenders, thereby providing the lenders with funds to lend to additional clients. The issuers sell the securities that represent interests in the pools of mortgages to the marketplace. Regardless of the type of issuer, they all have the same basic functions:

- Purchase qualified mortgage loans that are originated by financial institutions

- Securitize loans

- Distribute the securities through the dealer community

- Provide different levels of guarantees to investors

The agencies that are most commonly involved in the issuance of MBS are:

GNMA (Ginnie Mae)

The Government National Mortgage Association, also called Ginnie Mae, was created in 1968. It is a U.S.-based corporation that is owned by the government and managed by the Department of Housing and Urban Development (HUD) that recycles mortgages. GNMA buys mortgages from banks, thereby giving banks more money to lend for more mortgages, packages the securities into mortgage backed securities, and guarantees them.

The minimum denomination of GNMA certificates is $25,000. While these securities are designed to mature in 40 years, their average life is approximately 12 years because of mortgage prepayments.

The principal and interest payments that are collected by GNMA on specific pools of mortgages are *passed through* to GNMA investors after service and guaranty fees are deducted.

FNMA (Fannie Mae)

Congress established the FNMA, also called Fannie Mae, in 1938 as a government agency to provide a secondary market for FHA and VA-guaranteed mortgages. Although FNMA is an independently owned corporation, it is still considered a quasi-governmental agency since the government guarantees its bonds. FNMA adds liquidity to the residential mortgage market by buying mortgages from original lenders and selling securities that represent interests in pools of mortgages.

By law, mortgages granted under Fannie Mae must have at least a 20% down payment, or be covered by some other form of mortgage insurance.

Read as 100 and 9 / 32nds

U.S. Government Agency Issues				
FNMA Issues				
Rate	Maturity	Bid	Asked	Ask Yield
3.50	9 04	100:07	100:09	1.01
1.88	12 04	100:00	100:02	1.70
7.13	02 05	102:23	102:25	1.81
3.88	03 05	101:04	101:06	1.92

Source: Wall Street Journal

Read as 1.92 %

Figure 274 - Example of US Government Agency Issues Prices

This excerpt shows the rates for a federally sponsored agency issue that is posted in daily newspapers, and shows the following information:

- Coupon rate that is on the original certificate
- Maturity date for the issue
- Bid and asked prices, expressed as a percent or original face value
- Yield-to-maturity
- Change in asking price from the previous day

FHLMC (Freddie Mac)

The Federal Home Loan Mortgage Corporation, also called Freddie Mac, was established in 1970. It is chartered by Congress, and owned by stockholders. The securities that it issues are primarily backed by conventional home mortgage loans, and the government does not guarantee these securities.

By law, mortgages granted under Freddie Mac must have at least a 20% down payment, or be covered by some other form of mortgage insurance.

Federal Agricultural Mortgage Corporation (Farmer Mac)

The FAMC was established in 1988 to provide a secondary market for farm mortgages.

Student Loan Marketing Association (Sallie Mae)

Sallie Mae packages and distributes student loans.

Private Label Mortgage Securities

In addition to the U.S. government agencies issuing mortgage backed securities, there are other firms in the U.S. that issue MBS. Some investment banks and financial institutions can also package various groups of mortgage loans and mortgage pools that are issued as private-label mortgage securities.

Investors

Mortgage backed securities provide a slightly higher return than U.S. Treasury securities for virtually no increase in risk since the U.S. government guarantees most MBSs. The downside is that these securities continuously repay principal throughout the life of the security and the final paydown of the security cannot be precisely determined since it is based upon the paying dynamics of the individual mortgagees.

Individuals, corporations, commercial banks, life insurance companies, pension funds, trust funds and charitable endowments all invest in MBSs.

Certificate Form

All mortgage backed securities are issued in registered form.

Classifications

Mortgage Backed Securities

Mortgage backed securities are bonds that are a general obligation of the issuing agency or institution and are also collateralized by a pool of individual mortgages. Mortgage backed securities were created to:

- Remove assets from the banks' balance sheets
- Provide investors with another form of instrument
- Distribute risk away from a single bank and across multiple investors

The most basic mortgage securities, which are known as pass-through securities or participation certificates (PCs), represent a direct ownership interest in a pool of mortgage loans.

When investors buy a pass-through mortgage backed security, they will receive portions of multiple home mortgage payments, which include the interest and the principal that homeowners make each month. When individuals pay off the remaining principle and close out their mortgages, the investors get the principle as it is repaid.

Although most MBS are backed by fixed-rate mortgage loans, adjustable-rate mortgage loans (ARMs) can also be pooled to create securities.

Collateralized Mortgage Obligations (CMOs or REMICs)

The Collateralized Mortgage Obligation (CMO) was developed in 1983 to expand the market for mortgage securities by creating a new instrument that would appeal to investors with various investment time frames and cash-flow needs. A CMO is a special type of pass-through mortgage backed fixed income instrument that gives the buyer an interest in, but not ownership of, the underlying mortgage assets as do regular MBSs.

The Tax Reform Act of 1986 permitted mortgage securities pools to be taxed as a Real Estate Mortgage Investment Conduit (REMIC), and since then, most new CMOs have been issued in REMIC form because they provide tax and accounting advantages for the issuers.

- In a REMIC, the issuer can use multiple classes of pass through securities.

- The REMIC eliminates the opportunity for tax free arbitrage by banks.

Although the terms are often used interchangeably, CMOs and REMICs are similar, but slightly different types of securities. Each type allows cash flows to be directed to create different classes of securities with different maturities and coupons. Both types may be collateralized directly by mortgage loans or by securitized pools of loans. In the rest of this section, we will use the market convention and refer to both CMOs and REMICs as CMOs. The differences are described later in this chapter.

In a typical mortgage backed security, the investor owns a share of the underlying mortgages proportionate to their investment and receives repayment of principal and interest as it occurs. The investor does not know when the mortgage holders may elect to pay off their mortgages and therefore pay-down the MBS. A CMO is a special form of pass-through security that has been repackaged by the issuer in order to minimize the pre-payment risk.

To manage this risk, CMOs are divided into various segments, or tranches, each of which is assigned a unique CUSIP number. CMOs are designed so that investors in the earlier tranches are repaid their principal in full before the owners of the later tranches are paid any principal. This helps the investor determine when they wish to be repaid and eliminates the risk of early pre-payment for investors who do not wish to have an early repayment.

There are at least five tranches in a CMO, and no limit on the maximum number. Some CMOs have had more than 50 tranches. While the approximate date to complete each tranche is estimated by the issuer, it is not guaranteed and can vary as economic conditions change.

The final tranche of a CMO is often called a Z-bond, which is also known as an accrual bond or accretion bond. The holders of these final tranches receive no cash until the earlier tranches are all paid in full, and while the other tranches are outstanding, the regular interest earned by the Z-bond is added to the initial face amount of the bond but is not yet paid to investors. When all of the other tranches are repaid and retired, the Z-bond receives the interest payments, plus the final principal prepayments from the underlying mortgage loans.

CMOs may be collateralized by

- Ginnie Mae, Fannie Mae or Freddie Mac pass-through issues

- Unsecuritized mortgage loans insured by the Federal Housing Administration or guaranteed by the Department of Veterans' Affairs

- Unsecuritized conventional mortgages

A new *callable pass-through* was created in the mid 1990s, and other types of CMOs exist.

Callable Pass-Through

A callable pass-through CMO is created by splitting a regular MBS pass-through into two classes that meet different investors' needs, which are:

- A Callable Class which receives all of the principal and interest from the underlying collateral

- A Call Class which receives no principal or interest, but which has a right to call the underlying pass-through at a stated price (usually par plus accrued interest) from the Callable Class holders at a specific point in time.

Floating-Rate CMO Tranches

Floating-rate CMO tranches, which are also called floaters, pay a variable rate of interest which has been usually tied to the London Interbank Offered Rate (LIBOR), and which will probably be tied to EURIBOR in the future.

Other types of CMOs

As the CMO has evolved additional classes have been created, including:

- Planned Amortization Class (PAC)
- Targeted Amortization Class (TAC)

These classes were created to reduce an investor's prepayment risk by establishing a sinking-fund structure so that investors will receive payments over a predetermined time period under various prepayment scenarios. With these instruments, the prepayment risk is not eliminated; it is transferred away from the PAC to the TAC holders.

Derivatives

Strips

Stripped mortgage securities were first introduced in 1986, and have been created by segregating the cash flows from the underlying mortgage loans or mortgage securities to create two or more new securities. Each new security can contain a specific proportion of the underlying security's principal payments, interest payments or a combination of interest and principal.

For example, all of the interest could be distributed to one type of security, called an interest-only (IO) security, and all of the principal could be distributed to another instrument, which is known as a principal-only (PO) security. Also, hybrid securities could be created which mix different proportions of interest and principal.

Comparison of Pass-Through Mortgage Securities [96]

The various MBS that are generally available are similar but differ in their guarantee, minimum investment and payment methods, as shown in the following chart.

Security	Guaranteed by:	Minimum Investment	Payment Date
Ginnie Mae I and II	Full-faith-and-credit guarantee of the U.S. Government	$25,000 minimum $1 increments	15th or the 20th of the month for Ginnie Mae I and II pools, respectively, following the record date and every month thereafter
Ginnie Mae Platinum	Full-faith-and-credit guarantee of the U.S. Government	$25,000 minimum $1 increments	"
Fannie Mae MBS	Fannie Mae	$1,000 minimum $1 increments	25th of the month following the record date and every month thereafter
Freddie Mac PC (75-day PC) [97]	Freddie Mac	$1,000 minimum $1 increments	15th of the second month following the record date and every month thereafter
Freddie Mac Gold PC	Freddie Mac	$1,000 minimum $1 increments	"

Figure 275 - Comparison of Pass-Through Mortgage Securities

---

[96] Source: Bond Market Association

[97] A Participation Certificate is a type of a mortgage backed security that represents an interest in a group of mortgages that have been purchased by a mortgage corporation. PCs trade like to GNMAs, but within a much smaller market.

Comparison of CMO / REMIC Mortgage Securities [98]

The leading CMOs and REMICs are also similar, with some slight differences as shown in the following chart.

Security	Guaranteed by:	Minimum Investment	Payment Date
Ginnie Mae REMIC	Full-faith-and-credit guarantee of the U.S. government	$1,000 minimum $1 increments	16th of the month for Ginnie Mae I and the 20th for Ginnie Mae II
Freddie Mac REMIC	Freddie Mac	$1,000 $1 increments (most dealers, require a minimum investment of $1,000 or more)	15th of the month following the record date and every month thereafter
Fannie Mae REMIC	Fannie Mae Fannie Mae "G" series is also backed by the full faith and credit of the U.S. government	$1,000 minimum $1 increments	18th or the 25th of the month following the record date and every month thereafter
Agency-Backed Private Label CMO/REMIC	Ginnie Mae, Fannie Mae or Freddie Mac without a government guarantee	Varies	Varies; may be monthly, quarterly or semiannually; with or without payment delay
Whole Loan Backed Private Label CMO/REMIC	Credit support provided by some combination of issuer or third-party guarantee, letter of credit, over collateralization, pool insurance, and/or subordination. Generally rated AA or AAA	Varies	"

Figure 276 - Comparison of CMO / REMIC Mortgage Securities

Characteristics

Trading

Mortgage backed securities are offered in minimum amounts of $1,000 to $25,000, depending on the issuer, and are traded OTC between broker/dealers and market makers.

There is an active primary market for dealers and a secondary market for institutions and retail investors.

[98] Source: Bond Market Association

Transaction Costs

Transaction costs are generally shown as a mark-up or a mark-down that is combined with the traded price.

Liquidity

There is a national network of securities dealers that are involved in the purchase and sales of MBS in the primary market, and which make a market for other investors. There is a sizable and active secondary market for pass-through mortgage backed securities and a moderate secondary market for CMOs and REMICs that are issued or guaranteed by Ginnie Mae, Fannie Mae, or Freddie Mac, and by private-label mortgage securities issuers.

Pricing

The return on a MBS is determined by the prevailing market interest rates and by the anticipated remaining life of the security, which is estimated as an average life remaining, rather than an actual number of years remaining till maturity.

Maturity

MBS securities can be created with a stated maturity of up to forty years; however, maturity is generally stated as 30 years. An increasing number have maturities of 5, 7, or 15 years. On average, even the longest securities are retired after only twelve years as the homeowners pay off their mortgage loans.

Interest

Interest on mortgage backed securities is defined for each issue.

Payment Periods

Mortgage backed securities usually pay interest and principal monthly, with some paying quarterly or semiannually.

Yield

Investors in mortgage securities earn a coupon rate of interest and receive repayments of principal routinely over the life of the security as the underlying mortgage loans are paid off, rather than in a single lump sum at maturity.

Calculating the yield on a mortgage security investment is similar to other fixed income instruments in that the yield depends on the purchase price, the coupon rate and the length of time the principal is outstanding. Since the remaining life is uncertain, investors must make assumptions regarding the potential prepayments, based on historic prepayment rates. The most widely used prepayment assumption is the Standard Prepayment Model of The Bond Market Association.

This Prepayment Model was designed to help investors standardize the measurement of prepayment risk. "The model assumes that for new mortgage loans the probability of prepayment increases as the mortgage 'seasons,' or ages, eventually reaching a constant rate at 30 months. Both projected and historical prepayment rates are expressed or quoted as a *percentage of PSA* (Prepayment Speed Assumptions)." [99]

---

[99]   Source: Bond Market Association

Interest Accrual

Mortgage backed securities are also traded with accrued interest included.

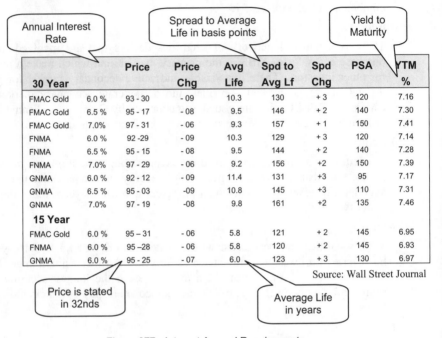

		Price	Price	Avg	Spd to	Spd	PSA	YTM
30 Year			Chg	Life	Avg Lf	Chg		%
FMAC Gold	6.0 %	93 - 30	- 09	10.3	130	+ 3	120	7.16
FMAC Gold	6.5 %	95 - 17	- 08	9.5	146	+ 2	140	7.30
FMAC Gold	7.0%	97 - 31	- 06	9.3	157	+ 1	150	7.41
FNMA	6.0 %	92 -29	- 09	10.3	129	+ 3	120	7.14
FNMA	6.5 %	95 - 15	- 08	9.5	144	+ 2	140	7.28
FNMA	7.0%	97 - 29	- 06	9.2	156	+2	150	7.39
GNMA	6.0 %	92 - 12	- 09	11.4	131	+3	95	7.17
GNMA	6.5 %	95 - 03	-09	10.8	145	+3	110	7.31
GNMA	7.0%	97 - 19	-08	9.8	161	+2	135	7.46
15 Year								
FMAC Gold	6.0 %	95 – 31	- 06	5.8	121	+ 2	145	6.95
FNMA	6.0 %	95 –28	- 06	5.8	120	+ 2	145	6.93
GNMA	6.0 %	95 - 25	- 07	6.0	123	+ 3	130	6.97

Source: Wall Street Journal

Figure 277 - Interest Accrual Requirements

Processing

There are two parts to the processing of MBS:

Processing of Payments

The issuer or the servicer of pass-through securities collects the monthly payments from the homeowners whose loans are in a given pool, and passes-through the cash flow (interest plus repayment of principal) to investors in periodic payments.

Purchase and Sale of MBS

Primary Market

The settlement for new FHLMC and FNMA MBSs and CMOs is through the Fed Wire system, and is conducted through member banks.

Settlement occurs once a month for all MBS, but on different days for different categories of MBS. Between the time of the trade and the settlement, the value of each pool continues to change. The issuer calculates the actual value of each pool once a month, just prior to the official settlement date. The issuers must notify all of the participants of the factor that is used to calculate the actual value, for each category of MBS 48 hours prior to the settlement date.

A factor is the current value of the pool stated as a percentage of the original face value of the pool. For example, if an investor bought $1,000,000 of a

7.5% GNMA, the investor would want to receive an investment worth $1,000,000. However, it is unlikely that the seller will have a pool available that exactly matches the investment. Under market rules (PSA Guidelines), the seller can deliver up to three pools per million dollars to satisfy the sale. Since it is also unlikely that any combination of pools will exactly equal $1,000,000, the seller is allowed to deliver pools that are within +/- 2% of the contracted amount, and the buyer is obligated to pay the actual amount/value of the settlement

In our example, the seller may decide to deliver two pools:

Pool Number	Face Amount	Factor	Actual Value
123456X	$1,000,000	.912345678	$ 912,345.68
123457X	$ 100,000	.891544000	$ 89,154.40
	$1,001,500		$1,001,500.08

Since +/- 2% would be a range of $980,000 to $1,020,000, the total amount due for the two pools ($1,001,500) is within the PSA guidelines.

Secondary Market

Almost all ABSs, MBSs and CMOs are cleared through the MBSCC, while they can settle differently.

GNMA securities are issued in registered form only, and settle at the Participant Trust Company (PTC), which was absorbed by the DTC in 1998 and is now called the MBS Division of the DTC.

Many ABSs and CMOs also settle through the DTC, although not all have sufficient volume to be eligible for the depository. The remaining issues are settled physically between the buyer and seller.

Risks

Pass-through mortgage securities that are issued and/or guaranteed by Ginnie Mae, Fannie Mae or Freddie Mac are rated AAA. MBS issued by other entities are generally privately issued and are usually rated AAA or AA.

While the payments of interest and principal on MBS are considered secure, the cash flow will vary from month to month, based on the actual prepayment rate of the underlying mortgage loans.

Prepayment Risk

To account for the pre-payment risk, mortgage securities are normally priced at a higher yield than Treasury and corporate bonds with a comparable maturity.

Market Risk

MBS prices will fluctuate in response to changing interest rates like other fixed income securities: when interest rates fall, prices rise, and vice versa.

Decreases in market interest rates will also cause homeowners to consider re-financing their mortgages early, and repay their original loans sooner than expected. The investor will receive the principal and will only be able to reinvest at the new, lower interest rates.

Credit

There is very little credit risk in MBS. The issuers are typically very selective in choosing the mortgages that go into their pools, and the security itself is usually guaranteed by Ginnie Mae, Fannie Mae and Freddie Mac as well as the implied guarantee of the U.S. government for Ginnie Maes.

Although Fannie Mae's and Freddie Mac's guarantees are not backed by the U.S. Government, each entity has a line of credit to the U.S. Treasury. The credit markets consider the securities of both entities to be nearly equivalent to those issued by agencies that have the full-faith-and-credit guarantee.

Private-label mortgage securities; however, have a different credit risk. These instruments are the obligation of their issuer and are not guaranteed by any governmental entity. However, if the private label security is a CMO, and the CMO is based on MBSs issued or guaranteed by Ginnie Mae, Fannie Mae or Freddie Mac, the collateral backing these CMOs also carries the respective agency's guarantees.

Taxation

Interest

Interest payments are taxable as regular income at the interest rate of the investor.

Principal

That portion of the payments that includes a repayment of principal is not taxable.

Gains and Losses

Gains and Losses on the purchase or sale of the security are taxable as regular income at the interest rate of the investor.

Original Issue Discount (OID)

An OID exists if a mortgage security is issued at a discount from its face value. As with all other OID issues, the investor will be taxed on the annual increase in value over the life of the security at the regular income tax rate of the investor.

G. MONEY MARKET INSTRUMENTS

Marketplace

The money market is an over-the-counter, telephone-based process of trading short-term (less than one year) fixed income instruments. There are several different classifications of short-term instruments, all of which are considered money market instruments.

Purpose

Money market instruments are used by issuers and investors to maximize their liquidity and manage their cash flows while obtaining a return on their money.

Regulators

The market for money market instruments is not regulated by the Securities and Exchange Commission since the instruments are all short-term.

Issuers

The issuers of money market instruments are U.S. and non-U.S. based corporations, and the classification of the instrument depends upon the issuer and their needs.

Investors

Money market instruments give investors a guaranteed interest rate for a short-term investment. Investors in money market instruments could be individuals and institutions from anywhere in the world.

Money market instruments are purchased and sold by investors, mutual funds and the Treasury departments of corporations.

Types of Money Market Instruments

Most commercial money market instruments are issued in physical form as a receipt, not as a certificate.

Classifications

There are several different classifications of money market instruments.

Banker's Acceptances

A Bankers' Acceptance is an irrevocable bank draft for a future import/export of merchandise that is guaranteed by the bank and by the borrower. As a negotiable instrument, it can be traded in the secondary market, and is usually traded in a discounted form.

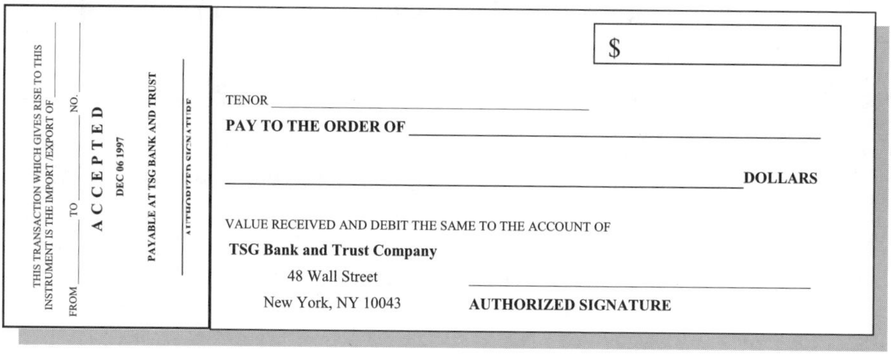
THIS TRANSACTION WHICH GIVES RISE TO THIS INSTRUMENT IS THE IMPORT /EXPORT OF ____
FROM ____ TO ____ NO. ____
ACCEPTED
DEC 06 1997
PAYABLE AT TSG BANK AND TRUST
AUTHORIZED SIGNATURE

$

TENOR ____
PAY TO THE ORDER OF ____
____ DOLLARS
VALUE RECEIVED AND DEBIT THE SAME TO THE ACCOUNT OF
TSG Bank and Trust Company
48 Wall Street
New York, NY 10043
AUTHORIZED SIGNATURE

Figure 278 - Example of a Banker's Acceptance

A Banker's Acceptance is usually issued by an importer's bank in anticipation of goods that have been ordered but not received. The BA gives the seller the protection that if the goods are delivered as ordered, the seller will receive the appropriate payment.

A BA is issued as a physical receipt that is transferred from the seller to the receiver as it is traded in the secondary market. Maturities can range from any number of days (usually 30, 60 or 90) up to a legal maximum of 180.

BA's are liquid, and are becoming a more popular instrument for institutional investors.

As a result of an SEC rule change, they are now eligible for book-entry processing at the DTC, where an accepting bank can assign a single CUSIP number to a group of BAs that are issued at a discount and which have a common maturity date.

Certificates of Deposit (Negotiable)

Negotiable Certificates of Deposit are issued by a financial firm, such as a bank. They are sold directly or through financial intermediaries in denominations of over $25,000, and can be traded on the secondary market until they mature. These are different from retail CD's which are discussed later in this chapter.

Negotiable CD's can be issued in book-entry form or as a physical receipt, and are eligible for deposit in the DTC. As of December, 1998, the DTC supports 179 issuers, which were valued at that time at $260 billion.

When a CD program is processed as book-entry-only, a single master note represents all of the CD's in the issuer's program.

Commercial Paper

Large commercial firms with excellent credit ratings issue Commercial Paper, usually for very short periods of time, and rarely for more than 270 days to avoid registration with SEC under the 1933 Act. Commercial paper is typically bought by other large firms or pension plans.

Commercial paper is issued as a physical receipt as shown below, and since there is only a small secondary market, it is usually held by the broker or the custodian in their vault until it matures. Commercial paper can be held at the DTC.

$ 100,000.00 Haverty Furniture Company
Atlanta, GA Oct. 6 , 19 96

Seventy Days after the above date, we agree to pay to the order of

BEARER .

Dollars

THE FIRST NATIONAL BANK OF CHICAGO, CHICAGO, IL

Payable at FULTON NATIONAL BANK, MAIN OFFICE, ATLANTA, GA 30302

P A I D
Dec 15, 1996
FIRST NATIONAL
BANK OF CHICAGO

Value Received HAVERTY FURNITU
NOT VALID UNLESS AUTHENTICATED BY By //Original Sig
THE FIRST NATIONAL BANK OF CHICAGO Senior Vice President and Treasurer
AS ISSUING AGENT

No: -12- . Date: Dec 15, 1996 . First National Bank of Chicago

Figure 279 - Example of Commercial Paper

The amount and the term are structured between the borrower and the lender. Commercial paper usually is sold at a discount; however, it can be sold as principal plus interest that is paid at maturity.

Repurchase Agreements

A Repurchase Agreement (Repo) is short-term contract (frequently overnight) that is used to finance government and money market inventory positions by agreeing to sell and subsequently repurchase specific securities (usually government securities) at a specified date and price. Structured as a short-term loan, the U.S. government collateral makes these instruments very safe.

- The Repo market in the U.S. is a highly liquid market with over $2.5 trillion traded daily.

- A Reverse Repo is an agreement to buy and subsequently resell specific securities.

Money Market Examples

The institutional money market consists of a variety of very short-term instruments, each of which is traded separately and at different rates. The next table shows the closing rate for various money market instruments.

Money Market Rates

Instrument Type	Rate	Effective Date	Instrument Type	Rate
Prime Rate	4.25	07/01/04		
Discount Rate	2.25	6/30/04	Certificates of Deposit	
			30 Days	1.47
			60 Days	1.65
			180 Days	1.94
Federal Funds			Bankers Acceptances	
Target Rate	1.250	06/30/04	30 Days	1.42
High	1.344		60 Days	1.51
Low	1.000		90 Days	1.61
Effective Rate	1.290		120 Days	1.70
			150 Days	1.81
			180 Days	1.90
Call Money	3.0	07/01/04	Overnight Repo Rate	1.33
Commercial Paper			Dealer Commercial Paper	
30 – 41 Days	1.41		30 Days	1.47
42 – 65 Days	1.48		60 Days	1.56
66 – 86 Days	1.54		90 Days	1.64
87 – 116 Days	1.62			

Source: Wall Street Journal

Figure 280 - Money Market Rates

The categories shown in this table are the:

Prime Rate

The prime rate is the rate that is charged by the leading U.S. banks to their best clients.

Discount Rate

The discount rate is the rate on overnight loans made by the Fed to its member banks.

Federal Funds Rate

The Fed Funds rate is the rate that Fed member banks charge to each other to loan/borrow their Fed reserves overnight. The minimum amount for a loan is $1 million.

This rate is based upon the discount rate and it is used as a benchmark rate for the industry. The Fed sets the discount rate, which influences the Fed Funds rate and therefore affects other near-term rates such as the 3 month T Bill rate.

Call Money

The call money rate is the rate for loans to brokers when their own securities portfolio is used as collateral.

Commercial Paper

Commercial paper consists of short-term certificates representing unsecured loans that are issued by leading corporations.

Certificates of Deposit

These certificates of deposit are negotiable CD's sold in the primary market. The rate shown is the average interest rate at which they are offered by major New York banks. The minimum amount is $1 million.

Bankers Acceptance

A Bankers Acceptance is a negotiable instrument, issued by a bank that is normally used to finance an import/export order.

Overnight Repo Rate

The overnight repo rate is the interest rate set between dealers for the sale and repurchase of U.S. Treasury instruments.

Dealer Commercial Paper

Dealer commercial paper consists of short-term certificates representing unsecured loans by major corporations that are sold through dealers.

Retail Money Market Products

The most common forms of money market instruments that are sold in the retail market are:

Certificates of Deposit (Non-Negotiable)

A Non-Negotiable CD is issued by a bank to a specific individual who is a retail client. It is issued for almost any amount and cannot be transferred. The bank issues a certificate that represents the ownership, and interest is generally accrued and paid when the CD matures.

The following example of a six month CD was issued at 4.86%.

Figure 281 - Example of a Non-Negotiable CD.

Insured Money Market Account (IMMA)

An insured money market account is a Money Market Fund that has been established by a bank, and which the bank has insured. It is very similar to the money market mutual funds that are issued by managed investment companies.

These accounts are also called Insured Market Rate Accounts (IMRA).

Money Market Funds

Money Market Funds are discussed in the chapter on Fund Products.

Characteristics

Trading

The money market is a telephone-based marketplace that involves corporate Treasuries and dealers.

Transaction Costs

Most of the instruments are sold at a net discounted price. The seller discounts the instrument based upon the current market conditions, the credit worthiness of the borrower, the length of the instrument, and includes the costs and profit in the calculation.

Liquidity

In general, the money market is a very liquid market, although some categories of instruments are issued and held to maturity with very little secondary market interest.

Pricing

All money market instruments are very sensitive to interest rates, and their price depends upon market conditions as well as the length of the loan and the credit worthiness of the issuer.

Maturity

Commercial money market instruments generally mature in less than one year, with the vast majority having a maturity of less than 270 days. Retail money market instruments can be established for longer periods of time.

Interest Payments

Most commercial money market instruments are sold at a discount and redeemed at the full face value (or par) at maturity, so there are no periodic interest payments as with most of the fixed income types of securities.

Retail instruments can be issued at a discount or with regularly scheduled interest payments.

Payment Periods

Most commercial money market instruments are sold at a discount and are redeemed at maturity for their full value.

Retail instruments can be issued at a discount or with regularly scheduled interest payments.

Yield

The yield on money market instruments is determined by current market rates and can change daily.

Interest Accrual

Money market instruments accrue in value from the time of issue to the time of maturity.

Processing

Purchases and sales of money market instruments are cleared between brokers on the street-side of the trade and settled directly between brokers and their client.

Risks

Credit

The primary credit-related risk that an investor in a money market security assumes is that the issuing firm will remain in business.

Interest Rate

Money market instruments also assume some interest rate risk, since the value of the instrument is very closely tied to interest rates and the overall credit rating of the issuer.

Taxation

Interest

Interest paid on money market instruments is taxable at the regular income tax rates of the investor.

Gains and Losses

Commercial money market instruments are, by their nature, short-term instruments, and any gains or losses are treated as ordinary income.

Retail instruments are not generally traded and therefore do not have a potential for a gain or loss.

H. DEBT OPTIONS

Debt-related options have some specific risks due to the fact that the vast majority of the trading activity in bonds and money market instruments takes place in a dealer market. While dealers typically maintain markets in all outstanding issues of Treasury securities, most of the activity and liquidity is in recently issued securities.

In addition, the minimum size of a lot in Treasury securities is $1,000,000, and most of the business is with institutions and other dealers, so there could be a shortage of the underlying security.

XV. Fund Products

According to the SEC, "an investment company is a business entity that issues securities and is primarily engaged in the business of investing in securities. An investment company invests the money it receives from investors on a collective basis, and each investor shares in the profits and losses in proportion to the investor's interest in the investment company. The performance of the investment company will be based on (but it won't be identical to) the performance of the securities and other assets that the investment company owns." 100

The federal securities laws categorize investment companies into three basic types:

- Mutual funds (legally known as open end companies)
- Closed end funds (legally known as closed end companies)
- UITs (legally known as unit investment trusts)

In this chapter we will examine each of these types of funds, and separately review a new type of mutual fund, the Exchange Traded Fund (ETF).

A. MUTUAL FUND MARKETPLACE

There has been an incredible growth in the number and size of mutual funds over the last 15 years. Although mutual funds were originally created to simplify the investment process, there are now over 125,000 Mutual Funds offered worldwide, with more than 13,000 mutual funds offered in the U.S. Moreover, there are now more funds available than there are equities listed on the New York Stock Exchange.

This has caused the selection of a mutual fund as an investment to become even more complex than choosing a single equity. Despite this, as of 2003, over 95 million individuals (representing almost 50% of the households in the U.S.) have invested nearly $6 trillion in U.S. based funds.

Purpose

In addition to making investment simpler, mutual funds were created to provide access to professional money management for individuals. Investors' cash is pooled to purchase a portfolio of stocks or bonds, the funds have lower processing costs as they buy in larger quantities, and the investor realizes a reduction in risk through diversification of investments within the funds. Mutual Funds also provide the investor with other benefits:

- Automatic reinvestment of dividends
- Liquidity, and ease of investment and withdrawal (called subscription and redemption)
- Investment strategies that would not otherwise be feasible, such as buying bonds that only sell in very large denominations
- Families of funds that offer a variety of investment alternatives and minimal switching costs

Regulators

The Securities and Exchange Commission regulates the investment company

---

[100] Source: SEC

industry.

Investment companies are regulated primarily under the Investment Company Act of 1940 and the rules adopted under that Act. Investment companies are also subject to the Securities Act of 1933 and the Securities Exchange Act of 1934.

Issuers

Mutual funds are issued by managed investment companies, which were discussed in the chapter on Securities Industry Participants, and which are formed to create, manage and distribute the funds. When a fund is registered, it must have a(n):

- Board of directors
- Management company
- Investment manager
- Custodian
- Transfer agent
- Independent auditors
- Underwriter (Except for No Load funds)

The funds are permitted to absorb and charge various fees as they calculate the Net Asset Value (NAV) of the fund. The NAV is determined by subtracting the fund liabilities from the assets and dividing the total by the number of shares in the fund. Liabilities include:

- Management fees
- Custodian fees
- Transfer agent fees
- Sales and marketing charges
- Other fees

Investors

Investors in U.S. mutual funds can be individuals and institutions from anywhere in the world.

Registration

The Securities Exchange Act of 1934 requires that any publicly offered security be described by a prospectus, and that the prospectus be delivered to anyone considering purchase of the security. In 1998 the SEC revised what must be included in an open end fund prospectus to include:

- Front and back cover pages
- Risk/return summary: investments, risks, and performance
- Fee tables
- Investment objectives, principal investment strategies, and related risks
- Management's discussion of fund performance
- Management, organization, and capital structure

- Shareholder information
- Distribution arrangements
- Financial highlights information

The registration process requires the open end fund to submit and regularly update SEC Form N-1A, which details the fund's organization and investment objectives. Form N-1A has three parts:

Part A: The Prospectus

Part A contains information that regulators believe is essential for an investor to make an informed purchasing decision and therefore is required to be distributed before a purchase.

Part B: The Statement of Additional Information (SAI)

Part B contains information that the SEC has concluded is not necessary for investor protection, but some investors may find useful.

Part C: Other Information

Part C is required by the SEC, but is not typically distributed to investors.

In addition, a Profile Prospectus is a four-page condensed and simplified version of the prospectus that some fund companies provide to prospective investors.

Information Sources

There are three primary sources of information about Mutual Funds:

- Investment Company Institute (ICI) collects data on mutual fund activity/sales, redemptions, reinvestments, net exchanges, and other items, and publishes this data monthly.
- Morningstar provides investors with information, analysis, and research, including ratings and other comparative data for mutual funds.
- Lipper provides fund information to fund families.

B. TYPES OF MUTUAL FUNDS

There are several different types of mutual funds that are based upon their investment objectives. For the purposes of this book it is not necessary to understand the exact investment objectives of each of these funds that are described below; however, it is important to note that there are different types of funds. When investing, it is critical to understand the stated purpose of the fund and the investment objectives.

Stock and Bonds Funds

Funds can be established to hold any type of securities that the fund identifies in its prospectus. The investors should thoroughly understand the stated purpose of the fund before investing.

Balanced Funds

Balanced funds are designed to provide a balance of income and growth. This is usually accomplished through a mixture of stocks and bonds, which is based upon the concept of asset allocation that was described in the Introduction chapter.

Bond Funds

Bond funds only invest in fixed income instruments, but since the funds is constantly buying and selling bonds, the fund itself does not have a fixed interest rate or a fixed maturity date. The value and interest paid by the fund varies along with the market's interest rates.

Capital Appreciation Funds

Capital appreciation funds invest in instruments that the fund manager believes will grow in the future, rather than provide current income. This usually means equities.

Equity Funds

Equity funds will only invest in equities, and can be subdivided into categories such as small cap (funds invest only in firms with a small capitalization), mid cap (middle capitalization firms), and large cap funds.

Growth Funds

Growth funds are similar to capital appreciation funds and only invest in instruments that the fund manager believes will grow quickly in the future. This usually means equities.

Growth/Income Funds

Growth/income funds are similar to balanced funds, and will rely on asset allocation to guide their mixture of stocks and bonds.

Income Appreciation Funds

Income appreciation funds are designed to invest in instruments that will provide current income for the investor, which could include interest and/or dividends.

Leveraged Funds

Leveraged funds typically invest some portion of the fund in leveraged instruments, such as derivatives, and the remaining amount in very safe instruments, such as government bonds. The idea here can range from being extremely leveraged, with a high degree of risk and anticipated gains, to a fund that will buy a sufficient amount of U.S. government zero coupon bonds that will accrete in value to provide the investor with a compete return of their investment (without any interest) at a specified point in time. And the remaining investment will be used to buy options that the fund hopes will increase rapidly in value and provide a large gain.

Market Neutral Funds

The objective of a market neutral fund is to try to participate in the market when it goes up and limit losses when it goes down. These funds buy an equal number of promising stocks to keep and unpromising stocks to sell short, to hedge against volatile equity markets.

Municipal Bond Funds

Municipal bond funds only invest in munis. These funds are usually geographically specific to take advantage of the tax exempt status for residents.

Option Income Funds

Option income funds typically use the income from a portfolio to buy options.

Specialized Funds

Specialized funds only invest in certain, defined industry sectors, such as technology, or a segment of the technology market.

Tax Exempt Funds

Tax exempt funds only invest in instruments that are tax exempt for the investor.

Index Mutual Funds

An index mutual fund is composed of securities intended to replicate the movement of a specific securities index.

An index fund is considered a passive investment since the portfolio manager does not have to decide between various investment alternatives. The manager knows the securities that make up the index and their relative weights in the index, and the manager's goal is to match it.

Because there is little active management, the expenses and transaction costs are low. The following chart shows that the expense ratio for an average index fund is lower than for several other types of actively managed funds.

Type of Fund	Lipper Average Expense Ratio (2003) [101]
S&P 500 Index Fund	0.81%
Balanced Fund	1.47%
Equity Income Fund	1.62%
Growth Stock Fund	1.62%
Income Fund	1.37%

Figure 282 - Comparison of Index Fund Expense Ratios to Other Funds

Limitations

The main limitations are that the manager must buy all of the securities in the index, even if the market *knows* that a particular security in the index is going to go down.

Benefits

The main benefit is that since most mutual funds do not beat the index anyway, the investor has a greater chance of at least matching the industry averages.

Structure

The various methods used to construct the indexes themselves are discussed in the chapter on Equity Products. An index mutual fund is designed to mimic the performance of the actual index and may involve buying all of the securities in the index or a set of securities that behave like the index.

---

[101] Source: Lipper, a Reuters Company

Processing

As an index fund receives subscriptions, it generally reserves about 3 to 5% of the mutual fund's value in cash to cover potential redemptions and to assemble block orders. This cash is often temporarily invested in short-term futures contracts for the same index in which the fund is currently invested. The purpose is to use the leverage associated with futures to counteract the fact that the Index Fund has expenses that need to be deducted from the performance of the fund. Unless another investment for the uninvested cash is found, the fund could never exactly match the index.

Money Market Funds (MMF)

Money Market Funds were first introduced in 1972, and are unique because they maintain a constant Net Asset Value of $1.00. As the investor subscribes and redeems shares, the number of units they have increases or decreases, but the NAV is constant.

Since 1998, to be classified as a Money Market Fund, these funds are required by the SEC to invest only in highly liquid fixed income instruments with an initial maturity of less than 90 days that will mature within a small number of days. The number of days to maturity, which identifies the firm's exposure to interest rate risk, is published for each Money Market Fund. These funds usually include U.S. Treasuries, certificates of deposit, and/or commercial paper, and could invest in municipal notes and bonds or other short-term fixed income instruments.

Funds with longer tenors, up to 270 days, are now called ultra-short bond funds.

The interest rate on a MMF is generally comparable to bank CD rates; however, the MMF interest rate varies along with the market's daily interest rates while the CD rate is fixed for the life of the CD.

Limitations

These funds are generally expected to have a low interest rate, but are considered to have very little risk. However, Money Market Funds, even if offered by a bank, are not FDIC insured, and are subject to interest rate and credit risk just like any other investments.

The funds could be insured by SIPC if they are a part of an account with a broker.

Benefits

Most people tend to use Money Market Funds today to replace traditional bank provided FDIC-insured savings accounts.

To counter this, banks have created an insured product, the insured market rate agreement, which acts like a traditional MMF with a slightly lower rate due to the insurance premiums.

Processing

Money Market Funds are generally processed just like any other funds. Any differences are due to the type of securities that are being purchased (which generally settle the same day or in one day) and the fact that the NAV is calculated to be $1.00. Not all systems have been constructed to do this calculation.

C. MUTUAL FUND CHARACTERISTICS

Mutual funds, also called open end funds, will continue taking in subscriptions for as long as investors wish to send them money.[102] These funds are valued daily and the purchase and selling price is the calculated net asset value (NAV). Open end funds constantly offer new shares for sale, which are redeemable on any business day at their NAV.

These funds cannot be listed on an exchange since they do not have a fixed capitalization. The fund can only issue one type of security, which represents all of the shares in the fund.

Trading

Mutual funds were initially sold to investors through brokers. Throughout the 1980's and 1990's, this shifted to a strategy where most funds marketed directly to the investors.

Increasingly, there are many different, competing distribution methods that can be used by funds to reach investors, including:

- Direct from the mutual fund
- Through investment management firms
- Through brokers, which may sell a small number of funds or a broad array of funds
- Through banks, which may sell a small number of funds or a broad array of funds
- Through insurance agents and financial advisors

Since 2000, the trend has shifted back to using brokers more frequently. Once the market started to improve in 2003, the funds didn't need the broker's selling support as much and began again to promote directly to the clients.

Transaction Costs

Mutual funds that are sold through an intermediary may have a sales charge imposed, while those that are sold directly have the marketing fee included in the NAV.

Sales Loads

An open end fund can charge a load, or a sales charge. This load can be taken at the beginning of an investment (Front End Load), where it decreases the amount of money that is actually invested for the investor, or at the end of the investment (Back End Load) when the investor redeems their shares.

Other funds are established as No Load funds, where the manager takes his fees and expenses from the fund itself each year, which reduces the annual return.

---

[102] The Magellan Fund grew so large in the late 1990's that it announced that it would no longer accept new investors, although existing investors could continue to add subscriptions.

Each of these types has specific advantages and disadvantages for the investor and the issuer, and each investor should understand how the differences relate to his/her objectives.

Redemption Fees

If a fund does not have a back-end load, it could still have a redemption charge that is imposed when the investor sells the mutual fund.

Management Fees

Funds typically charge a management fee of no more than 1%. This fee is used to compensate the fund for the portfolio management services it offers. In addition to the management fee, the fund can also charge other fees for administrative costs (called 12b-1 fees), and pass along out-of-pocket expenses for custody, auditing, etc. All of these fees affect the NAV of the fund.

The 12b-1 fee, currently capped at 1%, is divided into two parts:

- Marketing and advertising (0.75%)
- Service (0.25%) which is a continuing commission to the brokers who sell the funds.

It is critical for mutual fund investors to understand the expense structure of the fund. Whether the fund has a load or annual expenses, the efficiency of the fund should be carefully considered before investing. There is wide range of expense charges from fund to fund, and these expenses should be compared before investing.

Maturity

A mutual fund does not have a maturity date, unless it is a unit trust with a pre-defined expiration date. Regardless of the assets included in the portfolio, mutual funds are designed to continue indefinitely.

Income

Some funds are designed to generate income (interest and dividends) that can be paid periodically to the investor. Other funds are designed to either retain and reinvest the income, or to avoid income generating securities in favor of rapidly growing firms that usually do not pay income.

Pricing

Open end mutual funds are priced on a daily basis at their Net Asset Value, which is a combination of:

- The market value of all of the securities in the portfolio
- Plus cash and accruals, and minus expenses

Shares are sold to the public at NAV plus any sales charges, and shares are redeemed at NAV, less any redemption charges.

Liquidity

Open end funds are considered to be very liquid since they can be resold (redeemed) to the managed investment company that established the fund. Although the open end mutual funds are prepared to repurchase their shares, there are two characteristics of funds that can cause concern to investors.

- In the market adjustment of 1987, many investors were not able to contact their fund managers to redeem shares because so many people were trying to sell at the same time that the phone lines were jammed. Since then, the major funds have established disaster contingency plans that provide them with additional phone lines and additional operators in case of a dramatic surge in volume.

- The price that an investor sees posted in this morning's newspaper is the current price that was calculated yesterday. It is the price that was used for purchases and sales on the previous day. This is because the fund's position on a certain day, which is the price that an investor can buy and sell the fund, cannot be priced and calculated until the next day. It is only then that all of the information about the prior day's trading has been gathered, accruals calculated, expenses identified, etc.

For example, the fund's position on Monday normally cannot be calculated until Tuesday. The number that is reported, the NAV, must be calculated and reported to the industry by the end of business on Tuesday, using Tuesday's closing prices. While it could be available on the evening of Tuesday on the Internet or online, it won't be published in newspapers until Wednesday.

Reporting

The following example shows several of the key data elements that are routinely reported in daily newspapers, which include:

AMutl   American Mutual Fund
NE Co   New Economy Fund
SmCap   Small Cap Fund

NAV	% Change	Company	Fund Objectives	NAV YTD	NAV 4 Weeks	NAV Last 12 Months	Ranking	NAV 3 Years	Ranking	NAV 5 Years	Ranking	Max. Sales Comm.	Annual Expenses
American Funds													
31.31	-0.50	Amutl	GI	+8.6	+0.6	+15.9	C	+21.4	E	+17.1	E	5.75	0.58
24.14	-0.31	NE Co	GR	+21.1	+3.3	+32.2	A	+24.0	A	+18.1	D	5.75	0.81
27.43	-0.31	SmCap	GL	+5.6	+0,1	+5.9	D	+14.7	D	+15.1	C	5.75	1.07

Net Asset Value = Assets - Liabilities - Expenses / Number of Shares Outstanding

Figure 283 - Example of Information Available in Newspapers

The column headings from the previous example are shown in the following chart.

Column Headings	Definitions
Net Asset Value (NAV)	The NAV is calculated daily for open end funds.
% Change	The change from the prior close is shown.
Fund Name	The name of the fund is identified.
Fund Objectives	The objectives of the fund are stated in the prospectus, which could be growth, income, balanced, etc. The abbreviations that are used are normally found in a footnote in the newspaper.
NAV YTD	The year-to-date change in NAV is presented.
NAV 4 Weeks	The change in the NAV over the last four weeks is presented.
NAV Last 12 Months	The change in the NAV over the last twelve months is presented.
Ranking	The ranking for the fund's performance over the last twelve months, in quartiles, where A is the top quartile and D is the lowest is presented.
NAV 3 Years	The change in the NAV over the last three years is presented.
Ranking	The ranking for the fund's performance over the last three years, in quartiles, where A is the top quartile and D is the lowest.
NAV 5 Years	The change in the NAV over the last five years is presented.
Ranking	The ranking for the fund's performance over the last five years, in quartiles, where A is the top quartile and D is the lowest.
Maximum Sales Commission	The maximum sales commission that is allowed by the fund is presented.
Annual Expenses	The annual expenses that are being charged to the fund are presented.

Figure 284 - Column Heading Definitions

In addition to the information that is found in the daily and weekly newspapers, two vendors also publish information about funds: Morningstar and Lipper Analytical Services.

Processing

Most mutual funds can settle in three days through the NSCC or can be bought and sold directly from the fund. Mutual fund processing is discussed in the chapter on Mutual Fund Processing.

Risk

Interest

Mutual funds that invest heavily in fixed income securities can have some interest rate risk if the overall rates in the market change.

Credit

One of the benefits of mutual funds is that they invest in many different securities. If an individual firm in which a mutual fund has invested has a credit problem, it does not affect each investor as seriously as if the investor had made their entire investment in that firm's issues.

Credit risk is distributed over a large number of firms, and therefore the overall risk is lower.

Tax

One of the primary ways to differentiate between Mutual Funds is their tax efficiency. In boom years, the differences are negligible, but in normal years the difference between a tax efficient mutual fund and an inefficient fund makes a significant impact on the overall return of the fund.

Dividends

Mutual funds can pay dividends. These are the result of the firm's overall growth, which results from the net of gains and losses, interest, dividends, etc. These dividends are taxable at the current income tax rate of the investor.

Capital Gains

When a mutual fund is sold, the taxpayer will be subject to normal income tax rates for securities (either at regular or capital gains rates).

In addition, holders of a mutual fund could be responsible for the capital gains earned by the fund when the fund itself sells the securities in the portfolio. These gains and losses can be passed on to the taxpayer.

D. CLOSED END COMPANIES

Closed end companies, usually referred to as closed end funds, have a fixed number of shares outstanding, and identify a specific amount of money that they will collect for investment, and then stop taking subscriptions when they reach their stated goal.

Closed End Fund Investments

Closed end funds also are permitted to invest in a greater amount of *illiquid* securities than mutual funds. An illiquid security generally is considered to be a security that can't be sold within seven days at the approximate price used by the fund in determining NAV. Because of this feature, funds that seek to invest in markets where the securities tend to be more illiquid are typically organized as closed end funds.

Types of Closed End Funds

Closed end funds come in many varieties just as do mutual funds. They can have different investment objectives, strategies, and investment portfolios. They also can be subject to different risks, volatility, and fees and expenses.

Regulation

Closed end funds are subject to SEC registration and regulation, and are subject to numerous requirements imposed for the protection of investors. Closed end funds are regulated primarily under the Investment Company Act of 1940 and the rules adopted under that Act. Closed end funds are also subject to the Securities Act of 1933 and the Securities Exchange Act of 1934.

Trading

After the initial offering the investor buys these funds in the secondary market just like any other stock, and the price is based upon supply and demand. Shares of closed end funds are traded on exchanges or OTC and may trade at a discount or at a premium to the fund's NAV.

Closed end funds are traded on an exchange and their liquidity depends upon the demand for their shares, just as any other exchange listed security.

Transaction Costs

Since closed end funds are traded like stocks, they are charged a commission for purchases and sales.

Fees

The fees for closed end funds are charged to the fund, and since the trading price of the fund is a market price and not a NAV, these fees are less visible than for open end funds.

Maturity

Closed end funds do not have a fixed maturity date, although if they invest in fixed income instruments, they could have maturing bonds in the portfolio.

Income

Income that is earned by the investments is automatically reinvested in the fund and is not distributed to the shareholders.

Price

Closed end funds trade at the value placed on them by the marketplace, and the NAV is only calculated on a weekly basis. These funds can trade at a premium or a discount, based upon the market's perception of the value of the fund over the long-term.

A closed end fund calculates its NAV once a week, but this means little since the shares trade at a market price, and the price is based upon supply and demand. Therefore, the calculated NAV is only meaningful if the investment company goes out of business and liquidates the assets.

Liquidity

Closed end fund shares are not redeemable and therefore are not a liquid as open end funds. A closed end fund is not required to buy its shares back from investors upon request. Some closed end funds, commonly referred to as interval funds, offer to repurchase their shares at specified intervals.

Reporting

Since closed end funds are traded throughout the day, prices are constantly changing and are available along with other stock prices throughout the day and as a closing price at the end of the day.

Processing

The purchase and sale of a closed end fund occurs like a stock, except in the case of an interval fund that is being redeemed by the issuer.

Risk

Closed end funds are more risky than open end funds because of the types of investments they typically make and because f the lower liquidity.

E. COMPARISON OF MUTUAL FUNDS AND CLOSED END COMPANIES

Three characteristics distinguish open end funds from closed end funds:

Capitalization

The capitalization for a closed end fund is fixed when the fund is established, while the capitalization for an open end fund increases or decreases along with market demand for the fund.

Market Price

The market price for an open end fund is typically established daily as the NAV, while the closed end fund's market price varies throughout the day along with the market demand for the fund.

Subscription/Redemption

Open end funds are purchased from the mutual fund and are redeemed by returning them to the mutual fund, while a closed end fund is bought and sold in the open market to another investor.

F. UNIT INVESTMENT TRUSTS (UIT)

A Unit Investment Trust is an investment that offers an interest in a fixed portfolio of equities and/or fixed income securities. The securities are usually self-liquidating, or are scheduled to be sold at a certain point in time, and do not have to be actively managed. This reduces the cost of administering the portfolio.

A UIT consists of a group of securities that are purchased at one time and which are held until the trust matures, usually in one year, but not more than three years. They are normally created along with a story, where for example, a broker might point out that the market expects $x Billion to be spent in the next y years for Homeland Security. It could then assemble a small portfolio of firms that are likely to benefit from the governments purchases and create a new UIT.

UITs can be defined by their creators in any way that they wish. Brokers create these products as a marketing tool, and then promote them to their clients.

UITs can be traded in the secondary market, and can often be sold back to the broker that issued them. UITs are not listed in the newspapers and are not tracked by the regular mutual fund tracking services such as Lipper and Morningstar.

- Most municipal and corporate bond UITs generally require a minimum investment of $5,000.

- Most equity UITs require a minimum purchase amount of $1,000.

Brokers like this product because it requires very little maintenance and they can charge a large load.

Investors like this product because it is easy to understand and usually has minimal risk.

- Most fixed income UITs are either insured or are rated investment grade. Details are stated in the prospectus for each trust.

- Units of the UIT represent a pro rata share of a diversified portfolio of securities, and diversification can help minimize the credit risks of investing in individual securities.

- With a few exceptions, an investor can sell a UIT every business day at its liquidation price in the secondary market. Like mutual funds, UITs have a public offering price (POP) and a net asset value (NAV).

- If there is no public market, the shares are redeemable by the issuer.

- Fixed income UITs are designed to pay a consistent distribution amount each payment period until the bonds in the trust are retired and their capital investment is repaid.

However, UITs are not without risk.

- As with mutual funds, share prices fluctuate daily and there is no guarantee that the price, when redeemed, will equal or exceed the purchase price.

- Many UITs are insured for the payment of interest and principal, and similar to insured municipal bond, insured UITs usually have a lower yield than an uninsured UIT because of the extra cost involved in purchasing a policy.

- Fixed Income UITs are vulnerable to fluctuations in interest rates. If interest rates rise, bond prices within the trust will decline despite the lack of change in bond coupons and maturities.

- If any of the bonds within a UIT are called, the par value of the trust will drop and the principal will be paid out directly to the unit holder just like a regular bond. UITs are unlike mutual funds because when a mutual fund has a bond called, or if it matures, the principal is used to buy additional bonds for the portfolio. UITs pay the cash distributions directly to the unit holders and there is no reinvestment.

- There are some cases when an investor cannot sell a UIT back to its sponsor. If it is near maturity and the price per unit is very low then the sponsor will probably no longer accept liquidations on the trust and the investor will have to wait until maturity to redeem their shares.

G. EXCHANGE TRADED FUNDS (ETFS)[103]

An exchange traded fund is an investment company with the investment objective of achieving the same return as a particular market index. An ETF is similar to an index fund in that it will primarily invest in the securities of companies that are included in a selected market index. An ETF will invest in either all of the securities in an index or a representative sample of the securities included in the index.

Currently there are about 100 ETFs available for trading, ranging from SPDRS to Diamonds, tracking both broad and narrow exchange indexes.

ETF Type	Full Name	Tracks
DIAMONDs	Diamonds Trust Series I	Dow Jones Industrial Average
FITRs	Fixed income exchange traded securities	Various treasuries (including 1, 2, 5 and 10-year)
HOLDRs	Holding company depository receipts (marketed by Merrill Lynch)	Narrow industry groups. (Each initially owns 20 stocks)
iShares	iShares - possibly "index shares"	Group of ETFs marketed by Barclays Global Investors
QUBEs	NASDAQ-100 tracking stock (QQQ)	NASDAQ-100 index
SPDRs	Standard & Poor's' Depository Receipts (called Spiders)	Track a variety of Standard & Poor's' indexes
StreetTracks	StreetTracks - State Street Global Advisor ETFs	Various indexes, including Dow Jones style indexes and Wilshire indexes.
VIPERs	Vanguard Index Participation Receipts	Several Vanguard index funds

Figure 285 - Examples of Exchange Traded Funds

Although ETFs are legally classified as open end companies or Unit Investment Trusts (UITs), they differ from traditional open end companies and UITs in several ways.

Issuance

An ETF, like any other type of investment company, must have a prospectus which must be provided to all of the investors that purchase Creation Units. Some ETFs also deliver a prospectus to secondary market purchasers. ETFs that do not deliver a prospectus are required to give investors a document known as a Product Description, which summarizes key information about the ETF and explains how to obtain a prospectus.

- ETFs that are legally structured as open end companies (but not those that are structured as UITs) must also have statements of additional information (SAIs).

- Other open end ETFs must provide shareholders with annual and semi-annual reports.

---

[103]   Source: SEC

- The Exchange Traded Fund manager does not sell individual shares directly to investors and only issue their shares in large blocks (blocks of 50,000 shares, for example) that are known as "Creation Units."

- Investors generally do not purchase Creation Units with cash. Instead, they buy Creation Units with a basket of securities that generally mirrors the ETF's portfolio. Those who purchase Creation Units are frequently institutions.

Trading

Creation Units are normally split up and sold as individual shares in the secondary market. This permits other investors to purchase individual shares (instead of Creation Units).

Investors who want to sell their ETF shares have two options:

- They can sell individual shares to other investors on the secondary market

- They can sell the Creation Units back to the ETF

In addition, ETFs generally redeem Creation Units by giving investors the securities that comprise the portfolio instead of cash. So, for example, an ETF invested in the stocks contained in the Dow Jones Industrial Average (DJIA) would give a redeeming shareholder the actual securities that constitute the DJIA instead of cash.

Advantages/Disadvantages

Because of the price inefficiencies with mutual funds that have led to abuses, some institutional investors have switched to ETFs. ETFs are largely immune to the market-timing abuses which are currently being investigated by state and federal industry regulators. Unlike mutual funds, which have their prices set once a day at 4 p.m. EST, an ETF trades continuously on exchanges.

As they are similar to stocks, exchange traded funds offer more flexibility than a typical mutual fund.

Advantages of ETFs	Disadvantages of ETFs
ETFs can be bought and sold throughout the trading day, allowing for intraday trading - which is rare with mutual funds	Commissions are similar to stocks, and trading exchange traded funds can become more expensive than mutual funds
Traders can sell short or buy ETFs on margin.	
Low annual expenses are similar to the cheapest mutual funds.	Unlike mutual funds, ETFs don't trade at the net asset values of their underlying assets; they trade at market prices which could be at a premium or a discount.
Due to SEC regulations, ETF are more tax efficient than mutual funds	
ETF trading is not subject to the uptick rule, which restricts traders to selling stocks short only when the last trading activity in the stock pushes its price up	As with stocks, there is a bid-ask spread
Over the long term, the S&P 500 Index beats the returns of 80% of actively managed funds.	

Figure 286 - Comparison of ETFs to Mutual Funds

Summary of Advantages and Disadvantages

Investing directly with a mutual fund company is generally better than ETFs for:

- Non-taxable accounts because of the tax advantages of ETFs

- Small investments with dollar cost averaging where mutual funds do not require a commission and stock purchases would involve a commission (or a spread)

- Active trading, where some mutual funds (Rydex, Profunds and Potomac Funds) encourage trading with no commissions vs. commissions for stock trades

H. HEDGE FUNDS

A Hedge Fund is a fund that has a small group of investors, and which is not regulated by the SEC. This means that the restrictions on regular mutual funds do not apply and the fund manager can invest in significantly more risky instruments.

The number of participants in each hedge fund was limited to 99 investors until 1996, when Congress passed an amendment that raised the maximum to 499 so long as the total investable assets exceed $500 million. Participation in the fund is restricted to individual and institutional investors with significant available assets. Private individuals (which make up over 82% of hedge fund investors) are usually required to have at least $1 million in net worth, an annual income of over $200,000, and a minimum investment of $250,000.

In December 1998, there were approximately 3,000 hedge funds, managing $200 Billion. As of 2004, there are approximately 8,350 hedge funds with assets of over $875 billion industry and the hedge fund segment of the industry is growing at about 20% per year.

Hedge Fund Investing

Hedge Funds utilize a variety of investment strategies, some of which use leverage and derivatives while others are more conservative and employ little or no leverage. Many hedge fund strategies seek to reduce market risk specifically by short selling equities or buying/selling derivatives.

These funds can be very risky, but they can deliver an excellent return to the investor in good times. The funds will also provide an incredible return to the fund managers if the managers do a good job since the funds usually charge a fee of about 1% of the assets in order to pay their expenses, and then receive up to 20% of the annual profits. For example, the minimum a fund with 499 investors should have is $500 million in investments. For instance, if the fund goes up only 10% and the managers get 20% of the gain, their share is $10 million.

Hedge Fund Regulation [104]

Hedge funds generally rely on Sections 3(c)(1) and 3(c)(7) of the Investment Company Act of 1940 to avoid registration and regulation as investment companies. To avoid having to register the securities they offer with the SEC, hedge funds often rely on Section 4(2) and Rule 506 of Regulation D of the Securities Act of 1933. As of June, 2004, nearly 50 % of all Hedge Funds are already registered.

In 2004, the Securities and Exchange Commission published for comment a proposed new Rule 203(b)(3)-2 that would require hedge fund advisers to register with the Commission under the Investment Advisers Act of 1940. The Commission also voted to propose related rule amendments.

Registering Hedge Funds under the rule would permit the Commission to:

- Collect and provide to the public basic information about hedge funds and hedge fund advisers, including the number of hedge funds operating in the United States, the amount of assets, and the identity of their advisers;

- Examine hedge fund advisers to identify compliance problems early and deter questionable practices. If fraud does occur, examinations offer a chance to discover it early and limit the harm to investors;

- Require all hedge fund advisers to adopt basic compliance controls to prevent violation of the federal securities laws;

- Improve disclosures made to prospective and current hedge fund investors; and prevent felons or individuals with other serious disciplinary records from managing hedge funds.

---

[104] Source: SEC

XVI. Other Products

In addition to the equities, fixed income instruments, derivatives and mutual funds that are bought and sold every day in the U.S., there are several other types of securities that are used in the U.S. markets.

A. FUTURES CONTRACT

A futures contract is standardized, and traded on an exchange. It is not an option to buy or sell, it is an *agreement* to buy or sell. If the contract is held through the last day of the month, the buyer must accept delivery and the seller must deliver.

Since the contracts are standardized, the amount, commodity, month, and number of locations for delivery are specified. A contract typically requires a fraction of the total amount to be placed as margin, and the balance is due upon the execution of the contract.

If the contract is held through the last day of the month in which the contract matures, the buyer must accept delivery and the seller must deliver. Less than 5% of contracts actually involve delivery, with the vast majority closed out by offsetting contracts.

Foreign currency futures are quoted in the U.S. in dollars, and several interest rate futures (IRFs) are available for:

- U.S. Treasury Bonds, Notes and Bills
- GNMAs
- Euro-Dollar Deposits

Other types of futures contract were discussed in the chapter on Buying and Selling Securities.

B. FORWARDS CONTRACT

A forward contract, which is an agreement to buy or sell a security at some point in the future, is not traded on an exchange, and while somewhat standardized, each contract can be unique.

C. SWAPS

A swap is a very customized form of derivative instrument, and most swaps are processed individually. The term *swap* can be used in either one of two ways.

- A swap can simply be the sale of one security in order to purchase another security with similar features. This form of swap is not a specific instrument; it is a portfolio management technique that is performed between an investment manager's accounts.

- The form of swap that is a new instrument involves the exchange of different futures instruments, or two similar futures instruments with different features. Swaps generally exchange one type of cash flow or asset for another with prearranged rules, with the obligations of each underlying instrument managed by an intermediary.

For following example shows that an Interest Rate Swap is the simultaneous exchange of a fixed rate obligation for a variable rate obligation.

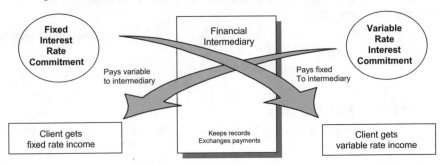

Figure 287 - Example of an Interest Rate Swap

There are many different types of swaps, including:

- Forward Rate Agreements
- Interest Rate Swaps
- Currency Swaps
- Commodity Swaps
- Equity Swaps
- Caps, Collars, Floors and Swaptions

D. AMERICAN DEPOSITORY RECEIPT

An American Depository Receipt is issued as a registered security in the U.S. and is backed by a related amount of the security in a non-U.S. market. ADRs can be backed by equities or fixed income instruments.

Investors who buy ADRs in the U.S. are making an indirect investment in the underlying security, but actually buy the ADR using U.S. dollars and settle in the U.S. using U.S. rules.

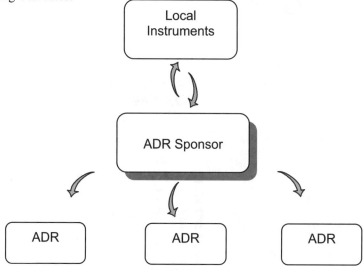

Figure 288 - ADR Relationships

As shown in the previous chart, an ADR depository bank can be selected as a sponsor that will act as the intermediary between the U.S. investors and the local market of the underlying security.

Depository banks are responsible for several functions:

- Receiving dividends from the issuer and redistributing them
- Creating the new instrument in the U.S.
- Ensuring that the U.S. instruments have sufficient underlying shares backing them
- Transferring or issuing additional shares as required
- Assisting the issuer in promoting the ADR shares in the U.S. as a good investment

There are two different ways depository banks become involved with the ADR process:

Sponsored ADR

With a sponsored issue, the issuer selects the depository bank and agrees to work exclusively with it. Depository banks aggressively seek to be appointed as the sponsors of ADR issues if they think that the issue will sell well in the U.S. The banks are compensated by the issuer, based upon the volume of transactions in the ADR.

Figure 289 - ADR Equity Tombstone

Unsponsored ADR

Any depository bank can issue an ADR as an unsponsored issue, merely by buying a sufficient number of shares in the local country and holding them in a local custodial account as the collateral for the ADRs sold in the U.S.

This does not generate any fees; however, unsponsored issues can generate trading volume and commission for the brokers involved in the process. Unsponsored issues are usually initiated by brokers for their clients; however, there is very little unsponsored activity.

Trading

If a U.S. investor approaches their broker and asks them to purchase an ADR. The broker has two options:

- Purchase an outstanding ADR from a counterparty on the U.S. exchange on which the security is listed.

- Purchase underlying shares in the home country of the issue and deliver the shares to the appropriate depository bank, which will issue the relevant ADR.

Trading Sponsored ADRs

When an investor buys a sponsored ADR they are buying a U.S. security just as they buy any other listed security. It is up to the depository bank to maintain a sufficient supply of shares, which they will obtain in the local market as required.

Since the ADR has been issued, it can be lodged in the DTC and traded in book-entry form. If additional ADR shares are required, the depository will issue them and deliver them to the DTC.

E. INSURANCE PRODUCTS

Insurance Policies

While an insurance policy itself is not a security, the insurance company that issued the policy usually has invested in a variety of security instruments in order to accumulate the funds that are needed to repay the insurance policy if/when it matures.

Annuity Contract

An annuity contract is an investment contract between a life insurance company and a subscriber. The subscriber agrees to pay the insurance company a specific amount (in one lump sum or partial payments) and the insurance company agrees to make periodic payments to that party beginning at a specific point in time for a specific amount of time or for as long as he lives.

If the payout is to be over the remaining life of the subscriber, the insurance industry's mortality tables are used by the insurance company to determine the amount of the deposit, which depends on the amount the investor wants to receive as well as the age and sex of the subscriber. Payments are guaranteed for the lifetime of the annuity, even if the investor outlives the tables.

Fixed Amount Annuity

For years, insurance companies have offered a fixed annuity contract. The policy was designed to supplement other forms of insurance that paid out on the insured's death.

- The fixed annuity could be purchased by depositing a lump sum or through the payment of premiums over a period of years.

- The fixed annuity allows for the fixed dollar amount payout over the lifetime of the annuitant. It has been used primarily as a supplement to other retirement benefits.

The insurance company usually invests the amounts received from the investor in fixed income securities, real estate, and mortgages, and the amount a fixed annuity pays can be increased if the subscriber has a participating clause.

A lifetime fixed annuity contract periodically pays a fixed amount over the life of the annuitant and has been, by far, the most popular form of annuity. Arrangements could also be made for a surviving spouse so that the spouse could continue to receive the payments for his/her remaining life.

Mortality Risk

Insurance companies based their payment guarantees on a continuing study of life expectancy. If the insured is fortunate enough to live longer than the tables, the insurance company must continue to pay. The mortality risk is borne by the insurance company.

Investment Risk

Investment risk is also borne by the insurance companies. If the value of their investments decline, they still must pay the pre-agreed upon amounts.

Inflation Purchasing Power

A person who buys an annuity contract 20 years before retirement thinking that $200 per month will be sufficient is subject to inflation risk, since the fixed amount remains the same. Because of this risk the variable annuity contract was born.

Variable Annuity

When the contract is initiated, the investor makes a lump sum or begins a series of periodic payments to the insurance company. The insurance company invests this money in a portfolio of securities, which usually includes mutual funds. The value of this investment fluctuates as the prices of the underlying securities rises or falls. At a predetermined point in time, such as when the investor becomes 65, the insurer begins making annual payments to the investor. A variable annuity pays varying amounts that are based upon how well the insurance company has invested the money.

Income tax on the income earned from the investment is deferred until the money is withdrawn. There are a number of costs, including sales charges, administrative charges, and asset charges, and a management fee.

The variable annuity contract was designed as a way for the insured to participate in the growth of the stock market. In 1959, the Supreme Court ruled that since variable annuity contracts passed the risk on to the annuitant, they were subject to the Federal securities regulations. Therefore, variable annuities must be registered with the SEC under the Securities Act of 1933 and under the Investment Act of 1940 as an open end investment company.

Variable annuities are set up in a separate account so as not to be mixed with the assets of the insurance company's straight-life and fixed annuity contracts.

XVII. Vendors

There are many different categories of vendors providing services to the securities processing industry. Some direct industry participants, such as banks and brokers are also vendors when they sell their services to other firms, and other businesses are indirect participants that provide software and other forms of products and services.

The different categories of vendors that will be covered in this chapter are:

Software Applications Vendors:

      A. Front Office Applications

      B. Middle Office Applications

      C. Back Office Applications

Information Vendors:

      D. Market Data Vendors

      E. Bond Rating Vendors

Processing Support:

      F. Third-party Insurance Companies

Services:

      G. Systems Integrators

      H. Newsletters

      I. Education Providers

A. FRONT OFFICE APPLICATION VENDORS

The vendors supporting the front office can be segmented according to the types of applications they provide, such as:

- Registered Representative Support
  - Financial Planning
  - Client Management
  - Investment Decision Support
  - Prospecting and Sales Support
  - Tax Planning and Calculation
- Institutional Sales Support
  - Client Management
  - Prospecting and Sales Support
- Trade Order Management for Buy-Side firms
- Order Management for Sell-Side firms
- Portfolio Management

Each of these categories can also be sub-divided into additional categories based upon the securities instruments they cover, such as equities, fixed income, etc., as well as the markets they support such as private banks, brokers, managers, etc.

Also, there is no clear line that separates the categories, and most vendors provide different combinations of functionality and instruments, which makes it difficult to directly compare one application to another.

The advantage that these vendors have is that they are selling to the front office. The front office is more likely than the back office to have the budget to buy applications and services since it is easier to justify purchases that support revenue increases than it is to support expense reduction. The marketplace and the vendors' approach to the market are very different for the vendors selling to the middle and back office.

Again, because the complexity of the tasks, each of these individual vendors tends to focus on a specific niche opportunity and has connected a subset of the firms in the marketplace with a subset of functionality for a subset of instruments. While these vendors can provide very efficient solutions for their specific area of interest, they are not able to provide a comprehensive solution, and are finding it difficult, yet increasingly mandatory, to interface with each other.

Different User Requirements

Each group of financial intermediaries uses similar systems but has different detailed requirements.

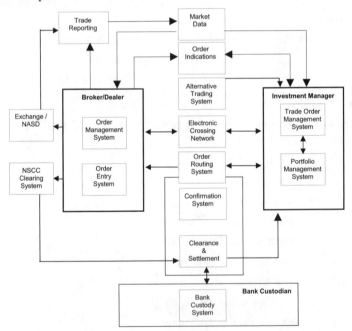

Figure 290 - Broker and Investment Manager Interfaces

Investment Manager

As shown in the previous flow chart, the investment manager is often involved with many of these interfaces.. An active investment manager must get information from marketing vendors, order indication systems, order routing systems, alternative trading systems, electronic communication networks, confirmation systems, and have an interface with at least one custody system. To manage this information flow, investment managers are either buying or building trading systems to manage their workflow, and have portfolio management systems that are used for their primary reporting and analysis.

Broker/Dealer

Brokers find themselves in an even more complex situation because they have to interface with multiple vendors in each classification in order to support multiple investment manager clients. Rather than deal with one order indication system, for instance, brokers may find themselves with interfaces to *all* of the order indications systems, as well as to *all* of the order routing systems and *all* of the confirmation systems.

Banks

Banks deal with multiple investment managers and must be prepared to accept input from them in a variety of formats and protocols. Banks also need high-speed connections to the DTC for settlements.

Trade Order Management Systems/ Trading Systems

Trade Order Management System vendors focus their resources on supporting an investment manager's front office functions, and provide the functions of order entry, order routing and order execution. The successful vendors present data elegantly and have robust interfaces to systems such as portfolio management, back office processing, security master file and pricing. Trade Order Management Systems are also being connected to the emerging Alternative Trading Systems and Electronic Communications Networks.

Some of the leading systems and vendors [105] are:

Firm	Product Name
Advent Software	Moxy
Charles River Development	Charles River IMS
Eze Castle Software	Traders Console
Financial Models Company	FMCModel, FMCTrade
INDATA	Precision Trading
Latent Zero	Capstone
Linedata Services	LongView Trading
Macgregor	XIP
OM (US) Inc.	TCAM
Sanchez Computer Associates, Inc.	Wealthware
SS&C Technologies	Antares
SunGard Investment Management Systems	Decalog
Thomson Financial	Oneva Trade EQ (Formerly Open Trader)

Figure 291 - Trade Order Management Systems

---

[105] Vendors mentioned as "leading vendors" hold these positions as of the writing of this book, and are subject to rapid change.

These systems are also used by banks and brokers for their proprietary trading activities.

Order Management Systems (OMS)

Order Management Systems are used by brokers to connect to exchanges, NASDAQ, Alternative Trading Systems (ATS) and Electronic Communication Networks (ECN), which are described in a later section in this chapter.

Order Indication Systems

An Order Indication System is used to send position information and advertise possible trades to potential counterparties. The FIX standard has opened up this market significantly by allowing brokers and managers to send indications electronically to each other in an agreed-upon format. The most entrenched vendors of these systems are AutEx and Bridge.

Order Routing Systems

Order Routing Systems allow investment managers to route their orders directly to a broker's order system, which then has its own version of order routing that sends the trade to an exchange floor, to NASDAQ or to their in-house traders. The vendors in this area are fairly entrenched since order routing interfaces are complex and truly real-time.

Order Entry

Order Entry systems are used by registered representatives or their assistants to begin the process of entering client trades into their firm's Order Management System. Most of these systems were developed in-house by the broker.

Alternative Trading Systems

As presented in the chapter on Buying and Selling Securities, there are four types of Alternative Trading Systems:

- Electronic Communications Networks
- Cross-Matching Systems
- Crossing Networks
- Call Markets

Some of the leading ATS vendors are presented in the following sections.

Electronic Communications Networks

The ECN process is usually in three steps:

- Look for a match on the ECN
- Look for a match on the other ECNs
- Send the order to an exchange or market maker

Some of the leading ECNs in the U.S. are:

Archipelago LLC (ARCA)

The Archipelago ECN was formed in 1996 by major Wall Street firms and is one of the four original ECNs approved in January 1997 by the Securities and Exchange Commission. It is an order entry and execution system for

NASDAQ and listed stocks, with anonymous access for all NASDAQ market participants.

Archipelago uses a proprietary algorithm to find the best price for orders and provides an open limit order book for NASDAQ and listed stocks. Archipelago is available to subscribing institutions, NASDAQ Market Makers, broker/dealers and professional trading accounts. Archipelago has Exchange status following its merger with the Pacific Exchange in July 2000.

Attain (ATTN)

Attain, a subsidiary of Domestic Securities, began operations in 1998 as an order display alternative to the traditional market making price quote system on NASDAQ. It provides direct access electronic trading for individual clients who trade their own accounts as well as for broker/dealers, institutions and hedge funds.

Bloomberg Tradebook

Bloomberg Tradebook is a global ECN offering clients direct access to eleven national equity exchanges around the globe and potential access to 65 total markets world-wide.

Brass (BRUT)

Brut ECN was established in 1998, and provides proprietary access to the NASDAQ market. It was recently acquired by NASDAQ.

GlobeNet (GNET)

GlobeNet displays and internally matches a variety of order types for NASDAQ's National Market, Small Cap and Bulletin Board orders, including Limit, Market, Stop, Stop-Limit, Sell-Short, Sell-Short Exempt, Post, Smart Post, Reserve Order Size, Sweep Orders and the ability to Cancel/Replace quickly and easily.

Instinet Corporation (INCA)

Founded in 1969, Instinet was the first ECN and has been providing investors with electronic trading solutions for 35 years. Instinet started as a platform for brokerages to display bid and ask prices for North American securities and was first used by institutions to buy/sell from each other.

Instinet and The Island ECN merged to form INET.

INET

INET was formed by the merger of the Instinet ECN and The Island ECN.

It offers U.S. broker/dealers access to NASDAQ equities, U.S. exchange-listed securities, and routing access to other major U.S. trading venues.

Market XT (MKXT) (LSPD)

Market XT only supports limit orders, and changed its symbol to LSPD.

NexTrade (NTRD)

NEXTrade was started in 1997, and was the first ECN to offer 24-hour trading to retail investors through participating broker/dealers. Today its clients include mutual funds, hedge funds, market-makers, traditional broker/dealers, online broker/dealers and professional trading companies.

In 1999, NexTrade officially applied with the SEC to become a registered, fully-electronic, 24-hour securities exchange.

Spear, Leeds & Kellogg (REDI)

REDIPlus supports U.S. equities, options, and electronic futures, plus European equities and electronic futures markets, and includes quotes, news, charts, order management, and position management. REDIPlus' clients include mutual funds, hedge funds, market makers, floor traders, professional investors and investment managers.

Redibook merged with Archipelago in 2002.

Strike Technologies (STRK)

Strike merged with BRUT in 2000.

The Island ECN (ISLD)

The Island started with the concept that everyone placing a NASDAQ order on Island is on equal ground, through the Island Order Book, which lists all of the bid and ask orders for each individual stock.

Instinet and The Island ECN merged to form INET.

Track Securities (TRAU)

The Track ECN is a division of Track Data Securities Corp.

Cross-Matching Systems

SelectNet

SelectNet is a negotiating system primarily used for trading between market makers. As a negotiating system, market makers are looking for the best price, not execution speed and may or may not execute an order immediately as on an ECN.

GlobeNet ECN

GlobeNet provides a single point of access for the trading of all NASDAQ NMS, NASDAQ Small Cap, and OTCBB equity securities.

Pipeline

The Pipeline ATS was developed in 1999 and includes an anonymous order book that allows institutions to negotiate large blocks of NYSE-listed securities, NASDAQ stocks, and Exchange Traded Funds (ETFs).

TradeWeb

TradeWeb's dealer-to-client platform provides a pool of liquidity for fixed-income products with 27 of the world's leading primary dealers and over 1,500 of the largest buy side institutions. Since its inception in 1998, more than $46 trillion in bond trades have been executed over the TradeWeb network. Over $150 billion in securities has changed hands through TradeWeb on a single day.

TradeWeb supports the execution of the following products:

- U.S. Treasuries
- Agencies
- Agency Discount Notes

- TBA-MBS
- Corporates
- Commercial Paper
- Euro Commercial Paper
- European Government Bonds
- Pfandbriefe/Covered Bonds

Trade Express

TradeXpress is an Internet-based network that can send trade allocations to dealers and receive confirmations for each fixed income trade ticket.

AccountNet

AccountNet is an online, central depository of settlement instructions that links broker/dealers, institutions, custodians and ECNs.

BrokerTec

BrokerTec was originally founded in January 1999 by 14 of the world's largest financial services companies to create a global fixed income wholesale trading platform, and in May 2003 BrokerTec was acquired by ICAP Plc.

TheMuniCenter

TheMuniCenter is an established electronic marketplace created for live anonymous fixed income trading across multiple asset classes for broker/dealers and investment managers. Founded by a consortium of major broker/dealers[106] and operational since 1999, TheMuniCenter has conducted business with more than 7,500 users at over 750 firms.

TheMuniCenter's trading platform enables users electronically to trade secondary market municipal, corporate, and agency securities, and to enter orders on new-issue Medium Term Notes (MTN's), Certificates of Deposit (CD's), and equity-linked notes.

The marketplace is supported by full two-way price negotiation where users can post bids, offerings, and counter offers on every item listed.

MarketAxess

MarketAxess was formed in April 2000 as a single trading platform with easy access to multi-dealer research, new issues, and competitive pricing in a wide range of credit products.

MarketAxess offers fully-disclosed trading in U.S. high-grade corporates, emerging markets, and Eurobonds for 19 broker/dealer clients and 575 institutional investor firms as of December 31, 2003.

MarketAxess' institutional investor clients include investment advisers, mutual funds, insurance companies, public and private pension funds, bank portfolios, and hedge funds.

---

[106] Salomon Smith Barney, Merrill Lynch, Morgan Stanley Dean Witter and Chapdelaine & Co., Lehman Brothers and Financial Security Association Inc.

Crossing Network

E-Crossnet

E-Crossnet is a crossing network for European equities, and membership is restricted to large institutional fund managers.

Trade Reporting

Trade Reporting is a function that is required of brokers and exchanges. The prices of securities that are traded on an exchange or NASDAQ are automatically captured; however, over-the-counter transactions outside of NASDAQ must be separately reported. If a security is traded on an exchange and is also traded OTC, the broker must report the OTC trades to the exchange.

Portfolio Management

Portfolio management systems are used to track trading activity and update positions. Successful portfolio management systems have interfaces to many different data sources and to their TOMS to allow for decisions to be implemented immediately and electronically.

Some PMSs also include accounting functionality which increases the number of interfaces for the application and the complexity.

Some of the leading portfolio management systems are:

- Croesus Finansoft
- DST International
- Eagle Investment Systems Corp.
- Effron Enterprises
- Financial Computer Software
- Financial Models Company
- Global Investment Systems Ltd.
- INDATA
- Integrated Decision Systems
- Princeton Financial Systems
- Sanchez Computer Associates, Inc.
- State Street Portfolio Accounting System
- SunGard Investment Management Systems
- SunGard Investment Management Systems / Decalog
- Thomson Financial
- x.eye

B. MIDDLE OFFICE APPLICATION VENDORS

There are many different categories of vendors that provide specific types of middle office applications to a number of niche markets.

Allocation Applications

A significant percentage of investment managers' trades are blocks, which must be allocated to the appropriate portfolios. Once the manager knows how many shares of the block were purchased/sold, and at what price, the manager must tell the broker which portfolios are affected. This information is either sent by fax or by an allocation system.

This can be performed by various Omgeo applications or the functionality could be built into the firm's TOMS.

Once the broker has received the allocation information, the broker must create a separate confirmation for each settlement.

Electronic Trade Confirmation Applications

The Electronic Trade Confirmation (ETC) systems are designed to support connectivity and routing of messages between the parties to a trade, and are primarily used for cross-border transactions. The original ETC providers that were established in the UK were TRACS, SEQUAL and Global OASYS.

The SWIFT approved ETC Providers as of April 2004 are:

- SIA S.P.A. - Italy
- Nomura Research Institute - SmartBridge Dept. - Japan
- City Networks - U.K.
- Cross Border Exchange Corp. - U.S.
- Depository Trust Clearing Corp. - U.S.
- SunGard Data Systems / e-Sourcing SB - U.S.

Risk Management Applications

As was discussed in the chapter on Post-Trade Processing, the concept of risk management is very broad. Risk can refer to the amount of risk assumed by a portfolio, including market, credit and performance risk. Risk systems can be used to identify and avoid risk by helping the firm:

- Choose between investment alternatives
- Better understand the potential gains/losses for types of investments or asset classes as market conditions such as interest rates change
- Monitor the level of exposure the firm has to individual traders, countries, industry segments, countries, etc.

These systems have different purposes for different categories of firms.

- Managers are concerned about market, credit and performance risk, and their risk monitoring functions are sometimes built into their portfolio management systems or trading systems.
- Brokers and banks that are trading for their own account are concerned about trading risk, as well as market, credit and performance risk. Managing trading risk is generally performed in the front office, in the trading systems that accumulate information about the firm's positions and the positions of individual traders.
- Brokers are also concerned about credit and margin risk for their clients, and if a client does not pay for a position, they become concerned about market and performance risk for the specific position.

- Banks are most often concerned about processing and fiduciary risk when they are supporting their clients.

Each of these different concerns requires different categories of information and different techniques to evaluate the information. Many of these risk systems need to accumulate information from various other internal systems, often across geographical boundaries.

Some of the existing risk management systems are:

- Algorithmics Incorporated
- Barra, Inc.
- Cicada
- FAME Information Services, Inc.
- Financial Engineering Associates
- FNX Limited
- Summit Systems, Inc.
- SunGard Trading and Risk Systems

Compliance Applications

Compliance involves ensuring that each firm is doing what it is allowed to do according to regulation or by its clients, in contrast to risk management which is often more concerned about ensuring that firms correctly decide what to do or avoid making mistakes.

Compliance differs for different types of firms, such as institutional accounts, mutual funds, brokers and custodians, and these systems can all be incorporated into trading systems, portfolio systems and/or record keeping systems.

These systems have different purposes for different firms.

- Investment managers wish to ensure that they comply with their fund's or client's investment objectives, as well as applicable processing regulations and rules. An investment manager's compliance system should identify if a proposed trade is inappropriate before the trade is made.

- Brokers have the same objectives in preventing inappropriate trades by their traders and clients, and in evaluating what was done after the trade to ensure that all of the appropriate processing regulations and rules are followed.

- Banks, unless they are trading for their own account, are generally more concerned with ensuring that processing is accomplished correctly within the banking regulations, as well as the specific regulations that govern the conduct of the various categories of clients.

C. BACK OFFICE SYSTEM VENDORS

The back office systems used by brokers, banks and investment managers are described in their respective chapters on processing.

The back office marketplace is also fragmented. The general rule is that most of the largest firms have proprietary systems or buy vendor applications for specific departments. Mid-range firms tend to buy applications and small firms often outsource. This does differ by market segment.

- Most large brokerage firms have in-house applications for their main processing systems, either proprietary or vendor-supplied, while some use central applications. Mid-size and small broker/dealers normally use a correspondent clearer.

- Most investment managers still acquire applications, and only a few of the largest build proprietary systems. There is an increased trend towards outsourcing of the entire back office process.

- The largest custodians usually use a series of proprietary and vendor-provided applications while the mid-size firms use vendor applications and the smaller firms outsource the custody process.

D. MARKET DATA VENDORS

Firms in the financial industry use several types of securities-related data, delivered in either real-time, batch or historical feeds. Data falls broadly into two types: Prices and Notifications. The data are required by both front- and back-office systems in order to process transactions correctly.

- Real-time pricing data (also called 'quotes') are generally used by traders and brokers who must make investment decisions quickly and on the most recent information possible. Real-time data is collected by vendors through feeds with various stock exchanges and ECNs and can be delayed a few minutes, giving the vendor time to validate and compare the information before disseminating it to clients.

- Batch information, which is generally received once per day, is satisfactory for the back-office for most processes. Batch prices are end-of-day ('closing') prices that are typically used to value portfolios, determine net asset values of mutual funds, and mark collateral to market. Batch notifications are notices of corporate events, such as dividends or corporate actions (mergers, tenders, etc.), which have longer windows in which to make decisions or process transactions.

  Batch data is usually transmitted via high bandwidth Internet connections, though a decreasing number of firms still require the data on tape.

- Historical data is batch information that reflects data over long periods of time. It is generally used by research analysts to look for trends and predict future price movements or economic activity.

	Front Office		Back Office	
	Prices	**Notifications**	**Prices**	**Notifications**
Real Time	X	-	-	-
Batch	-	-	X	X
Historic	X	-	-	-

Figure 292 - Market Data Usage Summary

The consequences of incorrect or missing data, either prices or notifications, can be so severe that most firms use multiple sources of information. Historically, this was accomplished by subscribing to two or more vendor data feeds for the same information, comparing them in-house and manually reconciling any discrepancies. While many firms still use this method, over the last few years the concept of 'data scrubbing' has become popular. In this method, a single vendor collects data from different sources, reconciles the discrepancies and delivers to the client a single clean batch, called a 'golden copy,' of the data.

There has been a significant amount of consolidation in this segment of the industry, and the current participants are entrenched. While the sources of market data are widespread, an increasing number of providers are using the same sources, as well as re-branding data from their competitors, a situation that is frequently unknown by their clients.

Real Time Data (Quote) Vendors

The major real time data vendors are:

- Bloomberg
- Comstock
- E-Signal
- North American Quotations
- Reuters
- SunGard
- Telekurs
- Thomson

Batch Data Vendors

The major batch data vendors are:

- CCH Incorporated – Corporate Actions
- Financial Information Incorporated – Corporate Actions
- Interactive Data – Corporate Actions, Income, Pricing
- JJ Kenny – Fixed Income Pricing
- Mergent – Corporate Actions, Income
- Standard and Poor's – Income, Corporate Actions, Pricing
- Telekurs – Income, Corporate Actions, Pricing
- Xcitek – Corporate Actions

Reference Data Vendors

Another type of data that is used by both the back office and the front office is reference data. Reference data is relatively static information about securities (e.g., type of security, settlement method, paying agent, transfer agent, income payment frequency, etc.) or clients (address, payment histories, ID numbers, etc.). Reference data has gained in popularity with the passing into law of the USA Patriot Act, which requires financial firms to have faster and more accurate access to information.

As processors have come to understand how critical it is to maintain accurate reference data, firms have identified several ways to improve their processing:

- Reduce or eliminate manual entry
- Avoid redundant data storage
- Eliminate inconsistent business rules

79% of the respondents in a recent survey by Reuters, Tower Group and Capco agreed that inconsistent, inaccurate and incomplete reference data is the major cause of failure to achieve internal STP.

Many banks are establishing a separate department to manage reference data.

The major reference data vendors are:

- Asset Control
- Cicada Corporation
- CUSIP Service Bureau
- Eagle Investment Systems
- FT Interactive data
- Fame
- Fidelity ActionsXchange
- Financial Technologies International
- Standard & Poor's
- Telekurs Financial
- Xcitek

Market Data Survey

The Summit Group conducts an annual survey of data vendors through its subsidiary, Securities Operations Forum, which measures the vendors on accuracy, reliability and coverage. The results of the survey can be found on TSG's website (www.tsgc.com).

There are three generic issues that are identified by the respondents to the survey year after year:

- Lack of coverage on foreign corporate actions
- Lack of coverage on thinly traded securities
- Inconsistent information between vendors

E. BOND RATING VENDORS

Bond rating vendors evaluate the credit risk associated with specific vendors and specific issues. The ratings that are established by these vendors differ slightly; however, the methodologies are very similar so that securities that are rated by different vendors can usually be compared according to the ratings.

The vendors are selected and paid by the issuers to perform this service, and are very competitive. The primary rating agencies in the U.S. are shown in the following chart:

Definition	Duff & Phelps	Fitch	Moody's	S&P	DBRS [107]
Highest Rating	AAA	AAA	Aaa	AAA	R1 High
Very Strong	AA	AA	Aa	AA	R1 Middle
Strong	A	A	A	A	R1 Low
Adequate	BBB	BBB	Baa	BBB	R2 High
Uncertain	BB	BB	Ba	BB	R2 Middle
Vulnerable	B	B	B	B	R2 Low
High Risk	CCC	CCC	Caa	CCC	R3 High
		CC	Ca		R3 Middle
		C	C		R3 Low
Default	DD	D, DD, DDD		D	D
Further modifiers for each rating			1,2,3	+ or -	

Figure 293 - Bond Rating Vendor Abbreviations

---

[107] Dominion Bond Rating Service

While it isn't perfect, the rating system has been successful in identifying potential defaults, S&P has reported the following results over a fifteen year period.

Original Rating by S&P	Actual Default Rate
AAA	0.52%
AA	1.31%
A	2.32%
BBB	6.64%
BB	19.52%
B	35.65%
CCC	54.38%

Figure 294 - S&P Default Results

F. THIRD-PARTY INSURERS

The issuer pays the premium for third-party insurance, so that specific issues can have some coverage beyond that provided by the issuing firm. Insurance is usually used on municipal issues to increase the investors' feeling of safety, and the premium reduces the yield.

The fact that an issue is insured does not totally guarantee that it will be repaid, since it is possible that in extreme circumstances, the issuer and the insurance company can both default.

The primary insurers in the U.S. are:

- MBIA (The letters are used exclusively today, although they originally stood for Municipal Bond Investors Assurance)
- AMBAC (The letters are used exclusively today, although they originally stood for American Municipal Bond Assurance Corporation)
- FGIC (Financial Guaranty Insurance Company)
- FSA (Financial Security Assurance)

G. MIDDLEWARE VENDORS

There is an on-going industry need to move messages from application to application rather than moving files. This increase in the use of messaging has driven the need for flexible applications that can reformat and reroute these messages so that they can be easily read and understood by the appropriate systems.

Messaging involves individual transactions that are sent from point to point as they occur. The message is a single transaction that is sent by itself to another application for further processing, while a file typically contains many transactions.

Messaging is generally associated with real time processing, where the actual processing occurs as soon as the transaction is received. The opposite of real-time processing is batch processing, where a file of transactions is held until the system is ready to process them. While the industry trend is towards increased use of real time processing (or near real time) and messaging, there is still a definite place for batch processing to support operations.

It is clear that an order for a trade must be sent and processed quickly, and therefore messaging and real time processing are appropriate. It is also clear that in today's environment, we can easily process transactions such as dividends in an overnight batch, so not every transaction needs to be converted to real time processing.

Most firms have a technology architecture that evolved as users defined their changing needs, specific applications were acquired and as new technologies were developed. Efficient and high quality processing is increasingly requiring the movement of data in the form of messages between these legacy applications, new applications and to/from other firms and industry utilities. This increase in the use of messaging has increased the need for flexible applications that can reformat and reroute these messages so that they can be read by the appropriate systems.

To make messaging work efficiently in the past, the industry has accepted the challenge to develop message standards. SWIFT, ISITC-IOA and FIX have supplied, and are continuing to supply, a variety of useful message formats. When both sides to a transaction use the same format, the chances of a misunderstanding are reduced, and the processing is more efficient.

As the potential use of messaging has increased, so has the need for a new category of application, often called Middleware, which is shown in the following graphic, This layer of code sits between the processing applications and the network and performs three basic functions, reformatting, routing and protocol connectivity. Some of the leading vendors are MQ Series, Tibco, Vitria, Mercator, CheckFree and webMethods.

In the past, each programmer wrote specific code that generated the application's output in a specified format and told the network where to send it. This worked fine when there were only a few applications and a few end points. However, as the number of both has increased, it has become more and more difficult to maintain the hard coded instructions, and the need for a flexible application has increased. Middleware eliminates the need to hard code these connections between applications or firms.

In addition to routing and formatting, systems developers have had to contend with various telecommunications protocols, which describe the technical points of connectivity. To provide true Middleware functionality, an application must also support the transfer of a message from one protocol to another while routing and formatting.

External Connectivity (In/Out)

Format   Route   Protocols   Reconciliation

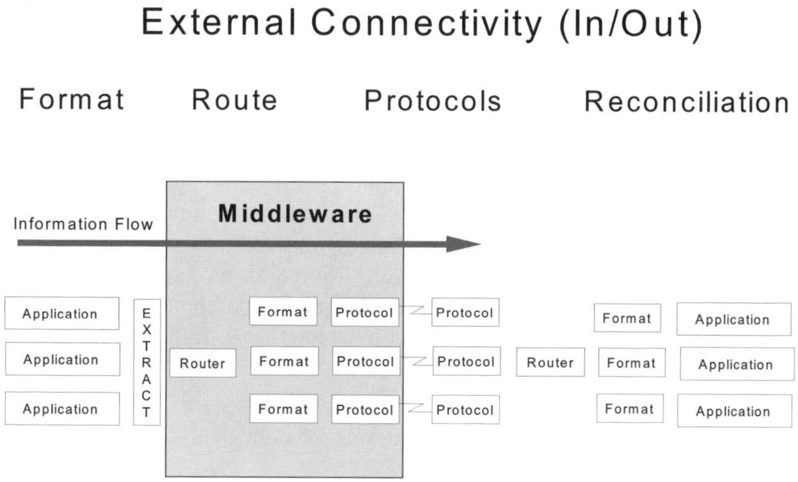

Figure 295 - Middleware Architecture

The use of Middleware will continue to expand as real time processing and messaging become more prevalent, as developers realize that it is not economical to hard code every interface between applications and firms, and as the number of different points of connectivity continues to increase.

H. SYSTEMS INTEGRATORS

There are many different systems integrators that support the securities industry, and which provide a variety of services, including:

Design and Development

Systems integration has become so complex that in-house resources often need some specific additional support in order to succeed. Information Technology (IT) consultants can assist in designing, building, and implementing system solutions through mainframes, client/servers or distributed computing.

These consultants are skilled at matching the appropriate technology to a business's needs by using a range of techniques, from simple programming languages to advanced technologies. Most system integrators will also be able to support their clients with project management, requirements definition, system design and development, testing and conversions, and documentation and training.

Outsourcing / Off-Shore Development

Increasingly, firms are using outsourcing to maintain and enhance their legacy systems and for certain types of de novo development. Most firms providing this service have a staff in the U.S., and can call upon resources in other countries for additional, cost effective resources when necessary. When a firm has a proven offshore development methodology, they can take responsibility for complete projects that will be developed in a low cost environment; or they can bring highly skilled individuals or teams into the U.S. to work with their clients' staff.

Testing and Conversions

Also, today's complex systems require a different approach to testing and conversions. The traditional file-to-file conversions and manual testing activities of the past are no longer able to efficiently and effectively support complicated system migrations or on-going testing. Some firms have developed tools to automatically build a test deck of business conditions which significantly reduces the effort involved in conversions and testing, and dramatically increases the quality of the resulting system.

The Summit Group has written a book on *Software Testing for Financial Services Firms* that is available on Amazon.com or through the SOF website (http://www.soforum.com).

I. NEWSLETTERS

There are a number of publications that serve the U.S. securities industry. Each one focuses on some specific aspect of the industry. Some examples are:

Publication	Published By:
American Banker	American Bankers Association
Pension and Investments	Crain Publications
Journal of Securities Operations	Securities Operations Forum *(The Summit Group)*
Securities Industry News	Thomson Financial Services
Operations Management	Institutional Investor
Securities Operations Letter	Securities Operations Forum *(The Summit Group)*
Wall Street Technology	Miller Freeman

Figure 296 - Industry Publications

J. EDUCATION

Several industry support groups, including non-profit and for-profit organizations, provide securities industry professionals with educational opportunities through training and conferences.

Training

The leading education providers for securities processing are:

Securities Operations Forum (The Summit Group)

SOF offers a wide range of classroom training, custom training at the client's location and eLearning courses for securities operations professionals. These courses and programs are described at http://www.soforum.com/training/

American Bankers Association

The ABA offers a Certified Securities Operations Professional (CSOP) program that is described at

http://www.aba.com/ICBCertifications/CSOP.htm

ISITC-IOA

The ISITC-IOA in partnership with Securities Operations Forum has sponsored a Securities Industry Professional (SIP) Credential that covers all aspects of securities processing, and which is described at http://www.soforum.com/training/SIP_index.php

FT Knowledge

FT Knowledge conducts a number of basic operations courses for industry professionals.

Cannon

Cannon provides several classroom courses on trust and banking.

NASD Securities License Training

There are several firms that offer training for the various NASD licenses, including:

- CCHWall Street
- Boston Institute of Finance
- American Investment Training

CFA Training

There are several firms that offer training for the various NASD licenses that were described in the chapter on Regulators and Legislation, including:

- Boston University (available through Securities Operations Forum)
- PassPro
- Wallace Cititraining
- Stalla

Key Trade Shows

Trade shows are sponsored by different industry organizations for their members and for interested participants. The major trade shows for the securities operations industry are:

Trade Show	Sponsor	Purpose
ABA Operations Conference for Securities, Brokerage & Trust	ABA	Trust processing and bank securities processing
ISITC Update	ISITC-IOA	Quarterly updates and working groups
BDUG (Bank Depository Users Group)	DTC	Depository users forum
SIA Securities Operations Conference	SIA	Securities Operations Update
Sibos	SWIFT	Annual Conference
NICSA (National Investment Company Service Association)	NICSA	Annual investment company update

Figure 297 - Industry Trade Shows

Conferences

There are several different conference organizers, and many of the associations that are discussed in the chapter on Industry Owned Organizations conduct their own annual conferences or trade shows for their members and guests. The major organizers for general purpose securities operations conferences are:

- International Business Communications
- Institute for International Research
- Securities Operations Forum (*The Summit Group*)
- Wall Street Technology Association

These conferences cover topical subjects such as STP, Reconciliations, corporate actions, etc.

XVIII. Industry Owned Organizations

The organizations that are owned by financial firms that support securities processing fall into four categories:

- Industry Associations
- Standards Making Organizations
- Self-Regulatory Organizations (Covered in the chapter on Regulators and Legislation)
- Joint Ventures (New businesses established to provide common processing for firms)

Standards Organizations and Industry Associations are covered in this chapter with a special emphasis on three of the primary organizations:

- SWIFT
- FIX
- ISITC

A. INDUSTRY ASSOCIATIONS

There are several significant industry associations, with minimal corporate and/or individual membership fees, which can help industry professionals keep in touch with developments in their segment of the industry.

American Bankers Association (ABA) [108]

The American Bankers Association (ABA) provides publications, training, conferences and lobbying support for all U.S. banks.

- ABA Bank Membership, including banking, savings, and trust Institutions
- Service Membership, including vendors and non-financial companies
- Associate Membership, which includes non-U.S. banks

There are also state bankers associations in most states that bring a more local focus to the lobbying and educational efforts of the associations.

Since the ABA covers all banks, large and small, it only focuses a small portion of its effort on the securities businesses of banks.

Asset Managers' Forum (AMF) [109]

The Asset Managers Forum was formed, in cooperation with The Bond Market Association by securities processing professionals affiliated with various asset management firms. The Forum focuses on the opportunity for sell side and bayside operations professionals to jointly pursue the development of mutual industry-wide securities processing or operations projects and enhancements.

The primary mission of the Forum is to give the bayside a unified voice in addressing major securities operations, accounting, legal and regulatory compliance, and market practices initiatives.

---

[108] Source: American Bankers Association

[109] Source: Asset Managers' Forum

Bank Insurance & Securities Association (BISA) [110]

Gramm-Leach-Bliley formally paved the way for depository institutions to actively integrate their securities and insurance programs, and led to the merger of the Bank Securities Association and the Financial Institutions Insurance Association into BISA.

The single goal of the BISA is the advancement of profitable wealth and risk management solutions through banks, thrifts and credit unions by:

- Providing members with the knowledge and support to grow their businesses through enhanced productivity, professionalism and service to their clients, and

- Working to assure a legislative and regulatory environment that is healthy for future growth.

The Bank Insurance and Securities Association (BISA) was formed in October 2002 as a result of the Bank Securities Association (BSA) and the Financial Institutions Insurance Association (FIIA) merger.

- Founded in 1987, The Bank Securities Association (BSA) is dedicated to serving the needs of those responsible for marketing securities, insurance and other investment products through commercial banks, trust companies, savings institutions, and credit unions. The membership includes financial institutions of all sizes, their broker/dealer and mutual fund subsidiaries, and firms providing products and/or services to support these operations.

- Founded in 1989, the Financial Institutions Insurance Association (FIIA) is comprised of financial institutions, insurance companies, third-party marketers, service providers and state banking trade associations active in the marketing of insurance and annuities. The FIIA's membership included bank holding companies, national banks, state-chartered banks, thrifts, card issuers, credit unions, mortgage companies, and finance companies that sell insurance to consumers and businesses.

The Bond Market Association (TBMA) [111]

The Bond Market Association is the trade association represents the $17 trillion debt markets. TBMA speaks for its bond industry members, represents their interests in New York; Washington, D.C.; London; Frankfurt; Brussels and Tokyo; and with issuer and investor groups worldwide.

The Association represents securities firms and banks, whether they are large, multi-product firms or companies with special market niches.

- 30% of the Association's members specialize in a particular bond market.

- Seventy-percent of the member firms are headquartered outside of New York City, while approximately 20% are substantially owned by foreign institutions.

- 10% are predominantly American-owned multinationals.

The Association's membership collectively accounts for approximately 95% of

---

[110]   Source: Bank Insurance & Securities Association

[111]   Source: The Bond Market Association

the nation's municipal bond underwriting and trading activity, and the membership also includes all primary dealers in U.S. government securities, as recognized by the Federal Reserve Bank of New York, and all major dealers in federal agency securities, mortgage- and asset-backed securities and corporate bonds, as well as money market and funding instruments.

The Bond Market Association is a lobbyist for the bond industry and has several goals, including:

- Working as an industry advocate
- Keeping members informed of relevant legislative, regulatory and market practice developments
- Providing a forum through which the industry can review and respond to current issues
- Striving to standardize market practices and commonly used documentation
- Promoting efficiency to reduce costs
- Helping members solve common problems and develop more efficient management, operations and communications methods
- Educating legislators, regulators, the press and investors on the size and importance of the bond markets by publishing books, brochures, manuals and other educational materials, and sponsoring seminars, conferences and informational meetings
- Compiling and tracking various industry-related statistics on an historical basis and disseminating the information through published research reports

Membership is open to any bona fide debt securities dealer, as long as the firm supports the Association's objectives of promoting fairness and efficiency through open access to the bond markets throughout the world.

CFA Institute (Formerly the Association for Investment Management and Research (AIMR)) [112]

AIMR was founded in January 1990 from the merger of the Financial Analysts Federation (FAF) and the Institute of Chartered Financial Analysts (ICFA). In May, 2003, AIMR changed its name to CFA Institute to better reflect its mission, which is to serve its members and investors as a global leader in educating and examining investment managers and analysts and sustaining high standards of professional conduct.

AIMR's worldwide members are employed as securities analysts, portfolio managers, strategists, consultants, educators, and other investment specialists who work in a variety of fields, including investment counseling and management, banking, insurance, and investment banking and brokerage firms.

AIMR offers three categories of services to its members: Education through seminars and publications; Professional Conduct and Ethics; and Standards of Practice and Advocacy.

---

[112] Source: CFA Institute (Formerly AIMR)

Financial Information Services Division (FISD) [113]

The Financial Information Services Division is a part of the Software and Information Industry Association, which is discussed later in this chapter.

The Financial Information Services Division of the SIIA provides a forum for exchanges, market data vendors, specialist data providers, brokerage firms and banks to address and resolve business and technical issues related to the distribution, management, administration and use of market data. Participants use the forum to exchange ideas, build business relationships and improve the business climate associated with the worldwide flow of financial information.

Members are responsible for their own strategic and commercial interests. FISD's role is to act as a neutral facilitator of the discussion and manager of the consensus agenda that emerges as a result. FISD was founded in 1985 and is governed by a 27-member Executive Committee consisting of equal numbers of exchanges, vendors and market data user firms.

The agenda of FISD is organized into the following broad activities:

- Market Data Business/Commercial Issues
- Market Data Definition Language (MDDL)
- Symbology and Reference Data
- Facilitation and Industry Representation

Futures Industry Association (FIA) [114]

FIA, with more than 180 corporate members, represents organizations that participate in the futures market through two classes of membership:

- Regular members are futures commission merchants, which are responsible for more than 80% of the client business transacted on U.S. futures exchanges
- Associate members include international exchanges, banks, legal and accounting firms, introducing brokers, commodity trading advisors, commodity pool operators and other market users, and information and equipment providers headquartered in the U.S. and abroad

Investment Company Institute (ICI) [115]

The Investment Company Institute, founded in 1940, is a national association for the investment company industry. ICI membership, which reaches over 86.6 million individual shareholders and manages $7.4 Trillion in assets, includes:

- Mutual Funds (8,633 members)
- Closed End Funds (622 members)
- Exchange-Trade Funds (126 members)
- Sponsors of Unit Investment Trusts (5 members)

ICI represents its members regarding legislation, regulation, taxation, public

---

[113]   Source: Financial Information Services Division

[114]   Source: Futures Industry Association

[115]   Source: Investment Company Institute

information, economic and policy research, business operations, and statistics.

Investment Counsel Association of America (ICAA) [116]

The Investment Counsel Association of America represents the interests of federally registered investment adviser firms. The Association was founded in 1937 and played a major role in the enactment of the Investment Advisers Act of 1940 which regulates the investment adviser industry. The ICAA consists of more than 300 investment adviser firms that collectively manage in excess of $4 trillion in assets for a wide variety of institutional and individual clients.

The purposes of the Association are:

- To promote high standards of integrity, public responsibility, and competence in the profession of the investment adviser industry for the benefit of all member firms and their clients and to promote the objectives of rendering professional, informed, unbiased, and continuous advice to clients based on investment analysis.

- To provide effective, exclusive, and quality representation of the investment adviser industry at all levels of government for the development, formulation, and enactment of appropriate legislation relating to investment advisers and promulgation of rules and regulations thereunder.

- To provide benefits, services, and products that assist and add value to member firms.

International Financial Services Association (IFSA)

The International Financial Services Association supports firms involved in international transaction processing, and its members include U.S. and non-U.S. banks with offices in the U.S.

International Swaps and Derivatives Association (ISDA) [117]

Chartered in 1985, the International Swaps and Derivatives Association, with over 600 members worldwide, is a global trade association which represents participants in the privately negotiated derivatives industry, a business which includes swaps and options across all asset classes (interest rate, currency, commodity and energy, credit and equity).

The goals of the ISDA are:

- Promoting practices conducive to the efficient conduct of the business, including the development and maintenance of derivatives documentation
- Promoting the development of sound risk management practices
- Fostering high standards of commercial conduct
- Advancing international public understanding of the business
- Educating members and others on legislative regulatory, legal, documentation, accounting, tax, operational, technological and other issues affecting them

---

[116]   Source: Investment Counsel Association of America

[117]   Source: International Swaps and Derivatives Association

- Creating a forum for the analysis and discussion of, and representing the common interest of its members on, these issues and developments

Managed Funds Association (MFA) [118]

Managed Funds Association is a U.S.-based association representing professionals in the global alternative investment industry. With approximately 750 members worldwide, MFA represents professionals in futures, hedge funds and other alternative investments, as well as brokers, exchanges, and all the other services which support the industry.

Founded in 1991, MFA promotes:

- A beneficial regulatory environment
- Growth of the alternative investment industry
- Improved public relations
- Increased member and investor knowledge

National Association of Insurance Commissioners (NAIC) [119]

NAIC, established in 1871, is an organization of insurance regulators from all 50 states, the District of Columbia and the four U.S. territories. NAIC provides a forum for the development of uniform policy when uniformity is appropriate. NAIC helps state regulators protect the interests of insurance consumers by establishing shared objectives of financial and market conduct regulation.

The mission of the NAIC is to:

- Protect the public interest
- Promote competitive markets
- Facilitate the fair and equitable treatment of insurance consumers
- Promote the reliability, solvency and financial solidity of insurance institutions
- Support and improve state regulation of insurance

National Investment Company Services Association (NICSA) [120]

The National Investment Company Services Association was founded in 1962 to provide support for operations and shareholder servicing professionals in the mutual fund industry. Members include representation from nearly 400 companies in the U.S. and other countries, and include mutual fund complexes, investment management companies, custodian banks, transfer agents and independent providers of specialized products and services.

North American Securities Administrators Association (NASAA) [121]

Established in 1919, the North American Securities Administrators Association is the oldest international organization devoted to investor protection. Members of the association consists of state, provincial, and territorial securities

---

[118] Source: Managed Funds Association
[119] Source: NAIC
[120] Source: National Investment Company Services Association
[121] Source: North American Securities Administrators Association

administrators in the 50 states, the District of Columbia, Puerto Rico, Canada, and Mexico. In the United States, NASAA is the voice of state securities agencies responsible for efficient capital formation and grass roots investor protection.

The association conducts its affairs through standing committees organized into four sections in the areas of broker/dealer and investment adviser regulation; state, provincial, and territorial enforcement; corporate finance; as well as administration and technology. NASAA also coordinates and implements training and education seminars for the industry.

Options Industry Council (OIC) [122]

The Options Industry Council, formed in 1992, consists of the Options Clearing Corporation and the four exchanges trading options in the U.S., which are the:

- American Stock Exchange
- Chicago Board Options Exchange
- International Stock Exchange
- Pacific Stock Exchange
- Philadelphia Stock Exchange

REDAC [123]

The Reference Data Coalition (REDAC) was formed to:

- Ensure that the multi-dimensional and complex data requirements for STP automation are well defined and clearly articulated to all involved parties
- Facilitate coordination among the various reference data initiatives
- Promote the development of practical solutions that are aligned with global industry objectives

The overall goal is to define the data elements and the essential industry standards that are needed to precisely describe assets and account entries required for global trade cycle processing. The primary objectives of REDAC are:

- To act in coalition with other industry bodies to ensure that data reference requirements for STP are well defined and clearly articulated to all involved parties, specifically related to multiple-listed and other "non-traditional" securities. The goal is to resolve the information needed for instrument, client/counterparty, trade-specific and accounting identification [throughout the security lifecycle (creation, research, trade, confirmation, settlement, clearing, reporting)] as well as how it will be collected, disseminated and implemented by industry participants.
- To evaluate and promote coordination among the standards activities affecting reference data. REDAC will help ensure that standards bodies are aligned with industry requirements and will help drive these standards toward implementation on a global basis.

---

[122]   Source: Options Industry Council

[123]   Source: Financial Information Services Division

- – Standards for identification - including numbering schemes, instrument symbology, sector codes and business entity relationships required for unique and precise identification
- – Standards for content - to ensure that there is a common understanding of all reference data attributes needed to describe assets and account entries (market data ontology) particularly within security master files
- – Standards for communication – focusing on trade messages and standing settlement instructions

- To act in coalition with other industry efforts to define the entities responsible for providing the information required (roles and responsibilities) throughout the information chain and help identify alternative sources of required information.

- To ensure that the operational challenges associated with implementation of solutions are well defined and viable – and ensure that the commercial models are not an impediment to global electronic commerce.

- To coordinate reference data activities and ensure broad participation by all segments, functions, groups and entities (i.e. asset managers, broker/dealers, custodians, vendors, exchanges, depositories, standards bodies, regulators and numbering agencies) involved in the transactions lifecycle.

Securities Industry Association (SIA) [124]

The Securities Industry Association, established in 1972 through the merger of the Association of Stock Exchange Firms (founded in 1913) and the Investment Banker's Association (founded in 1912), represents about 600 U.S. securities firms which are active in all securities markets and all phases of corporate and public finance, including:

- Investment banks
- Broker/dealers
- Specialists
- Mutual fund companies

The SIA is organized into various divisions for professionals who work in specialized areas of activity, which are:

- Compliance and Legal
- Credit
- Client Account Transfer
- Data Management
- Dividend
- Financial Management
- Internal Auditors
- Reorganization

---

[124]   Source: Securities Industry Association

- Securities Lending
- Securities Operations
- International Operations

Securities Market Practices Group (SMPG) [125]

In July 1998, SWIFT sponsored the organization of the Securities Market Practice Group (SMPG), which resulted in the establishment of National Market Practice Groups (NMPG) in more than 35 geographic markets that are comprised of broker/dealers, investment managers, custodian banks, central securities depositories and regulators.

The membership of the SMPG and the NMPGs are committed to the vision that standards in conjunction with defined market practices will bring the industry closer to its goal of achieving STP.

The SMPG is a tactical initiative focused on enhancing the current securities industry practices. This group realizes the benefit of industry utilities and other industry groups in dictating conformance to standards and market practices. As such, there is active dialogue between the SMPG and other similar initiatives (.i.e., FIX, OMGEO, European Central Securities Depositories Association, ISITC-IOA, etc.), in order to ensure that the tactical work of the SMPG provides a first step toward the restructuring of the securities industry.

Securities Industry Automation Corporation (SIAC) [126]

SIAC was established in 1972 as a subsidiary of the NYSE and AMEX to run the computer systems and communications networks that support the two exchanges and to disseminate U.S. market data worldwide.

This system's organization and data center is responsible for ensuring that sufficient capacity exists to process the rapidly increasing volume of securities transactions. In the 1960s, when the volume grew to over 11 million shares per day, the industry closed one day a week to process the related paper. In the 1990s, SIAC was able to process over 200 million shares in the first seven minutes of single trading day, and today is even faster.

Software and Information Industry Association (SIIA) [127]

The Software & Information Industry Association is the principal trade association for the software and digital content industry. SIIA provides global services in government relations, business development, corporate education and intellectual property protection to the leading companies that are setting the pace for the digital age.

The SIIA goals are to:

- Promote the common interests of the software and digital content industry as a whole, as well as its component parts.
- Protect the intellectual property of member companies, and advocates a legal and regulatory environment that benefits the entire industry.

---

[125] Source: Securities Market Practices Group
[126] Source: Securities Industry Automation Corporation
[127] Source: Software and Information Industry Association

- Inform the industry and the broader public by serving as a resource on trends, technologies, policies and related issues that affect member firms and demonstrate the contribution of the industry to the broader economy.

B. FINANCIAL INFORMATION EXCHANGE (FIX) [128]

The FIX protocol was, initiated in 1992 by a group of institutions and brokers with a goal of streamlining the trading process. The group created an open message standard that can be structured to match the business requirements of each firm for electronic communication of indications, orders and executions. The FIX committee defines the benefits as:

- FIX provides institutions and brokers a means of reducing the clutter of telephone calls and paper, and facilitates targeting high quality information to specific individuals

- FIX provides an open standard that leverages the development effort so that firms can efficiently create links with a wide range of counterparties

- FIX provides ready access to the industry, which reduces vendors' marketing effort

FIX is a totally open system, which encourages vendors to use the standard. FIX will work with leased lines, frame relay, Internet, etc., and with multiple security protocols.

The FIX Steering Committee currently consists of:

Committee Member	Committee Member
American Century	JF Asset Management
Citigroup	Jordan and Jordan
Credit Suisse First Boston	Lehman Brothers
Gartmore Investment Management plc	Merrill Lynch
Hitachi, Ltd.	Peter Randall & Associates
Implementation Solutions LLC	UBS Investment Bank
Instinet Japan Ltd	

Figure 298 - FIX Executive Committee

FIX, originally defined for U.S. domestic equity trading with messages moving directly between principals, supports a variety of business functions such as cross-border equity, foreign exchange, and limited fixed income trading.

FIX can be used with many different communications protocols (X.25, asynch, TCP/IP, etc.), and the protocol is defined at two levels: session and application. The session level is concerned with the delivery of data while the application level defines business related data content.

FIX Message Format and Delivery

The following section summarizes the general specifications for constructing and transmitting FIX messages.

---

[128]   Source: FIX

Session Protocol

A FIX session is a bi-directional stream of ordered messages between two parties within a continuous sequence number series. A single FIX session can exist across multiple physical connections, and parties can connect and disconnect multiple times while maintaining a single FIX session.

The FIX session protocol is based on an optimistic model where normal delivery of data is assumed (i.e., no communication level acknowledgment of individual messages) and errors in delivery are identified by message sequence number gaps.

Message Format

The general format of a FIX message is a standard header followed by the message body fields and terminated with a standard trailer. Each message is constructed of a stream of fields where <tag> = <value>, and over 200 fields have been identified.

There are several different categories of messages included in the FIX format:

Indications of Interest

Indication of interest messages identify securities which the broker is either buying or selling, for their own firm or as an agent. The indications can have specific expiration times/dates and a specific expiration value.

News

The news message is a general free format message that can be initiated by the broker or the investment manager.

Email

The email message is intended for private use between two parties.

Quote Request

Investment managers can use this message to request quotes from brokers prior to placing an order for securities or forex.

Quote

The quote message is the response to a Quote Request message and can also be used to publish unsolicited quotes.

Order messages can be generated based on quotes.

New Order - Single

The new order message type is used by institutions wishing to electronically submit a single order for securities and Forex orders to a broker for execution.

Orders can be submitted with special handling instructions and execution instructions. Handling instructions refer to how the broker should handle the order as it is traded, and execution instructions contain explicit directions as to how the order should be executed.

Execution Reports

The execution report message is used to:

1. Confirm the receipt of an order
2. Confirm changes to an existing order (i.e. cancel and replace)

3.   Relay order status information

4.   Relay fill information on working orders

5.   Reject orders

Don't Know Trade (DK)

The Don't Know Trade (DK) message notifies a trading partner that an electronically received execution has been rejected.

Order Cancel/Replace Request (Order Modification Request)

The Order Cancel/Replace Request is used to change the parameters of an existing order. Only a limited number of fields can be changed via the cancel/replace request message. All other fields should be retransmitted as sent in the original order.

Order Cancel Request

The Order Cancel Request message requests the cancellation of all of the remaining quantity of an existing order. The request will only be accepted if the order can successfully be pulled back from the exchange floor without executing.

Allocation

The allocation record instructs a broker on how to allocate executed shares to the investment manager's sub-accounts. The allocation record can also be used as a confirmation message through which third parties can communicate execution and settlement details between trading partners.

In addition, the allocation record can be sent by the broker to communicate fees and other details that can only be computed once the sub-account breakdowns are known.

Settlement Instructions

The settlement instructions message provides either the broker's or the manager's instructions for trade settlement. This message has been designed so that it can be sent from the broker to the institution, from the institution to the broker, or from either to an independent *standing instructions* database or matching system.

New Order List

The new order list message type is used by institutions wishing to electronically submit a list of related securities or Forex orders to a broker for execution.

FIX Vendors

There are several categories of vendors that provide applications supporting FIX, including:

- FIX Engines
- FIX Applications
- Communications

A list of FIX-approved vendors can be found FIX website (http://www.fixprotocol.org).

Future Plans

FIX's flexibility with the flexible tag-value message format creates problems in other areas since it does not impose structural constraints on a message, which requires all validation to occur at the application level.

FIX has proposed an evolution of the FIX application messages to FIXML, which is defined as a structured, validated message using an Extensible Mark-up Language (XML) and derived grammar that is contained within the standard FIX message. This format will leave the FIX session handling protocol intact and is intended to minimize the impact on existing implementations.

As an XML-derived language, FIXML messages can be validated by standard parsers and take advantage of the following points, according to FIX: [129]

The benefits are:

Session and application layers that evolve independently

The separation of application and session layers creates opportunities to break away from the traditional methods of implementing FIX. Session and security levels can develop unconstrained without affecting application level messages. A new security model could be embraced or the session layer could be implemented using off-the-shelf technology.

Improved communication

A DTD-based protocol language (one based on XML) offers improved communication over written documentation alone.

Improved evolution and extensibility

A DTD-based language provides a better communication model for software and users.

Structure and content validation

DTD-based structural and content validation eliminates imprecision over current procedural-based software implementations.

Evolutionary, not revolutionary

XML offers an evolutionary model for future improvements to the FIX protocol, allowing the protocol to evolve naturally and in a controlled way.

Reduce duplication of effort

XML is becoming widely used and well-respected in the software industry. Basing FIX on XML will provide commonality with other initiatives outside the FIX community and help to reduce duplication of effort in achieving mutual goals. In forums such as EDI, SWIFT, OFX, and ISITC, dictionaries are being built that describe the varieties of price, quantity, security, etc. XML allows these groups to share results and save effort by leveraging each other's work. Over time, this may also establish a basis for convergence and interoperability of these various message standards. The ultimate benefit will be a common data dictionary for the financial community that helps pave the way for straight through processing.

---

[129]   Source: FIX

C. INTERNATIONAL SECURITIES ASSOCIATION FOR INSTITUTIONAL TRADE COMMUNICATION – INTERNATIONAL OPERATIONS ASSOCIATION (ISITC-IOA) [130]

ISITC-IOA is a global working committee of over 1,500 securities operations professionals who represent 350 custodian banks, investment managers, brokers, and vendors, with a goal of fostering alliances and advocating standards that promote straight through processing (STP) of securities transactions.

ISITC-IOA believes that STP is an important industry objective for the following reasons:

- The continued trend toward globalization of assets has increased the complexities of trading and settling investments across borders. Lack of standards and automation increases costs and risks to the industry.

- A move to a shorter settlement cycle in various countries is likely. As soon as a trade is executed, it must be affirmed and recorded in the custodian's SMAC system for settlement. There will be no time for end-of-day batches, faxes, or duplicate keystrokes.

- Firms are under continuous pressure to grow their business without increasing costs or risk. Consolidation in all markets continues to redefine the term 'big' This has changed the nature of the business, and has introduced an expanded product base to firms previously operating in a much narrower niche. It is increasingly difficult to support an ever increasing array of manual processes.

- Good support staff is hard to find, expensive to train, and have very different workplace expectations than employees entering the business in prior years. People are no longer willing to work unlimited overtime on routine processing. Operations professionals need to create an environment where the staff can become problem solvers rather than paper shufflers. The only way to accomplish these goals is via STP.

ISITC-IOA promotes industry-wide STP by defining short and long-term objectives, and establishing working committees that will focus on solving specific industry problems.

- In the short term, the group will ensure that we have the standards in place to implement STP within each organization.

- Longer term, the ISITC-IOA is working with industry utilities and vendors, as well as other initiatives like FIX and SWIFT, to ensure that STP can be achieved across the entire trade life cycle, on a global basis.

These working groups help ISITC-IOA's members keep up to date with the industry initiatives, as well as participate in the documentation of Market Practice.   The primary working groups are:

- Marketing
- Market Practice:
    - Settlements, Treasury and Cash

---

[130] Source: ISITC-IOA

- Reconciliation
- Corporate Actions
- Trade Initiation and Confirmation
- Securities Lending

- Reference Data

- Technology and Standards

- Claims and Compensation

- Education

The working groups define the data elements that are required to electronically communicate between participants, and they support the ISO15022 data dictionary for securities messages and ISO7775 for cash/foreign exchange messages. The working groups highlight how to communicate information based on the type of asset or transactions and the best way to ensure STP, and how this information is communicated.

While the ISITC-IOA is a global organization, each region focuses on issues that will yield the greatest impact for its member firms, and thus the entire industry. Each ISITC-IOA region is organized to resolve messaging and technical issues, as well as to discuss crucial industry-wide topics.

Individual initiatives within each group are approved by a global executive committee and have clearly defined objectives, scope, team leadership and active team members. This allows the ISITC-IOA to utilize its members' expertise in the most effective way, and allows all members to directly influence the attainment of STP.

ISITC-IOA North America is organized into three major working groups:

STP Solutions

The STP Solutions group develops the business case for standard message formats.

Technology

The technology group focuses on the technical issues surrounding STP like security, communications networks, and assisting members in implementing the standards.

Communications

The communications group educates members, executes programs to increase membership, and communicates ISITC-IOA initiatives in a consistent way.

Additionally, ISITC-IOA provides its members with a venue to get updates on what is going on in the industry both domestically and globally. They work closely with several other industry groups (including SIA, BMA, AMF, SMPG) to ensure consistency and to provide support.

The success of ISITC-IOA has always been its membership's depth of expertise and diversity of industry background. It is one of a few associations that has members who are operations professionals from banks, investment managers, brokers, vendors and industry utilities.

D. SWIFT [131]

Introduction

SWIFT (Society for Worldwide Interbank Financial Telecommunication) provides financial data communication and message processing services to support the business activities of worldwide financial institutions for securities, payments, foreign exchange, derivatives and money markets, as well as trade finance. Its dedicated telecommunications network guarantees the rapid, cost-effective, secure and reliable transmission of financial data using a range of ISO-compliant standardized messages that have been developed by SWIFT in conjunction with its users and industry organizations.

Originally designed to eliminate the need for paper-based processes in the world-wide financial markets, SWIFT has also lowered costs, increased productivity and helped reduce risk in the securities industry by providing several of the key elements necessary for the automation of the settlement process, and by providing a reliable and secure global financial messaging network.

History

SWIFT began live operations in May 1977, to help banks electronically move large numbers of fund transfers from bank to bank across borders securely and efficiently. When brokers were admitted in 1987, the members created and began using the Category 5 (CAT 5) message standards to structure settlement instructions, confirmations and safekeeping information for securities transactions.

As of June 2004, over 7,500 institutions use SWIFT to communicate with each other 24 hours a day. SWIFT operates in 200 countries and processes over 2 billion messages each year, with an average daily message volume of over 9 million messages.

Owned by approximately 2,300 of its user banks broker/dealers and investment managers, SWIFT also connects other categories of non-bank financial institutions engaged in the securities industry, such as:

- Securities exchanges
- Central domestic securities depositories and clearing organizations
- Central cross-boarder securities depositories and clearing organizations such as Clearstream, Sega/Intersettle, and Euroclear
- Trust Companies and fiduciary service providers
- Custody and nominee services providers
- Registrars
- Transfer agents
- Fund Administrators
- Market Data Providers

---

[131]   Source: Extracted from a booklet prepared by H. McIntyre for SWIFT, dated 1999, and significantly updated by Chuck Wiley in 2004.

- Securities Electronic Trade Confirmation (ETC) Service Providers.[132]

Purpose

SWIFT plays an important role in increasing the efficiency of the international financial markets. In addition to its worldwide telecommunication network and the increasing number of message standards for financial instruments, SWIFT offers software and network-compatible interfaces, as well as several applications that can be used with the network to reduce costs and risk.

The central organization establishes numerous user committees to refine the standards, and holds a conference (Sibos) for its members each autumn to review what has been accomplished and to set the priorities for the following year.

Allowing investment managers to become participants in 1992, and to attain member/shareholder status as of 2002, were critical steps in extending the use of the SWIFT securities standards (and potentially the SWIFT network) beyond banks and brokers. This expansion of SWIFT's role is significant for individual investment managers, as well as for the entire securities industry.

There has been a significant growth in the usage of the SWIFT CAT 5 series of messages since they were introduced. While all of the banks and brokers have not yet established a full electronic SWIFT connection for securities, almost all can send and receive some of the SWIFT CAT 5 message types. As of April, 2004, over 3.08 million CAT 5 messages flowed over the SWIFT network each day, out of the total network traffic of 9.399 million messages.

Due to the industry's trend toward message standardization and automated, electronic counterparty connectivity, securities messages have represented SWIFT's fastest-growing market segment for the 1999-2002 period and again in 2003 and early 2004. Over 4,000 banks, broker/dealers and investment management firms sent nearly 660 million securities messages through the SWIFT network in 2003, accounting for 32% of the total network message traffic. In 2004, as shown in the following chart, securities traffic is again expected to grow by over 15% to 760 million messages.

---

[132] Securities ETC Service Providers are defined as organizations, other than SWIFT member or sub-member banks that function as an ETC provider for banks, broker/dealers, investment management institutions or other regulated institutions, any of whom themselves are eligible to join SWIFT.
Through their connection to SWIFT, Securities ETC Service Providers must perform all of the following principal functions:
1. Receipt of securities electronic trade confirmations from broker/dealer counterparties trading securities for market-side clearing and/or a broker/dealer counterparty for clearing purposes with the investment management institutions settlement agent.
2. Electronically match or affirm broker/dealer counterparty securities market-side trade confirmations and/or investment management institution's allocation instructions against broker/dealer's trade confirmations.
3. Report the status of matching and/or confirmation/affirmation activity to the appropriate trading and settlement parties.

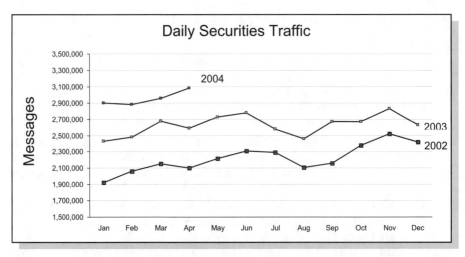

Figure 299 - Growth in SWIFT Securities Message Traffic since 2002

For most of the past ten years, the securities industry has been shifting away from the use of free-format messages in favor of specific settlement, reporting and custody-related messages. The use of formatted messages which are encrypted, validated and authenticated by SWIFT as part of a firm's overall message routing process, leads to more efficient and reliable communication between parties and increased back office automation where fewer errors and investigations will mean more timely reconciliation.

Strategy

SWIFT's current strategy is to position itself to support all aspects of the securities processing value chain from issuance to issue servicing, by extending the scope of the message standards and by introducing new products and services under the SWIFTNet brand. This puts SWIFT potentially into competition with other service organizations such as the DTCC and with vendors such as Thomson and other application vendors.

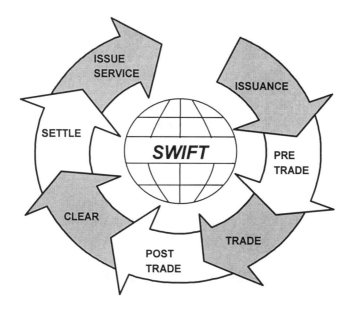

Figure 300 - Securities Processing Value Chain

As SWIFT began supporting securities firms several years ago, it concentrated on adding new broker and investment manager users to the network. More recently, while continuing to add new users, the emphasis has shifted to helping existing participants use SWIFT more effectively. To do this, SWIFT has:

- Increased is emphasis on working with application vendors

- Established a process to measure and report each participant's traffic (Traffic Watch)

- Established a process to measure and report on each participant's STP rates when using SWIFT (STP Watch)

- Implemented a new TCP/IP based network that will allow real-time transmission of certain categories of messages, as well as supporting a new set of messaging protocols

Products and Solutions

SWIFT offers its members a set of standards, a modern telecommunications network, network compatible terminals/interfaces, some software based services and increasingly relies upon third-party application providers to deliver value-added products to the industry. Firms can use the standards for free and decide if they want to use the network and the applications provided by SWIFT's vendor partners.

Standards

As one of the primary organizations creating international standards for financial services firms, SWIFT works closely with ISO (International Standards Organization), ISSA (International Society of Securities Administrators), ISITC (Industry Standardization for Institutional Trade

Confirmation), FIBV (Federation Internationale des Bourses), and FIX to support and enhance the SWIFT CAT 5 series of securities message types.

There are ten major categories of SWIFT messages that support all of the processing activities of SWIFT's members:

Category	Name
0xx	General Information
1xx	Customer Transfers and Checks
2xx	Financial Institutions Transfers
3xx	Financial Trading (FX, Loans, SWAPS, etc.)
4xx	Collections and Cash Letters
5xx	**Financial Trading (Securities)**
6xx	Precious Metals Trading and Syndications
7xx	Documentary Credits and Guarantees
8xx	Traveler's Checks
9xx	Cash Management and Client Status

Securities firms can use these messages for transactions involving securities, cash, and foreign exchange.

The SWIFT ISO Securities Messages that are listed below cover the complete life cycle of a securities transaction, from trading to settlement, including custody and reporting. The messages that support securities processing are in the SWIFT CAT 5 series, which consists of eight general groups. These groups cover all facets of securities processing, from trading to settlement and safekeeping. The eight groups are:

- General Messages
- Trade Orders and Confirmations
- Securities Lending and Borrowing
- Settlement Instructions and Confirmations
- Corporate Actions
- Capital and Income
- Inter-depository and Clearing Institutions
- Statements

SWIFT has released new versions of the securities message formats over the past three years, and the entire life cycle of the securities transaction (with the exception of the pre-trade Indications of Interest phase) can now be standardized with one or more of these ISO 15022-compatible messages.

For instance, Trade Order and Confirmation messages were implemented on the SWIFT network in November 1995. The November 1996 Standards Release delivered a new third-party foreign exchange confirmation message and additional changes to the Swaps message standards. In 1998, new securities settlement, reconciliation and corporate events messages were released onto the network under the ISO 15022 Data Dictionary umbrella

Network

SWIFT has two networks that are used by its participants: the existing X.25 network, which is being phased out by the end of 2004 and a new IP-based network, branded as SWIFTNet

X.25 Network

The SWIFT network uses a protocol, called X.25, which sends information in separate packages of information and functions over leased or dial-up lines. Packet switching networks of this type are designed to ensure accurate transmission of messages and files over lines of differing telecommunication quality such as those found in many emerging countries. SWIFT also supports messages and file transfers through the use of a *Store and Forward* standard, called CCITT X.400.

Messages and file transactions are processed by SWIFT immediately, with automatic verification and authentication. If the sender and the receiver are both connected online, a message transfer typically takes less than 20 seconds, even for cross-border message transfers.

By automating the sending and receiving of messages, firms can obtain significant productivity gains that will enhance their profitability and processing controls. SWIFT's *black box* architecture gives each firm a network connection, and a consistent methodology for interfacing with their own applications.

SWIFT provides a financial guarantee for the delivery of all FIN messages sent over its network. There is a full audit trail, and the system is available 24 hours a day, 7 days a week.

This current process is most effective for operationally-oriented messages that are not time sensitive in today's settlement environment. However, as the worldwide settlement cycles continue to be shortened to reduce risk, and as the trade processing activities increasingly require connectivity to the front office's systems, SWIFT has developed an interactive, real-time network to support this new level of message traffic.

SWIFTNet

SWIFT is currently deploying a TCP/IP-based communications network that permits real-time, interactive services that will be used to facilitate SWIFT's role in a variety of global market infrastructure projects   SWIFTNet comprises a portfolio of products and services enabling the secure and reliable communication of mission-critical financial information and transactional data.   SWIFTNet Single Window provides an overview of these various solutions, all accessible through a re-usable messaging and communications platform.

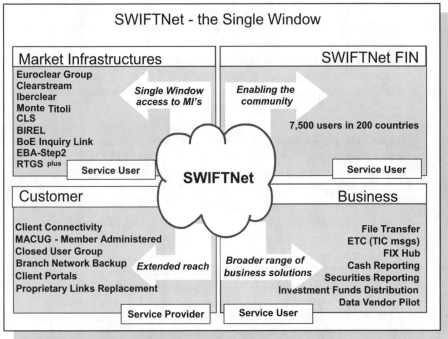

Figure 301 - SWIFTNet – the Single Window

A re-usable communications platform comprised of interface software, security infrastructure and physical network connections permits access to multiple service providers, correspondents and clients.   SWIFTNet Messaging Overview provides a diagrammatic representation of this multi-layered business and technical solutions platform.

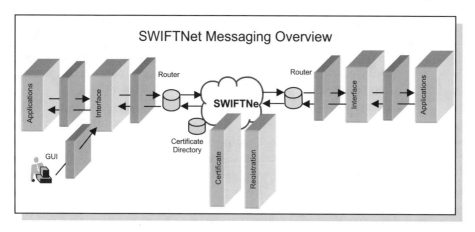

Figure 302 - SWIFTNet Messaging Overview

Full redundancy, advanced recovery mechanisms and first class operations and client support services ensure continuous network availability for SWIFTNet services. Users are offered a wide choice of connectivity options (see SWIFTNet connectivity options) that combine throughput and resiliency factors, and range from low-cost dial-up to fully resilient, high bandwidth configurations.

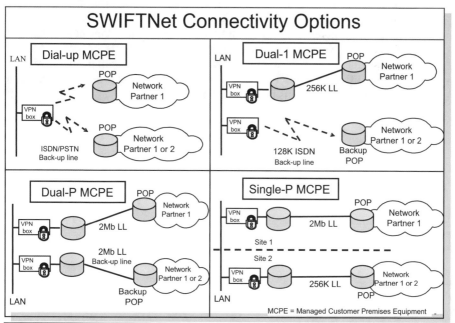

Figure 303 - SWIFTNet Connectivity Options

SWIFTNet offers access to four complimentary messaging services that provide SWIFT's users with a range of communication solutions, including:

- **SWIFTNet FIN** – SWIFT's traditional Store-and-Forward messaging with guaranteed message delivery in a many-to-many environment now incorporating over 7,500 end-users in 200 countries.

- **SWIFTNet InterAct** – SWIFT's real-time, query-response based messaging protocol

- **SWIFTNet FileAct** – SWIFT's bulk file transfer protocol, now supporting both real-time and store-and-forward based file transfer activities, and

- **SWIFTNet Browse** – SWIFT's human-t0-computer based messaging protocol, based on the use of standardized IP-based browsers such as Microsoft's Internet Explorer and Netscape Navigator.

SWIFTNet security is assured through Public Key Infrastructure (PKI), for which SWIFT provides such services as the management of the certificate directory, as well as acts as the certificate authority and registration authority for the service. SWIFTNet PKI guarantees users authenticity, integrity and non-repudiation of emission and reception at the message level.

SWIFTNet service inter-operability is achieved through a unique underlying software module called SWIFTNet Link (SNL), which encapsulates transport, service management and security technologies. SNL is used in conjunction with SWIFT's SWIFTAlliance family of interface products, or vendor equivalents, to integrate users' applications with the SWIFTNet messaging services. This is typically done through either SWIFTAlliance Gateway, which focuses on automated application-to-application integration with SWIFTNet and any of its core messaging protocols, or SWIFTAlliance Webstation, which is a browser-based interface enabling an operator to access different SWIFTNet business solutions in an integrated human-to computer manner. This is illustrated below.

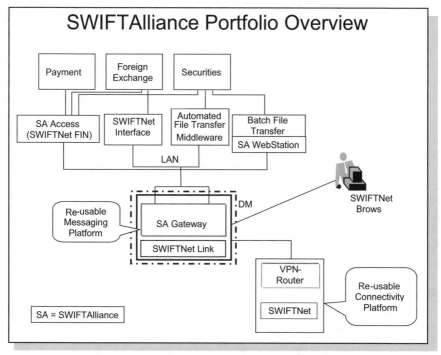

Figure 304 - SWIFTAlliance Portfolio Overview

Network Compatible Terminals (Interface Devices)

SWIFT has developed and supported several different platforms over the years, and has now implemented its latest generation of software for PC-based and UNIX-based applications. These products provide electronic interfaces to the network, and make it possible for participants to have a fully automated system.

The Interface Devices that are available from SWIFT to connect users to the SWIFT network are branded under the name SWIFTAlliance. This is SWIFT's newest interface product line, which consists of the UNIX-based Alliance Access and the Windows/NT-based Alliance Entry products for accessing the SWIFTNet FIN service, and the SWIFTAlliance Gateway and SWIFTAlliance Webstation for controlling access, generically, to other SWIFTNet-based messaging protocols such as InterAct, FileAct and Browse

SWIFTAlliance Access

SWIFTAlliance Access provides multi-network connectivity, focusing on SWIFT, fax, and telex, as well as national clearing system and private networks. SWIFTAlliance Access provides user-configurable security and is scaleable to accommodate a full spectrum of message volume needs. SWIFTAlliance Workstation (SAW) is also available to permit remote access to the SWIFTAlliance Access server for message input, validation, exception management and administration.

SWIFTAlliance Access uses a Motif-compliant graphical user interface (GUI) which can be easily learned by users experienced with Windows or

Mac software. SWIFTAlliance Access fully supports SWIFT's USE (User Security Enhancement) software and hardware that provide the foundation for Secure Login and Select (SLS) and Bilateral Key Exchange (BKE).

SWIFTAlliance Access is based on Open Systems Architecture, and runs today on the following hardware platforms:

- IBM RS/6000
- Sun Sparc
- Windows 2000

SWIFTAlliance Entry

SWIFTAlliance Entry is SWIFT's entry-level interface and is targeted at institutions which are new to SWIFT or which have relatively low message volumes up to about 1,000 messages per day.

SWIFTAlliance Entry runs on standard personal computers running the Microsoft Windows 2000 Operating System, and the hardware and software are priced to minimize capital and operating costs.

SWIFTAlliance Gateway

SWIFTAlliance Gateway (SAG) concentrates SWIFTNet message traffic (for FIN, FileAct, InterAct and Browse, in a secure environment that enhances security through the centralization of management and monitoring of functions related to SWIFTNet Link (SNL). Concentrating SWIFTNet message traffic through the SAG helps to simplify the telecommunication infrastructure, such as the configuration of firewalls and network address translation devices, which reducing the cost of software and administration costs and optimizing the scalability of a user's SWIFTNet environment.

SWIFTAlliance Webstation

SWIFTAlliance Webstation (SAB) facilitates human-to-computer interaction with SWIFTNet-based services, inclusive of the administration of SWIFTNet services via SWIFTNet Link (SNL). SAB is the basis for the SWIFTNet Browse service, which is conducted through SWIFTNet Service GUIs (Graphical User Interface) screens which are customized to the particular SWIFTNet service requirements. SAB can run as a standalone service module or as concentration access points through SWIFTAlliance Gateway. This later configuration allows several operators to share the same SWIFTNet PKI profile when accessing a SWIFTNet service.

Value-Added Applications

While SWIFT has reduced its emphasis on developing proprietary software, there are a growing number of services and products that are only available directly from SWIFT, and there are many applications available from third-party vendors which are integrated with the SWIFT network both from a standards and an interface perspective.

SWIFT Products

With the introduction of SWIFTNet, SWIFT has started to release a number of software applications and SWIFTNet-based Business Solutions, including:

SWIFTNet Accord - Financial Trading Matching and Netting

Accord is SWIFT's service for the matching - and where appropriate - bilateral netting of financial transactions. When a deal involving one of the financial trading instruments shown below has been struck between two counterparties, both parties confirm by sending the appropriate MT3xx message via SWIFT:

- MT300 - Foreign exchange confirmation
- MT305 – Foreign Currency Option confirmation
- MT320 - Fixed loan/deposit confirmation
- MT330 - Call/notice loan/deposit confirmation
- MT340 - Forward rate agreement confirmation
- MT341 - Forward rate agreement settlement confirmation
- MT360 – Single Currency Interest Rate Derivative confirmation
- MT361 – Cross Currency Interest Rate Swap confirmation
- MT362 – Interest Rate Reset/Advice of Payment
- MT392 - Request for cancellation

If at least one of the deal counterparties is an Accord subscriber, SWIFT copies the confirmation messages to the Accord central matching system. Accord then validates the integrity of the message contents (including valid value dates for each currency) and attempts to match it with a counterparty confirmation, based on the message type involved.

Confirmations are classified as *Matched* if their contents follow the matching criteria specified in Accord. Confirmations are classified as *Mis-Matched* if they almost, but not quite, match. All confirmations for which corresponding confirmations cannot be found are classified as *Un-Matched*.

Accord's reporting facilities enable reports to be generated based on the type of match up to several times per day in order for users to react to problems associated with Mis-Matched and Un-Matched confirmations during normal business hours.

Access to SWIFTNet Accord is facilitated either through the SWIFTAlliance Webstation-based Graphical User Interface (GUI), or through the SWIFTNet Accord Application Programming Interface (API), which permits real-time access from third-party applications to the Accord server.

Traffic Watch

Traffic Watch was developed by SWIFT to help participants manage their network traffic. Users of this service can see the details of all of the messages sent or received by BIC code, counterparty, country and message type. This information helps firms identify opportunities to reduce or re-route traffic to control telecommunications expenses.

SWIFNet FIX

Launched in December 2002 and powered by Financial Fusion, the SWIFTNet FIX messaging solution comprises a hub hosted on SWIFT's secure IP network that routes, monitors and manages FIX message traffic, ensuring the high degree of security and reliability required to relay live trade information. SWIFTNet FIX supports FIX versions 4.0, 4.1, 4.2, 4.3 and 4.4, using a FIX Connector software that interfaces to a user's FIX engine to communicate with the SWIFTNet FIX hub.

The service also provides for automated certification of counterparties' FIX capabilities, and enables smaller users without FIX engines and sophisticated Order Management Systems to communicate with the SWIFTNet FIX hub through a lightweight order entry facility. Pricing for the service, unlike SWIFT's traditional message-based pricing, is based on a monthly service fee and, for sell-side institutions, a monthly counterparty connectivity fee that is tiered based on the number of counterparties.

SWIFTNet FUNDs

SWIFTNet FUNDs is a SWIFT-sponsored business solution which combines connectivity, standards and messaging services as a foundation for automating investment funds transactions. Catering to the universe of constituents in the investment funds business - including fund managers, distributors, transfer agents, fund administrators, processing hubs and custodian banks - SWIFTNet FUNDs offers the industry a solution which can help control processing and reporting costs while supporting growth in the midst of declining margins.

Phase 1 of the FUNDs initiative focuses is based on SWIFTNet FIN and uses several ISO15022-based message templates which cover the main transaction flows, including subscriptions, redemptions, switches and reporting on balances. Phase 2 of the initiative began in 2Q2004 and will use the first tranche of a newly released set of XML messages, in conjunction with SWIFTNet InterAct, as the messaging infrastructure for the service. Over the next 18 months, a total of nearly 40 XML-based messages will be released to support the standardization needs of the investment funds business.

Software from Other Vendors

Software that is compatible with SWIFT's message standards and data network is also available from approximately 300 third-party providers. Network interfacing, Middleware, message processing, financial applications, and reconciliation represent only a few of the different types of *SWIFT-enabled* applications available from third-party software providers. A complete list is available from SWIFT, which has a vendor marketing group dedicated to increasing the number of software packages that can electronically send or receive SWIFT messages.

SWIFT's Partner Solutions group co-operates with application vendors in three categories under the SWIFTReady accreditation program. This accreditation process assesses the compatibility of vendor products and services with SWIFT solutions. Depending on the degree of compatibility, products are awarded gold and sliver labels. SWIFT also accredits service providers based on their ability to guarantee certain service levels and knowledge of SWIFT

The key strategy for Partner Solutions is to influence the development plans of the partner products by assigning SWIFTReady labels according to an objective public set of criteria. Products satisfying relevant criteria are given either a SWIFTReady Silver label or a SWIFTReady Gold Label.

There are different criteria according to the market and positioning of the product which relate only to SWIFT's services, products and message standards. SWIFT's Partner Solutions group does not attempt to qualify the quality or fitness of any product; however, SWIFT does require a minimum of five installed client sites in any of the following areas before any label can be assigned:

- SWIFT Interface Connectivity
- Support of SWIFT Value-Added Services
- Support of SWIFT Operational Information Services and Straight Through Processing guidelines
- Support and Automation of SWIFT Message Standards

The three Partner Solutions relationship/accreditation categories are:

SWIFTReady Gold

This represents the highest level of accreditation for third-party vendors by Partner Solutions. The Gold label indicates the highest level of full compliance and proactive implementation of new standards and services.

SWIFTReady Silver

The Silver label conveys a level of SWIFT-compliance that gives the client a sufficient business solution in a SWIFT environment.

SWIFT-Accredited Professionals

There is a separate but parallel initiative within Partner Solutions to promote and support those external vendors who provide consulting, systems integration and training services to SWIFT members.

E. INDUSTRY STANDARDS ORGANIZATIONS

In order for the securities industry to function efficiently, the participants have agreed upon a series of standards, and various organizations have been established to define and, where necessary, enforce the standards.

American National Standards Institute (ANSI) [133]

The American National Standards Institute (ANSI) is the overall administrator and coordinator for the U.S.'s private sector voluntary standardization efforts, and is a private, nonprofit membership organization. ANSI consists of members from approximately 1,000 companies, organizations, government

---

[133] Source: American National Standards Institute

agencies, and institutions.

ANSI does not itself develop the standards. Instead, it facilitates the development of standards by helping qualified groups reach a consensus, by using three principals:

- Consensus
- Due process
- Openness

ANSI is the only U.S. representative to the International Organization for Standardization (ISO) and was a founding member of the ISO. ISO is an organization supported by the United Nations and based in Geneva. ANSI is one of five permanent members of the governing ISO Council, and is active in the governance of ISO.

ANSI's primary benefit to the U.S. securities industry is the creation of numbering systems (CUSIP) and message standards (SWIFT).

Association for Investment Management and Research (AIMR) [134]

Founded in January 1990, the Association for Investment Management and Research is a global, nonprofit organization of more than 60,000 investment professionals from over 100 countries worldwide. AIMR's name was recently changed to the CFA Institute (CFAI).

CFAI's goal is to:

- Provide knowledge to investment professionals
- Promote a high level of standard, ethics and professionalism

CFAI was created from the merger of the Financial Analysts Federation (FAF) and the Institute of Chartered Financial Analysts (ICFA). The FAF was originally established in 1947 as a service organization for investment professionals in its societies and chapters. The ICFA was founded in 1959 to examine candidates and award the Chartered Financial Analyst (CFA) designation.

CFAI's members are employed as securities analysts, portfolio managers, strategists, consultants, educators, and other investment specialists who practice in a variety of fields, including investment counseling and management, banking, insurance, and investment banking and brokerage firms.

The Chartered Financial Analyst (CFA) Program is a globally recognized standard for measuring the competence and integrity of financial analysts. Its curriculum develops and reinforces a fundamental knowledge of investment principles. Three levels of examination measure a candidate's ability to apply these principles at a professional level.

Federal Trade Commission (FTC)

The FTC has regulatory oversight over standards in the U.S.

---

[134]   Source: Association for Investment Management and Research

Financial Accounting Standards Board (FASB) [135]

The SEC is authorized by the Securities Exchange Act of 1934 to establish the accounting and reporting standards for publicly held companies. Since 1973, the Financial Accounting Standards Board has been the official private sector organization that establishes standards for accounting and reporting and which is accepted as an authority by the Securities and Exchange Commission and the American Institute of Certified Public Accountants.

The stated mission of the Financial Accounting Standards Board is to establish and improve standards of financial accounting and reporting for the guidance and education of the public, including issuers, auditors, and users of financial information.

To accomplish its mission, FASB acts to:

- Improve the usefulness of financial reporting
- Keep standards current to reflect changes in methods of doing business
- Consider promptly any significant areas of deficiency in financial reporting
- Promote the international comparability of accounting standards
- Improve the common understanding of the nature and purposes of information contained in financial reports

Information Infrastructure Standards Panel (IISP)

The IISP, formed in 1994, has a goal of accelerating the development of standards that are needed to deploy information infrastructure products and services. Sponsored by ANSI, the IISP is an open forum for a broad range of firms affected by the distribution of information technology products, including companies, government agencies, standards and specifications developing organizations, industry associations, etc.

International Organization for Standards (ISO)

ISO, which is a part of the United Nations, develops standards for various industries, including financial services.

International Organization of Securities Commission (IOSCO)

IOSCO develops standards for international risk assessment and measurement.

Internet Engineering Task Force (IETF)

IETF develops standards for the Internet, including TCP/IP.

National Standards Systems Network (NSSN)

NSSN, located at www.nssn.org, provides an online reference of standards.

Reuters Ticket Output Feed

Reuters is responsible for maintaining the standard for the Ticket Output feed that goes from the exchanges and NASDAQ to vendors and users of the information.

---

[135]   Source: Financial Accounting Standards Board

F. CUSIP

In 1962, the New York Clearing House Association started the Securities Procedures Committee to identify how the United States could establish common numbering system, and subsequently asked the American Bankers Association's (ABA) Department of Automation to develop the numbering system.

In July 1964, the ABA's Committee on Uniform Security Identification Procedures (CUSIP) set the following goals:

- Develop specifications for a uniform security identification system
- Devise a format for imprinting the identification number on bond/stock certificates in man/machine-readable type font
- Establish an agency to administer the identification system according to specifications

CUSIP is managed by S&Ps CUSIP Service Bureau, and the CUSIP Technical Subcommittee established several goals for the new number, which should:

- Contain as few characters as possible
- Be linked to an alphabetic sequence of issuer names
- Meeting future as well as present operating requirements
- Be adaptable to the internal systems of all users, to communications systems, to automated document reading
- Allow each user to assign numbers to securities or other assets carried by them but not covered by the CUSIP System

The numbering system announced by the ABA in 1967, consists of nine digits:

- The first six numbers uniquely identify the issuer and have been assigned to issuers in alphabetic sequence
- Two characters (alphabetic or numeric) identify the specific issue
- The ninth digit is the check digit

CUSIP numbers are provided for several different categories of instruments:

Corporate Issues

- Public Offering of Equity or Debt
- American Depository Receipts
- Bank Holding Company
- Bankers Acceptances
- Certificates of Deposit
- Church Bonds
- Commercial Paper (Book Entry only)
- Medium-Term Notes (Book Entry only)
- Publicly Traded Limited Partnerships
- Mutual Funds
- Right Offerings
- Rule 144A Securities
- Shelf Registrations Supplements
- Unit Trusts

Municipal Issues

- Negotiated Issues
- Competitive Issues
- Private Placements
- Short-Term Notes

Canadian Issues

Canadian issues are given CUSIP numbers.

International Issues

Some international issues can be given a CUSIP number, but most are assigned a nine character CUSIP International Numbering System (CINS) identifier that conforms to the nine-character CUSIP System. Together, CUSIP/CINS identifies securities for U.S. markets. However, when securities trade internationally they require a twelve character ISIN identifier. The CUSIP Service Bureau, acting as the U.S. National Numbering Agency conforms to the ISO rules for ISIN assignments by using the 'US' prefix, to identify United States securities, and embeds the CUSIP/CINS identifier in the middle. A new check digit is calculated to create the twelve character ISIN number.

ISIN and ISO are described elsewhere in this chapter.

CUSIP also provides several products and services, including:

- CUSIP_db Master Service
- Mortgage Backed Securities files
- CUSIP Access, an Internet service
- CUSIP CD-ROM
- International Securities Identification Directory (ISID) – cross references: CUSIP/CINS, to other National Numbering Agencies such as Common Code, Sedol, Valor, etc.
- Crosswalk, a risk management tool

G. INDUSTRY STANDARDS

The standards organizations described in the earlier section have produced a variety of standards that are used by the securities industry, such as:

CUSIP

In the U.S., the primary numbering system is CUSIP, which has the following characteristics:

- Unique for each issuer (first 6 digits)
- Unique for each security (next 2 digits, plus a check digit)

CUSIP numbers are available for most equity, debt and government securities and those that are of interest to the securities marketplace, such as TBA's and Syndicated Loans.

CUSIP is described in detail earlier in this chapter.

International Securities Identification Number (ISIN)

ISIN is used as the unique numbering system for non-North American securities. It is used to a degree in the U.S. when trades in U.S. securities are executed abroad, and is different from CUSIP in that it has twelve digits:

- Prefix (2 letters designating the country of issue)
- Basic Number (9 digits that is the existing national number)
- Check digit

Financial Identification Numbering System (FINS)

There are other numbering systems in use, such as FINS, which is an ISO-based standard that is used to uniquely identify every financial firm in the world. DTC is an administrator for FINS numbers, and they can be requested on the www.dtc.org web site.

Bank Identification Code (BIC)

Financial firms use BIC to identify each other when using the SWIFT network.

- SWIFT
- DTCC Hub
- ISITC/SMPG Best Practices

SWIFT is the secretariat for BIC codes.

Other Standards

There are many other types of standards that can affect the securities industry, including:

Standard	Title	Application
ebXML	E-Business eXtensible Markup Language	e-Commerce
FinXML	Financial eXtensible Markup Language	Financial Instruments
FIXML	Financial Information eXchange Markup Language	FIX Applications
FpML	Financial Products Markup Language	Derivatives
Funds-XML	Funds eXtensible Markup Language	Investment Funds
GXML	Global eXtensible Markup Language	Global Market Data
IndeXML	Index Fund eXtensible Markup Language	Index Funds and ETFs
IRML	Investment Research Markup Language	Investment Research
irXML	Investor Relations eXtensible Markup Language	Investor Relations
MDDL	Market Data Definition Language	Market Data
MarketsML	Markets Markup Language	Reuters (Internal)
NewsML	News Markup Language	News Transmission
NTM	Network Trade Model	SunGard Products
OFX	Open Financial eXchange	Financial Data
RIXML	Research Information eXtensible Markup Language	Securities Research
SAML	Security Assertion Markup Language	Authentication/Authorization

SFXL	Securities Financing eXtensible Language	Securities Financing
SLML	Securities Lending Markup Language	Securities Lending
STPML	Straight Through Processing Markup Language	STP Facilitation
SWIFTML	SWIFT Markup Language	SWIFT Messages
VRXML	Vendor Reporting eXtensible Markup Language	Market Data Billing
XBRL	eXtensible Business Reporting Language	Financial Reporting
XML	eXtensible Markup Language	Generic
CUSIP	Committee on Uniform Securities Identification Procedures	Securities Numbering
ISO 6166	Securities Numbering Standard	ISIN Numbering
FIX	Financial Information eXchange	Securities Transactions
TWIST	Treasury Workstation Integration Standards Team	Foreign Exchange
ISO 15022	International Standards Organization - 15022 Messaging	Financial Messaging
ANSI - X9D	American National Standards Institute - X9D Committee	Securities Processing

Figure 305 - Standards Affecting the Securities Industry

Index

About the Author

Hal McIntyre - hal@tsgc.com

Hal has over 30 years of management experience, including 16 years at Citibank. He founded The Summit Group in 1991. Prior to establishing The Summit Group, Hal managed numerous banking and securities functions for Citibank, including marketing, operations, and technology. During his last four years at Citibank, he managed a systems division of over 300 people who supported Citibank's worldwide securities processing applications.

While at Citibank, he worked for four years in Zurich as the head of Operations and Technology for Citibank's Swiss Investment and Private Banks, and was the Chief Administrative Officer for Citicorp Investment Bank.

Hal is a Managing Partner of The Summit Group, which, with over fifty employees, is active in consulting to major banks, brokers, investment managers, and other financial institutions, and provides comprehensive services in Management Consulting, Market Research, and Systems Integration.

Securities Operations Forum, a subsidiary of The Summit Group, is a leading supplier of information and training to the securities industry. Securities Operations Forum publishes two newsletters for over 4,000 readers worldwide: *Securities Operations Letter* focuses on the U.S. industry, and *Global Custody News* concentrates on international securities processing. Securities Operations Forum also conducts open enrollment and customized training for over 2,500 people each year throughout the U.S. on processing topics such as Derivatives, Corporate Actions, etc., and annually presents several major conferences on key securities industry issues. SOF offers a wide range of eLearning courses and a credential program sponsored by ISITC-IOA.

A former Air Force officer, Hal has a Bachelor of Arts in Industrial Psychology from Miami University and an MBA from Southern Illinois University. He has taught graduate and undergraduate courses at Fairleigh Dickenson University, and has been a guest lecturer at the University of Massachusetts. He is frequently quoted in publications such as American Banker, Trends and Institutional Investor, is a regular speaker at securities industry conferences around the world.

Hal is the author of several other books, including the *Securities Operations Glossary, Software Testing for Financial Firms* and *Straight Through Processing for Financial Firms.*